Shakespeare Companies and Festivals

Shakespeare Companies and Festivals

An International Guide

**Edited by Ron Engle,
Felicia Hardison Londré,
and Daniel J. Watermeier**

GREENWOOD PRESS
Westport, Connecticut • London

Library of Congress Cataloging-in-Publication Data

Shakespeare companies and festivals : an international guide / edited
   by Ron Engle, Felicia Hardison Londré, and Daniel J. Watermeier.
         p.   cm.
   Includes bibliographical references and index.
   ISBN 0–313–27434–7 (alk. paper)
   1. Shakespeare, William, 1564–1616—Dramatic production—
Directories.   2. Repertory theater—Directories.   3. Drama
festivals—Directories.   I. Engle, Ron.   II. Londré, Felicia
Hardison.   III. Watermeier, Daniel J.
PR3091.S35   1995
792.9′5—dc20   94–32786

British Library Cataloguing in Publication Data is available.

Library of Congress Catalog Card Number: 94–32786
ISBN: 0–313–27434–7

First published in 1995

Greenwood Press, 88 Post Road West, Westport, CT 06881
An imprint of Greenwood Publishing Group, Inc.

Printed in the United States of America

The paper used in this book complies with the
Permanent Paper Standard issued by the National
Information Standards Organization (Z39.48–1984).

10 9 8 7 6 5 4 3 2 1

Contents

Preface   vii
Introduction   xiii

The United States of America
  Alabama   1
  Arizona   10
  California   12
  Colorado   89
  Connecticut   100
  District of Columbia   108
  Florida   115
  Georgia   126
  Hawaii   134
  Idaho   134
  Illinois   137
  Iowa   150
  Kentucky   151
  Maine   161
  Maryland   171
  Massachusetts   176
  Minnesota   192
  Missouri   194
  Montana   200
  Nebraska   202
  Nevada   206
  New Jersey   207
  New Mexico   216
  New York   218

North Carolina   255
Ohio   259
Oklahoma   266
Oregon   275
Pennsylvania   290
Rhode Island   299
Tennessee   306
Texas   308
Utah   343
Vermont   349
Virginia   353
Washington   366
Wisconsin   372

International Companies and Festivals
Australia   381
Canada   383
China   403
France   413
German-Language Shakespeare: Austria, Germany, Switzerland   421
Great Britain   446
Japan   491
New Zealand   498
South Africa   504
Spain   507

Appendix A: List of Abbreviations   509
Appendix B: List of Companies and Festivals by Geographical Location 511
Appendix C: List of Companies and Festivals in Alphabetical Order   519
Selected Bibliography   523
Index of Names   533
About the Editors and Contributors   565
Photographs follow page 380

Preface

This reference profiles over 150 Shakespeare companies and festivals worldwide. Each company or festival is described in a separate essay. In light of the differences among the various companies and festivals and the fact that the essays were written by a number of contributors, the authors have never intended to be uniform in style. Nevertheless, each profile narrative does follow a general format, describing the history of the particular festival or company, its organization, including staffing and budgeting, its physical facilities and performance site, the demographics of its audience and the community where it is located, and its approach to producing Shakespeare's plays. Most of the essays also include a brief review of one or more performances witnessed by the contributor. The essay is preceded by a "headnote" containing essential information about the company or festival, including its name, mailing address, site, administrative office phone number, box office phone number, ticket prices, length of season, number of productions and performance starting times, principal staff members, physical facilities, audition procedures and location, Equity status, annual budget, annual attendance, date of its founding, and the name of its founder. The essay is followed by a chronological summary (Production History) of the Shakespeare plays (in most cases, all plays) produced by the organization and by Research Resources, a guide to further information, including, when available and pertinent, a listing of selected publications.

Please note that when a category has been omitted from a headnote, this is not due to an oversight; rather, the information was either unavailable (rarely the case) or not applicable. Thus, for example, Shakespeare festivals that do not charge admission, which are "free," usually do not have a "box office." Hence, this category would be omitted for such festivals. For the most part, we have listed in the Production History section all plays, both Shakespearean and non-Shakespearean, presented by a company or festival since its founding. In a few instances, however, when a company or festival has a long history of presenting numerous non-Shakespearean plays, we have chosen to list only the Shakespearean plays. Similarly, with a few companies for which a published comprehensive historical calendar of productions is easily available—as in the case of the Stratford Festival or the Royal Shakespeare Company—we have chosen to list only those seasons omitted from the published calendars (such calendars are cited in Research Resources).

In Research Resources, we have noted the presence of archives or collections pertinent to each respective festival or company. Some festivals have well-established formal archives, while many others have informal collections housed in the festival office or in the home of the founder. For the most part, we have listed only publications that can be easily accessed in libraries or through interlibrary loans, such as books or articles in nationally or internationally distributed periodicals. We have generally not listed articles in strictly local publications, for example San Francisco's *Tenderloin Times*. For readers or students wishing additional information about a company or festival, Research Resources is intended to be a helpful starting point, not a definitive bibliography or research guide.

At the outset of this project, we committed ourselves to actually visiting every Shakespeare company and festival we intended to cover. We would interview key personnel, examine archives, tour physical plants, observe audiences, and review productions at first hand. Indeed, this was the only way to obtain the information needed to write the sort of essay described above. We enthusiastically divided up the United States and Canada: Ron Engle took Canada and the Upper Midwest, Felicia Londré took the South and Midwest, and Dan Watermeier took the West Coast and New England. Festivals abroad did not seem to pose a particular problem. We already had personal familiarity with the Royal Shakespeare Company, Ron was well acquainted with Shakespeare in Germany, and Felicia had some knowledge of a festival or two in France. We were confident that we could accomplish our task in a relatively short period of time.

In 1989, however, we little understood the vast scope of the Shakespeare festival phenomenon, particularly in North America but abroad as well, nor did we appreciate that the two years allotted for the project would prove woefully inadequate to the task. It is not that we were total innocents to research on Shakespeare production. The three of us had already worked on the 970-page *Shakespeare Around the Globe: A Guide to Notable Postwar Revivals*, edited by Samuel L. Leiter (Greenwood, 1986). We were familiar with the 1975 book, *The Shakespeare Complex*, by Glenn Loney and Patricia MacKay (Drama Book Specialists), which described the twenty-six American and Canadian Shakespeare festivals in existence at that time. We were avid Shakespearean playgoers both in this country and abroad. We simply did not realize how fast and how far the grass-roots appeal of Shakespeare had spread in only fifteen years. Soon our territorial boundaries crumbled, and our world view expanded.

Each of us ended up visiting all parts of the United States, and our essentially Euro-American point of view broadened to include Japan, China, South Africa, and the Antipodes. Our list of festivals rapidly grew, and, out of necessity, we recruited contributors to assist us. Still, we and our contributors managed over a four-year period (1990-1993) to visit most of the festivals covered in this book. Finally, our deadline having been extended twice, with only a few secondary or minor festivals remaining and feeling anxious to bring the project to closure, lest our information become dated, we relied on telephone interviews and printed information supplied by individual companies or festivals. We have indicated at the end of entries the date of our site visitations and interviews. The omission of such a citation indicates that the information was collected "off site" or from a previous visit before the conception of this book.

What constitutes a Shakespeare company or festival has not always been easy to determine. Most German theatre companies, for example, have two or more Shakespeare productions in their repertories at all times; unless Shakespeare production is designated as central to the mission of the company, however, these have not been given individual essays. Similarly, many English provincial theatres and companies include one Shakespeare play in their annual seasons. Some American companies do this as well. For example, the Guthrie Theatre in Minneapolis has included two Shakespeare plays each season for the past several years, and the Actors Theatre of Louisville has been including a Shakespeare production annually for the past several seasons. Nevertheless, for our purposes, in order to be designated a "Shakespeare festival or company," either a substantial portion of a company's annual season had to be dedicated to producing Shakespeare's plays or Shakespeare was designated as central to the company's artistic mission. Most major festivals, for example, present as many (sometimes more) non-Shakespearean plays as Shakespearean plays, but they all acknowledge Shakespeare's plays to be the foundation, the core, on which their repertoires rest. Even so, we have made an occasional exception. For example, we have included an entry on the Great Lakes Theatre Festival (GLTF), although in recent years it has included only one Shakespeare play in a season of four or five productions. Founded originally as the Great Lakes Shakespeare Festival, it has a history of presenting distinguished productions of Shakespeare's plays, which justified inclusion for us. We have also included several Shakespeare companies and festivals that produce on an irregular basis due to funding difficulties or other circumstances, as well as a few recently defunct companies in order to preserve their history, such as the American Shakespeare Festival in Stratford, Connecticut, which was a major American festival until its demise in 1982.

When we started the project, the most obvious purpose of a book with the working title *The Shakespeare Festival Handbook* was to serve as a field guide for the itinerant Shakespeare enthusiast—and we soon discovered that there are indeed hundreds (at least) of indefatigable theatregoers who spend their summers on individually devised circuits of favorite outdoor festivals. The example of *The Shakespeare Complex*, however, taught us that the useful life of such a handbook might be a matter of only a few years. There is no escaping the fact that any guidebook to theatre companies will be somewhat outdated even as it goes to press. We determined, therefore, to produce a work that would remain informative and useful for a number of years after publication, despite season-to-season changes and the constant cycle of death and birth of companies committed to Shakespeare production. For that reason, the essays in this book emphasize historical development, organizational structure, and artistic philosophy. We also tried to set each festival or company within the context of its community. From the great mosaic of Shakespearean producing groups, large and small, commercial and admission-free, year-round and seasonal, housed in magnificent complexes or in a public park, the reader—whether playgoer or scholar—should be able to get an overall picture of the prominent place of Shakespeare not only in North America and the United Kingdom, but also in several other countries around the world.

While some of the information, such as budgets and that on annual attendance, for example, will probably be somewhat dated by the time of publication, we have made every effort to bring at least the Production Histories up through 1993 and 1994. Most entries have been reviewed for factual accuracy by company or festival personnel, but we take responsibility for any errors that may still remain. We have tried to be inclusive, covering every operating festival, regardless of its size or significance, that we knew about or that came to our attention during the period 1990 to 1994. A few festivals ceased operation before we could cover them, such as the Indianapolis Shakespeare Festival in 1991, for example. Even as we go to press, we have seen a notice that several new festivals would be inaugurated in summer 1994; the Tulane Summer Shakespeare Festival in New Orleans, for example, and the African-American Shakespeare Company in San Francisco. Undoubtedly, despite our efforts, we may have omitted some festival. If so, please call its absence to our attention. A revised edition of *Shakespeare Companies and Festivals* may be justifiable in the future.

This five-year endeavor has been gratifying to us in many ways. We have had the pleasure of seeing the great variety of Shakespeare production in the United States and abroad. During a fourteen-week stay in Japan, for example, Felicia Londré saw twelve Shakespeare productions. In Germany, Ron Engle visited the Bremer Shakespeare Company and dozens of other companies. Dan Watermeier became an habitué of the Stratford Theatre Festival in Ontario, seeing most (often all) of its productions every season. All of us published articles and reviews and delivered conference papers based upon our research in progress. Felicia helped to found the Shakespeare Theatre Association of America at a meeting of Shakespearean artistic directors, organized by Sidney Berger (of the Houston Shakespeare Festival) and held in Washington, D.C., in January 1991. Numerous artistic directors, managing directors, and promotion and development directors, some of whom are named below, assisted in furnishing information for entries on their respective organizations. They offered us with unstinting generosity complimentary tickets, advised us on lodging and restaurants—sometimes even making reservations for us—and supplied us with audience survey data, programs from previous seasons, financial reports, and photographs. For their interest and cooperation we are most grateful. Without it, this book would have been impossible. The most personally rewarding result of our undertaking was getting to know so many talented and dedicated theatre professionals, who have chosen to devote themselves to Shakespeare production, sharing with contemporary theatregoers a love of great language, provocative ideas, complex characters, and action-packed stories.

Each of the three editors of this volume has many people to thank. Ron Engle would like to especially thank the entire ensemble of the Bremer Shakespeare Company, Andreas Höfele, Richard Fotheringham, and Adrian Kiernander for their contributions to this book. The helpful assistance of Barbara Engle during this extended project has been most appreciated. He would also like to thank Dean Bruce C. Jacobsen for his support and Dan Plato for his support of scholarly and creative endeavors. Finally, he is most appreciative to the University of North Dakota Faculty Research Committee for its financial support.

Felicia Londré is grateful to the University of Missouri-Kansas City for two Faculty Research Grants (1990 and 1991). The interest, support, kindness, and generosity of many individuals made this project immensely rewarding and enjoyable for her. Among them, she would particularly like to acknowledge Fred Adams, Jessica Andrews, Kathy Barber, Sidney Berger, Jess Borgeson, Eve Brennan, William T. Brown, Raymond Caldwell, T. Carmi, Douglas Cook, Suzanne Croucher, Norio Deguchi, Richard Devin, Kevin Dressler, Louis Fantasia, Buck Favorini, Charles Fee, Julia Gábor, Jean Gurr, Richard Garner, Michael Greenwald, Steve Hemming, Osamu Hirokawa, Sally Homer, Péter Huszti, Michael Kahn, Eri Kawano, Randall Duk Kim, Alan Klem, Yoshiteru Kurokawa, Kimie Imura Lawlor, Eusebio Lázaro, Gyorgy Lengyel, Kristin Linklater, Georgianna Londré, Venne-Richard Londré, Adam Long, Mike Markey, Jennifer Martin, Reed Martin, Ada Brown Mather, Michelle Moraine, Toshio Murakami, Neal Newman, Kathryn Huey O'Meara, Pat Patton, Jamie Peck, Cindy Phaneuf, Louis Rackoff, Bill Rudman, Peter Sander, Hassell Sledd, Marilyn Strauss, Zdenek Stríbrny, Curt Tofteland, Jim Volz, the Shakespeare Theatre Association of America, the Shakespeare Oxford Society, and the late Bill Eaton and Sam Wanamaker.

Dan Watermeier would like to acknowledge the early contributions to this project by four University of Southern California graduate theatre students: Scott Atkinson, Dawn Ferry, Paul Jeffers, and Todd Hansen. Travel to a number of festivals in the summer of 1991 was supported in part by a

University of Toledo Faculty Research Fellowship Grant. His department also absorbed many other incidental research costs; including photo duplication, mailings, phone calls, and faxes. His wife, Roberta Kane, and son, Ethan, accompanied Dan on several of his research journeys. He was particularly grateful for their company during a three-week trip from Los Angeles to Ashland, Boise, Salt Lake City, Boulder, and back to Toledo, with many festival stops on the way. Ethan served as an able technician, recording interviews and taking photographs. Gigi Whittaker, his department's exceptionally gracious, diligent, and patient secretary, whose word-processing skills are impressive, typed and retyped, formated and reformated numerous entries. Without her assistance, Dan probably would never have completed his portion of this project.

Introduction

In Europe, the "festival" performance of plays in a formal setting, in the sense of a religious festival, can be traced back to performances of Greek drama and the festival of Dionysus; in a more modern context, the medieval guild and religious festivals, as well as the court masques and elaborate Jesuit productions produced on special occasions during the Renaissance and Baroque periods, all continued this kind of performance. David Garrick is usually credited with initiating the idea of the modern festival. In September 1769, Garrick organized a Shakespeare Jubilee in Stratford-upon-Avon; three days of fireworks, processions with townsfolk costumed like characters in Shakespeare's plays, banquets, orations, and a costume ball on the banks of the Avon River. Curiously, the celebration did not include the staging of a play by Shakespeare. But it proved sufficiently popular among the townspeople that the Jubilee became an annual event. Not until 1830, however, when Charles Kean presented *Richard III* in a new theatre in Stratford, were performances of Shakespeare's plays included as part of the celebration.

The next major stage in the development of a Shakespeare festival in Stratford occurred in the 1870s and 1880s, when Charles Flower, a leading citizen of Stratford, the owner of a long established brewery, organized annual performances of Shakespeare's plays in a theatre he had built expressly for this purpose, the Shakespeare Memorial Theatre. Flower's efforts and those of his grandson, Archibald, eventually become, in 1961, the Royal Shakespeare Company (RSC), undoubtedly the best known Shakespeare company in the world.

Annually, millions of Shakespeare fans from around the globe journey to Stratford, especially during the summer months, to see one or more of a dozen different productions staged in Stratford by the RSC and to tour Shakespeare's birthplace, the Anne Hathaway Cottage, New Place, and other historic sites associated with the Bard of Avon. Indeed, the RSC has become such a dominant and pervasive influence in post-war Shakespearean productions, that it may very well have impeded the development of comparable festivals or Shakespeare companies, at least on the continent.

This is not to say that Shakespeare is not a very popular playwright in the non-English speaking world. He is in fact the most produced playwright in the world theatre. In April 1991, the Shakespeare Globe Centre (USA) sponsored a week-long celebration of Shakespeare in translation for a multicultural America. The Los Angeles event, titled "Shakespeare in the Non-English Speaking World," brought together Shakespearean artists and scholars from around the world for performances, film screenings, lectures, panel discussions, and social gatherings. Among the participants were such luminaries as poet T. Carmi (Israel), actor Péter Huszti and director Gyorgy Lengyel (Hungary), director Atul Tiwari (India), producer Kamen Kostov (Bulgaria), director Roberto Javier Hernandez (Mexico), professor Kimi Imura (Japan), and translators Jean-Claude Carrière (France), Tsegaye Gabre Medhin (Ethiopia), and Zdenek Stríbrny (Czechoslovakia).

We know that Shakespeare's plays are widely produced in South America by companies like the Gran Circo Teatro in Chile and the Ornitorrinco company in Brazil, but these are not exclusively Shakespearean companies. Likewise, the Italian company, Teatro Due di Parma is known for its Shakespeare productions. Our research revealed relatively few foreign language Shakespeare festivals or companies that are committed *exclusively* or even mainly to producing Shakespeare's plays. The Bremer Shakespeare Company in Germany is a notable exception, and the China Shakespeare Festivals of 1986 and 1994 remain singular events in the context of foreign language festivals.

In 1981, there was a Shakespeare festival organized in Yerevan, Armenia, which brought together productions from Lithuania, Latvia, Estonia, Georgia, Azerbaijan, Moscow, and Leningrad. The distinguished Russian Shakespearean Alexei Barthoshevitch reported in some detail on this festival in *Theatre International* ("Feast and Celebration," 9 (1983): 25-41). The festival was so enthusiastically received that the organizers believed that it would "lay the foundation of a wonderful and lasting tradition." But despite a strong interest in Shakespeare in many of the former Soviet republics, a second festival never materialized, undoubtedly because of traumatic social and political upheavals.

Beginning in the early decades of the twentieth century, North American theatre producers began to embrace Shakespeare as an organizing principle for a summer festival. They had as models not only the Shakespeare Memorial Theatre, but also numerous pageants and folk dramas produced in outdoor theatres. These pageants, often referred to as "masques," were reenactments of early historical events in American history, such as Civil War battles, colonial life, early explorers and trappers meeting Native Americans.

In 1916, Shakespeare became the focus of outdoor pageants that celebrated the tercentenary of his death. In New York City, Percy MacKaye's adaptation of *The Tempest*, entitled *Caliban by the Yellow Sands*, was performed in the City College Stadium for ten performances. Isadora Duncan danced, and Robert Edmond Jones designed the costumes (*New York Times*, 19 March 1916, and David Glassberg's *American Historical Pageantry*. See also Charles Shattuck's *Shakespeare on the American Stage*, Vol. II). In St. Louis, *As You Like It* was performed in the Forest Park amphitheater. Also in 1916, in Grand Forks, North Dakota, Frederick H. Koch, who is best known as the founder of the Carolina Playmakers, presented Shakespeare in his Bankside Theatre, named after the location of the original Globe Theatre in London. Koch, who founded the Dakota Playmakers at the University of North Dakota, actively produced outdoor pageants in the 1910s before moving to North Carolina in the 1920s. Koch had produced *Twelfth Night* outdoors on the campus of the university as early as 1910; the permanent open-air Bankside Theatre was dedicated in 1914, situated on the bank of a natural curve of a stream to separate the stage from the auditorium. Within this "horseshoe" was the stage, and, on the opposite side, a rolling slope provided a natural seating area for several thousand people. *The Taming of the Shrew* and *As You Like It* were produced in the new Bankside Theatre in 1914 and *Twelfth Night* in 1915. In 1916, for the Shakespeare tercentenary, *Shakespeare the Playmaker*, a compilation of scenes, attracted national and international interest. The Bankside Theatre was written up in the *London Times*, and production reviews appeared in major newspapers and magazines, including the *Boston Transcript*. Photographs of the audience at the Bankside Theatre look uncannily similar to many contemporary outdoor Shakespeare festivals and "in the park" performances.

Numerous theatre companies with Shakespeare in their repertories toured the United States in the 1910s and 1920s, most notably the Ben Greet Players, Julia Marlowe and E. H. Sothern, the Coburn Shakespeare Players, the Robert Mantell company, and others. Charles Coburn with his wife, Ivah Wills, founded the Coburn Shakespeare Players in 1906 and toured an extensive repertory of Shakespeare's plays. But perhaps the closest thing to the formation of a "festival" as we know it today was a project conceived by Fritz Leiber, who had acted with Mantell and also toured Shakespeare with his own company. In 1929, Leiber created the Chicago Civic Shakespeare Society, which continued presenting, in resident-theatre fashion, several Shakespeare productions in the Chicago Civic Theatre each year. Although the productions served primarily as a vehicle for Leiber and his wife, Virginia Bronson, they were an annual event devoted exclusively to Shakespeare.

There was also considerable regional interest in Shakespeare before World War II. In 1934, Thomas Wood Stevens, founder of the theatre department at Carnegie-Mellon University (then Carnegie Institute of Technology), collaborated with English director Ben Iden Payne to reconstruct a conjectural Globe Theatre at the Chicago World's Fair, where abbreviated versions of Shakespeare's plays were presented. This theatre was rebuilt the following year at the Pacific National Exposition in Balboa Park in San Diego, eventually giving rise to the Old Globe Theatre. Margaret Webster toured Shakespeare productions, as did Katherine Cornell and her husband, director Guthrie MaClintic. Undoubtedly, the Federal Theatre Project also set the stage for the postwar interest in Shakespearean production and in the founding of Shakespeare festivals.

But the modern idea of a "festival" of Shakespeare plays seems to have been initiated by Angus L. Bowmer, a professor at Southern Oregon College in Ashland, who founded the Oregon Shakespeare Festival (OSF) in 1935. Today the OSF is the oldest surviving Shakespeare festival, the premier festival, and the largest resident repertory company in the United States. In several respects, it also is the parent of the numerous other Shakespeare festivals in North America. Every region in our country—indeed, almost every state—has at least one festival.

Following the establishment of the OSF and the Old Globe Theatre (which began regular Shakespeare production in 1949), festivals sprang up at Antioch College in Yellow Springs, Ohio (1952), in Phoenix, Arizona (1957), in Boulder, with the Colorado Shakespeare Festival (1958), in Stratford, Ontario, with the Stratford Shakespearean Festival, now called the Stratford Festival of Canada (1953), in New York, with the New York Shakespeare Festival (1954), and in Stratford, Connecticut, with the American Shakespeare Theatre (1955). In 1950, the Hofstra University replica of the Globe Theatre was completed and became the site for an annual Shakespeare festival. By 1964, the quadricentennial of Shakespeare's birth, bolstered undoubtedly by a burgeoning regional theatre movement, there were dozens of Shakespeare festivals in the United States. A publication entitled *Shakespeare in North America*, issued by the Shakespeare Anniversary Committee in 1964, lists a dozen festivals with their founding years, in addition to those above, including the Southern Shakespeare Repertory Theatre at the University of Miami in Coral Gables (1961), the Great Lakes Shakespeare Festival in Lakewood, Ohio (1962), the Cincinnati Shakespeare Festival (1961), the Shakespeare Summer Festival staged at the Sylvan Theatre on the sloping lawn of the Washington Monument (1961), the Champlain Shakespeare Festival in Burlington, Vermont (1958), the Irish Hills Shakespeare Repertory Festival in Onsted, Michigan (1961), the Victoria Shakespeare Festival in Victoria, Texas (1964), the San Francisco Shakespeare Festival (1961), the Southeastern Shakespeare Festival in Atlanta (1960), the Utah Shakespearean Festival (1961), the Marin Shakespeare Festival in Ross, California (1960), and the Ravinia Shakespeare Company in Highland Park, Illinois (1964). Some of these festivals for a variety of reasons lasted only a season or two or three, but many are still in operation, and new festivals were continually opening. Throughout the 1970s and 1980s, there was a net increase, never a net decrease, in the number of Shakespeare festivals in the United States. Indeed, since we began this project in earnest in the summer of 1990, some festivals have ceased operation—for example, the Indianapolis Shakespeare Festival in 1991—while others have come into being—for example, the Heart of America Shakespeare Festival in 1993. On balance, there are more festivals as we go to press than when we started.

American festivals fall into two broad categories: "destination" festivals and "community" festivals. "Destination" festivals include the Oregon Shakespeare Festival in Ashland, Utah Shakespearean Festival in Cedar City, and the Stratford Festival in Ontario. They have developed over several decades. They are large, fully professional operations, employing several hundred artistic, managerial, and technical personnel. In most cases, they operate virtually year-round, although peak attendance is usually during the summer months. They simultaneously operate two or more theatre facilities. Even though several of these "destination" festivals are located in comparatively small, rural towns, their constituency is truly nationwide. The Oregon Shakespeare Festival, for example, boasts an annual attendance of over 350,000, while the local population numbers only about 30,000. Their budget figures are in the millions, and they have a significant economic impact on the communities in which they are located.

"Community" Shakespeare festivals comprise the bulk of the festivals in North America. The size and organization of these festivals ranges widely, from operations that are almost as large, well-funded, and professional as the Utah Shakespearean Festival to very small, mostly amateur operations mounting only one production each summer in a municipal park. A few festivals or companies are not located in any permanent venue but travel from place to place. This is the case of the Shenandoah Shakespeare Express, the University of Maryland-Baltimore's Shakespeare-on-Wheels, and Montana's Shakespeare in the Parks.

There are numerous differences between destination festivals and community festivals—differences in physical facilities, budget, staffing, and the type of patron they attract. Destination festivals are patronized by people who have the interest and the money to travel several hundred miles to see plays. Eighty-eight percent of the Oregon Shakespeare Festival's audience travels over 25 miles to Ashland; almost 17 percent come from the populous Bay Area, over 350 miles away. The Stratford Festival draws nearly 40 percent of its audience from Michigan, Ohio, New York, Pennsylvania, Indiana, and Illinois. The Utah and Alabama festivals can claim similar out-of-state patronage. If one takes into account the cost of traveling to the festival, spending two or three days in a hotel, dining out during that period, and, of course, buying tickets, which could range from $20 to $50 each, a weekend in Ashland or Stratford could easily run to several hundred dollars. Demographic surveys conducted by these destination festivals—and our own on-site observations—confirm that their audiences are generally affluent, middle-class, well-educated, and middle-aged. In this respect, destination festival audiences are no different from audiences for American commercial theatre in general.

In contrast, community festivals tend to draw their audiences from the local population. Many of these festivals, moreover, are free, and, even when there is a charge for tickets, they are more modestly priced than at the destination festivals. At the admission-free festivals especially, one observes in the audience many more university students, children, young families, senior citizens, and more ethnic diversity than at the destination festivals. Furthermore, the audiences at the free festivals can be very large. The Houston Shakespeare Festival audiences can reach 7,000 on weekends; Toronto's free festival, called the Dream in High Park, regularly plays to 2,000–2,500 a performance. When Washington D.C.'s The Shakespeare Theatre offers free performances in the summer at the Carter Barron Amphitheatre in Rock Creek Park, attendance is regularly about 4,000 people, and the New York Shakespeare Festival's 1,932 seat Delacorte Theater in Central Park is normally full even with the threat of rain. Thus, over the course of a three- or four-week run, these free festivals can easily play to a total of between 40,000 to 50,000 spectators.

Both community and destination festivals share in common a concerted effort to create an ambience which is relaxed, informal, and "festive." Their very locations in parks or park-like environments encourage theatregoers to dress casually and to picnic before, and even during, the performance. The festive atmosphere is often reinforced with pre-show performances of Renaissance music and dancing or sometimes a pre-show lecture on the grounds. Sales of souvenirs—T-shirts, coffee mugs, posters, postcards, books about Shakespeare and the theatre—not only generate income for the company, but also add to the carnival milieu.

The Shakespeare festival phenomenon rests upon a blending of cultural idealism and wholesome popular entertainment. One experienced festival artistic director, Buck Favorini of the Three Rivers Shakespeare Festival in Pittsburgh, has called festival-going America's "second favorite summer pastime," after baseball. And indeed, there is probably no other comparable cultural experience in America through which, without much effort, one can be simultaneously educated, edified, and entertained—often for free. While American festivals seem to promote Shakespeare—or his plays—as a cultural ideal, what the Shakespeare ideal means and how it is interpreted varies from festival to festival. The destination and the other more established festivals tend to take a fairly conservative approach. For them, Shakespeare represents tradition—traditional drama and traditional humanistic and aesthetic values. This idea of Shakespeare is summarized by Jerry Turner, former artistic director of the Oregon Shakespeare Festival and one of America's most experienced Shakespearean directors:

> The vitality of a play depends neither on its historical interest nor upon its capacity to capture the social issues of the moment. . . . Theatre at its best defines the human condition in roles both traditional and relevant. . . . Thus *King Lear* is neither about prehistoric Britain, nor Elizabethan society, but about loyalty and betrayal in the face of growing old. We and the author share a

common understanding through a theatrical image of it. (Brubaker, *Golden Fire*, p. 13)

Turner is not ignorant of the insights of the new historicists and critical theorists, but he is not particularly interested in realizing productions inspired by such insights. Even a director noted for avant-garde productions, JoAnne Akalaitis, seems to be rather conservative when approaching Shakespeare. "Shakespeare [in Central Park]," she is quoted as saying, "is part of the essence of being a cultured person in New York City. It is relaxing, warm, open and democratic." When Bill Patton, long-time executive director of The Oregon Shakespeare Festival, was asked why Shakespeare is so popular, he replied, "it's certified as good for you, so audiences can congratulate themselves on their intellectuality" (quoted by William A. Henry III in "Midsummer Night's Spectacle," *Time* [24 August 1992]: 60-61). That is exactly the kind of message that attracts the patrons of the destination and larger, established festivals. It is a message that is projected not only in the quasi-Elizabethan design of their theatres and the carefully controlled "festival" ambience, but also, and more importantly, in what might be called the "festival production style." This style is characterized first by fidelity to the text—that is, few cuts, rearrangements, or adaptations. The performances are carefully rehearsed by skilled directors and enacted by an ensemble of skilled performers, all essentially working in a representational, "realist" mode of theatre that emphasizes Shakespeare's drama of character and conflict. This mode is frequently enhanced by the use of experienced, bravura performers. Production at the established festivals is also often distinguished by lavish historical costuming, spectacular scenic and lighting effects, artfully crafted properties, and cinematic, mood-enhancing original musical scores. It might even be argued, ironically, that for the spectator the visual text of these productions takes precedence over the verbal text of the Bard. That is, Shakespeare—generally acknowledged to be the greatest writer of the English language—is actually consumed in strongly visual terms. The larger festivals also market plays in visual terms, via brochures, posters, and lavishly illustrated souvenir programs.

In contrast to the destination festivals, many of the newer, smaller, and especially the free festivals mount productions that are less spectacular, less polished and "rougher," but perhaps more playful, fresh and engaging. Managers of these festivals say that they want to make Shakespeare accessible to a large "popular" audience. In fact, their funding from community-minded corporations, foundations, and municipal agencies (such as park and recreation commissions) often is tied to their ability to attract large audiences representative of the entire community, although this latter goal is more an ideal than a reality. To this end, artistic directors of such festivals adhere to standard Shakespearean texts, but they are not averse to cutting and rearranging the text so that a performance runs no more than two hours without an intermission. A few artistic directors have even confessed to a modest amount of rewriting, such as by substituting modern words or phrases for the archaic Shakespearean original. With budgets significantly smaller than the establishment festivals, community festivals use settings that are often minimalist and utilitarian. Costuming tends toward modern dress or simplified quasi-Elizabethan costuming. Sometimes costumes, settings, even theatrical business, and the entire *mise-en-scène*, are designed to evoke parallels to popular movies (*Star Wars*, *The Godfather* or *Mad Max*) or to sporting events. Acting companies at these festivals are often composed of young, aspiring professionals or talented but untrained amateurs. Youthful enthusiasm and energy substitutes for professional technique, experience, and depth. In fact, the performance style in these popular outdoor festival theatres is often much more physical and kinetic than in the established theatres.

American Shakespeare festivals, in general, however, do not move very far away from "tradition." The gap between a "populist" production style and an "establishment" style is really rather narrow, a matter of degree, of surface rather than substance. We saw very few truly radical, overtly politicized, or deconstructed productions of Shakespeare at festivals in the United States. What Alan Sinfield has written about Shakespeare in England may be equally true of Shakespeare in America:

> It may be that we must see the continuous centering of Shakespeare as the cultural token which must be appropriated as itself tending to reproduce the existing order: that however the plays are presented, they will exercise a relatively conservative drag, that any radical influence can hardly extend beyond the educated middle class, that in practice conservative institutions are bound to dominate the production of such a national symbol, and that one cultural phenomenon to have such authority must be a hindrance to radical innovation. (*Political Shakespeare*, p. 133)

In contrast, German Shakespeare productions have been quite radical and have often been drastically re-interpreted on the German stage. In light of this, we have included Andreas Höfele's essay which surveys recent trends in Shakespeare production in Germany.

Certainly, the great number of American festivals and productions—as evidenced in this book—argues for Shakespeare's having been appropriated, ironically, as an American national symbol. Yet, at the same time, Shakespeare is truly international. During the China Shakespeare Festival, for example, performances of Shakespeare's plays, some modified by traditional Chinese theatre practices, demonstrated how Shakespeare has been assimilated into foreign theatrical conventions.

The United States of America

ALABAMA

ALABAMA SHAKESPEARE FESTIVAL. MAIL: #1 Festival Drive, Montgomery, AL 36117. SITE: The Carolyn Blount Theatre in the Winton M. Blount Cultural Park, just off East Boulevard on Woodmere Boulevard. ADMINISTRATION: 205/271-5300. BOX OFFICE: 1-800/841-4ASF. ADMISSION: ranging up to $22; subscriptions $110–$170 for 10 shows (1993). SEASON: 12–15 productions, November to August. 7:30 p.m., Tues.–Thurs. and Sun.; 8:00 p.m., Fri.–Sat.; 2:00 p.m., Sat.–Sun. PRINCIPAL STAFF: Kent Thompson, artistic director; E. Timothy Langan, managing director; Beau Williams, general manager. FACILITY: Festival Stage (capacity 750); The Octagon (capacity 225). AUDITIONS: scheduled through casting agents. STATUS: LORT C and D. ANNUAL BUDGET: $6.0 million (1993). ANNUAL ATTENDANCE: 195,341 paid, 300,341 total (1992). FOUNDED: 1972, Martin L. Platt.

In its first thirteen years, the Alabama Shakespeare Festival (ASF) grew from an inaugural performance attended by only two people in a stifling high school auditorium to a 13-play season in a $21.5 million facility. Its second decade brought a new artistic director and significant changes in ASF's mission.

ASF's founder, Martin L. Platt, was a 22-year-old graduate of Carnegie-Mellon University who came to Anniston (population 30,000) in 1971 to direct the community theatre there and stayed to create what was to become (in 1977) the official "State Theatre of Alabama." Platt's idea for a Shakespeare festival arose from his own desire for summer employment and from the realization that there was no Shakespeare-producing organization in the southeastern United States at that time. Platt won the support of state arts council representatives, wrote to existing Shakespeare festivals for information, and borrowed $500 from his mother to launch the endeavor in the summer of 1972.

He directed the original company of eleven men and four women in all four plays, which were given a total of 31 performances in the auditorium cum basketball court of the former Anniston High School. Without air conditioning, temperatures often reached into the 100s. The two who attended the opening night performance of *The Comedy of Errors* (and had to wait for a 45-minute-late curtain while costumes were still being stitched) were a critic and his wife. Somehow the first season almost broke even, losing only $34 on an $8,000 budget, while boasting an attendance of 3,000 and enough local enthusiasm to carry the venture over to a second summer.

Anniston's location, two hours northeast of Montgomery, on the main highway between Birmingham and Atlanta, not far from Chattanooga, meant that the festival did not have to rely entirely on the local population to keep the box office busy. Calhoun County businessmen and arts supporters soon realized, however, that they were sitting on a cultural gold mine. A board of directors was formed in 1973, and ASF moved to the new Anniston Educational Complex (capacity 1,000) for its second summer. The ASF Guild was also formed in 1973, and its volunteers regularly logged over 7,000 hours each season in activities supporting the festival.

Directing all 16 productions of the first five seasons, Platt created a recognizable house style, based on bold interpretive choices while adhering closely to Shakespeare's texts. Thus, the 1973 season included a rock musical version of *As You Like It* and a *Much Ado About Nothing* inspired by *Gone With the Wind*. Placing the emphasis on the actors, Platt aimed "to revive the original spirit of Shakespeare, the spirit of entertainment, of amusement" (Volz, *Shakespeare Never Slept Here*, p. 18). *A Birmingham News* story on the 1974 season referred to the festival's "athletic, bawdy, robust, noisy Shakespeare" (Volz, 19). By the mid-1970s, however, Platt was moving toward more traditional, Elizabethan-period productions.

In 1976, ASF hired its first Equity actor (Charles Antalosky) and its first guest director (Bruce Hoard). A major tour was launched in 1978, sending *The Taming of the Shrew* to seven states in six weeks. By 1980, with FEDAPT guidance, ASF had become a fully professional theatre and inaugurated a conservatory training program for young actors. Peripheral programs were added: a classic film series, Shakespeare Sundays (church services with Elizabethan music and pageantry), Elizabethan concerts, pre-show discussions, and so forth. In 1981, a second performance space, known as the ACT Theatre (capacity 100), opened in downtown Anniston.

As ASF entered its second decade, it faced a mounting deficit, partly as a result of too-rapid growth. At the same time, it was impossible to expand the season beyond the summer months, because the facility was needed for educational uses during the remainder of the year. The company's continuing existence was assured when Winton M. "Red" Blount and his wife, Carolyn Blount, contributed $130,000 to pay off the debt and offered to build ASF a new theatre of its own, provided the festival would move from Anniston to

Montgomery and expand to a year-round season. The agreement reached in 1982 between the former U.S. postmaster general/entrepreneur and the ASF administration called for the continuation of the summer festival in Anniston until January 1985 or until the completion of the new facility.

The impressive, postmodern, brick theatre complex, designed by architects Tom Blount and Perry Pittman finally opened to national press coverage in December 1985. Winton Blount's contribution of 250 acres of land and $21.5 million make this the largest single gift to a playhouse in American theatre history. The beautifully landscaped Winton M. Blount Cultural Park is an idyllic setting for the elegantly proportioned 97,000 square-foot, eight-level theatre complex. Facing the building from a wooded area and across a manicured expanse of green is a bronze sculpture of Puck. Other sculptures, including some very lifelike grazing sheep, enhance the approach, as do the live swans gliding in a man-made pond. Among the flags above the facade is that of the **Royal Shakespeare Company**: ASF is the only American theatre authorized to fly it.

The facility houses the 750-seat Festival Stage and the 225-seat Octagon, two rehearsal halls, administrative offices, costume and scene shops, a snack bar and gift shop, a three-story lobby with curvilinear staircases and balconies, a tastefully appointed patrons' room, and "a box office that more resembles an upscale hotel check-in desk" (Filichia, 11). The foyer is dominated by a bronze replica of the statue of Shakespeare in New York's Central Park; exceptional permission was granted to ASF for this second casting from the original mold, because Blount set up an endowment for the maintenance of the Central Park statue in perpetuity. The Festival Stage has a modified thrust stage with a 34-foot-wide proscenium opening. The 69-foot-deep stage is trapped in four-foot sections and served by eight-three counterweighted linesets. The auditorium is equipped with an infrared sound system, and all sections are wheelchair accessible. The Octagon can be adapted to a proscenium, thrust, or arena configuration. In addition to the intimate-scale and experimental ASF productions mounted there, the Octagon is used for the graduate student training program. ASF's professional actor-training program is a cooperative venture with the University of Alabama's Master of Fine Arts program in theatre.

With the switch to a year-round season in the new facility, ASF's budget jumped in one year from $800,000 to $4.2 million, while contributions grew from $511,000 to over $2 million. Eight months before the opening of the first production in the new theatre (*A Midsummer Night's Dream* on Friday, 13 December 1985), ticket sales had surpassed $250,000. The staff also grew considerably during the transition years. One of Platt's luckiest moves was to hire Jim Volz as managing director, beginning in January 1983; Platt credits Volz with taking on the festival "at its lowest ebb" and guiding it through "the choppy waters of change and growth." Board member Austin Letson has commented: "Jim inherited a floundering Festival and almost single-handedly turned the situation around. Through his expert leadership and guidance, the Festival was brought into the black and developed into a year-round theatre, which became designated as the official State Theatre by the State of Alabama. He continually amazed the Board with his ability to solve difficult problems." Volz stayed with ASF until 1991, when he left to join the theatre faculty at California State University, Fullerton.

Another staff member who played an instrumental role in the transition was Carol Ogus. As director of ASF touring programs, she booked and coordinated the two-month tours that went out after the summer season ended in Anniston. The tours covered most of the southeastern United States and attracted about 50,000 theatregoers. Ogus worked to expand the educational programs that went with the tour, including a major artist-in-education program that she initiated in 1983. When ASF moved to Montgomery and began performing at home for eleven months of the year, the tour necessarily became a smaller component of the total operation, and a new position—that of educational services director—was created for Ogus. In that role, she created the SchoolFest program, which brings students from all over the state to see mid-morning performances of the same productions—not condensed or bowdlerized ones—that are seen by adult audiences in the evening. With Coca-Cola USA's underwriting, every schoolteacher of English, speech, and drama in the state of Alabama, whether he or she ever comes to SchoolFest or not, is supplied with a study kit that includes a poster with the dates of SchoolFest performances, booking information, and a 24-page booklet with essays and suggested classroom activities on each of the seven plays in the program. By 1990, over 120,000 Alabama students from grades 7 through 12 had attended perform-ances by the official State Theatre of Alabama. Other educational ventures include Theatre in the Mind, the scholar/actor program, the scholar lecture program, and the seminar program.

Ogus then became ASF's marketing director until 1991, when she was succeeded by Barry Colfelt. The job entails balancing two constituencies: the local audience and the out-of-town audience. The City and County of Montgomery provide funds for the general operation of the theatre, but the local population base is only 200,000. The disparity between the total annual attendance figures and the number of paid tickets (see data in the header above) reflects the great number of free programs available to residents of the community and the state. In order to fill 250,000 seats each season, ASF relies heavily upon theatregoers from across the nation. To that end, Colfelt arranges package deals with nearby hotels, offering discount rates for tourists attending ASF productions. According to Ogus, ASF's commitment to rotating repertory is its greatest marketing asset, because it allows the out-of-state ticket-buyer to purchase a package. "One year we tried a season doing stock instead of rep," Ogus has commented, "and it was the worst season we've ever had." Volz has reiterated ASF's firm commitment to rotating repertory, "because it helps you attract a much stronger company. Otherwise, it's hard to get the best actors to fill the medium-size and smaller roles. And to see Willie Loman opposite Richard III in rotating repertory, for example, gives greater meaning to both of those tragic figures."

Dramaturg Susan Willis coordinates Theatre in the Mind, along with her other duties. The Theatre in the Mind (TIM) began in 1984 as a project developed by the Alabama Humanities Foundation and funded by a $74,760 grant from NEH. One of only seven national projects chosen by NEH for an Exemplary Award, TIM is the umbrella title for a wide range of public humanities programs designed to complement and enhance plays in the ASF season. It includes seminars in public libraries around the state, a speaker's program, pre-show discussions, films, exhibits, and an adult study-guide publication called *Prologue*. All TIM programs are free and open to the public. Willis also travels around the state as the "scholar" half of the scholar/actor programs.

Volz's book *Shakespeare Never Slept Here* chronicles ASF's history up to the opening of the new theatre facility in December 1985. Picking up where that book's narrative leaves off, Volz has called the move to Montgomery "a tremendous success story." The site, once surrounded by cow pastures, now boasts nine new hotels and a number of restaurants. The local chamber of commerce and the state's department of tourism and travel "love the festival, because it's turned Montgomery into a major tourist attraction." It was estimated that in 1990, ASF was pumping close to $20 million into the local economy. Volz claims that approximately 1,000 articles about ASF are published each year, some in publications as distant as the London *Financial Times*. He also credits much of ASF's success to:

> the remarkable pride that the community takes in the theatre and what the theatre gives back to the community. Our artists and company members have embraced the community, so it's a mutual relationship. For example, as soon as we moved to Montgomery, there was a volunteer force of 200 people who sought us out and offered to help: they raise funds, cook dinners for actors, put actors up in their homes, open up their lake houses to artists, and throw endless holiday parties. In return, our company members deliver meals on wheels, read for the blind, donate blood, and find many ways to use their artistic skills to give something back to the community.

In 1989, Martin Platt resigned as artistic director. The theatre had grown to a size that was in a sense artistically confining for him, and he took the opportunity to indulge his passion for opera by becoming director of the Birmingham Opera. An international search for Platt's replacement brought in hundreds of applications and led to the hiring of "the best of the bunch." According to Volz, 38-year-old Kent Thompson emerged as an "exciting, vibrant director who could lead the theatre into the future. He combines a solid background of American and English training in Shakespeare with a sensitivity to the South and a strong national reputation." Asked to elaborate upon his "sensitivity to the South," Thompson explained that he was born, raised, and educated in the South before going on to study at the Guild Hall School of Music and Drama in London, and elsewhere.

> I understand a lot of the issues that are going to either provoke or cause problems or be very enlightening to our audience. And I understand the people in the community. But I feel like the ten years away have given me a fresh perspective, so I can see how things are changing. I have a strong desire to discover Southern voices in the theatre. And we are incorporating African-American experiences and black artists, and developing plays based on black writing about the South—like *All God's Dangers*, a one-man play with Cleavon Little. We didn't develop it here, but we worked hard to get it after its Cricket Theatre premiere, because it's based on the story of a black sharecropper who lived 30 miles from here. For that production, we hired a black marketing firm, and we're making an effort to contract with black-owned businesses in town.

Volz estimates that ASF probably has the largest number of African-American subscribers of any Shakespeare festival in America, and he estimates that of the 170,000 annual ticket-buyers, perhaps 24,000 to 26,000 are black audience members. In addition, black children make up about 50 percent of the 30,000 who participate in SchoolFest each year. Despite the difficulty of recruiting classically trained black actors to come to Montgomery, Thompson stands firmly committed to both minority casting and nontraditional casting. "It would be unconscionable to bring those schoolchildren in to see a European classic play without black performers in it," adds Thompson. "Socially, culturally, and politically, nontraditional casting is a necessity, because we live in a multiracial, multicultural society."

The ASF mission statement proposed by Thompson in April 1991 serves as a succinct summation of his continuing commitments and of new directions for the company:

> The Alabama Shakespeare Festival is first and foremost committed to artistic excellence in the production and performance of classics and outstanding contemporary plays, with the works of William Shakespeare forming the core of our repertoire. This is best achieved through a commitment to a company of resident artists. The Festival is also dedicated to creating theatre in repertory style, which we believe to be the most demanding, stimulating and rewarding form of theatre.
>
> The artistic staff of the Alabama Shakespeare Festival is fiercely committed to making these texts directly relevant to a Southern audience. Rather than imposing a sweeping conceptual rule such as traditional Shakespeare or radical updating of text, we will produce our classics in a variety of styles, periods, and concepts, each chosen to illuminate the particular play and stir greater awareness and identification in our audiences. Most importantly, these plays should provide us with a renewed perspective on our lives and the times in which we live.

Without undermining our principal commitment to Shakespeare, we have focused our attention on plays which deal with our own culture and society: American classics, plays by African-American writers, plays by Southern writers. We will also offer annual performances of a Children's Theatre play or musical. We are committed to non-traditional casting, achieving diversity in the hiring of staff personnel, and presenting plays which speak directly to minority audiences.

Finally, we have developed The Southern Writers' Project to identify southern or African-American writers or works which we hope to commission for the stage. This project will provide a voice in professional theatre for the artists of our region.

In 1992, ASF received a $1 million grant from the Lila Wallace-Reader's Digest Fund to expand its efforts to increase cultural diversity at the theatre. The funding primarily targets audience development, but the five-year initiative also provides for adding more African-American artists, board members, staff members, and MFA students.

Actors likely to be hired at ASF are described as "classically trained repertory actors." Of the 35-member resident company, up to 15 are new company members each season. "Of course, everybody likes to come back," says Volz, "but we have an interest in refreshing the company every year, as well as hiring for specialized casting demands." Contracted by the season, actors arrive in October and remain through mid-July. Auditions are held in Chicago, Los Angeles, and New York, and special auditions can be set up at the theatre. For Thompson, however, the key to hiring is seeing an artist's work at other theatres; he travels extensively to visit other professional repertory companies.

The ASF/University of Alabama two-year MFA training program takes a classical approach to conservatory training but recognizes that the actor must be capable of performing in a wide variety of production styles each season. The 15 actors in the MFA program form an ensemble company called The MFA Company, which presents two or three productions each season, including a Shakespeare; those actors may also participate in the mainstage productions as understudies or in the smaller roles.

For the 1990 production of *Measure for Measure*, directed by Gavin Cameron-Webb and designed by Harry Feiner, an imposing gray stone facade with a monumental staircase filled center stage. Carved in the stone above the up-center doorway at the top of two flights of stairs was the motto "JVSTVS DEVS STATVS," signifying this locale's identification with public justice and authority. To either side of the central steps were shabby billboards and neon signs. Among the fanciful modern-dress costumes, the low-life characters were particularly colorful. Isabella, Juliet, and Marianna all appeared to be very sweet and wholesome characters in a corrupt environment. The production abounded with powerful dramatic gestures: Angelo's kneeling to pray on the stairs after Vincentio's transfer of power to him; Isabella's white wimple ripped off to reveal her closely cropped red hair during Angelo's violent attempt to seduce her; Claudio (played by black actor Derrick Lee Weeden) holding the infant born to him and Juliet, cradling it in his arms all during the final moments of the action and the curtain call.

Monica Bell, who played Isabella in *Measure for Measure*, gave another compelling performance as Viola in *Twelfth Night*. The glamour of the lavish Regency-period costuming was enhanced by a setting full of shiny silver, copper, and brass reflective elements. The myriad mirrored surfaces suggested that these characters related primarily to superficial images (of themselves as well as of others). The pranksters who eavesdrop on Malvolio hid behind a standing mirror, which, when turned around, became transparent glass. Philip Pleasants as a black-garbed, spit-curled Malvolio generated some wonderful humor by his hilarious mugging and milking of lines. Another outstanding performance was that of Kent Gash as Feste. Directed by Kent Thompson, *Twelfth Night* elicited from its audience warm laughter, an occasional hoot of recognition at the characters' foibles, and a standing ovation at the final curtain.

Production History: **1972**: *Err., Ham., Hedda Gabler, TGV*; **1973**: *AYL, Mac., Ado, Tartuffe*; **1974**: *MND, Rom., Shr., The School for Scandal, Mandragola*; **1975**: *Fitting for Ladies, R2, Tmp., TN, Ralph Roister Doister*; **1976**: *Lr., Wiv., The Miser, WT*; **1977**: *Ham., The Hollow Crown, The Imaginary Invalid, LLL, Rosencrantz and Guildenstern Are Dead*; **1978**: *Clarence Darrow, A Lover's Complaint, MM, MV, Oth., Private Lives, Shr.*; **1979**: *AYL, Clarence Darrow, Err., The Country Wife, Oh, William!, TN*; **1980**: *Cym., The Importance of Being Earnest, Rom., Tartuffe, TGV*; **1981**: *1H4, MND, Ado, Oh, Coward!, Servant of Two Masters, The Marowitz Hamlet, The Importance of Being Earnest*; **1982**: *Ham., Junebug Jabbo Jones, Red Fox/Second Hangin', Err., TN, Rom.*; **1983**: *AWW, Arms and the Man, Lr., Mass Appeal, Shr., LLL, Err.*;

1984: *Billy Bishop Goes to War, LLL, Mac., Oh, Mr. Faulkner, Do You Write?, She Stoops to Conquer, Arms and the Man*; **1985-86**: *MND, Wiv., R3, Death of a Salesman, Pygmalion, A Flea in Her Ear, The School for Scandal, The Glass Menagerie, The Cherry Orchard, The Imaginary Heir, Betrayal, The Beaux Stratagem, The Changeling*; **1986-87**: *Rough Crossing, Terra Nova, Master Harold...and the Boys, Misalliance, Shr., Tmp., TN, The Royal Family, Oth., Hedda Gabler, Pump Boys and Dinettes, Zelda*; **1987-88**: *Ham., The Sea, Hay Fever, Painting Churches, You Never Can Tell, Long Day's Journey into Night, AYL:, A Bold Stroke for a Wife, Little Shop of Horrors, The Playboy of the Western World, Wild Honey, A Streetcar Named Desire, A Month in the Country*; **1988-89**: *Rom., Candida, Ado, Per., WT, Tit., A Christmas Carol,*

Steel Magnolias, Les Liaisons Dangereuses, Cyrano de Bergerac, On the Verge, The Road to Mecca, The Beggars' Opera; **1989-90**: *All God's Dangers, Cat on a Hot Tin Roof, Noises Off, Major Barbara, The Immigrant, Driving Miss Daisy, Mac., TN, Tartuffe, MM*; **1990-91**: *Season's Greetings, Fences, AWW, I'm Not Rappaport, The Cherry Orchard; JC, TGV, Inherit the Wind, Lend Me a Tenor*; **1991-92**: *The Misanthrope,* *Peter Pan, Miss Evers' Boys, The Little Foxes, Arms and the Man, Lr., Err., R2, Shadowlands, Lend Me a Tenor*; **1992-93**: *Big River, I Hate Hamlet, Our Town, A Raisin in the Sun, Heartbreak House, MND, Blithe Spirit, 1H4, 2H4, Dumas*; **1993-94**: *Peter Pan, Holiday, Grover, Flyin' West, How the Other Half Loves, Tmp., Oth., Light Up the Sky, Dancing at Lughnasa, H5.*

Research Resources: The Alabama Shakespeare Festival has no formal archives, but complete press files and promptbooks are kept in the stage management office.

Filichia, Peter. "Shakespeare Down South." *TheaterWeek* (15-21 June 1992): 11.

Jones, Chris. "Welcome to Alabama." *American Theatre* (October 1992): 70-1.

Kelly, Dennis. "Culture overtakes sports at box office." *USA Today* (12 September 1988): 1.

Loney, Glenn, and Patricia MacKay. *The Shakespeare Complex.* New York: Drama Book Specialists, 1975.

"Montgomery, The Jewel in the Crown." *Horizon* (December 1985): 29-31.

Volz, Jim. *Shakespeare Never Slept Here: The Making of a Regional Theatre; A History of the Alabama Shakespeare Festival.* Atlanta: Cherokee Publishing Co., 1986.

Site visit and interviews: 10-11 July 1990.
Felicia Hardison Londré

DAPHNE RENAISSANCE FESTIVAL. MAIL: P.O. Box 400, Daphne, AL 36526. SITE: May Day Park in Daphne. ADMINISTRATION: 205/621-2823. ADMISSION: $3 adults, $1 children. SEASON: 1 Saturday in April, performances at 9:30 a.m. and 2:00 p.m. PRINCIPAL STAFF: Judy Sims, director. FACILITY: open-air platform stage and benches. ANNUAL ATTENDANCE: 2,000 (1992). FOUNDED: 1992.

Sponsored by the Daphne Recreation Department, the Daphne Renaissance Festival (DRF) is a one-day event that incorporates Shakespeare performances (as well as other plays), musical entertainments, children's activities, and exhibitions of acrogymnastics, archery, and fighting with wooden staffs.

Sections of the park are set aside for the Children's Cove, the Wyldwood Stage, and the Treetop Theatre, the latter being the site for continuous dramatic presentations. At the 1992 festival, Daphne's Puzzled Peasant Players, a youth company under the direction of Judy Sims performed *A Midsummer Night's Dream* from 9:30 to 11:00 a.m. At 2:00 p.m., the Firehouse Theatre from nearby Mobile offered preview scenes from its upcoming production of *Two Gentlemen of Verona*.

The success of the first DRF ensures its continuation as an annual event. But the organizers have resolved to resist the temptation to expand too rapidly, preferring to consider it a local affair. A Renaissance-period production of Shakespeare will certainly remain a centerpiece of DRF, and it is expected that one of the Firehouse Theatre's two annual Shakespeare productions will be hired each year.

Production History: **1992**: *MND*, *TGV*(excerpts).

Information supplied by Carl D. Doehring; telephone interview with Judy Sims, 26 August 1992.
Felicia Hardison Londré

ARIZONA

SOUTHWEST SHAKESPEARE FESTIVAL (formerly **ARIZONA SHAKESPEARE FESTIVAL**). MAIL: P.O. Box 44672, Phoenix, AZ 85064-4672. SITE: Mesa Amphitheater, Mesa; Mountain View High School auditorium, Mesa. ADMINISTRATION: 602/954-0656. BOX OFFICE: Mesa Community and Conference Center, 602/644-2560. ADMISSION: $6–$12 (1992-93). SEASON: 3 shows, 6–9 performances of each. October, February, April. 7:30 p.m., Thurs.–Sat. PRINCIPAL STAFF: Randy Messersmith, artistic director; Kevin Dressler, associate artistic director/marketing director. FACILITY: outdoor amphitheatre with covered stage (capacity 3,800). AUDITIONS: Phoenix metro area in August, November, and February. STATUS: 1–3 Equity Guest Artist contracts, 6–10 interns, apprentices. ANNUAL BUDGET: $100,000 (1992-93). ANNUAL ATTENDANCE: 12,000 (projected, 1992-93). FOUNDED: 1992.

The Arizona Shakespeare Festival (ASF) was founded in January 1992 at the request of several actors who were taking a workshop in Shakespearean acting from Randy Messersmith. A recent arrival in the Phoenix metro area, Messersmith had been a founding member of the **American Globe Theatre** in New York. Asked to create a new festival in Phoenix and to serve as its artistic director, Messersmith agreed, provided that he could enlist the help of his longtime associate, Kevin Dressler. Soon a board of directors was formed, non-profit status was applied for, and a season was planned. The idea became a reality.

The 14 member board is an active, working group. Each member heads or works on a committee, drawing upon a pool of 75 volunteers. Current committees are in the areas of finance, volunteers, development, and marketing. Artistic decisions are made by Messersmith or Dressler. Small stipends are paid on a show-by-show basis to most artistic and technical staff, but all administrative work is coordinated through the board without compensation.

The Mesa Amphitheater was built in 1978 as part of a unified community and conference center in downtown Mesa. Owned by the city, it is adjacent to the Sheraton Mesa Hotel and surrounded by numerous restaurants and shops. The complex, with its southwestern-style adobe band shell over the stage area, was designed by a team of architects influenced by Frank Lloyd Wright. The amphitheatre is sunken into the ground. It has an elevated 60 by 40 foot stage and a terraced hillside with an audience capacity of 3,800. For ASF perform-ances, 500 portable chairs are set up, complete with sections, row letters, and seat numbers. When these are sold out, 300 lawn chairs are also available for use. Numerous light trees are located on the outside perimeter of the amphitheatre grounds. The April and September productions are performed here, with a 7:30 p.m. curtain in compliance with a city ordinance restricting outdoor amplified sound in the later evening. The January production is presented in the auditorium of Mountain View High School at the corner of Lindsay and Brown roads (2700 East Brown) in Mesa.

Mesa is a bedroom community of 300,000; many of its residents are em-ployed in Phoenix, Tempe, and Scottsdale. One of the fastest-growing communities in the United States, Mesa nearly doubled in population in the 1980s. Median household income is $34,500, and the average home costs $85,000. The city is recognized as having one of the best public school systems in the country, a thriving community college, an active parks and recreation program, and spring-training facilities for the Chicago Cubs; nonetheless, there is no permanent professional theatre company. ASF thus clearly fills a need in its community.

In its first year of operation, ASF adopted two simple marketing strategies. First, ASF Founding Memberships guarantee permanent recognition in ASF programs for a donation of $100 or more; there are over 100 founding members. The second strategy has been to build a solid subscriber base, primarily through subscription parties. Each board member hosted a party at which some short scenes or monologues were performed; Messersmith or Dressler spoke about their dreams for ASF, and then memberships were sold. Over 1,000 subscribers were signed up at about twenty-five parties. Although the parties were labor-intensive in terms of volunteer hours, the number of sales made them cost effective.

The ASF is currently working with city officials, Fighting for the Arts in Mesa (FAME), and the Mesa Downtown Tomorrow Committee for the creation of a permanent performing arts facility that could be designed with ASF's needs in mind. It is hoped that ASF will grow into a facility that can house both indoor and outdoor productions. The biggest challenge facing ASF is to convince the population of Mesa that high-quality, visible arts will benefit the city economically.

The ASF plans to produce three relatively traditional Shakespearean productions annually for its first two years of operation. The company is dedicated to "wordsmithing," the notion that a playwright crafts and works with words in much the same manner as other craftspeople mold and form their respective media. Eventually, other playwrights deemed to be "wordsmiths" will be added to the repertoire.

A *Phoenix Gazette* review by Kyle Lawson (30 September 1992) found ASF's first production, *The Taming of the Shrew*, "much better theater than expected." He noted that Messersmith "presents Shakespeare fairly and cleanly, without trendy gimmicks to confuse the issue. Audiences leave this Shrew with the feeling they've understood it all, no small accomplishment with a 400-year-old script."

Production History: **1992-93**: *Shr., Mac., Tmp.*; **1993-94**: *Wiv., Rom., WT.*

Research Resources: Archives are informally maintained at the Arizona Shakespeare Festival administrative office.

Kevin L. Dressler

ARIZONA SHAKESPEARE FESTIVAL. See **SOUTHWEST SHAKE-SPEARE FESTIVAL.**

CALIFORNIA

ACTER (A Center for Theatre, Education and Research). MAIL: ACTER, 2723 South Hall, University of California, Santa Barbara, 93106. ADMINI-STRATION: 805/893-2457, 893-2911. PRINCIPAL STAFF: Homer Swander, director; Teresa Ragsdale, general manager; associate directors, Tony Church, Sam Dale, Lisa Harrow, Vivien Heilbron, Elizabeth Huddle, Bernard Lloyd,

David Rintoul, and Patrick Stewart. ANNUAL BUDGET: $295,660 (1989-90). FOUNDED: 1967, Homer Swander.

ACTER is a unique Shakespearean producing, educational, and research organization. It was founded in 1967 by Homer Swander, a Shakespearean scholar at the University of California–Santa Barbara (UCSB) to organize annual study tours for students and teachers to attend plays presented by the **Royal Shakespeare Company** (RSC) in Stratford-upon-Avon and London. After almost a decade of successful study tours, Swander began to explore the feasibility of touring a small group of RSC actors to American college and school classrooms to share their knowledge and experience of Shakespeare with students and teachers. His expressed aim was "to take Shakespeare away from the literary people" and return him to the arena of the stage. Swander hoped that, by introducing professional Shakespearean actors of the highest calibre into the classroom, he could focus attention on Shakespeare as a writer of "scripts" intended for performance, rather than, as was too often supposed, "dramatic narratives" to be read or studied. Indeed, through various ACTER programs Swander aimed specifically at undermining traditional literary approaches to Shakespeare's plays. He articulated the mission of ACTER as follows:

1. An *alliance* of American and British academics (teachers, scholars, critics) and theatre professionals (actors, directors, playwrights); and—on an institutional level—of colleges, research universities, and theatres in the United States and England.

2. A *theatrical* activity that hires, prepares, directs, and tours distinguished professional actors from England and America who perform all over the United States and in several other countries—for example, Spain, Turkey, Egypt, Malaysia, the Philippines.

3. An *educational* activity with the goal of radically improving the teaching of Shakespeare and other drama in classrooms on all instructional levels throughout the English-speaking world.

4. A *research* activity with a core group of four "research associates" (three Shakespearean scholars and one director) who meet frequently to stimulate, evaluate, and develop research projects at the forefront of advances in the theory, practice, and teaching of drama.

In 1975, ACTER initiated the first of an annual series of tours of "Actors From the RSC," as the program was called. A small company of five actors was booked into a number of colleges and universities to present an "anthology program" of scenes from Shakespeare and to offer classroom demonstrations, workshops, and lecture-recitals. In 1983, the "anthology program" was replaced by a full-length presentation of Shakespeare's *Merchant of Venice*, still utilizing, however, only five actors, no scenery, few properties, and but a suggestion of costuming. It was an unusual academic-theatrical approach, but it proved sufficiently successful to set a pattern for all the subsequent ACTER tours.

The ACTER performances are not for every Shakespearean playgoer or taste. As Alan C. Dessen has observed, "not all members of an audience are engaged by the doubling and tripling of roles necessitated by this out-minimalized Shakespeare" (1989). Moreover, "given minimal or no costumes and properties, these shows have obvious limitations, particularly for the playgoer who would rather look than listen." He noted one playgoer's comment: "This is definitely *not* entry-level Shakespeare" (1991). June Schlueter and James P. Lusardi also have complained that "the presence of only five actors to do the play-within-the-play scene [in *Hamlet*] proved a distinct loss, for an audience could not simultaneously see the play-within and the onstage audience's reaction to it" (1988).

But, for many academic playgoers, the ACTER performance style has had distinct rewards. In a 1992 overview of 14 different ACTER productions he had seen to date, Dessen observed that "to watch five-actor Shakespeare is to confront striking and unmistakable evidence for the pivotal role of the audience in helping to create theatrical effects and meanings." He found, for example, the storm scene in the 1987 rendition of *The Tempest*

> unusually effective, for the sounds and movement were generated by the ensemble huddled together, with the speakers emerging to deliver their lines but otherwise remaining part of the swaying, wind-driven, sound-producing group. From the opening line of the play, the playgoer was, therefore, being asked . . . to aid in "creating" a sense of a storm and a ship in distress.

Dessen has cited similar moments in other ACTER productions that rely almost solely on the inventiveness of the performers and the imaginative participation of the playgoer.

It should be noted, however, that ACTER five-actor productions have varied widely in their minimalist approach to realizing the script. Some groups have left everything to the playgoer's imagination: no properties, costumes, or weapons whatsoever. Other groups have opted for fairly elaborate costumes or costume pieces and properties. The performance space also can contribute significantly to the experience or reception of ACTER performances: the five-actor format does seem to work better in small, intimate spaces than in large auditoriums. The format is not equally effective for every script. Dessen (1992), for example, has expressed reservations about five-actor tragedies. By contrast, where "magic" or "wonder-amazement-admiration" is strongly evoked—for example, in *A Midsummer Night's Dream* or *The Tempest*—he has found the minimalist five-actor approach to be an asset, "a way of realizing a dimension of the play easily blurred or buried in more sumptuous productions." After viewing several productions Cary M. Mazer (1990) found that the ACTER groups had "perfected a simple, highly conventionized and extraordinarily effective means" of presentation.

Moreover, despite whatever reservations critics and scholars may have about the five-actor format, audiences—comprised mostly of college students at an "entry level" in their experience of Shakespeare on stage—have been very receptive. By 1993, ACTER five-actor tours had played at well over 100 American universities, colleges, schools, Shakespeare festivals, and other cultural institutions. Many of these sponsoring groups, in fact, have invited an ACTER tour back as often as five times.

During the first few years, ACTER tours operated as the official educational and scholarly agent for the RSC in the United States. In 1985, however, ACTER tours became entirely independent, utilizing actors affiliated not only with the RSC, but nonaffiliated British performers as well. The touring program was renamed "Actors from the London Stage" (ALS). It has continued to operate essentially as one of the research units of UCSB..

In 1993-94, the fee for an ACTER ALS one-week residency, including three performances, two to three lecture-recitals, and five days of workshops and discussions was $16,750. (This fee remained unchanged since 1990.) Typically, workshops and discussions aim to incorporate the actors into various academic courses and might include sessions on "Reading Verse," "Characterization" using one of the texts being performed, or "Movement and the Actor" or a session in which the actors describe their own experiences working in various productions. (See Millard et al. for a detailed description of residencies at LaSalle University and at the University of Pennsylvania in 1983 and 1984 respectively.) This fee covers actor's salaries, rehearsal pay, and ACTER's administrative costs both in the United States and the United Kingdom as producer of the tours. As producer, ACTER, through the collaboration of the director, the associate directors, and the general manager, hires actors, organizes and supervises rehearsals in London, designs special workshops and programs for the tours, arranges all travel, living accommodations, and educational and performance schedules, formulates the educational philosophy, and supervises the instructional practices that define the tours.

In 1993-94, actors were paid about $1,350 a week while on tour and $625 a week during the four week rehearsal period. Administrative costs include transportation from the United Kingdom to the United States and return, transportation costs while on tour, office, printing, and mailing expenses, and salaries and employee benefit costs. The general manager's salary was paid by UCSB for a number of years, but, in 1990-91, ACTER absorbed this cost. UCSB does provide office space to ACTER without charge, however. Salaries for a half-time secretary, four student assistants, and two to six student fellowships for study in London also are included in ACTER administrative costs. Director Swander has never taken any salary for his ACTER involvement. In 1989-90 the total ACTER operating budget was $295,660 for two tours, one from mid-September to mid-November and another from mid-

January to mid-March, each tour visiting up to eight or nine different host institutions. Of this total operating budget about $85,000 was allocated for administrative costs while the remainder went mostly for actor salaries.

The residency fee does not include local promotion and advertising costs for the event, technical expenses, and local transportation costs. Thus, the total cost to a host institution for a ALS residency can exceed $20,000. Usually a portion of these costs can be offset with income from the three performances, but normally the host institution subsidizes from one-third to one-half the total residency costs. Through 1990, the ALS tours have paid for themselves, so that additional fund-raising efforts to cover a potential operating budget deficit or even to increase the residency fee charges have been unnecessary; still, ACTER has organized some fund-raising projects and has received contributions for student scholarships.

Although the ALS tours are its most visible program, ACTER also has organized a number of Shakespearean research conferences, workshops, and lecture programs, including educational activities for the **Oregon Shakespeare Festival** and the Mark Taper Forum in Los Angeles. In 1990, its "research associates" were noted Shakespearean scholars Alan Dessen, Phyllis Gorfain, and Steven Urkowitz and Shakespearean director and cofounder of the **Shakespeare Santa Cruz Festival**, Audrey Stanley. ACTER also continues to sponsor an annual "Theatre in England" study tour. In 1987, ACTER initiated the first of an annual series of tours and workshops in England for British students.

How influential ACTER has been in changing the academic approach to studying and understanding Shakespeare's plays is difficult to determine, although an increasing number of American scholars have embraced a performance-oriented methodology in recent years (See Paul). ACTER, however, has provided opportunities for thousands of American students and mature playgoers to experience high-quality, insightful performances of Shakespeare's plays, and, in so doing, it undoubtedly has contributed significantly to the popularity of staged Shakespeare in America.

Production History: Spring 1975/May-June: *He That Plays The King, Shall I Compare Thee?* **Actors**: Tony Church, Susan Fleetwood, Mike Gwilym, Ian Richardson, Robin Weatherall. **Institutions**: UCSB, UC-Davis, UC-Berkeley.

Winter 1976/January-February: *He That Plays The King, Shall I Compare Thee? Actors at Work: Scenes in the Making, Groupings/Gropings, The Hollow Crown.* **Actors**: Church, Lisa Harrow, Charles Keating, Bernard Lloyd, Patrick Stewart. **Institutions**: UCLA, Alan Hancock College, UCSB, UC-Santa Cruz, Santa Barbara City College, University of Hawaii.

Winter **1977**/January-February: *Lovers and Madmen: A Shakespearean Frenzy, Groupings/Gropings, Wooing, Wedding and Repenting: Shakespeare and Marriage.* **Actors**: Shelia Allen, Juliet Aykroyd, Ben Kingsley, Richard Pasco, Stewart. **Institutions**: UC-Irvine, UC-Riverside, College of Santa Fe, UCSB, UCLA, Simon Fraser University, California State University-Long Beach, Shakespeare Festival of Dallas.

Fall **1977**/October-November: *He That Plays The King, Groupings/Gropings, Love, Love, Nothing But Love.* **Actors**: Bill Homewood, Estelle Kohler, Lloyd, Sebastian Shaw, David Suchet. **Institutions**: Rockhurst College, William Jewell College, Drake University, Northwestern University, University of Illinois, University of Iowa.

Winter **1978**/January-February: *This Great Stage of Fools, The Green-Eyed Monster: Scenes from Shakespeare, Pleasure and Repentance: A Light-Hearted Look at Love.* **Actors**: Aykroyd, Church, Terrence Hardiman, Homewood, John Kane, Barbara Leigh-Hunt. **Institutions**: California State University-Northridge, UCSB, College of Santa Fe, Shakespeare Festival of Dallas, University of Houston, UC-Irvine, Santa Barbara City College.

Fall **1978**/October-November: *Lovers and Madmen, Sigh No More Ladies: An Anthology of Shakespeare's Lovers, Groupings '78, Actors at Work: Working Not Conjuring.* **Actors**: Allen, Kane, Keating, Kingsley, Shaw. **Institutions**: Southern Oregon State College, Santa Barbara City College, Brandeis University, Vanderbilt University, Oberlin College, University of North Carolina-Chapel Hill.

Winter **1979**/January-March: *Actors at Work: On Shakespeare's The Tempest, Play the Villain: A Rogue's Gallery of Portraits, The Bird in the Gilded Cage: An Ironic Look at the Victorian Age.* **Actors**: Harrow, Richard Johnson, Keating, Lloyd. **Institutions**: College of Santa Fe, UCSB, UCLA, California State Universities at Long Beach, Fresno, and Northridge.

Fall **1979**/October-November: *Shakespeare Lady: Fanny Kemble, Passionate Victorian, Merry England, Song of Songs, Who's Afraid of the Sonnets.* **Actors**: Aykroyd, Homewood, Barry Ingham, Kohler, Paul Shelley, Stewart. **Institutions**: Middlebury College, University of Oklahoma, University of Dallas, Shakespeare Festival of Dallas, University of Texas, University of Oregon, University of Santa Clara.

Winter **1980**/January-March: *Shakespeare and the Actors: Signals Through the Flames, Murder Most Foul, Ariel: Shakespeare's Sweet Power of Music.* **Actors**: Martin Best, Ann Firbank, John Nettles, Richardson, Shaw. **Institu-**

tions: California State University-Humboldt, William Jewell College, UCSB, University of Delaware, Folger Shakespeare Library, Kennedy Center, Library of Congress.

Fall **1980**/September-November: *The Tarnished Phoenix, Shakespeare and the Actors: Brief Chronicles of Our Time, The Measure of Our Days: Shakespeare's Great Stage*. **Actors**: Firbank, Geoffrey Hutchings, Nettles, Shaw. **Institutions**: University of Puget Sound, UCLA, UC-Santa Cruz, Cuesta College, University of Maryland, Brandeis University, University of Southern Maine.

Winter **1981**/January-March: *Under Milkwood, Shakespeare and the Actors: Brief Chronicles of Our Time, Wise Enough to Play the Fool*. **Actors**: Jeffrey Dence, Geoffrey Hutchings, Lloyd, Cherie Lunghi. **Institutions**: Oberlin College, Furman University, University of Houston, Old Dominion University, Northwestern University.

Fall **1981**/October-November: *Under Milkwood, Troubador's World, Borrowed Robes and Seeming Truths*. **Actors**: Best, Megan Cole, Brian Cox, Fleetwood, James Laurenson. **Institutions**: UCSB, UCLA, California State Universities at Long Beach and Dominguez Hills, California State Polytechnic University-Pomona, U.S. International University (San Diego), Pasadena City College, Pepperdine University.

Winter **1982**/January-March: *Under Milkwood, Shakespeare Lady: Fanny Kemble, Love, Love, Love, Nothing But Love*. **Actors**: Nicholas Grace, Homewood, Kohler, Edwin Richfield, Susan Tracy. **Institutions**: Pennsylvania State University, University of Pennsylvania, University of Rochester, University of Nebraska, University of Florida, Goucher College.

Fall **1982**/September-November: *The Hollow Crown, Pleasure and Repentance, The Loving Voyage: Shakespeare and Marriage*. **Actors**: Allen, Best, Domini Blythe, Keating, Paul Whitworth. **Institutions**: Oberlin College, University of Arizona, University of Maryland. (A separate residency was held this Fall at Scottsdale Center for the Arts.)

Winter **1983**/January-March: *The Hollow Crown, The Loving Voyage, Behind Our Scenes*. **Actors**: Best, Blythe, Julian Curry, Firbank, Whitworth. **Institutions**: Drake University, California State College-Bakersfield, California Institute for the Arts, University of Wyoming, University of Texas, William Jewell College, UCLA.

Fall **1983**/September-November: *MV*, *Under Milkwood*. **Actors**: Heather Canning, Kane, Christopher Ravenscroft, Richfield, Jennie Stoller. **Institutions**: California State University-Fresno, Lafayette College, LaSalle College, Riverside Shakespeare Company, NYC, Pennsylvania State University, University of Maine, Indiana University, University of Arizona.

Winter **1984**/January-March: *TN*, *Pinter This Evening*. **Actors**: Trevor Baxter, Blythe, Patrick Godfrey, David Gwillim, Louise Jameson. **Institutions**: Lawrence University, University of North Carolina-Chapel Hill, University of Pennsylvania, Rice University, UCSB, California State University-Long Beach, Scottsdale Center for the Arts.

Fall **1984**/September-November.: *TN*, *Pinter This Evening*. **Actors**: Marjorie Bland, Canning, Homewood, Stephen Jenn, Richfield. **Institutions**: Oberlin College (2 weeks), Wake Forest University, University of Tennessee-Knoxville, Navarro College, the Greenwich (Connecticut) High School District, Northern Illinois University, Florida Atlantic University.

Winter **1985**/January-March: *AYL*, *Beckett This Evening*. **Actors**: Lynsey Baxter, Alan David, Godfrey, Gerard Murphy, Stoller. **Institutions**: Vanderbilt University, Rice University, Montclair State College, Lawrence University, Occidental College, California State University-Fullerton, University of North Carolina, Furman University.

Fall **1985**/September-November: *Lr.*, *Pinter This Evening*. **Actors**: Allen, John Burgess, Julian Glover, Pippa Guard, David Rintoul. **Institutions**: Lafayette College, Annenberg Center, University of Pennsylvania, Pennsylvania State University, University of Arizona, Mount St. Mary's College.

Winter **1986**/January-March: *MM*, *Beckett This Evening*. **Actors**: Curry, Harrow, Jenn, Joe Marcell, Whitworth. **Institutions**: UC-Davis, Indiana University, UCLA, Texas A & M University, UCSB, Mills College, University of South Carolina.

Fall **1986**/September-November: *Ham.*, *An Evening With Noel Coward*. **Actors**: Burgess, Vivien Heilbron, Rintoul, Michael Thomas, Philip Voss. **Institutions**: University of New Hampshire, Memphis State University, Goucher College, University of Southern Maine, Lawrence University, LaSalle University, Rice University, Brandeis University.

Winter **1987**/January-March: *Tmp.*, *Pinter This Evening*. **Actors**: Bruce Alexander, Trevor Baxter, Sarah Berger, Tom Manion, George Raistrick. **Institutions**: Kansas State University, Susquehanna University, Occidental

College, University of North Carolina-Chapel Hill, Georgia Southern College, Texas A & M University, California State University-Los Angeles, Furman University.

Fall 1987/September-November: *TN, George Bernard Shaw This Evening*. **Actors**: Sam Dale, Heilbron, Clifford Rose, Richard Simpson, Julia Watson. **Institutions**: University of New Hampshire, Pennsylvania State University, University of Puget Sound, Clark University, University of Maryland, College of Charleston, Indiana University, Mount St. Mary's College, San Francisco State University.

Winter 1988/January-March: *MND, Throwing Stones at Shakespeare (Hosted by George Bernard Shaw)*. **Actors**: Selina Cadell, Elizabeth Estensen, Allan Hendrick, Phillip Joseph, Thomas. **Institutions**: UC-Davis, Millikin University, Dartmouth College, Lafayette College, LaSalle University, Stanford University, UCSB, Rice University.

Fall 1988/September-November: *Ado, Under Milkwood*. **Actors**: Blythe, Richard Cordery, Allan Hendrick, Paul Moriarty, Dudley Sutton. **Institutions**: University of New Hampshire, University of Southern Maine, University of Maryland, Goucher College, College of Charleston, Pennsylvania State University, Lawrence University, University of Texas-San Antonio.

Winter 1989/January-March: *Lr., Stoppard This Evening*. **Actors**: Geoffrey Church, Heilbron, Lloyd, Patti Love, Rose. **Institutions**: Stephens College, Memphis State University, California State University-Fresno, Rice University, Texas A & M University, Portland State University, California Polytechnic University-Pomona, University of Tennessee-Knoxville, University of Nebraska.

Fall 1989/September-November: *WT, Stoppard This Evening*. **Actors**: Dale, Firbank, Tim Hardy, Eunice Roberts, Richard Simpson. **Institutions**: University of New Hampshire, Southwest Texas State University, University of Puget Sound, Clark University, UCSB, Michigan Technical University, Santa Monica College, Occidental College, Annenberg Center, University of Pennsylvania.

Winter 1990/January-March: *WT, Pinter This Evening*. **Actors**: Henry Goodman, Richard Johnson, Gemma Jones, Shelley, Auriol Smith. **Institutions**: University of Wyoming, Texas A & M University, Stanford University, College of Charleston, Portland State University, University of Texas-San Antonio, Rice University, California State University-Fullerton.

Fall **1990**/September-November: *AYL, Sons & Daughters of Cathleen ni Houlihan*. **Actors**: Geoffrey Church, Miranda Foster, David Howey, Jenn, Alison Skilbeck. **Institutions**: University of Richmond, Stetson University, Texas Woman's University, Memphis State University, Florida Atlantic University, Kansas State University, University of Notre Dame.

Winter **1991**/January-March: *AYL, Sons & Daughters of Cathleen ni Houlihan*. **Actors**: Clive Arundell, Jane Arden, Kane, Rose, Celia Bannerman. **Institutions**: Millikin University, UC-Santa Cruz, Central Oregon College, Lafayette College, Pacific University, University of Texas-San Antonio, Michigan Technical University.

Fall **1991**/October-November: *MND, Under Milkwood*. **Actors**: Bruce Alexander, Geoffrey Beevers, Dale, Joanna Foster, Eunice Roberts. **Institutions**: Santa Monica College, Occidental College, University of North Carolina, Chapel Hill, Brandeis University, Lafayette College, University of Pennsylvania.

Winter **1992**/January-March: *Ado, The Tarnished Phoenix*. **Actors**: Trevor Baxter, Meg Davies, John Dougall, Lloyd, George Raistrick. **Institutions**: Middlebury College, Stanford University, Denver Center Theatre, UC-Santa Barbara, University of Texas, San Antonio, Berea College, Rice University, Clemson University, Furman University.

Fall **1992**/September-November: *Tmp*. **Actors**: Stephen Jenn, Katherine Schlesinger, Peter Grayer, Dougall, Clive Arundell. **Institutions**: University of New Hampshire, Michigan Tech University, Memphis State University, Southwest Texas State University, Lawrence University, University of North Carolina-Chapel Hill, University of the Ozarks, DePauw University, University of Pennsylvania, Edison College.

Winter **1993**/January-March: *Tmp*. **Actors**: Arden, Beevers, Stephen Rashbrook, John Fraser, Gareth Armstrong. **Institutions**: University of Wyoming, Hillsdale College, Clemson University, Stephen F. Austin University, University of Wisconsin-Madison, Northeastern University, University of Texas-San Antonio, Denver Theatre Center, Santa Monica College.

Fall **1993**/September-November: *Ham*. **Actors**: Dale, Jonathan Donne, Miranda Foster, Howey, William Russell. **Institutions**: Lafayette College, Juniata College, University of Delaware, University of Richmond, Rice University, University of Notre Dame, University of Pennsylvania, Berea College.

Winter **1994**/January-March: *TN*. **Actors**: Cordery, Geoffrey Church, Eunice Roberts, Hugh Sullivan, Suzan Sylvester. **Institutions**: UC-Santa Barbara, El Camino College, Rutgers University, University of North Carolina-Chapel Hill, University of Toledo, Clemson University, University of Texas-San Antonio, Southwest Texas State, Whittier College.

Research Resources: Archival materials are informally maintained at the ACTER offices. See also the following selected publications.

Deese, Helen. "*Twelfth Night.*" *Shakespeare Bulletin* (March/April 1988): 18-19.

Dessen, Alan C. "Exciting Shakespeare in 1988." *Shakespeare Quarterly* (Summer 1989): 198-207.

————. "Adjusting Shakespeare in 1989." *Shakespeare Quarterly* (Fall 1990): 352-65.

————. "Resources and Images: Shakespeare in 1990." *Shakespeare Quarterly* (Summer 1991): 214-24.

————. "Wonder and 'Magic' in the ACTER Five-Actor Comedies." *Shakespeare Bulletin* (Winter 1992): 7-9.

Mazer, Cary M. "*The Winter's Tale.*" *Shakespeare Bulletin* (Winter 1990): 27.

————. "*As You Like It.*" *Shakespeare Bulletin* (Summer 1991): 22-23.

Millard, Barbara, Georgiana Ziegler, and Geraldine Custer. "'Playing Out the Play': Actors, Teachers, and Students in the Classroom." *Shakespeare Quarterly* 35 (Special Issue 1984): 609-15.

Richard, Jeremy. "ACTER at Greenwich." *Shakespeare Bulletin*. (March/April 1985): 7.

Schlueter, June, and James P. Lusardi. "*As You Like It.*" *Shakespeare Bulletin* (March/April 1985): 18-19.

————. "*The Tempest.*" *Shakespeare Bulletin* (May/June 1987): 18.

Interview at ACTER Office, 15 June 1990.
Daniel J. Watermeier.

CALIFORNIA SHAKESPEARE FESTIVAL (formerly Berkeley Shakespeare Festival). MAIL: 2531 Ninth Street, Berkeley, CA 94710. SITE: The Lt. G. H. Bruns III Memorial Amphitheater–Siesta Valley near Orinda. ADMINISTRATION: 2531 Ninth Street, Berkeley, CA 94710, 510/548-3422. BOX OFFICE: 510/548-9666. ADMISSION: $10–$25 (1991). SEASON: approximately 90 performances, rotating repertory, from mid-June through early October. 8:00 p.m., Wed.–Sat., 11:00 a.m., 4:00 p.m., Sun. PRINCIPAL STAFF: Michael Addison, artistic director; Marcia O'Dea, managing director. FACILITY: outdoor, open stage (capacity 550). AUDITIONS: Local Bay Area and other West Coast cities in February/March. STATUS: LORT D (EMC). ANNUAL BUDGET: $1.6 million (1994). ANNUAL ATTENDANCE: 40,250 (1991). FOUNDED: 1973 by Mikel Clifford, Myron Schreck, Robert Eldred Schneider and others.

The California Shakespeare Festival (CSF) was founded in 1973 when a group of Bay Area actors who called themselves the Emeryville Shakespeare Company offered a summer season of *Hamlet, As You Like It,* and August Strindberg's *The Father.* The plays were staged in an outdoor amphitheatre—actually little more than a natural hollow ringed with trees at the bottom of which was a laid asphalt circle—in Berkeley's John Hinkel Park. Costumes, scenery, and properties were minimal, fairly "rag-tag," and designed and constructed by the actors themselves. About this company Stephen Booth (1976) wrote that, while they "could probably be classed as semi-pro, they are amateurs in the purest sense. They ask a two dollar donation, but only from those members of the audience who find it perfectly convenient to donate: this company literally gives its plays." Presumably the Emeryville players were sufficiently encouraged, however, to offer a second season of four Shakespearean and one non-Shakespearean production (Michel de Ghelderode's *Pantagleize*—41 performances in all, over an 11-week period from mid-June to early October. After their second season, the group voted to incorporate as a membership organization called the Berkeley Shakespeare Festival, to be managed in monthly meetings of the entire company. It continued to be managed in this manner through the fifth season (1978).

In 1975, CSF expanded to 80 performances over a 16-week period. John Hinkel Park, however, is a relatively small park with extremely limited parking surrounded by a middle-class residential neighborhood. Complaints from the neighbors about the crowds and the cars persuaded the Berkeley City Council to limit subsequent seasons to 12 weeks (65 performances). Performances also were required to end not later than 10:00 p.m.

Despite these limitations, CSF continued to develop. By 1977, its income was large enough to pay several actors. Receipt of a federal CETA grant also allowed the hiring of a full-time administrator. At the end of the 1978 season, the company voted to elect a board of directors composed of theatre professionals and community leaders. They also appointed one of their own members to serve as artistic coordinator on an annual basis and signed an Equity "guest artist" contract.

The overall artistic quality of CSF productions also improved steadily. Stephen Booth (1978) commented, for example, that the festival "continued its fast, steady progress from the benign local embarrassment it was four years ago toward a position as an established mid-coast peer" of San Diego's **Old Globe** and the **Oregon Shakespeare Festival**. Although "not yet at parity" with these older West Coast festivals, "at its present rate it should get there soon." He complained that both *Romeo and Juliet* and *Richard III* were completely presented but dull, but he praised the *Much Ado About Nothing* as "gracious" and "lively" and the *Measure for Measure* as "tight, authoritative...and always entertaining, sometimes moving, and always moving forward purposefully." In 1979, Jacobs waxed enthusiastic about *Pericles,* which used only nine actors: "I loved this production." So did an audience that "included children, stray old couples,...and groups of young people who, before the play started, insisted loudly...to one another that they had neither liked nor understood any of their high school or college Shakespeare. Everyone in the audience followed the story, knew who was who, laughed and cried in the right places, and seemed as generally delighted as I was." Indeed, *Pericles* won an Outstanding Production Award from the Bay Area Drama Critics Circle. Jacobs noted that, in 1980, the group's "tickets were the hot item in the San Francisco theatre scene. People without tickets came anyway—to wait in line for cancellations. Festival audiences are generous; they squeezed together and made room; part of the audience even sat in the trees around the amphitheatre." Artistically this was a strong season, with Richard E. T. White's production of *Merry Wives of Windsor*—"a tableau of Elizabethan town life," according to Jacobs (1981)—winning a second Outstanding Production Award for the festival.

Bolstered by this success, in 1981, the festival increased its Equity guest artists to three and mounted a visually spectacular post-modern production of *Cymbeline* staged by former **Royal Shakespeare Company** director Patrick Tucker. The season ended with a Christmastime production of *Twelfth Night,* staged indoors at the Great Hall of the Veterans Memorial Building in a style to suggest the Christmas revels in an Elizabethan hall. A Festival Institute also was founded in 1981 to develop a range of educational activities, including outreach programs for children, courses for theatre professionals, lectures on Shakespeare and the Elizabethan Age, and workshops on directing, acting, design, and technical theatre for high school students. In 1987, the Institute was renamed the Conservatory. In 1994, Dick Butterfield, formerly the Conservatory Dean of San Francisco's American Conservatory Theatre (ACT) was appointed CSF director of educational programs with responsibility for managing a wide range of educational and out-reach programs, including CSF's *Shakespeare Fantasy Camp,* a weekend-long training and performance program for Shakespeare buffs and amateur actors, and a very successful *Summer with Shakespeare* teen program.

In 1983, Dakin Matthews was hired as the first full-time artistic director, and the season was expanded to six productions including an experimental production of *Ivanhoe,* adapted by the company from Sir Walter Scott's novel. But this rapid expansion may have been too ambitious: "too much, too soon." At the end of the season the festival was left with an undisclosed but sizable debt. To eliminate this debt and reduce future financial risks, the board of directors mandated stricter budgeting practices and initiated a series of marketing strategies to increase ticket sales. The size of the board also was increased, contributions were more aggressively solicited, and the season was cut back to three productions.

In 1984, the Equity company was increased to seven actors and a stage manager and an Equity apprentice program was introduced. With increased ticket sales and contributions, both the 1984 and 1985 seasons were financially successful. Brooks called the CSF "one of the finest Shakespeare Festivals around." Indeed, the 1985 season was virtually sold out. The award of a grant from the California Arts Council to support a statewide tour of *Macbeth* also contributed to CSF's fiscal recovery.

Early in the 1986 season, a ceremony was held on stage to retire the festival's debt publicly. This season also proved to be a financial success with sold-out performances and a second well-received tour of *The Tempest*. (CSF has continued to tour one of its productions throughout California each year in late October.) The festival expanded to full LORT-D status with 11 Equity contracts, and the board of directors began to lay plans for acquiring a new, larger performing site, since clearly the festival had outgrown the 350-seat capacity of the Hinkel Park amphitheatre.

In 1987, Michael Addison replaced Matthews as artistic director. In his first season, Addison once again expanded to four productions, daringly mounting the first tetralogy of Shakespeare's history plays from *Richard II* through *Henry V*; the latter was presented indoors in late September and early October in Berkeley's Julia Morgan Theatre (capacity, 380). This pattern of presenting a fourth production at the Morgan Theatre continued through the 1990 season. Addison's initiative paid off both artistically and financially, and, under his leadership, CSF has continued to develop. Artistic standards have remained high, management has become fully professional, and seasons have been virtually sold out. In 1991, CSF employed a full-time staff of seven, which more than doubles during the season. The professional company of 16 to 18 actors is supported by nationally recognized directors, designers, and a complement of technicians, composers, stage combat specialists, choreographers, voice consultants, and eight to ten acting apprentices. About 75 percent of the over $1.2 million annual budget is generated from ticket sales, with the remainder raised from private and government sources. The number of season subscribers has steadily increased to over 5,600 in 1991.

In 1987, a capital campaign was launched to raise $2.9 million for a new theatre in a new location. After examining numerous possible locations in the Bay Area, a site was selected in Siesta Valley in Contra Costa County near Orinda, immediately on the east side of the Caldecott Tunnel on Highway 24. The site was one of the original land holdings of the East Bay Municipal Utility District, had never had any commercial or residential development, and had been preserved as a watershed area with minimal grazing use. The Utility District agreed to lease the land for 50 years to CSF and to open it to the public for performances, but at all other times, the land would remain restricted private property, thus preserving its virtually unspoiled quality. This site, moreover, was convenient to a freeway exit and there could be ample parking. A BART (Bay Area Rapid Transit) station was located in nearby Orinda, only a short distance from the site. It also was outside the Bay fog zone, with an average temperature 10° warmer than Hinkel Park. In every respect, it was an ideal location.

Gene Angell, who had designed the Berkeley Repertory Theatre and the Eureka Theatre, was commissioned to design a new theatre, and, in 1991, the renamed California Shakespeare Festival moved into its new home. Angell's outdoor amphitheatre is simple and functional. Its open circular configuration sweeping around a thrust stage suggests the intimate actor/audience relationship of an Elizabethan public theatre. Indeed, no seat is more than 75 feet from the front of the stage. Elements of the design also hint at Elizabethan half-timbering, but in materials, theatrical technology, and production capability, it is a completely modern theatre.

A unique feature of the design is the "Shakespeare Wall." Patrons were offered the opportunity to purchase a colorful hand-painted tile on which would be inscribed their name, their choice of a Shakespeare quotation, and the name of the play or the sonnet number; prices ranged from $250 to $5,000. These tiles mounted on the interior walls of the amphitheatre reinforce the sense of a genuinely "community theatre." During my 1991 visit, I observed numerous patrons reading the tiles before the performance or at intermission, searching for their tile, that of a friend's, or their own favorite quotations.

The amphitheatre is approached along a path that winds up a hill from the parking lot through a grove of eucalyptus and California live oak. Patrons who cannot walk up the hill are bused to the top. BART users also are bused at no charge from and back to the Orinda station. At the top of the hill is a "picnic meadow." The food kiosks sell not only light refreshments but also "gourmet boxed meals" and a variety of California wines, local beers, and bottled waters. A fair number of patrons take advantage of this informal, festive atmosphere and the otherwise inaccessible beauty of Siesta Valley's rolling golden hills to picnic before the performance. According to the managing director, CSF audiences are drawn from numerous communities in the populous greater Bay Area, but their demographic composition is not yet known. Certainly the audience I observed seemed typical of many Shakespeare festival audiences—affluent, well-educated, and, despite the ethnic diversity of the Bay Area, predominantly white.

The Sunday matinee performance of *All's Well That Ends Well* that I attended on 18 August 1991 was completely sold out. It was handsomely costumed in Napoleonic-era dress. The functional, minimalist scenery consisted mainly of a skeletal two-storied tower situated on a small revolving stage. By rotating the tower and adding a few decorative pieces, the setting was effectively changed from Rosillion to Paris to Florence without breaking the flow of the action. In a program note, director Julian López-Morillas implied that his production was intended to explore "the painful and sometimes violent misunderstandings that plague man-woman relationships in the play." Outdoor, daylight performances do not, however, readily accommodate approaches that might require a degree of naturalistic nuance and subtlety. In realization, the production seemed to foreground the romantic and especially the comedic, rather than the psycho-social elements of the action and characters.

Overall, it was a lively, clearly staged production, altogether competently performed by a cast consisting mostly of seasoned professionals. Sam Gregory and Nancy Carlin were a handsome and charming Bertram and Helena, and veteran Shakespearean Tobias Smollett was a dignified and authoritative King of France. Marco Barricelli, who in 1990 had played both Prince Hal and King Henry in *1* and *2 Henry IV* and *Henry V* for the **Oregon Shakespeare Festival** and in *Richard III* for the Missouri Repertory Theatre, was particuilary forceful as an energetic, swashbuckling Parolles. But it was perhaps Howard Swain, playing Lavatch mostly for laughs as an effeminate "closet transvestite," who stole the show. At one point early in the performance, for example, he placed two apples in his coat breast pockets so that he looked as if, indeed, he had breasts. At another point, the Countess opened Lavatch's valise to discover it filled with fancy lingerie. Finally, in the penultimate scene, Lavatch entered completely cross-dressed in a black and white lace *peignoir*, completely made-up, and with a voluminous black chiffon scarf around his head. Twirling a long-stemmed red nose, he literally swished off stage. While Swain's interpretation may be questionable, it was very popular with the audience. Indeed, the entire performance was received with full attention, appropriate laughter, and, at the curtain call, enthusiastic applause.

Although the amphitheatre was complete in 1991, the entire site was not finished. In June 1992, however, CSF announced that it had successfully completed its capital campaign and was now the debt-free owner of its new amphitheatre "lock, stock and sonnets." Moreover, a portion of the funds raised would be used "to put the finishing touches on the theatre, including installing a water system, permanent fully plumbed restrooms, and when drought conditions allow, completing the landscaping." Clearly, CSF is an established cultural institution offering high-quality Shakespearean productions to residents of the greater Bay Area.

Production History: 1973: *Ham., AYL, The Father*; 1974: *AYL, MND, Tmp., AWW, Pantagleize*; 1975: *TN, R2, MND, LLL, Per.*; 1976: *Mac., TN, Tro., Shr.*; 1977: *Rom, Ado, R3, MM.*, 1978: *Ham., Err., 1H4, AYL*; 1979: *Per., MND, The Duchess of Malfi*; 1980: *Wiv., Tmp., Lr.*; 1981: *Shr., JC, Cym., TN*; 1982: *Ant., AWW, WT, Ham.*; 1983: Ado, *Rom., Jn., TGV, Mac., Ivanhoe*; 1984: *MV, LLL, Oth.*; 1985: *MND, TNK, R3*; 1986: *AYL, Cor., Tmp.*, 1987: *R2, 1H4, 2H4, H5.*, 1988: *Err., Tro., Tim., JC.*; 1989: *Shr., Rom., MM, Ado*; 1990:

Wiv., Oth., Cym., TN., **1991**:
MND, Lr., AWW, Ant.; **1992**: *MV,*
Tmp., Mac., TGV; **1993**: *WT, Jn.,*

AYL, Ham.; **1994**: *Rom., R2, Shr.,*
Err.

Research Resources: Archives are informally maintained at California Shakespeare Festival administrative offices. See also the following selected publications.

Booth, Stephen. "Shakespeare in California, 1974-75." *Shakespeare Quarterly* (Winter 1976): 94-108.

_____. "Shakespeare in the San Francisco Bay Area." *Shakespeare Quarterly* (Spring 1978): 273-75.

Brooks, Phyllis. "Berkeley Shakespeare Festivals: Summer 1985." *Shakespeare Quarterly* (Autumn 1986): 393-99.

Jacobs, Laurence H. "Shakespeare in the San Francisco Bay Area." *Shakespeare Quarterly* (Spring 1979): 248-51.

_____. "Shakespeare in the San Francisco Bay Area," *Shakespeare Quarterly* (Summer 1980): 274-76.

_____. "Shakespeare in the San Francisco Bay Area. *Shakespeare Quarterly* (Summer 1981): 264-65.

_____. "Shakespeare in the San Francisco Bay Area. *Shakespeare Quarterly* (Autumn 1982): 396-98.

Site visits and interviews: 3 July 1990 and 18 August 1991.
Daniel J. Watermeier

CARMEL SHAKE–SPEARE FESTIVAL. MAIL: Pacific Repertory Theatre, P.O. Box 222035, Carmel, CA 93922. SITE: Forest Theatre, Carmel. ADMIN-ISTRA-TION: Golden Bough Playhouse, Monte Verde, Carmel, 93922; 408/622-0700. BOX OFFICE: 408/622-0700 or 408/622-0100. ADMISSION: (1992) $8–$10; previews, $5. SEASON: approximately 25 performances, rotating repertory, from early September through mid-October. 8:00 p.m., Thurs.–Sun. (2:00 p.m., Sun., for readings and discussions). PRINCIPAL STAFF: Stephen Moorer, executive director and founder; Julie Hughett, business manager. FACILITY: outdoor, open stage (capacity 500). AUDI-TIONS: Monterey area in February/March. STATUS: non-Equity. ANNUAL BUDGET: $50,000 (1992). ANNUAL ATTENDANCE: 3,000 (1992). FOUNDED: 1990, Stephen Moorer.

The Carmel Shake-speare Festival (CSF) was founded in 1990 as a community outreach program of the GroveMont Theatre, itself founded in 1982 by Stephen Moorer. In 1983, the GroveMont Theatre was incorporated and invested with a board of directors and began producing in various locations around the Monterey Peninsula, including Carmel's historic Forest Theatre. The GroveMont Theatre Arts Center in Monterey came into being in 1986 in the form of what is now a 99-seat theatre. In 1991, the GroveMont Theatre refurbished and opened the Monterey Playhouse in downtown Monterey as a second and larger performance venue. In 1994, GroveMont changed its name to the Pacific Repertory Theatre and acquired, in addition to the Forest Theatre, a new indoor theatre, the historic Golden Bough Playhouse built in 1907. For over a decade, Moorer has provided the Monterey Peninsula with a summer outdoor festival of theatre and theatrical entertainments, consisting of children's plays, musicals, and plays by Shakespeare, Molière, and other classical dramatists.

The Forest Theatre Society of Carmel was formed in 1910 and created the Forest Theatre, the first outdoor amphitheatre west of the Rockies. Among the early members of the society were such literary lights as George Sterling, Mary Austin, and Jack London. The Forest Theatre is built into a natural amphitheatre surrounded by trees, with a large raised stage and open fireplaces on either side of the seating area. Underneath the stage is an enclosed area where the Carmel Children's Experimental Theatre (CET) is conducted and where, during the winter months, the Staff Players Repertory Company offers productions. After several years of performing at the Forest Theatre, the GroveMont initiated the CSF there in 1990 with a production of *A Midsummer Night's Dream* and went on in 1991 to offer *Romeo and Juliet*. In 1992, the CSF presented *Othello* and *Macbeth* in repertory and included Sunday afternoon sessions devoted to "knowledge and discovery" as they explored the "Shake-speare Authorship Question." Moorer is an unabashed supporter of Edward De Vere, the seventeenth Earl of Oxford, as the true author of Shakespeare's plays—hence the hyphenated "Shake-speare." But Moorer has a refreshing sense of humor about the issue. In 1990, for example, CSF staged a dramatized Human Chess Game that pitted Shakespeare against De Vere in an entertaining farcical romp; De Vere won the match. The CSF has also offered staged readings of pre-Shakespearean dramas, such as the anonymous *Famous Victories of Henry V* (1570s), as part of its educational mission.

Though the festival company is not composed of Equity actors, most of the actors are paid, and the entire operation of the company is highly professional. There is a fair amount of theatrical activity on the Monterey Peninsula, so Moorer has had little difficulty in attracting experienced and well-qualified actors even for minor roles. Occasionally guest artists are contracted from outside the community to fill major roles. Careful scholarship goes into the interpretation of the plays, and the productions are skillfully mounted. The stage lighting, for example, is usually fairly sophisticated, and the sets are often elaborate.

Whether it is a clear moonlit night or the fog is rolling in from the nearby ocean, there is a kind of magical atmosphere to the Forest Theatre. The seating consists of long benches built into the side of the hill. These benches were not designed for comfort, but most of the theatregoers solve that problem by bringing their own seating cushions and robes for warmth. The fires in the fireplaces on either side of the audience add to the rustic ambiance. Members of the audience are encouraged to bring food and drink into the seating area, further contributing to the informal, communal atmosphere.

The opening production of *A Midsummer Night's Dream* in 1990 made maximum use of the theatre's size, flexibility, and forest environment. Although the setting was romantic, poetic beauty was sacrificed somewhat to emphasize the farcical elements in the action. This approach delighted the audiences. The production of *Romeo and Juliet*, in 1991 represented a significant artistic improvement over the CSF's first season. The actors, in particular, provided sensitive and imaginative performances, and the audience responded with great enthusiasm. Thus encouraged, the CSF mounted two productions in 1992—*Othello* and *Macbeth*. *Othello* was perhaps the more successful of the two. With the exception of some prolonged combat scenes, it concentrated appropriately on the development of the major characters and the conflict inherent in the plot. *Macbeth*, on the other hand, was skewed by its preoccupation with the witches. There were few artificial effects in the *Othello;* the director confined himself to some freeze-action moments during a few long speeches, which proved very effective. *Macbeth*, by contrast, was full of smoke, explosions, and musical sounds that were occasionally impressive, but also distracted from the development of the plot and character relationships. In both plays, small roles as well as major ones were performed with conviction and style. Both plays utilized a constructivistic unit set, involving high-level ramps that could be rolled into various positions. Lighting, sound effects, costuming, and properties were all given care and attention. The audiences at both productions were receptive and attentive.

In the program for the 1992 season, the philosophy of one of the founders of the Forest Theatre, Herbert Heron, was quoted: "The aims, ambitions, hopes of the Society are that we may find and point worldwide a play—say many plays—worthy of general knowledge; that we may discover a star-dream and help give it to the lovers of dreams of genius; that we may be the link between unrecognized inspiration and the rewarding public." This seems to represent, in part, the philosophy of the GroveMont Theatre. The aim of the CSF was perhaps more clearly enunciated by Moorer when, in directing *Othello*, he told the cast that what he wanted was for Shakespeare to be truly communicated to the audience. In this respect, he wanted the cast to remember that Carmel's audience was not comprised especially of Shakespearean aficionados. The Monterey Peninsula contains a large proportion of scholars and sophisticated theatregoers, but it also attracts many tourists and others who have little acquaintance with Shakespeare. Moorer cares about his scholarship, but his primary objective is to reach the general public.

Plans for next year (1993) are in progress, and I quote from the 1992 program:

In the spring of next year, look forward to the "1993 Carmel Shake-speare Festival Informance," a combination informational gathering and preview performance of selected scenes from the 1993 season. Fine food and drink will be on hand for this special event which honors our valued supporters. Play titles for next year will be drawn from the following works of Shake-speare (tentative): *Hamlet, Henry V, Richard III.* "Shake-speare Authorship West" will continue to promote the Oxfordian Theory and to explore the Shake-speare Authorship Question.

Indeed, in October 1994, CSF hosted the annual meeting of the Shakespeare Oxford Society.

The CSF production staff members, paid and unpaid, take their responsibilities very seriously. The actors are remarkable for their teamwork. They obviously enjoy working together, and they support each other with an enthusiasm that exceeds that of many more established repertory companies. The audiences are also very supportive. All of this bodes well for the continued development of the festival.

Production History: **1990**: *MND*; **1991**: *Rom.*; **1992**: *Oth., Mac.*; **1993**: *R3, Ham.*; **1994**: *JC, H5, The Mikado.* CSF also offered readings; **1990**: anonymous version of *Famous Victories of Henry V* (1570s); **1991**: Arthur Brooke's adaptation of *Romeo and Juliet* (1560s); **1992**: *Taming of the Shrew* (anonymous 1570s), *The Bad Quarto Hamlet* (1603).

Research Resources: An informal archive for the Carmel Shake-speare Festival is kept at the GroveMont Theatre offices. See also, Wendell Cole's "Myth Makers and the Early Years of the Carmel Forest Theatre, in *Theatre West: Image and Impact,* Dunbar H. Ogden, ed. Amsterdam and Atlanta: Rodopi B.V., 1990.

Site visits, interviews, and festival participation: 1990–1993.
Philip B. Clarkson

GLOBE PLAYHOUSE OF LOS ANGELES/SHAKESPEARE SOCIETY OF AMERICA. MAIL/SITE: 1107 North Kings Road, Los Angeles, CA 90069. ADMINISTRATION/BOX OFFICE: 213/654-5623. ADMISSION: varies. SEASON: 10 to 12 productions mounted consecutively for 20 performances each between September and June. FACILITIES: Globe Theatre, (capacity 99). PRINCIPAL STAFF: R. Thad Taylor and Jay Uhley. AUDITIONS: open in Los Angeles. STATUS: Equity waiver. FOUNDED: 1965, R. Thad Taylor.

R. Thad Taylor founded the Globe Playhouse of Los Angeles/Shakespeare Society of America (GPLA) in 1965 as an organization dedicated to educating the public and entertaining the public with the works of Shakespeare. The society presented lectures, published a newsletter, and occasionally produced plays in an old, rented, Tudor-style mansion, "the SSA Shakespearean Centre," on Alta Loma Road. When the Alta Loma property was razed in 1972 to make room for a high rise, Taylor began the search for a new theatre location. His dedication to seeing Shakespeare's plays performed led Taylor in 1974 to erect his own theatre inside a large "Quonset hut"-style building on North Kings Road in West Hollywood.

Drawing on a number of well-known historical documents, Taylor created his own version of the original Globe. The octagonal shape and "huts" of Taylor's Globe, for example, were inspired by Claes Jansz Visscher's 1616 panoramic view of London. The dimensions were borrowed from the Fortune Theatre contract of 1600, the shape of the "heavens" and upper stage from the Johannes de Witt drawing of the Swan Theatre (1596), the thrust stage from the *Roxanna* (1632) and *Messalina* (1640) frontispieces, and the inner stage, columns, and proscenium doors from Taylor's reading of Shakespeare's plays themselves. Taylor, by profession an electrical engineer, financed and built the theatre himself. The building also contains a corner suite where Taylor lives and his extensive collection of Shakespeareana.

In 1974, the Globe Playhouse opened with a production of *Henry V.* The cost of the production was approximately $3,500. Tickets were priced at $3.50 for adults and $2.50 for students. The box office proceeds were then used to finance the next play. Taylor continued to operate in this fashion, generally producing one play every month, for the next 15 years. In 1976, Taylor began to stage the entire Shakespearean canon in the order in which they were presumably written, a task he completed with a production of the *Tempest* in 1979. He would complete the canon for a second time in 1985.

For his productions, Taylor used volunteer actors and directors, but nearly all were professionals eager to showcase their talents in a Shakespearean play. In addition to the box office receipts, Taylor likewise relied on volunteers, in-kind services, private donations, and his own financial resources. He has never had a city, state, or national grant.

With performances five nights a week, Taylor has estimated that the average attendance was about 80 percent of capacity. The majority of the audience (70 percent) was comprised of students and educators. Reviews of GPLA productions have generally been favorable, although, considering the haste in which the many plays were mounted and the changeable and sometimes uneven casts, the quality of productions naturally varied. Thus, reviewing the ten plays and one opera presented in 1977, UCLA Shakespearean scholars A. R. Braunmuller and William L. Stull, writing in *Shakespeare Quarterly* (Spring 1978), had warm praise for *King Lear*, calling the distinguished veteran actor George Coulouris "masterful" in the title role. They called *1 Henry IV* "one of the Globe's best productions." The interracial interpretation of *Romeo and Juliet*, directed by Taylor himself, had some directorial flaws but it "made Shakespeare our contemporary," "revitalized the play's imagery," and "made the nature of the 'ancient grudge' clearer than ever before." On the other hand, Braunmuller and Stull characterized *2 Henry IV* as "dismal," *The Taming of the Shrew* as "weak," and *Troilus and Cressida* as "more problem than play." Joseph H. Stoddard and Lillian Wilds (*Shakespeare Quarterly*, Summer 1980) had similar responses to the 12 productions GPLA mounted in 1979. *Henry V*, for example, they described as "a sparkling, compact version of the play, evenly balancing battles, lovemaking, and comedy." *The Merry Wives of Windsor* they thought "a robust, vividly projected romp." *The Two Noble Kinsmen,* in their view, "shone with unexpected brilliance among the more familiar and accepted plays of the canon." Indeed, *Two Noble Kinsmen* won two prestigious Los Angeles Drama Critics awards for best production and best performance by an actress (Suzanna Peters as the Jailer's Daughter). By contrast, Stoddard and Wilds found *Richard II* and *Henry VIII* "uneven in some respects." Taylor's own multicultural, nontraditional interpretation of *The Tempest* (which completed his ambitious goal to present the entire canon in three and a half years) produced a decidedly mixed response: "The results were occasionally banal but the attempt was no less worthwhile." Audiences were enthusiastic, however: *The Tempest* had its run extended three times. Over the years, moreover, there is no doubt that the overall quality of GPLA productions steadily improved, attracting an increasingly knowledgeable and dedicated patronage, including leading Shakespearean scholars and prominent actors and directors like Charlton Heston, Gloria Grahame, and Delbert Mann.

After 1985, Taylor devoted much of his time to the staging of Shakespeare's apocryphal plays, of which he calculates there are sixteen. With *The Merry Devil of Edmonton*, the Globe's most recent production (August/September 1989), Taylor had staged all but four of these plays.

To meet the rising costs of production—*The Merry Devil of Edmonton*, for example, cost an estimated $17,500—ticket prices were increased periodically. By 1989, the price of a general admission ticket was $12.50, box seats $17.50, and student tickets $8.50. To mount a similar production in 1990 would cost an estimated $20,000 to $25,000, but Taylor was determined to meet this challenge.

In September of 1989, he temporarily closed the Globe Playhouse to mount a campaign to raise $500,000 for a season of six to eight plays. And, after 25 years, Taylor also wanted to start paying actors at least the minimum Equity scale of about $125.00 a week. Taylor also has applied for governmental, corporate, and private funding. But he is adamant that sponsorship will not change his agenda; he will finish staging the apocryphal plays and continue "to enable the community to view the plays of Shakespeare in that way the Elizabethan audiences would have enjoyed them."

Production History: 1965-73: n/a; 1974: *H5*; 1975-1976: n/a; 1977: *AYL, Lr., 1H4, 2H4, Tit., AWW, Shr., Jn., Tro., Rom, The Merry Wives of Windsor* (Nicolai opera). 1978: *WT, 1H6, TGV, Oth., Ham., Per., Ant, Tim., TN, Shakespeare's Manuscripts?* (an original play by Taylor); *Romeo and Juliet* (Gounod opera) and *The Merry Wives of Windsor* (Nikolai). 1979: *2H6, 3H6, MND, MM, H8, TNK, H5, Tmp., Wiv., Cor.* (Two different productions of *Coriolanus* were mounted this season. The first, presented from 7 to 15 March, mixed Shakespeare with Bertolt Brecht. Taylor decided that it could not qualify as canonical, so he then mounted a more traditional production from 24 October to 10 November.) 1980: *Shakespeare's Sonnets Act One and Act Two, Tmp., MND, Err.*; 1981-1983: n/a; 1984: *Sir Thomas More*. 1985: *AYL, Arden of Faversham, Duchess of Malfi*. 1986: *The Puritain, The Raigne of King Edward III, The London Prodigal, Thomas Lord Cromwell, Sir John Old Castle*. 1987: *Tim., Mucedorus, MND, Mac., Rom., The Alchemist, A Yorkshire Tragedy*. 1988: *Marlowe, An Elizabethan Tragedy, Tamburlaine the Great, Dr. Faustus, The Birth of Merlin, Edmund Ironside, TN*, 1989: *Edward II, The Merry Devil of Edmonton*. 1990: *The Rape of Lucrece*.

Research Resources: This essay is based mainly on information provided by R. Thad Taylor. Globe Playhouse/Los Angeles productions were reviewed in the following issues of *Shakespeare Quarterly*: 28 (1977), 239-42; 29 (1978), 259-67; 30 (1979), 232-38; 31 (1980), 257-61; 32 (1981) 255-56; 38 (1978) 243-48; 39 (1988), 232-38; 41 (1990), 268-72;43 (1992), 86-89.

Site visit and interview: 10 June 1990.
Daniel J. Watermeier

GROVE SHAKESPEARE FESTIVAL. (Ceased operation in 1993.) SITE: Village Green Arts Complex in downtown Garden Grove. ADMISSION: $16–$25. SEASON: year-round. 8:30 p.m., Wed.-Sun. (amphitheatre); 8:00 p.m., Wed.–Sat.; 7:30 p.m., Sun.; 3:00 p.m., Sat.–Sun. (Gem). PRINCIPAL STAFF: W. Stuart McDowell, artistic director; Jules Aaron, associate artistic director. FACILITIES: Festival Amphitheatre (capacity 542); Gem Theatre (capacity 172). AUDITIONS: various sites. STATUS: LOA and SPT. ANNUAL BUDGET: $800,000 (1992). ANNUAL ATTENDANCE: 30,000 (1991). FOUNDED: 1979 as Grove Theatre Company operating the Grove

Shakespeare Festival, Thomas F. Bradac and Sondra Evans; Grove Shake-speare Festival, 1989-1993.

In affluent Orange County, the city of Garden Grove has had the reputation of being a poor stepchild, even to the point that it has been called "Garbage Grove." But it was the city itself that pulled together to give its residents a cultural arts complex. Beginning in the early 1970s, Sondra Evans, director of community services, worked with the city council and various architects to get a federal grant to renovate the elegant and intimate Gem Theatre, a 1920s *art déco* movie house. The next step was to build an adjacent open-air amphi-theatre. That project was on the drawing board in 1979, when Thomas F. Bradac was hired by the city of Garden Grove to manage what was envisioned as a community theatre. Bradac, an Equity actor, had produced summer stock in the east while dreaming of starting a Shakespeare festival. He won the city's permission to take the theatre to a level of greater professionalism, and, although the plays had already been chosen when he was hired, he slipped *Romeo and Juliet* into the third slot of the opening season and heralded it as the Grove Shakespeare Festival at the Gem Theatre (GSF). GSF took its place alongside the Gem Theatre series as programs of the Grove Theatre Company. The company's other offerings ranged from standard community-theatre fare to more challenging selections. The latter productions caused a furor in reaction to the four-letter words spoken on stage, whereas the Shakespeare, directed by Bill Purkiss, was warmly received. In May 1980, the Gem/GSF programs separated from the city, which contracted the theatre's management to the non-profit Village Green Fine Arts Association.

Encouraged by the success of *Romeo and Juliet*, the board of trustees approved two Shakespeare productions in rotating repertory for the summer of 1980, and two Equity guest artists were hired. The summer of 1981 brought the opening of the amphitheatre. Because of concerns that Shakespeare might not fill the larger theatre, the two-play Shakespeare repertory was sandwiched between two musicals. *A Midsummer Night's Dream* not only outdrew both musicals, but it also won a review in the *Los Angeles Times*.

Instrumental to the early success of GSF was a liaison forged in 1982 between the theatre management and Rancho Santiago Community College. Burt Peachy, then dean of fine arts at the college, initiated an agreement whereby the college contributed $155,000, rehearsal space, construction facilities, and college staff assistance in exchange for opportunities for student involvement with GSF. The extra funding enabled Bradac to hire well-established professional directors, Lee Shallatt and Kristoffer Tabori. Despite cutbacks in city funding, the festival prospered in its relationship with the college, and the agreement lasted, with periodic revisions and adjustments from 1982 to 1988. Citing inadequate acknowledgement of its contribution, insufficient opportunities for students, and budgetary cutbacks from the state, the college withdrew its support after 1988.

The musicals were dropped from the summer season in 1985. As GSF became more visible, the Gem Theatre series was gradually upgraded, and some classics began to be staged there. Bradac sees 1986 as a milestone year in that GSF's Equity status changed from guest artist contracts to LOA, and *The Merry Wives of Windsor* became GSF's first *Los Angeles Times* "Critic's Pick." In 1987, the board hired Richard Stein as the theatre's first managing director, a position he held until 1990. The 1988 summer season boasted three Shakespeare plays. By 1989, the board of trustees had consented to the Grove Theatre Company's officially adopting the name of its offspring, GSF, which had continued in use for the summer Shakespeare series.

Nonetheless, the economic climate was changing in California in 1988, as cities began to feel the crunch from Proposition 13. The Garden Grove City Council gave GSF less than 30 days' notice that its regular $80,000 contribution would not be forthcoming. Meanwhile, GSF faced a large insurance payment that was due and the prospect of closing down. One city councilman made a statement to the press to the effect that "Garden Grove is a hard hat community, and hard hats don't like Shakespeare." This unleashed a storm of press coverage, including CNN and NPR. On the opening night of the festival, 50 or so audience members showed up wearing hard hats, and Bradac appeared in a hard hat for his pre-curtain speech. As a *cause célèbre*, GSF suddenly received more money from individuals and corporations than ever before, making up about $50,000 of the $80,000 shortfall. The city eventually provided the remainder.

GSF survived, but the experience had been debilitating, and it initiated four seasons of barely getting by. The board of trustees, appointed by the city council, found itself strained by divided loyalties—to the city and to the theatre. With Stein's departure, Bradac and the board asked Barbara Hammerman, J.D., a volunteer board member since 1987, to fill the managing director position. In 1990, Bradac requested and received a part-time sabbatical from the theatre, as he had accepted a full-time teaching position at Chapman College. A year later, when he renewed his request for part-time employment, the board requested and received Bradac's resignation as artistic director. This action occurred just two weeks into the summer season. Guest director Jules Aaron, who was then rehearsing *Measure for Measure*, agreed to serve as acting artistic director until a permanent appointment could be made. Hammerman eased the transition and spearheaded a new fund-raising drive. That summer brought the largest grossing audiences in GSF history and three rave reviews from Sylvia Drake of the *Los Angeles Times*.

Hammerman negotiated an unprecedented five-year, no-fee lease agreement with the city for use of the theatres. Under prior contracts, the company could have been asked to vacate with only 30 days' notice. In cooperation with the Children's Theatre Ensemble, an organization now incorporated into the Grove operations, Hammerman started the Grove Theatre School, which offered classes for all ages. In 1992, the GroveShakespeare Family Theatre series presented guest company productions, programed by Michele Roberge, who also inaugurated school outreach programs. These expanded educational and volunteer operations were made possible when Hammerman obtained 1,500 square feet of office space rent-free for two years in the commercial Main Street Pavilion.

W. Stuart McDowell was appointed as artistic director and made his GSF directorial debut with the 1992 annual summer benefit. "A Midsummer Night's Eve III" was also a tribute to Joseph Papp. Tyne Daly, Sally Kirkland, Michael Learned, Donna McKechnie, Loretta Swit, John Vickery, and other artists lent their support by interacting with benefactors at the dinner and performing songs, sonnets, and scenes in the amphitheatre.

The Village Green Arts Complex, which includes the Gem and the amphitheatre, is located in downtown Garden Grove at the center of three major freeways (Interstate 5, the 22, and the 57), near Disneyland and Knotts Berry Farm. Orange County (population 2.4. million) is about 60 percent white, with a large Korean and Vietnamese component and a considerable number of Latinos. African-Americans comprise less than 2 percent of the population. Within Orange County, there are three major universities and nine community college campuses. Although GSF draws from Los Angeles and Riverside, about 90 percent of the audience is from Orange County.

GSF's season has evolved from two separate seasons (one for the Gem and one for the amphitheatre) to an integrated season in both houses, running from April to December. Hammerman left GSF in 1993 to pursue other interests. McDowell and the board faced continuing financial challenges, but McDowell was optimistic: "Since we don't have much money, we'll just have to be brilliant."

According to a report in *American Theatre* (November 1993), however, GSF suspended operations in June, "leaving more than 1,400 subscribers without refunds and creditors with $250,000 of unpaid bills." With a July vote of confidence from the city council, granting it continued free use of the Gem and the Festival Amphitheatre, GSF was expected to return for the 1994 summer season.

Production History: **1979-80**: *Anything Goes, Arsenic and Old Lace, Rom., Mame, Pippin, One Flew Over the Cuckoo's Nest, Hot L Baltimore, Sleuth, Once Upon a Mattress*; **1980-81**: *Shr., Ado, The Robber Bridegroom, The Cold Wind and the Warm/Pillar of Fire, Cabaret, The Shadow Box, Private Lives, Dames at Sea*; **1981-82**: *South Pacific, AYL, MND, Grease,* *Company, The Miracle Worker, No Mother But Jazz, Ladyhouse Blues, Scapino!, Man of La Mancha, Boy with Goldfish*; **1982-83**: *Oliver!, Rom., TN, Side by Side by Sondheim, The Fantastiks, On Golden Pond, A Christmas Carol, Charlie's Aunt, A Man for All Seasons, The Real Inspector Hound*; **1983-84**: *Tintypes, Mac., TGV, Rodgers and Hart, Hay Fever, Bus Stop, A*

Christmas Carol; Starting Here, Starting Now, The Elephant Man, Chapter Two; **1984-85**: *Tartuffe, Ado, Ham., Err., Bleacher Bums, Annie, California Suite, Tribute, Of Mice and Men, They're Playing Our Song*; **1985-86**: *The Rivals, Tmp., Shr., Shakespeare 1614, Alive!, Going to See the Elephant, Some Enchanted Evening*; **1986-87**: *Crimes of the Heart, The Dresser, A Moon for the Misbegotten, What the Butler Saw, 1H4, LLL, Wiv., Quilters, A Child's Christmas in Wales* (revived every season subsequently); **1987-88**: *True West, The Show-Off, Devour the Snow, A Life in the Theatre, JC, The Imaginary Invalid, MND,* *Sherlock's Last Case*; **1988-89**: *Vikings, Mrs. California, Trinity, The Price, Pump Boys and Dinettes, R2, Err., Lr., MV, And A Nightingale Sang*; **1989-90**: *Lily Dale, Acting on Rollerskates, Requiem for a Heavyweight, Tomfoolery, Rom., The Songs of War, Cyrano de Bergerac, Heathen Valley, TGV, The Scoundrel*; **1990-91**: *TN, The Miser, Ado, MND, Oth., The Importance of Being Earnest*; **1991-92**: *MV, MM, MND, Shr., Les Liaisons Dangereuses, Tomfoolery, Our Town*; **1992-93**: *The Dining Room, Mac., Tmp., Wiv., Long Day's Journey into Night, Falling in Love, William of Stratford, The Fantasticks.*

Research Resources: "Acknowledging a Debt to the Theater," *Los Angeles Times* (1 September 1991): B8; Michele Pearce, "Road to Recovery or Road to Nowhere?" *American Theatre* (November 1993): 68; Thomas O'Connor, "Rebirth of Grove Falls Short," *Orange County Register* (3 January 1993): 5, 27.

Interviews: 9 and 11 January 1992.
Felicia Hardison Londré and Daniel J. Watermeier

THE LOS ANGELES SHAKESPEARE COMPANY. MAIL: 15752 Enadia Way, Van Nuys, CA 91406. SITES: various. ADMINISTRATION: 818/989-7221. ADMISSION: $10–$20. SEASON: six productions a year in two three-play seasons, from January to June and July to December; each production runs eight weeks, four weeks in each location below; 8:00 p.m., Wed.–Sat. PRINCIPAL STAFF: Geoffrey G. Forward, artistic director. FACILITIES: Union Labor Temple, 42 E. Walnut Ave. (at Raymond), Pasadena, flexible (capacity 99-seat); Richard Basehart Playhouse, 21208-B Victory Blvd., Woodland Hills, proscenium (capacity 99-seat). AUDITIONS: Los Angeles. STATUS: Equity LOA. ANNUAL BUDGET: $40,000 (1993). ANNUAL ATTENDANCE: 2,400 (1993). FOUNDED: 1992, Geoffrey G. Forward.

The Los Angeles Shakespeare Company (LASC) was founded in February 1992 by Geoffrey G. Forward, an actor, director, and acting teacher with a keen interest in Shakespeare. He is a resident reader at the renowned Huntington Library in San Marino and formerly worked with the **Globe Playhouse of Los Angeles/Shakespeare Society of America** in West Hollywood.

Forward opened his first season on 5 August 1992 with a production of *The Taming of the Shrew*. This was then followed by a production of *Richard II*. Both productions proved sufficiently successful that in January 1993, LASC mounted its first full season.

Reviews of LASC productions generally have been favorable. *Much Ado About Nothing*, for example, set in a "Roaring Twenties" milieu was commended by *Drama-Logue* reviewer Larry Jonas (14-20 January 1993) for being well cast and for Forward's flair and creativity as a director. Ray Loynd in the *Los Angeles Times* (10 June 1993) praised LASC's *A Midsummer Night's Dream* for its "deft and even brisk" direction (by Eric Liddell, who also played Theseus), for its "inventive and sublime contemporary" costumes, and for the generally solid, energetic performances, especially the "playful, sexy and infectious" sets of lovers.

Forward has also organized a performance workshop at The Huntington Library and Botanical Gardens. Every Saturday morning from 10:00 a.m. to 12:00 noon, interested actors assemble at the lily ponds to work on such matters as diction, movement, scansion, phrasing, and the historical context of Shakespeare's plays. The workshop is open to the public, and, according to Forward, many visitors to the Huntington Gardens stop for a few minutes, or longer, to observe the actors at work. Many of the actors for LASC productions have been drawn from this workshop.

To date, Forward has relied solely on earned income to finance the LASC. He is adamant in his belief that theatres do not need public or corporate funding to survive. "A theatre," he says, "is defined by its audience. That's why we're relying on, and building upon, a base of subscribers. This is a popular meeting. If the seats are empty, why are you doing the play? If Shakespeare's own Globe Theatre didn't sell tickets, the show closed" (*Los Angeles Times*, 31 July 1992). Forward has steadily built his mailing list from 1,600 to over 3,200.

Although LASC is currently a modest Shakespearean venture, Forward hopes to build on his successes to become a fully professional Equity company, performing throughout the populous greater Los Angeles area.

Production History: 1992: *Shr.*, *R2.*; **1993**: *Ado*, *Lr.*, *MND*, *Wiv.*, *Rom.*, *TN.*

Research Resources: Forward maintains a file of reviews and other materials concerning Los Angeles Shakespeare Company. This essay is based on information supplied by him.

Telephone interview: 11 February 1994
Daniel J. Watermeier

MARIN SHAKESPEARE COMPANY. MAIL: P.O. Box 4053, San Rafael, CA 94913. SITE: Forest Meadows Amphitheatre, Dominican College, San Rafael. ADMINISTRATION: 415/499-1108. BOX OFFICE: 415/456-8104. ADMISSION: $10–$16. SEASON: 20 performances, mid-August through mid-September; 8:00 p.m., Thurs.–Sat.; and some 4 p.m., Sun. PRINCIPAL STAFF: Robert S. Currier, producing director; Lesley Schisgall Currier, managing director; Ann Brebner, consultant. FACILITY: outdoor, open stage (capacity 550). AUDITIONS: San Francisco Bay Area; Equity actor pre-cast. STATUS: Equity Guest Artist. ANNUAL BUDGET: $120,000. ANNUAL ATTENDANCE: 5,000 (1993). FOUNDED: 1989, Robert S. Currier, Lesley S. Currier, Ann Brebner, and Robert Egan.

The Marin Shakespeare Company (MSC) can trace its beginnings to one of the San Francisco Bay Area's oldest Shakespearean production groups. In 1961, He and Ann Brebner formed the Marin Shakespeare Festival. John had earlier worked with the **Oregon Shakespeare Festival** (OSF) and took his inspiration from that experience. After several successful seasons at the Marin Art and Garden Center, parking problems and performance noise began to irritate the center's neighbors increasingly. Nearby Dominican College offered the group a refuge and retained an architect to build an outdoor theatre on their 26-acre student picnic grounds. The plans featured a sweeping concrete stage (which bridges a creek) with a reflecting pool in front. The audience area, a semicircular ring of redwood benches with backs, was surrounded by an earthen wall that improved acoustical conditions. In 1967, the festival opened at Dominican College and for the next several years, its reputation grew as the group presented Shakespearean productions, occasional musical comedies, and performances for children. In the early 1970s, a fire destroyed much of the festival's costume and properties stock. The fire, together with a growing deficit caused in large part by a lavish production of *Antony and Cleopatra*, eventually led to Dominican College's withdrawing from the festival. The Brebners attempted to continue their efforts at the San Francisco Palace of Fine Arts, but finally disbanded after two seasons.

In the late 1980s, Robert Egan, who had actually been the first performer to set foot on the new stage at Dominican College as Feste in *Twelfth Night* in 1967, remembered the festival's successes and believed that Marin County would welcome a return of Shakespeare productions. Now Chair of the Department of Dramatic Arts at the University of California-Santa Barbara, Egan, together with Ann Brebner, began to explore reviving the festival. They invited Robert S. Currier to become the first producing director of the new MSC. Currier's successful work with the Woodstock Opera House and the Ukiah Players Theatre and his expertise in many facets of production made him and his wife, Lesley Schisgall Currier (another OSF alumna), a good team to initiate the enterprise. According to Jean Schiffman's 1991 survey of summer festivals in *Callboard*, the pair developed a very successful fund-raising formula: "The Curriers jumped in, raised over $43,000 in community donations with some money from the Marin Arts Council and the Fireman's Fund and generated a third of their budget through ticket sales during their first production."

"Shakespeare Under the Stars" is how the MSC officially describes the experience of seeing a production at Forest Meadows. The large stage, surrounded by trees and a pond that often reflects the moon as it rises in the background, provides a striking natural setting. The company, now in its third year of performing one Shakespearean play each summer, has increasingly garnered the support of many Marin County businesses and individuals.

Ann Brebner herself provided a link with the past as the director of the inaugural production of *As You Like It* in August 1990. The *San Francisco Chronicle* reviewer (Gerald Nachman) enthused over the "idyllic" backdrop that the theatre provided (15 August 1990). He pronounced the production "as romantic and moonlit as the sylvan setting itself." This enthusiasm was echoed in a comment in the local *Marin Independent Journal* that it was an "auspicious beginning" (15 August 1990). Opening night was enhanced by a pre-curtain "Feast of Good Will," at which, for a contribution of $50 to the festival, patrons were entertained in the fashion of an Elizabethan feast. The feast proved so successful that it has become an annual event.

The production of *Macbeth* in 1991 was directed by Patrick Kelly and featured Eric Zivot, a professional actor, in the title role. The *Marin Independent Journal*'s reviewer called this effort "spellbinding," "poetic and eerie" with "exceptional acting" (20 August 1991). He noted that the production "incorporates the surroundings and brings life into the forest." Jim McKie, who served as both lighting and setting designer, created a towering wall with doors for the different scenes. The special effects—cauldron smoke, the appearance and disappearance of the witches and Banquo's Ghost—received praise from all. The show played without an intermission to emphasize the "focused single-mindedness" of Zivot's Macbeth. The sound effects, featuring everything from birds to military flourishes, was credited with achieving an atmosphere the *Chronicle* termed "frequently striking" (20 August 1991).

Playing on the mistaken identity theme and following the lead of some recent productions, director Robert Currier for the 1992 *Comedy of Errors* cast one actor for the twin Dromios and one for the twin Antipholuses, but he fooled some critics and audience members into thinking that there were actually two sets of twins! Using fake names and biographies in the program, as well as costumed stand-ins for those few times when both Dromios and Antipholuses must appear together, Currier solved a major difficulty presented by the comedy: how to find look-alike performers. To his credit, the *Chronicle*'s critic, Steven Winn, had the grace to admit that even he had been fooled (20 August

1992). The "twin" hurdle overcome, a very capable cast navigated the plot's twists and turns with youthful comic zest.

Jim McKie's set was a witty variation on the conventional Roman street scene. Elaborate two-story recreations of the Antipholus home and the courtesan's house featured windows and shutters, half-doors and ladders, abetting the demands of the farce's chase scenes at the climax of the story. The shipwrecked Argos loomed at stage left near the Priory, reminding the audience of the past. To get to the setting, actors crossed from the auditorium to the stage on gangplanks over the pond (the pond itself inspired some slapstick business). Hucksters, spies bent on foreign intrigue, a snake charmer, and a troupe of *commedia* players created the atmosphere of an exotic, bustling marketplace. Scimitars, turbans, exotic robes, jewels, fezes, pantaloons, and veils flashed from the stage at every opportunity, contributing further to this "Turkish delight" of a production. The sound system, which constantly punctuated the action with comic effects, provided a splendid musical subtext that helped clarify characters and incidents. Though the theatre is located quite near a major freeway, the meadow with its huge parking area, provided a very effective noise buffer. The hushed quiet, the comfort and beauty of the surroundings, and a delightful "big production" of a Shakespearean comedy were a disarming combination. The 1994 production of *A Midsummer Night's Dream* featured members of the well-known San Francisco-based Pickle Family Circus with Jeff Raz playing Bottom and Diane Wasnak playing Puck.

Production History: **1990**: *AYL*; **1991** *Mac.*; **1992**: *Err.*; **1993**: *Tmp.*; **1994**: *MND*.

Research Resources: Archives for the Marin Shakespeare Company are maintained on an informal basis at the company's administrative office. See also: Jean Schiffman. "The Shakespeare Festivals." *Callboard* (June 1991): 3-7.

Site visit and interviews: 17 and 22 August 1992, and 18 September 1992. Patricia M. McMahon

NEW SHAKESPEARE COMPANY. (Ceased operation in 1991.) SITES: varied. ADMINISTRATION: 771 5th Avenue #4, San Francisco, CA 94118. PRINCIPAL STAFF: Margrit Roma, artistic director; Clarence Ricklefs, producer. STATUS: non-Equity. FOUNDED: 1964, Margrit Roma and Clarence Ricklefs.

The New Shakespeare Company (NSC) is the oldest Shakespeare company in California. Swiss-born Margrit Roma trained with Max Reinhardt and worked in Bertolt Brecht's company in Berlin before meeting her social worker husband, Clarence Ricklefs, in Southern California in the early 1960s. Moving to San Francisco, they began producing shows in 1965 at Trinity Episcopal Church. When audiences increased beyond the capacity of the church in 1969, they moved to Golden Gate Park, where they presented Shakespeare outdoors on Saturdays and Sundays in the spring. The success of the weekend performances prompted the troupe to begin touring productions to other California locales. In 1971, a grant from the San Francisco Foundation permitted the New Shakespeare Company to begin a one-year actor-training program and to tour their productions across the United States to high school, college, and university stages. During the summer months, they would reprise their productions at Sugar Pine Point State Park, at Sand Harbor State Park at Lake Tahoe (see **Shakespeare at Sand Harbor**), and at other popular California recreation areas. After a decade of this schedule, drastic federal and state cuts in education budgets in 1981 forced the NSC to cancel its touring productions. Declaring bankruptcy, Roma and Ricklefs dissolved the NSC. Nonetheless, as "Shakespeare–San Francisco," they continued to showcase productions in Golden Gate Park, even though philosophical differences within the new organization led to the eventual withdrawal of Roma and Ricklefs. The **San Francisco Shakespeare Festival**, as it was called, continued to mount an annual production in Golden Gate Park, while, once again as the NSC, Roma and Ricklefs presented various productions both in Golden Gate Park and other locales until 1990.

Jean Schiffman's article on local Shakespeare festivals for *Callboard* (June 1991) neatly sums up the NSC's contribution: "Most local actors who aspire to classical theatre have started their careers by putting in a season on the mainstage or touring with the 25-year-old New Shakespeare Company, founded and run entirely by Margrit Roma and Clarence Ricklefs, better known as Rick and Roma." This production team can also boast about being the first to foster interracial casting as a standard company policy (1966), the first to present free Shakespeare productions in Golden Gate Park (1969), and the first to bring summer Shakespeare shows to California state parks and recreation areas (1971).

Roma prefers to work with neophyte performers who recognize the social values, as well as the artistic aspects, of their productions. In Jennifer Wright's appraisal in *The Tenderloin Times* (August 1989), the director shared her views on training: "Most actors have learned to play Shakespeare in a boring, self-conscious way.... prefer untrained actors because untrained actors will perform Shakespeare with what's inside them." Most critics commend Roma's work for its striking energy, inventiveness, and clarity.

For 28 years in over 80 productions, the New Shakespeare Company has primarily concentrated upon eight Shakespearean plays: *As You Like It, Hamlet, Macbeth, The Merchant of Venice, A Midsummer Night's Dream, Romeo and Juliet, The Tempest*, and *Twelfth Night*, as well as Brecht's *The Threepenny Opera* and a selection of classic children's plays. The team is now looking for original work to produce as well as compiling their experiences in a book-length retrospective of their producing career.

Production History: **1967**: *Rom., Alice in Wonderland, MND*; **1968**: *Alice in Wonderland, MND, The Wizard of Oz*; **1969**: *Rom., MND*; **1970**: *MND, AYL*; **1971**: *Rom., AYL, MND*; **1972**: *Rom., MND*; **1973**: *Threepenny Opera, Rom., MND, AYL*; **1974**: *MV, MND, AYL*; **1975**: *Ham., MV, MND, AYL*; **1976**: *Tmp., Ham., AYL, MND*; **1977**: *Tmp., Ham., AYL, MND*; **1978**: *MND, TN*; **1979**: *TN, Mac.,* *Rom.*; **1980**: *Rom., AYL, MV*; **1981**: *MND, AYL*; **1982**: *Alice in Wonderland, TN*; **1983**: *Tmp., Rom.*, **1984**: *Alice in Wonderland, AYL*; **1985**: *Alice in Wonderland, MND. Ham.*; **1986**: *MV* (two different productions), *Rumpelstilt- skin*; **1987**: *The Good Woman of Setzuan, The Wizard of Oz*; *Rom.*; **1988**: *Rom., TN, The Wizard of Oz*; **1989**: *TN, The Wizard of Oz*; **1990**: *Good Women of Setzuan.*

Research Resources: Archives for the New Shakespeare Company are maintained by the company producer and by the San Francisco Performing Arts Library and Museum.

Interview: 17 March 1993.
Patricia M. McMahon

OJAI SHAKESPEARE FESTIVAL THEATRE COMPANY. MAIL: P.O. Box 575, Ojai, CA 93024. SITE: Libbey Bowl Outdoor Theatre, Libbey Park, in downtown Ojai. ADMINISTRATION: 805/646-2917. BOX OFFICE: 805/646-WILL. ADMISSION: $7–$12, Fri., Sun.; $7–$15, Sat. SEASON: first three weekends in August. PRINCIPAL STAFF: Paul Backer, artistic director; Geoff Foley, executive producer and managing director. FACILITY: outdoor amphitheatre (capacity 675 seated, 300 lawn/blanket). AUDITIONS: advertised locally. STATUS: Equity Guest Artist and non-Equity. ANNUAL BUDGET: $48,000 (1993). ANNUAL ATTENDANCE: 3,500 (1992). FOUNDED: 1982, as Royal "Shake-speare" Revels, by Patricia (Tish) Winkworth.

Ojai Shakespeare Festival Theatre Company (OSFTC), as the company is now called, began as the Royal "Shake-speare" Revels (RSR). Founded in 1982 by Patricia (Tish) Winkworth, who functioned as general director of the community organization, RSR was launched in June 1993 with four perform- ances of *A Midsummer Night's Dream* and an Elizabethan Faire in Libbey Park. A message from Winkworth in the program explained the spelling of the company name at that time. The hyphenation in "Shake-speare" reproduces the name as it appeared when 12 of the plays were published for the first time in

1598, which in turn raises questions about the identity of the author behind the name. The 1983 program also included information about Edward De Vere, seventeenth Earl of Oxford, as a likely candidate for the authorship, as well as information about the Shakespeare Oxford Society. Because the authorship question alienated some subscribers, however, the company gradually deemphasized its Oxfordian identification. Changing the name to OSFTC helped to stress the location and to give a greater sense of community involvement in a festival activity.

Producing one play each summer, RSR concentrated on the comedies for the first six years in order to get the audience more readily involved in the Shakespearean form and language and thus build up a following. Although the first five productions lost money, the company was sustained by several large contributions by corporations, as well as by a prominent Oxfordian, Ruth Lloyd Miller. By 1989, RSR was ready to depart from the comic tradition, and its *Winter's Tale* drew a record 1,700, including about 150 children. The policy of free admission for children under age 13 (when accompanied by an adult) boosted the child audience to 450 by 1992. Originally drawing primarily from the Ojai Valley and Ventura County, the company now boasts regular theatregoers from San Francisco, Sacramento, and several New England states. Although about half of the audience comes from outside the immediate area, it is the local constituency that is named in RSR's mission statement, which emphasizes the preservation of the Shakespearean cultural heritage through community involvement in production and in educational outreach. Over 100 volunteers work on the annual productions. Even senior citizens get involved by "set sitting" for the daytime portion of the 24-hour security guard needed during the run of the play.

With the appointment of artistic director Paul Backer, the community theatre gained a reputation for professionalism in production quality. Budgetary setbacks—such as suddenly having to pay $3,000 in 1989 for the rental of lighting equipment that had previously been borrowed—were weathered, but fund-raising continues to be a year-round effort, especially since the organization is committed to offering scholarships for high school students to enroll in the acting and stagecraft training programs. Since 1992, OSFTC has offered two productions in rotating repertory. A broad comedy is given lawn show matinees on Saturday and Sunday, while Friday and Saturday evenings are devoted to stage shows (usually a more serious work). The Shakespeare for Kids program takes Shakespeare programs into Ventura County elementary school classrooms. The Madrigal Revelers provide pre-performance entertainment and often present their Renaissance concerts in nursing homes and for civic groups.

Mary Wolk, managing director until 1994, notes that "expanding the programs and audience base has provided a transition from the original Oxfordian posture, but our mission continues to promote the culture and educational aspects of Shakespeare's time, while also continuing to include discussion of the authorship question, as evidenced in program and director's notes."

Production History: **1983**: *MND*; **1985**: *Shr.*; **1986**: *Wiv.*; **1987**: *TN*; **1988**: *Ado*; **1989**: *WT*; **1990**: *MV*; **1991**: *Mac.*; **1992**: *1H4, TGV*; **1993**: *Shr., MM.*; **1994**: *TN, Oth.*

Research Resources: Company archives are maintained at the Ojai Shakespeare Festival Theatre Company office in Ojai.

Felicia Hardison Londré

OLD GLOBE THEATRE. MAIL: Box 2171, San Diego, CA 92122-2171. SITE: Simon Edison Centre for the Performing Arts, 1363 Old Globe Way in Balboa Park, San Diego. ADMINISTRATION: 619/231-1941; Fax: 619/231-5879. BOX OFFICE: 619/239-2255. ADMISSION: $17.50–$30 (1992). SEASON: December– October, 12 to 13 productions in three theatres, 8:00 p.m., Tues.–Sat.; 7:00 p.m., Sun.; 2:00 p.m., Wed., Sat., Sun. PRINCIPAL STAFF: (1992) Jack O'Brien, artistic director; Thomas Hall, managing director; Craig Noel, executive producer. FACILITIES: Old Globe Theatre, flexible (capacity 581); Cassius Carter Centre Stage, arena (capacity 225); Lowell Davies Festival Stage, outdoor amphitheatre with thrust stage, (capacity 612). AUDITIONS: nationally through Equity. STATUS: LORT C2-B+. ANNUAL BUDGET: $8.5 million (1992). ANNUAL ATTENDANCE: 250,000 (1992, all programs). FOUNDED: 1935, Thomas Wood Stevens; 1947, Craig Noel.

The Old Globe Theatre (OGT) began as an entertainment attraction at the 1935-36 California Pacific International Exposition held in San Diego's Balboa Park. A temporary replica of Shakespeare's Globe Theatre, seating 580, was erected on the exposition site. In this roofless "wooden O," audiences viewed 50-minute versions of Shakespeare plays adapted and directed by Ben Iden Payne, a noted Shakespearean scholar, director of the Shakespeare Memorial Theatre [see **Royal Shakespeare Company**], and specialist in Elizabethan staging techniques, and by Thomas Wood Stevens, founding director of Chicago's Goodman Theatre and the designer of the Globe Theatre replica. Indeed, Payne and Stevens had also collaborated to produce abbreviated versions of Shakespeare's plays in a Globe Theatre replica at the 1934 Chicago World's Fair.

The structure was to be torn down at the exposition's close, but a group of local citizens raised some $10,000 to arrange for a remodeling of the structure and of two adjacent buildings (Ye Old Curiosity Shoppe and Falstaff Tavern) to meet state fire and structural codes. A charter was granted by the state to the San Diego Community Theatre, as the producing organization for the theatre to coordinate the renovations and fund raising. The San Diego Community Theatre leased the land and buildings from the city of San Diego, an arrangement that continues to this day. Because the theatre company was, from the outset, popularly known as the Old Globe, in 1958 the San Diego Community Theatre officially changed its name to the Old Globe Theatre, Incorporated.

On 2 December 1937, the newly remodeled OGT opened with a production of John Van Druten's *The Distaff Side*. In the cast was a young actor by the name of Craig Noel, who would be named full-time director of OGT in 1939 and artistic director in 1947. As a community theatre, OGT continued to operate successfully, presenting popular dramatic fare until 1941; shortly after the bombing of Pearl Harbor, however, the U.S. Navy occupied Balboa Park for military purposes. The theatre, along with other exposition buildings, was occupied, and all its records and equipment were removed. The organization continued to mount occasional performances, however, at Dartlee Hall in San Diego's Hillcrest area and, through the USO, at local military installations. In 1947, the navy returned Balboa Park to the city of San Diego. A new lease agreement between the city and OGT was approved, and theatre operations resumed in October 1947 with a production of William Saroyan's *The Time of Your Life*.

In 1949, OGT joined with San Diego State College (now San Diego State University) to present a summer production of Shakespeare's *Twelfth Night*, directed by Payne. This cooperative venture was sufficiently successful that two Shakespearean plays were presented under the rubric of the San Diego National Shakespeare Festival each summer for the next three summers (1950-52). In 1953, a production of *Mister Roberts* was presented instead of Shakespeare. For the next season, however, OGT assumed sole responsibility for producing the Shakespeare festival, which expanded to three productions, presented for 15 performances each, using talented young actors who received subsistence scholarships of $250. This laid the foundation for OGT's long-standing commitment to presenting the plays of Shakespeare and set the pattern for its annual programing. In the winter, OGT presented a season of modern and contemporary plays and then, in the summer, two to three Shakespearean productions or a combination of Shakespeare and other "classics." Beginning in 1959, Equity actors were contracted for the summer Shakespeare festival, although the winter season continued to operate mainly as an amateur community theatre. As it raised its artistic standards, OGT began to gain a regional and even national reputation. In 1964, for example, it was invited to tour its productions of *Macbeth* and *Much Ado About Nothing* to Stanford University as part of a gala festival to celebrate the quadricentennial of Shakespeare's birth.

Even earlier, in 1961, OGT had been invited by the La Jolla Museum of Contemporary Art to produce a spring season of three plays at Sherwood Hall in La Jolla. To offer a broader range of theatre than had been presented in San Diego, Noel mounted works by Edward Albee, Jean Anouilh, Luigi Pirandello, and others. The program was successful at the box office, but it was soon discontinued because of inadequate staff and logistical problems created by producing so far from the Old Globe Theatre. San Diego's appetite for more experimental theatre, however, had been aroused. Noel, who had long envisioned a second stage at the Old Globe, began producing alternative or less popular dramas in the Falstaff Tavern in 1963. In 1969, the tavern was remodeled into the 225-seat arena-style Cassius Carter Centre Stage, named after the late San Diego arts patron and Shakespeare scholar, Cassius Carter. The Carter Centre Stage remains a venue for theatrically challenging avant-garde plays, new scripts, small cabaret musicals, or experimental stagings of classic works.

In 1964, OGT received its first funding from an outside source. The Combined Arts and Educational Council of San Diego County (COMBO), a fund-raising umbrella for arts organizations, allocated funds to OGT to expand and improve its facilities. Completed in 1966, the construction included space for new dressing rooms, new public restrooms, shops, business offices, and a rehearsal hall. The late 1950s and 1960s generally represented a period of artistic growth for OGT, as it increased its number of productions and performances, and expanded its facilities. Its repertoire also became more diverse, with offerings not only of popular Broadway comedies and dramas, such as *Life with Father*, *Come Blow Your Horn*, or *Inherit the Wind*, but also of plays by Harold Pinter, Ugo Betti, Arthur Kopit, Brian Friel, Jean Genet, Alexei Arbuzov, Bertolt Brecht, and others. The Shakespeare festival also mounted some of Shakespeare's less popular and more difficult plays, such as *Antony and Cleopatra*, *2 Henry IV*, *The Winter's Tale*, *Henry VIII*, and *King John*. In 1974, OGT played to its 100,000th patron and was widely regarded as a major cultural institution in the San Diego area.

In the 1970s, OGT also began a number of initiatives that reached out into the local and regional community. Globe Educational Tours, founded in 1974, provides an introduction to Shakespeare and the classics to city and county school children in grades K-12. Community Acting Workshops were established in 1975, providing classes in theatre disciplines for adults and youth. The Play Discovery Program, founded in 1976, administers an extremely popular readings series. From its initial Play Discovery Festival in 1986 emerged Reuben Gonzalez's acclaimed *The Boiler Room*, given its world premier at the Globe in 1988. As an extension of the San Diego National Shakespeare Festival, summer tours to Scottsdale, Arizona, in association with the Arizona Shakespeare Association, took place from 1977 through 1980.

The late 1970s, however, were to prove critical years for OGT. On the morning of 8 March 1978, a fire, the work of an arsonist, destroyed the landmark Old Globe Theatre. Fortunately, the fire was confined to the mainstage; production and administrative facilities and the Cassius Carter Centre Stage remained intact. News of the fire elicited a nationwide outpouring of support for OGT. Nearly $500,000 in unsolicited donations were received in the first 30 days. Over the next 20 months, contributions grew to $6.5 million to rebuild the theatre. After the fire, OGT was able to continue its winter productions by moving to other theatres in San Diego, at first to the Spreckles Theatre and later to the California Theatre. For the summer Shakespeare festival, a new outdoor stage was constructed in a mere 52 days. Located in a wooded canyon adjacent to the ruins of the Old Globe Theatre and named the Festival Stage, this award-winning performance space soon became a permanent fixture of the organization. When the new Old Globe Theatre was completed in 1982, the three-theatre complex was named the Simon Edison Centre for the Performing Arts, after the late husband of Helen Edison whose donation to the rebuilding fund was at the time the largest single private donation ever made to a performing arts organization in San Diego. The complex, surrounded by eucalyptus groves and gardens and adjacent to San Diego's natural history and art museum and its world-famous zoo, is among the more attractive theatre sites in the United States. To inaugurate the new theatre, Noel staged a production of *As You Like It*, employing the first winter-season Equity company in the 45-year history of the Old Globe. Now a year-round fully professional theatre, OGT began a pattern of producing Shakespeare at any time during the year, not just during the summer months. And, to reflect this change, OGT stopped using the designation "San Diego National Shakespeare Festival."

Earlier in 1981, the board of directors had established an artistic/administrative triumvirate to manage and lead the new complex. Noel was named executive producer. Nationally acclaimed director Jack O'Brien, who had returned to stage eight productions following his 1969 OGT directorial debut, was named artistic director. Thomas Hall, a native San Diegan, who had extensive administrative and production experience, including several seasons at the **Oregon Shakespeare Festival**, was named managing director. Over a decade later, this arrangement continues to be a very effective one for OGT. Indeed, OGT's managerial staff has been remarkably stable. William B. Eaton, for example, joined OGT as a volunteer in 1948. He became production coordinator in 1956, subsequently business manager, and then public relations director, a post he held until his death in 1994. Such commitment undoubtedly has contributed significantly to OGT's organizational and artistic success.

After the opening of the new complex, several events focused additional national and regional attention on OGT. In January 1983, Thornton Wilder's *The Skin of Our Teeth* was telecast on PBS's American Playhouse live from the stage of the theatre. Directed by O'Brien, it was the first live telecast of a theatrical stage production in the 25-year history of the Public Broadcasting Service (PBS). Also in 1983, Queen Elizabeth II visited to dedicate a bronze bust of Shakespeare now permanently on display in the lobby. In January 1984, O'Brien conceived and directed a critically acclaimed revival of Cole Porter's *Kiss Me, Kate*, which broke all previous records with a total attendance of 27,906. This record was overturned two years later by another musical, *Pump*

Boys and Dinettes, which played to a total of 40,000 patrons. In 1984, to honor OGT upon the occasion of its Jubilee Year (1985), PBS television's local affiliate, KPBS, prepared an award-winning, nationally aired documentary that chronicled the theatre's history.

On 29 October 1984, however, OGT suffered another setback, when the Festival Stage was destroyed by yet another early-morning arson. But OGT's board of directors vowed to rebuild the theatre in time for the June 1985 festival season. Groundbreaking took place on 6 March 1985, and, on 7 June, *A Midsummer Night's Dream*, directed by O'Brien, opened in the new theatre, now renamed the Lowell Davies Festival Theatre in honor of the late Mr. Davies who had been a board officer for 40 years, including service as president of the board from 1945 to 1976.

A milestone was achieved during OGT's Jubilee Year: Combined winter and summer season subscriptions topped 50,000 for the first time, providing OGT with the largest subscriber base of any not-for-profit theatre in the nation. In 1985, OGT mounted its 500th production: *Richard III* directed by John Housman.

In the late 1980s, OGT also embarked on a series of collaborations with several notable American playwrights to mount world premieres of plays, many of which have subsequently been produced on Broadway, off-Broadway, and at leading regional theatres. Among OGT's world premieres have been Neil Simon's *Rumors* and *Jake's Women*, A. R. Gurney's *Another Antigone*, *The Cocktail Hour*, and *The Snow Ball*, and Stephen Sondheim's and James Lapine's Tony Award-winning musical, *Into the Woods*. Additionally, OGT has mounted productions in cooperation with other theatre companies. The **Great Lakes Theatre Festival** and OGT, for example, produced a splendid revival of Federico García Lorca's *Blood Wedding* in 1989. OGT and Yale Repertory Theatre also have collaborated on a number of productions, including August Wilson's *The Piano Lesson* and *Joe Turner's Come and Gone*. These cooperative ventures have allowed both companies to spread the costs of mounting productions and have made productions, particularly of new plays, available to a wider audience. To date, however, OGT has not tried to coproduce a Shakespeare production, mainly because of the expense and logistical organization required, but such a collaboration has not been ruled out for the future.

The 1980s saw a major new outreach effort launched, called Teatro Meta. Initiated by Noel, it is a program designed to explore the resources, history, and talent emanating from the region's sizable Hispanic community. With support from the California Council for the Humanities and the Ford Foundation, Teatro Meta has presented classic and contemporary Hispanic plays in both Spanish and English in various venues in the San Diego area, including the Old Globe complex. Teatro Meta also sponsors an in-schools program of performances and workshops, a Latino Play Discovery Series to encourage Latino playwrights, and The Spanish Golden Age Street Theatre Fest. In 1989,

Raul Moncada became the head of Teatro Meta, and OGT incorporated the program into its ongoing educational and artistic efforts. In the future, Teatro Meta plans to broaden its cultural outreach to include the Asian, African-American and American Indian communities. Despite the fact that the greater San Diego area has a significant Hispanic population, with sizable African-American, and Asian-American populations, patrons, especially subscribers, tend to reflect the demography of American theatre audiences in general—that is, affluent, well-educated, white, and middle-aged. Through Teatro Meta and "Adopt an Audience," a program launched in 1991 that asks current subscribers to contribute the price of a ticket for someone who cannot afford one, OGT hopes to bring more of San Diego's ethnic minorities into the theatre.

In 1987, OGT entered into a joint agreement with the University of San Diego, a private Catholic college, to create an MFA actor-training program, essentially to provide a future core of classically trained performers not only for OGT but for regional theatres in general. To date, this program has proven very successful for both institutions.

Generally, OGT presents 12 to 13 productions annually—646 performances. Roughly 50 percent of its recent productions have been new works—world, American, or West Coast premieres. At least two and sometimes three Shakespeare plays are included in the season. The Shakespeare plays can be presented in any of the three theatres, but they continue to be presented in the summer in a "festival atmosphere." Since 1935, more than a 100 different Shakespeare productions and over 400 productions of plays by other playwrights have been presented. With the exception of *Pericles, Titus Andronicus*, and the three parts of *Henry VI*, OGT has staged all of Shakespeare's plays

OGT has a year-round staff of almost 100, including a full panoply of administrative and production personnel. Rather than hiring a seasonal company, OGT's policy is to obtain the best possible artistic personnel for each production. Thus, actors, directors, and designers are drawn from a nationwide pool. Over the years, however, OGT has built a core of actors, directors, and designers who are regularly contracted for various productions. In recognition of their contributions to the development of OGT, a number of prominent actors, directors, designers, and playwrights have been named Associate Artists of the Old Globe, including actors Jacqueline Brooks, Ellis Rabb, Ken Ruta, David Ogden Stiers, Sada Thompson, and Paxton Whitehead; playwrights Stephen Metcalfe and A. R. Gurney; and designer Douglas Schmidt. Actors, directors, designers, and playwrights who at one time or another have worked at the Old Globe literally comprise a "Who's Who" of the contemporary American stage.

Playing to an average of 95 percent of capacity, OGT earns over 65 percent of its annual budget through ticket sales. Like most regional professional theatres, the remainder of its income comes from federal, state, and municipal grants and from private and corporate support. OGT has generally been very successful in building widespread community support for its programs. In 1989, OGT launched the Advancement Campaign to build a substantial endowment that would assure future growth, development, and financial stability.

We had opportunities to visit OGT on two separate occasions: In 1988, we saw the late director John Hirsch's production of *Coriolanus,* which set the action in a contemporary Latin American country. Powerfully and clearly directed with a strong ensemble cast, headed by Byron Jennings as Coriolanus, and lavishly staged, it was altogether an impressive production. In 1990, we saw productions of C. P. Taylor's bittersweet World War II drama *And A Nightingale Sang* in the Old Globe Theatre and Lanie Robertson's *Lady Day at Emerson's Bar and Grill,* a study of the great blues singer Billie Holiday, in the Carter Centre Stage. Both productions were skillfully directed and designed, with solid performances by casts of experienced professional actors. Taken collectively, these three productions represent the artistic quality and range of OGT and the reason why it clearly merits its reputation as one of the nation's leading professional theatres.

Production History (Shakespeare and classics only; abbreviations in parentheses refer to performance venues other than the Old Globe Theatre; refer to the key below): **1935**: 50-minute versions of *JC, Shr., Ham., Ado, Err., WT, AYL, Mac., MND, AWW, TN, Wiv., Doctor Faustus*; **1936**: 50-minute versions of *Tmp., H8, TGV, Rom., Err., Life and Death of Falstaff (1* and *2H4)*; **1937-38**: *Wiv., MND*; **1938-39**: *Shr*; **1939-40**: no Shakespeare productions; **1941-47**: no productions during these war years; **1947-48**: no Shakespeare productions; **1948-49**:*TN*; **1949-50**: *Shr., Rom.*; **1950-51**: *Ado, Wiv.*; **1951-52**: *AWW, AYL*; **1952-53**: no Shakespeare productions; **1953-54**: *Oth, TN, MV*; **1954-55**: *MM, Ham., Shr.*; **1955-56**: *MND, R3, Volpone*; **1956-57**: *Tmp., Lr., Knight of the Burning Pestle*; **1957-58**: *Mac., Ado, Ant.*; **1958-59**: *1H4, Rom., LLL*; **1959-60**: *JC, AYL, Ham.*;

1960-61: *TN, MV, R3*; **1961-62**: *Shr., 2H4, Oth.*; **1962-63**: *MND, WT, Ant.*; **1963-64**: *Ado, Mac., MM*; **1964-65**: *Wiv, H8, Cor.*; **1965-66**: *Rom., Tmp., TGV*; **1966-67**: *TN, AWW, Oth.*; **1967-68**: *Ham., AYL, Jn.*; **1968-69**: *JC, Err., Mac.*; **1969-70**: *Ado, R2, Cym.*; **1970-71**: *MND, Shr., Ant.*; **1971-72**: *Wiv., LLL, R3*; **1972-73**: *MV, TGV, Lr.*; **1973-74**: *TN, Rom., 2H4*; **1974-75**: *Tmp., Ado, MM*; **1975-76**: *AYL, Oth., Tro.*; **1976-77**: (FS) *Ham., Shr., Tim*; **1977-78**: (FS) *H5, MND, WT*; **1978-79**: *JC, Err., Mac.*; **1979-80**: (FS) *Rom., TGV, LLL*; **1980-81**: (FS) *Lr., Ado, MM*; **1982**: *AYL,* (FS) *Shr.*; **1983**: *TN,* (FS) *1H4,* (CC) *Mac.*; **1984**: *Oth.,* (FS) *Wiv.*; **1985**: *R3,* (LD) *MND*; **1986**: *R2,* (LD) *Ado,* (CC) *JC*; **1987**: *Ant.,* (LD) *Err.*; **1988**: *Cor.,* (LD) *LLL,* (CC) *Tim,*; **1989**: *MM,* (LD) *Rom.*; **1990**: *Ham.,* (LD) *AYL*; **1991**: (LD) *MV, Tmp.*; **1992**: *WT,* (LD) *TGV*; **1993**: *Lr.,*

(LD) *AWW*, **1994**: (LD) *TN, 1H4,*   *2H4.*

Key:
CC: Cassius Carter Centre Stage
FS: Festival Stage
LD: Lowell Davies Festival Stage

Research Resources: This essay draws on materials furnished by Old Globe Theatre and obtained in interviews. OGT does not maintain official archives. The San Diego State University library has a collection of press-books, programs, and promptbooks. Some materials are kept in the administrative offices at the Simon Edison Centre for the Performing Arts. The Thomas Wood Stevens archives are at the University of Arizona. Old Globe Shakespearean productions were regularly reviewed in issues of *Shakespeare Quarterly* between 1950 and 1986. See also Glenn Loney and Patricia MacKay, *The Shakespeare Complex* (New York: Drama Book Specialists, 1975) on the San Diego National Shakespeare Festival.

Site visits and interviews: August 1988; 31 May and 9 June 1990.
Felicia Hardison Londré and Daniel J. Watermeier

REDUCED SHAKESPEARE COMPANY. MAIL: P.O. Box 1564, Big Bear Lake, CA 92315-1564. SITE: touring. ADMINISTRATION: 909/866-2162; Fax: 909/866-2168. ADMISSION: varies, from free to $30.00. SEASON: approximately 215 performances per year. PRINCIPAL STAFF: Scott Ewing, company manager. STATUS: commercial. ANNUAL BUDGET: $250,000. ANNUAL ATTENDANCE: 175,000. FOUNDED: 1981, Daniel Singer.

The beginnings of the Reduced Shakespeare Company (RSC) were as impromptu as its high-spirited performances appear to be. The company's one-show repertoire—a free-wheeling abridgment of all 37 Shakespeare plays plus the sonnets, athletically performed by three men in Converse high-tops and an assortment of wigs—came about almost haphazardly after six years of fooling around with the Bard.

The origins of the fun might be traced back to a Department of Dramatic Art production of Tom Stoppard's *The (15-Minute) Dogg's Troupe Hamlet*, which gave Jess Borgeson his first role at the University of California, Berkeley. He used that material the following summer to audition for a half-hour *Hamlet* (same idea, different script) at a renaissance fair. Cast as Hamlet in that four-person version by Daniel Singer, Borgeson had performed for about three weekends when Singer called to say that the next week's performances would be canceled because the actress who played Gertrude and Ophelia had stepped into a ditch and broken her ankle. Borgeson suggested filling in the part with a friend who had been attending performances and was a quick study. "Great! What's her name?" Singer asked. "Well, that's the thing," Borgeson replied "We're going to need a wig." Adam Long has been wearing the female wigs ever since.

After a season of playing the four-person *Hamlet* at renaissance fairs, Singer went to the University of Washington, Borgeson returned to Berkeley, and Long transferred to the Portland Center for the Performing Arts. Singer and Long teamed up the following summer to tour a two-person *Romeo and Juliet* that they had coauthored by mail. Eventually Borgeson rejoined them and was integrated into *Romeo and Juliet*, while *Hamlet* reshaped itself into a three-man play. At first, they worked for salaries up to $40 a day, until a group of jugglers took the trio under its wing and taught them some tricks of the trade. Singer, Borgeson, and Long learned that passing the hat would bring in five or six times as much as any wages the fairs could pay them. They learned the importance of establishing an intimate connection with their audience, and they discovered a definite relationship between fast pacing, the laugh quotient, and the number of dollars that went into the hat at each performance. This realization, says Borgeson, spurred them to develop their breakneck, laugh-a-second pace. But Long claims a loftier motivation: "We had a mission based on studies of how laughter cures cancer, experiments showing the healing properties of comedy, especially when it's Shakespeare."

Soon the RSC was getting bookings not only at renaissance fairs but also at weddings and as warm-up for groups like the High Rollers in Reno. With a 15-minute version of *Romeo and Juliet* and a 20-minute version of *Hamlet*, the trio suddenly got the bright idea of writing 35 minutes worth of additional material based on Shakespeare's other 35 plays and taking the show to the Edinburgh Festival's Fringe as *The Complete Works of William Shakespeare (Abridged)*. The larval hour-long version was first performed on 19 June 1987 on the Old West set of Paramount Ranch in Agoura, California, and was taken to Edinburgh, where it was given a 10:00 a.m. performance slot. The Reduced Shakespeareans did well, despite the disadvantage of playing to audiences exhausted from late-night theatregoing. And watching the Doug Anthony All-Stars—"a three-man singing and audience assault group from Australia"—taught them how much further they could go in tangling with their audiences.

After Edinburgh, they had intended to "call it quits and stop dressing in tights," but bookings began to pour in. Suddenly their weekend hobby had turned into a thriving business, and a formal partnership was set up in 1988. In 1989, however, Singer left the company to take a job at Walt Disney Studios. Since the show was so closely based upon their personalities, Borgeson and Long were hesitant about continuing the venture. But Borgeson remembered a classmate from Berkeley who had been on the road for two years as a clown with Ringling Brothers Circus. Reed Martin had topped off his Berkeley B.A. in theatre and political science with an M.F.A. in theatre, a Bachelor of Fun

Arts from the Ringling Brothers-Barnum and Bailey franchise, and an umpire degree from the Bill Kinnaman Umpire School in St. Petersburg, Florida. Borgeson tracked Martin down by telephone and sounded him out. Nine days later, Martin was putting his own imprint on *The Complete Works*.

Return visits to the Edinburgh Fringe inspired refinements that expanded the production to about two hours, more or less, depending upon what happens in the audience-participation segment. The team's success there led to a three-month tour of England, Scotland, Wales, and Ireland in 1990, a four-week engagement at the Lilian Baylis Theatre in London in December-January 1990-91, a seven-week tour of England in 1991, and an open-ended run at the Arts Theatre in London's West End, beginning 23 March 1992. Besides performing at festivals in New York City, Montreal, Tokyo, and Dublin, they have toured to Singapore and Australia; they would have gone to Israel in 1992 if the West End opportunity had not come up. In Belfast, they performed at the opera house across the street from the Europa Hotel, which was bombed a week after they left. "It was obviously meant for the Reduced Shakespeare Company," Long observes, and Borgeson chimes in: "Yeah, their timing was off."

The Reduced Shakespeare Company is a profit-making, five-person, limited partnership, composed of the three performers plus Sa Thomson (billed in the program as "backstage dresser/costume and prop goddess") and company manager Scott Ewing. Having joined the venture in 1987 to relieve Daniel Singer of the pressure of business details, Ewing holds the fort at the Los Angeles headquarters and handles bookings. After going nonstop for so many years, the company has decided on a policy of taking six weeks off each season. The five partners share all decisions, with only an occasional breakdown in communications between Los Angeles and "the road." Borgeson offers a favorite example of the kind of mix-up that can occur: During a visit to Stratford-upon-Avon ("to make sure Bill was not, as many a journalist has suggested, spinning in his grave over our work"), the performers saw a beautiful sepia-toned linen tea-towel printed with a facsimile of the Folio table of contents. They called Ewing and suggested he have some made for them to sell. The new merchandise awaited them on their return to Los Angeles: it was "a dishrag with a list of plays on it." "And the price is exorbitant," says Long, "just as for other dishrags." The RSC souvenirs are always in demand, but the troupers resist becoming overburdened with them, as they travel mostly by air with their entire set, props, costumes, and personal items as checked baggage. Other merchandise items are a cassette single with their "Rap Othello" and tank tops with the company's "Screamin' Bill" logo, designed by Singer.

The company owns three drops, two of them brightly painted with the same design: a stylized Elizabethan theatre facade with a wide, curtained central doorway. In front of this, they easily adapt their playing to a proscenium or thrust stage. The third drop, for use in smaller spaces, depicts a generic Shakespearean landscape: a forest, a river, a village, and a castle. Karl Hamann, whose connection with the group goes back to Berkeley, travels with the performers as technical director. He calls himself "the hired help," but, Long adds, "he also offers spiritual guidance." Thomson recalls that she linked up with the others just before the first Edinburgh engagement: "They asked, 'Can you make this costume?' and I said, 'I don't know. I'll try.'" Before *Hamlet* and *Romeo and Juliet* were absorbed into *The Complete Works*, the actors had done their own costume changes; but the more complex show required lightning-fast changes and some backstage organization. Thomson does her work on roller skates, enforcing discipline and dispensing humor behind the scenes. Indeed, Thomson has contributed such gems to the script as "Omelette the Danish" and "Titus Androgynous."

Although the RSC's success is built upon what some would see as "trashing the Bard," there is at the core a genuine love and respect for Shakespeare's work. Indeed, the three performers all harbored aspirations toward legitimate Shakespearean acting and hint that they have not renounced such hopes for the future. Borgeson, who earned his B.A. in English at Berkeley, suspects that he might end up teaching Shakespeare "when this old body can't handle playing thirteen roles in one evening." Martin's pre-circus credentials include acting Shakespeare at the **Old Globe Theatre**, La Jolla Playhouse, and Berkeley [now **California] Shakespeare Festival**; even when he was in the circus, he was reading everything he could get his hands on about Shakespeare. Long also acted with various California Shakespeare festivals and tells about going to Ashland to audition for the **Oregon Shakespeare Festival**: "I went up there three consecutive years, and every year they sent me a rejection letter. The fourth year I decided not to audition, and they sent me a rejection letter anyway!"

Pressed for a statement of artistic philosophy, Martin posits: "To put the 'shake' back in Shakespeare." "We're returning Shakespeare to the groundlings," Borgeson told Glenn Collins (*New York Times*); "More importantly, we feel that Shakespeare went too far and wrote too many words. So we get right to the sex, the fighting, and the killing." According to Long, the RSC started out with no more philosophy than that of the jugglers who were passing the hat on the street: to make some money and make people laugh. "It has a lot to do with just getting through to an audience in whatever way we can," he says. "And if that means eating fire or playing the accordion, then we do it." "We don't make fun of Shakespeare," adds Martin, "we make fun of the pompous, overblown productions of Shakespeare that sort of make people sick of him. We try to make him fun and accessible." Borgeson comments: "When people have 'Shakespeare fear,' it has nothing to do with the quality of the plays, but with the middleman—whether it's a teacher or a theatre company." But when Long claims that "I've never seen a Shakespeare production that I found in any way boring," the others nod in acknowledgment, recalling how Long sat absolutely spellbound during a four-hour production in Romanian at the Dublin Theatre Festival.

The script for *The Complete Works of William Shakespeare (Abridged)* is credited to Borgeson, Long, and Singer, with additional material by Martin. Although the basic format has changed little since 1987, they manage to keep the show looking fresh and spontaneous. "We involve the audience so much in the show that we never know exactly what's going to happen from one show to the next," says Long. According to Borgeson, "You might say we live for those times when things go wrong. Some of our best material has come from times when somebody screws up on stage and we're forced to think on our feet and come up with something new on the spot." Bits that were once improvised get incorporated on a regular basis as long as they work. Looking over the script every once in a while reminds the actors of ideas that have been dropped or added along the way. "We seem to rotate things in and out," Borgeson notes, "using a joke until it dies, as all jokes eventually do." Along with ever-changing topical references to names in the news, they try to inject local allusions. They credit the Doug Anthony All-Stars with showing them that "you can get away with insulting people if you insult everybody, including yourself." "So we try to be egalitarian," adds Martin," offend everybody equally."

The action begins with Borgeson as an evangelical professor challenging the audience's knowledge of Shakespeare and conscripting a callow know-it-all audience member who turns out to be Long. They quickly move into *Romeo and Juliet*, followed by quick clips from the other plays. *Titus Andronicus*, done as a cooking show, blends slapstick and verbal humor ("Bone appétit!"). *Othello* is a rap song, *Troilus and Cressida* brings together a mechanical Godzilla and an inflatable dinosaur, and the history plays compress into a football game between the Reds and the Whites. Since all the comedies and romances have the same basic ingredients (and the tragedies are funnier anyway), everything from *As You Like It* to *The Merchant of Venice* is amalgamated into one fantastic plot that can be dispatched in a moment. An index card, bearing all 154 sonnets printed in reduced type, is passed around in the audience. By the end of Act 1, the trio has dealt with every play but the big one. Long sees what's coming for him and heads for the hills with Borgeson in pursuit, so Martin calls an intermission.

Martin's finest moment comes after intermission, when he desperately employs his circus skills—fire-eating, accordion playing, tapping out the William Tell Overture on his windpipe—to hold the audience's interest until Long and Borgeson return to launch into *Hamlet*. The three performers whiz through the plot in a flurry of props (a mini-ghost lowered in on a string, Yorick's bouncing skull, a life-size ragdoll representing Ophelia's corpse), wigs (also serviceable, in a pinch, as beards), and costume pieces (like Gertrude's monumental pink falsies). An audience participation segment breaks the narrative, as two spectators are conscripted to stand in for Ophelia and her "ego on the run," while the actors lead sections of the audience in chanting the conflicting instructions of her id, ego, and super-ego. At the performance I attended in Houston, the surrogate Ophelia was a game student actress who had actually played Ophelia. In Kansas City, a woman in an advanced stage of pregnancy was unwittingly chosen; her husband was hauled in as a shadow figure. Just when the "high-speed, roller-coaster condensation" would appear to be skidding out of control, there is an abrupt change of pace and mood: Long renders Hamlet's "What a piece of work is man" soliloquy in a breathtakingly simple and direct manner. Following the half-hour *Hamlet*, the company offers a 47-second reprise, then a three-second encore, capped by the 47-second version played backwards, "so you can hear the subliminal satanic messages." The ghost's "BOO" flashcard now reads "OOB." For Ophelia's reverse-action drowning, Long spews out a mouthful of water.

Certainly, there are some who have little patience for the RSC's skewing of the Bard and his work, but they cannot say they weren't warned. The program includes the disclaimer: "not recommended for people with heart ailments, back problems, English degrees, inner ear disorders, and/or people inclined to motion sickness. The Reduced Shakespeare Company cannot be held responsible for expectant mothers."

In the two years since the foregoing essay was written, several changes have occurred. The RSC's summer 1992 booking in London's West End was successful enough that the run was extended to October. During that time, Borgeson retired from performing, married Sa Thomson, moved back to Los Angeles, and adopted the name J. M. Winfield, under which he writes screenplays. He also edited the book version of the RSC's *Complete Works of William Shakespeare (Abridged)*. His role in the show was adeptly taken over by Austin Tichenor, "another old Berkeley pal." Tichenor continued working with Long and Martin to develop *The Complete History of America (Abridged): From the New World to New World Order*. Doing for American history very much what they had done for the Bard, the troupers were booked solidly for the show's 1993-94 American tour.

Production History: **1981**: Half-hour *Ham.*; **1982**: Half-hour *MND* (cast of six); **1982-87**: Reduced *Rom.* and *Ham.*; **1988**: Abbreviated Ballet Theatre (ABT)'s *Lucinda, Wood Nymph of the Glade*; **1987-92**: *The Complete Works of William Shakespeare (Abridged)*; **1993**: *The Complete History of America (Abridged)*.

Research Resources:

Borgeson, Jess, Adam Long, and Daniel Singer. *The Reduced Shakespeare Company's The Complete Works of William Shakespeare (Abridged)*. Edited by Professor J. M. Winfield. New York: Applause Books, 1994.

Collins, Glenn. "The Shoehorn School of Doing Shakespeare." *New York Times* (13 June 1991): B1, B4.

Gussow, Mel. "Shakespeare Writ Small, As You Might Like It." *New York Times* (15 June 1991).

J. H. "Party Dude Shakespeare." *TheaterWeek*, 4: 44 (10 June 1991): 32.

Londré, Felicia Hardison. "These Guys Do 'Hamlet' Backwards." *American Theatre* (April 1992): 54-55.

Magruder, James. "Judicious Howl." *The Village Voice* (18 June 1991): 89.

Peterson, Jean. "The Complete Works of William Shakespeare (Abridged)." *Shakespeare Bulletin* (Summer 1991): 24-25.

Interview: 1 February 1992. Performances attended: 11 and 31 January 1992; 10 December 1993.

Felicia Hardison Londré

SAN FRANCISCO SHAKESPEARE FESTIVAL. MAIL: P.O. Box 590479, San Francisco, CA 94159-0479. SITES: Golden Gate Park, San Francisco; St. James Park, San Jose; Lake Merritt, Oakland. ADMINISTRATION: Lone Mountain Theatre, 330 Parker Street, San Francisco; 415/666-2222. ADMISSION: Free. SEASON: 24 performances; Sat., Sun. afternoons, August through October. PRINCIPAL STAFF: Bobby Winston, producer; Jill Linwood, associate producer; Russell Blackwood, tour and internship director. FACILITY: No permanent facility; outdoor, open stages erected in parks. AUDITIONS: San Francisco Bay Area, Equity/non-Equity, in May. STATUS: Equity-LOA. ANNUAL BUDGET: $579,000 (1993). ANNUAL ATTENDANCE: 40,000 (1993). FOUNDED: 1982, Bobby Winston.

Since 1983, the San Francisco Shakespeare Festival (SFSF) has presented "Free Shakespeare in the Park" for all who find their way into the various performance venues on weekend afternoons in late summer. For the festival's tenth anniversary season (1992), *Romeo and Juliet* drew exceptionally large crowds to Liberty Tree Meadow in Golden Gate Park. To discover the architect of such a successful program, I met Bobby Winston, the producer, not the artistic director, of the company. As local critic Robert Hurwitt noted in his November 1988 article in *American Theatre*, "SFSF is the only regularly operating theatre company in the Bay Area—and one of the few in the country—without an artistic director." Winston makes this unusual arrangement work because he hires experienced directors as contract employees and then makes no further intrusion into rehearsal and production. The director is free to choose the play, the cast, and the production style. Winston manages the budget and is usually able to raise whatever funds are needed to realize the production. Winston has little time to sit and talk about the work he does to promote and nurture Shakespeare in an urban climate. The morning I interviewed him, he was preparing for the afternoon's performance by checking a balky body microphone, rushing through lunch, and transporting cans of gasoline to the park, since there are no electrical plugs, only gas-guzzling generators. "I do gas, water, and garbage," he quipped.

The SFSF emerged from the **New Shakespeare Company** (NSF), an organization founded by Margrit Roma and Clarence Ricklefs in 1964. In the 1960s and 1970s, the NSF's performances in Golden Gate Park functioned as dress rehearsals for their nationwide tours to college campuses during the academic year. In 1982, philosophical differences split the NSF into two groups. Winston joined the group that soon became the SFSF. He laughs about how early failures only sharpened his appetite to make the venture work. He notes that a review of *The Tempest* in 1983 was titled "Shakespeare and a Snooze in the Park." Winston now leads a very successful organization that stages a major production in San Francisco; the production then travels for two-week runs at St. James Park in San Jose and at Lake Merritt in Oakland. The SFSF also mounts a "Shakespeare in the Schools" program that annually tours two different hour-long plays to schools and groups across California. While SFSF usually presents only one major production a year, the routine has occasionally changed. In 1984, for example, Bertolt Brecht's *Mann ist Mann* joined *The Taming of the Shrew*; in 1987, director Albert Takazauckas paired *Much Ado About Nothing* with Beaumarchais's *The Marriage of Figaro*; and in 1991, the vaudeville group Fratelli Bologna's version of *Medea* alternated with *The Tempest*.

The mission of the SFSF, according to the 1992 program, is to expand the audience for the classics through their presentations—"an irresistible mix" of great performances and a beautiful setting. The organization cannot afford an "artistic vision," because the focus is on mounting the best, most accessible productions possible for spectators who are more accustomed to rock concerts than to Shakespeare. The festival must lure the uninitiated into trying something new. Since there are no ticket sales, it is difficult to know precisely who the audience is, but Winston has noted that the audiences for *Romeo and Juliet* were younger than in past years—ages 25 to 30, rather than 35 to 40 years of age. My own observations would indicate that the SFSF draws from a genuine cross-section of the highly diverse Bay Area population.

In guiding the SFSF from a less than $5000 budget in 1982 to its present half-million-dollar level, Winston works ceaselessly to raise money and to find donors for supplies and services. He attempts to be as creative administratively as the production is artistically. "Attract resources and manage them wisely" is his creed. There are two boards of directors, one an honorary slate and the other an active unit each of whose members donates some particular expertise to fueling the festival's momentum. "A la carte, à la park," the annual SFSF benefit, features music and a lavish spread of food and wine. Clearly Winston and his colleagues have found a formula that works. The SFSF is a well-regarded organization among Bay Area actors and directors. After ten seasons, the SFSF has also become an established institution for Bay Area theatregoers.

For SFSF's "Shakespeare in the Schools" program, five or six actors tour California with a one-hour version of one of Shakespeare's plays. SFSF works hard to make sure that the production articulates with the school curriculum. In

1992, "Shakespeare in the Schools" gave 350 performances at 275 schools across California. Prisons, parks, and shopping malls have also begun to request appearances. In 1992, for example, the tour played in twelve different malls.

The scenery for *Romeo and Juliet* was set on three separate stages arranged in a semi-circle around the meadow in Golden Gate Park. The scenery suggested ruined neoclassical stone buildings, covered with contemporary graffiti and three to four levels of scaffolding. The largest structure, which faced the audience directly, served as the Capulet residence and had several large platforms and staircases. The audience had to turn left to watch the action at Friar Laurence's cell—a platform with an arched doorway at the rear, a few steps, and a simple white metal cabinet for herbs. On the audience's right was a public monument, a column whose disrepair hinted at the thematic thrust of the play—the clash between the traditional and the contemporary, between youth and adulthood.

Director Dennis Bigelow chose to set the play in our own time to reinforce the relevance of the action. Costume designer Beaver Bauer's creations were outstandingly witty commentaries on the generational gap the play emphasizes. The older Montagues and Capulets, as well as the Nurse and Friar Laurence, were all very smartly turned out in 1960s fashion, but their garb contrasted sharply with the striking, contemporary leather outfits and torn jeans of the younger crowd.

The opening scene underlined the generational conflict when the romantic pre-curtain music was suddenly interrupted by the noisy appearance of opposing groups of young men. The ensuing rumble was very physical. The two groups battled with garbage can lids, swords, and chains; Tybalt cracked a bull whip. Sirens and rock music blared as the actors, who managed to be both funny and menacing, pushed through the audience to get at one another. The actors all wore body mikes, an absolute necessity in such a boisterous production in a large urban park. In an interesting instance of cross casting, Escalus was played by Ingrid Berstmann as a take-charge and capable female corporate executive.

Mercutio (Charles Shaw Robinson) was in several respects the pivotal character in this production. He was the master of the gangs that prowled the sets, and, after he died, the production never returned to the high level of energy his presence had projected. "Are you ready for some football?" he bawled at his entrance. His "Queen Mab" speech was not so much a verbal *tour-de-force* but instead a thoughtful progression of insights ending with a muted, sad premonition of his violent death. When the fatal fight scene began, Mercutio used a banana as his weapon as he kissed Tybalt; then he climbed the scaffold to "moon" him and the audience. The crowd's laughter was instantly halted by the deaths that followed. Waiting police, ambulance sirens, and Romeo's anguished "I am Fortune's fool" shocked all into silence. Lady Capulet's (Lura Dolas) shrill cries for vengeance as she raised her bloodied hands over her nephew's corpse provided another numbing moment. The action ended as the audience's attention was drawn to the sight of Tybalt's bloody back as he was slowly carried out.

The second half of the performance was no match for the first segment in terms of energy and frenetic pace. The acting remained excellent, especially in moments that featured a more mature Juliet (Maura Vincent) and a Friar Laurence (Robert Sicular) whose rich tones impressively heightened the sense of tragic loss for both families, but the tone was somber and muted. Still the huge crowd clearly appreciated Bigelow's contemporizing approach as they responded with laughter and applause throughout the afternoon. The production ended with a short speech by one of the actors asking for donations. The entire cast then plunged into the audience with collection baskets. Getting to meet the performers in such a manner seemed like a very pleasant way to end the afternoon.

Production History: **1982**: *TN*; **1983**: *Tmp.*; **1984**: *Shr., Mann ist Mann*; **1985**: *Shr.*; **1986**: *Wiv.*; **1987**: *The Marriage of Figaro, Ado*; **1988**: *AYL*; **1989**: *MND*; **1990**: *R3*; **1991**: *Tmp., Medea* (with Fratelli Bologna); **1992**: *Rom.*; **1993**: *TN*; **1994**: *Shr., Oh, Kay.*

Research Resources: Archives for the San Francisco Shakespeare Festival are informally maintained at the festival administrative offices. See also the following publications: Robert H. Hurwitt, "SFSF Blooms, Takes Root in Golden Gate Park," *American Theatre* (November 1988): 34-35; Jean Schiffman, "Shakespeare Festivals," *Callboard* (June 1991): 3-7.

Site visit and interview: 26 September 1992.
Patricia M. McMahon

SHAKESPEARE AT BENBOW LAKE. MAIL: P.O. Box 365, Garberville, CA 95542. SITE: Benbow Lake State Park, Garberville, CA. ADMINISTRA-TION: 707/923-2211; Fax: 707/923-9364. BOX OFFICE: 707/923-2613. AD-MISSION: $12–$15. SEASON: one week, with three plays presented in repertory. PRINCIPAL STAFF: Dana Dimmick, managing director. FACIL-ITY: outdoor stage (capacity 450). ANNUAL BUDGET: $40,000 (1993). ANNUAL ATTENDANCE: 2,100 (1993). FOUNDED: 1983, Judith Sutton, Jim Hibbert.

Shakespeare at Benbow Lake (SABL) was initiated in 1983 when the foun-ders of Saratoga's Valley Institute of Theatre Arts (VITA) suggested to Jim Hibbert, head of district parks in Humboldt County, that VITA tour three productions from its regular season at the Paul Masson Winery to Garberville. (VITA also toured to Sand Harbor at Lake Tahoe; see **Shakespeare at Sand Harbor**.) Hibbert endorsed the suggestion, and, with the support of the Garberville community, VITA's visit to Benbow Lake became an annual event.

The success of SABL is a tribute to the people of the area and to the guiding spirits of the organization, Dana and John Dimmick. She is SABL's part-time managing director, while he manages its finances. SABL is governed by a board of directors that generally follows the lead of its administrators in making its decisions. Dana Dimmick describes SABL as "a volunteer organization dedicated to bringing professionally produced theatre to our rural resort area." Other unpaid volunteers act as concession stand operators, ushers, and so on, while members of the Garberville Volunteer Fire Department put up banners advertising the festival and erect stage lighting. The management of the Benbow Inn provide an opening night party, and Garberville residents house and help to feed the visiting performers. SABL is thus a community effort. It is understandable that the community has its own agenda for SABL. According to a grant proposal made by the organization in 1992, SABL is "part of a concerted area-wide effort to move from a lumber-based economy to a tourist/fine arts-based economy."

The theatre site in Benbow Lake State Park, easily accessible from U.S. Route 101, is located at the water's edge and across a road from the venerable but comfortable Benbow Inn, a National Historic Landmark. Promotional literature refers to audiences watching "egrets, ospreys, and herons fly up the river to their nesting sites." In July, at the beginning of the season, 250 padded theatre chairs (reserved seats) and 200 folding chairs (general admission seats) are set up on the turf facing a platform stage built and maintained by the Rotary Club since 1985. Lighting and scenery are provided by the touring company. Drinks and light refreshments are available at a nearby concession stand, and a catered "Picnic in the Park" is offered for $10 a person from 5:30 to 7:30 p.m. on each performance night. Attendees are advised to dress warmly and/or to bring a blanket, since summer evenings can be cool. Those who plan to stay overnight are urged to make reservations at the Benbow Inn or a nearby motel as early as possible.

Although it has operated without a deficit since 1986, SABL has weathered a few organizational crises. In 1985, for example, rain nearly washed out a performance of *The Count of Monte Cristo*. Perhaps the most serious crisis occurred in 1991, when VITA, under new management after the departure of the founders the previous year, disbanded and cancelled all performance plans. A replacement production was quickly arranged: A San Francisco Bay Area theatre offered to present *A Midsummer Night's Dream* in a 1960s setting. But in June, that group withdrew its offer, and it seemed like the end of "Shakespeare at Benbow Lake." At the last moment, however, the VITA founders rescued their adopted community by forming a new production company, assembling a troupe of professional actors, borrowing sets and costumes, and mounting a production with only three weeks of rehearsal time. "Ad-hoc acting troupe pulls off a miraculous *Comedy of Errors*," enthused the local *Times-Standard* critic (30 August 1991) about the newborn **Shakespeare Theatre Arts Repertory** (STAR). In 1992, California Theatre Center's **Sunnyvale Summer Repertory** brought *Love's Labour's Lost* and *Dracula* to Benbow Lake to complement STAR's *Charley's Aunt*.

Surviving difficult and unexpected challenges has only strengthened Garberville's resolve to maintain this yearly theatrical tradition. When director Dana Dimmick tried to cancel the 1991 season because it looked as though there would be no show, few business underwriters wanted their money back. And, she adds, "It's Shakespeare that sells—the other productions do well, but the really large audiences flock to his plays." In some respects, SABL resembles the **Oregon Shakespeare Festival** (OSF) as it was thirty years ago, particularly the involvement of community volunteers, businesses, and other organizations. There are, however, significant differences. Unlike the OSF, SABL produces no plays; instead, it contracts companies. As a presenting rather than a producing organization, SABL has only limited artistic control. SABL's artistic philosophy is to present the best performing groups available and the most artistically responsible productions. SABL would seem to have succeeded in this goal. Randy Omer-Sherman (Eureka *Times-Standard*, 11 September 1992) wrote of SABL's accomplishment that "Shakespeare has come a long way in 10 years, from its one-time haphazard seating and bare set, to its current well-designed and professional productions."

The OSF in its formative years was closely connected to academic institutions, in particular Southern Oregon State College in Ashland and Stanford University in California, which provided personnel and support, acted as stabilizing influences, and encouraged continuance and growth. SABL has no similar connections. Without such influences, SABL's continuing growth and development may be more limited. Though significant, these differences are less important in 1993 than the fact that the plays at Garberville have for a decade attracted audiences averaging 2,100 for a five-night run. SABL and the people who support it are to be congratulated on the success of their efforts in bringing Shakespeare to northern California.

Production History: **1983**: *LLL, AYL, The Three Musketeers*; **1984**: *MV, Shr., Robin Hood*; **1985**: *TGV, MND, The Count of Monte Cristo*; **1986**: *MV, Err., Don Quixote*; **1987**: *AYL, Tmp., Charley's Aunt*; **1988**: *Ado, Mac., Tom Jones*; **1989**: *MND, TN, Cyrano de Bergerac*; **1990**: *Wiv., 1H4, The Beaux' Stratagem* (**1983-1990** productions mounted by VITA); **1991**: (STAR) *Err.*; **1992**: (SSR) *LLL, Dracula*; (STAR) *Charley's Aunt*; **1993**: (STAR) *TGV, The*

Liar (Goldoni); **1994**: (Festival Theatre Ensemble) *MND, Per.,*   *Mister Toad Rides Again.*

Research Resources: Dana Dimmick maintains an informal collection of materials about Shakespeare at Benbow Lake.

Johnson, Ronna. "Outdoor Theatre Offered *As You Like It* at Benbow." *Times-Standard* [Eureka, CA] (13 August 1987): A-3.

"Shakespeare at Benbow Is a Truly Quality Effort." *Times-Standard* [Eureka, CA] (2 August 1990): no page.

Shakespeare at Benbow Lake, "Organizational Support Program Application 1992-93." Unpublished grant proposal, 1992.

Trauth, Beti. "Ad-hoc Acting Troupe Pulls Off a Miraculous *Comedy of Errors*." *Times-Standard* [Eureka, CA] (30 August 1991): 23.

Site visits and interview: 9 May 1992 and 25 September 1992
Patricia M. McMahon and Hassell B. Sledd

SHAKESPEARE FESTIVAL/LA. MAIL: 411 W. 5th Street, Suite 815, Los Angeles, CA 90013. SITE: various. ADMINISTRATION/BOX OFFICE: 213/489-1121. ADMISSION: tickets for performances in Los Angeles are free with a donation of canned food; performances at the South Coast Botanical Gardens and Descanso Gardens, $5–$12. SEASON: two productions, playing in the evenings for six weekends at several locales from late June to late August. PRINCIPAL STAFF: Ben Donenberg, artistic director; Stacy Brightman, associate director; Heather McQuarrie, administrative associate. FACILITIES: Citicorp Plaza, outdoor temporary stage (capacity 350); Japanese Gardens, West Los Angeles Veterans Administration Hospital grounds, outdoor temporary stage (capacity 1,000); South Coast Botanical Gardens, Palos Verdes, outdoor temporary stage (capacity 1,000); Descanso Gardens, Antelope Valley, outdoor temporary stage (capacity 1,000). AUDITIONS: Los Angeles and New York. STATUS: LOA. ANNUAL ATTENDANCE: 25,000 (1993). FOUNDED: 1986, Ben Donenberg.

The Shakespeare Festival/LA (SFLA) was founded in 1986 by Ben Donenberg to offer productions of Shakespeare that would be accessible to people of all economic means in Los Angeles. Like the charitable organizations that produced plays in seventeenth-century Spain, Donenberg's mission is social as well as theatrical. Admission is free to SFLA performances in Los Angeles, but playgoers are asked to bring cans of nonperishable food in exchange for a ticket. The food is then donated to organizations like the Salvation Army and AIDS Project Los Angeles. In 1993, for example, SFLA collected food valued at over $100,000. A Los Angeles supermarket chain, Vons, then matched this sum two to one. (By now, SFLA has been a conduit for over $1 million worth of food.)

Donenberg studied at the Second City in Chicago, the **National Shakespeare Company**, and the Juilliard School, and, in the early 1980s, he performed with the **New York Shakespeare Festival**. He came to Los Angeles in 1983 with his production *Starship Shakespeare*, a spoof that mixed characters from Shakespeare and the popular *Star Trek* television series. First staged at New York City's Lincoln Center Out-of-Doors Festival, *Starship Shakespeare* proved very popular in Los Angeles where it played in three theatres over a ten-month period and was named "Cult Classic" by the *Los Angeles Times*.

With a donation from Lenore Gershwin, the widow of lyricist Ira Gershwin, for whom he was doing some part-time archival work, Donenberg launched SFLA in June 1986 with a production of *Twelfth Night*. It played for a total of eight free performances on consecutive Saturday and Sunday afternoons on a makeshift outdoor stage in Pershing Square in downtown Los Angeles. About 800 playgoers attended the production, and Donenberg was sufficiently encouraged to continue the project. By 1989, SFLA had expanded to five weekends, with performances in both the afternoons and evenings in three different venues, at Citicorp Plaza in downtown Los Angeles, in the John Anson Ford Amphitheatre in Hollywood, and at the Long Beach Rainbow Lagoon.

In 1989, SFLA launched *Shakespearience!*, a special introduction to Shakespeare for elementary school students. Through authentic dance and music, a puppet show adaptation of a Shakespeare play, and live interviews with historical Elizabethan figures played by actors, each and every child involved participates in activities that might have been common to Elizabethan children. Mounted at the Los Angeles Children's Museum, the initial *Shakespearience!* played to over 2,500 children drawn from elementary schools and children's centers throughout Los Angeles. In 1993, SFLA created two additional educational outreach programs. One called "Will Power to the Youth" is an innovative program that employs 15 teenagers from the inner city; over a six-week period, the program guides them through a series of intellectual, emotional, and physical activities that culminate in a performance of a one-hour adaptation of *Romeo and Juliet*. For Donenberg, the program was an opportunity "to demonstrate that the arts can be a source of job creation and education and, through the intense process that these young people are engaged in, build their self-esteem and enrich their appreciation for theatre and the great things in life" (as quoted in *Inside*, the official newsletter of Rebuild LA, August 1993). The second program is designed to train teachers to introduce Shakespeare into an English as a Second Language (ESL) curriculum.

Described by associates as "incredibly dogged" and "very tenacious and strong willed," Donenberg over the years has proven to be very successful at raising private, corporate, and foundation support to finance SFLA as a free Shakespeare festival and educational organization.

The artistic quality of SFLA productions has steadily improved with each successive season. Reviews of SFLA productions have generally been very favorable. The reviewer for the weekly *Downtown News*, for example, wrote about SFLA's 1991 *Love's Labour's Lost*, set in a 1950s "beatnik" milieu, that "the staging is lucid and acute, the acting at times superb and the whole affair completely engaging" (29 July 1991). The inventive 1992 *A Midsummer Night's Dream* evoked not a bucolic, enchanted forest but the environs of post-riot Los Angeles. The setting featured chunks of freeway, weeds, and assorted pieces of urban debris, including the last four letters of the famous "Hollywood" sign. Characterizations complemented the setting. Oberon and Titania, for example, "were a dashing couple: he a mustachioed, roustabout in a tired white suit; she a tan-skinned blond voluptuary: King and Queen of the streets." *Los Angeles Times* critic Sylvie Drake had some minor reservations about the urban *mise-en-scène* but praised the production overall for its "post-modern impudence," which gave *A Midsummer Night's Dream* "an immediacy and purpose hard to beat that made "us see things as they are and diffuse the menace with laughter" (13 July 1992).

In 1993, SFLA expanded to two productions playing in various Los Angeles venues and also at the South Coast Botanical Gardens on the Palos Verdes Peninsula and at the Descanso Gardens in Antelope Valley. Since its founding, SFLA undoubtedly has become an increasingly visible, respected, and significant institution in the cultural life of greater Los Angeles.

Production History: **1983**: *Starship Shakespeare*; **1984-1985**: n/a; **1986**: *TN*; **1987**: *TGV*; **1988**: *Err.*; **1989**: *AYL*; **1990**: *Ado*; **1991**: *LLL*; **1992**: *MND*; **1993**: *Rom.*, *TGV*; **1994**: *TN*, *Err.*, and a one-hour Youth Theatre production of *Rom.*

Research Resources: An informal archive of reviews, programs, and photographs is maintained at the SFLA offices. This essay is based on material supplied by Shakespeare Festival/LA.

Daniel J. Watermeier.

SHAKESPEARE IN THE PARK. MAIL: P.O. Box 5108, Chico, CA 95927. SITE: Cedar Grove in Bidwell Park, Chico. ADMINISTRATION/BOX OFFICE: 916/343-5210. ADMISSION: $9–$4. SEASON: 25 performances, late July through August, 7:30 p.m., Wed.–Sun.; pre-show at 6:30 p.m. PRINCIPAL STAFF: Robin Trenda, president, Wall Street Center for the Arts; Christine Myers and Dan DeWayne, producers. FACILITY: outdoor, natural amphitheatre. AUDITIONS: mid-April in Chico area. STATUS: non-Equity. ANNUAL BUDGET: $75,000 (1994). ANNUAL ATTENDANCE: 6,000 (1993). FOUNDED: 1990, Wall Street Center for the Arts.

Begun in 1990, the month-long Shakespeare in the Park (SIP) is produced by the Wall Street Center for the Arts and partially funded by the city of Chico. The goal of Shakespeare in the Park, according to producer Dan DeWayne, is "to provide an opportunity for the development of professionally presented community theatre in a beautiful out-of-doors setting." The inaugural offering in 1990 was *Romeo and Juliet*, directed by Brad Moniz. The following year, the producers' use of the Cedar Grove area of Bidwell Park earned the following description: "Picture if you will a massive oak in a small clearing, towering over a pale white disk of a stage." Paula Munier Lee went on to observe how the director of *A Midsummer Night's Dream*, Robert Taylor, "capitalized" on "the extraordinary beauty of the setting" (Chico *Enterprise-Record*). In 1992, Moniz returned to direct *The Taming of the Shrew*, which played for three weeks. Subsequently, Donna Breed, a professor of theatre at California State University at Chico guided a two-week run of Thornton Wilder's *Our Town*. Larry Mitchell, a reviewer for the *Enterprise-Record*, wrote: "I was impressed by what I found. Everyone involved is to be congratulated for this endeavor, bringing outdoor theatre to the park."

The Chico community has wholeheartedly embraced SIP, demonstrating their appreciation by increased attendance and participation. The pre-show entertainment, which begins at 6:30 p.m., features an array of local talent who perform as strolling minstrels, costumed musicians, jugglers, and dancers. Local restaurants provide a wide variety of foods and drink for sale on site for picnickers who arrive early to enjoy the lovely wooded setting skirted by Big Chico Creek.

Future plans for Shakespeare in the Park include expanding the play offerings and pre-show entertainment and increasing the use of the outdoor setting to encourage exploration of Bidwell Park. Another feature of SIP's program is the Special Audiences Night. The group supplies transportation to and from Cedar Grove for those with special needs. On-site sign language interpretation and Braille play synopses are also available.

Production History: 1990; *Rom.*; **1991**: *MND*; **1992**: *Shr.*, *Our Town*; **1993**: *Tmp.*, *Robin Hood*; **1994**: *AYL*, *Count Dracula*.

Research Resources: Archives are informally maintained by the Shakespeare in the Park producers.

Interview: 20 July 1992.
Patricia M. McMahon

SHAKESPEARE ORANGE COUNTY. MAIL: P.O. Box 923, Orange, CA 92666. SITE: campus of Chapman College in Orange. ADMINISTRA-TION/BOX OFFICE: 714/744-7016; Fax: 714/744-7015. ADMISSION:

$18–$23. SEASON: June–September, 8:00 p.m.,Thurs.–Sun.; 8:00 p.m.; 2:00 p.m., Sun. PRINCIPAL STAFF: Thomas F. Bradac, producing artistic director. FACILITY: Waltmar Theatre (capacity 256). AUDITIONS: announced in *Drama-logue*. STATUS: SPT. ANNUAL BUDGET: $195,000 (1993). ANNUAL ATTENDANCE: 10,000 (1993). FOUNDED: 1991, Thomas F. Bradac.

After 13 seasons as founding artistic director of the **Grove Shakespeare Festival**, Thomas F. Bradac left that position to join the communications faculty at Chapman College in Orange. Within six months, he had founded another festival, Shakespeare Orange County (SOC) and had launched the publicity for the inaugural season in summer 1992. Billing it as "a new theatre with old friends," Bradac enlisted a founding company of five actors who had worked with him at the Grove: Daniel Bryan Cartmell, Michael Nehring, Elizabeth Norment, Kamella Tate, and Carl Reggiardo. Lee Shallatt, another Grove Shakespeare Festival veteran, directed the opening production, *The Winter's Tale*, which Bradac followed with *Hamlet*.

SOC is a nonprofit corporation supported by an active volunteer group, Will's Guild. Subscribers enjoy a quarterly newsletter, *Good Will*. Since the festival is based at a college, educational programing supplements the productions. For example, Charles Vere, Lord Burford, was engaged to speak on the Shakespeare authorship question during his 1992 lecture tour.

The 256-seat Waltmar Theatre is located at Center Street and Palm Avenue on the Chapman College campus in the historic city of Orange. The campus is easily accessible from the 22, 55, and 57 freeways and from Interstate 5. The grounds offer a lovely setting for picnicking before the performance, and a Renaissance pre-show is presented on the Schweitzer Mall Outdoor Stage.

Marketing for SOC's inaugural season made canny use of photographs to let the Orange County theatregoing public know that these were artists they recognized, offering a level of artistry they could trust. Bradac's excitement is evident when he speaks of his liberation from commercial constraints. In 13 seasons at the Grove, only 19 of Shakespeare's plays were produced. "Shakespeare's greatest hits" were relied upon out of economic necessity; *Much Ado About Nothing* and *The Taming of the Shrew* were each mounted three times. Now, Bradac says, "I'm doing it more out of love. I'll do the more challenging plays."

Elaborating on his philosophical approach to the new festival, Bradac says he has always believed that the inspiration comes from the text. "If the text could stand the concept, then it was fine. If the concept overwhelmed the text, then it wasn't fine. But the new theatre will be much more conventional in that the concept really is going to take a back seat to the text. The more I produce Shakespeare, the more I realize that if the text is clear and investigated, the inspiration really springs out of it and sings."

Production History: 1992: *WT, Ham.*; **1993**: *Ado, JC*; **1994**: *Alms for Oblivion* (an original one-man show on life of Shakespeare), *TN, Lr.*

Interview: 9 January 1992.
Felicia Hardison Londré and Daniel J. Watermeier

SHAKESPEARE SANTA CRUZ. MAIL: Performing Arts, University of California–Santa Cruz, (UCSC), Santa Cruz, CA 95064. SITE: Performing Arts Complex at UCSC. ADMINISTRATION: 408/459-2121. BOX OFFICE: 408/459-4168 (April–August only). ADMISSION: $12–$20 (1992). SEASON: 72 performances, including previews of four plays in rotating repertory, from late July to 1 September (seven weeks). 8:00 p.m., Tues.–Sat.; 2:00 p.m., Wed., Sun.; 7:30 p.m., Sun. PRINCIPAL STAFF: Danny Scheie, artistic director; Paul B. Hammond, managing director. FACILITY: Performing Arts Theatre, an indoor, flexible stage (capacity 537); Karen Sinsheimer and Audrey Stanley Festival Glen, an outdoor natural amphitheatre (capacity 700); Concert Hall Theatre, an indoor, proscenium stage (capacity 230). AUDITIONS: open auditions in New York, Chicago, Denver, San Diego, Los Angeles, San Francisco, and Santa Cruz. EQUITY STATUS: Equity Guest Artist. ANNUAL BUDGET: $800,000 (1991). ANNUAL ATTENDANCE: 34,000 (1993). FOUNDED: 1981, Karen and Robert Sinsheimer, Audrey Stanley.

The founding of Shakespeare Santa Cruz (SSC) was prompted by the death in early 1980 of University of California–Santa Cruz professor C. L. "Joe" Barber, a distinguished Shakespearean scholar whose *Shakespeare's Festive Comedies: A Study in Dramatic Form and its Relation to Social Custom* (1959) remains an important, influential study. Barber's colleague, theatre professor and director Audrey Stanley, was approached by UCSC's chancellor, Robert Sinsheimer, to organize a Shakespeare festival in Barber's memory. Indeed, Stanley and Barber had discussed the idea of a Shakespeare festival in Santa Cruz as early as 1975. From the spring of 1980 through early 1981, Stanley organized several faculty and community members into "Shakespeare Santa Cruz" to support a summer festival. Stanley was familiar with several American festivals, having been the first woman to direct Shakespeare at the **Oregon Shakespeare Festival** and having directed at the **Colorado** and **California** (formerly, Berkeley) **Shakespeare Festivals** as well. Indeed, her original training and theatre experience had been with the **Old Vic** and the **Royal Shakespeare Company** in her native Britain. As she has recalled, "I mixed in things from all three [American festivals] to try and extract what was the best for our situation." The nascent organization considered various "festival" ideas, including inviting the Berkeley Shakespeare Festival and the RSC to tour one or more of their productions to Santa Cruz and even creating a "Camp Shakespeare," a summer immersion program in Elizabethan living.

But, in February 1981, a proposal was submitted to Chancellor Sinsheimer for a 1982 festival at UCSC, to include productions of *King Lear* and *A Midsummer Night's Dream*, seminars, workshops, and films. Sinsheimer approved the plan and provided a significant start-up grant of $50,000.

Stanley has said that she was motivated in part to select *Lear* because Michael Warren, another English emigré and a distinguished UCSC Shakespearean scholar, was then working on a comparative study of the *Lear* quarto and folio texts and was eager to serve as a textual consultant for a production. She thought "a very exciting program would be to begin with the greatest play and in many ways the toughest—to say this was a serious festival—and perform it inside [in the Performing Arts Theatre] and somewhere outside perform *A Midsummer Night's Dream*: the two supreme examples of tragedy and comedy." Stanley also used her RSC connections to draw English actors Tony Church and Julian Curry to the first season as guest artists and to teach classes during the summer sessions. To test community support for a festival, in the summer of 1981, SSC invited the **Will Geer Theatricum Botanicum** company from Los Angeles to present a performance of its spirited, updated version of *The Taming of the Shrew* outdoors at UCSC. According to Stanley, "the audience seemed to come out of the woodwork, and the forests. There was a tremendous sense of Santa Cruz support. It made us think our own festival might be feasible."

Buoyed by this success, SSC proceeded with its planning and mounted its inaugural season. In keeping with its scholarly and serious intentions, and at Warren's urging, the standard, conflated, hybrid *Lear* text was tossed aside in favor of the First Folio version. Church and Curry performed Lear and the Fool respectively, supported by a cast of talented graduate students and community actors. *Lear* was staged indoors on a somber set suggesting black spikes; the actors performed in Napoleonic-era costumes. *A Midsummer Night's Dream*, in contrast, was performed outdoors, in a glen surrounded by redwoods, in an 1890s "Coney Island" style. The two productions attracted an attendance of 7,716 and brought in over $50,000 in ticket revenue. Critical reaction to this new venture was sparse, but Glen Lovell, theatre critic for the *San Jose Mercury News*, wrote: "If this is the quality of theatre that artistic director Audrey Stanley can deliver in her inaugural season, the mind races at the possible treasures awaiting us next year."

For her second season, Stanley mounted a production of *Macbeth* featuring Curry in the title role. She also hired a newly appointed UCSC theatre professor, Michael Edwards, an Australian emigré with a masters degree in directing from UCLA, to direct a production of *The Merry Wives of Windsor*. Edwards has said that he wanted the play to say something to an American audience of today and, at Stanley's suggestion, he relocated the play from Elizabethan England to the Plymouth Colony in the 1640s. Both productions were very successful with attendance increasing to 8,375 and income to over $53,000.

In a lengthy, and very detailed review in *Shakespeare Quarterly* (Spring 1984), Mary Judith Dunbar, a University of Santa Clara Shakespearean specialist, praised Stanley's "penetrating" *Macbeth,* based on an uncut folio text and performed without an intermission. She praised Curry for his generally "cerebral" Macbeth, marked by consistently "clear and intelligent choices," "daring contrasts," and "sharp focus and timing." Edwards' *Merry Wives* was compared very favorably to Terry Hands' celebrated 1968 RSC production (revived in 1975 and 1976) for balancing realism with farce and for "maintaining a continuous flow of action and an impression of communal life." Dunbar also commended the value of the scholarly conference organized to complement the productions. "Clearly this Festival in its second year," she concluded, "shows exceptional potential both in quality of productions and in possibilities for bringing the academy and the theatre together in collaboration." In fact, several ancillary educational programs were initiated in 1983. "Weekend with Shakespeare" offered an opportunity to go "behind the scenes" for a closer look at the plays, their backgrounds, and the SSC productions. Included in the weekend were discussions with directors, actors, and scholars. The 1983 scholarly conference eventually developed into an educational program called "Focused Research Activity in Shakespeare" (FRA), a consortium of UCSC scholars and performers who are invited to use the Shakespeare Santa Cruz productions to analyze the deep connections between text, interpretation and performance. Often the results of this research are presented in public lectures during the festival and throughout the year. Michael Warren serves as the director of the FRA program.

Stanley has also been particularly interested in getting young people involved with Shakespeare, and area teachers had expressed interest in having Shakespearean scenes performed in their classes. In 1983, Sue Warren guided the festival into a Shakespearean workshop for children, out of which Stanley was able to recruit child performers for both *Macbeth* and *Merry Wives.* In the following season (1984), the children's workshop expanded into "The Company of Little Eyases," named after the children's acting troupe mentioned in *Hamlet.* This program continues to provide live performances of one-hour versions of Shakespeare's plays by child actors between the ages of eight and fifteen. Following a winter or spring workshop open to children from schools throughout Santa Cruz County, auditions are held; the children's company is organized and the play rehearsed. It is then toured countywide during late June and early July. All performances are free and open to the public and are supported by various Santa Cruz County businesses. In 1985, another program, called "Shakespeare To Go," evolved to meet the needs of area schools. Essentially, Shakespeare To Go is an educational program touring scaled-down 45-minute versions of Shakespeare's plays. Following the model of the **ACTER** program, the productions are presented by only nine actors, with minimal costuming, scenery, and properties. The actors are drawn from among UCSC theatre students and directed by a UCSC Theatre Arts faculty member.

The production is rehearsed during the winter quarter academic term and, then tours to high schools, junior highs, and community venues during the spring quarter. In 1991, Shakespeare To Go gave 31 performances in Santa Cruz County.

For SSC's third season, the Performing Arts Theatre was unavailable because it was being earthquake-proofed (Santa Cruz is near several major geological faults). Although there were those who suggested that the festival "go dark" for a season, Stanley wanted to keep the momentum going. She opted to produce an experimental version of *The Tempest* in the small Performing Arts Concert Hall and to do *1 Henry IV* in the outdoor theatre. Director and designer Bradford Clark adapted various Balinese theatrical conventions, including shadow and rod puppets, masks, and gamelan music for his production of *The Tempest*. Although Dunbar (Winter 1984) found moments of this experiment visually "fascinating" and "impressive," she frequently missed "the power of the acted word." Edwards, assisted by designer Norvid Jenkins Roos, updated the action of *1 Henry IV* to our own time, with the men of the court wearing dark business suits, Falstaff sporting a leather motorcycle jacket, and Prince Hal in his madcap role styled after the British punk rock star, Boy George. In the latter part of the play, however, Hal appeared as a crew-cut army recruit wearing combat fatigues. The set was a stripped-down replica of Shakespeare's Globe theatre with a crashed military helicopter protruding from the roof. Through such a *mise-en-scène*, Edwards aimed to make "strong connections between contemporary social and theatrical conventions and conventions inherent in Shakespeare's play" (Dunbar, Winter 1984). With strong performances by Paul Whitworth as Hal, Tony Church as Falstaff, and Canadian actor Neil Freeman as Henry IV, this production proved an immense popular and critical success. Dunbar reported (Winter 1984) that Alan Dessen, Shakespearean scholar and an authority on Shakespearean staging, thought the Santa Cruz production better than the three most recent productions he had seen of the play by the **Stratford Festival**, the **Oregon Shakespeare Festival**, and the RSC. Local critics called it a "hit" and gave it four stars. (It should be noted that Edwards' production preceded British director Michael Bogdanov's celebrated contemporized staging of *The Henry's* by four years, although Bogdanov had staged contemporized versions of *Hamlet* and *Romeo and Juliet* even earlier. See **English Shakespeare Company**.) To complement *1 Henry IV*, Stanley staged four performances of a studio reading of selections from *2 Henry IV*, entitling it *Hal and Falstaff* and using only five actors in multiple roles. But, despite the popularity of this production, attendance and revenue declined in 1984 to 7,728 and $47,693, respectively.

The 1984 season, however, set the direction for the future development of the festival. At the end of the season, Stanley appointed Edwards associate artistic director, after the 1985 season, he succeeded her as artistic director. The successful collaboration between Edwards and Paul Whitworth also continued through numerous productions, including *Hamlet* (1985), *Richard II* (1986),

Henry V (1987), *Amadeus* (1990), and *Measure for Measure* (1991). In 1990, Whitworth was appointed associate artistic director of SSC, as well as professor of theatre at UCSC. Edwards' productions of *Merry Wives* and *1 Henry IV*, furthermore, became a hallmark of the SSC approach to staging Shakespeare's plays. Edwards has said that he is "completely uninterested in doing museum theatre." His productions aim:

> to be vivid and alive and . . . to connect with contemporary culture. . . . This doesn't mean just contemporizing the plays in terms of setting and costume, although that is how people superficially would recognize that aim. . . . It's in the examination of the behavior of relationships that makes it modern. . . . Modern means to be modern in performance as well as in a commitment to clarity and sense in the speaking of the text. . . . Modern means making the language clear as well as setting the plays in worlds that release the play in sometimes dangerous and unexpected ways.

In 1985, SSC initiated the practice of producing two Shakespearean plays along with a non-Shakespearean, modern play. By the end of this season, both attendance and income had doubled compared to the previous season. With the hiring of Brian Payne in 1986 as managing director, the management of the festival also became more professional. A concerted effort began to attract private and corporate contributors to the festival, including the underwriting of individual productions. From its beginning, the festival had employed visiting RSC actors, but such underwriting allowed the addition of Equity guest artists, supported by talented graduate students recruited from across the country and San Francisco Bay Area actors. In 1991, SSC employed eight Equity guest artists in addition to Paul Whitworth.

In 1988, SSC mounted "contemporized" productions of *Titus Andronicus*, *Julius Caesar*, and *Antony and Cleopatra*, as well as *The Comedy of Errors* presented in a 1930s-style barnstorming rag-tag company. Scott Rosenberg, theatre critic of the *San Francisco Examiner*, wrote in a lengthy and judicious review that, with this season, SSC "made strides in consistency and imagination that place its work well within the same league as longer-established regional festivals like the Oregon Shakespeare Festival. . . . The company is still relying on RSC visitors for some of its leading roles, but they are better integrated into the productions, and they're fully balanced by several American Equity actors who can match them soliloquy for soliloquy." In the following season, Judith Green of the *San Jose Mercury News*, called SSC "the best Shakespeare Company in the Bay Area and (except for the Oregon Shakespeare Festival which it often equals) on the West Coast. . . . a model of scholarship, artistry and production values." In 1989, SSC also won a number of awards presented by *Drama-Logue*, a West Coast theatre journal, including an award to Mark Rucker for his direction of *Romeo and Juliet* and to David A. Baker for his performance as Romeo. (Other recipients of *Drama-Logue* performance awards that season included such notable performers as Topol, Ben Vereen, Andrea Marcovicci, and Nehemiah Persoff.) Attendance in the 1988 and 1989 seasons also increased to over 23,000, while ticket revenue increased to over $250,000.

The 1990 season was seriously jeopardized by the disastrous earthquake of October 1989 that struck many Central Coast and Bay Area cities, including Santa Cruz. While SSC's facilities were undamaged, many Santa Cruz businesses were devastated. (As of the summer of 1991, many of the destroyed or badly damaged buildings in downtown Santa Cruz had still not been rebuilt.) Earned income accounts for about 70 percent of the revenues needed for SSC's annual operating expenses. The remaining 30 percent comes from a modest grant from the UCSC chancellor's office and, largely from business underwriting of production and advertising and from private contributions. Faced with significant losses, local business and individuals were not in a financial position to support SSC for the 1990 season. A number of corporate foundations and arts agencies in the area, however, succeeded in persuading the U.S. congress to appropriate, through the National Endowment for the Arts (NEA), about $635,000 in immediate emergency relief for arts programs in the earthquake-stricken region. Subsequently, an NEA matching grant generated an additional $2.4 million for regional arts organizations. The Cultural Council of Santa Cruz County alone raised $220,000, an indication of the significance of the arts in this area. A grant of $22,000 from the Arts Recovery Fund enabled SSC to play a full three-play season in 1990. The San Francisco Opera also contributed significantly by donating costumes for SSC's production of *Amadeus*.

Although SSC is a coproduction of the Santa Cruz county community and UCSC, in terms of its management, artistic philosophy, and budget, it operates as an autonomous, professional, nonprofit theatre company, governed by its own 26-member board of directors. But, like other festivals associated with a university (the Colorado Shakespeare Festival, for example, with which SSC shares several similarities) SSC is fairly dependent on various resources provided by UCSC. Edwards, Stanley, Warren, and Whitworth, for example, are professors during the academic year at UCSC. The festival technical director is also production technical director for performing arts at UCSC during the academic year. The festival, of course, uses UCSC facilities, equipment, utilities, and certain other services, although it does pay a rental fee of $12,000 (1990) for this use. The university, moreover, provides an outright grant to the festival—about $65,000 in 1990. Students from the university provide a pool from which to draw additional performance, production, dramaturgical, and administrative personnel (lighting technicians, cutters, painters, box office staff, etc.). Without such direct and indirect support, SSC undoubtedly would find it more difficult financially to maintain its high level of production quality and organizational management and to pay all its personnel, including student performers and technicians (a total payroll of 178 in 1991), on an annual operating budget of about $800,000. In return for its support, UCSC does gain community good will and an important educational and cultural program for its students. To date, the arrangement seems mutually advantageous. Edwards, for example, despite his desire to develop an increasingly strong professional company and to expand the season beyond the summer, believes that the festival should remain at UCSC. In fact, a proposed MFA program in theatre at UCSC, which Edwards himself will head, will likely complicate but also strengthen the connections between the university and the festival, between scholarship, training, and performance.

In 1991, to celebrate its tenth anniversary, SSC expanded to four productions and 74 performances, including two performances in early September at Villa Montalvo in Saratoga, about 30 miles to the north of Santa Cruz. In fact, SSC's experiments in touring had been initiated during the 1990 season, with six performances at Villa Montalvo and another performance at Foothill College's Performing Arts Festival in Los Altos. Edwards would like to expand this touring program through the month of September to integrate SSC more fully into the cultural life of the region. At the same time, Edwards wants to maintain a commitment to "vivid and provocative interpretations" of Shakespeare, as well to the production of new and contemporary plays, all complementing and informing one another, particularly "at the level of acting."

The two Shakespearean productions that I observed in 1991 certainly adhered to Edwards' programatic ambitions. *A Midsummer Night's Dream*, for example, was staged outdoors in the Festival Glen. The setting consisted of a series of rough-hewn platforms, ramps, tree houses, and a network of ropes and pulleys arranged between and among the towering redwood trees at the bottom of the glen. (The program noted that the set was built "in close consultation with the UCSC Campus Facilities Tree Crew to assure that no harm would be done to the redwood trees.") The costumes were designed to suggest a range of contemporary styles and to reinforce characterization. The lovers, for example, wore clothing that evoked 1950s teenage fashion. The "mechanicals" were dressed like contemporary skilled workers in jeans, coveralls, work boots, and so forth. On their first entrance, they sang "Heigh-ho, heigh-ho, it's off to work we go" from *Snow White and the Seven Dwarfs*. Theseus wore a gaudy military uniform suggestive of some Latin American dictator; while Hippolyta, attired in a leather outfit with a distinctly German air, suggested a stereotypical, mannish, contemporary Valkyrie.

As he had done in his 1988 *Comedy of Errors* production, director Danny Scheie mocked traditional perceptions of gender roles and relationships by cross-casting and cross-dressing key characters. Megan Cole played both Hippolyta and Oberon, while Michael Rogers played both Theseus and Titania, exchanging his uniform for tights and a brightly hued ballerina's tutu. The respective fairy attendants also were cross-cast and cross-dressed. Titania's fairy court, for example, was entirely male and dressed in brightly colored high-top sneakers, tutus, wigs, and diaphanous wings, like a rag-tag Ballet de

Trocadero. Hilarious in itself, the costume convention stimulated numerous comic gestures and business satirizing the absurdity of gender stereotyping.

The production, indeed, was marked by an exuberant physicality. Hermia, for example, at one point energetically "manhandled" a docile Demetrius, tweaking his ears, pummeling him, dropping him on his head, and even slamming him into a tree. At another point, Lysander and Demetrius executed a series of athletic handsprings. On-stage physicality was complemented by the activities of the off-stage flying crew, completely visible to the audience, as they manipulated the various ropes, pulleys, and winches that flew, with varying degrees of success, Titania's tutu clad fairies, as well as Puck, played with aplomb by sexagenarian Audrey Stanley. Overall, it was a skillfully directed and acted production that, despite program notes alluding to the sexual darkness inherent in the dramatic action and language, clearly aimed to be and succeeded as a festive farce.

In contrast, director Edwards highlighted decadent sexuality, political intrigue, and corruption in his contemporized production of *Measure for Measure*. The unit setting, for example, initially suggested the kind of unsavory street or district found in most modern cities–42nd Street in New York or San Francisco's Broadway. Flashing neon light signs advertised "Adult Theatre," "Topless," "Male Revue," and "Sex Acts." Steam wafted through two grates in the floor, as from below a city street. In the background, a set of clear plastic boxes were illuminated to reveal leather-clad disco dancers writhing to an "Enigma" recording. The costumes generally suggested an artful synthesis of contemporary and Jacobean modes of dress. Inventive stage business, furthermore, often reinforced the connections between the dramatic action and contemporary culture. Entrance to the prison, for example, was gained through a hi-tech handprint identification plate; while in Act IV, scene 3, the provost brought in Ragusine's head packed in a styrofoam picnic cooler.

Indeed, Edwards' approach to *mise-en-scène* often reminded me, though not in every detail, of Bogdanov's *Measure for Measure* for the Stratford Festival in 1985, the most effective production of the play I have ever seen. By comparison to the Bogdanov production, the SSC production faltered, though only to a certain degree, and in the areas of performance subtlety, nuance, and especially depth. Overall, the direction was nevertheless assured and the performances creditable, with Whitworth especially authoritative as Vincentio; the interpretation was clear and engaging.

Both productions, moreover, were very well received by capacity audiences. Although concrete demographic data is unavailable, the SSC audiences I observed seemed affluent, well-educated, and probably mostly in the 40-to-60 age range. While the majority of the audience is drawn from Santa Cruz County (51 percent), almost 30 percent come from adjacent Santa Clara County and 10 percent from other Bay Area counties north of Santa Cruz. The remaining 9 perecnt or so come from other parts of California and out of state. (At *A Midsummer Night's Dream*, for example, I sat next to a dentist from Ann

Arbor, Michigan who volunteered that he had regularly attended the festival since its founding.) Despite the multiethnic composition of the population in the region and SSC's commitment both to recruiting and casting across ethnic lines—Theseus/Hippolyta was played by a black actor, for example—and to connecting with the entire community, the audiences I saw were overwhelmingly white.

In ten years, however, SSC has developed a fairly high level of professional attainment. Growing from a community/university-organized event, it now has widespread regional, national, and even some limited international recognition. With an expanding financial base, a clear sense of mission, and solid community support, it will undoubtedly continue to enrich its various patrons for decades to come. It should be noted that in 1992 Scheie succeeded Edwards as artistic director and that in 1994, Paul Hammond, formerly associate producer of South Coast Repertory, replaced Payne as managing director.

Production History: **1982**: *Lr.*, *MND*; **1983**: *Wiv.*, *Mac.*; **1984**: *1H4*, *Tmp.*; **1985**: *AYL*, *Ham.*, *Rosencrantz and Guildenstern Are Dead*; **1986**: *R2*, *TN*, *A Life in The Theatre*; **1987**: *Ado*, *H5*, *Company*; **1988**: *Err.*, *JC*, *Tit.*, *Ant.*; **1989**: *LLL*, *Rom.*, *Once in a Lifetime*; **1990**: *WT*, *Oth.*, *Amadeus*; **1991**: *MND*, *MM*, *Our Town*, *Waiting for Godot*; **1992**: *Shr.*, *Mac.*, *A Doll's House*; **1993**: *Err.*, *AWW.*, *Dr. Faustus*, *Damn Yankees*; **1994**: *Wiv.*, *MV*, *The Rape of Tamar*.

Research Resources: Archival materials are housed in the Shakespeare Santa Cruz administrative offices at UCSC. See also the following selected publications.

Dessen, Alan C. "Staging Shakespeare's History Plays in 1984: A Tale of Three Henrys." *Shakespeare Quarterly* (Spring 1985): 75-79.

———. "Exciting Shakespeare in 1988." *Shakespeare Quarterly* (Summer 1989): 201-03.

Dunbar, Mary Judith. "Shakespeare/Santa Cruz." *Shakespeare Quarterly* (Spring 1984): 107-12.

———. "*Henry IV* and *The Tempest* at Santa Cruz." *Shakespeare Quarterly* (Winter 1984): 475-79.

———. "*Hamlet* and *As You Like It* at Santa Cruz." *Shakespeare Quarterly* (Summer 1986): 241-44.

———. "*Richard II* and *Twelfth Night* at Santa Cruz." *Shakespeare Quarterly* (Summer 1987): 220-24.

Esta, A. J. "San Francisco Bay Area." *Drama-Logue* (October 1989): 29.

Foley, Kathy. "Shakespeare Santa Cruz Festival, 1991." *Theatre Journal* (May 1992): 229-33.

Green, Judith. "Bay Area Summer Guide to the Bard." *The San Jose Mercury News* (21 July 1989): 16-E.

Morgan, Gwyn. "Shakespeare at Santa Cruz." *Drama: The Quarterly Theatre Review*, 1 (1989): 7-9.

Rosenberg, Scott. "Shakespeare Santa Cruz Takes Big Strides." *San Francisco Examiner* (20August 1988): C-1, 11, 12.

————. "Shakespeare's Youthful Passions, Youthful Follies." *San Francisco Examiner* (2 August 1989, B-1, 10.

Winn, Steven. "The Bard's Provocative Pair." *San Francisco Chronicle* (1 August 1989): E-2.

Site visits and interviews: 30 June 1990 and 17 August 1991.
Daniel J. Watermeier.

SHAKESPEARE THEATRE ARTS REPERTORY. MAIL: 926 Hedegard Avenue, Campbell, CA 95008. SITE: Sanborn-Skyline County Park. ADMINISTRATION/BOX OFFICE: tickets by phone order only: 408/379-7208. ADMISSION: $8–$15. SEASON: June and September at Sanborn-Skyline County Park. 8 p.m., Thurs.–Sat.; 3:30 p.m., Sun.; July on tour in Northern California. PRINCIPAL STAFF: Judith Lyn Sutton, John B. Swartz, Bill Peck, producers. FACILITY: outdoor stage (capacity 400). AUDITIONS: local South Bay area. STATUS: non-Equity. ANNUAL BUDGET: $25,000 (1992). ANNUAL ATTENDANCE: 5,000 (1992). FOUNDED: 1991, Judith Lyn Sutton, John B. Swartz, Bill Peck.

The Shakespeare Theatre Arts Repertory (STAR) was established by the Valley Institute of Theatre Arts (VITA) founded in Saratoga, CA, in the late 1970s by Judith Lyn Sutton, John B. Swartz, and Bill Peck to demonstrate their belief that "the arts provide life, vitality, spirit to the community." The trio formed VITA to create a source of professionally produced and performed classics for South Bay Area audiences and a theatre-training program for students of all ages. In 1979, the VITA Shakespeare Festival opened its initial season at the Villa Montalvo Center for the Arts in Saratoga. In the following year, they moved to the Paul Masson Mountain Winery in Gonzales, where they used the magnificent Renaissance-style facade of the winery to provide a backdrop for their outdoor productions. In later years, they also performed at the Forest Theatre in Sanborn Park in Saratoga, at Benbow Lake in Garberville, and at Sand Harbor near Lake Tahoe (see **Shakespeare at Benbow Lake** and **Shakespeare at Sand Harbor**). VITA created a very popular summer formula by combining two Shakespearean selections with the production of a related "classic," such as *Cyrano de Bergerac* or *Robin Hood*. In ten years, audiences grew from about 3,000 to 37,000, according to *Sunset* magazine, but, in early 1989, the three founders withdrew from the management of VITA, and the following year the organization disbanded.

Responding to calls and letters from former patrons, however, Sutton, Swartz, and Peck established a new organization in 1991 called STAR, which was originally an acronym for Summer Theatre Arts Renaissance. The suggestion of rebirth was aptly demonstrated when, in three weeks time, the company assembled a production of *The Comedy of Errors*, using a troupe of professional actors and borrowed sets and costumes. STAR won an enthusiastic reception from the citizens of Garberville when the new group arrived to rescue Shakespeare at Benbow Lake's 1991 season. Subsequently renamed the Shakespeare Theatre Arts Repertory, the aims of the company echo VITA's original mission: "to nurture the arts of theatre through the revival of the classics" and to create a conservatory for high school and college students (and soon, for those of all ages and levels of training). STAR participants are professional performers, veterans of stage, television, and film, the majority of whom have elected to remain non-Equity in part because of the dearth of consistent union employment in the South Bay Area and also because they wish to remain eligible to act in those plays that spark their interest. *The Comedy of Errors* played at Sanborn Forest Theatre as well as at Benbow Lake. In 1992, *Charley's Aunt* was presented in Garberville and then moved to open-air performances at Saratoga High School while the Sanborn Park facilities were being upgraded. In 1993, STAR planned to present Shakespeare's *Two Gentlemen of Verona* as well as Carlo Goldoni's *The Liar* in a series entitled "Love Italian Style." According to Peck, the series is intended to explore "the betrayal, deceit and double dealing all too often involved in love's pursuit." Both plays will open in Saratoga and then alternate in repertory for the six performances at Benbow Lake.

Production History: **1991**: *Err.*; **1992**: *Charley's Aunt*; **1993**: *TGV, The Liar*.

RESEARCH RESOURCES: Archives are informally maintained at the Shakespeare Theatre Arts Repertory administrative office. See also "Open Air Shakespeare," *Sunset* (May 1989): 80-84. Jean Schiffman, "The Shakespeare Festivals," *Callboard* (June 1991): 3-7.

Interview: 19 March 1993
Patricia M. McMahon

SONOMA VALLEY SHAKESPEARE FESTIVAL. MAIL: Odyssey Theatre, P.O. Box 727, Sonoma, CA 95476. SITE: Gundlach Bundshu Winery, 2000 Denmark Street, Sonoma. ADMINISTRATION: 2510 Claremont Drive, Santa Rosa, CA 95405. BOX OFFICE: 707/575-3854. ADMISSION: $15; children under 12 free. SEASON: 24 performances, July–September: 6:30 p.m., Sat., Sun. PRINCIPAL STAFF: Carl Hamilton, executive/artistic director; Jamie R. Smith, business and box office manager. FACILITY: outdoor, open stage (capacity 600). AUDITIONS: local and San Francisco Bay Area in February. STATUS: non-Equity. ANNUAL BUDGET: $50,000 (1992). ANNUAL ATTENDANCE: 4,800 (1992). FOUNDED: 1992, Carl Hamilton.

The Sonoma Valley Shakespeare Festival (SVSF) is a recent initiative of the Odyssey Theatre, which was founded in the early 1980s by Carl Hamilton. After almost a decade of producing contemporary plays such as Christopher Durang's *Beyond Therapy,* Tom Stoppard's *The Real Thing,* and John Patrick Shanley's *Danny and The Deep Blue Sea,* Hamilton persuaded the Gundlach Bundshu Winery's owner, Jim Bundshu, to let him mount a summer Shakespearean production on the grounds of the winery. With funds raised from local individuals and an NEA grant, Hamilton opened his first SVSF production on 11 July 1992.

The grounds open for playgoers at 5:30 p.m. on Saturdays and Sundays, leaving an hour for dinner before the performance begins. Picnic tables are set up in an area where patrons can purchase wine, desserts, T-shirts, and visors, or can rent beach chairs. A short distance beyond this area, ushers collect tickets and direct patrons to the nearby hillside performance site.

At the base of the hillside is a large, stepped platform stage, designed by California State University—Sonoma professor Peter Maslan. Permanent wooden screens surround the stage and provide several up-and downstage exit and entrance possibilities. These large and handsomely crafted flats are stained in colors that richly complement the vineyards surrounding the site. Musicians are on hand to entertain before, during, and after the production.

The Merry Wives of Windsor was a judicious choice to open a new theatrical venture in a vineyard setting. Actor John Reid's age, girth (padding added, but not obviously so), witty by-play, and hilarious physical discomfort as Falstaff made him a solid center for this fast-paced and effective ensemble production. In contrast, *Pericles, Prince of Tyre,* which joined the season's repertory the week of 18 July, seemed like a more risky selection. Director Roy Jimenez told Gary Peterson (*The Press Democrat,* 16 July 1992) that he viewed the play as "a spectacular theatrical event" and as "a wide open romantic fantasy with pirates, magicians, sailors, lords and shipwrecks." Sonoma audiences were treated to an entertaining, often amusing, and gripping adventure story. The costuming offered striking color combinations and suggested exotic locales with clever motifs and simple touches that communicated instantly. The final offering for the 1992 season, an adaptation by James McClure of John O'Keefe's *Wild Oats,* transported the action to the American Wild West, winning the praise of local critics and audiences. For 1993, Hamilton plans to stage five productions: three Shakespeare plays, a Greek comedy, and an American classic.

Production History: **1992**: *Wiv.*, *Per.*, *Wild Oats* (James McClure's adaptation of John O'Keefe's original); **1993**: *Err.*, *MND*, *The Servant of Two Masters*; **1994**: *TN, Mac.*, *A Funny Thing Happened on the Way to the Forum, Tartuff.*

Research Resources: Archives for the Sonoma Valley Shakespeare Festival are informally maintained by the Odyssey Theatre.

Site visits and interview: 23 August and 12 September 1992.
Patricia M. McMahon

SONOMA VINTAGE THEATRE—SHAKESPEARE IN THE VALLEY OF THE MOON. MAIL: Sonoma Vintage Theatre, P.O. Box 312, Sonoma, CA 95476. SITE: B. R. Cohn Winery, Glen Ellen. ADMINISTRATION: 18121 Barrett Street, Sonoma, CA 95476. BOX OFFICE: 707/939-1369. ADMISSION: $11–$13, children under 12 free (1994). SEASON: early August to late September, 7:00 p.m., Sat.–Sun., grounds open at 5:30 p.m. PRINCIPAL STAFF: Nancy Nollen, artistic director, Mark Staley, managing director, Kathy Mason, executive producer. FACILITY: Winery courtyard area, audience at picnic tables. AUDITIONS: Bay Area/Sonoma Valley in May. STATUS: non-Equity. ANNUAL BUDGET: $8,000 (1992). ANNUAL ATTENDANCE: 2,400 (1992). FOUNDED: Sonoma Vintage Theatre 1978 by Charles Bearsley; Shakespeare at Buena Vista, 1980; Shakespeare in the Valley of the Moon, 1993.

Shakespeare in the Valley of the Moon (SVM), named after the larger Sonoma Valley where it is located, is part of Sonoma Vintage Theatre's (SVT) regular season. Profits from their summer venture provide production financing for the fall through spring season when SVT performs in Andrews Hall, Sonoma Community Center. SVM originally began in 1980 as Shakespeare at Buena Vista, an experiment to see if presenting scenes from Shakespeare plays in the courtyard of California's oldest winery would attract an audience. The experiment proved very popular and each summer for 12 years, a full-length production of one of Shakespeare's comedies was presented each Sunday evening in September at the Buena Vista Winery. In 1993, however, SVT moved to the B. R. Cohn Winery because Cohn offered a better venue with more flexibility in scheduling that Buena Vista was willing to offer. In 1993, they departed from Shakespeare to offer a production of Aristophanes' *Lysistrata*. But in 1994, now renamed Shakespeare in the Valley of the Moon, a production of *Romeo and Juliet* was performed for two weekends throughout the months of August and September.

In 1992, SVT's production of *The Taming of the Shrew* was staged in the courtyard space in front of the three story, ivy-clad Buena Vista Winery facade. The setting for *The Taming of the Shrew,* for example, was minimal: a pair of screens, an occasional table, a carpet on the courtyard pavement, and assorted properties. Downstage, a large fountain, a permanent feature of the winery courtyard, gurgled continuously. The Elizabethan-style costuming, however, was striking, and the lighting was technically sophisticated. Patrons sat at picnic tables in a large, roughly semicircular ring around the fountain. SVT board members coordinated backstage duties and produced additional tables when new patrons arrived unexpectedly. Late-summer Sunday evenings, picnic dinners, local wine, and Shakespearean comedy must seem like a splendid combination because large, enthusiastic crowds are invariably in attendance.

Simplicity and a clear focus on the courtship-versus-marriage relationships were the outstanding aspects of SVT's *Shrew*. Returning for her fourth year, director Kate Kennedy omitted the Induction scene and opened with Shakespeare's Act I, scene 1. According to local critic Laura Horton, "it was as if assembled picnickers were suddenly treated to a performance in the round in the middle of an Italian street." The pace of the show was rapid, and the cast used the fountain and the surrounding audience in clever, inventive ways.

While SVT is an amateur community-theatre organization, the performers clearly understood their roles. Kate (Ruth Tackes) and Petruchio (John Gavignan) were mature, seasoned performers who effectively handled the witty, aggressive debates about their relationship without resorting to the mindless gymnastics often found in other productions of *Shrew*. Both revealed a softer, more vulnerable side behind their verbal fireworks. Audience members became a part of the action as characters picked up bits of their dinners, took sips of their wine, patted and pinched their cheeks, or sat in their laps or beside them. Kennedy added a number of contemporary touches to point up the relevancy of the comedy. For example, at one point Kate threw water balloons at Bianca. Bianca's serenade was the theme from the popular television series *The Love Boat*, and one character waved his ATM card.

The climactic moment of the comedy essentially captured the spirit of SVT's Shakespearean productions. For the banquet scene, the winery doors were thrown open, and the interior champagne caves were richly illuminated. A table, center stage, was laden with food and flanked by long, brocade-covered benches. Kate dutifully lectured Bianca and the Widow about wifely duties but, in full view of the audience, she crossed her fingers behind her back. Thus, a sumptuous, satisfying ending was achieved with very simple means. The care and thought lavished upon this straightforward, stripped-down, but very funny interpretation of *The Taming of the Shrew* was appreciated by the audience, which registered its wholehearted approval with laughter during the performance and enthusiastic applause at the curtain call.

Production History: 1980: Scenes from Shakespeare; **1981**: *AYL*; **1982**: *TN*; **1983**: *MND*; **1984**: *Err.*; **1985**: *Shr.*; **1986**: *Err.*; **1987**: *TN*; **1988**: *TGV*; **1989**: *AYL*; **1990**: *MND*; **1991**: *Ado*; **1992**: *Shr.*; **1993**: *Lysistrata*; **1994**: *Rom.*

Research Resources: Archives are informally maintained by the Sonoma Vintage Theatre.

Site visit and interviews: 20 September 1992 and 30 September 1992.
Patricia M. McMahon

SUNNYVALE SUMMER REPERTORY (CALIFORNIA THEATRE CENTER).

MAIL: P.O. Box 2007, Sunnyvale, CA 94087. SITE: Sunnyvale Community Center Theatre. ADMINISTRATION: 408/245-2978. BOX OFFICE: 408/720-0873. ADMISSION: $13–$16. SEASON: 40 performances in Sunnyvale in June and July, 8:00 p.m., Tues.–Sat. PRINCIPAL STAFF: Gayle Cornelison, general director; Will Huddleston, resident director. FACILITY: proscenium (capacity 200). AUDITIONS: resumes and photos accepted throughout the year. STATUS: Equity Guest Artist. ANNUAL BUDGET: part of the larger CTC budget. ANNUAL ATTENDANCE: 6,000-7,000 (Sunnyvale 1993). FOUNDED: 1982, Gayle Cornelison.

Sunnyvale Summer Repertory (SSR) is a part of the California Theatre Center (CTC). Founded in 1976, CTC's main focus during the school year is the Theatre for Young Audiences series. From October through June, productions (16 for the 1992-1993 season) originate on the Community Center stage; then six to eight of these shows tour nationwide to high schools. CTC has appeared at international festivals, hosted guest artists from around the world, and presented as many as 400 performances a season to approximately 160,000 students. Since 1982, CTC has used the school vacation period to develop the Sunnyvale Summer Repertory and to maintain a large program of theatre classes for students aged 8 to 18. Some of these conservatory students develop the skills necessary to work with the adult performing group.

In 1991, CTC was invited to present a production of *A Midsummer Night's Dream* at the **Shakespeare at Sand Harbor** program at Lake Tahoe. In 1992, CTC's Summer Repertory toured productions of *Love's Labour's Lost*, *The Comedy of Errors*, and *Dracula* to Sand Harbor for a three-week run. *Dracula* played for six additional performances at **Shakespeare at Benbow Lake**. SSR directors, both resident and the occasional guest, believe in trying a wide variety of styles in approaching Shakespearean texts. *Love's Labour's Lost*, for example, featured 1920s dress and manners. Resident director Will Huddleston reports that the company aims to produce lively, entertaining productions that run about two hours. A new $25 million-dollar performing arts center is planned for Sunnyvale, and CTC is likely to become the resident professional company at the center.

Production History: **1991**: *Tmp.*, *The Miracle Worker*, *The Lion in* *Winter*, *MND* (at Lake Tahoe only); **1992**: *Err.*, *LLL*, *Dracula*,

Mass Appeal; **1993**: *Stop the World I Want to Get Off, Shr., Rom., Arms and the Man*; **1994**: *A*   *Walk in the Woods, Little Mary Sunshine, MND, Tom Sawyer.*

Research Resources: Archives for the Sunnyvale Summer Repertory are informally maintained at the California Theatre Center administrative office.

Site visit and interview: 15 April 1992.
Patricia M. McMahon

WILL GEER THEATRICUM BOTANICUM. MAIL: P.O. Box 1222, Topanga, CA 90290. SITE: 1419 North Topanga Canyon Boulevard, Topanga, CA 90290. ADMINISTRATION: 213/455-2322. BOX OFFICE: 310/455-3723. ADMISSION: $8.50–$12; children under 12 free (1993). SEASON: June–September, three productions presented in repertory for 13 to 15 performances each, 8:00 p.m., Fri.; ; 3:30 p.m., Sat.; 3:30 and 7:30 p.m., Sun. PRINCIPAL STAFF: Ellen Geer, artistic director; Kathy Schutzer, general manager; Susan Angelo, educational director. FACILITY: outdoor amphitheatre (capacity 350). AUDITIONS: Los Angeles area. STATUS: Equity LOA. ANNUAL BUDGET: $291,000 (1993). ANNUAL ATTENDANCE: 13,000 (1993). FOUNDED: 1973, Will Geer.

As the name indicates, the **Will Geer Theatricum Botanicum** (WGTB) was founded by Will Geer (1902-1978), a very successful featured actor in theatre, film, and television for over 40 years, but probably best known in the latter part of his career for his role as Grandpa on the popular 1970s television series, *The Waltons*. Throughout his life, Geer was also committed to various humanitarian activities and causes. In the 1930s, for example, he toured migrant farm workers camps with folk singers Burl Ives and Woody Guthrie. He founded the New Theatre Group in Los Angeles, which presented a number of politically oriented plays, and he also appeared with the Labor Stage, the Mercury Theatre, and the Federal Theatre Project in New York. Because of these activities, Geer was accused in 1950 of leftist leanings (which he denied) and subpoenaed by the House Un-American Activities Committee. He refused to testify, invoking his Fifth Amendment rights. Like many other actors, directors, and writers who refused to testify, Geer found himself blacklisted by Hollywood film producers. Although he had been very active in films since the 1930s, he was unable to secure a film role for over ten years. Geer continued to work in the theatre, however, appearing in both character and leading roles in classical and contemporary plays at the **American Shakespeare Theatre**, the **Old Globe Theatre**, the APA-Phoenix, and on Broadway. In 1962, he finally returned to films in *Advise and Consent*.

Following his blacklisting, Geer conceived the Theatricum Botanicum. Initially it was an informal actor's workshop held at his own home located off the Topanga Canyon road, roughly halfway between Malibu Beach and Ventura. (Although less than a one-hour drive from downtown Los Angeles, Topanga Canyon remains a rugged, almost wilderness, area, valued by Angelinos for a variety of outdoor recreational uses). Here, in a secure, supportive environment, fellow blacklisted actors could either gain an initial exposure to classical techniques or hone these skills that were so rarely applied in films and television. In the early years of the workshop, Geer, along with such friends as Robert Ryan and Woody Guthrie, would gather at Geer's rustic retreat under a giant sycamore to sing songs and recite poetry. Over the years, however, an extended company of amateur and professional actors formed around the Geer family nucleus. Geer's wife, Herta Ware, was also an actress, and daughters Ellen and Kate and son Thad soon followed in their parents' footsteps.

Geer had a long-standing interest in Shakespeare and in classical theatre, having toured with the famous Sothern and Marlowe Shakespeare Company in the 1920s. He also had a degree in botany from the University of Chicago and was an exceptionally knowledgeable, avid gardener. Both interests were combined in his Theatricum Botanicum. A Shakespearean Garden, following Geer's design, gradually developed on the Topanga Canyon site, leading to a rough-hewn, hillside, outdoor amphitheatre. There, beginning in earnest in 1973, the plays of Shakespeare were performed free of charge to all comers on Sunday afternoons throughout the summer months. Although advertisement was only by word of mouth, a steadily growing and knowledgeable audience was attracted to these Sunday afternoon performances. In 1977, for example, University of California—Los Angeles (UCLA) Shakespearean scholars A. R. Braunmuller and William Stull reported in *Shakespeare Quarterly* (Spring 1978) that WGTB's production of *The Merry Wives of Windsor* "deserves special consideration, since it redeemed a play that has come in for much scorn in recent years". Giving *Merry Wives* "the two things it requires, room and ham," according to Braunmuller and Stull, the production was "rollicking and satisfying."

Following Will Geer's death in 1978, his daughter Ellen, an accomplished classical actor in her own right, succeeded her father as artistic director of the WGTB. She set out to build a fully paid summer repertory company, based on the principle, as stated in WGTB's "General Statement of Purpose," that "paying actors was not only requisite to the creation of quality theatre, but a matter of moral commitment." The WGTB's Summer Repertory Theatre came into existence in 1983, presenting at least one Shakespearean play, one modern classic, and one new work, which usually aimed to address "current social and moral issues in a pertinent language, delineating viable alternatives to social avarice and apathy." (A series of musical concerts, including annual blues and reggae festivals, complements the theatrical performances.) Since 1979, the number of paid actors in the company steadily increased to over 30 under contract by the early 1990s. WGTB productions, furthermore, have generally received very favorable reviews: "worthy of a far wider audience than those who normally trek into the woodsy canyon," as Jan Breslauer noted in the *Los Angeles Times* (7 July 1993).

Beginning in 1979, WGTB also initiated a number of educational outreach efforts. WGTB's "Academy of Classics" eventually encompassed an extensive range of programs for children, teenagers, and adults. The Intensive Shakespeare Seminar (ISS), for example, was begun in 1979 to offer advanced training in Shakespearean performance techniques for a small group of committed actors. The Shakespeare Scene Study/Monologue Class was established in 1983 in response to the needs of ISS students for an opportunity to study particular roles in greater depth. WGTB employs a number of distinguished actors and specialists in voice, movement, textual study, and stage combat to teach these classes. The Summer Youth Drama Camp was founded in 1981 to provide training in basic theatre techniques for children ages eight through fifteen. The Youth Drama Saturdays on Playwriting and Performing grew out of an expressed desire on the part of Youth Drama Camp students. WGTB usually offers at least two annual sessions of these various educational programs, either at its Topanga Canyon location or at locations in Granada Hills and Hollywood.

In 1979, WGTB also began the School Days Field Trips. During the month of May, students from area public and private schools are bused to the Topanga Canyon amphitheatre to participate in a variety of theatrical workshops and to attend a theatrical performance, usually of a Shakespeare play such as *A Midsummer Nights Dream* or *Romeo and Juliet*. Preparation for this field trip begins months in advance: Educational materials and an in-service program are provided for each participating classroom teacher. An actor/teacher visits each classroom to prepare the students for the field trip. The number of students participating in this program each year has expanded from 460 in 1979 to over 7,000 in 1990. It is estimated that over 50,000 students have participated in the School Days Field Trip program since its inception. Supplementing this program, WGTB recently initiated Classroom Enrichment, a series of educational programs designed to augment and strengthen the teacher's curriculum. Classroom Enrichment combines specialized teaching techniques with drama, music, poetry, and song to examine particular historical periods, individuals, or works of classical literature. There are programs, for example, that dramatize the lives of Shakespeare, Abraham Lincoln, Martin Luther King, or Harriet Tubman, the civil rights movement, and scenes from various novels, plays, or the great myths.

WGTB operates with a year-round staff of three and depends on a core of dedicated volunteers for the myriad tasks involved in managing its various programs. In addition to earned income, WGTB relies on contributions, ranging from $10 to over $5000 from numerous individual and corporate sponsors. Its School Days program is supported by grants from the City of Los Angeles Cultural Affairs Department and the Los Angeles Unified School District.

In 1990, I attended a production of *A Midsummer Night's Dream* at the WGTB. The amphitheatre is situated in a small glen just a short walk from Topanga Canyon Boulevard. Huge logs placed in a hillside serve as benches. The stage is a large wooden platform perhaps 30 feet wide by 20 feet deep. Pathways running up the hill behind the stage serve as natural exit and entrance ramps. The amphitheatre is surrounded by California live oaks, pine trees, and mountain laurel. Patrons are invited to picnic on the grounds before and after the performance, and, in fact, several were doing so on this Sunday afternoon. The atmosphere was casual, relaxed, friendly, and festive with many families enjoying the occasion.

For *A Midsummer Night's Dream*, the stage was set with a giant stump on one side and a simple facade on the other, with two doors and a series of steps leading up to a second level. The costumes for the "mortals" mixed pastel-colored "Athenian" dress with modern sandals. The fairies wore tie-dyed (batik) leotards and chiffon scarves. Some wore multicolored, abstract half masks or abstract makeup, evoking an image of exoticism or other-worldliness. The acting style was physically vigorous. Puck, for example, regularly swung, Tarzan-like, on a rope attached to an enormous tree overhanging the stage. Taking advantage of the natural setting, both the lovers and the fairies frequently ran up, down, and around the wooded pathways. Bottom's mock heroic suicide in the Pyramus and Thisbe scene was filled with hilarious, inventive slapstick.

Presented with a modest amount of cutting in about two and one-half hours of playing time, including a 15-minute intermission, the production overall was well executed, clear, and forceful. What it lacked in subtlety was balanced with unpretentious charm and energy, altogether appropriate for the setting and the festive atmosphere. The audience, including many children, was very enthusiastic at the performance's conclusion.

Production History: 1973: *AYL, WT, Rom.*; **1974**: *AYL. Rom., WT., Americana*; **1975**: *Tmp., AYL, WT, TN, Americana, Rom.*; **1976**: *Tmp.., TN, Wiv., The Glass Menagerie, Of Mice and Men, Lysistrata*; **1977**: *Rom., Shr., Voices, Wiv., MND*; **1978**: *TN, Lysistrata, The Seagull, Voices*; **1979**: *MND, TN, Lysistrata, The Seagull, Voices*; **1980**: *Barnyard Sweets, The House of Atreus, Tmp., Shr.*; **1981**: *Cym., The Skin of Our Teeth, Gammer Gurton's Needle*; **1982**: *Three Sisters, Wiv., One Acts*; **1983**: *Our Town, Lysistrata, Rom.*; **1984**: *Shr., The Trojan Women, Women & Other People, Americana*; **1985**: *TN, Dory! A Musical Portrait, The Skin of Our Teeth*; **1986**: *WT, Suddenly Last Summer, The Tavern*; **1987**: *Tmp., Two Character Play, Pie in the Sky*; **1988**: *Cym., Heir Transpar-*

ent, *Toys in the Attic*; **1989**: *Per.*, *Americana*: *Saints and Sinners*, *Night of the Iguana*; **1990**: *MND*, *Huckleberry Finn*, *Three Sisters*, *Workers USA*; **1991**: *AYL*, *Workers USA*, *The Hunchback of Notre Dame*, *Dory!*; **1992**: *Ham.*, *TN*,

The Miracle Worker; **1993**: *TGV*, *A Streetcar Named Desire*, *The Caucasian Chalk Circle*, *Ham.*; **1994**: *Mac.*, *MND*, *Educated Women* (an adaptation of Molière's *Les Femmes Savantes*), *The Glass Menagerie*.

Research Resources: An informal archive for the Will Geer Theatricum Botanicum is maintained by Ellen Geer. This essay is based on material supplied by WGTB.

Site visit and interview: 24 June 1990.
Daniel J. Watermeier

COLORADO

COLORADO SHAKESPEARE FESTIVAL. MAIL: Box 261, University of Colorado, Boulder, CO 80309-0261. SITE: Mary Rippon Theatre and University Theatre on the University of Colorado campus. ADMINISTRATION: 303/492-1527. BOX OFFICE: 303/492-8181. ADMISSION: $12–$28 (1992). SEASON: 65 performances, rotating repertory, from late June to mid-August; 8:00 p.m. (outdoors), 8:30 p.m. (indoors), 2:00 p.m. matinees Tues., Sun. PRINCIPAL STAFF: Richard Devin, producing artistic director; Anne Thaxter Watson, personnel and development director; Patti McFerran, director of public relations; Joel Fink, casting director; Stephanie Young, production manager. FACILITY: Mary Rippon Theatre, an outdoor, open stage (capacity 1,004); University Theatre, an indoor, proscenium stage (capacity 416). AUDITIONS: open auditions in New York and Los Angeles and at selected universities with professional actor-training programs. STATUS: Equity Guest Artist. ANNUAL BUDGET: $985,136 (1992). ANNUAL ATTENDANCE: 43,000 (1991). FOUNDED: 1958, J. H. Crouch.

Although the Colorado Shakespeare Festival (CSF) was officially inaugurated in 1958, it can trace its roots as far back as 1897, when a Shakespearean play was produced outdoors on the campus lawn by the University of Colorado's (CU) senior class as part of its Commencement or Class Day celebrations. As this event became an established tradition, popular support grew. In 1902, for example, a special train from Denver was chartered to bring audiences to performances that for the first time were presented in the evening, illuminated by hundreds of incandescent lights. In 1907, a performance of *The Winter's Tale* reportedly played to over 1,000 patrons. These outdoor Class Day performances of Shakespeare continued regularly until the outbreak of World War I.

Another phase in the development of the festival came in 1935 with the death of Mary Rippon, CU's first woman professor and long-time head of the German language and literature department. A committee of university women was formed to solicit contributions for a memorial to Professor Rippon. Perhaps influenced by their memories of the class day plays, the women proposed the construction of an open-air theatre as a suitable memorial. Funds raised by the committee were used for building supplies and labor was provided under the auspices of a Works Progress Administration (WPA) program. Although the original completion date was delayed by other university construction projects, the Mary Rippon Theatre, a handsome amphitheatre that looked more like an ancient Greek theatre than an Elizabethan playhouse was finally finished in 1939.

Except for an occasional concert or chapel program, however, the theatre lay virtually unused until the summer of 1944 when James Sandoe, a CU librarian with a love of theatre, decided to stage *Romeo and Juliet* there. The event was sufficiently popular to encourage annual summer Shakespearean productions for the next 14 years. In 1947, English professor J. H. Crouch took over from Sandoe. (In the late 1940s and 1950s, Sandoe also became a regular and influential director with the developing **Oregon Shakespeare Festival**.) For a decade, Crouch lobbied university officials for money to mount three plays in repertory over the summer months. In 1957, John Little, dean of the summer session and director of the creative arts program, gave Crouch $1,500 in scholarships for ten college actors who, along with some local extras and three directors, became the first Colorado Shakespeare Festival company. Crouch was named the CSF's executive director, and the premiere season opened on 2 August 1958 with productions of *Hamlet, Julius Caesar*, and *The Taming of the Shrew*. Tickets were $1.50 each, and over 7,000 patrons attended the 13 performances offered. Indeed, public response to this season was so favorable that, for the next year, the number of scholarships was increased to 18 and two more performances were added. In 1959, more than 13,000 people attended the performances, and the production of *Macbeth* was sold out.

The CSF's first decade focused mainly on expanding the company and the number of performances and on improving the overall quality of the productions. In 1961, for example, Howard M. Banks' production of *Henry V* was filmed for television; in the same year, Crouch's *King Lear* and Sandoe's *Love's Labour's Lost* played to sold-out audiences. In 1964, public demand required an extra performance of *As You Like It*, and, by 1966, the season was extended to 16 performances. In 1964, Albert H. Nadeau succeeded Crouch as executive director, but Crouch remained active in the festival as a director and actor through the 1980s. In 1966, Richard Knaub was named executive director. By the end of its first decade, the CSF had produced 26 of the 37 plays in the canon with only one duplication, *Hamlet* in 1965.

Through 1966, the Mary Rippon Theatre was used in its original state—a three-level stage facing an open amphitheatre with permanent sandstone benches. Scenery consisted of a few set pieces, mainly thrones and banquet tables, and two small, temporary platforms constructed in front of and atop the two side wings of the upper stage, to provide spaces for an "inner above" or "below". In 1967, however, the university authorized several improvements to the theatre, including permanent platforms and stone walkways along the sides of the auditorium. A permanent stone forestage with steps leading down to the audience was constructed in the original grass-covered semicircle. (In 1970, the remaining grassy space was covered in Astroturf.) In 1968, two large light towers were installed about halfway up the sides of the house.

During its second decade, the CSF emphasized completing the canon and further improving the space and production capabilities of the Mary Rippon Theatre. In 1967, Knaub decided to begin a cycle of productions in which the less popular histories, romances, and minor tragedies would be incorporated with reprises of the more popular plays. This was a compromise solution that allowed the CSF to pursue completion of the canon while retaining audience support and financial solvency. In 1975, with its production of *Cymbeline*, directed by Crouch, the CSF became one of only seven companies in the world and, along with the University of Michigan, the only other university based theatre to produce the entire canon. For good measure, the CSF also mounted three performances of a staged reading of *Two Noble Kinsmen* that same season. In 1975, the CSF also presented Ben Jonson's *Volpone* (until 1991, CSF's only non-Shakespearean production). Throughout the 1970s, festival productions were characterized by an increasing use of scenery. In 1974, a multileveled, lowered-back, wooden unit set was designed, in part to return the productions to a single setting, but this set lasted but a single season. Unfortunately, during storage, elements were damaged or lost, so, for the next two years, the festival returned to its former open platform stage.

With his appointment as executive director in 1977, Daniel S. P. Yang continued efforts to improve the stage. He commissioned Dan Dryden to design a new "festival stage" that could be used for all three productions. Dryden's original design underwent several modifications over the years, but its central element, a 36-foot-wide raked disk, remained virtually unchanged. The Astroturf was covered over by extending the stage. In 1981, lighting designer Richard Devin altered the lighting towers and added other lighting bridges and positions, thus expanding the number of lighting instruments that could be used. The addition of a computerized light board also increased the potential for creating effective and imaginative lighting effects. Indeed, during Yang's tenure as executive producer, the overall artistic quality of CSF productions achieved a consistently high level. Yang began to hire professional designers, technicians, and directors with national reputations, such as Robert Benedetti, Audrey Stanley, Michael Kahn, and Tom Markus. He also began to recruit talented graduate theatre students from programs across the country, rather than just from CU or the immediate region. In 1982, he brought the first Equity actor to the CSF under a "guest artist contract." By 1989, five professional actors were employed as guest artists, supplemented by a company of student actors. By the late 1970s, the CSF was beginning to gain a national as well as a regional reputation. As Jerry Turner, the artistic director of the Oregon Shakespeare Festival observed about the 1979 season, the CSF "had stepped out of its academic cocoon" giving new emphasis to "decor as language" and a "non-historical approach to production" (*Shakespeare Quarterly*, Summer 1980, 251). Indeed, without neglecting performance, the CSF under Yang's direction became noted for its willingness to experiment with Shakespearean production style, ranging from, as Michael Mullin noted, "*Hamlet* in outer space, to topless witches in *Macbeth*, to a *commedia dell'arte Shrew*" (*Shakespeare Quarterly*, Summer 1989, 223).

The third decade of the CSF also saw the inauguration of several new programs and ventures. In 1978, for example, the CSF introduced a Young People's Shakespeare program that toured an abbreviated version of a Festival production to various informal venues in Boulder. The first year, a shortened version of *Twelfth Night* was staged in front of the courthouse in downtown Boulder. Although this abbreviated touring production was subsequently dropped, the Young People's program continued by offering high school students opportunities as apprentices in various aspects of production. In 1982, the CSF began its Dramaturg Program, recruiting CU doctoral candidates in theatre to serve as full-time dramaturgs for each festival production. CSF remains one of the few American Shakespeare festivals using full-time dramaturgs. A commitment to scholarship in the theatre was demonstrated even earlier when, in 1976, the CSF launched a new scholarly journal, the *CSF Annual*, under the editorship of Martin Cobin, who also served as interim producing director from 1982 to 1984. Subsequently retitled *On-Stage Studies*, the journal continues to publish essays on Festival productions or on Shakespearean performance written by directors, actors, designers, and scholars.

In 1989, Yang resigned from the CSF to assume the artistic directorship of the Hong Kong Repertory Theatre. After serving as acting producing director for the 1990 season, Devin was appointed as CSF's producing artistic director. In 1991, Devin expanded the CSF season to four productions: three Shakespeares, staged in the Mary Rippon Theatre and, for 1991, *The Importance of Being Earnest*, staged in the newly renovated, indoor University Theatre.

While Yang envisioned the CSF becoming a fully professional, nonprofit organization completely independent of the university, Devin does not believe this to be a likely development in the foreseeable future. In terms of its management, artistic philosophy, and operating budget, the CSF operates as an autonomous unit of the university's department of theatre and dance, but it is still very dependent on the resources of the university. For example, the CSF receives the use of the theatres and of ancillary support facilities and still very dependent on the resources of the university. For example, the CSF receives the use of the theatres and of ancillary support facilities and services—costume shop, business offices, electricity, and so on—at no cost. Devin himself is a member of the faculty of the department of theatre and dance, but his appointment allows him two-thirds "release time" from teaching and design duties to administer the CSF. As Devin has said, if the CSF had to rent its facilities or build its own theatre, its budget would "skyrocket." University support, however, allows the CSF to present visually impressive productions and to maintain a fairly large (162 in 1991) company of paid actors, technicians, and managerial personnel—a mixture of seasoned professionals and students—on a budget of about $1 million, at least 76 percent of which is earned income. In return for their support of the CSF, the university and the department of theatre and dance have a first-class, professional-quality training program for both undergraduate and graduate students, which gains widespread public recognition and significant community goodwill. Thus, the arrangement between the CSF and the university is regarded as mutually advantageous. Indeed, the CSF embraces training in the arts and crafts of theatre as a primary part of its artistic mission. Numerous CSF "alumni" have gained prominence in theatre, television, and cinema, including Michael Moriarty (1962), Karen Grassle (1964), Barry Kraft (1966), Joe Spano (1968), Annette Bening (1980), Jimmy Smits (1984), and Val Kilmer (1988).

For the present, in any case, the CSF aims to maintain its current organizational structure and its tradition of presenting Shakespeare's plays and, since the 1991 season, other world classics in a variety of production styles, ranging from the historical to contemporary post-modernism. The three productions that I saw in the summer of 1990 typified the CSF's philosophy, although not successfully in every instance.

Romeo and Juliet, for example, directed by Tony Church, was set in the mid-1600s. While the elaborate, authentically Baroque costumes were stunning, they suggested the world of *The Three Musketeers* more than the world of *Romeo and Juliet*. The handsome Italianate setting, the moody lighting, and the exciting swashbuckling duels could not entirely compensate for the competent but lackluster performances in the title roles. As if literally weighted down by long, curly wigs and thick silks, brocades, and laces, this Romeo and Juliet were unable to take flight; their adolescent passion remained stilted and earthbound. Several supporting cast members, however, were able to overcome the heavy costumes and the production's generally somber tone. Bruce Orendorf, for example, was an energetic, forceful Mercutio, while veterans Dudley Knight and Sean Hennigan brought sensitivity and depth to their roles of Capulet and Friar Laurence, respectively.

In contrast to this historical *Romeo and Juliet*, director Jack Clay placed *As You Like It* in a world that eclectically mixed a variety of icons drawn mainly from contemporary American popular culture. Frederick and his courtiers, for example, wore costumes suggestive of Darth Vader and his troops. The century "mountain men," with fringed leather jackets, fur caps, and Indian blanket capes and cloaks. Corin and Silvius were dressed like cowboys and had appropriately twangy accents. Phebe looked like Dolly Parton, while Audrey and William were straight out of *The Beverly Hillbillies*. As Act III opened, the wintry, monochromatic, generally stark Forest of Arden literally blossomed into an idealized summery Southern Californian ambience, complete with palm trees, bright blue sky with a few white clouds, and multihued flowers scattered about the ground. Finally, in the last scene, a model spaceship, out of *Close Encounters of the Third Kind* flew down from the rear of the theatre. As the ensemble gazed upwards, the godlike "voice" of Hymen (Tony Church) was broadcast, as if from the spaceship, uniting the various couples.

Despite this smorgasbord of pop references and *coups de théâtre*, Shakespeare's play survived mostly intact, thanks to some very solid performances. Nance Williams as Rosalind, for example, exuded intelligence and a romantic, wistful, utterly winning charm; Barry Kraft, doubling as Frederick and Duke Senior, brought authority and clarity to both characters. Sean Hennigan was a riveting Jacques, melancholy, rueful, but never morose or sarcastic. Indeed, the performances overall were so vital and infectious that one tended to overlook the silliness of the concept.

Director Joel Fink's *Much Ado*, like A. J. Antoon's celebrated 1972 **New York Shakespeare Festival** production (which undoubtedly influenced Fink's approach in several respects), was set in turn-of-the-century America, with Claudio and Benedick returning victorious from the Spanish-American War. Beatrice and Hero were dressed like Gibson girls and Dogberry and the Watch like Keystone Kops. The setting consisted mainly of a Victorian-style garden gazebo. The entire "Gay 'Nineties'" milieu, moreover, was reinforced by sprightly ragtime tunes and barbershop quartets. Falling somewhere between the Baroque decor of *Romeo and Juliet* and the campy tendencies of *As You Like It*, *Much Ado*'s *mise-en-scène* was perhaps the most successful in complementing the play's inherent elegantly, high-comedy action. A practical Keystone Kops chase scene, accompanied by strobe lighting to suggest "silent film" movement, seemed out of keeping with the dominant production style, however. I was also jarred at one point when Bruce Orendorf's Don John gave himself an intravenous injection of morphine, presumably to ease the pain of the "war wound" that had given him a noticeable limp and perhaps contributed to his moments of almost manic behavior. Still, overall Orendorf's Don John, drawn from the mold of nineteenth-century melodramatic "plain dealing villains," was a magnetic, skillful interpretation. Indeed, as with *As You Like It*, the entire ensemble shone in this graceful, sparkling production, especially Nance Williams as Beatrice, Dudley Knight as Leonato, Sean Ryan Kelley as Benedick, and Barry Kraft as Don Pedro. And, despite my criticisms, on balance these were Shakespearean productions of a fairly high caliber, altogether professionally presented, inventive, and engaging.

The CSF seems to have found an effective artistic and organizational formula since, for the last several seasons, it has played to over 93 percent capacity, drawing about a third of its audience from the Boulder area and almost 50 percent from the remainder of the state; about 9 percent comes from out of state and about 9 percent from outside the United States. The CSF audiences, furthermore, are unusually well educated and affluent. College graduates comprise 40 percent of the audience, while almost 40 percent have graduate degrees. Over 40 percent have incomes in excess of $50,000 per year, and 15 percent have incomes between $75,000 and $95,000 a year. The audiences I observed were clearly entertained and engaged by the performances, especially the *As You Like It*, to which they responded with frequent laughter and bursts of enthusiastic applause.

Production History: **1958**: *Ham., JC, Shr.*; **1959**: *MND, R3, Mac.*; **1960**: *1H4, Ant., TN*; **1961**: *H5, Lr., LLL.*; **1962**: *Rom., Err., Oth.*; **1963**: *MM, R3, Ado*; **1964**: *AYL, Jn., Tro.*; **1965**: *Ham., Tmp., 2H4*; **1966**: *MV, Cor., Wiv.*; **1967**: *MND, 1H6, Tit.*; **1968**: *Mac., TGV, 2H6*; **1969**: *Rom., Shr., 3H6*; **1970**: *Oth., R3, AWW*; **1971**: *Lr., H8, LLL*; **1972**: *Volpone, Ant., WT*; **1973**: *TN, Ham., Per.*; **1974**: *Mac., MND, Tim.*; **1975**: *Cym., AYL, Rom.*; **1976**: *Err., Tmp., Jn.*; **1977**: Ado, *MV, R2.*; **1978**: *TN, Oth., 1H4*; **1979**: *MND, Lr., 2H4*; **1980**: *LLL, Ham., H5*; **1981**: *Shr., JC, AWW*; **1982**: *Mac., AYL, WT*; **1983**: *R3, MM, Err.*; **1984**: *TN, R2, Oth.*; **1985**: *Ant., Wiv., Rom.*; **1986**: *Lr., TGV, 1H4*; **1987**: *Tmp., Mac., MV*; **1988**: *MND, Ham., Tit.*; **1989**: *Shr., Oth., LLL*; **1990**: *AYL, Rom., Ado*; **1991**: *R3, JC, Err., The Importance of Being Earnest*; **1992**: AWW; *H5, WT; The Rivals*; **1993**: *Wiv., Tmp., Lr., Per.*; **1994**: *TGV, Mac., Ant., TN.*

Research Resources: Colorado Shakespeare Festival archival materials are housed in the University of Colorado–Boulder library. CSF seasons have been reviewed on an almost annual basis in issues of *Shakespeare Quarterly* (*SQ*), from 1959 through 1989. Issues of the CSF annual, *On-Stage Studies*, also provide valuable information, including essays by various CSF actors, directors, designers, and dramaturgs, as well as reproductions of design sketches, renderings, and production photographs.

Site visit and interview 12-14 July 1990.
Daniel J. Watermeier

LAKE DILLON SHAKESPEARE FESTIVAL (Ceased operation in 1993). SITE: Lake Dillon Amphitheatre. ADMISSION: free. SEASON: late July–early August. PRINCIPAL STAFF: Gary J. Mazzu, artistic director; Lorrie

Schottleutner, managing director. FACILITY: outdoor amphitheatre (capacity 700). FOUNDED: 1991, Gary J. Mazzu.

The Lake Dillon Arts Guild (LDAG) had been operating as a nonprofit organization for nearly two decades, and the Lake Dillon Amphitheatre had been in existence for several years, when the right person came along to devote these resources to the formation of a Shakespeare festival. Gary Mazzu had been directing renaissance festivals and knew a lot of entertainers with unusual talents, like fire-eating and sword-swallowing. When LDAG booked a one-man show that he had directed, Mazzu was asked if he might fill another evening in August 1991 with "some Shakespeare." Since there was not sufficient time to mount a Shakespeare production, Mazzu put together an evening of women entertainers. He was an experienced director of Shakespeare, however, and it had long been one of his goals to start a Shakespeare festival. Following the success of his two evenings, Mazzu began discussions with the president of LDAG about developing a Shakespeare festival.

Lake Dillon Shakespeare Festival (LDSF) presented its first productions, *A Midsummer Night's Dream* and *The Taming of the Shrew*, for two performances each in July and August 1992. The board of directors and LDAG supported Mazzu's plans to build up LDSF gradually into a major festival, perhaps eventually developing an Elizabethan "village" with crafts demonstrations and strolling performers for daytime entertainment. Summit County is a popular ski resort area, which includes Copper Mountain, Breckenridge, Keystone, and Arapahoe Basin. It is hoped that LDSF will bring the winter tourists back again in the summer.

The beautifully situated, 700-seat Lake Dillon Amphitheatre has excellent acoustics but only minimal stage facilities at present. LDSF already has an architect's proposal for its development into an indoor/outdoor facility with sliding panels.

LDSF's mission was "to develop an annual festival celebrating the works of Shakespeare, utilizing a professional company comprised of local, regional, and national artists." LDSF ceased operation in 1993.

Production History: 1992: *MND, Shr.*

Interview: 11 January 1992.
Felicia Hardison Londré and Daniel J. Watermeier

THEATREWORKS SHAKESPEARE FESTIVAL. MAIL: University of Colorado–Colorado Springs, P.O. Box 7150, Colorado Springs, CO 80933-7150. SITES: variable. ADMINISTRATION: 719/593-3240; Fax: 719/593-3582. BOX OFFICE: 719/593-3232. ADMISSION: free to the public. SEASON: 21 performances in August. PRINCIPAL STAFF: Murray Ross, artistic director; Whit Andrews, producing director; Margaret Patterson, production coordinator; Sharon Andrews, head of acting program/staff director; Robert Pinney, voice instructor/staff director. FACILITY: tent, thrust stage (capacity 227). AUDITIONS: various professional training schools throughout the country. STATUS: Equity guest artists. ANNUAL BUDGET: $75,090. ANNUAL ATTENDANCE: 6,000. FOUNDED: 1982, Murray Ross.

Since 1976, Theatreworks, a theatre organization associated with the University of Colorado–Colorado Springs, had been producing plays in repertory, combining the talents of local community actors and students. Murray Ross, founder of Theatreworks, had for many years included a Shakespeare play as one of the year's offerings in the repertory. In 1982, the Colorado Springs Parks and Recreation Department invited Ross to present *A Midsummer Night's Dream* free to the public outdoors in Monument Valley Park near downtown Colorado Springs. On a cold, damp summer evening, Ross arrived at the site to inform his acting company that no audience could possibly turn out in the harsh conditions, only to find 700 people seated on a hillside, eagerly anticipating the evening's performance. A Shakespeare festival was about to be born.

On a budget of only $6,000, six performances of *The Comedy of Errors* were offered in 1983, marking the initial season of advertised free Shakespeare. Encouraged by the enthusiastic response to the first season, Shakespeare-in-the-Park, now Theatreworks Shakespeare Festival (TWSF), has continued to grow and contribute to the summertime festivities in one of Colorado's prime tourist areas.

TWSF has always limited its season to one Shakespeare play, typically performed during the month of August in a large tent. Exceptions were *Twelfth Night* in 1987 and *Othello* in 1988, which were performed in the Pike's Peak Center, a performing arts auditorium with a seating capacity of 2,600. Though indoors, the performances remained free to the public. Although Ross, who has directed all the productions for the festival, has experimented with various performance spaces, he believes that a large tent configuration works the best in Colorado Springs. "Why didn't we stay there [Pike's Peak Center]? Well, it felt a little too much like an institution."

Theatreworks mounts approximately four productions each season, but Shakespeare, Ross emphasizes, is "the primary mover." Other university staff in full-time positions include Whit Andrews as producing director, Margaret Patterson as production coordinator, and Sharon Andrews and Robert Pinney as staff directors. An advisory board of 16 members links the desires of the community to the staff at the university but is not responsible for executive decisions.

Since its inception, TWSF has grown steadily in its budget and size of company. Ross prefers to direct the majority of expenditures for the festival into the hiring of an acting company. In 1990, about 17 actors were employed, mostly from outside the community. For *As You Like It* in 1991, the company expanded in size to 21, with about half the company from outside the community. Out-of-town actors are paid between $1,000 and $1,500 for three to four weeks of rehearsals and approximately three and one-half weeks of performances, with one day off each week. Housing and transportation are also provided. Local actors and students at the university are paid between $500 and $2,000, depending on skill level and the size of the role.

Ross conducts auditions during the months of February and March at various universities with professional theatre-training programs. Several actors each season are also recruited from the Theatre Conservatory in nearby Denver. Ideally, Ross likes to employ about four or five Equity guest artists, five or six conservatory students, and local actors to fill the remainder of his company each year. Generally, a large house is provided where actors can use the kitchen to cook their own meals. One year, the Colorado Springs Hilton Hotel provided six rooms for out-of-town company members.

The annual budget for the Shakespeare component of Theatreworks is approximately $75,000, with an additional $20,000 of in-kind contributions. From $25,000 to $30,000 is spent on company wages. Approximately 75 percent of funding is provided by local corporate support, with additional revenues provided by the city of Colorado Springs and the university. Individual contributions are accepted, but Ross admits that much work still needs to be done to increase support from the private sector. Because reservations for each performance are so much in demand, in 1991, Ross began to sell about 50 of the 275 available seats at $10 a seat to individuals who did not wish to wait in line to reserve a space for the evening performance. The tactic has worked well, and yet Ross can still consider the festival to be free to the public. As the audience leaves the tent at the close of each evening's performance, donations are solicited.

The performance sites and theatre facilities for TWSF are bound by no set rules or regulations. Ross attempts to locate the performance site in the locale that best suits the offering for that particular summer. In addition to a tent in Monument Valley Park and the cavernous Pike's Peak Center, TWSF has performed a 1940s black-and-white version of *Hamlet* in a local movie theatre that had a similar *noir* atmosphere. In the near future, Ross would like to produce *King Lear* at the Garden of the Gods, an area of natural rock formations located on the foothills of nearby Pike's Peak. Rehearsals are conducted in a nearby abandoned warehouse where the sets are constructed and then taken intact to the performance site. Office space for the festival is donated in-kind by the university.

Local residents and tourists comprise the majority of the audience for TWSF, which averages about 6,000 per season for 21 performances. The festival does not attract a large number of spectators from other areas of the state or country. Ross is particularly proud that various age groups attend the performances each summer: "I see little children sitting next to senior citizens all the time, and I think that's great." As of yet, however, the festival has had less luck attracting a wide range of minorities to its space. In an area with a large Hispanic population, Ross would like to encourage their attendance by hiring more Hispanic actors in the future. Any reviews are generally from the local news media. Despite positive reviews in *Shakespeare Quarterly* and good verbal responses from NEA observers, Ross has had little luck in attracting reviewers from the metropolitan Denver market located 70 miles to the north.

Ross admits that the TWSF takes a somewhat nontraditional approach to the performance of Shakespeare's plays. Due largely to budgetary limitations and his own philosophy that "our job is to find how American actors can own this language, to actually make it seem that its their own," the festival works in the spirit of an ensemble, almost collective, approach that honors the text but explores the unlimited range of possibilities suggested by the poet's imagination. "I like Shakespeare because he was not afraid to take chances. I think he probably would have flunked playwriting." In that spirit, Ross adapts most of the scripts himself. Text and actors come first; sets, lighting, and costumes are coordinated with what is available after the company is established.

Future plans for Ross include touring to rural communities that do not otherwise have the opportunity to view the performing arts, as well as to the more affluent tourist areas such as Vail and Aspen. In the foreseeable future, the TWSF will remain with its pattern of one Shakespeare play per season.

The 1991 production of *Pericles*, performed in the tent, used a bare stage, except for a crude ship's mast at center and an upstage balcony accommodating various musical instruments and electronic devices. The enthusiastic audience consisted of people of all ages. Just as the performance was about to commence, the artistic director darted eagerly onto the stage and announced that the actor playing the role of Pericles was ill and would not be able to perform that night. He regretted that there were no understudies but suggested that, rather than canceling the performance, the part of Pericles would be read first by the stage manager and later by another actor in the company; he asked the audience for their support. As my mind conjured up images of the worst in community theatre, the performance began, and, by the end of the evening, I must admit that I was quite pleasantly surprised and indeed, very well entertained.

The level of acting talent varied greatly, and the costumes were at best pieced together from what was available at little or no cost, yet this play progressed from beginning to end with nary a dull moment. The production was lively and vibrant. Murray's concept and nontraditional approach to the script was successful. The inhabitants of Antioch appeared to be survivors of a post-nuclear holocaust. This Tarsus was a land not unlike what one sees in 1950s Biblical movies, and the fishermen whom Pericles later visits could very well have been one's obnoxious next-door neighbors. For me, those images were what made this production work. The live music ("sound" might be a better word) provided for the ensemble by Mark Arnest and Gregg Johnson was fittingly eclectic, as were the costumes designed by Elizabeth Ross, to effect a patchwork of various styles (and probably past theatrical productions). Nonetheless, they were appropriate for the concept and suggested a range of emotions, from the sensuous (Antiochus' daughter's dancing garb left little to the imagination) to the ridiculous (fishermen with trout flies on their hats).

Production History: **1983**: *Err.*; **1984**: *MV*; **1985**: *Tmp.*; **1986**: *Shr.*; **1987**: *TN*; **1988**: *Oth.*; **1989**: *Ham.*; **1990**: *AYL*; **1991**: *Per.*; **1993**: *Ado.*

Site visit and interview: 23-24 August 1991.
Alan Klem

CONNECTICUT

AMERICAN SHAKESPEARE THEATRE. Stratford, Connecticut (Ceased operation after the 1982 season).

The American Shakespeare Theatre (AST) operated for 27 years, from 1955 to 1982, producing 27 of Shakespeare's plays, some as many as four and five times, as well as twelve plays by nine other playwrights from William Wycherley to Tennessee Williams. The AST mounted a number of notable seasons and productions, although it ultimately failed in its fundamental mission to establish an American approach to Shakespeare, along with a school to teach it and an ensemble to perform it. Perhaps the chief reason for AST's eventual failure can be attributed to a board of directors. The members committed themselves personally to the venture but never were able to relinquish artistic control or to raise sufficient monies to bridge the inevitable gap between the costs of running a professional repertory company and earned income. The Festival Theatre itself, where the AST performed, also posed an impediment to AST's success.

The AST was started in the early 1950s by Lawrence Langner, the cofounder of the Theatre Guild. To assist him in the enterprise, he enlisted Lincoln Kirstein, cofounder of the New York City Ballet Company, and Joseph Verner Reed, a wealthy arts patron and successful producer. The decision to locate in Stratford was made only after attempts to establish the AST in other southern

Connecticut towns closer to New York City had failed. On 24 October 1954, actress Katherine Cornell broke ground for a new theatre, located on 12 acres in Stratford overlooking the junction of the Housatonic River and Long Island Sound. The Festival Theatre was completed in mid-July 1955. The exterior of the building, handsomely finished in imported teak, suggested the configuration of Shakespeare's Globe, but the interior was closer to that of a modern Broadway theatre, with a banked fan-shaped auditorium and an essentially proscenium-arch stage, in front of which was a fairly wide and shallow thrust or forestage. Neither a truly Shakespearean theatre, nor entirely a proscenium arch theatre, the Festival Theatre, with its 1,550 seats, was too large and acoustically inadequate. The stage configuration, furthermore, was to prove a formidable challenge for actors, directors, and designers alike. The first season was mounted in 1955, when Denis Carey, formerly of the **Old Vic**, directed *Julius Caesar* and *The Tempest,* with Canadian actor Christopher Plummer featured as Antony and Ferdinand. John Burrell, a former co-artistic director of the Old Vic, was placed in charge of the AST Academy or training school; during the premiere season, he directed a company of apprentices in a production of *Much Ado About Nothing,* intended primarily for student audiences. Also under the auspices of the AST Academy, neighboring Yale University conducted a three-week summer seminar, which was repeated the next year.

Beginning with the 1956 season and continuing through 1959, John Houseman served as artistic director of the AST, with Jack Landau as his assistant. Reed became chairman of the board for a year until he resigned to take a post as cultural adviser in the U.S. Embassy in Paris. Langner and Kirstein then moved up from the board to replace him. These were very successful years artistically, bringing such notable performers as Katherine Hepburn to play Portia, Beatrice, and Cleopatra; Alfred Drake to play Iago and Benedick; and, most significantly, Morris Carnovsky to play Shylock. Carnovsky's Shylock and his later performances as King Lear stand, along with Plummer's Antony and later Iago, as the most critically acclaimed and popular performances in the history of the AST.

By 1960, after disagreements with board officers, Houseman left the AST. He was replaced by Landau, who was given the titles of associate producer and director of the academy. During his tenure, Houseman had built attendance from 90,000 in 1956 to 147,000 in 1959 and had turned deficit seasons into profitable ones. The 1958 season, for example, ended with a $40,000 surplus. The AST was, nevertheless, reorganized in 1960 to reflect professional theatre practice in New York City, with commercial producers making artistic decisions and hiring directors for specific productions. Generally, Shakespeare festival theatres have not prospered with such an approach. The uneven history of the AST reflects a constant struggle between its boards of directors and its artistic directors. The AST boards never learned the difference between governance, which was their true responsibility, and administration, which was the responsibility of the professional staff. The boards also never learned how to raise money effectively, an essential responsibility of a nonprofit arts board. They did, however, continually interfere in artistic decision making, causing the departures of their most talented artistic directors.

In 1962, Reed returned from Paris to assume the title of executive producer. He contracted Allan Fletcher to direct *Richard II,* Douglas Seale to direct *1 Henry IV,* and Warren Enters to direct Helen Hayes and Maurice Evans in something called *Shakespeare Revisited.* The production of *1 Henry IV,* with a then relatively unknown Hal Holbrook as Hotspur, proved popular, but the 1962 season still ended with a $45,000 deficit. With Langner's death in December 1962, Reed also assumed the duties of chairman of the board.

By 1962, the AST Academy had virtually ceased to exist, but, in 1963, the Ford Foundation invested $500,000 for two years to revive the Academy training program, with Fletcher and Seale as codirectors. The Ford Foundation also paid $180,000 to assist in retiring the theatre's mortgage. As both producer and chairman of the board, Reed consolidated his control over the operation, which had been steadily losing its critical and popular following since Houseman's departure. The AST continued to suffer from the absence of sustained, effective artistic leadership. Still, 1963 was to produce one of the theatre's most successful seasons ever—both artistically and financially. New records were set for attendance and box office receipts. The critical reception for Seale's *commedia*-style *The Comedy of Errors,* Carnovsky in *King Lear,* and AST's first non-Shakespearean production, G. B. Shaw's *Caesar and Cleopatra,* directed by Ellis Rabb with George Voskovec as Caesar and Carrie Nye as Cleopatra, was enthusiastic.

The next year, 1964, was the Shakespeare quadricentennial, and Will Steven Armstrong, who had designed the Carnovsky *Lear,* returned to design a new raked stage over the old, flat one. It was yet another attempt to compensate for the excessive size of the stage and the house and the inadequacy of their acoustics. The productions were *Hamlet, Much Ado About Nothing,* and *Richard III,* with Philip Bosco as Claudius and Benedick, and Douglas Watson as Richard. The Yale student season again attracted large audiences, but the main summer season lost $37,000.

In 1965, Reed himself committed $100,000 to the current season and gave Fletcher the title of artistic director. The Ford Foundation contributed $200,000 and renewed its commitment to the actor training program for two additional years. The University of Bridgeport offered two five-week summer courses for graduate students at its Shakespeare Institute. But the most significant event of the season was a revival of the 1963 *King Lear* with Carnovsky, who was even more impressive this time. *The Taming of the Shrew* and *Romeo and Juliet* received decidedly mixed reviews, but *Coriolanus* with Philip Bosco in the title role was well received. On the whole, however, the next two seasons were artistically disappointing.

The next major phase in the history of the AST began in 1967, when 29 old Michael Kahn was invited to direct *The Merchant of Venice,* again with Carnovsky as Shylock. Influenced by the European theatre of the 1950s and 1960s, Kahn's directorial approach was fresh and provocative. In 1969, he was appointed artistic director. The AST had accumulated a deficit of almost a half-million dollars; attendance was down, even in the student season, and fund raising continued to be ineffectual. The nation was consumed by the war in Vietnam, and Kahn believed that the theatre should not ignore it. For the next eight years, until his resignation in the canceled season of 1977, Kahn was to present a series of challenging interpretations of Shakespeare, underscoring the plays' contemporary relevance, including *All's Well That Ends Well* in 1970 and *The Winter's Tale* in 1975. Kahn succeeded in elevating the artistic standards and drawing critical attention to the AST.

In November 1973, the AST suffered a serious set back with the death of Reed, its most devoted and generous supporter. Because of Reed's personal generosity to AST, there had never been the need to develop a systematized approach to annual fund raising and endowment building. Nonprofit professional theatres in the United States typically earn only between 50 and 60 percent of their operating costs. The balance must be raised from corporations, foundations, and individuals in the form of gifts and grants. The AST somehow always managed to find money without a system. In 1974, for example, the AST received a $200,000 grant from Andrew W. Mellon Foundation and the next year received a five-year $975,000 pledge from the Ford Foundation. But, despite such grants and artistically successful seasons in the 1970s, debt continued to accumulate. The lack of a sustained fund-raising program would eventually affect the financial health of the AST significantly.

In 1974, Konrad Matthaei was appointed as the board's first paid president and chief operating officer. Harold Shaw, the theatre manager and producer, was elected chairman of the board. Kahn, perhaps wary of the administrative changes, accepted an appointment as producing director of the McCarter Theatre at Princeton University. The appointment provided Kahn with employment during the winter months and a potential opportunity to move McCarter productions to Stratford.

Hoping to recapture the extraordinary successes of Carnovsky's 1963 and 1965 performances as Lear, the AST scheduled another revival to open the 1975 season, with Anthony Page directing. The results, however, were disappointing. At 78 years of age, Carnovsky's new interpretation was subdued and lacked energy. It found little audience or critical favor. Futhermore, a major fund-raising campaign that attracted less than half the money projected also proved dispiriting. Consultants had forecast these results, noting that there was simply insufficient commitment from the board members to make the goal a reality. With cancellation of the 1976 season a possibility, Matthaei enlisted the support of the professional theatre community in a nationwide appeal for funds. An additional $300,000 was raised, and Matthaei announced that the

1976 season would be scheduled. Unintentionally, however, Matthaei's effort revealed that the theatre was indeed desperate for financial support and on the brink of insolvency.

The 1976 season was finally set only in the spring. Kahn decided to open with the previous season's relatively successful production of *The Winter's Tale*. The other productions were *As You Like It* and Arthur Miller's *The Crucible*, and, although they received generally favorable reviews, attendance was poor. Box office receipts were less than half of the budgeted amount, the 1977 season was canceled, and Kahn resigned. Aiming to resume the festival in 1978, the board decided to try to operate year-round, using the theatre as a road house during the winter to supplement revenues. This operation was named the Connecticut Center for the Performing Arts. William Goodman moved up to the chairmanship of the board, and, after an extensive search, Gerald Freedman was employed as artistic director. Freedman was a respected director with experience at Joseph Papp's **New York Shakespeare Festival** and Houseman's Acting Company. He arrived at Stratford convinced that by starting modestly, with a limited season, with a company of talented, young American actors, augmented by a few more experienced actors, with Stratford, Ontario, as a model, and with a goal of making Shakespeare entertaining, the AST could be successful.

For the 1978 season, Freedman mounted only one production: *Twelfth Night*. It was imaginatively designed by Ming Cho Lee, with Lynn Redgrave as Viola and Bob Dishy as Malvolio, and it received enthusiastic notices and popular support. With the board's approval, Freedman expanded the 1979 season to three plays: *Julius Caesar, The Tempest*, and a revival of *Twelfth Night* with a largely new cast. *Julius Caesar* was conceived as a contemporary media event, relevant to the political news of the day, but the AST's traditional audience avoided it. Kenneth Haigh, a British actor, played Brutus, Prospero, and Malvolio. Critics considered *Julius Caesar* audacious but misguided; *The Tempest*, by contrast, lacked definition and consistency but managed to attract audiences. The board, nevertheless, judged the season a failure because box office receipts were less than what had been projected. Freedman submitted his resignation. Before the season had begun, the board had agreed to raise more than a half-million dollars, but ultimately it raised only half that amount.

The 1980 summer season was decided by agreement with Roger Stevens, the noted producer and director of the Kennedy Center for the Performing Arts. He committed the Kennedy Center to share the costs of a production of *Richard III*, starring Michael Moriarty at the head of his own Potter's Field Company. A separate student season production of *Macbeth* was scheduled in May, but it was based upon an abridged text and directed without subtlety, angering many teachers who had brought their students. To complete the season, three touring musicals were booked from mid-June to mid-July.

Moriarty's *Richard III* was distinguished by his own fascinating but bizarre interpretation of Richard. As Roberta Krensky Cooper notes, "The reviews were among the worst in AST's history." Audiences came to see this controversial production, however. The season ended with only an $18,000 deficit. Still, the overall financial condition of the theatre probably had never been worse; even the touring operation lost money.

For the next season, British director Peter Coe was hired, and he engaged Christopher Plummer to play Henry V and Iago. Although Coe's straightforward but unimaginative interpretation of *Othello* received mixed reviews, the work of Plummer and James Earl Jones in the title role was widely admired. Subsequently the production opened to very favorable reviews for a limited Broadway engagement (redirected this time by Zoe Caldwell) in February. *Henry V*, with Plummer playing both Chorus and Henry, was generally considered "workman-like" at best.

The 1982 season began with new managing directors, Richard Harnes and Lynne Stuart, and the theatre in legal bankruptcy. Coe scheduled *1 Henry IV* and *Hamlet*. His company included Chris Sarandon as Hal, Roy Dotrice as Falstaff, and Christopher Walken as Hamlet. The critics found *1 Henry IV* as static as they had found *Henry V* the previous season. *Hamlet* was a disaster that even Coe did not wait to see open.

By the end of the 1982 season, the AST had accumulated almost $2.4 million in debt, including a half-million-dollar deficit from the past summer season. On 5 April 1983, Governor William O'Neill announced that the State of Connecticut would purchase the land and buildings for $1 million. The transfer of deed was effected on 21 July. Despite deliberations and a report by a task force comprising corporate officers and theatre professionals, as well as the commitment by the state of monies for the renovation and remodeling of the theatre, to date no new resident artistic efforts have been realized.

The task force issued its report in January 1987, outlining its objectives, mission, recommendations, and plans for implementation. Except for a proposed name change to American Heritage Theatre (based upon the incredible notion that "Shakespeare" was a liability) and flawed estimates of potential box office income, the task force report provided a useful tool for planning.

Problems followed when Governor O'Neill appointed the task force chair to head the implementation phase. Arthur Hedge, Jr., was experienced in real estate matters but had no prior experience with the arts. He enlisted a board comprised mainly of corporate officers with whom he had business connections. Few had any experience with nonprofit arts organizations. They quickly lost interest in meetings devoted largely to discussions of the property, and this board failed as miserably as had some of its predecessors.

Governor O'Neill, meanwhile, had asked the University of Connecticut to represent the state in an attempt to revive the AST. In 1988, University President John Casteen appointed Jerome M. Birdman, Dean of the University's School of Fine Arts, to the newly created position of Director, Stratford Institute, which was to become the AST's education, training, and research component. Birdman communicated with counterparts at Stratford-upon-Avon and Stratford, Ontario, to plan the coordination and exchange of educational programs. Nevertheless, it was obvious that Hedge wanted to reorient the theatre away from Shakespeare and its past. Birdman resigned from the Institute, and it ceased to exist. The University likewise discontinued its limited involvement and, shortly thereafter, Hedge dissolved the board.

The state, under newly elected Governor Lowell P. Weicker, Jr., established a new implementation committee, with representation from such state agencies as public works and the commission on the arts and headed by the deputy director of the department of economic development. The committee issued a request for a proposal (RFP) from anyone with the ability and resources to operate a revived AST. The RFP was to be accompanied by a deposit of $100,000; several proposals were received. In mid-1992, it appeared that an award might be made to a group headed by David Reed, former marketing director of the AST, purporting to represent Tony Randall's National Actor's Theatre. Birdman then wrote an essay for the Sunday editorial section of *The Hartford Courant*, the state's largest circulation daily (23 August). Birdman argued for the decision, based primarily upon qualitative considerations and the goal of making Stratford, Connecticut, comparable to the two other Stratfords in England and Canada.

The state's process of making an award was postponed, its guidelines for submitting proposals clarified, and a revised RFP issued. This resulted in a second application from Louis Burke, a theatrical producer from South Africa, now active in the United States, and a first proposal from Robert M. DelBuono, Jr., a Stratford real estate broker, who had supported Burke in his previous application. Burke proposed establishing the American Festival Theatre; DelBuono's group is called Stratford-upon-the-Housatonic, Inc. (SUTHI), and his proposal incorporates many ideas similar to Burke's. In support of his first proposal, Burke had enlisted Michael Price, the managing director of Connecticut's Goodspeed Opera House, who defected to the SUTHI group. DelBuono, who has no theatrical background, also lists as a consultant Ron Daniels, who recently left the **Royal Shakespeare Company** to join Robert Brustein as associate artistic director of the American Repertory Theatre at Harvard. DelBuono's plan calls for contemporary plays and musicals during the spring and summer and a 12-week season in the fall in collaboration with the American Repertory Theatre.

On 6 October 1993, the state committee voted unanimously to enter into negotiations with DelBuono's SUTHI group for revival of the theatre. The state also reaffirmed its pledge of 1988 to invest $7.8 million in capital improvements to the property. This decision was challenged almost immediately by Burke, who charged the committee with procedural irregularities and charged SUTHI with stealing aspects of his proposal. The state Department of Economic Development has disputed Burke's claims and expressed certainty that the state's auditors and attorney general would find no fault with the decision. On 3 June 1994, the Connecticut attorney general issued a finding free of fraud, corruption or favoritism on the part of the state committee, and upholding the selection of SUTHI as the theatre's developers. This step freed the Connecticut Department of Economic Development to release the first $3.5 million for renovation of the theatre and parking area. SUTHI's plan calls for expending $15-$18 million on theatre renovation.

Production History: **1955**: *JC*, *Tmp.*, *Ado*; **1956**: *Jn.*, *MM*, *Shr.*; **1957**: *Oth.*, *MV*, *Ado*; **1958**: *Ham.*, *MND*, *WT*; **1959**: *Rom.*, *Wiv.*, *AWW*, *MND*; **1960**: *TN*, *Tmp.*, *Ant.*, *MND*, *WT*; **1961**: *AYL*, *Mac.*, *Tro.*; **1962**: *R2*, *1H4*, *Shakespeare Revisited* (readings); **1963**: *Lr.*, *Err.*, *H5*, *Caesar and Cleopatra*; **1964**: *Ado*, *R3*, *Ham.*; **1965**: *Cor.*, *Rom.*, *Shr.*, *Lr.*; **1966**: *2H4*, *JC*, *TN*, *Murder in the Cathedral*; **1967**: *MND*, *MV*, *Mac.*, *Antigone*; **1968**: *R2*, *AYL*, *LLL*, *Androcles and the Lion*; **1969**: *H5*, *Ado*, *Ham.*, *The Three Sisters*; **1970**: *AWW*, *Oth.*; **1971**: *Wiv.*, *Tmp.*, *Mourning Becomes Electra*; **1972**: *JC*, *Ant.*, *Major Barbara*; **1973**: *MM*, *Mac.*, *JC.*, *The Country Wife*; **1974**: *TN*, *Rom.*, *Cat on a Hot Tin Roof*; **1975**: *Lr.*, *WT*, *Our Town*; **1976**: *WT*, *AYL*, *The Crucible*; **1977**: no productions; **1978**: *TN*, *Ado* (Goodman Theatre production, student season only); **1979**: *TN*, *JC*, *Tmp.*, **1980**: *R3*, *Mac.* (student season only); **1981**: *H5*, *Oth.*, *MND* (Acting Company production, student season only); **1982**: *1H4*, *Ham.*, *TN* (Acting Company production, student season only); **1983**: *Err.* (Shakespeare and Company production, student season only); **1984**: *Rom.* (Shakespeare and Company production, student season only); **1985**: *Shr.* (student season only).

Research Resources: Records are maintained by the Trustees of the American Shakespeare Theatre. For a comprehensive history of the AST, see Roberta Krensky Cooper, *The American Shakespeare Theatre: Stratford, 1955-1985* (Washington, D.C.: The Folger Shakespeare Library, 1986). See also: John Houseman, and Jack Landau, *The American Shakespeare Festival: The Birth of a Theatre* (New York: Simon and Schuster, 1959); articles by Frank Rizzo in *The Hartford Courant*, 30 July 1993 (A1, 8); 7 October 1993 (D1, 13); 3 November 1993 (D1, 11); and an editorial 9 August 1993 (C14); and David A. Rosenberg, "Conn. Investigating Stratford Theatre Selection Process," *Backstage* (20-26 August 1993): 4.

Jerome M. Birdman

DISTRICT OF COLUMBIA

THE SHAKESPEARE THEATRE. MAIL: 301 East Capitol Street, S.E., Washington, D.C. 20003. SITES: The Lansburgh, 450 7th Street, N.W., Washington, D.C., and Carter Barron Amphitheater in Rock Creek Park. ADMINISTRATION: 202/547-3230. BOX OFFICE: The Lansburgh: 202/393-2700. ADMISSION: $12–$45 (1993); Carter Barron presentations are free. SEASON: September–May, four productions presented consecutively at The Lansburgh; 8:00 p.m., Tues.–Sat.; 2:00 p.m., Sat.–Sun.; 7:30 p.m., Sun.; one production at Carter Barron, late May to mid-June; 7:30 p.m., Tues.–Sun. PRINCIPAL STAFF: Michael Kahn, artistic director; Jessica L. Andrews, managing director. FACILITIES: The Lansburgh, proscenium (capacity 449); Carter Barron, open-air amphitheatre (capacity 4,200). AUDITIONS: major cities nationwide and in Washington, D.C. STATUS: LORT C. ANNUAL BUDGET: $5.5 million (1993). ANNUAL ATTENDANCE: 130,000 (1992-93). FOUNDED: 1969, O. B. Hardison, Jr., and Richmond Crinkley as Folger Theatre Group; incorporated in 1985 as the Shakespeare Theatre at the Folger; in 1992, the name was changed to The Shakespeare Theatre.

The Shakespeare Theatre (ST) is widely recognized as one of the more important Shakespeare centers in the United States. It is committed not only to presenting productions of Shakespeare and other classics of the highest possible calibre, but also to promoting educational, audience development, and professional training programs. Each season, ST typically produces three Shakespeare plays and one other play from the ancient or modern repertoire. Throughout the year, it also offers a range of special performances, workshops, classes, and seminars, including a series of free, outdoor Shakespearean performance in Washington's Rock Creek Park. Much of its deserved reputation has developed since the mid-1980s thanks to the skillful leadership of artistic director Michael Kahn, his artistic and managerial associates, and the theatre's board of trustees. The roots of the present organization, however, can be traced back to the late 1960s.

When the Folger Shakespeare Library building was completed in 1932, it included a small auditorium that was designed to suggest, on a reduced scale, a model Elizabethan indoor theatre—the Blackfriars, perhaps. Originally it was intended only for lectures and for musical and dramatic recitals. In fact, it was not in compliance with the District of Columbia's building codes for a public theatre, and, hence, only rarely were stage productions mounted in the space—usually college productions presented for free. In the late 1960s, however, O. B. Hardison, Jr., the director of the Folger Library who was keenly interested in utilizing the auditorium as a public theatre, initiated a number of steps, principally treating the considerable amount of wood in the auditorium with flame-proofing chemicals, to bring the theatre into conformity with the building codes.

After permission was granted to operate it as a public theatre, Hardison began to explore various options for operating a theatrical company under Folger auspices. Neither a resident Equity company nor booking outside professional productions seemed practical because of the small seating capacity and the limitations of the stage itself which remained more Elizabethan than modern. To realize his ambitions, Hardison, together with Richmond Crinkley, a young theatre director and scholar, founded the Folger Theatre Group (FTG). This company was composed mainly of drama students drawn from universities in the Washington, D.C., area, complemented by some experienced area actors and technicians who had worked with the Arena Stage, the Washington Theatre Club, and other theatre companies. Within its resources, the FTG aimed to mount quality productions of classical, modern, and new plays and to explore innovative stagings adapted to the particular limitations of the Folger's Elizabethan Theatre, as it was called.

The FTG opened its first season in late August 1970 with a production entitled *Dionysus Wants You!*, adapted by Crinkley from Euripides' *The Bacchae*. This production, however, opened not in the Elizabethan Theatre, but in the air-conditioned St. Mark's Church across the street from the Folger Library. With its second production, *Natural and Unnatural Acts*, an original play about Lord Byron by Michael Menaugh, the FTG moved into the Elizabethan Theatre. During its first season, which included productions of Samuel Beckett's *Happy Days*, *Twelfth Night*, and Alexei Arbuzov's *The Promise*, the FTG played to about 12,000 spectators. *Twelfth Night*, directed by Crinkley and Louis Scheeder, was staged in contemporary dress in an abstract setting that included an aluminum geodesic dome and soft-rock incidental music. Sebastian and Viola were doubled by one actor, and Feste was played by a woman. The production generated some critical controversy, but it was very popular with audiences, and its one-month run was extended by a week. Indeed, this first season was sufficiently successful to warrant the continuation of the FTG enterprise.

At the end of 1973, Louis Scheeder assumed the artistic directorship of the FTG, Crinkley having resigned to assume a position at the Kennedy Center for the Performing Arts. Under Scheeder's leadership, the FTG gradually developed, over the course of the next ten years, a national reputation for its innovative, youthful interpretations of Shakespeare and its presentations of new, often provocative, contemporary American and British plays. Beginning with the 1975-76 season, Scheeder began to present three rather than two Shakespeare plays each year. By the mid-1970s, total box-office income had risen significantly from about $41,000 in 1973 to almost $184,000 by the end of 1976, with attendance for the 32-week season at near capacity. The number of subscribers had also increased, from about 2,000 to over 4,000, and FTG was attracting substantial support from governmental agencies and private foundations.

The 1977-78 season was in several respects a high point for the FTG. After some 32 productions in its seven years of operation, the FTG felt that it was ready to begin a systematic exploration of Shakespeare's major tragedies. It mounted a production of *Hamlet* that competed favorably with a *Hamlet* running simultaneously at Washington's well-established, professional resident theatre, the Arena Stage. This was followed by a very popular and critically well-received production of *Richard III*, which, in its final two weeks played to standing room only. The season contributed significantly to the FTG's reputation as an important Shakespearean theatre. National recognition was further enhanced in early 1978 by a nationwide, 64-performance, five-month tour of *Black Elk Speaks*. In 1977-78, with support from a grant by the District of Columbia Commission on the Arts and Humanities, the FTG also expanded its "Theatre in Schools" outreach program. It sponsored a week-long seminar entitled "Shakespeare in the Classroom" for a select number of area high school teachers, and a three-actor troupe visited more than 60 schools in the Washington metropolitan area. From its inception, the FTG had been committed to making its productions accessible to handicapped individuals. In the 1977-78 season, at least one performance of each of its productions was signed for deaf or hearing-impaired patrons. For its efforts in this area, the FTG was commended by the President's Committee on Employment of the Handicapped.

Nevertheless, the FTG's fairly rapid growth, coupled with rapidly rising production costs (principally the result of an inflationary economy during the mid-1970s), left the organization in a managerially and financially vulnerable position at the end of 1977-78 season. But, with the assistance of a substantial grant from the Ford Foundation, the FTG, working in consort with officers of the Ford Foundation, the Folger Shakespeare Library, and the trustees of Amherst College, who were ultimately responsible for the administration of all Folger Library programs, moved to stabilize and improve the organizational and fiscal position of the FTG. In the 1979-80 season, now operating under a LORT contract and with its own autonomous business office, the FTG expanded its season by offering two additional productions in the Terrace Theatre, located at the Kennedy Center. The production of *Custer* at the Terrace Theatre was extended for additional performances because of ticket demand and then moved to the Hartman Theatre in Stamford, Connecticut, for a virtually sold-out four-week run. *Charlie and Algernon*, the second Terrace Theatre production, became popular immediately and was subsequently transferred to the Kennedy Center's mainstage Eisenhower Theatre for a five-week run. The production eventually played to over 48,000 people.

Despite these successes, the FTG's financial position remained precarious. After only two seasons, the Terrace Theatre program was canceled for financial reasons. Believing that certain necessary adjustments in the budget for 1981-82 would compromise the FTG's artistic development, Scheeder resigned as artistic director. He was succeeded by John Neville-Andrews, who had been an actor with the FTG for four seasons. The 1981-82 season was one of "ups and downs." Productions of *Julius Caesar* and Aphra Behn's *The Rover* received mixed responses from the critics and were not as well attended as expected. On the other hand, *The Tempest*, featuring the noted actor Joseph Wiseman as Prospero, and a production of *The Comedy of Errors*, updated to the Levant of 1913, proved critical and popular successes. *The Comedy of Errors*, in fact, was extended for two weeks beyond its scheduled ten-week run and played to 98 percent capacity. A production called Playaround Shakespeare, a series of scenes from Shakespeare's plays linked by original dialogue and designed to introduce Shakespeare to young people, toured the Washington area, playing to over 3,000 children and college students. Subsequently, it was booked into the Smithsonian Institute Discovery Theatre where it played to capacity audiences; then it toured New York State for two weeks where it was seen by over 2,000 young people.

In an effort to raise artistic standards, Neville-Andrews established an FTG resident acting company and a conservatory and internship program for training theatre students. In the early 1980s, the FTG presented a number of imaginative productions that received, however, mixed receptions from audiences and critics. These included *King Lear*, Calderon's rarely seen *The Mayor of Zalamea* in a fresh translation by Adrian Mitchell, a strikingly handsome *Much Ado About Nothing*, and the American premiere of *Cinderella*, a traditional British pantomime. Box-office revenues continued to lag behind projections, due to falling subscriptions and poor notices. By the end of its fourteenth season, the FTG's debt had grown to almost $2 million. Faced with this deficit, which jeopardized the fiscal stability of the Folger Shakespeare Library, the Trustees of Amherst College announced that they would close the theatre on 30 June 1985, the end of its season and fiscal year.

The *Washington Post* and many prominent Washingtonians, including Senator Daniel Patrick Moynihan of New York, Elizabeth Hanford Dole, then secretary of transportation, and, especially, attorney R. Robert Linower, who became president of the board of trustees, led a successful campaign to rescue the theatre. The FTG was reorganized as The Shakespeare Theatre at the Folger, a not-for-profit theatre company that was financially independent of the library. Neville-Andrews was replaced by Michael Kahn, an experienced, widely respected director, particularly of Shakespeare's plays, who at various time had been the artistic director of the **American Shakespeare Theatre**, the McCarter Theatre Company in Princeton, New Jersey, and the Acting Company.

Kahn and his managerial associates (Mary Ann de Barbieri was the managing director from 1985-1990, when she was succeeded by Jessica L. Andrews) set about to strengthen the financial and organizational position of The Shakespeare Theatre, to elevate its artistic standards, and to build extensive and innovative educational and professional training programs. As its new name indicated, the theatre was to be even more clearly oriented toward Shakespeare, mounting three Shakespeare plays and one non-Shakespearean classic play each season. Kahn established a core company of veteran performers, including Emery Battis, Franchelle Stewart Dorn, Edward Gero, Ted Van Griethuysun, and Floyd King; he also brought new attention to the theatre by inviting classically trained actresses and actors who were best known for their film and television performances to play leading roles. As he was quick to point out, however, these "movie stars" also had proven themselves as gifted stage actors (*New York Times*, 16 September 1990). Stacey Keach, for example, was invited to play Richard III; over the course of three seasons, Kelley McGillis played Portia, Beatrice, Viola, and Isabella; the veteran comedienne Pat Carroll—in a fresh example of reverse gender casting—proved a very popular and critically acclaimed Falstaff in *The Merry Wives of Windsor;* and Sabrina Le Beauf of the popular television series *The Cosby Show* was an appealing Rosalind. Kahn also recruited talented directors and designers to complement his own reputation as a skillful, thoughtful director.

Under Kahn's directorship, The Shakespeare Theatre quickly began to build a reputation for innovative, thought-provoking, but also accessible productions. Writing in *Shakespeare Quarterly*, Miranda Johnson-Haddad, for example, called Kahn's 1989 production of *Twelfth Night*, provocatively set in the India of the British Raj, "one of the strongest productions" she had seen "in four years of regular attendance at The Shakespeare Theatre." Kahn's interpretation struck her as "profoundly different from other interpretations" she had seen, while McGillis' sensitive, vulnerable Viola caused her to reexamine her "long-held assumptions about this character and her position within the play." Johnson-Haddad was equally impressed by Kahn's more traditional *Richard III* (1990) in which Keach played Richard strongly and compellingly "in all his wonderful villainy." The production demonstrated that "traditional" does not necessarily mean "dull" or "unprovocative." In response to such productions and performances, audiences increased dramatically.

At the end of the 1990-91 season, The Shakespeare Theatre had balanced its $4.3 million budget, enrolled over 8,000 subscribers, and played to an average overall capacity of 103 percent (includes standing room). In the summer of 1991, The Shakespeare Theatre, with significant financial support from private foundations and government agencies, brought free, outdoor Shakespeare to Washington by remounting its production of *The Merry Wives of Windsor* (with Paul Winfield replacing Pat Carroll as Falstaff) in the Carter Barron Amphitheater in Rock Creek Park where it played to more than 30,000 people during a two-week run.

In 1992, a revival of Kahn's *As You Like It* played for three weeks at the Carter Barron Amphitheater to an estimated 45,000 people. Under the collective title "Shakespeare Free for All," a number of free ancillary educational programs complemented the performances, including a workshop called

"The Classics From Casting to Curtain Call" focusing on *As You Like It,* free performances of *The Two Gentlemen of Verona* by members of The Shakespeare Theatre's Intensive Classical Training Workshop for Professional Actors of Color (see below), and afternoon workshops and demonstrations concerned with stage combat, stage makeup, and voice and speech. Over 1,500 people took advantage of these offerings in summer 1992. The 1993 "Shakespeare Free for All," centering on *Much Ado About Nothing,* was equally successful.

To develop new and diverse audiences for classical theatre, The Shakespeare Theatre also began to expand its educational and community outreach efforts. Programs included special student matinees, discounted student tickets to regular evening performances, and free public school tours by The Shakespeare Theatre Young Company. A program called TEXT ALIVE! (Winter 1990-91) was created to provide area teachers with added resources to teach Shakespeare's plays, including study guides, free tickets to performances for both participating teachers and their students along with bus transportation to the theatre, and a range of workshops and seminars. Working in partnership with several universities, in particular the University of South Carolina, internships and fellowships were offered in acting, directing, dramaturgy, design, and theatrical administration and management. Concomitant with such opportunities, The Shakespeare Theatre also sponsored a 14-week educational program for high school students, a Summer Classical Acting Workshop, and an innovative Intensive Classical Training Workshop for Professional Actors of Color. (Kahn has long been an advocate of nontraditional casting and has regularly cast African-American actors in major Shakespearean roles.)

By the early 1990s, however, continuing development was clearly limited by the size of the 243-seat Elizabethan Theatre. Attendance actually slightly exceeded capacity, but earned income amounted to only 46 percent of the funds necessary to support The Shakespeare Theatre's artistic and related programs. Continued growth and development was assured, however, when, in 1992, The Shakespeare Theatre moved into a handsome, new, technologically advanced theatre in The Lansburgh, a complex of rental apartments and retail shops located in Washington's art district near the busy Federal Triangle area. (With the move, what had been The Shakespeare Theatre at the Folger became simply The Shakespeare Theatre.)

In 1991 and 1992, we had the opportunity to see two Shakespeare Theatre productions. The 1991 *Othello,* performed in the Folger's Elizabethan Theatre and directed by Harold Scott, opened and closed with the image of black and white bodies intertwined on a bed. In John Ezell's versatile unit setting of columns and levels, evocative of glittering Venetian interiors as well as sunlit Cypriot terraces, Avery Brooks' regal Othello succumbed to a raging jealousy that was painful to behold over his delicate, blond Desdemona (Jordan Baker). The show's most striking interpretation was that of André Braugher as Iago. Casting an African-American actor in the role made sense, in that Othello's implicit trust of him seemed only natural, as did Iago's resentment that a "brother" should be passed over in favor of Cassio. Gleefully relishing the evil he was working, Braugher exulted in his soliloquies, which he addressed directly to the audience. It was a bravura performance. (With a different cast and a somewhat different setting, Scott and Ezell reprised this interpretation in 1993 at the **Great Lakes Theatre Festival**.)

The following year, we saw *Measure for Measure* in the new theatre in The Lansburgh. Derek McLane's dark, multilevel setting, seemingly constructed of concrete slabs and iron pipe was appropriately stark, cold, and threatening. With the addition of a few select pieces of furniture, the set variously suggested a prison, a basement cabaret, or an office or study in some ancient fortress or castle. A full-scale reproduction of Jean Léon Gérôme's strikingly sensual *Pygmalion and Galatea* decorated Vincentio's study, visually emphasizing the repressed erotic desires underlying the action of *Measure for Measure*. Lewis Brown's handsome costumes evoked both official *fin-de-siècle* Vienna and its seamy underworld as well. Drawing on Brecht as much as on Shakespeare, director Kahn effectively created a believable "world," while simultaneously clarifying the character relationships and narrative significance of Shakespeare's difficult, troubling play. McGillis, in her fourth Shakespearean role for The Shakespeare Theatre, proved a magnetic and moving Isabella. Philip Goodwin, who has played several leading roles at The Shakespeare Theatre, including an award-winning Malvolio in 1989, captured the repressed prurience of Angelo. Keith Baxter, a veteran of numerous classical productions in England, Canada, and the United States, brought authority and depth to the role of Vincentio. These principals, moreover, were supported by a fairly strong ensemble, composed of seasoned veterans and young professionals. Kahn's production was not as original as Michael Bogdanov's memorable *Measure for Measure* at the Stratford Festival in 1985, nor did it have quite the subtlety and control of Michael Langham's 1992 production at Stratford, but, on balance, it was a skillful, often moving production at a very high level.

With the move into The Lansburgh, The Shakespeare Theatre has certainly entered another stage in its development as one of America's foremost Shakespearean companies. As Johnson-Haddad wrote in a review of the 1991-92 season (Winter 1992), The Shakespeare Theatre continues "to expand and diversify the classical theatre audience in Washington"; in her view, their productions overall "rivalled and in some cases surpassed" anything that she had seen in New York or Stratford, Ontario.

Production History: 1970-71: *Dionysus Wants You!, Natural and Unnatural Acts, TN; The Promise*; **1971-72**: *Landscape* and *Silence, The Revenger's Tragedy, Rom., Subject to Fits* (adaptation of Dostoyevsky's *The Idiot* by Robert Montgomery); **1972-73**: *Total Eclipse, The Complete Works of Studs Edsel, WT, Bartholomew Fair*; **1973-74**: *Creeps, Edward G., Like the Film Star, The Inspector General, LLL* (musical adaptation); **1974-75**: *The Farm, 1H4, He's Got* a Jones, Tmp.; **1975-76**: The Collected Works of Billy the Kid, Medal of Honor Rag, Err., H5, AWW; **1976-77**: The Fool, Mummer's End, Black Elk Speaks, Ado, MND; **1977-78**: Teeth 'N' Smiles, TGV, Ham., R3, Mackerel; **1978-79**: Whose Life Is It Anyway?, Wiv., R2, AYL, Benefit of a Doubt; **1979-80**: Mac., TN, Shr., Custer, Wild Oats, Love Letters on Blue Paper; **1980-81**: Charlie and Algernon (musical adaptation of Daniel Keyes' Flowers for Algernon), The Rivals, Museum, Crossing Niagara, How I Got That Story, MM, LLL, Rom.; **1981-82**: JC, Tmp., Err., The Rover; **1982-83**: Marriage à la Mode, MV, AWW, She Stoops to Conquer;

1983-84: Tro., H5, Cinderella (pantomime), School for Scandal, The Mayor of Zalamea; **1984-85**: Lr., Ado, Ham., MND, Crossed Words; **1985-86**: Oth., Wiv., TN; **1986-87**: Rom., WT, LLL, Mandragola; **1987-88**: AWW, Mac., MV, The Witch of Edmonton; **1988-89**: Ant., R2, AYL, The Beggar's Opera; **1989-90**: TN, Wiv., Tmp., Mary Stuart; 1990-91: Oth., R3, Lr., Fuente Ovejuna, Wiv. (at Carter Barron); **1991-92**: Cor., MM, Ado, AYL (at Carter Barron), Saint Joan; **1992-93**: Tro., Ham., Err., Mother Courage, Ado (at Carter Barron); **1993-94**: JC, Rom., R2, Err. (at Carter Barron), The Doctor's Dilemma.

Research Resources: The Shakespeare Theatre maintains various records dating from 1986 on, in its administrative offices. Materials concerned with the history of the theatre from 1969 through 1985 are collected in the Folger Shakespeare Library. This essay was based on annual reports, programs, and interviews with Jessica Andrews, Beth Hauptle, and Michael Kahn. Productions have been regularly reviewed in issues of Shakespeare Quarterly and Shakespeare Bulletin. See for example, review essays by Miranda Johnson-Haddad in Shakespeare Quarterly (Winter 1990): 507-20; (Winter 1991): 472-84; and (Winter 1992): 455-72.

Site visits and interviews: 15 December 1991 and 5 May 1992.
Felicia Hardison Londré and Daniel J. Watermeier:

FLORIDA

AMERICAN STAGE IN THE PARK, FREE SHAKESPEARE FESTIVAL. MAIL: 211 3rd Street South, St. Petersburg, FL 33731. SITE: Demens Landing. ADMINISTRATION: 813/823-1600. BOX OFFICE: 813/822-8814. ADMISSION: free, but must obtain a ticket in advance. SEASON: Shakespeare mid-April to mid-May. PRINCIPAL STAFF: Victoria Holloway, artistic director; John Berglund, executive director; Robert Jill, company manager/park coordinator. FACILITY: open-air proscenium on the St. Petersburg waterfront. AUDITIONS: contact business office for procedure. STATUS: AEA. ANNUAL ATTENDANCE: 40,000. FOUNDED: 1977 (company), Shakespeare Festival 1986.

The American Stage in the Park (ASP) company was founded in 1977 with a mission to promote "widespread interest in and study of live professional theatre." In 1979, the company renovated the Cameo Theatre on Central Avenue in downtown St. Petersburg into a 175-seat performance space and commenced a season of five productions. In 1984, the company moved into a former auction gallery in the downtown area and converted a portion of the gallery's 10,000 square feet into an intimate, 110-seat theatre. In 1986, the company became the first nonprofit theatre company in the Tampa Bay area to operate under a full contract with Actors' Equity. In 1987, the St. Petersburg City Council designated ASP as St. Petersburg's resident professional theatre company. In the 1990-91 season, the American Stage produced 270 perform-ances, reaching over 72,000 residents and winter visitors in the Tampa Bay area. The company is committed to provide a living wage for its artists and is known in the Tampa Bay area for its "commitment to compensating profes-sional artists for their craft." The company is a constituent of the Theatre Communications Group, the American Arts Alliance, and the Florida Professional Theatre Association.

The ASP festival with its free Shakespeare productions has become an annual spring event since its inception in 1986, and it attracts audiences from the entire West Central Florida area. The present mission is to "produce alive, challenging and enriching theatre, and to prosper as a cultural institution which represents and influences the life of its community through the art of live professional theatre."

Artistic director Victoria Holloway has established an American Stage School Tour Program, which takes selected scenes into area schools in the fall and spring of each year. This project is supported by the American Stage Forum, a support group for the touring program, and sponsored events held at American Stage. Holloway has also developed a New Play Reading Series for Florida playwrights and is a reader of new scripts for the NEA Theatre Program. Holloway was the costume designer for the film *Promised Land* and a founding member and associate producer of the **Idaho Shakespeare Festival** in Boise before joining ASP. Holloway notes that:

for the past decade we have sought the perfect union between personal artistic expression and realistic programming. We have responded on the one hand to our artistic needs, and on the other hand to the needs of our community. The balance between the two has insured our past success. At this time, our future is here . . . mirrored towers, growth management, transitory populations, high school dropouts, financial risks, cocaine babies, manatees and lots of sun.

And Holloway intends to keep free Shakespeare as a mainstay of their future.

Production History: **1986**: *Shr.*; **1987**: *MND*; **1988**: *Tmp.*; **1989**: *Err.*; **1990**: *TN*; **1991**: *MND*; **1992**: *Ado*; **1993**: *Wiv.*
Research Resources: Programs and clipping files about the American Stage in the Park are stored at the festival office.

Interviews: January and February 1993.
Ron Engle

FLORIDA SHAKESPEARE FESTIVAL. MAIL: 2304 Salzedo Avenue, Coral Gables, FL 33134. ADMINISTRATION/BOX OFFICE: 305/446-1116, Fax: 305/445-8645. ADMISSION: normally free. SEASON: six productions, August through May. PRINCIPAL STAFF: Ellen Beck, executive director; Rose McVeigh, artistic director. FACILITY: (temporary) Bayfront Park Amphitheater (capacity 2,600). AUDITIONS: contact business office. STATUS: AEA, under reorganization. ANNUAL BUDGET: n/a, reorganized. ANNUAL ATTENDANCE: n/a. FOUNDED: 1979, Gail Deschamps.

The Florida Shakespeare Festival (FSF), founded in 1979 as the South Florida Theatre Company, was renamed the FSF in 1983. A professional repertory company based in Coral Gables, the FSF performed Shakespeare in the Vizcaya Museum Gardens until 1987. The 273-seat Minorca Playhouse served as the FSF's home from 1987 until 1992, when the theatre was totally destroyed by Hurricane Andrew. Producing a variety of modern, original, and classical works as well as Shakespeare, in the final season before the hurricane FSF offered *Les Liaisons Dangereuses*, Noel Coward's *Hay Fever*, and Gilbert & Sullivan's *Princess Ida*. In spite of the heavy damage, the FSF assisted in relief efforts by taking a children's show, *Cinderella*, on tour to the tent city in Homestead and to other area residents and hurricane victims.

The FSF has served elementary, junior high, and senior high students throughout the area with special matinees of Shakespeare and the classics. Past productions have included *Twelfth Night*, *Romeo and Juliet*, George Bernard Shaw's *Pygmalion*, and Jean-Paul Sartre's *No Exit*. The FSF is committed to multiculturalism. According to artistic director, Rose McVeigh, in a recent adaptation of *America: The Dream*, titled *Poetic Justice*, students were taught:

to confront and confound prejudice of all types. Works written by women, Blacks, Hispanics, Asians, Native Americans, the elderly and the disabled are woven together with the works of Florida students to enlighten, educate, and entertain in a positive way. Similarly, the casting of minority and physically challenged actors provided the students with excellent role models.

With the loss of the theatre itself and with much of the lighting and sound equipment beyond repair, the entire 1992-93 season had to be canceled. The company was heavily in debt, but the Hurricane Andrew insurance money actually paid off most of the outstanding debts. In addition, the Metro-Dade County Commission approved $248,000 in hurricane relief funds for the FSF, part of which was used to assist in getting the company back on its feet. The former artistic director, Gail Deschamps, left the FSF, and Kathleen Toledo served briefly as artistic director. In mid-1993, Ellen Beck, who had served as both the director of development and public relations director, became the new executive director and set about the task of reorganizing and rebuilding the FSF. Beck invited Rose McVeigh, who was working in Europe at the time, to become artistic director. Both Beck and McVeigh are native to the Coral Gables area.

The reorganized FSF presented Ariel Dorfman's *Death and the Maiden* in August 1993 in El Carrusel Theatre as the "kick start" to their season. Still, anxious to return to staging Shakespeare, the FSF negotiated with the City Park Trust to waive a portion of the rent for the 2,600-seat Bayfront Park Amphitheater, where, in early 1994, they staged a cowboy version of *The Comedy of Errors*, in "Tex-Mex" style. Enthusiastic crowds greeted FSF's first Shakespeare production since Hurricane Andrew, and both Beck and McVeigh look forward to rebuilding the FSF and finding a new, permanent home for the company.

Production History: **1993-94**: *Death and the Maiden, Bloody Poetry, Voices of Christmas, Err., Shades.*

Research Resources: Informal archives are maintained at the Florida Shakespeare Festival administrative office.

Telephone interviews: January and February 1994.
Ron Engle

NEW RIVER SHAKESPEARE FESTIVAL (The Public Theatre of Greater Ft. Lauderdale, Inc.) MAIL: 2301 N.E. 26th Street, Fort Lauderdale, FL 33305. SITE: Broward County Main Library Theatre, 100 S. Andrews Ave. ADMINISTRATION/BOX OFFICE: 305/564-6770. ADMISSION: $10–$14.50 (1991). SEASON: approximately 28 performances, three productions, straight runs, from mid-October through November, 8:00 p.m., Wed.–Sat.; 2:00 p.m., Sat., Sun. Also guest engagements in area theatres. PRINCIPAL STAFF: Vince Rhomberg, artistic and executive director; Mark DeMoranville, associate producer. FACILITY: proscenium, large apron (capacity 292). AUDITIONS: Fort Lauderdale, annual basis; regional actors, directors should apply to administrative office. STATUS: SPT. ANNUAL BUDGET: $60,000 (1991). ANNUAL ATTENDANCE: 5,400 (1991). FOUNDED: 1990, Vince Rhomberg.

A need for more classical theatre productions in the Fort Lauderdale area prompted Vince Rhomberg to establish the New River Shakespeare Festival (NRSF) in 1990. Rhomberg has since developed an audience for quality classical theatre in the greater Fort Lauderdale area. His artistic philosophy is to keep Shakespeare accessible by focusing on clear enunciation and by emphasizing Shakespeare as entertainment for a broad audience including children. Rhomberg recognizes a need to vary the artistic approach in each of the three productions presented during the festival, so that audiences will be exposed to a diversity of styles and provided with variety in the season. Thus, one production will usually be staged in a period setting and one out of period. For example, NRSF's *Midsummer Night's Dream* was staged with an Arabian Nights flavor. Rhomberg also believes that the scripts should be edited and cut down to a running time of approximately two to three hours. With this philosophy, Rhomberg has been successfully staging three Shakespeare productions a year to near capacity crowds.

The productions are currently staged in the Broward County Main Library Theatre, located in downtown Fort Lauderdale and not far from the beaches. The theatre was originally designed as a lecture auditorium with seating for 292. The 40-foot proscenium has a large apron and provides an intimate atmosphere. Rhomberg's five-year plan includes audience development and moving the festival outdoors (or perhaps into the just-completed Broward Center for the Performing Arts).

The NRSF's outreach program includes touring productions to nearby cities and a special group of actors touring the local schools. One production toured as a guest engagement to the Coral Springs City Center and the Miami Shores Theatre. The school touring group, "Shakespeare Speaks," features Shakespeare speaking as himself about his work and life. Shakespeare is accompanied by five other actors who are "cast" by him in various scenes that are then acted out before the students. A lecture series has also been established that is presented before the Saturday night performances. The short lecture/presentation focuses on the artistic concept of the production with a brief history of the work.

For the festival, Rhomberg hires a staff of 60 performers, mostly regional actors, as well as 15 technicians. The permanent staff includes Rhomberg as artistic director, plus an associate director and marketing director. Directors are hired for the productions on an individual basis. The company has Small Professional Theatre (SPT) status and is unionized. The budget for the festival is approximately $60,000 with a total annual attendance of 5,400.

A unique aspect of the NRSF is the People's Choice Award. Season tickets are available on a subscription basis for all three productions, and audience members who see all three plays receive ballots to vote for the People's Choice Award. The winning production is then revived as a "command performance" in the spring for free public performances presented at the annual Renaissance Fair.

As the NRSF grows and additional funding is secured, Rhomberg envisions a number of high-visibility guest actors appearing in leading roles and the expansion of the touring program. He notes that the population base is large and that the area attracts a number of winter visitors interested in Shakespeare festival activities.

Production History: 1990: *Shr.*, *MND*, *Oth.*; **1991**: *MV*, *Mac.*, *AWW*.

Research Resources: Informal archives are maintained at the New River Shakespeare Festival administration office.

Site visit and interview: April 1992.
Ron Engle

ORLANDO - UCF SHAKESPEARE FESTIVAL. MAIL: 30 S. Magnolia St., Suite 250, Orlando, FL 32801. SITE: Walt Disney Amphitheater at Lake Eola Park. ADMINISTRATION: 407/423-6905; Fax: 407/423-6907 BOX OFFICE: 407/841-9787. ADMISSION: $6–$25 (1994). SEASON: two productions, presented in rotating repertory for 14 performances each, including school performances, in April. 8:00 p.m. Weds.–Sun; on two Sundays during the season, a 1:00 p.m. matinee is also presented. PRINCIPAL STAFF: Stuart E. Omans, artistic director; Kristin Lindfors, business manager. FACILITY: open-air amphitheater (capacity 930). AUDITIONS: New York and locally. STATUS: Equity LOA. ANNUAL BUDGET: $550,000 (1993). ANNUAL ATTENDANCE: 21,500 (1994). FOUNDED: 1989, Stuart Omans.

The Orlando - UCF Shakespeare Festival (OSF) had its beginnings in 1987 when Stuart Omans, a professor of English Renaissance literature at the University of Central Florida in Orlando, initiated an arts and humanities outreach program in downtown Orlando. The program was a response in part to a series of criticisms in *The Orlando Sentinel* that the university was not as involved as it should be in the cultural life of the Orlando community. With sponsorship from the university and the Florida Humanities Council, Omans organized a series called "Windows into the World of the Renaissance Artist," which was designed to emphasize the connection between the Renaissance and our own time. The series sponsored a variety of events, exhibitions, and lectures by prominent Renaissance scholars, performances by Renaissance music groups, and classes in acting Shakespeare. The first series in 1987 proved to be very popular, attracting as many as 400 people for particular events. In 1988, another equally popular series was organized. The success of these programs led Omans to believe that his long-held dream of organizing a festival of Shakespearean productions might be feasible.

With the encouragement of the late Shakespearean scholar, O. B. Hardison, Jr. (see **The Shakespeare Theatre**) and the assistance of Jim Volz, then managing director of the **Alabama Shakespeare Festival**, Omans began to recruit a board of directors, draft a budget prospectus, and raise start-up funds for a festival. A 1950s-style band shell in Orlando's downtown Lake Eola Park was identified as a potential performance site. Except for the band shell, the park had recently undergone a $3.5 million renovation. The city had budgeted $400,000 to rebuild the band shell, but it was estimated that to convert the band shell into a facility suitable for staging plays would cost $900,000. The city solicited the Walt Disney Company, located in nearby Lake Buena Vista, for assistance. Disney officials offered to assume the band shell renovation project. Disney architects designed a new amphitheater at no cost to the city and the Walt Disney Company contributed technical advice for lighting and sound installations, as well as on-site supervision during construction.

During the months of construction, which began in February 1989, Omans continued to raise funding support from the local community to strengthen his board of directors, and to prepare for the inaugural season by recruiting directors, actors, designers, and so forth. The university hired a full-time business manager and a publicist. The Orlando Shakespeare Festival Guild, a volunteer organization, was organized to assist in the myriad tasks of operating the festival. With support from the Florida Humanities Council, another "Windows into the World of the Renaissance Artist" was organized for the winter and early spring of 1989. Finally, after months of preparation, the OSF opened its premier season with productions of *The Tempest* and *The Taming of the Shrew*, running in rotating repertory for five performances each from 17 November to 3 December. Tickets for this inaugural season were distributed free. Between 8,000 and 10,000 playgoers attended the Festival, many standing around the fringe of the amphitheater when all of the seats were gone.

Immediately following this successful opening, preparations began for the next season. New board members were added and a campaign initiated to raise $150,000 so that the festival could expand from ten to 27 performances. November and December can be rainy and cool in Central Florida, so the next season was scheduled to open in late March and run through April when the days are usually sunny and dry with balmy evenings—an ideal time for an outdoor festival. The OSF also moved to new offices in a downtown office building just a few blocks from the Walt Disney Amphitheater. Omans had directed *The Tempest* himself, but, for the second season, he decided to contract two professional directors. He also contracted with three Equity guest artists, to be supported as before by talented non-Equity performers recruited mostly from university theatre programs and the local community. (With such nearby attractions as Universal Studios, Walt Disney World, MGM-Disney Studios, and the Epcot Center, the OSF can draw on a fairly large pool of local performers, musicians, and theatrical technicians.) The OSF board of directors voted to assess a modest charge for tickets, ranging from $5 to $25 for the second season, but the board also decided to provide 5,000 seats—about 25 percent of the total seats available for the season—free to members of the community who otherwise might not be able to attend the festival. In addition, they offered discounts to senior citizens and students. OSF is determined to keep the festival a popular event. This commitment to the community, however, meant that while ticket revenue would become significant to its operating budget, the festival would continue to depend on individual and corporate support. It should be noted, moreover, that while OSF was incorporated as an independent, not-for-profit institution, it continues to have strong ties with the University of Central Florida, which provides 30 percent of its annual operating budget. Omans, for example, remains a full-time, active faculty member, with half of his duties being the administration of the festival. The festival also offers internship opportunities for university students in theatre, communications, English, education, and management. Indeed, in 1994 the University became a full partner in the festival and its name officially changed to the Orlando - UCF Shakespeare Festival.

The 1991 season was both a popular and critical success. Attendance topped 20,000. The critic for the *Orlando Sentinel* (21-22 March 1991), for example, generally viewed both productions very favorably, commending the direction, "fine ensemble acting," and the strong performances of guest artists Sybil Lines as Lady Macbeth and Maria, Joseph Culliton as Macbeth and Malvolio, and Eric Hoffmann as Toby Belch. Richard L. Coe, critic emeritus of the *Washington Post*, writing in *Theatre Week* (27 May- 2 June 1991) was, as one might expect, more judicious in his assessments, but he still found both productions "decidedly sturdy and, without going to extremes for 'relevancy,' often original." He commended, in particular, the *Macbeth* director's casting of the three witches as a grandmother, daughter, and a boy to suggest "the subliminal result of evil through the ages," which Coe thought added "depth to the several recurring scenes." He also praised the "scampering comedy" in the *Twelfth Night* duel between Aguecheek and Viola. The staging of both productions was generally traditional and conservative. As the festival has matured, however, the productions have explored other styles while remaining true to the texts. *A Midsummer Night's Dream* (1992) featured construction worker mechanicals who arrived in an early model Volkswagen "Beetle", a Renaissance music ensemble that played bebop and jazz, and a semi-surrealistic scenic design. *The Comedy of Errors* (1993), set in a mythical Byzantine Turkey, presented an almost comic-book effect in its bold scenic and costume design. By a special arrangement, OSF rents its costumes from the **Royal Shakespeare Company**.

The quality of costuming is therefore far superior to what one might expect from a mid-size, developing Shakespeare festival.

The Walt Disney Amphitheater is a handsome, art deco-style structure but with a fairly wide and deep seating area completely open to the surrounding park, Lake Eola, and a major downtown street. There is interference from automobiles, overhead airplane traffic, and other park users—joggers, strollers, boaters, and others. The festival has addressed these sound difficulties by providing state-of-the-art body microphones for all actors and a sound system that can, if need be, compete with most ambient noise.

In keeping with the educational mission established in 1989, the OSF offers a variety of school programs, public educational activities, and other events. The 1993 season marked the fourth year that OSF prepared and distributed an interactive study guide to middle and secondary school students, the fourth season that company members have presented workshops and lectures in a week-long national Elderhostel program, and the third season for discounted student matinee performances. In 1992, OSF established The Young Company, a multicultural, multiethnic student theatre troupe, dedicated to bolstering the self-esteem of inner city youth by providing a supportive environment in which to create. The Young Company doubled in size and received four major grants in its first two years. Additionally, OSF has organized a series of ancillary lectures, Renaissance concerts, symposia, fully produced original scripts, screenings of Shakespeare on film, and an art exhibition by Florida artists who were commissioned to create works inspired by quotations from Shakespeare's plays.

Since 1992, OSF has operated under an Equity Letter of Agreement contract and employed six Equity members. With continuing strong support from the university and the community and a clear mission, OSF is as the *Orlando Sentinel*'s critic observed, "on solid ground" for continuing growth and development.

Production History: **1989**: *Tmp.*; *Shr.*; **1991**: *Mac.*; *TN*; **1992**: *Rom.*; *MND*; **1993**: *Err.*; *AYL*; **1994**: *Ham., Ado.*

Research Resources: An informal archive is maintained in the Orlando - UCF Shakespeare Festival offices.

Site visit and interviews: 27-28 March 1991.
Daniel J. Watermeier

PALM BEACH SHAKESPEARE FESTIVAL. MAIL: 353 South U.S. Highway 1, Suite F 103, Jupiter, FL 33477. SITES: Carlin Park, Jupiter; Palm Beach Community College North, Palm Beach Gardens; Gruber Hall, Kaplan Community Center, West Palm Beach. ADMINISTRATION/BOX OFFICE:

407/575-7336. ADMISSION: $5–$21 (1993). SEASON: two productions presented at Carlin Park and two-three productions on tour at Palm Beach Community College North or Gruber Hall. PRINCIPAL STAFF: Kermit Christman, executive producing director; Jacqueline Siegel, managing director. FACILITIES: outdoor open space at Carlin Park (capacity 5,000); outdoor amphitheatre at Palm Beach Community College North (capacity 750); indoor theatre at Gruber Hall (capacity 300). AUDITIONS: New York and locally through Florida Professional Theatre Association. STATUS: Equity Guest Artist; SPT; URTA. ANNUAL BUDGET: $250,000 (1993). ANNUAL AT-TENDANCE: 30,000 (1993). FOUNDED: 1990, Kermit Christman, Jacqueline Siegel.

The Palm Beach Shakespeare Festival (PBSF) is the brainchild of its foun-der Kermit Christman. Christman, an actor and director trained in England, had performed in classical plays with several leading actors, including Charlton Heston, Vanessa Redgrave, and Richard Chamberlain, and at a number of American Shakespeare festivals. On holiday in the Palm Beach area, he met Jacqueline Siegel, a musician and program director for Young Audiences, Inc., an educational organization that arranged performances and lecture/demonstrations for area primary and secondary schools. Siegel contracted with Christman for a series of Shakespearean lecture/demonstrations for a Young Audiences tour. This experience, his growing familiarity with the area, and his long-standing interest in Shakespeare suggested to him that a local Shake-speare festival might prove a successful venture.

Working in consort, Christman and Siegel incorporated The Palm Beach Shakespeare Festival as a not-for-profit arts and education theatrical organization, aiming to provide "accessible cultural events to enhance the quality of life for visitors to and residents of Palm Beach County." In April 1990, the PBSF opened its first season with *Macbeth* staged at Palm Beach Community College. The success of this performance encouraged the PBSF to mount five performances of *Twelfth Night* in September. The venue chosen was outdoors in Carlin Park, a large but underutilized and underdeveloped county park located directly across highway A1A from Jupiter Beach, one of the finest public beaches on the South Florida coast. The park area surrounding the stage was transformed into a fair, dubbed the "Greenshow," which offered pre-performance variety entertainment—jugglers, strolling musicians, "court jesters," children's games, craft exhibits, and mock sword fights. Local restaurants set up booths and offered a range of food and drink for informal *al fresco* dining. The reviewer for the *Palm Beach Post* hailed both the Green-show activities and the performance. "Christman," the reviewer wrote, "had taken one of the Bard's most talky and confusing (albeit funny) plays and turned it into a fast-moving medieval version of *Charley's Aunt*." After the run in Carlin Park, *Twelfth Night* was staged for two more performances in a park in the nearby town of Stuart. Following *Twelfth Night*, Christman mounted his own adaptation of Ray Bradbury's *The Martian Chronicles*, renamed *Rocket Summer: The First Expedition*, in a small theatre called the ARTSBAR in West Palm Beach. He and Siegel began to plan and raise money for their next "Shakespeare by the Sea" season.

The Tempest opened in early March 1991 and played for eight performances over two consecutive weekends. The *Palm Beach Post*'s reviewer called it "the best entertainment bargain in town." On 1 and 2 June, the PBSF organized Kids Fest, a series of arts events specifically designed for children and often performed by children as well. According to the Palm Beach *Courier Journal*, over 5,000 people attended Kids Fest, including 600 children under the age of three. In September, the PBSF presented eight performances of *A Midsummer Night's Dream*. A popular and critical success, *A Midsummer Night's Dream* was named one of the Top 10 productions in South Florida for 1991.

In April 1992, the PBSF presented the Florida premiere of *Dinner and Drinks*, described by author and director Christman as "a murder mystery dedicated to the Golden Age of Hollywood's style, wit and elegance." This was produced at Theatre at the Harbour, an indoor venue at the Harbour Shops complex in Palm Beach Gardens. At Carlin Park, *Richard III* ran for 20 performances in May. In November, a production of *As You Like It*, using only five actors to play all the roles (similar to the **ACTER** model), was presented for six performances in Carlin Park; it then toured to the Ann Norton Sculpture Gardens in West Palm Beach for eight more performances. The Kids Fest was reprised in mid-April 1993. The major project in 1993 was a musical version of Ray Bradbury's popular *Dandelion Wine*, with music by Grammy award winner Jimmy Webb. It opened on 5 March at the Palm Beach Community College Amphitheatre.

Although Shakespeare remains at the center of Christman's interest, by presenting a range of entertaining musical comedies and dramas, such as a tour of Albee's *Zoo Story* with the television actor William Katt, and utilizing several different sites, the PBSF clearly wants to make a variety of live theatre attractive to a broad cross-section of Palm Beach County residents and visitors. Indeed, Christman deliberately aims to popularize Shakespeare, making the plays as entertaining and as accessible as possible. He confesses, for example, to "ruthlessly cutting" the text to a two-hour running time. His version of *A Midsummer Night's Dream* was set in a style that evoked the atmosphere of Robin Hood movies. That the film *Robin Hood, Prince of Thieves*, starring Kevin Costner, was being screened almost simultaneously in the South Florida area undoubtedly contributed to the popularity of the PBSF production. Similarly, his *Richard III* was set in a futuristic time and deliberately evoked parallels with the popular *Mad Max* and *Terminator* movies. *The Tempest* was staged to suggest the late seventeenth-century settlement of Florida, a context probably familiar to most PBSF audience members. While critics and scholars may have reservations about Christman's approach, it has proven very popular with PBSF audiences, whom Christman describes as a "family audience." In three years, the festival has tripled its number of performances, and attendance at Carlin Park is regularly 1,000 or more spectators per performance.

The PBSF is essentially a two-person operation. Christman and Siegel manage the various programs, and Christman directs most of the productions. He hires Equity actors for major roles and recruits his supporting cast from the community and from the theatre programs at universities, like Florida Atlantic University in Boca Raton, the Palm Beach County School for the Performing Arts, and film star Burt Reynolds's Institute for theatre training at Florida State University in Tallahassee. Non-Equity performers are paid at the rate of $150 a week. Instead of hiring individual designers and technicians, Christman contracts with local firms for costumes, scenery, and lighting design. Thus far, this arrangement has proven very satisfactory. For the future, Christman and Siegel are working closely with the town of Jupiter and the Palm Beach County Parks and Recreation Department to implement a plan to improve Carlin Park, which would include a permanent, 1,000-seat amphitheatre. This is scheduled to open in the summer of 1994. With such a facility, Christman and Siegel could expand their operation to include a wide range of musical and theatrical presentations. The PBSF is a young, developing festival, but it already has had a significant impact on the cultural climate of South Florida, and its future growth is promising.

Production History: **1990**: *Mac.*, *TN*; *Rocket Summer, The First Expedition*; **1991**: *Tmp.*, *MND*, *Vampire Lesbians of Sodom, Hell's Broke Loose!*; **1992-93**: *R3, AYL, Dandelion Wine, Dinner and Drinks, Zoo Story*; **1993-94**: *Rom.*, *Ham.*

Research Resources: An informal archive is maintained in the Palm Beach Shakespeare Festival offices.

Site visit and interview: 24 March 1993.
Daniel J. Watermeier

GEORGIA

ATLANTA SHAKESPEARE COMPANY. MAIL: P.O. Box 5436, Atlanta, GA 30307. SITE: Atlanta Shakespeare Tavern, 499 Peachtree Street, Atlanta, GA 30308. ADMINISTRATION: 404/874-9219. BOX OFFICE: 404/874-5299. ADMISSION: $14 general; $8 students. SEASON: August–June, 7:30 p.m., Wed.–Sat. PRINCIPAL STAFF: Jeffrey Watkins, artistic director; Tony Wright, associate director. FACILITY: tavern-style seating (capacity 175), facing a stage; cafeteria and bar at the rear. AUDITIONS: open call and invitation to local actors. STATUS: SPT, Category 3. ANNUAL BUDGET: $278,000 (1992). ANNUAL ATTENDANCE: 12,000. FOUNDED: 1979, Atlanta Shakespeare Association.

Seeing Shakespeare performed in a tavern may be as close as today's audiences can get to the atmosphere of Elizabethan London's Globe Theatre. The concept works for the Atlanta Shakespeare Company (ASC), although it developed almost haphazardly. The company's origins may be traced back to the Atlanta Shakespeare Club, which began in 1975 and was incorporated in 1979 as the Atlanta Shakespeare Association (ASA). The nonprofit group, led by Elisabeth Lewis Corely and Jane Tuttle, produced *An Evening with Will Shakespeare*, an anthology of music and scenes from Shakespeare, at the Five-Point Pub. That effort was followed by readings of the plays and poetry at various coffeehouses. Eventually, they presented six full-length plays, although they lost money on *Love's Labour's Lost*.

Jeffrey Watkins became the artistic director in January 1984 and produced *As You Like It* for a three-week run at Seven Stages Theater. It soon occurred to him, however, that the Bard might be well served in the raucous, no-frills atmosphere of nearby Manuel's Tavern (634 North Highland Avenue). There, surrounded by photographs of prominent Democrats and paintings of nudes, a lively clientele ranging from policemen to students mingled over beer and cheeseburgers. Owner Manuel Maloof, a cracker-barrel politician who was campaigning for reelection as chair of the county commission, welcomed Watkins' proposal to present *As You Like It* in the back room. The enthusiasm that greeted the four saloon performances (applause interrupting the show 23 times) led to a feature story in the *Wall Street Journal*. When NBC News called, the show had closed; but Watkins revived it for a two more weeks of performances to capacity crowds.

Watkins quickly realized that he had found the right vein for producing Shakespeare, and he decided to build his career and his theatre company on that close, mutually acknowledging relationship of actors and audience. He made a virtue of financial necessity, using the same sets and costumes repeatedly, because that was also the reality of Elizabethan theatre. By 1985, the company was producing two plays in rotating repertory and regularly packing Manuel's Tavern to the rafters. Yet it was difficult to pay Equity and non-Equity salaries while working in a 105-seat house. For five years, Manuel's Tavern served as home to the company, while they also toured to other venues in the area. "After the joy of playing Shakespeare in a tavern," Watkins has commented, "taking a show into an 1,100-seat school auditorium really points up how wrong most twentieth-century theatres are for Shakespeare."

The year 1987 marked a turning point in the company's fortunes. In January, under the leadership of board chairman Richard V. Morse, ASA was reincorporated as the Atlanta Shakespeare Company. A highly acclaimed production of *Twelfth Night* reinvigorated Watkins' determination to persevere with the financially unstable venture. The company leased an 8,800-square-foot studio space for rehearsals, storage, and construction. In 1989, $270,000 was raised to renovate a space that would serve as a permanent home for the ASC, but construction delays put the opening 12 weeks behind schedule and brought a $58,000 deficit. The still-unpainted facility, with "Jiffy Johnnies in the back," opened with *The Tempest* in May 1990. Since then, the Atlanta Shakespeare Tavern at 499 Peachtree Street has seen steady improvement. The ASC began to hit its stride with *Much Ado About Nothing* in September, and G. B. Shaw's *Saint Joan* in December was a palpable hit with a three-week extended run in January 1991. The latter success also brought two foundation grants. Still, the budget was 80 percent earned income in 1992.

A FEDAPT consultancy assisted the ASC articulating a mission statement and in establishing sound operating procedures. By 1991, the deficit had been reduced by 70 percent. Although the ASC employs only two full-time staff members, the large casts required for classical plays mean hefty payrolls, and Watkins is committed to paying actors as much as possible. "The ability to make a living in the arts is at the core of what we are," he says. "Artists have a right to a home and family, and must be remunerated for their work." Five or six Equity actors are hired per show. Others are paid on a sliding scale, ranging from $25 to $250 per week, with the higher rates going to those who have worked longest with the company. Both the assistant stage manager and Watkins himself play small roles. Watkins usually takes a part in the middle of the play, leaving himself free to greet audience members in the lobby before and after performances. ("I work them like a minister," he says.) In *As You Like It* in 1992, for example, he played Jaques and designed the lights.

The Atlanta Shakespeare Tavern is accessible by public transportation; from the MARTA stop at the Civic Center, a four-block walk to Peachtree and Pine brings one in sight of the theatre's blue awning in the middle of the block. Parking is available in a lot nearby. From the main entrance, a flight of stairs leads down into the spacious lobby. Dressing rooms, green room, and offices are all located off the lobby. The theatre itself retains the tavern format. Small tables and chairs seat up to 175 comfortably, but an audience of 50 can seem like a full house; 190 is the upper limit. The house opens at 6:30, an hour before curtain time. Reasonably priced pub food and ales (average $6.00 for a light dinner) are sold at the food and beverage bars at the back of the house; only the beverage bar reopens at intermission. Until the 1992 season, a 20-minute pre-show was presented. Performed by five actors, these sketches were usually comic spoofs of the tragedies, such as *The Really Bad Timing and Rotten Luck of Romeo and Juliet* or *How MacBeth Murdered All His Friends*. As audiences have grown, however, the dining and drinking have distracted from the pre-show, so it has been discontinued.

The 14 by 30-foot stage has a traditional half-timbered look. It has a central doorway, a balcony at stage right, five side entrances, and a backstage thunder sheet. In keeping with the philosophy of tavern theatre, actors do not keep their places on the stage but step down to move about among the audience, frequently making eye contact and delivering asides to the spectator cum tavern customer. Watkins takes a "back to basics" approach to production. "I play it straight," he says. "I don't monkey around with the material. It's excellent. It doesn't need improving." Nor will he use electronic sound effects. All the drums, trumpets, and madrigal singers are live.

"Radically committed" to Shakespeare, Watkins studied under Paul Baker at Trinity University. His easygoing manner barely conceals a missionary zeal for artistic fulfillment for himself, his company, and his present and future audiences. In addition to his regular duties as director, actor, stage designer, and carpenter, he has worked as a singer, magician, juggler, and mime; he plays the saxophone, flute, clarinet, piano, guitar, recorder, and nose flute. His biggest challenge was learning business management. Fortunately, his wife is a certified public accountant, so the ASC has not needed to hire a general manager.

With the move to the Atlanta Shakespeare Tavern, ASC lost about half of its Manuel's Tavern clientele. When Watkins does recognize a face from the old days, he'll ask, "Why did it take you two years to find us here?" They usually become regulars again. About one-quarter of the audience is composed of students, many from Emory University; 30 percent of the students belong to ethnic minorities, including many Hispanic individuals. The multicultural makeup of the audience might be traced back to the 1984 *Romeo and Juliet*, in which seven African-American actors were featured in the cast, including the two title roles. About 20 percent of the ASC's audience is also on the Alliance Theatre's mailing list. Its volunteers tend to be older single people. The tenor of the ASC's reviews suggests that Atlantans are proud of "the only Elizabethan performance tavern in the U.S." Marilyn Dorn Staats observed that "after a show, it is not unusual for the audience to gather together at the bar, order a beer, and use the company's T-shirt slogan as a toast: 'This Bard's for you!'"

Production History: **1984**: *AYL, Rom.*; **1985**: *Ado, Ham.*; **1986**: *MND, MV*; **1987**: *TN*; **1988**: *TGV*; **1989**: *Shr.*; **1990**: *Tmp., Ado, Saint Joan*; **1991**: *Wiv., Commedia dell'* *Shakespeare, An Elizabethan Christmas Carol*; **1992**: *The Lion in Winter, Rom., AYL*; **1993**: *JC, Tit.*

Research Resources: Atlanta Shakespeare Company archives are maintained at the Atlanta Shakespeare Tavern offices. See also:

Ricci, Claudia. "In Atlanta, Manuel's Tavern Mixes A Bit of the Bard With Its Drinks."*Wall Street Journal* (21 May 1984).

Schmidt, William E. "Atlanta: Beer and the Bard."*New York Times Magazine* (7 October 1984).

Staats, Marilyn Dorn. "Theater: It's Supposed To Be Fun." *Atlanta Magazine* (July 1987).
Youngers, Laurie. "Offering of Faith." *Creative Loafing* (8 December 1990).

Site visit and interview: 4 August 1992.
Felicia Hardison Londré and Daniel J. Watermeier

GEORGIA SHAKESPEARE FESTIVAL. MAIL: 4484 Peachtree Road N.E., Atlanta, GA 30319. SITE: festival tent at Oglethorpe University. ADMINISTRATION: 404/233-1717. BOX OFFICE: 404/264-0020. ADMISSION: $16–$20. SEASON: approximately 50 performances in rotating repertory, mid-June to mid-August, 8:00 p.m., Tues.–Sun., with pre-show 7:00 p.m. PRINCIPAL STAFF: Richard Garner, producing director; Margaret Conant Dickson, managing director; Maureen Kelly, administrative director. FACILITY: 110-foot tent (capacity 399). AUDITIONS: Atlanta, Southeast Theatre Conference, North Carolina School of the Arts. STATUS: LOA Equity contract. ANNUAL BUDGET: $500,000 (1990). ANNUAL ATTENDANCE: 14,000 (1990). FOUNDED: 1985, Lane Anderson, Richard Garner, and Robert Watson.

Two of the three founders of Georgia Shakespeare Festival (GSF) were undergraduates together in the 1970s. When their careers took them to opposite coasts, Lane Anderson and Richard Garner vowed to work together some day. Several years later, had switched coasts and both had worked with Shakespeare companies, but they had not found the joint venture they sought. Eventually, Anderson settled down to teach in the Department of Drama at Oglethorpe University in Atlanta. When the university's president solicited ideas for drawing people to the campus in summer, Anderson seized the opportunity. Garner joined him in conducting a feasibility study in 1984 to determine whether Atlanta would support a Shakespeare festival. The third GSF co-founder, Bob Watson, had worked with Anderson at a North Carolina outdoor historical drama and had run a small theatre company for new plays in Atlanta. When that company folded, Watson had its name legally changed from the Atlanta Stage Company to the Georgia Shakespeare Festival, allowing anyone from the old board who had no interest in Shakespeare to resign. This saved the eight months it would have taken to incorporate a new non-profit company.

During the year and a half leading up to the inaugural 1986 season, the co-founders sought advice from the staffs of about 30 different Shakespeare festivals in the United States. A 17-member board was formed and became very active at fund raising. There were many small parties at private homes, where people would write checks for as little as $5.00. GSF went into production with a budget of $120,000. One of the riskier decisions was to start with an Equity company. The College Apprentice Program also dates to the inaugural season.

For the first two summers, the student actors were expected to work on set and costume construction and to help in the box office, but, by the third season, they had become "true acting apprentices," taking acting classes as well as playing small roles.

Originally the cofounders saw themselves as a triumvirate of directors. Garner kept the best personal checkbook, so he functioned as managing director, while Anderson, with the best technical background, served as production manager, and Watson directed the first season's productions. Watson left the company midway through the second season. Anderson and Garner then made the decision to discontinue in-house directing and to hire the best directors they could afford. Notably, Sabin Epstein of the American Conservatory Theatre directed *Much Ado About Nothing* (1987), *The Winter's Tale* (1988), and *As You Like It* (1990) and subsequently became artistic associate on the festival staff. After the third season, Anderson left to work on a degree in arts management. Garner has since headed the company. In 1990, the permanent year-round staff was expanded to four, with the addition of Maureen Kelly as administrative director, Sara B. Looman as director of development and marketing, and Gina Marks as administrative assistant. The summer company numbers around 70.

The GSF's relationship with Oglethorpe University is informal, but very strong. In effect, the university hosts the festival on its grounds and provides free office, shop, and rehearsal space, as well as photocopying and mailing privileges. Oglethorpe also provides housing for about 20 out-of-state actors, technicians, and apprentices. Garner speaks glowingly of Oglethorpe's generous support: "They're all goodwill ambassadors on behalf of the festival." The festival site has been located on various parts of the campus over the years, but there is always a picnic area outside the festival tent. Banners and colorful imagistic signs lend a festive air to the grounds. The tent gives the festival an outdoor atmosphere while offering protection from the frequent summer rains. The first season's tent, a 60 by 90-foot rectangle, proved inadequate, so a round tent with seating for 350 was used for the second and third seasons. In 1989, a larger round tent with seating for 399 was made for GSF, which has a five-year contract on renting it. The rent is about $18,000 for the summer. A unit setting on the shallow stage can be easily modified to suit the three plays in rotating repertory. The GSF owns the chairs placed on risers in the semicircular auditorium. Overhead ceiling fans and good sightlines from all seats create a pleasant atmosphere for the audience. The souvenir programs (60 pages in 1990) are attractively designed with ample illustrations and text.

Oglethorpe University is situated in the fairly affluent Buckhead area in the northern part of the city. It is accessible by public transportation: bus 23 goes to Lenox Station, where one transfers to bus 25, which stops across from the Oglethorpe gatehouse; alternatively, one can take MARTA to Lenox (N7) and from there a short taxi ride ($2.00) to the GSF. Garner admits that the GSF has been slow to target particular constituencies and develop sophisticated marketing techniques. By comparison with other Atlanta arts groups, it is apparent that the GSF draws a youngish audience. The GSF has always practiced multiracial casting, and that ethnic makeup is gradually beginning to be reflected in the audience.

Asked what distinguishes the GSF from other Shakespeare festivals, Garner is quick to emphasize that it is designed to make the educational component interactive with the artistic endeavor. At the first company meeting, he urges the professional actors to think of themselves not only as teachers of the apprentices, but also as company members who may learn from their students. "To continue to learn—that is the philosophy I try to encourage everyone to embrace. There's a mutual teaching and nurturing going on."

The popular Camp Shakespeare outreach program begun in 1988 is a series of one-day programs for children from ages five to eleven. Offered Tuesdays through Saturdays for three weeks, it reaches a multicultural audience through schools, social service agencies, and church groups. For $2.50 per child, the apprentices perform scenes from Shakespeare, conduct creative dramatics, and lead backstage visits. GSF's high school tour also uses scenes from Shakespeare to stimulate teenagers' enthusiasm for Shakespeare; a study guide is distributed to teachers.

When the cofounders were developing their initial mission statement, Garner wanted to specify a "bold" production style, while Anderson and Lane held out for "traditional" work. The first season was "straightforward Shakespeare," Garner recalls, but "after our second season, we've done very few traditional productions." He tells directors (who are hired primarily on the basis of their ability to work with actors) that they can set the play in any period as long as it enhances the story for the audience; he does not want concepts for concepts' sake. He describes the 1989 *Comedy of Errors* (so successful that it was revived in 1990) as a "perfect example" of the house style. Directed by Luis Q. Barroso, it was set in 1940s postwar Italy, with "real swagger and machismo" and pastel zoot suits. "The concept integrated so well into the production," Garner says, "that it really illuminated the characters and the relationships and situations."

The set for the 1990 *Macbeth*, directed by Stephen Hollis, took the rough form of an Elizabethan stage with central balcony and inner below, but it was a metallic patchwork with rusted oil drums at the sides. A metal stair unit rolled out for the castle scenes. The witches were three small children playing eerie singing games and often creeping about on the periphery of the main action, occasionally even clinging to one of the adults. Lane Davies was a low-key, introspective Macbeth, opposite a vibrant red-headed Lady Macbeth (Stephanie Kallos). Their costumes, designed by Douglas J. Koertge, both moved beautifully and looked impressive in silhouette. Koertge's costumes also contributed superbly to the eclecticism of *As You Like It*. Rosalind's disguise as Ganymede was especially delightful: she wore a 1900s-era beige linen suit with straw boater, her pretty face charmingly adorned with a brown handlebar moustache. John Ammerman as Jaques and Clark Taylor as Touchstone turned in the outstanding performances; indeed, Ammerman in the small role of Ross in *Macbeth* brought more genuine emotion and credibility to that play than did any of the principles.

The 1992 production of *Hamlet, Godfather of Brooklyn* was guaranteed to offend purists, but it offered a genuinely entertaining evening to those capable of enjoying it on its own terms. Set among the Italian Mafia controlling Club Elsinore in 1930s Brooklyn, the production was cleverly adapted and directed by John Briggs. A prologue in which Claudius and Old Hamlet played billiards, ending with Claudius' stabbing Old Hamlet with an icepick hidden in the handle of a cue stick–was spoken entirely in Italian. In the subsequent scene, when Hamlet (a young seminarian) paid his respects at his father's coffin, the corpse of Old Hamlet rose from the pool table and crossed to appear to Hamlet as a ghost. The court scene, mingling a Cardinal of the church among short-skirted cocktail waitresses, opened with Claudius addressing his dialogue to reporters. Hamlet's friend Horatio was a nun in full habit. In contrast to the polished speech of Hamlet's family, Polonius' family spoke in strongly nasal Brooklyn accents. This worked especially well for interpolated lines like Ophelia's exclamation when Hamlet tried to take some liberties before the players' scene (having already slapped her around in his mad scene): "You gotta lotta noive, Hamlet!" The players were the corniest of vaudevillian stand-up comics, while Rosencrantz and Guildenstern stood out at Elsinore as Jewish Mafia intruders. Claudius' prayer was spoken to a priest in the confessional, after which Claudius scourged himself while his henchmen quietly garrotted the priest. Hamlet enjoyed a restaurant meal of red wine and spaghetti during "your worm is your only emperor for diet." (making appropriate use of the spaghetti). By the time Hamlet and Laertes dueled at billiards, Hamlet was carrying two guns in his pockets. Laertes' stabbing at Hamlet with the pool-cue icepick triggered flashes of gunfire that left almost everybody dead. Claudius, however, managed to put a pistol to Hamlet's head, but even that gun battle was topped by the image of the nun Horatio picking up the gun Hamlet had dropped and quaveringly shooting Claudius. Although Ammerman as Hamlet got to deliver his soliloquies straight, the production delivered more laughter than emotion. Undeterred by the reviewers' reservations, the audience at the performance I attended was clearly having a wonderful time.

Production History: **1986**: *Shr.*, *Lr.*; **1987**: *Rom.*, *Ado*; **1988**: *MND*, *WT*; **1989**: *TN*, *Err.*; **1990**: *Err.*, *Mac.*, *AYL* ; **1991**: *R3*, *TGV*, *The Three Musketeers*; **1992**: *LLL*, *Tmp.*, *Hamlet*, *Godfather of Brooklyn*; **1993**: *JC*, *Rom.*, *Cyrano de Bergerac*; **1994**: *Shrew: The Musical*, *MND*, *MV*, *The Imaginary Invalid*.

Research Resources: Archives are maintained at the Georgia Shakespeare Festival company offices.

Site visit and interview: 18-19 July 1990; 2 August 1992.
Felicia Hardison Londré

HAWAII

HILO SHAKESPEARE FESTIVAL. MAIL: P.O. Box 46, Hilo, HI 96721. SITE: in or near historic Kalakawa Park in downtown Hilo. ADMINISTRATION: 808/935-9155. ADMISSION: free. SEASON: July–August. PRINCIPAL STAFF: Paul Mark Clark, executive director.

Hilo Shakespeare Festival (HSF) is a project of Hilo Community Players.

Production History: 1978: *MND*; **1979**: *Tmp*.; **1980**: *Shr*.; **1981**: *AYL*; **1982**: *Ham*.; **1983**: *Rom*.; **1984**: *Err*.; **1985**: *Oth*.; **1986**: *TN*; **1987**: *JC*; **1988**: *Wiv*.; **1989**: *Ant*.; **1990**: *MV*; **1991**: *R2*; **1992**: *1H4*; **1993**: *2H4*; **1994**: *H5*.

IDAHO

IDAHO SHAKESPEARE FESTIVAL. MAIL: P.O. Box 9365, Boise, ID 83707-3365. SITE: 400 E. Park Center Blvd., Boise, ID. ADMINISTRATION/BOX OFFICE: 208/336-9221. ADMISSION: $12.50 (1990). SEASON: appoximately 80 performances during the summer, including previews 8:00 p.m., Tues.–Sun. PRINCIPAL STAFF: Charles Fee, artistic director; Mark Hofflund, managing director. FACILITY: outdoor, natural amphitheatre (capacity 600). AUDITIONS: open auditions in Seattle, San Francisco, Los Angeles, and Boise. STATUS: Equity SPT: ANNUAL BUDGET: $400,000 (1993). ANNUAL ATTENDANCE: 21,000 (1992). FOUNDED: 1977, Doug Copsey.

The Idaho Shakespeare Festival (ISF) was founded by Doug Copsey using several local actors in 1977 as a business venture. Copsey approached the owner of a downtown Boise restaurant, Ray's Oasis (located in a new building, One Capital Center), with a proposal to present a production in the courtyard section of the restaurant during the summer. Although the play originally proposed was the musical *Hair*, the first production was actually *A Midsummer Night's Dream*. Its success led to another Shakespearean production in 1978. By 1980, under the name "Doug Copsey Productions," the season had expanded to three Shakespearean productions, was attracting over 3,000 spectators, and was returning a modest profit. In 1980-81, however, the restaurant was sold to a new owner who wanted to change its ambience and had no interest in continuing the Shakespearean productions.

Determined to continue the enterprise, Copsey and his associates moved to a leased outdoor setting located at the Plantation Country Club. Incorporated as the not-for-profit Idaho Shakespeare Festival, they continued their practice of presenting three Shakespearean productions in rotating repertory for about 12 weeks during the summer. In 1983, the Plantation decided to develop condominiums on the performance site, and the festival was forced at short notice to find another new home. Fortunately, the Ore-Ida Company offered a site in a park along the banks of the Boise River adjacent to the corporate headquarters, and the festival continued.

At the end of the 1983 season, Copsey resigned as artistic director. He was succeeded by Mark Cuddy as producing director. In the fall of 1984, Cuddy hired Vangie Osborn as general manager. The abrupt move from the Plantation to Park Center in 1984, with its attendant costs, and a season in which expenses were greater than income left the festival almost $58,000 in debt. Under the leadership of Osborn and Cuddy, however, the management of the festival was reorganized. Individual and corporate sponsors, as well as state arts funding agencies, were solicited, and new members were appointed to the board of trustees. Cuddy and Osborn also set out to raise the artistic quality of the festival by recruiting performers, directors, designers, and technicians from outside of the immediate area. Gradually, attendance and income increased, expenses declined, and the debt decreased. By the 1988 season, the debt had been completely eliminated, and the festival was attracting nearly 20,000 spectators per season.

In 1988, Rod Ceballos succeeded Cuddy as artistic director. Ceballos brought freshness and daring to the festival with provocative, contemporized productions of *Troilus and Cressida, Titus Andronicus,* and *The Merchant of Venice.* The festival also expanded to include, on a regular basis, an indoor production in the fall in cooperation with the Boise State University Department of Theatre; indeed, Ceballos was appointed to an adjunct professorship during the off-season. In 1986, the ISF, with the support of the U.S. West Corporation and the Idaho Humanities Council, initiated a statewide tour of schools from January through April. It was called "Shakespearience," which involved three actors doing scenes from Shakespeare and offering workshops and demonstrations as well. Through 1992, Shakespearience had played to over 153,000 students in Idaho.

In 1991, Charles Fee succeeded Ceballos as artistic director, and, in 1992, Osborn was succeeded by Mark Hofflund. With only three full-time staff members (an artistic director, a managing director, and a marketing/publicity director), ISF is a relatively small organization. Nonetheless, it has a clear sense of mission and widespread, strong support in the community and across the state. At present, the festival leases its performance site and portions of a downtown Boise building for administrative offices, production facility, and storage, both on a month-to-month basis. For the future, the ISF hopes to mount a capital campaign to build a permanent theatre, with ancillary and adjacent shops, rehearsal spaces, and offices. The ISF operates as an Equity SPT company, also employing a large number of non-Equity artists. All out-of-town personnel are provided with transportation and housing in addition to their wages. As the base budget has increased, the ISF has increased its salaries and stipends and plans to continue to do so.

The production of *The Merry Wives of Windsor* that I attended in 1990 began at 8:45 p.m., rather than at the usual curtain time of 7:30 p.m., because the Ore-Ida Women's Challenge, a major cycling road race, had booked the theatre for its awards ceremony at 7:30 p.m. following the conclusion of the race. Although many of the race observers remained for the performance, the audience was about half its usual size, undoubtedly because of the late curtain.

Most spectators arrived at the festival site early, bearing lawn chairs, blankets, and picnic hampers. The concessions stands and ticket booth, constructed to suggest miniature Elizabethan half-timbered houses, sold a variety of desserts, soft drinks, wine, beer, coffee, and tea to complement picnic suppers. The theatre itself is located in a natural amphitheatre sloping down toward the river. A wall constructed of pressure-treated finished logs, simultaneously evoking the circularity of Elizabethan public theatres and nineteenth-century frontier forts, encircles the upper part of the amphitheatre. A series of park benches are arranged in a fixed semicircle at the top of the amphitheatre, but most patrons prefer setting up their own blankets and lawn chairs on the slope. The audience as a whole seemed fairly young, in the 25-40 age range, and affluent. (One couple, for example, sipped Chandon champagne from crystal flutes during the performance.) Several steel towers for lighting instruments and audio speakers are located at the rear and sides of the amphitheatre. The setting consisted of a large, two-leveled stage, at the rear of which was a unit set with a fairly large, curtained, inner below at its center, with additional curtained openings at the right and left. Black-curtained "wings" that jutted out at both sides served as a "tiring house" and masked entrances and exits. It was not a particularly attractive arrangement, but it proved functional for the production of *Merry Wives* and, one assumes, for the other productions mounted this season.

Merry Wives was costumed in a style suggesting Elizabethan dress, although the brightly colored, heavy upholstery material (donated by a local merchant) made the costumes look, not inappropriately, comically overblown. Director Cynthia White (a dramaturg and an occasional director at the **Oregon Shakespeare Festival**) clearly aimed for a production, as she noted in the program, with "a strong sense of fun, of the bawdy and the ridiculous." The production was thus marked by a broad, vigorous, physical style of acting. It offered a distinct contrast to *The Merry Wives of Windsor* at the Oregon Shakespeare Festival that I had seen the previous evening. The Oregon production, set in Windsor in the period immediately after World War II, was polished and professional in terms of production values and overall acting skill but also somewhat dull, with occasional *longeurs* in the action—more like Noel Coward than Shakespeare. The ISF production was more rough-hewn but often funnier and truer to the comedic rhythm of Shakespeare's play. In its own way, it was an entertaining, energetic performance. Certainly the audience seemed to enjoy it. At the curtain call (well past 11:00 p.m.), the cast was enthusiastically applauded.

Production History: **1977**: *MND*; **1978**: *TGV*; **1979**: *Wiv.*, *Rom.*; **1980**: *Err.*, *Shr.*, *MV*; **1981**: *Tmp.*, *Ado*, *AYL*; **1982**: *Ham.*, *TN*, *MND*; **1983**: *1H4*, *LLL*, *Wiv.*; on tour, *AYL*; **1984**: indoors, *Billy Bishop Goes to War*, *Sister Mary Ignatius Explains It All For You*, *Crimes of the Heart*; outdoors, *Lr.*, *Shr.*, *Robin Hood*; on tour, *The World of Shakespeare*; **1985**: *Robin Hood*, *TGV*, *R3*, *WT*, *Waiting for Godot*; **1986**: *MND*, *Oth.*, *AWW*, *Pendragon*; on tour, *Shakespearience*; **1987**: *Rom*, *Err.*, *Per.*, *The Adventures of Sherlock Holmes*, *Mark Twain*, *Hisownself*; on tour, *Shakespearience*; **1988**: indoors, *Mac.*, *What the Butler Saw*; outdoors, *AYL*, *MM*, *Tit.*, *Quilters*; on tour, *Shakespearience*; **1989**: indoors, *A Touch of the Poet*; outdoors, *Ado*, *R2*, *Tro.*, *Waiting for the Parade*; on tour, *Shakespearience*; **1990**: indoors, *The Skin of Our Teeth*; outdoors, *H8*, *Wiv.*, *MV*, *A Woman of Means*; on tour, *Shakespearience*; **1991**: indoors, *The Crucible*; outdoors, *Tmp.*, *TN*, *Mac.*; on tour, *A Woman of Means*, *Shakespearience*; **1992**: outdoors, *Rom.*, *Shr.*, *R3*, *Scapino*; on tour, *Shakespearience*. **1993**: *Quilters*, *MND*, *Err.*, *Tartuffe*; **1994**: *Ado*, *JC*, *AYL*.

Research Resources: Archival materials are informally maintained at the administrative offices of the Idaho Shakespeare Festival.

Site visit and interviews: 8-9 July 1990.
Daniel J. Watermeier

ILLINOIS

ILLINOIS SHAKESPEARE FESTIVAL. MAIL: P.O. Box 6901, Normal, IL 61761-6901. SITE: Ewing Manor, corner of Towanda and Emerson Streets in Bloomington, IL. ADMINISTRATION: 309/438-7314. BOX OFFICE: 309/438-2535. ADMISSION: $8–$13; Fri. subscription (all three plays) $19–$34; student, child, and senior citizen discount. SEASON: 39 performances, rotating repertory, late June to beginning of August, 8:00 p.m.,

Tues.–Sat., 2:00 p.m., Sun. PRINCIPAL STAFF: John Sipes, artistic director; John Stefano, managing director; Barbara Felmley Funk, executive director; Peter Guither, general manager. FACILITY: thrust-stage, open-air Elizabethan-style theatre on the grounds of Ewing Manor (capacity 390). Sunday matinees and inclement weather performances at Westhoff Theatre at Illinois State University. AUDITIONS: January—March: regional U/RTA auditions and visits to pre-professional programs. STATUS: special Equity guest actor contract. ANNUAL BUDGET: $210,000, (1991). ANNUAL ATTENDANCE: 11,000. FOUNDED: 1978, Cal Pritner.

In 1973, Cal Pritner, then chairman of the Department of Theatre at Illinois State University, proposed to president of the university, David Berlo, the idea of a summer Shakespeare festival in Bloomington. Pritner suggested that such a festival could be located on the grounds of the beautiful Ewing Manor estate in Bloomington, which had recently been willed to the university for use as a museum. Five years later, thanks to the support of key administrative officials at the university and consultation with Doug Cook, associate producer of the **Utah Shakespearean Festival**, Pritner's dream of a professional summer Shakespeare festival in central Illinois became a reality. In 1977, construction began on a wood-frame, open-air, Elizabethan-style theatre on the Manor site where an unused tennis court had once stood. In the summer of 1978, the Illinois Shakespeare Festival (ISF), with an acting company consisting largely of acting students from Illinois State, presented *As You Like It*, *Macbeth*, and *Twelfth Night* in repertory to enthusiastic audiences from the Normal, Bloomington, and surrounding plains communities of central Illinois. Fourteen years later, thanks to the solid foundation established by Pritner, who retired in 1990, and to the excellent acting program at Illinois State (most famous for the origins of the Steppenwolf acting company, now located in Chicago), the summer festival remains a popular event. Still closely associated with the theatre department at Illinois State University, the ISF presents three Shakespeare plays in repertory in mid-summer. With minor renovations through the years, the "temporary theatre facility" still accommodates the performances. Nonetheless, according to John Sipes, who succeeded Pritner as artistic director after the 1990 season, the Ewing advisory board has granted permission to the festival to begin plans and fund raising for a permanent theatre facility that will include an improved sound system, additional and more comfortable seating, and aesthetic improvements to the building's facade.

Although the format of performing three plays in repertory has remained consistent, strict adherence to the Shakespearean canon has not always been observed. Concerned with a decline in attendance from near capacity to about 80 percent, Pritner included productions of *She Stoops to Conquer* and *The Rivals* in the 1989 and 1990 seasons, respectively. While not opposed to producing non-Shakespearean drama, Sipes' plans for the near future include adherence to the canon and the presentation of one history play per season, beginning with *Richard II* in 1993 and continuing in historical progression through the Henry plays to *Richard III*. To prepare the audience with appropriate background information pertaining to each historical drama, Sipes envisions a lecture series presented by scholars from various disciplines.

While continuing the tradition of a three-play repertory at the Ewing Manor, Sipes also plans for a separate wing of the festival to produce one experimental or radical interpretation of Shakespeare each season, beginning in 1993 with a two-person adaptation of *King Lear*. A long-time advocate of experimental drama, Sipes foresees the radical interpretations developing over several years for performance in the university's Allen Theatre during the run of the regular festival.

The ISF functions largely through the year-round efforts of artistic director Sipes and managing director John Stefano, as well as a full-time executive staff, which includes general manager Peter Guither and executive director Barbara Felmley Funk; all of them are associated with and compensated for their work on the festival by Illinois State University. The dean of fine arts at the university hires the managing and artistic director for the festival. The managing director, responsible for all budgetary and marketing operations, works in close harmony with the artistic director, who is responsible for all artistic visions and policies. Publicity is the primary responsibility of the general manager. For the 1992 season, Sipes plans to add an additional part time position of production manager, who would be responsible for the rehearsal scheduling as well as coordinatingfestival events.

Throughout the winter, Sipes and his staff recruit young actors and technicians, primarily from pre-professional acting programs at academies and universities throughout the country. A final acting company of approximately 12 full company members and eight associate company members is selected and scheduled to report in mid-May. The three directors are chosen either from within the theatre department at Illinois State University or nationwide, from professional theatre programs with strong emphasis on Shakespearean production. Each director then selects a cast through auditions from within the acting company. Once roles are assigned to the satisfaction of the directors and artistic director, the actors begin a six-week rehearsal process, ten hours a day, six days a week, to prepare for the festival. The three productions in rehearsal rotate the three-hour morning and afternoon time slots at the Westhoff Theatre on the campus (which includes an exact replica of the festival stage and serves as an auxiliary performing space during inclement weather) and the four-hour evening rehearsal period on stage at the Ewing Manor estate.

Directors are at the top end of the pay scale with $3,600 contracts. Each member of the acting company is paid a $1,400 stipend for a ten-week commitment of rehearsals and performances, while associate company members (who generally play supporting roles) are paid $700 plus the opportunity to enroll for up to nine hours of college credit. Travel expenses for out-of-state performers and staff members are negotiable. Although it is a nonequity company, the ISF contracted Equity guest artist Johnny Lee Davenport to play the title role in *Othello* during the 1991 season. It is one of Sipes' major goals to improve the professional quality of the festival by hiring additional Equity performers within the company. In 1990, the Douglas Harris Actors' Equity Fund was established to help toward that goal.

The Ewing Manor estate, located in the heart of Bloomington at the corner of Towanda and Emerson streets, provides a secluded and pastoral setting for the ISF, which pays $60 per night in rent for its use. Patrons can arrive as early as 6:00 p.m. to enjoy a relaxing picnic on the estate grounds adjacent to the theatre facility. At 7:00 p.m., madrigal singers and Moonie the Magnificent, a popular comedic entertainer and juggler who was also a member of the 1991 acting company, entertain on the lawn until the theatre opens at about 7:45 p.m. The audience can also tour special Shakespearean exhibits within the manor house itself. The walls of several rooms are adorned with posters, photographs, and paintings of historical interpretations of the three productions being offered that particular season. A nearby room has videotape monitors running constantly with the PBS versions of the three current Shakespearean plays. A souvenir and refreshment table is located in a courtyard along with the box office and ticket booth. At 7:45, a recorded horn flourish invites the evening's audience into the theatre complex itself. Built of wood, the Elizabethan-style open-air theatre seats 386 playgoers around a multilevel thrust platform approximately 20 feet wide. At the back of the stage, two stair units on either side lead first to doors on a second level of both stage left and right and then up to a balcony directly above the inner below. There is an opening at upstage center that can accommodate exits and entrances onto the balcony. The performance space is compact but practical. Simple plastic folding chairs surround the stage on three sides and extend from stage level on a steep incline about seven rows to the back of the house. The ISF offers price variations to fit the various seating options. The side chairs are the most economical at $8.00. Between the side chairs and the center or premium seats are the intermediate chairs, which sell for between $11 and $12, depending on the night of the performance. The premium seats are the most expensive, ranging from $13 to $15. Due to the rather steep incline of the seating area as well as the proximity of the auditorium to the stage, sight lines are good to excellent from any seat in the house. At times, however, projection is a problem, particularly for the side seats. Plans are underway for a major renovation of the "temporary" theatre facility that would include improved acoustic elements and seats, as well as cosmetic changes to the theatre structure.

The blue-gray walls of the stage facade, with its various levels, entrances, and stair-units, provide the basic backdrop for all three productions. Scenic elements are adapted to the basic facade to enhance and correspond to the various production concepts. Tapestries and curtains of various colors and textures are used to dress and trim the walls and the openings of the multilevel set. Set pieces help to suggest the desired historical period and concept for each production. At the completion of the evening's performance, the set crew immediately tends to the "turn-around" trim for the following evening's performance.

According to artistic director Sipes, the ISF makes every effort to perform outdoors at the Ewing Manor estate. But, if weather reports suggest a good possibility of inclement weather, the festival officials in charge of operations for that particular day decide at 5:00 p.m. if the performance will be held indoors at the Westhoff Theatre. Local radio and television stations are then notified of the change, and an attendant remains on hand at the estate to guide uninformed patrons to the Westhoff. If unexpected weather conditions are deemed dangerous during an outdoor performance, the play is stopped. If the play is stopped before intermission, patrons can redeem their ticket stubs for a future makeup performance during the last week of the festival in early August. If the play is stopped after intermission, the evening is considered complete, and there are no refunds.

Approximately 60 percent of ISF's subscribers come from Bloomington and Normal. According to Sipes, these communities, located in the fertile farm belt of central Illinois, are made up of predominantly Caucasian middle- to upper-middle- class affluent people with few social problems. His mission is to bring "to this community influences that we normally don't experience." To accomplish this goal, Sipes intends to incorporate into his acting company artists of various races and creeds to help the community understand Shakespeare's words as felt and understood by people of all backgrounds and cultures. Communities within a 100-mile radius of Bloomington-Normal—including Peoria, Champaign-Urbana, Decatur, and Springfield—contribute an additional 30 percent of festival subscribers, while Chicago and the rest of the state make up much of the remaining audience base. Out-of-state visitors are estimated at 1.1 percent. According to a festival fact sheet, numerous national travel guides include the ISF as an important Illinois attraction, and articles about the festival have appeared in papers as far away as the *New York Times*.

The ISF is a nonprofit organization dedicated to the production of the works of Shakespeare and other classical authors, with major emphasis placed on actor and text rather than on spectacle and concept. The ISF operates on a budget of approximately $200,000 per year and performs to near capacity (over 90 percent) houses. Approximately 50 percent of its income is generated through ticket sales with financial support from the Fine Arts College and the theatre department comprising an additional 25 to 30 percent. A grant from the Illinois Arts Council, an individual patrons' organization called The Illinois Shakespeare Society, and souvenir and concession sales generate most of the remaining income for the festival. In addition to expanding corporate support (which is currently minimal) to secondary status after ticket sales as a source of income, marketing strategies for the future include increasing the price of tickets in 1992 for premium seats (while still maintaining $8 for the cheapest seats) and creating an increasing awareness of the festival among young people. Sipes maintains that "if you can get to young people when they're still easily influenced and not frightened by Shakespeare, so that they don't feel you have to have a Ph.D. to understand it, they will enjoy it; they will eat it up." Future plans to encourage younger audiences include the addition of spring workshops and educational outreach programs, especially the video series that in the past has generated sizable income for the festival. The non-Equity company of young actors (MFA candidates or recent graduates) that I saw in 1991 was technically very accomplished, capable of handling Shakespeare's language well, both vocally and physically. The direction was, for the most part, quite good from conception through performance. The three productions together represented three vastly different approaches to Shakespeare.

The Taming of the Shrew directed by Penny Metropulos was, I believe, the festival's strongest production in 1991 for two reasons. First, the production most closely captured the conceptual spirit that the director attempted to achieve. Second, Metropulos made maximum use of the acting company itself, highlighting individual strengths and camouflaging weaknesses. In her director's notes, Metropulos suggested that *Shrew* is considered in this day and age to be a "problem play." "We cannot approach it as the straightforward comedy (based on an old folk tale) it may have been four-hundred years ago, or we risk rightful condemnation from every person who has ever fought for women's equality." Yet, bravely, "straightforward" is the approach Metropulos and her ensemble took, and it worked beautifully. The production was set in early twentieth-century Italy. Petruchio and Grumio entered wearing riding goggles and knickers, perhaps straight from an unfortunate encounter between their Packard driving machine and a roadside tree. The costumes, designed by Nancy Pope, illustrated well the humor and exquisite wealth of the period. The famous exchanges between Kate and Petruchio seemed freshly interpreted, to reveal two wacky individuals who were undeniably "right" for each other. The fun of this production was watching them discover that fact for themselves. The climax seemed to occur in the "blessed moon" sequence of Act IV, scene 6. In a wonderful pause after Petruchio's "I say it is the moon," Kate suddenly put the pieces of the puzzle together. That pause seemed to say that "this man is not trying to trick me or 'train' me" (as is the usual interpretation), but rather that "this man is slightly left of center by nature, and he is naturally amusing himself as much as anyone. Come to think of it, I'm slightly left of center myself, so instead of fighting each other, perhaps we could enjoy each other." Kate and Petruchio do so, and this *The Taming of the Shrew* succeeds as a true romance, beyond the usual battle of the sexes. Both Deanne Lorette as Kate and Robert Caisley as Petruchio excelled as the comedic pillars of this production.

Director Patrick O'Gara suggested in his production notes for *Antony and Cleopatra* that this interpretation would concentrate on psychological aspects of the leading characters. "Thus, in this trio of characters (Antony, Cleopatra, and

Octavius Caesar) . . . exists the moral conflict of Antony and Cleopatra; the conflict (existing in each of us and in all of human history) between the world of the spirit and the world of material conquest; ultimately, between good and evil." The actors playing these pivotal characters, Philip E. Johnson as Mark Antony, Keytha Graves as Cleopatra, and Thomas Kelly as Caesar, while technically proficient, lacked the adequate life experience to illustrate the director's vision and bring the characters to total believability. The two leading actors looked good together, but the electricity was not quite there. Set in Jacobean England, the production did boast some opulent costumes designed by Steven Miller and Frank Vybiral; Antony's forces wore red, while Caesar's were in light blue. Cleopatra and her world were robed in soft and natural colors.

The ISF's *Othello* boasted a first for the festival: the use of an Equity actor on a Guest Artist contract. Johnny Lee Davenport offered a very good interpretation of the jealous Moor. His Othello was a soft-spoken man who is calculating and intelligent, but who also incorporates an element of danger, a side to the character that is missing from many interpretations. This production had a contemporary setting, using Operation Desert Storm camouflage uniforms, red berets, and so forth. The love relationship between Othello and Desdemona was for the most part convincing, thanks to the work of Deanne Lorette as the unfortunate heroine. Kim Pereira did an excellent job of clipping off Iago's famous metered lines of Machiavellian calculation, and one saw in his eyes a cold and evil stare. Still, one was never sure of the passion and whence it originated. The passion was clear for Davenport, however, especially in his love for Desdemona, and that is what made this production a success. Davenport was not technically the most proficient Othello I have ever seen, but he ranks as one of the most passionate and individualized.

Production History: 1978: *AYL, Mac., TN*; 1979: *Ham., 1H4, Shr.*; 1980: *Wiv., MND, Rom.*; 1981: *Err., JC, WT*; 1982: *2H4, LLL, Oth.*; 1983: *Mac., Ado, TGV*; 1984: *Per., MV, Shr.*; 1985: *Cym., Lr., MND*; 1986: *AYL, Ham., Tmp.*; 1987: *MM, Rom., TN*; 1988: *AWW, Err., R3*; 1989: *H5, Wiv., She Stoops to Conquer*; 1990: *JC, Ado, The Rivals*; 1991: *Ant., Oth., Shr.*; 1993: *R2, Per., MND*; 1994: *Rom., 1H4, TGV*.

Research Resources: Archives are informally maintained in the Illinois Shakespeare Festival's administration office.

Site visit and interview: late July 1991.
Alan Klem

OAK PARK FESTIVAL THEATRE. MAIL: P.O. Box 4114, Oak Park, IL 60302. SITE: Austin Gardens in Oak Park. ADMINISTRATION/BOX OFFICE: 708/524-2050. ADMISSION: $12–$15, discount for students and seniors. SEASON: 39 performances, July 1–mid-August; 8:00 p.m., Wed., Thurs., Sun.; 2:00 p.m., Sun.; 8:30 p.m., Fri.–Sat. PRINCIPAL STAFF: Tom Mula, artistic director; Mark Rosenbush, managing director. FACILITY: temporary, outdoor 30 by 20 feet platform stage. AUDITIONS: March, in Chicago. STATUS: Equity CAT (Chicago Area Theatre) and non-union contracts. ANNUAL BUDGET: $125,000 (1991). ANNUAL ATTENDANCE: 6,000 (1991). FOUNDED: 1975, Marian Karczmar.

The Oak Park Festival Theatre (OPFT), founded in 1975, owes its existence to the dreams of community leader Marian Karczmar. Karczmar was on the board of the St. Nicholas Theatre, whose artistic membership included David Mamet, Stephen Schacter, William H. Macy, and Linda Kimbrough. Karczmar hired St. Nicholas Theatre artists to produce *A Midsummer Night's Dream*. This pilot project was successful enough to produce a second season. The third year, the organization moved to a park setting in the western Chicago suburb of Oak Park, where it produces one Shakespeare play each summer season.

OPFT hires three to ten Equity actors and one Equity stage manager per season. Auditions, consisting of a two-minute monologue, are held in Chicago each March. Permanent staff members include artistic director Tom Mula and managing director Mark Rosenbush. Both work part time during the off-season and full-time during the summer. The board of directors consists of 12 to 18 people whose main job is to raise funds. Joan Herbert Mulvany serves as the president of the board. Lacking any "heavy hitters," the board plans multiple fund-raising events in addition to obtaining local grants and private donations. Events such as raffles and educational trips to Stratford, Canada, have netted worthwhile profits ($8,000 and $5,000, respectively). The board also works with the artistic director in choosing the play to be presented.

The 1991 budget was $125,000. Ticket sales and concessions account for 50 percent of earned income, while the remainder comes from local grants and donations. Major contributors include the Illinois Arts Council ($5,000), the city of Oak Park ($10,000), and First Chicago of Oak Park Trust ($2,500). The lovely park setting provides the major scenery for the event. A temporary platform stage (30 by 20 feet) is erected each summer. Audience members bring blankets or chairs or rent chairs for $1.00. The level audience area can accommodate 350. Dressing and makeup rooms are housed in a barn behind the audience area. A gate through the park fence allows a single table and chair to serve as the box office. Lights are hung on temporary scaffolding. Local spaces are rented for rehearsals, and the sets are built on-site. Costumes are constructed utilizing the resources of the designer. A standard Chicago playbill gives company biographies, director's notes, and plot synopses.

Oak Park is located near downtown Chicago off Interstate 290 and is best known as the home of Frank Lloyd Wright. Several Wright-designed homes are available for tours. What used to be a very exclusive area now houses people from all walks of life and supports several community theatres and a dance company. The majority of the audience (70 percent) are local people from Oak Park and the surrounding suburbs. About 3,000 people (50 percent of the audience) are loyal patrons who come every year. In 1991, the theatre strengthened its community connection by offering free tickets to seminars and a special family-day performance of *Richard III* to children accompanied by a parent. This event proved to be very popular, and additional "family days" are planned for future seasons.

Marketing begins in February with news releases announcing the season. Newspaper and occasional radio advertising are the primary marketing tools. Posters and flyers blanket the surrounding neighborhoods. The mailing list for brochures, which go out in May, includes 20,000 names. The performances are listed in the Oak Park and Chicago newspapers as well as in *Chicago* magazine. Reviewers from all the Chicago papers are invited, and The *Chicago Tribune*, *Chicago Sun Times*, The *Learner Papers*, and *Oak Leaves* all provide good coverage.

The strengths of the festival include the lovely park setting, a rich talent pool in Chicago, and the determination of the board to see that the professional festival continues. Mula states the OPFT's future goals as expanding the season to more than one play, adding Equity contracts, and providing additional rehearsal time. One difficulty that the theatre faces is recruiting minority actors. Despite the abundance of minority actors in Chicago, very few audition. In some seasons, the festival has had all white casts. For the 1991 and 1992 seasons, however, minority cast members were successfully recruited.

The OPFT's stated mission is "to present the greatest plays of our language as they were meant to be appreciated: as thrilling, living, popular theatre, in a pastoral setting that mirrors the beauty of the poetry." Mula chooses plays from the center of the canon, as the OPFT's primary interest is in the entertainment value of Shakespeare's work. He elaborates, "It is not our job to do archival productions or the little known plays." Mula first came to Shakespeare as an actor, playing Caliban and several of the clowns. When asked why he chooses to do Shakespeare, he states, "I feel there is a magic in the words—that the words bless and heal both the person who listens and the person that says them."

Production History: 1975: *MND*; 1976: *TN*; 1977: *Rom.*; 1978: *Oth.*; 1979: *Shr.*; 1980: *AYL*; 1981: *MND*, *Dr. Faustus*, *The Twins*; 1982: *Ham.*; 1983: *TN.*; 1984: *Tmp.*; 1985: *JC*; 1986: *MV*; 1987: *Shr.*; 1988: *Err.*; 1989: *AYL*; 1990: *Falstaff*; 1991: *R3*; 1992: *Dr. Faustus*.

Research Resources: The archives of the Oak Park Festival Theatre are informally maintained by Marian Karczmar.

Site Visit: 19 August 1990, interview with Tom Mula: 15 February 1991
Cindy Melby Phaneuf

SHAKESPEARE ON THE GREEN. MAIL: 700 East Westleigh Road, Lake Forest, IL 60045. SITE: front lawn of the Barat College campus located at the corner of Sheridan and Westleigh Roads. ADMINISTRATION: 708/234-2620. ADMISSION: free. SEASON: one production presented for six performances during the last two weekends in July. 8:00 p.m., Fri.–Sun. PRINCIPAL STAFF: JoAnne Muth, producing director; Karla Koskinen, artistic director; Steve Carmichael, managing director. FACILITY: open stage, outdoors (capacity 2,000). AUDITIONS: May, in Chicago. STATUS: non-Equity. ANNUAL BUDGET: $40,000 (1992). ANNUAL ATTENDANCE: 6,000 (1992). FOUNDED: 1992, Steve Carmichael, Karla Koskinen, JoAnne Muth.

Shakespeare on the Green (SOTG) was founded in 1992 by three members of the theatre faculty at Barat College, a private liberal arts college in Lake Forest, Illinois. Steve Carmichael, who chairs the theatre department, and Karla Koskinen, head of the acting/directing program, joined forces with JoAnne Muth, a producer of outdoor summer events in Chicago. Muth joined the theatre faculty in 1990 with experience in fund raising, and she was able to help Carmichael and Koskinen realize their long-term goal of presenting a professional outdoor Shakespeare festival, free to the public. In the summer of 1992, SOTG mounted its first production, *A Midsummer Night's Dream.*

The campus at Barat College is an idyllic setting for SOTG. It is located in suburban Lake Forest, a North Shore community of 17,000, located 29 miles north of Chicago. The picturesque campus has 30 acres of lawns, woods, and ravines, and is situated a half-mile from Lake Michigan. SOTG has enjoyed capacity attendance, and the enthusiasm of the community, the surrounding suburbs, and the local and Chicago press is beginning to attract a wider urban audience as well.

Koskinen is the artistic director for SOTG and has directed the two productions that have been offered to date. Muth operates as producer, handling festival marketing and fund raising. Carmichael serves as managing and technical director and lighting designer; he is responsible for the design and construction of SOTG's traditional Shakespearean stage, modeled after the main stage in Stratford, Ontario. Typically, the acting area is simply and minimally dressed, allowing ornate costumes rented from the **Stratford Festival of Canada** to have maximum impact.

A paid cast for SOTG is chosen in May of each year by auditioning professional actors from the Chicago metropolitan area. Each production has a six-week rehearsal period. Performances are held the last two weekends in July. The atmosphere at SOTG is relaxed, convivial, and unpretentious. Seating is on a first-come, first-served basis. A large grassy area in front of the stage is reserved for blankets, with lawn-chair and bleacher seating located immediately behind this space. People are encouraged to arrive early, picnic, and enjoy a live pre-performance musical show. Local restaurants provide an array of food and beverage tents. Picnic tables and a large open play area for children are also available.

SOTG is produced in cooperation with the City of Lake Forest. The festival relies heavily on in-kind services from the college, which provides security, free parking, maintenance, festival workers, print and mailroom facilities, and a host of volunteers. Major sponsors include American Airlines, Coca-Cola, Pioneer Press, WNUA-Chicago Radio, and Carmichael Leasing. Local businesses, individual donors, alumni, and friends of SOTG complete the sponsorship base.

A modest box office staff helps market the production, and "the local support of the press has really been an asset to us," says Muth. "With pre-opening press coverage and a glowing review, I wasn't surprised to see 6,000 people in attendance over a six evening run." Carmichael adds that "the fact that the production is free is very important. People are surprised by the quality and professionalism we offer, and extremely appreciative of the fact that it is free of charge."

As director, Koskinen is occasionally faced with the dilemma of presenting Shakespeare to a large outdoor audience while simultaneously keeping the integrity of the play intact:

> I sometimes find it necessary to cut a script in order to accommodate the type of audience an outdoor festival attracts. My main objective is to clarify and distill the action. An outdoor setting provides us with less ability to control audience perception and sometimes Shakespeare's longer poetic passages do not work well. That can make for difficult choices, but it is also exciting to try to provide something for everyone with an audience so diverse. I look to strengthen aspects of a play which make Shakespeare universal.

The SOTG staff is committed to setting Shakespeare's plays in time periods that set them apart from contemporary life and will continue to choose Shakespeare's more accessible works in order to build a solid audience base. They also feel strongly that, in a time of economic recession and dwindling resources for the arts, it is more important than ever to present free Shakespeare. Particularly important to them is the idea that Shakespeare be accessible not only to experts, scholars, and those who can afford the theatre, but also to those who might not ordinarily consider it, including children, young adults, people with limited income, and especially those who think they probably won't like it.

In the future, SOTG would like to increase sponsorship to fund the hiring of Equity actors. Another long-term goal is to continue to strengthen audience development so that SOTG can eventually present some of Shakespeare's more challenging works.

Production History: 1992: *MND*; 1993: *Ado*; 1994: *TN*.

JoAnne Muth

SHAKESPEARE REPERTORY. MAIL: 820 N. Orleans, Suite 345, Chicago, IL 60610. SITE: Ruth Page Theater, 1016 N. Dearborn. ADMINISTRATION: 820 N. Orleans, Suite 345. 312/642-9122; Fax: 312/642-8817. BOX OFFICE: 312/642-2273. ADMISSION: $16–$30 (1994). SEASON: approximately 200 performances, four productions in repertory, from late August (free in Grant Park), and October through May, 7:30 p.m. Tues.–Thurs.; 8:00 p.m., Fri.; 8:30 p.m., Sat.; 1:30 p.m., Wed.; 4:00 p.m., Sat.; 3:00 p.m., Sun. PRINCIPAL STAFF: Barbara Gaines, artistic director; Criss Henderson, producing director; Marilyn J. Halperin, director of education and communications. FACILITY: indoor, thrust (capacity 330). AUDITIONS: Chicago, early spring and summer; information available from main office. STATUS: CAT, AEA. ANNUAL BUDGET: $1,600,000 (1994-95). ANNUAL ATTENDANCE: 70,000 (1994). FOUNDED: 1986, Barbara Gaines.

Shakespeare Repertory (SR) was founded by Barbara Gaines in 1986 with a production of *Henry V* on the "rooftop" of a northside Chicago English pub. Gaines, a graduate of Northwestern University, was concerned about the lack of classical theatre productions in Chicago, especially productions of Shakespeare. SR became the first professional theatre company in Chicago dedicated exclusively to the works of Shakespeare since Fritz Leiber's Chicago Civic Shakespeare Society productions in the early 1930s. The company started with a $6,000 budget in 1986; this has grown to a budget of $1,600,000 in 1994-95. The first major production of the SR in its present home, the Ruth Page Theatre, came in October 1987 with *Troilus and Cressida*, which was nominated for several Joseph Jefferson Awards. In the 1989-90 season, SR hired a managing director and director of development. Criss Henderson, as producing director of the company, expanded its programs to include student matinees and launched a touring performance program along with workshops in the schools and seminars. "Shakespeare's Greatest Hits" featured selected interconnected scenes from Shakespeare's plays and "counterpointed" to the greatest hits of music, from Beethoven to the Rolling Stones, in a 70-minute performance for grade levels six through twelve. The company now produces one abridged "curriculum play" each year, specially for student audiences. The company offers 25 performances of this 75-minute abridgment at the Ruth Page Theater and on tour regionally for two weeks. In 1993, SR's young audience reached 20,000.

The 1989-90 season expanded to two productions, *Cymbeline* and "Shakespeare's Greatest Hits," the success of which required extended performances and resulted in a doubling of the previous year's income. The company now (1994) maintains ten permanent staff members in addition to the artistic director. Positions include: producing director; director and assistant director of development; director of education; group sales manager; accounting manager; technical director; a ticket manager; and lighting, set, and sound designers.

The artistic philosophy of Shakespeare Repertory "is based on the premise that only through the exploration of human behavior can we redefine, refocus and enrich our own lives. Shakespeare understood the human condition, all of our lives, our pain and joy better than any other writer." Thus, "his work surmounts any racial, religious or cultural barrier. Accordingly, SR's productions reflect Chicago's rich cultural diversity through color-blind casting." True to its philosophy, the ensemble includes Asian, black, Hispanic, and white members who are frequently cast in nontraditional roles. Shakespeare Repertory prides itself on being a leader in multicultural casting. The company size varies: the 1991 company for *Macbeth* and *Pericles* included 25 actors, 14 of whom were paid Actors' Equity wages. Another unusual aspect of SR is its dedication to producing many of the less frequently produced plays of Shakespeare, such as *King John, Cymbeline,* and *Pericles.* SR has become the fastest-growing company in the Chicago area. In 1989-90, both the *Chicago Tribune* and *Chicago Sun-Times* declared SR's *Cymbeline* production one of the ten best productions of the season.

The performance site, the Ruth Page Theater, lies in the heart of the near north Chicago area, close to the Newberry Library, and it is easily accessible with two parking garages in the immediate area. For travelers, the location is close to the major shopping centers of North Michigan Avenue and a short affordable cab ride from the downtown Loop district. The physical plant is an older theatre building that houses the distinguished Ruth Page School of Dance and an intimate auditorium arranged into a thrust stage (sometimes arena) with seating for approximately 330. The company's sound and lighting equipment, including the control board, and even the portable heating units for the backstage area not included in the theatre rental costs and are rented. Costumes are rented from other Shakespeare festivals, such as the **Stratford Festival of Canada**, the **Royal Shakespeare Company**, and Britain's National Theatre.

In 1992, Czechoslovakian director Roman Polak directed SR's *Macbeth* as part of Barbara Gaines' long-range plan to bring "world-class" directors to Chicago. Polak is the former artistic director of the Theatre of Martin in Bratislava and recently debuted a production of Kafka's *The Trial* at the International Drama Festival in Berlin. Gaines aspires to establish the SR as a national and international center for the performance and study of Shakespeare. She is dedicated to producing exclusively Shakespeare each year, at least for the next five years, when she may consider the production of other classics during the season. Shakespeare Repertory has established a reputation in Chicago as a major cultural center and tourist attraction. The company also supports other local arts groups and fund-raising events. In the summer of 1994, SR presented *Macbeth* as "Free Shakespeare" in Grant Park. Talks are continuing in the search for a permanent home for SR, perhaps on Navy Pier.

Production History: **1986**: *H5*; **1987**: *Tro.*; **1988**: *Ant.*; **1989**: *Cym.*; **1990-91**: *Jn., Ado*; **1991-92**: *Mac., Per*; **1992-93**: *Shr., Lr.*; **1993-94**: *Cym., Shr., MM*; **1994-95**: *Mac., WT, Tro., AYL.*

Research Resources: Informal archives are maintained at the Shakespeare Repertory administrative office.

Site visits and interviews: August 1990, February 1991, February 1992, February 1993.
Ron Engle

IOWA

THE IOWA SHAKESPEARE PROJECT. MAIL: 2330 E. P. True Parkway, #8, West Des Moines, IA 50265. SITE: "The Farm," Raccoon River Valley, near Adel. ADMINISTRATION/BOX OFFICE: 515/222-0124. ADMISSION: $1–$3. SEASON: two weeks in July. PRINCIPAL STAFF: Brian R. Lynner, artistic director; Lisa Norris, associate director. FACILITY: open-air platform. STATUS: non-Equity. ANNUAL BUDGET: $20,000 (1992). ANNUAL ATTENDANCE: 5,000 (1992). FOUNDED: 1992, Brian R. Lynner.

As a professional actor, Brian Lynner had performed at the **Oregon** and **New Jersey Shakespeare Festivals**. He had also owned and operated Soap Opera, a South Des Moines laundry business. The turning point in his career came in the fall of 1991 when a friend who taught English at Roosevelt High School asked him to come to her class and present a Shakespeare workshop. After a week of such sessions, the positive response of the students convinced Lynner of his calling: to take Shakespeare into classrooms all over Iowa. Soon he had reached over 3,000 students with a program he called "Shakespeare and You."

In the summer of 1992, Lynner organized the first annual Iowa Shakespeare Conservatory, a one-week pre-professional training program for 14- to

18-year-old young people. After five eight-hour days of classes in voice, ballet, movement, stage combat, singing, acting, text analysis, and Elizabethan culture, the students presented a demonstration program at the training site in Raccoon River Valley. Joined in his efforts by Lisa Norris, Lynner incorporated an umbrella organization, the Iowa Shakespeare Project (ISP), with an ambitious set of educational, artistic, and community service goals.

Summer 1993 brought the worst flooding in Iowa's history. ISP's rehearsal space and shops were inundated, as was the supplier of lighting and sound equipment. Nevertheless, the 40-member company of professional actors and student interns from the conservatory somehow managed to present all 15 of the scheduled performances of *Much Ado About Nothing* and *Macbeth* at nine different locations in and around Des Moines. The company used its portable outdoor stage for all but four performances (the latter had to move indoors to school auditoriums due to the weather). Company members also participated in flood relief efforts.

With ISP performances and classroom outreach activities well underway, Lynner has already begun to raise funds for the construction of a replica of Shakespeare's Globe Playhouse in Iowa. He sees it not only as a cultural attraction for the state but, even more importantly, as directly addressing a problem that he has observed among young people of the video-game generation: "the impoverishment of verbal abilities and a malnutrition of values." Plans for the 1994 season include a winter production of *Hamlet* in addition to the two summer offerings.

Production History: 1992: scenes and sonnets; **1993**: *Ado, Mac.*; **1994**: *Ham., MND, Lr.*

Research Resources: Joan Bunke, "Onto the Iowa Scene with a Bound: The Iowa Shakespeare Conservatory," *Des Moines Register* (19 July 1992); "Iowa Shakespeare Project survives Midwest Flood," *Quarto* 3:2 (Fall 1993): 8.

Felicia Hardison Londré

KENTUCKY

DEVOU PARK SUMMER CLASSICS THEATRE. (Ceased operation at the end of the 1992 season.) SITE: Devou Park in Covington. ADMISSION: free. SEASON: approximately 40 performances from mid-June through late August. PRINCIPAL STAFF: Ken Jones, artistic director; Roger Augé II, managing director. FACILITY: outdoor, open stage. STATUS: non-Equity. ANNUAL

BUDGET: $70,000 (1992). ANNUAL ATTENDANCE: 27,500 (1991).
FOUNDED: 1990, Ken Jones, Roger Augé II.

The Devou Park Summer Classics Theatre (DPSCT) was founded in 1990
by two local Covington businessmen with an interest in theatre, Ken Jones and
Roger Augé II. They hoped that an annual summer theatre would contribute to
the revival of Devou Park, an 800-acre municipal park situated on the bluffs
above the Ohio River immediately across from downtown Cincinnati. The band
shell in the park had been the site of numerous concerts from the late 1930s
through the 1950s, featuring many popular entertainers and orchestras. In the
1960s and 1970s, both the band shell and the park as a whole had fallen into
disuse. In the late 1980s, however, the Cincinnati Symphony Orchestra (CSO)
presented a series of well-attended free summer concerts in the band shell.
    Encouraged by the CSO concerts, Jones and Augé produced *A Frontier Tale*
in the bandshell in 1988 to celebrate the Kentucky bicentennial. An estimated
4,500 spectators saw this performance, and it was videotaped for broadcast on a
statewide cable television system. In 1989, Jones' play *A Red Eagle Falling* was
presented for three performances in August to a total of 9,000 spectators, and
another cable television system videotaped a performance for future broadcast.
Bolstered by these two successful dramatic presentations, Jones and Augé
incorporated the DPSCT as a nonprofit organization and secured a ten-year
lease of the band shell from the Devou Park Advisory Board to present plays,
concerts, and children's theatre. Augé had fond memories of outdoor
Shakespeare presentations at Cincinnati's Edgecliff College in the 1970s. He
thought that a revival of free outdoor performances of Shakespeare would be
attractive to playgoers in the greater Cincinnati area. With support principally
from the Kentucky Arts Council and the Greater Cincinnati Foundation, Jones
and Augé mounted their first season of *A Midsummer Night's Dream*, *Macbeth*
and *Jesus Christ Superstar* in the summer of 1990 . Approximately 36,000
people attended this opening season. In 1991, Jones and Augé presented
productions of *Romeo and Juliet* and *Richard III*; they also contracted with Art
Reach of Ohio, a touring children's theatre based in Cincinnati, for performances of dramatic adaptations of *The Legend of Sleepy Hollow*, *Sword in the
Stone*, and *Huckleberry Finn*. But, perhaps because there was no musical that
summer and because neither *Romeo and Juliet* nor *Richard III* is a comedy,
attendance declined to 27,500.
    Augé has conceded that the Summer Classics Theatre is a fledgling organi-
zation trying to find an identity and an effective programing format. In 1992,
for example, he changed the format of previous seasons by mounting
productions of *The Winter's Tale*, an original play developed by area high
school students involved in an outreach "apprentice" program, and an
American classic, Arthur Miller's *All My Sons*. This program, however, proved
to be the least popular season to date. Attendance was also hurt by the
unusually rainy, cool summer, and a number of performances were canceled

because of inclement weather. By the opening of *All My Sons* in mid-August, attendance was running about half of previous years.

Augé was optimistic, however, about the future of the DPSCT and of Shakespeare presentations. At the end of the 1992 season, for example, he was planning to present not only another Devou Park season in 1993 but also an additional production of Shakespeare in Cincinnati in the Season Good Pavilion, an attractive location adjacent to Cincinnati's noted Art Institute. The 1992 season, however, ended with a considerable deficit. This problem, combined with a lack of municipal support, ended the Devou Park operation. It is not likely that a Shakespeare festival will return to the greater Cincinnati area in the near future.

Production History: **1990**: *MND, Mac.*, and *Jesus Christ Superstar*; **1991**: *Rom.*, and *R3*; **1992**: *WT, All My Sons*.

Research Resources: Augé has personally maintained an informal archive of reviews, programs, demographic surveys, correspondence, and so on.

Site visit and interview: 13 August 1992
Daniel J. Watermeier

KENTUCKY SHAKESPEARE FESTIVAL. MAIL: 520 West Magnolia Avenue, Louisville, KY 40208. SITE: C. Douglas Ramey Amphitheatre, Central Park, 4th and Magnolia. ADMINISTRATION: 502/634-8237; Fax: 502/636-1480. ADMISSION: free. SEASON: approximately 30 performances, mid-June to early August. 8:00 p.m., Tues.–Sun. PRINCIPAL STAFF: Curt L. Tofteland, producing director; Kathi Ellis, administrative associate. FACILITY: outdoor amphitheatre in a park (capacity 1,500). AUDITIONS: Louisville; Southeast Theatre Conference, Mid-America Theatre Conference; University of Delaware; Temple University; Penn State University; University of Illinois. STATUS: Equity LOA Developing Theatre. ANNUAL BUDGET: $250,000 (1992). ANNUAL ATTENDANCE: 15,000-20,000 (1992). FOUNDED: 1960, C. Douglas Ramey; Kentucky Shakespeare Festival since 1984.

Community pride has sustained the company that is now the Kentucky Shakespeare Festival (KSF) through its evolving identities and recurring financial difficulties over more than four decades. The festival originated as a community theatre group, the Carriage House Players, founded in 1949 by C. Douglas Ramey to produce classics, Broadway hits, and even experimental pieces by local playwrights, in the converted carriage house of his residence on Kentucky Street in Old Louisville. Among many flourishing community theatres, the Carriage House Players distinguished themselves as the most active and ambitious of several such groups, and, long before the regional professional theatre movement brought Jon Jory and Actors Theatre of Louisville, Ramey's company was credited with the development of an audience for serious theatre in Louisville. Among the actors who started with Ramey and went on to achieve national recognition in the theatre are Mitch Ryan, Ned Beatty, and Warren Oates. In that first decade, performances were given at the Brown Hotel Roof Garden, the Terrace Room of the Kentucky Hotel, the Crescent Theatre, Scaccia's Restaurant, and the Parkmoor Bowling Lanes. In 1959, with the financial support of Barry Bingham, Sr., a carriage house on South Fifth Street (three blocks from Central Park) was remodeled as a theatre for the troupe.

In August 1960, the Carriage House Players were invited to perform at an arts fair in Central Park. Over 300 people sat in the rain to watch an admission-free performance of a one-hour version of *Much Ado About Nothing*. That experience convinced Ramey that Louisville had an audience eager for Shakespeare, and he committed himself to developing a free classical theatre in the inner city. A committee was formed of community leaders and representatives of Metro Parks and Recreation, as well as Louisville Central Area, a downtown business association. Dr. Judith Bringham, a professor at Indiana University Southeast and a founder of the Louisville Shakespearean Society, had attended the **Stratford Festival**, and she played an important leadership role in bringing about Kentucky's first Shakespeare festival, a season of three Shakespeare plays that opened in the spring of 1961 and subsequently achieved a total of 101 performances to average audiences of 1,000.

A 1962 summer season of four plays in rotating repertory was presented on seven consecutive Friday and Saturday evenings, sponsored by the Louisville Shakespeare Society, Louisville Central Area, and Metro Parks and Recreation. Attendance held steady at about 1,000 people per performance. With free admission as a proviso, the parks department approved the use of Central Park and provided a makeshift performance space, consisting of a portable boxing ring, a circus wagon, and extra park benches. Area businesses contributed $1,000 toward production costs.

The Committee for Shakespeare in Central Park was incorporated in 1963, with Ramey as its executive director. A permanent stage modeled after the festival theatre of Stratford, Ontario, was constructed by the parks department on the present site. That year, the city of Louisville contributed $5,000 toward production costs. This allowed Ramey to hire eight salaried actors at $65 per week; among them were Pamela Brown and Jack Johnson, who later became associated with Actors Theatre of Louisville. Ramey settled into a pattern of presenting three plays for a six-week summer season. Each of the three plays in turn would have a Thursday-through-Saturday run, followed by a repeat of the three-week cycle. Funding, however, did not follow any dependable pattern. City funding was withdrawn in 1966. Although the state government bailed out the theatre with grants of $7,500 in 1966 and again in 1967, it became clear that Shakespeare in Central Park could not depend upon future subsidies. The committee's drive for private contributions included an especially successful "Pennies for Shakespeare" day in public and parochial schools. Even so, the final week of the 1967 season had to be canceled for lack of funds.

The 1969 season brought a new crisis. The wooden backing of the stage had to be torn down due to termite infestation. Although the parks department furnished the materials to rebuild, the Shakespeare company had to finance the labor. The parks department finally began funding the festival in 1974 with a grant of $10,000, which in turn drew other grants from Jefferson County and the Kentucky Arts Council. Over the years, however, support from the parks department has been complicated by separate budgets for city and county parks—what producing director Curt Tofteland calls "a two-headed beast." He explains that "we would occasionally get operational money from the county and occasionally get money from the city, but never with any sort of regularity." In 1976, $40,000 from the City of Louisville financed improvements to the amphitheatre, but problems of erosion and drainage continued for years afterward. Corporate donations reached a high of $9,000 by 1981. By 1984, when the Kentucky legislature changed the company's name from Shakespeare in Central Park to the Kentucky Shakespeare Festival, the annual budget had jumped to $120,000. Since 1985, the budget has not dipped below $200,000. Another renovation of the amphitheatre, completed in 1988, increased the capacity to 1,000, created permanent terracing for the benches, solved the drainage problems, and improved the lighting and sound systems. That $400,000 project was underwritten by the Mary and Barry Bingham, Sr., Fund ($150,000), the City of Louisville ($150,000), and Jefferson County (in-kind services worth $75,000), but cost overruns forced the festival to borrow an additional $25,000. Trying to maintain a quality product while running a deficit has necessitated cutting back to only two full-time staff positions. As one of 17 organizational members of the Greater Louisville Fund for the Arts (which administers a fund-raising campaign), KSF has at least one steady source of income (30 percent of its budget), but even that has been a mixed blessing, for that funding has enabled the mayor to justify cutting off all arts support except to the Fund for the Arts.

Festival founder Ramey was, says Tofteland, "a remarkable man." He left his highly paid position with the Reynolds Tobacco Company to become an actor, director, and playwright. Until 1967, he directed every production mounted by the company, but failing health forced his gradual withdrawal. By 1975, when he directed his last production, he had to work with an oxygen mask on his face. In 1976, the city named the Central Park amphitheatre after him. Ramey died of emphysema in 1979, nearly penniless in his last years. Nevertheless, Tofteland comments, "he lived a very rich, fulfilled life." In 1990, for the thirtieth anniversary of the Shakespeare festival, Tofteland organized a tribute to Ramey. He called people who had been with the festival over the years (including an actress who had worked with Ramey in 1949, when she was 15) and asked them to contribute to an oral history. Much of the festival's recorded history was lost when Ramey's papers were destroyed in a fire; thus the company archives date back only to the mid-1970s.

Bekki Jo Schneider succeeded Ramey as producer in 1980, and she oversaw a period of rapid growth during her four-year tenure. From 1985 to 1989, C. Hal Park served as producing director. Tofteland was hired as artistic director in 1989 but soon took over administrative duties as well. He had come to Louisville in 1979 to work with Stage One, an Equity children's theatre; by 1982, he had risen through the ranks to become its associate artistic director. Meanwhile, he was acting in the Shakespeare festival and working with its outreach program. After freelancing for a few years, he jumped at the chance to direct KSF, an organization he loved and a position that seemed right for his capabilities. His enthusiasm remains high, despite the fact that the administrative demands of the job take so much time that they sometimes rob him of artistic gratification.

Though the KSF now operates in the black, fiscal problems remain a dominant concern for Tofteland. He takes pride in the grass-roots support that the festival has always enjoyed. "People feel committed," he says, noting that the audience is drawn from every zip code of Jefferson County and southern Indiana, including a substantial representation of minorities. With only a small advertising budget, Tofteland relies upon public service announcements and word of mouth to draw patrons. Tofteland keeps a close watch on the demographics of his audience, and his current concern is that he is seeing fewer elderly people. His strategy for luring them back is to offer escorts to walk with them to their cars after performances. By contrast, he finds that economically disadvantaged people return repeatedly to watch both rehearsals and performances. The overall level of audience commitment is strong, as evidenced by on-site donations and spending, averaging $1.30 per person in 1992. Thus, each season generates about $12,000 in on-site donations, and the sale of concessions and souvenirs brings an additional $10,000 per season in earned income.

Central Park is located in the heart of Old Louisville, an "inner city" neighborhood of mixed ethnic composition and decaying gentility. The festival's administrative offices are located in a three-story former residence about 1,000 yards from the performance site. In the park, the stage is set off from its surroundings by large trees. The terraced amphitheatre is provided with park benches that seat about 1,000. Seating on blankets and lawn chairs at the sides and back bring the total capacity to 1,500. The city owns 150 benches, and the festival owns 200. Occasionally the benches will be moved into the picnic area or under a tree, but none has been stolen. Problems of vandalism have been minimal, Tofteland believes, because the community feels "a sense of ownership." For the 1990 production of *The Taming of the Shrew,* the open stage boasted an elaborate and well-designed setting with stair units. Traditionally, the neighborhood children have played on the Shakespeare festival sets during the day. Because of all the stairs on the *Shrew* set, however, Tofteland worried that someone might get injured and sue the festival for maintaining an "attractive nuisance." He therefore put up politely worded signs asking people to stay off the set. The following day, he found both signs destroyed, the mangled pieces placed in a neat pile on the ground, but the set had not been touched. The signs have not been replaced.

For the 1992 season, Tofteland had a new, permanent stagehouse designed and built at a cost of $35,000. The new facility offers a flexibility that will allow KSF to schedule performances in rotating repertory in 1993. It is also designed to keep the focus on the actor and the actor's relationship with the audience, which has always been a guiding principle at KSF. Most of the festival's supporting roles are played by actors in the Intern Company who are just finishing their MFA degrees in theatre. Tofteland attends auditions at the Southern and Midwestern regional theatre conferences as well as at certain schools that have a track record of turning out the kind of actors he likes. His Louisville casting call is usually in January, but he is open to auditioning actors any time they might come through town. He auditions about 1,300 actors annually for six to eight intern positions (four to six actors, one ward-robe/stitcher, and one stage manager). All else being equal, he gives priority to Louisville artists, who usually make up about 50 percent of the company. He enjoys the healthy spirit of cooperation among Louisville's various theatre companies. "There's little territorial instinct," he says. "We help each other."

Tofteland does not consider himself a "conceptual" director, but he gives free rein to the directors he hires (and he hires only directors whose work he knows well), as long as the concept helps the audience connect with the work. He does, however, choose his season with a thought to what's happening in today's society. For example, he produced *Macbeth* in 1990 because the story of a man who had so much going for him and yet just could not wait for Duncan's natural death seemed analogous to today's youth who "come out of college and don't want to pay their dues. They don't want to learn their craft. They want fame and fortune right now."

In 1989, Tofteland set up a pilot outreach program. He and a professional actress toured a performance workshop entitled "Boy Meets Girl Meets Shakespeare" around the state, playing to over 3,000 middle-school students in small groups of no more than a hundred. Although study guides were distributed in advance, experience showed that the presentation had to stand on its own. Four scenes were performed, each one followed by student responses to the content and dialogue with the actors. The program has proved wildly successful and attracted foundation support outside the festival budget. "Shakespeare is for everyone," Tofteland declares with missionary fervor:

> Part of my motivation in going to the schools is to counteract the way kids have been turned off to the work. I'm there to turn them around. And to me the joy of that fifty-minute program is to hear them say they never knew Shakespeare was

so funny or so exciting or–all those things. And that's what it's all about: opening up that alley where there was no interest whatever. And then they'll find that there's something in themselves that only the arts could reach.

In 1992, Tofteland wrote, directed, and cast himself in a new, fifty-minute, one-man performance workshop called, "Shakespare's Clowns: A Fool's Guide to Shakespeare."

The 1990 production of *The Taming of the Shrew* was a brisk, *commedia dell'arte*-influenced riot of color and comic action. The bright hues, with red, gold, and turquoise predominating, set the tone for lots of inventive business. Many of the lazzi (comic "bits") involved moneybags and gold coins. The skilled performances of Lee E. Ernst as Hortensio, Brian Russell as Petruchio, and Pamela Parenteau as a gorgeous spitfire Kate kept the comic by-play and mugging genuinely funny and never at odds with characterizations. Petruchio's introduction to Kate began with her offstage scream, bringing a wonderful grimace to his face. Then Gremio staggered in with a mandolin smashed over his head and hanging about his neck. Petruchio and Kate took a long eyeful of each other as she stepped out onto the landing, and both seemed to be pleasantly surprised. Their physical and verbal sparring was played to perfection, while the audience's laughter during the scene was mingled with frequent vocal responses of astonishment and delight. At Petruchio's country house, a servant played by Craig Wallace won laughter with his suave demeanor as the other servants tossed a huge mutton roast, too hot to hold, from hand to hand, until Wallace calmly caught it on a tray. Capping off the action, back at Baptista's house, Kate dragged Petruchio up the stairs to bed.

Production History: 1960: *Ado*; 1961: *Oth.*, *Mac.*, *Ado*; 1962: *Oth.*, *JC*, *Mac.*, *Ado*; 1963: *JC*, *Tmp.*, *TN*; 1964: *Shr.*, *Mac.*, *AYL*; 1965: *MND*, *Ado*, *Oth.*, *Wiv.*; 1966: *Shr.*, *Ham.*, *TN*; 1967: *Rom.*, *1H4*; *Tmp.*; 1968: *WT*, *JC*, *MND*; 1969: *Mac.*, *Ado*, *MM*; 1970: *Cor.*, *AWW*, *Lr.*; 1971: *Tmp.*, *Wiv.*, *Ant.*; 1972: *WT*, *JC*, *TN*; 1973: *Rom.*, *R3*, *Shr.*; 1974: *MND*, *Cym.*, *Ham.*; 1975: *AYL*, *Mac.*, *MM*; 1976: *Ado*, *R2*, *TN*; 1977: *WT*, *Lr.*, *LLL*; 1978: *Shr.*, *Rom.*, *Per.*; 1979: *Tmp.*, *JC*, *Jn.*; 1980: *Mac.*, *WT*, *Wiv.*; 1981: *TN*, *Ham.*, *Ado*; 1982: *Rom.*, *AYL*, *Cym.*; 1983: *Oth.*, *Shr.*, *MM*; 1984: *Tmp.*, *R3*, *MV*; 1985: *Ado*, *1H4*, *Wiv.*; 1986: *Err.*, *Mac.*, *2H4*; 1987: *Lr.*, *MND*, *H5*; 1988: *Rom.*, *TGV*, *JC*; 1989: *TN*, *Ham.*, *WT*; 1990: *Mac.*, *Shr.*; 1991: *Wiv.*, *R3 (green show: Gammer Gurton's Needle)*; 1992: *Ado*; *Oth.*, (green show: *The Farce of the Worthy Master Pierre Pathelin*); 1993: *R2*, *MND*, *Les Plaideurs*; 1994: *Err.*, *1H4*, *Pantalone's Examination*.

Research Resources: Archives dating back to 1970s are maintained at the Kentucky Shakespeare Festival administrative office.

Site visit and interview: 1-2 August 1990.
Felicia Hardison Londré

LEXINGTON SHAKESPEARE FESTIVAL. MAIL: P.O. Box 2115, Lexington, KY 40594. SITE: Woodland Park in downtown Lexington. ADMINISTRATION: 606/269-1800. ADMISSION: free. SEASON: three productions presented consecutively for five performances each in mid-July. FACILITY: outdoor, natural amphitheatre (capacity 3,500-4,000). PRINCIPAL STAFF: Walter W. May, chairman, board of directors; Derik R. Mannon, business manager; Sully White, production manager. AUDITIONS: Lexington in Spring. STATUS: non-Equity. ANNUAL BUDGET: $60,000 (1993). ANNUAL ATTENDANCE: 33,000 (1993). FOUNDED: 1982.

The Lexington Shakespeare Festival (LSF) is an organization whose main purpose is to offer an annual, free Shakespearean festival. The LSF began in 1982 when local and regional theatre artists and interested community members united in association with the Lexington Parks and Recreation Department to offer classical theatre productions on the grounds of the Bell Mansion—an antebellum Southern mansion located in downtown Lexington. In 1984, operations were moved to Woodland Park, formerly part of the Henry Clay estate, to accommodate the increased audience and production demands. Since its founding, the LSF has continued to grow in terms of the number of community participants and the number of performances and special services provided, such as special provisions for audience members with vision, hearing, mental, and mobility difficulties. In 1993, the LSF became an independent, not-for-profit organization, but it is still connected with the parks and recreation department.

Though located in Lexington, the LSF actually serves the entire surrounding area—a mosaic of cities, towns, and rural communities. Most often associated with thorough-bred farms and racing, the "blue-grass" area also is rich in cultural organizations, including several symphony orchestras, a ballet, a modern dance troupe, a youth orchestra, a children's theatre, a living arts and science center, and a number of art galleries. It also has a long theatrical tradition, sustained by five studio theatre ensembles as well as the theatre department offerings of a number of area colleges and universities. The LSF, however, is the only organization that offers Shakespeare and modern classics during the summer in a location and setting that attracts a significant cross-section of the population in central Kentucky.

Informal, random surveys conducted by the LSF over the past five years reveal that its audience is drawn not solely from the Lexington metropolitan area. In fact, 40 percent of the audience comes from outside of Lexington; nearly 22 percent comes from the rural communities in the surrounding counties. The festival also draws patrons from nearby towns and cities, from other parts of the state and other states, and from a sizable international community temporarily residing in central Kentucky. The LSF audience mirrors the surprising demographic diversity of the region. The approximate breakdown of the 1993 audience of 33,000 included: 4,300 African-Americans, 60 American Indians, Eskimos, or Aleuts, 545 Asians or Pacific Islanders, 525 Latinos, 27,575 whites, 120 other races, 4,390 older adults, 17,000 women, and 3,275 individuals challenged physically or mentally. LSF surveys also reveal that the audience is comprised of: (a) artists (8 percent); (b) professionals in the arts, medicine, business, agriculture, public services, law, finance, education, sports, industry, and entertainment (30 percent); (c) service personnel—clerical, agriculture, maintenance, construction, manufacturing, equine, food and tavern, and utility (20 percent); (d) housepersons (15 percent); (e) retirees (12 percent); and (f) students (15 percent). This spectrum includes the full range of age groups—children (12 percent), youth (18 percent), young adults (25 percent), adults (30 percent), and elders (15 percent). The surveys further reveal that nearly 40 percent of the the LSF audience has never before attended a live theatrical production. The reasons given for not previously attending are: (a) the expense; (b) lack of what such patrons perceive as the proper clothing for such events; and (c) a belief that theatrical productions "belong to others"—typically meaning white, professional, affluent, highly educated individuals.

The LSF is governed by a 21-member volunteer board of directors. Board members are drawn from across the community in terms of their professions, gender, ethnicity, and interests. They are appointed to staggered three-year terms. The board's major function is to provide appropriate policies, procedures, and fiscal accountability. The work of the board is organized into a number of committees, including budget and finance, fund raising, marketing and promotions, concessions and memorabilia, and volunteer management.

In 1993, 128 community volunteers participated in the various committee activities. Although a mainly community-oriented and staffed organization, the LSF did employ 75 individuals for its 1993 season, including performers, directors, designers, and technicians. LSF derives 50 percent of its budget from concessions and sale of memorabilia (T-shirts, posters, etc.). Grants from the parks and recreation department and from other municipal and state agencies provide 30 percent of the budget, with the remaining 20 percent coming from the sale of advertisements in the festival program. The LSF's 1993 production of *Macbeth*, which tended to emphasize the erotic tensions between Macbeth and Lady Macbeth, was described as an "exciting evening" of theatre. Charles Fuller's *A Soldier's Play*, the first production by the LSF to feature a predominantly black cast, was "well-done," with the actor playing Private Memphis singled out for a "technically impressive" performance.

Production History: 1982: *AYL*; 1983: *Tmp.*, *The Diviners*; **1984**: *Ham.*, *Picnic*; **1985**: *R3*, *Shr.*, *To Kill a Mockingbird*; **1986**: *JC*, *TN.*, *A Streetcar Named Desire*; **1987**: *Mac.*, *MND*, *On Blue Mountain*;

1988: *Err., Rom.*; **1989**: *Lr., MV, Pippin*; **1990**: *H5, LLL, Godspell*; **1991**: *Ham., Tmp., All the King's Men*; **1992**: *Oth., Wiv., Inherit the Wind*; **1993**: *Mac., Shr., A Soldier's Story*; **1994**: *WT, MM, The Miracle Worker*.

Research Resources: An informal collection of materials is maintained by Lexington Shakespeare Festival's business manager. This essay is based on information provided by Derik R. Mannon and C. Alan Moorer.

Telephone interviews: October 1993.
Daniel J. Watermeier

MAINE

CAMDEN SHAKESPEARE COMPANY (ceased operation in 1989). SITE: Bok Amphitheatre, adjacent to the Camden Library. ADMISSION: $6.50–$8. SEASON: late June–August, 8:00 p.m., Tues.–Sun; 2:00 p.m., Sun. FACILITY: Bok Amphitheatre (capacity 200-250). AUDITIONS: New York and Camden. STATUS: non-union contract. ANNUAL BUDGET: $124,980 ((1982); $85,000 (1989). ANNUAL ATTENDANCE: 3,600 (1978), 9,000 (1985), 4,500 (1989). FOUNDED: 1978, Michael Yeager and Madelyn Theodore.

The Camden Shakespeare Company (CSC 1978-1989) was founded in 1978 by 25-year-old Michael Yeager and his girlfriend Madelyn Theodore as the William Shakespeare Company. Yeager and Theodore were Bowdoin theatre graduates with high ambitions and entrepreneurial spirits, and both personally put up $10,000 to begin the company. They convinced the town board of selectmen that a Shakespeare company in Camden was a good idea and assembled a strong board of directors made up of corporate executives and local people of means. Some town residents were suspicious of its merits; these included the guardians of the outdoor amphitheatre and the Camden library board, who feared drinking, drugs, and vandalism. After much debate, the library board agreed to allow the company to use the space, provided they follow strict rules: The season could not begin until July; no rehearsing in the space (one dress rehearsal was allowed); nothing could be set up until 4:00 p.m. on the day of performance (including the 30-foot light tower, lighting instruments, sets, and seating); with an 8:00 p.m. curtain, everything had to be struck and the site vacated by midnight (a policeman came by each night to enforce the curfew); and the company would pay for any damage done to the grass and grounds.

The company followed these procedures for several years, until it gained the trust of the library board and town residents. Yeager and Theodore stayed with the company for three years as artistic director and managing director respectively. They were replaced by Kirk Wolfinger and Mary Rindfleisch in 1981. The name of the company was changed from the William Shakespeare Company to the Camden Shakespeare Company in 1981 at the suggestion of Wolfinger. Casey Kizziah replaced Wolfinger as interim artistic director in 1982, followed in 1983 by William Kelly as artistic director and Julie G. Levett as managing director; they stayed until 1985. Board member and actor Terry Bregy says that financial troubles for the company began in 1985 due to a number of factors, including increased expenses, a significant reduction in donations, and inclement weather. Increased expenses resulted in part from a greater focus on design elements and increased salaries for artists. Competition from other arts groups resulted in donation cuts of 80 percent as more arts groups competed for limited funds. Two seasons in a row were plagued by rain and fog, giving the theatre a reputation for inhospitable weather. Despite the excellence of the actors, attendance plummeted from full houses to only a handful of people. The year 1986 was dark for the company. Bruce Hazard assumed both artistic and managerial responsibilities from 1987 to 1989, making a valiant effort to reestablish the company. By this time, however, the board was "tired," and the community lacked the resources to revitalize the event. The board decided to end Shakespearean productions after 1989, although in 1990 and 1991 the tradition of summer children's shows continued. These have been performed free of charge on Saturday afternoons in July and August at 2:00 p.m. Donations are collected and support the endeavor.

Both Wolfinger and Bregy say the potential is there to begin Shakespeare production again if an individual or group with tremendous energy and drive should come along. The board has retained the goodwill of the community and the library board. Bregy suggests that a festival concept, with its connotations of a special event, might be more successful than the ongoing sense of "company" that preceded it.

The first William Shakespeare Company was composed of non-Equity performers with varying degrees of experience, mainly from Maine and New York. Beginning in 1980, many of the company members were associated with the National Shakespeare Conservatory; critical reviews from that period show a marked improvement in quality and production. When William Kelly took over as artistic director, many of his students from Penn State followed. Auditions were held locally and in New York and other sites at the discretion of the artistic director. Actors were paid $107 plus housing per week in 1981 and were expected to do technical work, including set up and strike each evening. A few technicians were hired, but design elements were minimal, due to the beauty of the space and budget constraints.

In the peak years around 1981-82, the company received $10,000 from the Maine Arts Council and $2,000 from the National Endowment for the Arts.

About 40 percent of the budget came from earned income. An active working board also raised money through bake sales, fashion shows, dinners, and other "labor-intensive" activities.

The initial 1978 budget was $60,000, and, by 1982, it had more than doubled to $124,980. The budget for the final year of production was $85,000. Tickets were $7.00 in 1981 and $8.00 during the last season.

The gorgeous outdoor Bok Amphitheatre was built around 1905 and was landscaped in stages by nationally known architect, Parker Morris Hoover. The multitiered, grassy, terraced theatre provides ample playing areas, with an impressive staircase on one side and stone walls, trees, and boulders all around. Critic Herbert Coursen marveled at the simultaneity of action that the space allowed. One critic noted that the ideal setting included the harbor fog that rolled in on cue for *Macbeth*. Costume and technical shops were housed in Pine Point, a former boarding school, and in other borrowed buildings. The box office was housed in a 40-square-foot building across from the amphitheatre.

Camden is located on coastal highway 1 on Penobscot Bay, 60 miles north of Boothbay Harbor and 60 miles south of Bar Harbor. This attractive tourist town contains a scenic harbor and seacoast with the lovely mountains of the Camden Hills. The windjammer capital of the world, Camden claims to have the best sailing in the world, attracting large numbers of summer tourists. The CSC's audiences were made up from 40 percent local people and 60 percent tourists. Many New England city-dwellers choose to spend their summers in Maine, and they want to take their cultural tastes with them. Camden's summer population is, therefore, predisposed to classical theatre.

Local newspapers provided ample coverage of the CSC activities. It was regularly reviewed in the *Bangor Daily News*, the *Portland Press Herald*, *Preview*, and *Maine Times*. The *Boston Herald* came out once a season and the *New York Times* wrote two paragraphs on the CSC in 1984. *Shakespeare Quarterly* published a very favorable review of the 1981 season. Posters, flyers, and sandwich boards covered the town. Limited marketing dollars were spent on local newspaper advertising.

Yeager stated his dream in the 1980 program as follows: "to build the William Shakespeare Company into a major ensemble company on the scale of the Royal Shakespeare Company in England, making Camden the home base for productions playing all across the United States." Later artistic directors took a more modest and pragmatic approach, stating their goals as "to produce fine classical theatre in mid-coast Maine at ticket prices that will make their performances accessible to as large and varied an audience as possible." Emphasis was placed on making full use of the "arresting" space and focusing on actors and text. Artistic director Kelly put more focus on design elements.

Production History: **1978**: *Oth.*, *Rosencrantz and Guildenstern are Dead*, *MND*; **1979**: *Rom.*, *Tmp.*, *Tro.*, *The Scoundrel Scapin*, *The Jungle Book*; **1980**: *The Lion in Winter*, *Thieves Carnival*, *TN*,

Mac., Donkey Cabbages, Brave Little Iris; **1981**: *Oth., The Importance of Being Earnest, Ham., Cinderella*; **1982**: *Rom., Our Town, AYL, Beauty and the Beast*; **1983**: *Dear Liar, Shr., Tartuffe, JC, Androcles and the Lion*; **1984**: *R3, TGV, The Good Doctor, Dracula, The Dancing Monkey*;

1985: *The Glass Menagerie, Ado, Mac., Hansel and Gretel*; **1986**: dark (sponsored four fund-raising events and raised $58,700); **1987**: *MND, Frankenstein, Playboy of the Western World*; **1988**: *Shr., Peer Gynt, The Inspector General*; **1989**: *Rom., The Barber of Seville, AYL.*

Research Resources: Archives for the Camden Shakespeare Company are informally maintained by former board members Katrinka Wilder and Terry Bregy. See R. Herbert Coursen, "Shakespeare in Maine: Summer 1981," *Shakespeare Quarterly* (Spring 1983): 96-97.

Site visit and interviews with Kirk Wolfinger: 4 August 1991; telephone interviews with Terry Breghy, 9 September 1991; and with Julie Canniff, 4 December 1991.
Cindy Melby Phaneuf

THEATRE AT MONMOUTH. MAIL: P.O. Box 385, Monmouth, ME 04259. SITE: Cumston Hall, Main St., Monmouth, ME. ADMINISTRATION: 207/933-2952. BOX OFFICE: 207/933-9999. ADMISSION: $14–$16. SEASON: early June through August. PRINCIPAL STAFF: Richard C. Sewell, artistic director; Christopher Rock, artistic collaborator; Betsy Sweet, general manager. FACILITY: Cumston Hall, European court theatre, proscenium with forestage extension (capacity 250). AUDITIONS: spring at North East Theatre Conference, and in Augusta or Waterville, ME. STATUS: SPT. ANNUAL BUDGET: $200,000 (1991). ANNUAL ATTENDANCE: 10,000, plus 3,000 school children. FOUNDED: 1970, Richard C. Sewell, Robert Joyce.

The Theatre at Monmouth (TM) was designated the "Shakespearean Theatre of Maine" by the state legislature in 1973 and was cited for excellence by the New England Theatre Conference in 1981. Founder Richard Sewell traces the origin of the idea to his own childhood experience of seeing Gilbert and Sullivan operettas performed at the historic Cumston Theatre in Monmouth. In 1969, Robert Joyce, a Maine native and professor at the University of Wisconsin—La Crosse, produced Sewell's play, *Winter Crane*, at his university and invited Sewell to attend the final dress rehearsals and performances. Sewell was impressed with Joyce's staging of the play. Talking together far into the night, often of Shakespeare, the two decided to combine their talents and launch a classical theatre in Maine. Sewell already knew the ideal location—Monmouth. Joyce provided technical equipment and other resources, including skilled technicians. Joyce's brothers, licensed electricians, wired the theatre for very little money.

The early years were lean in terms of audience attendance, but critical acclaim for TM's 1975 production of *The Tempest* helped boost attendance. The theatre has since grown steadily and maintained a loyal following. Union professionals and college interns produce four plays in rotating repertory. The season normally includes three classical plays, two of which are usually Shakespeare, and one contemporary play. Performances are given in July and August, and an annual children's show is produced in June with 3,000 school-children bused in for the performances. A children's show for family audiences is added to the repertoire in August.

Throughout TM's history, various programs have been established. Among the most notable are the fall tours, a Portland season, an Elizabethan Festival week in mid-July, and a three-week Shakespeare workshop led by Robert Hapgood of the University of New Hampshire (held at Bowdoin College). Fall tours to small towns in Maine have included Sewell's *The Royal Throne of Kings* (a condensation of *Richard II* and *Henry IV*), *Walt Whitman*, a one-man show written by Sewell and company member John Fields, *The Wooden "O"*, and Ted Davis' adaptation of *Jane Eyre*.

TM is governed by a 15-member board of directors composed of teachers, attorneys, accountants, and other community leaders. The board sets policy and hire the artistic director and general manager. A hands-on board, the members do everything from cleaning the theatre before the season opens to providing food for receptions as well as raising money. TM employs Equity actors, although early seasons depended more on student and local talent, and occasionally budget deficits have forced TM to go non-Equity, though the intent has always been to have a core of Equity actors.

TM operates under a Small Professional Theatre Contract (SPTC). The 1991 company had ten Equity members who were paid $235 a week plus benefits. Eight college interns rounded out the casts and were paid $40 per week. Equity members are housed in attractive lake cottages rented from local owners. All meals are provided by the company in Grange Hall, which was purchased by the company in 1991 and serves as the rehearsal hall as well. Artistic director Sewell jokes, "As the cooking goes, so goes the season." Monmouth pays the company cook a salary of $3,900 and spends $10,000 on food for the summer. Auditions are held in Boston and Augusta or Waterville in mid-March, as well as at the New England Theatre Conference. Many company members return season after season. Personal contacts are also important in the casting process. Technicians and designers are paid similar wages to the actors, according to their experience level. The entire company is composed of 40 employees.

Permanent staff members include artistic director Sewell, a Colby College professor and playwright; artistic collaborator, Christopher Rock, artistic director of the Theatre of The Enchanted Forest; and general manager Betsy

Sweet, who is also a political consultant. All employees are seasonal, but Sweet is paid $14,000 for full-time summer and part-time off-season employment. Additional summer employees include a business manager, George Carlson, at $250 a week, a box office manager at $100 a week, and a house manager ($40 a week).

Although the philosophy of the theatre precludes hiring stars, actresses Mary Ann Plunkett and Cecile Mann are among the professionals who have roots at TM. Also worth noting are actors Jim Bodge, Jerry Kissell, Anne Menelaus Brown, and Michael O'Brien, who have been with TM off and on for its 22-year history. O'Brien was a fisherman and clammer in Lubec, who went from being an intern to playing major roles such as Richard II.

In 1991, TM's budget was $200,000 a year. Sweet reports that 80 percent comes from earned income and ticket sales, advertising, concessions, and souvenirs. The other 20 percent (roughly $40,000) comes from small individual contributions. Although TM lacks an "angel" to support the theatre with a major gift, it receives hundreds of small contributions. Sewell notes that "the soil in which the theatre has grown is nourished with the hundreds of $5, $10, and $20 donations it receives." The Maine Council on the Arts and Humanities provided support in the mid-1970s. Other major contributors include Digital Corporation, Marjorie Sewell, and Joseph Rich. Three times in its history, the theatre has been debt free and three times, due to debt, the theatre nearly folded. The company has carried a debt of $60,000 on and off again since its seventh season, and, most recently, after nearly closing its doors, ran up a $60,000 deficit in 1990.

Cumston Hall, the home of TM, is the center of the political and social life of the town. An impressive, unique, ornamental Victorian building, it dominates the main street of the town and "has aroused the interest of passers-by" since its dedication on 28 June 1900. Charles Cumston, former headmaster of Boston English High School, retired to Monmouth and decided to give his town a building to house the town hall, the public library, and a theatre. He chose his friend Harry Cochran, an untrained architect, to design the building. Cochran, Monmouth's own Renaissance man, came up with a design that experts have praised highly. Cumston Hall still serves all three of its original functions.

The theatre itself is an elegant and intimate Victorian opera house with seats for 265 people. The curving lines of the space add to the acoustically flawless sound. The proscenium opening is 17 by 19 feet, with a depth of only 10 feet. With virtually no overhead flyspace and minimal wingspace, design choices must utilize clean lines and simple decor. Boxes on either side of the stage are often incorporated into the playing area. A forestage extension build in 1973 allows more playing space downstage of the proscenium. According to a TM publicity handout on Cumston Theatre, "Much of the theatre's charm is due to the cherubic fresco Cochran himself painted on the ceiling, also to his carving and hand molded plaster work on the walls, the boxes, and proscenium arch." The dressing rooms and scene shop space in the basement of Cumston Hall are converted for summer use. The costume shop and administrative offices are housed across the street.

Monmouth, population 3,000, is located in central Maine, halfway between Lewiston and Augusta just off Route 202. Monmouth is known for its theatre, and the citizens are very proud of it. The town owns the building and allows TM to pay rent on a sliding scale. The entire community supports the theatre. One year, for instance, Earl Flanders, a local funeral director, donated space in the funeral parlor for the costume shop.

The audience for the theatre is extremely loyal and divides into three components. About one-third of the audience has come to the theatre for 22 years and will come to see anything the theatre produces, often more than once. One-third are natives or people with summer homes in Maine, who know of the theatre and want the cultural experience that theatre can offer. The final third are tourists who come from the coast and lakes to see Shakespeare. They drive as long as two hours to get to Monmouth. For that reason, TM tries to conclude its evenings of theatre by 11:00 p.m. Shakespeare and other classics are the best sellers, although there is little difference in sales between the comedies and the tragedies. Overall, houses average 65 percent of capacity, but August usually boasts full houses.

A special feature of the 1991 season was a "Thank You Monmouth" evening. Instead of the usual $16.00 tickets, Monmouth citizens were offered tickets to *The Comedy of Errors* and *The Liar* for only $3.00 each. One 72-year-old woman came to both performances, saying she had always wanted to go, but had not had the opportunity. The theatre also recruits an "incredible core of volunteers" who do everything from running the gift shop and concessions to ushering, parking cars, and procuring props.

A variety of marketing tools are used, although, with its limited budget, the theatre depends heavily on public service announcements and word of mouth. The mailing list for brochures numbers 5,000 names. The season is listed in *Maine Publicity*, *Down East Magazine*, the *Boston Phoenix*, and *American Arts* calendars.

Reviewers from the *Portland Press Herald*, the *Maine Times*, the *Lewiston Sun Journal*, the *Brunswick Times Record*, and the *Kennebec Journal* provide regular feature stories and reviews. According to Sewell, the theatre has grown steadily in attendance from some meager early years (12 invited nuns) to an overall 65 percent of capacity.

TM's assets include the community pride and support that surround the event, the "gem" of a theatre in Cumston Hall, and the strength and maturity of the core acting company. When asked how TM is able to attract such experienced and mature performers, Sewell laughingly notes that his friends are now older. Seriously, he says that the classical literature and quality of productions keep TM actors returning year after year. In addition, TM tends to cast against type, allowing the actors to stretch their abilities, thus contributing to their continued interest in the company.

In terms of long-range goals, Sewell notes, "Though we have grown as Monmouth has grown, and contributed to its growth, we are a small theatre and we want to be a small theatre." The out-of-town audience has grown steadily, but retaining affordability for the large local following is foremost in Sewell's mind: "I really believe that when a theatre ticket costs more than ten loaves of bread, that ticket costs too much. That won't happen at Monmouth."

Sweet concurs with Sewell's assessment: "We want to continue the high-quality classical theatre, but we don't intend to be bigger." She would like to raise more money by attracting larger audiences, starting a Friends of the Theatre at Monmouth, and tapping into the resources of some of the millionaires who have summer homes in Maine. Year-round special events and educational tours to expose rural students to classical theatre are also in the planning stages. When asked about multicultural goals for the company, Sewell and Sweet both note that there is less than 2 percent cultural diversity in Maine. They would welcome minority members to the company, but, unfortunately, few audition.

When asked how they would spend an additional $50,000, Sewell and Rock both reply "more rehearsal time." The theatre survives by paring rehearsal time to an absolute minimum. Its technical equipment is also in need of repair, especially the sound system. Sewell concludes: "My own hope for the coming years is not that we should grow bigger, or richer, or more famous. Only funnier, sadder, subtler. There is a whole universe to expand and grow into—and that universe is within us."

TM's incorporation papers state its mission as follows: "to engage, promote and present literary and theatrical programs, workshops, seminars, lectures, recitals and performances." More specifically, Sewell says that Monmouth exists because Maine needs a classical theatre. He notes that:

> We are at Monmouth because audiences here are not jaded. Some of our public is seeing these shows for the first time. There is no need to do a version or find a gimmick. Monmouth is not "Macbeth-as-Aztec-death-rite-with-witches-from-outer-space," nor an "all-male-Lysistrata-in-drag." We have an open-minded, intelligent audience that is willing to use its ears and imagination; we try to give them the plays pretty much as written not in slavish subjection to the texts, but with friendly admiration: we *like* these plays.

TM's aesthetic is further defined by the intimacy found in small playhouses, with the potential for subtle expression and carefully nuanced unamplified voices. According to Sewell, the emphasis is on "live actors, live music, a few props—always the sense that we are conjuring creatures of imagination that live in a world as real as our own." A certain continuity of style allows costumes to be reused. The ensemble concept, with people returning year after year, provides a freedom to create, unmatched by companies that lack such continuity.

TM's moving production of *King Lear* in 1991 played to enthusiastic full houses. The intimate theatre allowed a subtle and carefully nuanced approach to the inevitable destruction. The mature cast, attracted from major regional theatres across the country, were excellently suited to their roles, and the powerful sense of ensemble was a major strength. From the forceful opening moments to the agonizing closing scene, this *King Lear* riveted its audience.

The impressive staging by Christopher Rock made the complex story seem simple and clear, and scenes flowed without interruption. Rock's skillful direction and careful editing clarified character relationships as well as heightening domestic and political issues. The uniformly excellent cast of 18 provided many memorable performances. Sewell as Lear went from arrogance and self-indulgence to intense sorrow. His vulnerable and human Lear grew in self-knowledge as the play progressed. He was almost an ordinary man, symbolic of our continued inability to deal with our lack of vision. Lina Patel was effortlessly virtuous as Cordelia. A gorgeous young woman of Indian descent, she went from surprised confusion in the early scenes to deep compassion. Jim Finnegan as Kent used his excellent voice and great emotional depth to full advantage; he played his scenes with urgency. Jim Kissell as Edmund was a skillful manipulator, and his offhand delivery created an immediate and direct connection with the audience. Michael O'Brien was equally believable as Gloucester's loyal son and as mad Tom. Dee Pelletier as Lear's Fool was lively and animated but worked too hard to illustrate her words. Her performance lacked the seriousness that underlies the Fool's actions. The fight scenes, choreographed by Edward Eaton, were most effective when they were covered, such as the blinding of Gloucester. The "low budget" weapons were occasionally distracting. The Stonehenge-like setting, designed by director Rock, effectively suggested the decaying ruins of Lear's kingdom. The primitive sounding score was suggestive of the storm writhing in the man. The simple, unadorned costumes by Elizabeth Tobey enhanced the performances.

This production of *King Lear* left the audience with the thought that too often we do not learn from our mistakes until the damage is irrevocable. In the final moments of the play, Lear carried not only Cordelia's dead body, but also the full weight of his tragic choices.

In contrast to *King Lear*, *The Comedy of Errors* was played for broad humor, both physically and vocally, with little attempt to ground it in reality. Overall, the play suffered from generalized choices, most likely stemming from a lack of adequate rehearsal time. Director Sewell inserted minor variations into the text, such as "Dromio, Dromio. Wherefore art thou Dromio?" and "Mr. Anti Phallus" at times substituted for "Antipholus." Both sets of twins differed greatly in looks, age, and level of experience. These choices were never fully integrated into the action of the play. Charles Weinstein as Dromio of Syracuse got the most laughs from his "kitchen wench" speech. Dee Pelletier's Courtesan was clearly a Mae West imitation. The various merchants were cleverly distinguished by their ethnic garments from Venice, Moscow, Bombay, and Canton. The set, an imaginative two-dimensional city, was designed by Jim Thurston. The playful costumes, designed by director Sewell, utilized geometric shapes and vibrant colors.

Production History: **1970**: *The Lady's Not for Burning, Tmp., Rom., TN*; **1971**: *MND, Shoemaker's Holiday, Mac., MM*; **1972**: *Ado, Wiv., R2, An Evening of Pinter: The Room and The Lover*; **1973**: *AYL, JC, Tartuffe, WT*; **1974**: *MV, Shr., The Miser, Caesar and Cleopatra*; **1975**: *Tmp., Err., The Dark Lady of the Sonnets, Androcles and the Lion, Lr.*; **1976**: *Ant., 1H4, MND, The Imaginary Invalid*; **1977**: *TN, Oth., MM, She Stoops to Conquer*; **1978**: *Ham., Rosencrantz and Guildenstern are Dead, AYL, Volpone*; **1979**: *Great Expectations, Ado, R3, H5, A Cry of Players*; **1980**: *Goodly Creatures, Rom., The Servant of Two Masters, Shr., Ondine*; **1981**: *The Glass Menagerie, Tartuffe, Mac., The Lark, The School for Scandal*; **1982**: *MND, Juno and the Paycock, WT, The Master Builder*; **1983**: *Err., TN, Ham., Cyrano de Bergerac*; **1984**: *Jane Eyre, The Importance of Being Earnest, The Doctor in Spite of Himself, The Rivals, Tmp.*; **1985**: *Great Expectations, Caesar and Cleopatra, JC, AYL, Mary of Scotland*; **1986**: *The Miser, The Lion in Winter, And a Nightingale Sang, Wiv.*; **1987**: *The Imaginary Invalid, Oth., Ado, Uncle Vanya*; **1988**: *Taking Steps, TGV, R2, Jane Eyre*; **1989**: *Wenceslas Square, AWW, The Country Wife, The Hunchback of Notre Dame*; **1990**: *MV, Light Up the Sky, The Cherry Orchard, Brave New World*; **1991**: *The Liar, Err., Our Country's Good, Lr., The Musicians of Bremen*; **1994**: *Tmp., Shr., The Play's the Thing, Grannia, Toad of Toad Hall.*

Research Resources: Archives are informally maintained in Theatre at Monmouth's administrative offices. See also Glenn Loney and Patricia MacKay, *The Shakespeare Complex* (New York: Drama Book Specialists, 1975).

Site visit and interviews with Richard Sewell, Christopher Rock and Betsy Sweet: 3 and 4 August 1991.
Cindy Melby Phaneuf

MARYLAND

SHAKESPEARE ON WHEELS. MAIL: Department of Theatre, Room 467, Fine Arts Building, 5401 Wilkens Avenue, University of Maryland Baltimore County (UMBC), Baltimore, MD 21228-5398. SITE: 25 outdoor sites with adjacent rain sites (1992). ADMINISTRATION: 410/455-2917. Fax: 410/455-1070. BOX OFFICE: 410/455-2476. ADMISSION: free. SEASON: 48 performances, July–October, in Maryland, Virginia, Pennsylvania, West Virginia, and the District of Columbia (1992). PRINCIPAL STAFF: William T. Brown, executive producer; Sam McCready, artistic director. FACILITY: three-level stage, transported by flatbed truck. AUDITIONS: April–June, Department of Theatre, UMBC. STATUS: students and faculty. ANNUAL BUDGET: $65,000 (1992). ATTENDANCE: over 10,000. FOUNDED: 1985, William T. Brown.

Shakespeare on Wheels (SOW), a traveling theatre program sponsored by the University of Maryland, Baltimore County, has performed to an estimated 90,000 people in its eight summers (one play each season) on the road in Maryland, Pennsylvania, Virginia, West Virginia, and Washington, D.C. The 1992 season brought 48 performances to 24 sites in a three-month period. Founder William T. Brown originated the concept when he was a visiting technical consultant on a Rockefeller Foundation grant to help establish a school of drama at the University of Ibadan, Nigeria, in 1963-64. Theatre so interested the African students that they would go by station wagon to villages in the region, presenting scenes and skits, but the halls where they performed were never adequate to accommodate all who wanted to attend. To celebrate the four-hundredth anniversary of Shakespeare's birth, Brown thought it seemed appropriate to send the Bard's work on the road in Nigeria. He conceived the idea of a portable stage that would both evoke Elizabethan staging and allow an unlimited number of spectators. Drawing upon his design experience, Brown constructed a flatbed wagon with sides that folded down to make a stage, to which could be added a thrust, balconies, and side entrances. The cost was about $4,000, and the set-up time was about an hour. For five weeks, Brown and the students toured cities and villages in Nigeria, performing scenes from Shakespeare to audiences ranging from 400 to 5,000. Brown has told about a performance of *Hamlet* before 1,500 people on an athletic field. During the "to be or not to be" soliloquy, he heard what seemed to be an echo, although it was an open space where echoes were unlikely. Listening closely, he realized that the audience was reciting the well-known words along with the actor!
  More than two decades later, the director of summer school at the University of Maryland Baltimore County asked Brown (now a faculty member at UMBC) to revive his mobile Shakespeare project. Brown redesigned the fold-

out stage for a 40-foot flatbed trailer. The sides of the trailer become part of the stage floor, the rear of the trailer becoming the apron of the stage, while columns, stairs, and so on are erected on the stage from elements carried inside the trailer. A control room for sound and lights plus ladders to the balcony fit within the backstage area. With the set folded up for travel, its size (roughly 8 feet wide by 12 feet high) conforms to highway specifications. The performance configuration measures 40 by 24 feet. "It's all put together with bolts, pin hinges and nuts, and assembled like a jigsaw puzzle," Brown told Anne Bennett Swingle. Performers walk down a few steps to interact with audience members, who stand or sit on bring-your-own chairs in a semi-circle around the apron. Easy to set up and strike, the black, brown, and yellow multileveled set looks attractive even when empty.

From 1985 to 1992, SOW grew from performances at six sites to performances at 24. The budget increased from $8,000 to $65,000. While performances remain free to the public, 1992 brought a policy of asking host sponsors to pay $2,000 for two performances. Other funding comes from UMBC, the NEA, and Friends of Shakespeare on Wheels. The sale of T-shirts and buttons brings in an additional $3,000 or so each season.

Apart from Edie Catto (associate producer and assistant director), the members of the 1992 artistic staff—Brown (set designer), Sam McCready (director), Elena Zlotescu (costume and makeup designer), and Terry Cobb (construction engineer)—are UMBC faculty members. Actors, production staff, and crews are students. The crew erects the set, and actors and others assist in striking it. Asked if people outside the university might join the company, Brown has said that this is possible. Students chosen to participate receive a stipend. Rehearsals begin in June. The season runs from July to October, with performances confined to the weekends after classes begin.

Brown has said that he was drawn to Shakespeare not only by his experiences in Nigeria and, earlier, with the Karamu Theatre in Cleveland and at Howard University, but also because, in 1985, there was only one performance of a Shakespeare play in Baltimore. Remembering that many people who were required to read Shakespeare in school hated it, he wanted to interest them in Shakespeare but not compel them to stay if they were not enjoying the performance. "Quality will bring in an audience and hold them," he has remarked. His hopes for the future are to tour beyond Maryland's neighboring states, to enlarge the company, and to offer more than one play, perhaps even a contemporary play.

Brown lists four basic objectives for SOW: First, annually to bring live theatre to "the people" who could not or would not ordinarily have access to such an experience; second, to increase the availability of professional-quality Shakespeare productions in Baltimore City, neighboring counties, and adjacent states by giving community audiences the experience of seeing and enjoying live theatre performances free of charge; third, to give students the experience of touring a production and performing a Shakespearean play on the type of stage for which Shakespeare wrote; and fourth, to build an awareness of UMBC as an excellent educational and cultural resource in the state of Maryland.

The company has received national and state awards, and it was asked to take its 1990 production of *As You Like It* to the John F. Kennedy Center for the Performing Arts Open House Festival. The awards indicate recognition, but repeat engagements indicate acceptance by those who pay for the performances. Its 1992 appearance in Ocean City, Maryland, where I saw its production, was the fourth annual engagement there. Sharon Tebbut of the Ocean City Parks and Recreation Department expressed her satisfaction with the troupe's work, despite the fact that this production had to be moved indoors to a brightly lit basketball court in the city recreation building after the outdoor set was damaged by a storm only two hours before that evening's performance of *Othello*. In spite of the difficulties of playing in an overlarge, echoing space to which the actors were not accustomed, they and the production staff rose to the occasion. The performance so gripped audience members of widely divergent ages and backgrounds that nothing mattered but the exceptionally well-enunciated words and well-acted events on the improvised indoor stage. Brown later reported that "the cast and crew assembled the next day to rebuild the damaged wagon. We were able to continue our tour without further interruption."

"Rarely traditional," said the 1992 promotional brochure about SOW productions in general. The brochure described SOW's *Twelfth Night* as "Arabian Nights-inspired," its *The Comedy of Errors* as "vaudevillian," its *Macbeth* as "Kabuki-inspired," and *The Tempest* as "a futuristic, rock musical version." The *Othello*, however, was not heavily conceptualized. A more traditional approach was certainly justified by the casting of James Brown-Orleans, a native of Ghana and older than many other members of the company, to sustain the intensities demanded by the title role. The Renaissance costumes suggested the battle between good and evil for the soul of Othello; he was costumed in deep red, while Iago wore black and Desdemona white. One innovation was the unabashed use of microphones. Occasionally an actor lifted a microphone from its stand and moved into the audience to address the spectators directly. Textual alterations included the elimination of Gratiano and the clown, and the combination of the Duke of Venice and Lodovico into "Duke Lodovico." Most unusual was the introduction of a costumed interpreter for the deaf, who signed the speeches as she moved about the stage among the actors. Brown said that the signer, Marla Tibbels, a UMBC student, rehearsed with the actors from the beginning and chose the performers whose speeches she would sign.

Othello's set speeches were well delivered, the intensity of his emotions deepening during the performance. Iago's villainy was performed with bravura by the talented young John C. Hansen, although variations in his voice dynamics frequently seemed to be divorced from the meanings of the words. Bonnie Webster as Desdemona was at first lively, witty, and naive, but when

Othello struck her and she said "I have not deserved this" (Act IV, scene 2), she became pathetic. The success of the performance might be measured by the fact that, when the bed on which Desdemona was to die was thrust out onto the improvised stage by the recently murdered Rodrigo and three others, there was no laughter, just a continuation of the audience's quiet, intense attention to the events of the play. SOW had made a success of what could have been a severely damaged situation.

Production History: **1985**: *MND*; **1986**: *Rom.*; **1987**: *TN*; **1988**: *Err.*; **1989**: *Mac.*; **1990**: *AYL*; **1991**: *Tmp.*; **1992**: *Oth.*; **1993**: *Wiv.*; **1994**: *Ham.*

Research Resources: Archives for SOW are maintained by William T. Brown. See also:
Caspar, Jennifer. "Shakespeare on Wheels Renews Midsummer Nights' Themes." *Washington Post* (27 July 1989): 11.
Ingalls, Zoë. "From Parks to Prisons, Traveling Theater Brings Shakespeare's Plays 'to the People.'" *Chronicle of Higher Education* (11 September 1991): B5.
Swingle, Anne Bennett. "Shakespeare on Wheels." *The Messenger* (Towson, MD, 14 August 1985): 6-7.
White, Louise M. "UMBC Takes Shakespeare on the Road." *Maryland Today* 14 (October 1986): 1.

Site visit and interview: 21 July 1992.
Hassell B. Sledd

TRAVELLING SHAKESPEARE COMPANY. MAIL: St. Mary's College of Maryland, St. Mary's City, MD 20686. ADMINISTRATION: 301/862-0244. PRINCIPAL STAFF: Michael Tolaydo, artistic director/producer. FACILITIES: various. STATUS: non-Equity and guest artist. ANNUAL BUDGET: $25,000-$35,000. ANNUAL ATTENDANCE: 2,000-4,000. FOUNDED: 1992, Michael Tolaydo.

The Travelling Shakespeare Company (TSC) had its origin in 1988, when Michael Tolaydo, a professional actor, director, and professor of theatre at St. Mary's College of Maryland, founded the Maryland Shakespeare Festival to present an annual Shakespeare production at the college. Tolaydo mounted a production of *Romeo and Juliet*, which ran for 21 performances in the summer of 1988. Tolaydo was then invited essentially to remount this production for the Fairfax Family Theatre, an enterprise founded by Bob Mullin, an English teacher at Robinson High School in Fairfax, Virginia. Mullin had begun the Fairfax Family Theatre with funding from the Fairfax County public schools to bring a full-scale professional production of a Shakespeare play to his school, along with workshops for students, teachers, parents, and members of the community. While many productions touring to schools offer little if any direct interaction with students, Mullin intended the production he sponsored to be fully integrated into the daily life of the students for a two-week residency.

During the first week, students helped reconstruct the sets for the Robinson High School auditorium. Students were also responsible for hanging lights, running the lighting and sound control boards, and maintaining costumes and properties. A few students were also cast in small roles. Throughout the week, faculty and students were encouraged to observe rehearsals, ask questions, and volunteer to assist in the preparations. During the performance week, Mullin invited Peggy O'Brien, head of educational programs at the Folger Shakespeare Library, to offer a series of workshops during the school day focusing on the play and its production. On one Saturday during the residency, O'Brien offered a workshop for teachers that featured noted scholars, master teachers, and cast members. Although held at Robinson High School, the workshops were open to students and teachers from throughout the Virginia, Maryland, and District of Columbia area. As a consequence of the workshops and active engagement in the production process, the evening performances were invariably sold out to audiences of students, teachers, parents, and other members of the immediate community. In fact, the initial residency was sufficiently successful that Tolaydo and Mullin were encouraged to continue their collaboration with productions of *Twelfth Night* in 1989 and of *Hamlet* in 1990.

In 1991, because of financial exigencies, the state of Maryland reduced its arts funding, and as a consequence, The Maryland Shakespeare Festival, which had relied on state grants for much of its financial support, was forced to close. Mullin, believing that the Shakespeare program was too important to the Fairfax Family Theatre, asked Tolaydo to mount a production of *The Taming of the Shrew* independently for the January 1992 presentation. Tolaydo formed the TSC expressly for this purpose. Although the TSC planned a production of *A Midsummer Night's Dream* for the Fairfax Family Theatre in 1993, a subsequent reorganization of Fairfax County projects led to a cancellation of this production. In the interim, however, Janet Griffin, director of museum and public programing, had invited Tolaydo to present the production at The Folger Shakespeare Library's Elizabethan Theatre for a week of performances in February 1993, along with a series of complementary workshops. In 1994, the TSF presented its production of *Macbeth* at the Folger Library for 14 performances and at Robinson High School for the Fairfax Family Theatre. The TSF projects productions of *Richard III* or *As You Like It* in 1995.

Production History: As the Maryland Shakespeare Festival: **1988**: *Rom., The Mikado, The Rainmaker*; **1989**: *TN, Dracula, The Medium*; **1990**: *Ham., Dial M for Murder, Pentacost*. As the Travelling Shakespeare Company: **1992**: *Shr.*; **1993**: *MND*; **1994**: *Mac.*

Research Resources: Michael Tolaydo maintains a file on the Maryland Shakespeare Festival and the Travelling Shakespeare Company. See also Tolaydo's essay, "Three Dimensional Shakespeare," in *Shakespeare Set Free*, Peggy O'Brien, ed. (New York: Washington Square Press, 1993).

Telephone interview: January 1994.
Daniel J. Watermeier

MASSACHUSETTS

COMPANY OF WOMEN. MAIL: 791 Tremont Street, Box X, Boston, MA 02118. SITE: variable. ADMINISTRATION: 617/247-9646. ADMISSION: varies. PRINCIPAL STAFF: Kristin Linklater and Carol Gilligan, artistic directors; Maureen Shea, Daniela Varon, Frances West, Kim Whitener, associate directors. FACILITY: touring facilities. AUDITIONS: workshop participants eligible. STATUS: LOA. FOUNDED: 1990, Kristin Linklater, Carol Gilligan.

The Company of Women had its origin in a piece called *Mouthings from Beckett and Shakespeare* that Kristin Linklater put together after she had been working on Samuel Beckett's *Not I* while directing a production of *Hamlet* at the Massachusetts Institute of Technology. She recalls that "my brain was going crazy with these different rhythms, the dislocations and the jaggedness of Beckett juxtaposed with the smoothness and harmony of Shakespeare. I was so interested in what was happening in my own brain that I wanted to put this piece together, so I did. What kept erupting from Shakespeare was a lot of *Henry V* and other kings." While the piece fulfilled her own desire to play the kings, Linklater realized that many other women in theatre would also like to do the big speeches from Shakespeare—speeches written for male roles. Linklater and two associates, Frances West and Daniela Varon, then conceived a "Women Love Shakespeare" Day and sent invitations to Boston actresses, proposing that each prepare a speech and perform it in a small rented theatre on the designated day. About 75 women came and 40 of them presented monologues, some wearing robes and crowns they had rented, others in sweatpants with book in hand. The spirit and excitement of that venture led to a weekend exploration of scenes between men and women but all performed by women. It was then that Linklater noticed that hearing Shakespeare's speeches through women's voices brought out different information in them. She decided to experiment with scenes from Shakespeare on the basis of that observation."If we speak his words through the resonance of women's experience and women's voices," says Linklater, "then we are transforming the culture within its most central organ."

Spurred by the idea of using Shakespeare not only to strengthen female voices but also to enable women and girls to enter the world of power and authority through the demystifying process of make-believe, Linklater joined with well-known psychologist Carol Gilligan in 1990 to found The Company of Women. Linklater's work on the voice, as exemplified in her books *Freeing the Natural Voice* and *Freeing Shakespeare's Voice*, combined with Gilligan's work on the psychology of women and girls, proceeding from her influential book *In A Different Voice*, form the philosophical and programatic basis for the company. They developed a mission statement:

> The Company of Women's mission is to free and strengthen the voices of women and girls. The Company of Women will bring the fresh resonance of female voices into the mainstream of live theatre through all-women productions of the plays of William Shakespeare. Touring nationally and internationally, The Company of Women means to affirm the ancient power of theatre to illuminate and heal its community. The Company of Women will also create a network of Companies of Girls whose interaction with the Company of Women and with the works of Shakespeare will encourage them to speak out freely, respecting the value of their voices in the world.

Linklater and Gilligan share fund-raising responsibilities. They began by making their presentation in various Boston salons, generating many small individual contributions that totaled about $75,000 in the first two years—just enough to rent office space at a **Shakespeare & Company** rehearsal studio and to staff the office with two people two days a week.

The Company of Women's first workshop was held at the University of Southern Maine in Portland in June 1992. Twelve women participated in a two-week program that included training in voice, movement, stage combat, and Shakespearean verse speaking as well as exercises and discussions led by Gilligan on the psychology of women and girls. A three-day weekend in the middle of the 14-day workshop was set aside as a "theatre camp" for girls between the ages of 10 and 13, so that women and girls could interact through theatre games, Shakespeare scene playing, outdoor activities, and discussion. This interaction was designed to "explore authentic relationships between girls and women," as a reflection of the company's belief that "girls at the edge of adolescence possess a clarity of voice and vision that can teach their elders how to hear and see life from a different perspective."

Similar workshops and residencies (lasting between two and six weeks each) at girls' schools and women's colleges conducted by a faculty of experienced teachers and professional actors paved the way to the formation of a multiracial Equity company in 1993. The six members of this "Connection Company" began with a six-month residency at Smith College, where they worked on a production composed of scenes from Shakespeare. A full-scale 15-

actor production of *Henry V* is to be ready for a national tour by the spring of 1994. Plans for subsequent activities include the formation of a Company of Girls, continuing workshops, residencies, and educational outreach programs, and an international tour of *Henry V*. The choice of *Henry V* as the first full production is intended to allow the women to adopt the perspective of Shakespeare's men and thus to shed some light on the causes of confrontation in war and politics as well as the tactics of aggression and courtship. The experience demonstrates that conflict stems from breaks in relationships, whether between women and men, men and men, or nations and nations. As the apex of English-language culture, Shakespeare's plays show that "free voices in creative relationship can underscore our common humanity from the personal level to the political, and expose the out-of-relationship causes of violence and war that threaten our community."

Linklater and Gilligan acknowledge "a very strong political and social mission attached to the forming of the company." Through careful planning and a commitment to the project by hundreds of supporters, TCOW has progressed on a timetable remarkably close to that drawn up at the company's inception in 1990. Its founders look forward to having a "product" to tour in 1994.

Production History: 1994: *H5*.

Research Resources: Archives are maintained at the Company of Women administrative office.

Interview: 12 June 1992.
Felicia Hardison Londré

EVER THEATER. MAIL: P.O. Box 263, 208A Washington Street, Somerville, MA 02143. SITES: Emmanuel Church, Newbury Street, Boston; and on tour to other locations. ADMINISTRATION: 617/776-7782. PRINCIPAL STAFF: Charles Boyle, artistic director. AUDITIONS: local, announced in trade publications. STATUS: non-Equity. FOUNDED: 1993, Charles Boyle.

Fifteen years of research on Shakespeare and the Elizabethan period have convinced actor-director Charles Boyle that the plays and sonnets published under the name of William Shakespeare were actually written by Edward De Vere, 17th Earl of Oxford. Boyle believes that applying that awareness to Shakespearean productions results in far greater clarity for the actors and audience alike. The premise was tested in April 1991 when he directed an all-female cast of Lesley College students in a production of *Twelfth Night*. Boyle provided the cast with information on the historical background of the play, showing how the main characters could be identified as satirical portraits of real people at the court of Elizabeth I. Olivia, for example, may represent Queen Elizabeth, while Feste, her "allowed fool," is the author himself, who probably carried on a secret love affair with the queen; Malvolio is, according to this interpretation, a pointed caricature of the self-seeking and obsequious Sir Christopher Hatton. According to Boyle, "this sort of analysis affects the tone of the play right down to individual line readings. Faculty members who came to see our production were amazed that students who had never done Shakespeare before made the language so easy to understand and the story so much fun to follow. The program director for the Liberal Arts department called it 'miraculous.'"

The success of that experiment stimulated Boyle to found the Ever Theater (ET) in 1993. The name refers to De Vere's frequent habit, throughout the Shakespeare plays and sonnets, of punning on his name E. (Edward) Vere, as in sonnet 76: "Every word doth almost tell my name." ET is devoted to "seeing Shake-speare through Shake-speare's eyes," that is, focusing on the plays in terms of what the author was really saying subtextually. Productions are mounted in Elizabethan style: no set, general lighting, no high-concept directorial interpretation. Music is a major component of all productions, however, with musical effects taking the place of lighting effects. Boyle feels especially fortunate to have John Tyson as music director.

For ET's pilot season, Boyle staged two productions. *Twelfth Night* was presented at the national conference of the Shakespeare Oxford Society in October 1993 and then moved on to engagements at Harvard University and the Boston Center for the Arts. With *As You Like It*, ET became theatre in residence at Emmanuel Church on Newbury Street in Boston. That production ran two weekends and is available for tours to colleges and universities in the Boston area. Boyle envisions eventually taking his productions on tour all over New England. Although knowledge of Oxford is not necessary for enjoying ET's work, the program always includes pertinent information, and other Oxfordian literature is made available to the audience.

Production History: **1993-94**: *TN, AYL*; **1994-95**: *Ado, AWW*.

Telephone interview: 22 April 1994
Felicia Hardison Londré

HAMPSHIRE SHAKESPEARE COMPANY. MAIL: P.O. Box 825, Amherst, MA 01004-0825. SITE: Various locations in Amherst, principally the courtyard of the Lord Jeffery Inn (adjacent to Amherst Common, 30 Boltwood Ave.) and, beginning in Fall 1992, the Hampden Theatre on the campus of the University of Massachusetts. ADMINISTRATION: 256 North Pleasant Street, Amherst 413/256-4120; 800/473-7396. BOX OFFICE: 413/256-4120, 800/473-

7396. ADMISSION: $8–$12 (overnight packages are available at the Inn). SEASON: July–August, 8:00 p.m., Tues., Thurs.–Sat., 6:30 p.m., Sun. PRINCIPAL STAFF: Timothy Holcomb, artistic director; Brian Marsh, executive producer; Ljuba Marsh, managing director. FACILITY: no permanent facility. AUDITIONS: open calls in February. STATUS: Equity SPT. ANNUAL BUDGET: $45,000 (1992). ANNUAL ATTENDANCE: 4,000–5,000 (1992). FOUNDED: 1989, Brian Marsh, Timothy Holcomb.

The Hampshire Shakespeare Company (HSC), which is dedicated to the production of new works by regional playwrights and the works of Shakespeare, was originally the dream of playwright and executive producer Brian Marsh, who met artistic director Timothy Holcomb in the fall 1989. The two men desire to create a theatre much like Shakespeare's own—a theatre that emphasizes performers and texts, that plays to a specific community, and that promotes spontaneous interactions between the performers and their audience.

Marsh and Holcomb first collaborated in July 1989 on Marsh's play *The Search for Emily*, which featured Holcomb's wife, actress Christine Stevens, as Emily Dickinson. HSC was incorporated in the fall of 1989. In the summer of 1990, they produced an adaptation by Holcomb of Shakespeare's sonnets called *Love's Journey*. It was presented several times indoors at the Lord Jeffery Inn. It was well received by audiences, and local critic Chris Rohmann (*Valley Advocate*, 23 July 1990), declared it "an inventive and largely successful reinterpretation of the cycle." In 1991, the first Shakespeare Under the Stars season at the Lord Jeffery Inn featured *The Comedie* [sic] *of Errors*, directed by Holcomb in a kind of John Waters-Mel Brooks polyester-suburban New Jersey presentation. For the 1992 Shakespeare Under the Stars season at the Lord Jeffery Inn, Holcomb directed a Maxfield Parrish-Charles Ives-inspired "*A MIDSOMMER Nights Dreame*" [sic] and a contemporary "*Twelfe Night, Or what you will*" [sic], set in Hollywood. The company has also presented eight new plays, including three of Marsh's works. Marsh expects that the company will continue this pattern of presenting new works at various venues in Amherst, and Shakespeare's comedies at the Inn. The company also produces an original adaptation of *The Christmas Carol*, an annual event staged on Amherst Common with over 50 child and adult performers.

The company is operated informally, with Marsh and Holcomb sharing most of the fundamental decisions concerning the company's objectives, aesthetic values, and procedures. A board of trustees affirms the work of the company with solid funding and marketing support. Currently, the company covers its own expenses through box-office and advertising receipts, as well as individual contributions. The company uses both Equity and non-Equity actors, supplemented by amateurs. Most of the performers and technicians are from the Amherst area and remain involved with the company from one production to the next. Holcomb and Marsh draw small salaries, as do the professional actors, technicians, and staff.

Holcomb is committed to the techniques and aesthetics of improvisational and presentational theatre, and he has been greatly influenced by British stage director, Patrick Tucker. HSC's Shakespeare productions are rehearsed from the Shakespeare's Globe Acting Editions (edited by Tucker). These editions, which are based upon the First Folio text, have been created so that each actor has much the same material at hand at the beginning of rehearsal that an Elizabethan actor would have had. Each actor is provided with his or her own part only ("sides") and encouraged to create a scroll that is easily carried and used as a prop in rehearsal. Citing Tucker, Holcomb believes that Shakespeare's texts contained shorthand director's notes, which were necessary to stage so many plays very quickly. Aside from entrances and exits, actors need only know that, once on stage, they cross directly to whomever they are addressing. "You don't have to block these plays," declares Holcomb, "they sort themselves out." Though not all the company is equally convinced, Holcomb believes that having only one's own part available forces an actor to listen carefully and respond spontaneously on stage. Holcomb is clearly enthusiastic about these acting editions and is seeking to distribute them in the United States. The company is pursuing a grant to bring Tucker to Amherst for a series of workshops with company members and with performers from the community and nearby colleges.

In June 1992, I drove to Amherst to see "*A MIDSOMMER Nights Dreame.*" An audience such as one might expect to see in this historic university town (teachers and other professionals, their families and students, vacationers) was clearly disappointed when the performance was rained out. Fortunately, I was able to see an afternoon rehearsal of "*Twelfe Night.*" It was evident to me that the actors were having a good time with their broad outdoor acting style and had adjusted well to their individual scrolls. Fanning herself with her scroll, Christine Stevens' Olivia—a bored, too-rich-for-words, spoiled Hollywood girl—made me think of Peter Sellars' staging of Mozart's *The Marriage of Figaro.* The rehearsal promised a lively, amusing production.

Production History: **1989**: *The Search for Emily*; **1990**: *Blessed, Sour Grapes, Without Consent, Love's Journey* (Shakespeare/ Holcomb), *Three Poets and the Soldier*; **1991**: *Verging on the Mona Lisa, Err., Remembrance Day, The Passenger Pigeon*; **1992**: *MND, TN*; **1993**: *AYL, Rom., Tim., Tit., Lr.*; **1994**: *Ham., Tmp.*

Research Resources: Brian Marsh maintains a file of clippings for the Hampshire Shakespeare Company. Material pertaining to his own plays is kept at the Jones Library in Amherst.

Site visit and interviews: 30 June 1992
Maarten Reilingh

PUBLICK THEATRE. MAIL: 11 Ridgemont Street, Boston, MA 02134. SITE: Christian A. Herter Park, Soldiers Field Road, Boston (on the banks of the Charles River). ADMINISTRATION/BOX OFFICE: 617/782-5425. ADMISSION: $12–$16 adults; $10–$14 seniors; $7 youth. SEASON: three plays, early June to early September. 8:00 p.m., Wed.–Sun. PRINCIPAL STAFF: Spiro Veloudos, artistic director; Deborah Schoenberg, executive director. FACILITY: outdoor stage (seating capacity 200, with additional space on the grass). AUDITIONS: local in March. STATUS: AEA SPT contract. ANNUAL BUDGET: $120,000 (1992). ANNUAL ATTENDANCE: 6,000 (1992). FOUNDED: 1970, Donato Colucci, David Evans, David Blumenthal.

In the 1960s, there were hopes that a theatre project using a tent at the Metropolitan Boston Arts Center could become a Shakespeare festival on the order of the **Stratford Festival** in Ontario. When the parent organization, the Institute of Contemporary Arts, moved downtown, however, the neighborhood declined, the facility fell into disrepair, and the tent burned down. In 1970, Donato Colucci, David Evans, and David Blumenthal approached the Metropolitan District Commission about forming a company that would pursue the same goal as the tent theatre, only on a smaller scale. The commission agreed, since the site was not being used for anything else, and, in the summer of 1971, the Publick Theatre (PT) presented *The Comedy of Errors*, using a borrowed farm wagon for a set. Without any lighting equipment, the production began at 6:30 p.m. and ended before sunset.

For a decade, the PT was run largely as a summer hobby by Blumenthal, a Boston lawyer. During his tenure, some capital funds were raised to landscape the theatre's present site and to put in a stage and a lighting system. In 1979-80, the entire facility was reconstructed and bench seating added for the first time. The investment called for greater management responsibility than Blumenthal was able to devote to PT. Spiro Veloudos, who had once acted at the PT and was then touring with the National Theatre, was invited to assume the artistic directorship in 1981. Having also worked with the Boston Shakespeare Company (see **Shakespeare & Company**), he was concerned about establishing a separate identity for the PT and avoided Shakespeare for three seasons. In 1985, however, he directed *A Midsummer Night's Dream*, and its success was instrumental in the company's rededication to Shakespeare and the classics. PT has since established a practice of presenting a Shakespeare, a classic, and a musical each summer. The musical gets the best attendance and helps to pay for the rest of the season, but Shakespeare comes in second. Veloudos justifies calling the PT a Shakespeare festival, because the Shakespeare takes precedence in the planning of each season.

The PT operates in partnership with the Metropolitan District Commission. The PT is responsible for the stage area and provides 24-hour security at the site during the season; the commission maintains the grounds (mowing grass, picking up trash, etc.). The theatre, which is within easy walking distance from Harvard University, nestles in a wooded area, just a short walk down a winding path from the parking lot. As with any outdoor theatre, the weather can cause problems. Each season is budgeted to absorb a 25 percent rainout loss. Veloudos feels lucky if the PT gets to do 16 of the 20 scheduled performances of each play. He recalls a performance of *The Taming of the Shrew* when it began to rain just after Kate's arrival at Petruchio's house. The exhausted Petruchio sat down in his chair, looked out at the audience, looked up at the sky, and said his line: "Thus have I politickly begun my *reign*." It brought down the house.

Deborah Schoenberg, marketing and development director for 11 years and now executive director, counted close to 850 subscribers in 1992. Although most are from the immediate area, some come from New Hampshire, and one Mississippi family times its annual Boston summer vacation to coincide with the PT Shakespeare production. She sees the "free parking" as a major enticement beyond the obvious lure of Shakespeare under the stars. A 1992 survey of audience preferences produced a single unanimous response: "Keep the Shakespeare."

Veloudos takes particular pride in the PT's success at drawing young people to the Shakespeare productions. Wednesdays are "Brush Up Your Shakespeare" nights for youths of 16 and under. Those who can recite one line of Shakespeare and tell what play it is from get a free admission. Veloudos was warned that he would have to give away a lot of tickets to people saying nothing more than "To be or not to be," but, for every dozen who do that, he can recall instances like the small boy reciting the "seven ages of man," the 12-year-old girl doing the entire conjuration from *The Tempest*, or the family who had read *Romeo and Juliet* together so that each child could choose a different passage to learn. He sits at the entrance to hear the recitations, satisfied that the students are not only gaining familiarity with the language but also that they are learning the value of theatre by having to do something to earn admission.

The 1992 production of *As You Like It*, directed by Veloudos, was charmingly costumed in Edwardian style. For the wrestling scene, Orlando and Charles wore turn-of-the-century bathing suits with tights and sandals. The tall, strong-featured Rosalind (Katy Myre) was convincingly boyish as Ganymede in a three-piece brown tweed suit. Her courtship scenes with Orlando included a surprising amount of back-slapping and punches on the shoulder, as if to suggest a latent aggressiveness in her. Despite an uncommonly ugly stage setting, the production as a whole was deeply satisfying, largely because the line readings were so full valued, fresh, and intelligent. The amateurs in the cast held up beautifully opposite the three superb Equity actors: Bob Jolly as a most compelling Jaques, Phillip Patrone as Touchstone (whose "philosophy" scene with Corin was a gem), and Steve McConnell as the two dukes and a hilariously stupid William.

Production History (non-Shakespeare plays omitted): **1971**: *Err.*; **1972**: *TN*; **1973**: *Ado*; **1974**: *Tmp.*; **1975**: *MM*; **1976**: *Shr.*; **1977**: *LLL*; **1979**: closed for renovations; **1980**: *MV*; **1981**: *TN*; **1985**: *MND*; **1986**: *Tmp.*; **1987**: *Ado*; **1989**: *Shr.*; **1990**: *Err.*; **1991**: *Rom.*; **1992**: *AYL*; **1993**: *MND*; **1994**: *MV*.

Research Resources: The Publick Theatre's archives are maintained by Spiro Veloudos.

Site visit and interview: 9-10 June 1992.
Felicia Hardison Londré

ROXBURY OUTREACH SHAKESPEARE EXPERIENCE. MAIL: P.O. Box 2044, Jamaica Plain, MA 02130. SITE: Y.W.C.A., 7 Temple Street, Cambridge, MA 02139; and other facilities in the Boston area. ADMINISTRATION: 617/497-7404; Fax: 617/497-2686. ADMISSION: $5 children, $10 adults. SEASON: school year. PRINCIPAL STAFF: Decima Francis, artistic and executive director. AUDITIONS: varies. STATUS: non-Equity. ANNUAL BUDGET: $90,000 (1992). ANNUAL ATTENDANCE: 5,000 for productions; 7,000 for school and other programs. FOUNDED: 1988, Decima Francis.

The Roxbury Outreach Shakespeare Experience (ROSE) was founded in 1988 by Decima Francis as both a theatre company and a school outreach program. The company produces one Shakespeare play each year, which it performs on tour in the greater Boston area at various theatre facilities. In 1989, ROSE took its first production to the Edinburgh Fringe Festival. In 1991, it was in residence at the Massachusetts Institute of Technology.

Through its school programs, ROSE aims "to develop meaningful and lasting ways to bring the beauty and power of Shakespeare's work to inner city students; to encourage students to discover voice, movement, and Shakespeare on their own level; to provide teachers with the tools to continue the work in the classroom." All of the actors who work in the classrooms are personally trained by Francis, an actress and director who interrupted her career on the London stage to launch the Boston venture.

Francis was exposed to Shakespeare from childhood on her native island of St. Kitt's in the Caribbean. She used the West Indian accent for her acclaimed London performance of Lady Macbeth. She was among the first four women to direct at the Royal National Theatre of Great Britain. As a resident director there, she pioneered the practice of bringing together professional theatre artists and children from London's inner-city schools. After a meeting with Tina Packer of **Shakespeare & Company**, Francis participated in that company's summer program in Lenox, Massachusetts, and saw the opportunity for further work with minority artists in the area. "I love being in America," she said in 1988, "because America likes to try things out. They let you have a go and not have to 'wait your turn,' as you do in England."

Backed by **Shakespeare & Company** and the Boston Shakespeare Company, as well as by the Massachusetts Council on the Arts and the Eliot Bank, Francis inaugurated her venture with a school program titled "Introduction to Shakespeare," performed by six young black actors. A performance at a youth detention center earned the interest and appreciation of a tough audience of 14-to-17-year-olds who found that they could relate to Shakespeare as performed by black actors. For them, Francis explained, "the authority figure has always been white."

ROSE was incorporated in 1989 and went on to present an all-black, full-length production of *Macbeth* that fall at the University of Lowell and at the Strand Theatre in Dorchester. The production was given excellent press and was the basis for that year's in-classroom residencies and workshops. By 1990, Francis was bringing together an ethnic mix of African-American, Asian, Hispanic, Caribbean, and white actors for *King Lear*.

Production History: **1989**: *Smitty's Blues, Mac.*; **1990**: *Lr.*, *Sugar Hill*; **1991**: *Rom.*, *Bones and Boxes*; **1992**: *Blue Sky Thinking*, *A Raisin in the Sun*; **1993**: *Shr.*

Research Resources: Kay Bourne, "Shakespeare in inner city with school drama project," *Bay State Banner* (4 August 1988): 15.

Felicia Hardison Londré

SHAKESPEARE & COMPANY. MAIL: The Mount, Lenox, MA 01240. SITE: The Mount (Edith Wharton's estate) in Lenox. ADMINISTRATION: 413/637-1197. BOX OFFICE: 413/637-3353. ADMISSION: $15–$22.50. SEAS0N: 600 performances, including tours (1992), modified repertory, late May–August; Mainstage Shakespeare, 8:00 p.m., Tues.–Sun.; Wharton Theatre, 1:00 p.m., 5:00 p.m., Tues.–Fri.; 10:30 a.m., 1:30 p.m., and 5:00 p.m. Sat., Sun.; Stables Theatre, 8:30 p.m., Tues.–Sun.; noon, Sat., Sun. PRINCIPAL STAFF: nine permanent full-time staff, including Tina Packer, artistic director; Dennis Krausnick, managing director; Kevin Coleman, director of education; Christopher B. Sink, business manager; Stephen D. Ball, production manager. FACILITIES: Mainstage (outdoor wooden platform and natural setting; capacity 500); Wharton Theatre (drawing room; capacity 75–100), Stables (studio theatre; capacity 80–100); Court Theatre (outdoor Elizabethan style; capacity 250). AUDITIONS: Boston and New York in the spring. STATUS: Equity LOA (similar to LORT C contract). ANNUAL BUDGET: $1.2 million (1991). ANNUAL ATTENDANCE: 25,000 (summer), plus 40,000 (Arts in Education program), 100,000 approximate total (1992). FOUNDED: 1978, Tina Packer, Kristin Linklater, B. H. Barry, John Broome, Dennis Krausnick.

Shakespeare & Company (SC) was founded in 1978 by Tina Packer, Kristin Linklater, B. H. Barry, John Broome, and Dennis Krausnick. Experienced as an associate artist with the **Royal Shakespeare Company** and as a director with the National Theatre in England, Packer decided to start her own theatre in America that would combine the theories of the master teachers named as cofounders. Ford and C.B.S. Foundation grants allowed these artists to explore the roots of Elizabethan acting. This experience confirmed the group's commitment to create a permanent Shakespeare company in America that performed as the Elizabethans did—"in love with poetry; physical prowess through fighting and dancing; and an unlimited vision of man's ability to explore the universe" (Shakespeare & Company program notes). Biographer Helen Epstein has elaborated on Packer's vision in *The Company She Keeps*: "She wanted a year round classically trained, repertory company based on the English model but with an energy and emotional truth that she saw as distinctly American."

This multiracial, regional, Equity theatre company performs in Lenox, Massachusetts on the lush grounds of The Mount, Edith Wharton's former estate. The season at The Mount includes three mainstage outdoor Shakespeare productions, a series of new plays adapted from the works of Edith Wharton and Henry James, and contemporary plays. In 1984, Packer also became artistic director of the Boston Shakespeare Company after Peter Sellars unexpectedly resigned, leaving the theatre with a $150,000 debt. In 1986, Shakespeare & Company legally merged with and thereby subsumed the Boston Shakespeare Company. While SC currently has no permanent theatre building in Boston, the Boston Redevelopment Authority has designated Parcel 6, on the corner of Massachusetts Avenue and St. Botolph Street as the site for a new facility. During the winter months, socially relevant plays and works-in-progress are presented in Boston (see the production history).

In addition to performing, the SC is equally committed to professional actor training and to providing school programs. Classical training for professional artists and educators is offered in intensive workshops and intern programs that attract national and international attention. Bill Murray, Sigourney Weaver, and Richard Dreyfuss are among the hundreds of artists who have completed the program. SC's extensive arts-in-education program has served 280,000 students in grades 4-12 and has been featured on ABC's *Good Morning America* program. More recently, the training has been used in business management and labor organization "to help the lay person evolve more effective communication skills and positive self-image." In the fall of 1991, the company traveled to Russia to conduct training seminars.

SC is an actor-driven organization. The company's commitment to research and training extends into its management philosophy. The actors also direct, teach, and hold major managerial responsibilities. Recent financial constraints and an evolving aesthetic that includes actors running their own company has led SC to develop a unique arrangement with Actors' Equity. All actors have additional company responsibilities in such areas as house management, concessions, and education. In fact, the managing director and director of development also regularly act in SC productions. A special letter of agreement with Equity allows SC to pay $400 per week rather than the usual $525 of the LORT C contract. In addition to saving money, this actor/manager arrangement fits the company's holistic approach to theatre. Forty-two Equity actors, 20 young actors-in-training, and 12 administrative and technical interns comprised the 1991 summer company; 100 actor/teachers form the complete company membership.

The nine permanent full-time staff members include artistic director Tina Packer, managing director Dennis Krausnick, director of education Kevin Coleman, business manager Christopher B. Sink, and production manager Stephen D. Ball. A small board of trustees gives gifts of $5,000–$25,000 to SC, but does not interfere in governing the theatre. Fund-raisers have never been a company strength. Packer's reputation and personal magnetism are the major resources for raising money. In 1992, Neil B. Calvin was named as chairman of the board and was instrumental in developing program changes.

SC's budget was $1.2 million in 1991; 73 percent of its revenue comes from earned income and ticket sales, while 27 percent comes from foundations, corporations, and private contributions. Major contributors include the National Endowment for the Humanities ($500,000 grant for three years) and G. E. Foundation ($20,000). Of the $1.2 million, $550,000 covers the summer theatre productions, and $650,000 goes to training and education.

To help turn The Mount from a neglected estate into a usable performance space, a separate nonprofit corporation was founded, and much manual labor was expended by early company members. The Mount is a 50-acre estate that includes four theatres (three were operational in 1991). Its neo-Georgian mansion was built in 1901. The mainstage outdoor theatre is made of wooden platforms nestled on the edge of the woods. Temporary seats accommodate up to 500 people. The mansion, situated directly behind the audience, is used for scenes when appropriate, such as the balcony scene in *Romeo and Juliet.* Scenery is minimal and most often utilizes the natural surroundings. The intimate Wharton Theatre (capacity 75 to 100) is located in the drawing room of the Wharton home. Original adaptations of works by Wharton and her contemporaries are produced in this space. Tea and cookies are served at intermission, and tours of the mansion are available. The Stables Theatre (opened in 1991) seats 80 to 100 people and serves as a flexible studio theatre.

The rustic atmosphere is charming and informal, and the sightlines are excellent. The Court Theatre, a 250-seat outdoor Elizabethan theatre was closed for renovations in 1991. A 62-page program gives the company's history and aesthetic, biographies, director's notes, and photographs. The box office is a small temporary building near the entrance, while administrative offices are housed on the top floors of the Wharton mansion. Makeup and dressing facilities are located on site near each of the theatres. Housing for actors and staff is provided on the estate and in nearby towns.

Lenox is located in the Berkshires, a fashionable and expensive resort area renowned for its summer arts events. Tanglewood, Jacob's Pillow, Berkshire Summer Theatre, and Williamstown all help attract tourists to this corner of the state. The Berkshire area has a year-round population close to 100,000, but its fine reputation for summer arts festivals attracts audiences from throughout New England and Canada. This culturally aware population sees SC as a welcome addition to the arts community. Wealthy New England families donate to the theatre, but there is little corporate base in the area. The Boston metropolitan area, with its 3 million people and large corporations, provides the greatest potential for further expansion. Two plays directed by Packer, *As You Like It* and *Observe the Sons of Ulster Marching Toward the Somme*, have garnered awards for outstanding productions in Boston. Audiences for SC productions vary according to the type of play presented. The outdoor Shakespeare plays attract family audiences, while the Wharton series attracts people with a love for nineteenth- and early twentieth-century history and literature. The 1991 summer season played to 25,000 people.

Marketing strategies include connections with Tanglewood, the summer home of the Boston Symphony, which is only one mile down a country road. Newspaper advertisements begin in March. The international mailing list numbers 30,000, and the summer season is listed in the travel calendars of the *New York Times* and the *Boston Globe* as well as in all New England and Berkshire travel guides. At its peak of support, the plays were reviewed in 33 newspapers including the *Boston Globe* and the *New York Times*. Regular coverage is provided by the *Boston Globe*, *Boston Phoenix*, *Village Voice*, and all major regional newspapers.

The strengths of SC include artistic director Packer's effective leadership, the well-defined company aesthetic and purpose, and the beauty and location of the setting at The Mount. Packer's passion, charismatic personality, and vision inspire the company. Her energy, clarity, and credibility make her an effective fund-raiser. She has built a dedicated company that possesses the multiple skills and willingness to sacrifice to make the company a success. SC's fully developed training and education programs give the company a base from which to develop and choose its artists. The natural beauty of the Berkshires, and specifically of The Mount, makes the area a summer and fall tourist haven.

The major problem the company faces involves severe cutbacks in funding. The Massachusetts Council on the Arts, which used to provide $175,000 a year, told SC to expect no funding in 1992 due to state tax shortfalls. The NEA last provided funding in 1980. Due to its extensive training and education programs, the company is sometimes perceived as a corps of teachers rather than as a group of professional artists of exceptional standards. The lack of a big-city base limits corporation and foundation grants. In addition, the upkeep on the Wharton property and its four theatres is quite expensive. What looked bleak in 1991 has subsequently turned hopeful, however. The company is planning a major restoration project in conjunction with the Edith Wharton Restoration Society. The Mount's four theatres and its mansion will be restored on a five-year schedule. The Stables will include a visitors center and cabaret theatre. Improved sewer lines will allow for permanent toilet facilities and modernized dressing and makeup rooms. These improvements will be paid for by the advertisers of *Architectural Digest, Architectural Landscaping,* and *Interiors.*

Packer's long-range goal is to provide year-round employment for the company in two locations, the Berkshires and Boston. To accomplish this objective, she needs four times the money currently being raised. As part of this long-range vision, Packer wants to renovate the theatres and find money to train and retain minority actors. The lure of lucrative film contracts or better-known theatres has made it difficult to keep minority members in the company. Although minorities find the Berkshires beautiful, they also see the area as very "white." Lack of financial support has dried up minority scholarship funds. Packer thus sees minority recruitment as a major goal.

SC's statement of artistic philosophy reads:

> Shakespeare & Company is committed to creating a permanent American Shakespeare company which will perform with the same intense understanding of language and verse, the same physical grace in dance, the same exploration in violence, and the same lust for exploring universal truths as did the Elizabethans. At the heart of this commitment is the principal aesthetic upon which the company is founded—the aesthetic of language—its power, its import, its visceral impact on humankind's emotions and intellect.

The company's philosophy of training actors merges classical training with a contemporary emphasis on emotional truth. This technique includes an exercise called "dropping in": actors in unswerving eye contact with one another encounter each word of the text. The goal is to "restore the experience of thought and language to their sensory organic roots" in order to "create each moment as a revelation to themselves and to the audience."

Much of Packer's work is governed by questions involving myth and ritual. Although she says she is not a purist, she believes that real homage has to be paid to the text. Nonetheless, she cuts or transposes scenes when necessary. Costumes are usually created from an imaginary period. Political content is often heightened.

Two Shakespeare productions were persented during my site visit in 1991. *Twelfth Night*, directed by Cecil MacKinnon on The Mount's outdoor mainstage, was most successful in bringing out the play's romantic and festive elements. A spirited and appealing Viola, played by male actor Tod Randolph, was effectively swept into the sensuous, swirling world of Illyria. An exotic and seductive Olivia, played by Melinda Lopez, captured the audience's attention and enticed the spectators into this mysterious land. The most successful aspect of the design was the costumes for Olivia and her entourage. Designed by Marian Hose, the costumes were fanciful creations using flowing fabrics and silhouettes reminiscent of the exotic Middle East. The natural woods served as the major scenic element, with a small scenic piece used for the comic subplot. The tricky marriage between the plot and subplot was marred somewhat by a staging that was so spread out as to diffuse the energy and overall drive of the production.

Women of Will follows the development of the female psyche in Shakespeare's plays. It was conceived, developed, and performed by Packer, with Jonathan Epstein as the male characters. Following a chronological structure from Shakespeare's early plays forward, the work traces the maturation of Shakespeare's vision of women in a series of short scenes and narrative. Part I examines how women use power, from direct confrontation, through love/lust, bearing children, and, finally, in tentative negotiation. Part II is called "Going Underground" and shows how "women tell the truth and die or disguise and live." Part III, "The Maiden Phoenix," examines the intertwined themes of death, daughters, and rebirth in the later plays. Parts I and II were performed in 1992.

The title, *Women of Will*, refers at once to William Shakespeare, will as sexual power, and will as a way of influencing people. The work-in-progress asks important questions about male-female relationships, sex, power, and violence, as well as fundamental questions about the making of art. Accompanying Packer on this journey through the canon of Shakespeare's women invites audience members to reflect on their own life questions. The performance of *Women of Will* that I saw was a living example of SC's aesthetic philosophy in action, as each moment appeared to be "a revelation" to the actors and audience. Packer and Epstein both gave mature, dynamic performances characterized by clarity, precision, and an engaging chemistry between them. They moved effortlessly between widely diverse characters, such as Kate and Petruchio, Elizabeth and Richard III, and Romeo and Juliet with a dancelike physicality and a contagious joy.

Production History. Mainstage at the Mount: **1978**: *MND*; **1979**: *WT*; *Rom.*; **1980**: *Tmp.*; **1981**: *TN, AYL*; **1982**: *Mac., TN*; **1983**: *Err.* (in Brooklyn); **1984**: *Rom., MND*; **1985**: *Ado, Err.*; **1986**: *Ant.*; **1987**: *MND*; **1988**: *AYL*; **1989**: *Tmp*; **1990**: *AYL*; **1991**: *TN, Mac.*; **1992**: *Shr., Rom.*); **1993**: (all theatres) *MND, JC, Tro., TN, The Henry VI*

Chronicles; **1994**: (all theatres) *Err., R2, Mac., WT, Ham., Cym., MV, Custom of the Country, Dibble Dance, The Body Revealed, Laughing Wild, House of Mirth, Mrs. Klein, Fiary Rain, Xinsu, Souls Belated* (Edith Wharton novellas), *Careful, a Ghost Story*. Boston short seasons: In 1986 when Shakespeare & Company legally subsumed Boston Shakespeare Company, it did short seasons of modern plays for three years. Additional productions at The Mount include Edith Wharton and Henry James adaptations and student productions. For example, the complete 1991 season included *TN; Mac.; Wharton Series of One-Acts; The Aspern Papers; Ham.; Women of Will; Shirley Valentine*. The summer of 1992 saw an entire program change whereby 16 productions were produced in the four theatres at The Mount, including: outdoor Mainstage Shakespeare: *Shr.* and *Rom.*; Bare Bard Series, Stable Theatre: *JC* and *Ado*; Modern Play Series, Stables Theatre: *Shirley Valentine; A Life in the Theatre; Custer Rides; Duet for One; Women of Will; Tale of the Tiger*; Wharton Theatre Series, drawing room:: *The Inner House, The Mission of Jane,* and *A Love Story, Manners and More, Maisie*; Oxford Court Theatre (outdoor): *TGV* and *Tro*.

Research Resources: The Shakespeare & Company archives are maintained in the Edith Wharton house (administrative offices). See also Helen Epstein, *The Companies She Keeps: Tina Packer Builds a Theater* (Cambridge, MA: Plunkett Lake Press, 1985) and a Boston public television station WGBH video of a Shakespeare & Company workshop, 1985.

Site visit and interviews with Tina Packer and Dennis Krausnick: 27, 30, 31 July 1991.
Cindy Melby Phaneuf

VINEYARD PLAYHOUSE. MAIL: 10 Church Street, P.O. Box 2452, Vineyard Haven, MA 02568. ADMINISTRATION/BOX OFFICE: 508/693-2176. SEASON: six productions, including two Shakespeare, in summer; June through September. PRINCIPAL STAFF: Eileen Wilson, artistic director. FACILITIES: proscenium (capacity 100); studio (capacity 50); amphitheatre (capacity 100). AUDITIONS: contact administration office. STATUS: Equity, SPT. ANNUAL BUDGET: $180,000 (1993). ANNUAL ATTENDANCE: 7,000 (1993). FOUNDED: 1982, Eileen Wilson.

Each summer the Vineyard Playhouse produces two Shakespeare plays in an amphitheatre on the island of Martha's Vineyard. In 1982, Eileen Wilson founded the theatre company to make accessible for the young people living on an island, a wider spectrum of theatre experiences, including Shakespeare, where there had been no professional theatre available closer than Boston or Providence. The productions are well attended by the residents of Martha's Vineyard as well as the summer visitors to the island.

Production History (Shakespeare only): **1982-93**: *MND, TN, Ado, AYL, Err., MV, Rom.*; **1994**: *AWW, Oth.*

Daniel J. Watermeier

MINNESOTA

MINNESOTA SHAKESPEARE COMPANY. MAIL: P.O. Box 2787, Minneapolis, MN 55402. SITE: Metropolitan Minneapolis/St.Paul city parks. BOX OFFICE: 612/377-7895. ADMISSION: free. SEASON: 40-50 performances, mid-July through Mid-September, rotating repertory of two productions. PRINCIPAL STAFF: Mark DeKovic, artistic director. FACILITY: open air in city parks. AUDITIONS: area auditions in March, contact artistic director. STATUS: non-Equity. ANNUAL BUDGET: $20,000 (1993). ANNUAL ATTENDANCE: 8,500 (1993). FOUNDED: 1981, Mark DeKovic.

The Minnesota Shakespeare Company (MSC) was founded in 1981 by Mark DeKovic to provide "a productive artistic environment which will entertain, educate, and enrich our community, employees, and artists primarily through the works of William Shakespeare." To this end, the motto of the MSC has been "To hold, as 'twere, a mirror up to nature." As DeKovic explains the artistic purpose of the MSC, he emphasizes the theatre as a "deliberate collaboration between audience and artist that expects all participants to experience nature and the world" and, "through shared imagination, to examine and analyze the world and, ultimately, understand it."

For 12 years, the MSC has performed in selected parks throughout the Minneapolis-St. Paul metropolitan area, including suburbs such as Eden Prairie and Bloomington, from late July through mid-September. An ambitious schedule of 40 to 50 performances, run at 7:00 p.m. Wednesday or Thursday through Sunday and at 2:00 p.m. on Saturday and Sunday. An arena setting allows the actors to enter from all sides and enables the focus of the action to play to the crowd on all sides. At the beautiful Lake Harriet Rose Garden, the setting is at the base of a hill overlooking the gardens with Lake Harriet in the distance. Most of the audience spreads out on the hillside, many with baskets of food and drink, to participate in the MSC's feast of Shakespeare.

For MSC's 1992 *Macbeth*, entrances were timed so that characters or armies initiated their entrances far in the distance. The outdoor setting added to the environment of the witches' field and of the battle scene, which was staged in back of the audience with the actors surrounding the spectators. A few audience members brought complete meals and set up small tables with wine goblets matching the period of the production. The potential for audience participation was duly noted by the drunken Porter, who lifted up one of the goblets and drank from it. Located directly above a landing approach to the Minneapolis-St. Paul International Airport, actors pause with improvised business when airplanes pass overhead. One such pause resulted in a long passionate kissing scene between Lady Macbeth and Macbeth, adding a special erotic interpretation to the scene.

Education and training are important aspects of MSC's professional commitment to quality programing and community accessibility. As a form of outreach, the MSC has developed a compilation of scenes from Shakespeare, a fast-paced introduction to the world of Shakespeare that is designed for all ages. In 1991, the compilation was entitled *Whirligig of Time* and featured scenes of tragedy, comedy, love, and war, highlighting the "universal themes established in Shakespeare's most famous plays." In 1992, the compilation was entitled *Inexplicable Dumbshows and Noise*. The MSC has presented its productions in a dinner theatre setting on special occasions and for benefits.

The MSC seeks to expand its production program for the 1993-1994 season throughout the year and to open a permanent office in the downtown Hennepin Center for the Arts. The season will include one outdoor production from June to August, a repertory season of two plays from September through mid-October, a production in January, and a spring festival in May with a new production of *Romeo and Juliet*. The MSC has established itself in the cultural life of the Twin Cities and has gained a reputation for quality Shakespeare productions in the parks during the summer.

Production History: **1981**: *Wiv., TN*; **1982**: *Ado, Shr., The Doctor In Spite of Himself*; **1983**: *MND, Rom., AYL*; **1984**: *Shr., She Stoops to Conquer*; **1985**: *Tmp., Err.*; **1986**: *MND, The Dark Lady of the Sonnets, Ham., Rosenkranz and Guildenstern are Dead*; **1987**: *TGV, WT*; **1988**; *Rom., AWW*; **1989**; *AWW, American Bards*; *Voices of the New World, AYL, Mac., MM*; **1990**: *JC, TN, The Play's the Thing, Per.*; **1991**: *R3, LLL*; **1992**: *Mac., Ado*; **1993-94**: *Wiv., 1H4, MV, Rom., A Man for All Seasons*.

Research Resources: Informal archives for the Minnesota Shakespeare Company are maintained at the administrative office.

Site visits and interviews: July 1992, 1993, 1994.
Ron Engle

MISSOURI

HEART OF AMERICA SHAKESPEARE FESTIVAL OF GREATER KANSAS CITY. MAIL: 4800 Main Street, Suite 402, Kansas City, MO 64112. SITE: Southmoreland Park, at 47th and Oak Streets, near Nelson-Atkins Museum of Art. ADMINISTRATION: 816/531-7728. ADMISSION: free. SEASON: July; 8:15 p.m., Tues.–Sun. PRINCIPAL STAFF: Marilyn Strauss, founder/producer; Felicia Londré, honorary cofounder; Joe Wilson, director of business and development; Beth Coughlin, administrative assistant. FACILITY: open-air platform in a park, seating on the ground (capacity 2,000). AUDITIONS: local, mid-January. STATUS: LOA. ANNUAL BUDGET: $250,000 (1994). ANNUAL ATTENDANCE: 35,000 (1994). FOUNDED: 1991, Marilyn Strauss, Felicia Londré.

The initial inspiration behind the founding of the Heart of America Shakespeare Festival of Greater Kansas City (HASF) evolved from Felicia Londré's field visits to festivals while conducting research. Enchanted with the concept of admission-free festivals, Londré approached her colleague Dale A.J. Rose, former artistic director of the **Shakespeare Festival of Dallas** and now head of the actor training program at the University of Missouri—Kansas City, about the possibility of establishing a Shakespeare festival in Kansas City. Rose and Londré initiated talks with university administrators and also explored a collaborative venture with the Missouri Repertory Theatre; both those lines of inquiry met with delays and complications.

Meanwhile, a native of Kansas City, Marilyn Strauss, had been pursuing the idea of combining Shakespeare with musical comedy presentations and exploring the possibility of a festival with city officials, including the city's parks and recreation staff. Strauss, active in the New York theatre during the 1970s, had been the producer of the Tony Award-winning play *Da*. Her familiarity with Joseph Papp's **New York Shakespeare Festival** heavily influenced her desire to produce Shakespeare in Kansas City. Londré convinced Strauss that musical comedy was not a necessary component and that Shakespeare would succeed on his own. Both Strauss and Londré were committed to an admission-free festival and one accessible by public transportation.

Strauss devoted herself full time to laying the groundwork in a constant round of meetings with local arts supporters, while Londré regularly redrafted the written proposal to suit the immediate need. On 1 May 1991, Strauss and Londré signed incorporation papers for what was then called the Missouri Shakespeare Festival. As support for the festival grew on both sides of Kansas City's State Line Road, it became evident that a "Missouri" festival would not fairly represent the Kansas constituents, and so the name was changed to the Shakespeare Festival of Greater Kansas City. Eventually, a logo designed by Don Carlton, a finishing artist for "Doonesbury" cartoons, featured Shakespeare in the "Heart of America" and deemphasized "of Greater Kansas City."

Strauss suggested the establishment of a Shakespeare club to assist in building public interest and to develop a solid corps of volunteers. The "bard club" organizing group threw a party on Shakespeare's birthday in 1991, and those who attended were invited to vote on the name of the new club. "Strictly Shakespeare" won over "Spear-Shakers" and "Monday Night Shakespeare Club," among others. Club meetings, held every other month, are usually hosted by a local theatre-producing group. In June of 1991, Londré presented a slide lecture on the Shakespeare authorship question. The August meeting featured an idyllic lawn party with lake swimming and an elegant picnic. In September and August, local theatre companies performed Shakespeare. In April 1992, the club raised over $500 by charging nonmembers for a lecture by Charles Vere, Lord Burford, on the authorship question. Within a year, Strictly Shakespeare's membership had reached 250.

Crucial in the development of the festival was the formation of a board of directors headed by Rufus Crosby (Chris) Kemper III. After being recruited by Strauss, Kemper hosted a series of lunches at the United Missouri Bank to elicit interest among potential supporters. Londré presented slides that she had taken at various festivals, emphasizing the admission-free festivals. On 2 July 1992, the HASF board of directors held its first meeting to consider a site for the festival and to aid in the planning of a major fund-raising campaign.

Publicity concerning the festival brought Strauss an avalanche of mail. Bill Woodman, who had directed at the Missouri Repertory Theatre, expressed an interest in directing for the festival. Strauss replied that she first needed help in putting together a fund-raising event. Woodman asked Kevin Kline if he would lend his artistry to the cause, and the two subsequently collaborated on creating a one-man show composed of excerpts from Shakespeare and titled "Lovers, Soldiers, Princes, Kings." Dedicated to the memory of Joseph Papp on the first anniversary of his death, the production premiered on 31 October 1992 at Kansas City's Folly Theatre. The performance, followed by a dinner-dance for contributors, netted $150,000 and national publicity for the festival.

On a visit to **Westerly Shakespeare in the Park**, Strauss met designer Marcus Abbott and invited him to Kansas City as a consultant in selecting a site. A representative from the city department of parks and recreation showed Abbott a variety of venues, from Allis Plaza in downtown to Swope Park's famed Starlight Theatre. Abbott quickly selected Southmoreland Park for its location, charm, size, and orientation to the setting sun. The oldest public park in Kansas City, Southmoreland is located within walking distance of the Country Club Plaza and across the street from the Nelson Gallery's Theis Mall; it is an area well known to the public for outdoor events. Elongated in configuration and slightly sunken below street level, the park holds 2,000 people on blankets and lawn chairs. Its abundant trees could serve as light stands.

For the inaugural production, to take place 24 June-4 July 1993, Strauss originally chose Woodman to direct *The Tempest,* but, due to complications, he was unable to fulfill his duties. Strauss then brought in Eberle Thomas from New York to direct the production. Auditions were held in January, and a cast of local Equity and non-Equity actors was assembled. Approximately 15,000 people attended the festival during the ten nights of performance. About 75 individuals volunteered to work for the festival, and 12 companies and organizations supplied volunteers, with some contributors having the evening named after them, such as Sprint night or Watson Ess night. A local poster contest sponsored by the festival attracted 215 entries depicting scenes from *The Tempest,* and the winning posters were displayed at a local bookstore. The festival also sponsored a Shakespeare Speaker Series to explore and enhance the humanities content of the production. A shuttle bus service to and from the festival was made available at several different locations in the city, including the popular Country Club Plaza.

Opening night was marred by rainfall, but, the weather served to enhance the "Tempest" atmosphere of the play's setting. Mimes and jugglers entertained the audience as they found their blanket spots on the lawn. The environment of the park itself was drawn into the play, with Caliban roaming the far corners of the park to fetch wood for Prospero. At times, Miranda and Ferdinand strolled around the landscape, and, as one reviewer noted, the fireflies glowing in the air added to the "show's magical atmosphere." Jim Birdsall as Prospero and Melinda McCrary as Ariel were the favorites with audience members and reviewers alike. The production was well received by the local press, and the Southmoreland Neighborhood Association praised the festival for enhancing the area's cultural opportunities. The production was budgeted at $200,000, which included a donation of over $50,000 by Sprint and a sizable amount contributed by the Kansas City Neighborhood Tourist Development Fund. The initial success of a new Shakespeare Festival has prompted Strauss to dream of the day when HASF will have its own facility on the scale of the **Utah Shakespearean Festival**.

In 1994, Strauss engaged Vincent Dowling to direct *A Midsummer Night's Dream* for the HASF. Dowling, an actor, director, and former artistic director at the famous Abbey Theatre in Dublin, had worked with the Missouri Repertory Company in Kansas City in the 1970s. The *Midsummer* production was praised for its pageantry but critics were mixed on Dowling's decision to have Theseus and Hippolyta enter on horseback. Robert Trussell of the *Kansas City Star* (31 July 1994) found the production a "major advance in quality" over *The Tempest.* He also noted that the "Shakespeare festival, without question, occupies an important position on the local theatrical landscape . . . and attracts many viewers who rarely attend professional theater."

A series of 12 cartoon panels, drawn by Conger Bearsley Jr. and Don Carlton, appeared in the *Kansas City Star* over a period of two weeks. The cartoons detailed parts of the play's plot or told about one of the characters. The newspaper's recorded phone information service provided a summary of the play and each day featured an excerpt from the play. For example, on one day Theseus and Hippolyta explained why nothing in the world is more complicated than love; the following day featured Hermia's laments about love. Strauss has estimated that 35,000 people saw the production and that the festival cost $250, 000 to produce.

Production History: **1992**: *Lovers, Soldiers, Princes, Kings* (a fund-raising one-man performance by Kevin Kline); **1993**: *Tmp.*; **1994**: *MND.*

Research Resources: Notebook and memoranda by Felicia Londré, minutes and reports of Strictly Shakespeare, and official programs are all stored at the festival office. See also the following articles:

"Bard in the Park." [Photo spread] *Kansas City Star* (4 July 1993): G4.

"Bard in the Park." [Editorial] *Kansas City Star* (2 July 1994): A2.

Engle, Tim. "The Bard in the Park." *The Wednesday Magazine* (14 October 1992): 1, 4, 6.

Eveld, Edward M. "Marilyn Strauss." *Star Magazine* (27 June 1993): 4-6.

Hockadady, Laura. "Actor Kevin Kline sells out benefit." *Kansas City Star* (1 November 1992): B3.

Londré, Felicia. "K.C.'s Culture Gap." *The View* (8-21 February 1991): 8.

Loutzenhiser, James K. "Shakespearean dream team." *The Squire* (7 July 1994): 4.

Townley, Roderick. "Ten Topics in Kansas City." *Town & Country* (September 1992): J1.

Trussell, Robert. "The Work before the storm." *Kansas City Star* (23 May 1993): E1.

———. "Bard in the park. Could festival grow next year?" *Kansas City Star* (20 June 1993): I1, I12.

———. "'Tempest,' indeed: Elements test the mettle of audience." *Kansas City Star* (26 June 1993): E4.

———. "'The Tempest' is worth a second look." *Kansas City Star* (29 June 1993).

———. "Shakespeare in the evening and in the light." *Kansas City Star* (30 June 1993): F1, F4.

———. "Dowling does 'Dream' . . . again." *Kansas City Star* (1 July 1994): G19.

———. "A Midsummer Treat." *Kansas City Star* (7 July 1994): E5.

———. "Is 'Dream' waking up Kansas City theater?" *Kansas City Star* (31 July 1994): G4.

Trussell, Robert, and Robert W. Butler. "In our mind's eye, Kansas City." *Kansas City Star* (18 October 1992): J1.

Interviews: 21 February, 22 March, 24 September 1993, and 15 September 1994.
Ron Engle

ST. LOUIS SHAKESPEARE COMPANY. MAIL: P.O. Box 23327, St. Louis, MO 63156. SITES: Mallinckrodt Center Drama Studio at Washington University (summer), and Sheldon Memorial Ballroom, 3648 Washington, near the Fox Theatre (winter). ADMINISTRATION/BOX OFFICE: 314/664-7586. ADMISSION: $8–$10; $24 for a three-play summer subscription. SEASON: mid-July–mid-August, three plays in rotating repertory; late January, one play. PRINCIPAL STAFF: Donna Northcott, artistic director; Thomas McAtee, managing director. FACILITY: black-box theatre (capacity 145); ballroom theatre (capacity 175). AUDITIONS: mid-May, Xavier Hall, St. Louis University. STATUS: professional, non-Equity. ANNUAL BUDGET: $25,000 (1992). ANNUAL ATTENDANCE: 2,100 (1992). FOUNDED: 1985 (incorporated 1986), Donna Northcott.

After St. Louis University student Donna Northcott spent a summer attending Shakespeare and other classic plays while studying in England at the London Academy, she became keenly aware of Shakespeare's absence from the stage in her home town. In 1985, she and her friend Stoney Breyer rallied a group of enthusiasts to mount a spring production of *Twelfth Night*. The success of that effort led to incorporation as the St. Louis Shakespeare Company (SLSC) in May of 1986.

By its second full season, SLSC's pattern was set: a comedy and a tragedy/history by Shakespeare, along with some other classic from the world repertoire. The five-week summer season is composed of three plays in rotating repertory on a unit set; each play gets nine performances. In 1993, SLSC added a winter production—three public performances and three sold-out high school matinees, for a total attendance of 1,200—in the Sheldon Memorial's ballroom, near the city's historic Fox Theatre. The company also offers various one-hour programs, including scenes from Shakespeare, for local arts festivals. Shakespeare's birthday (number 428) was celebrated in 1992 with presentations of sonnets, scenes, and birthday cake, all offered free of charge at community centers in "under-served neighborhoods."

SLSC operates on 70 percent earned income and has always ended each season slightly in the black. This success can be attributed to sound management of its $25,000 annual budget along with the generous cooperation of the performing arts department at Washington University, which makes its scene shop and studio theatre available at an affordable rate for the summer seasons; in addition, St. Louis University offers audition and rehearsal space as well as some costumes. SLSC also receives financial assistance from the Missouri Arts Council and the Regional Arts Commission. Major corporate supporters include Maritz Corporation, Union Electric, Emerson Electric, and Southwestern Bell Foundation. Private donations make up 7.5 percent of SLSC's annual income. Staff salaries are contracted, while pay for the cast is allotted at the end of the season, though Northcott dreams of the day when she can offer regular salaries to everyone involved. Northcott now lives and works most of the year in Chicago, returning to St. Louis each May to gear up for the new season. She also directed the 1993 and 1994 winter productions. Tom McAtee manages the company on a year-round basis.

The company logo—a jolly-looking Falstaff figure with cape and sword—conveys a spirit of populist fun. "We approach Shakespeare as we would any contemporary dramatist," Northcott says. "We try to create three-dimensional characters and make them as entertaining as we can. Shakespeare is theatre, not just literature." Not averse to changing the historical period of the plays, Northcott directed a modern-dress *King John* employing topical references like a jar of jelly beans on the title character's desk, negotiations by telephone, a gum-chewing French lord Melun wearing aviator glasses, and other clever touches. "Recognizing the universality of power politics, the current production concentrates on the underlying motivation of Shakespeare's characters," commented reviewer Gerry Kowarsky (*St. Louis Post-Dispatch*, 1 August 1991). "The acting in this production is excellent, making the characters' motivations plain through the smokescreen of their arguments about succession and other matters."

A review by Bob Wilcox in the *Riverfront Times* (22 July 1992) suggests the kind of critical acclaim Northcott has earned: "Donna Northcott deserves some kind of prize for her work with Shakespeare's seldom-performed plays—first *Titus Andronicus*, then *King John*, now *All's Well That Ends Well*. The artistic director of the St. Louis Shakespeare Company has directed an intriguingly absorbing production of this problem comedy." Of her Titus Andronicus, Harry Weber commented (*Riverfront Times*, 25-31 July 1990): "Believe me, there isn't a movie in town that's as entertaining as *Titus Andronicus*; not often is there theater as lovingly, artfully, successfully performed. With this and their other two productions this season, the St. Louis Shakespeare Company has set a standard for intelligence and integrity that every other group in the area should study and emulate."

Production History: 1985: *TN, MND, Ham.*; **1986:** *MM, Mac., She Stoops to Conquer;* **1987:** *AYL, R3, A Flea in Her Ear;* **1988:** *Rom., Dogg's Hamlet/Cahoot's Macbeth, Shr.*; **1989:** *MV, Private Lives,* *Wiv.*; **1990:** *Ado, Tit., Les Liaisons Dangereuses;* **1991:** *Err., Jn., Lysistrata;* **1992:** *JC, AWW, The Importance of Being Earnest;* **1993:** *Mac., Oth., Cym., The School for Scandal;* **1994:** *MND.*

Research Resources: The Saint Louis Shakespeare Company archives are maintained by Missouri Historical Society, 225 S. Skinker, St Louis, MO (mail address: P.O. Box 11940, St Louis, MO 63112-0040. See also Harry Weber, "Stratford-upon-Avon Calling," *Riverfront Times* (1-7 August 1990): 26-28.

Information supplied by Tom McAtee.
Felicia Hardison Londré

MONTANA

MONTANA SHAKESPEARE IN THE PARKS. MAIL: Department of Media and Theatre Arts, Montana State University, Bozeman, MT 59715. SITES: city parks throughout state of Montana, and portions of Idaho, Wyoming, and Alberta. ADMINISTRATIVE OFFICE/BOX OFFICE: 406/994-3901. ADMISSION: variable. SEASON: 80 performances of two productions, rotating repertory, usually one non-Shakespeare. PRINCIPAL STAFF: Joel Jahnke, producer and artistic director, FACILITY: portable thrust stage, open air. AUDITIONS: area auditions in Winter; also Chicago, Seattle, and Denver Theatre Center auditions. STATUS: non-Equity. ANNUAL BUDGET: $180,000 (1992). ANNUAL ATTENDANCE: 25,000. FOUNDED: 1972, Bruce C. Jacobsen.

Now in its twentieth season, the Montana Shakespeare in the Parks (MSP) is one of the oldest and most successful regional touring Shakespeare companies. The MSP was established in 1972 by Bruce C. Jacobsen, formerly director of theatre at Montana State University in Bozeman, with the purpose of providing Shakespeare productions for the vast rural area of Montana. Now dean of the College of Fine Arts at the University of North Dakota, Jacobsen recalls that he was well aware of the need to "enrich the cultural environment of the state" after moving from Minneapolis to Bozeman. Influenced by the Guthrie Theatre resident company model, Jacobsen explored the possibility of a resident company but realized that the sparse population was spread out too thinly over a large territory. He knew that whatever his prospective company did had to be self-contained and not dependent on any sort of indoor facilities. Based on the concept of "strolling players," only with the assistance of combustion engines, a portable stage evolved. An all-volunteer company tested the idea by touring the first year to a dozen nearby communities, and Shakespeare emerged as the playwright who best appealed to Montanans young and old. The concept worked, and Jacobsen established a paid company that toured to over 20 communities, giving birth to the MSP.

The MSP travels thousands of miles to over 40 communities across the state of Montana as well as to neighboring states and Canadian provinces, which may give the MSP the distinction of being one of the few international Shakespeare companies in North America. The tour begins in late June and continues through late August. In 1992, the MSC traveled close to 7,000 miles, which sets a record for the most land miles traveled by any Shakespeare company performing in parks in the United States. With the exception of a few larger cities, such as Billings or Great Falls, most performances are one night stands in communities with populations under 10,000. The smallest community on the tour is Birney, south of Lame Deer, Montana. With a population of only 17, the annual performance draws a crowd of over 200 spectators. A truck carries the scenery with the portable platform stage, which is erected to provide the setting for the action. A few panels on either side cover entrances and exits. The stage is generally set up in a city park in front of a group of trees or a majestic mountain.

For many communities, the event is a festive occasion and is promoted as a family affair, complete with potluck dinners and beer. Local sponsors pay a small fee and provide lodging. In Big Timber, Montana, the 1991 production of *Twelfth Night* brought over 100 people with folding chairs, blankets, pets, and children. Plenty of western hats showed up among the spectators, and a long line of pick-up trucks filled the parking spaces. A potluck dinner preceded the event, and locals, as well as guests from ranches and farms, spread out on the grass. The actors were quick to pass the hat following the performance with what looked like a good response.

Joel Jahnke became producer and artistic Director of the MSP in 1980 and has expanded the touring sites and established an endowment for the company. The tradition of the MSP is well established in Montana communities and has become an annual summer event in the local cultural life. In 1991, the MSP received Montana's most prestigious award in the performing arts, the Montana Governor's Award.

As part of its outreach, the MSP publishes a newsletter, entitled *The Clarion* for its sponsors and patrons. Unlike similar companies in metropolitan areas, which move locally from park to park, the MSP is truly unique in the long distances and thousands of miles traveled during the summer to rural communities. The company depends on a network of local supporters and fund-raisers, as well as on state funding organizations. With foresight, the MSP has built up an endowment fund of over $120,000 to support its operating budget. The company will celebrate its one-thousandth performance on 28 July 1994 in Helena, Montana.

Jahnke's plans include the establishment of a resident Shakespeare company in Bozeman, beginning with the 1993 season. The plan is to expand the summer season from the spring into the fall. The MSP will be in residence in Bozeman for a four-day weekend, then go on the road for four weeks, return to Bozeman, and keep alternating between Bozeman and the road through Labor

Day. Jahnke also hopes to offer classes for young people of various ages to complement the Shakespearean repertory.

Production History: 1973: Scenes; 1974: *MV, Shr.*; 1975: *Err., Wiv.*; 1976: *TN, Devil's Disciple*; 1977: *TGV, The Servant of Two Masters*; 1978: *MND, The Miser*; 1979: *AYL, Cyrano*; 1980: *Ado, The Rivals*; 1981: *Shr., The Doctor in Spite of Himself*, 1982: *Wiv., The Imaginary Invalid*; 1983: *Err., The School for Wives*; 1984: *TN, Tartuffe*; 1985: *AYL, The Would-Be Gentleman*; 1986: *MND, Volpone*; 1987: *Rom., TGV*; 1988: *MV, The Rivals*; 1989: *Shr., The Miser*; 1990: *Ado, Engaged*; 1991: *TN, Scapina*; 1992: *Wiv., Cyrano*; 1993: *Err., H5*; 1994: *Mac., The Country Wife.*

Research Resources: Archives are maintained at the Montana Shakespeare in the Parks administrative office.

Site visits: July 1991, July 1992; interviews November 1992, January 1993, and February 1994.
Ron Engle

NEBRASKA

NEBRASKA SHAKESPEARE FESTIVAL. MAIL: Fine and Performing Arts, Creighton University, 24th and California Streets, Omaha, NE 68178. SITE: Elmwood Park, off Dodge Street. ADMINISTRATION: 402/280-2391. ADMISSION: free. SEASON: 12 performances, late June through early July, 8:30 p.m., Thur.–Sun. PRINCIPAL STAFF: Cindy Melby Phaneuf, producing artistic director; Michael Markey, administrative director. FACILITY: open-air temporary stage (capacity 2,500). AUDITIONS: New York, Chicago (Feb.); Omaha (March). STATUS: Guest Artist. ANNUAL BUDGET: $135,000 (1991). ANNUAL ATTENDANCE: 25,000. FOUNDED: 1986, Alan Klem, Cindy Melby Phaneuf.

When Alan Klem joined the performing arts faculty at Creighton University in 1986, he brought along his professional expertise as a founder of Shakespeare festivals, having worked with Sharon Benge to launch **Shakespeare in the Park** (Fort Worth), where he served as artistic director from 1978 to 1980. At Creighton, Klem's departmental chair recalled that there had once been summer Shakespeare productions in the university's Jesuit Gardens, and he suggested that Klem might revive that tradition. Klem had seen and admired a production staged by Dr. Cindy Melby Phaneuf at the University of Nebraska at

Omaha (UNO), so he called her to talk over the idea. (Klem and Phaneuf had met briefly when both were students at Texas Christian University.) They quickly decided to try to involve both of their universities in starting a Nebraska Shakespeare Festival (NSF). Phaneuf's dean and others in university administration readily agreed to the idea, and this heightened the interest of officials at Creighton. A series of meetings and luncheons led to NSF's incorporation on 26 September 1986. The following summer brought a first season of two plays, with a total attendance of 12,000 despite several rained-out performances.

That opening season set the pattern that has been maintained ever since: one traditionally staged production and one production that takes a more adventurous approach, each presented for four consecutive performances, followed by a third week of rotating repertory. In 1987, *The Taming of the Shrew* was presented in Elizabethan style, complete with induction, while *The Tempest* incorporated elements of Kabuki. In the second season, attendance reached over 3,000 at the final performance of *Hamlet*, which had shared the summer bill with a 1920s black-and-white art deco *Midsummer Night's Dream*. Average nightly attendance since 1986 has held steady at around 2,000.

Over the years, the two universities have contributed tremendous in-kind support. UNO provides rehearsal space, costume storage, dressing-room facilities, and the electricity to run the festival. Creighton provides dormitory housing for actors and office facilities for Michael Markey, the full-time administrative director who was hired in 1990. In addition, Klem's and Phaneuf's respective universities pay their salaries as stage directors (but no extra compensation for their codirection of the festival). Klem and Phaneuf were encouraged to form a separate nonprofit corporation so that they could raise funds independently of the two universities. In order to allow for an expanded sphere of activities in the future, the NSF was therefore incorporated as the umbrella organization. Its free outdoor Shakespeare performances are presented under the rubric "Shakespeare on the Green," a project of the NSF. The Omaha Parks and Recreation Department keeps the green mowed and provides picnic tables, but the NSF is responsible for spraying for mosquitos. The parks department has also granted the NSF a special dispensation that allows picnickers to bring wine and beer into the park on performance evenings.

Chief responsibility for fund raising was taken on by Harold Anderson, retired publisher of the *Omaha World-Herald*. He and his wife, Marian Anderson, have cochaired the NSF's board of trustees since the festival's inception. The newspaper contributes free advertising and the printing of the program. Memberships in the Bard's Club (an honorary group of NSF financial supporters) range in price from $100 to $1,000. Corporate sponsors ($3,500) are acknowledged with the company name on a banner at the sponsored performance, and a section is reserved for that company's employees. Benefits in 1991 and 1992 also raised substantial sums. The rapid proliferation of festival volunteers has led to the establishment of a community board to supplement the original Executive Board.

The NSF's mission is "to provide, free to the public, a summer season of professional Shakespearean productions in an outdoor atmosphere that offers wholesome, meaningful entertainment for the entire family." The festival operates on a guest artist agreement with Actors' Equity, allowing for four Equity actors each season in a company of 60 performers and technicians. There is an attempt to balance each season's casts between half local actors and half from out of state. In terms of their conceptual approach to staging Shakespeare, Klem and Phaneuf are open to anything that will work, as long as it is based in the text. "We're big on research and analysis, but we won't try to prove an academic point," says Phaneuf. "We're trying to excite popular audiences, but we won't play down to them. I've been really pleased that the audience has given us a lot of freedom and also let us know what's good and what's not."

The NSF's Shakespeare on the Green boasts what is surely one of the most beautiful outdoor performance sites in the United States. The natural slope of the land means that there is no need for segregation of lawn chairs and blankets; everyone can get a good view—unless attendance tops 2,500, forcing some to the fringes and behind lighting towers. Although the plentiful parking south of UNO's library is immediately adjacent to the park, the slope itself offers a vista of virtually uninterrupted greenery on all sides. The dressing-room trailers are well hidden behind the stage, which nestles in a clump of trees, and beyond them stretches the gently rolling terrain of a golf course.

One of Phaneuf's special projects is the small Shakespeare garden now well established at the entrance to the park. There, volunteers hand out free programs; more elaborate souvenir programs are sold for a dollar. Just inside the entrance, a bell-ringer in Elizabethan dress solicits donations. Concession stands sell T-shirts and substantial food items. Picnickers who arrive two hours before performances are invited to gather near the stage where some folding chairs are set up for a 20-minute "seminar" on the play, conducted by a couple of actors and perhaps a local scholar.

Audiences appear to be composed largely of families. The number of ethnic minorities in attendance has grown steadily. Some Omahans return each night for all 12 performances. Attendance would clearly warrant an extension of the season, but UNO presents an obstacle. During performances, UNO's cooling tower must be shut off, due to the noise it makes, and the resulting lack of air-conditioning in offices and classrooms at those times has brought strong objections from some faculty. Indeed, one irate faculty senate member generated a survey titled "Heat from Shakespeare." Despite the prejudicial tone of the survey, the response from UNO faculty was five to two in favor of Shakespeare. A wall to baffle the sound from the cooling tower could be built for $30,000-$50,000, but this solution has been blocked because it would seem to grant the NSF official sanction as a permanent presence at the site. A related obstacle is the university's having obtained legal clearance for new construction on the library parking site; thus, UNO's higher administration is now eager to see the festival move elsewhere. A committee has investigated dozens of sites in the area and found nothing comparable to the present location. Nonetheless, there is a long-range plan to renovate Aksarben (Omaha's famous racetrack), a project that would include the construction of a new outdoor amphitheatre. Until that amphitheatre becomes available, the NSF and UNO remain at an impasse.

As academics, Klem and Phaneuf have experienced the strain of the year-round commitment to the festival. Their spring breaks must be devoted entirely to casting. "It's not only the grant-writing and day-to-day tasks," Klem commented in 1990. "It's the mental energy, the constant brainstorming. You live with it 24 hours a day." Indeed, Klem took a leave of absence in 1991, and, in order to pursue other professional opportunities, resigned his position as co-artistic director in 1992.

The 1990 production of *The Merry Wives of Windsor* typifies the NSF's nontraditional approach. Setting the action in the Red Garter Saloon in the fictional town of Windsor, Nebraska, around 1885, allowed many clever touches in the setting, costumes, and general horseplay. A cigar-chomping Falstaff (Charles Carroll) cut a rotund and slovenly figure in his Union soldier's pants, red suspenders, and a cowboy hat with a large flap turned up in front. Kevin Barratt as Fenton contributed some hilarious physical comedy: falling down stairs, getting tangled up in a chair, being bashed by swinging doors, and indulging in low comic byplay with the Host. Anne Page was the tallest of six little Pages, all in blue and white striped outfits, a stairstep line-up following their mother and often shifting set props. Director Klem carried off the concept with only minor textual changes: "dollars" for "pounds," "River Platte" for "Thames," and so on.

Casey Kizziah, returning to Omaha for his third consecutive summer, played George Page in *Merry Wives of Windsor* as well as the title role in *Macbeth*, directed by Phaneuf. Resplendent in their blood-red Gothic-style costumes, the Macbeths were an attractive, even charismatic, couple; the production focused strongly upon their relationship. Macbeth's moral decline was finely nuanced in counterpoint to the blatant viciousness of the violence. The live music (harp, percussion, reed, keyboard) composed by Jonathan Cole underscored much of the action to good effect. Over 3,000 people rose in a standing ovation on the closing night of the performance.

Production History: **1987**: *Tmp.*, *Shr.*; **1988**: *MND*, *Ham.*; **1989**: *Rom.*, *Ado*; **1990**: *Wiv.*, *Mac.*; **1991**: *Oth.*, *AYL*; **1992**: *Err.*, *R3*; **1993**: *TGV*, *MV*; **1994**: *LLL*, *1H4*.

Research Resources: Archives are maintained in the festival office at Creighton University and at the University of Nebraska at Omaha library. See also Felicia Londré, "Shakespeare sans Sous," *American Theatre* (December 1990): 54-55.

Site visits: 7-8 July 1990; 2-3 July 1992. Interviews: 8 July 1990; 3 March 1992.
Felicia Hardison Londré

NEVADA

SHAKESPEARE AT SAND HARBOR. MAIL: Incline Village/Crystal Bay Visitors and Convention Bureau, 969 Tahoe Blvd., Incline Village, NV 89450. SITE: Sand Harbor State Park, Incline Village, NV. ADMINISTRATION: 702/832-1606. BOX OFFICE: 800/468-2463. ADMISSION: $12–$18. SEASON: one week in July, two weeks in August; one performance per evening at 7:30 p.m. PRINCIPAL STAFF: Vicki McGowen, executive director. FACILITY: outdoor amphitheatre on Lake Tahoe (capacity 1,000). ANNUAL ATTENDANCE: 15,000–17,000 (1992). FOUNDED: NTFAC, 1974; Shakespeare at Sand Harbor, 1978.

In 1994, Shakespeare at Sand Harbor (SSH) celebrated its sixteenth season. The annual two-week festival is held at one of the West's most popular tourist sites. Sand Amphitheatre in Sand Harbor State Park is located southeast of Incline Village on the Nevada side of the lake. The outdoor stage positioned along the shore affords a spectacular view of Lake Tahoe and the surrounding mountains.

For most of the company's history, the Shakespeare at Sand Harbor festival was produced by the North Tahoe Fine Arts Council (NTFAC). This organization essentially contracted professional touring companies from California to present one to three productions each season in the Sand Harbor amphitheatre. As producer, NTFAC organized ticket sales, advertising, made arrangements for lighting and sound, provided for volunteers to serve as ushers and technicians, secured lodging for visiting company members, and coordinated concession sales with officials of Sand Harbor State Park. For three seasons, the **New Shakespeare Company** played at Sand Harbor. In 1981, the New Shakespeare Company was forced to cancel this activity when the company lost its source of funding as a result of the drastic cuts in California's state education and arts budgets. The NTFAC was able to replace the company, however, with productions from the Valley Institute for the Arts (VITA; see **Shakespeare Theatre Arts Repertory**) in Saratoga, California. VITA brought productions to Sand harbor annually until 1990, when the organization disbanded. For two seasons, the **Sunnyvale Summer Repertory**, an operation of the California Theatre Center in Sunnyvale, presented performances. In 1993, the Sunnyvale Summer Repertory was replaced by the California Repertory Company from California State University at Long Beach. In late 1993, NTFAC disbanded following a legal dispute between the board of directors and the executive director. The Incline Village-Crystal Bay Visitors and Convention Bureau was awarded the contract for the use of the facilities at Sand Harbor by the Nevada State Parks, and assumed responsibility for continuing the Sand Harbor festival. In 1994, in addition to presenting theatrical performances, the festival featured a special "Renaissance in the Pines" event for three days in August. The event included an Elizabethan-style fair and "Falstaff's Feast," a lavish dinner complete with period costumed servers, madrigal music, and variety entertainment.

Surveys from the past two seasons indicate that fully 46 percent of audiences are visitors who stay an average of four days in the area. Local residents are very supportive of this special summer entertainment and arrive early for pre-curtain picnic suppers at the site. The high-altitude setting dictates warm clothing and blankets, in addition to flashlights and beach chairs, for the routinely chilly evenings after the sun goes down.

Production History: 1979-80: n/a; **1981**: (VITA) *MND, Rom., Err.*; **1982**: n/a; **1983-90**: VITA returns, see **Shakespeare at Benbow Lake** entry for schedule of offerings; **1991**: (CTC) *Tmp., MND, The Lion in Winter*; **1992**: *Err., LLL, Dracula*; **1993**: *Ham., Shr., Le Miracle de Piaf*; **1994**: *TN, AYL, Tom Jones, Robinson Crusoe.*

Research Resources: Shakespeare at Sand Harbor archives are maintained informally by the North Tahoe Fine Arts Council office.

Interview: 12 April 1993.
Patricia M. McMahon

NEW JERSEY

HAWORTH SHAKESPEARE FESTIVAL. MAIL: 430 Ivy Avenue, Haworth, NJ 07641. SITE: "The Pond" in Haworth. ADMINISTRATION/BOX OFFICE: 201/387-7421. Fax: 201/384-1401. ADMISSION: free, donations accepted. PRINCIPAL STAFF: Cindy Kaplan, artistic director. FACILITY: open-air grassy alcove near "The Pond" in Haworth. STATUS: none. ANNUAL ATTENDANCE: 2,000 (1992). FOUNDED: 1979, Cindy Kaplan.

"Haworth is like Brigadoon—it's a magical place, and there really are leprechauns at the Pond," explains Cindy Kaplan, who in 1979 chose the "Pond" site for the first Haworth Shakespeare Festival (HSF); "It was a natural for a stage setting. At first it was just a way to get work for two actor friends," she continues. But what started as scenes from Shakespeare in a grassy alcove evolved into full productions. "Haworth is really a one-street sleepy town, but the people came—several hundred people came. I thought it would be too esoteric," says Kaplan, "but the people became passionate." Kaplan refocused the lights, which are used to illuminate the Pond skating rink, on the alcove and the actors. According to Kaplan, the town supported the event by allowing the HSF "total artistic freedom." An occassional train passes through town close to the stage area but, as Kaplan has explained, the "audiences are very forgiving about the trains . . . we deal with them by using improvisational techniques."

Kaplan has been instrumental in bringing multicultural theatre to New York City as well as to the HSF. She worked closely with the Roger Furman Theatre to bring *Asinamli* (*We Have no Money*) by Mbongeni Ngema to Harlem and Broadway in 1986 and became a member of the Board of the Committed Artists of South Africa. In 1990, she produced Miriam Tlali's play *Crimen Injuria* in association with the Afro-American Cultural Center and the South African Research Program at Yale University.

The HSF strives to be an exemplary and pioneering multicultural, inter-racial American theatre "bridging all classes." Its recent production of *The Tragedy of Macbeth* featured the Committed Artists in Great Britain, an offshoot of Committed Artists of South Africa, in a guest performance at the New World Theatre in Amherst. The Committed Artists brought the leading black actors of the **Royal Shakespeare Company** and the Royal National Theatre of Great Britain to perform together for the first time in a production of *Macbeth* set in contemporary South Africa. Directed by Stephen Rayne of the Royal Shakespeare Company (who also had directed British actress Susanna York as Gertrude with Kevin Doyle as Hamlet at the HSF in 1990), the production premiered at the New York International Festival of the Arts in 1992. According to Kaplan "The collaboration between African, Caribbean, British, and American artists demonstrated that the arts can be used as a model of international cooperation and dialogue." The production subsequently toured to a number of cities in the United States. Daniel Watermeier viewed the production in October 1992 in Ann Arbor, Michigan. He recalls that the production had a:

contemporized sub-Saharan *mise-en-scène*, mixing traditional tribal dress with European modes of dress. The witches, for example, were costumed as African priestesses, while the soldiers wore contemporary ubiquitous battle fatigues and carried automatic weapons. African music and rituals enhanced an evocation of a specific milieu. Through the vehicle of *Macbeth*, director Rayne effectively suggested the volatile and tragic post-colonial politics of Uganda, Nigeria, Rwanda, or South Africa. On balance, however, it was a very uneven production. The meeting of Macbeth and Lady Macbeth was, for example, physically passionate, sexy, refreshingly compelling, and provocative. But Macbeth's encountering Banquo's ghost during the banquet scene was, on the other hand, so broadly played that it impressed many audience members as caricaturish, provoking laughter. At other moments, performances were so lacking in physical energy, although the vocal delivery was always clear, that one was lulled into inattentiveness. Indeed, the pacing, the rhythm of the entire presentation was remarkably lethargic. Still, this Africanized interpretation demonstrated the potential of cross-cultural, cross-racial approaches to Shakespeare. It also provided a still too rare opportunity for African, Anglo-African, and Afro-Caribbean actors to showcase their skills and talent in a Shakespeare play. The sold-out audience in Ann Arbor's Michigan Theatre was warmly enthusiastic at the curtain call.

Production History: **1979**: Scenes from Shakespeare; **1980**; Scenes from Shakespeare; **1981**: *MND*; **1982**; *The Belle of Amherst, My Astonishing Self*; **1984**: *Woza Albert*, Scenes from Shakespeare, *The Human Voice*; **1987**: *Mac.*, *Deathwatch*; **1988-89**: *Mac.* (tour); **1990**: *Ham.*; **1991**: *Mac.*; **1992**: *Shr. Mac.* (tour).

Research Resources: Programs, clipping files, and other material are stored at the festival office. See also:

Bell, Bill. "'Macbeth': Out of Africa and into New York's conscience." *Daily News* (nd): np.

Cacioppo, Nancy. "'Hamlet' in Haworth: Susannah York heads a 'royal' cast, outdoors and near Rockland." *Journal News* [Rockland County] (30 August 1990): C1.

Hampton, Wilborn. "A Contemporary 'Macbeth' Without Changing a Word." *New York Times* (18 June 1991): C13.

Kaplan, Mitch. "Haworth Festival is pure theater." *Suburban News* (24 June 1987): 2.

Klein, Alvin. "From Juilliard to Shakespeare at a Pond." *New York Times* (12 July 1992): np.

Meltzer, Deanne. "The midsummer night's dream goes on." *Haworth Suburbanite* (27 June 1984): np.

Siegel, Jessica. "She's building a rich life, stage by stage." *The Record* (6 January 1993): np.

Telephone interview: December 1992 and January 1993.
Ron Engle

NEW JERSEY SHAKESPEARE FESTIVAL. MAIL: care of Drew University, Route 24, Madison NJ 07940. SITE: Bowne Theatre on Drew University campus. ADMINISTRATION: 201/408-3278. BOX OFFICE: 201/408-5600. ADMISSION: season subscription, $55—$140; single ticket, $14—$28. SEASON: Seven productions presented from mid-June to mid-October; 8:00 p.m., Tues.–Sun.; 2:00 p.m., Wed., Sat., Sun. PRINCIPAL STAFF: Bonnie J. Monte, artistic director; Michael Stotts, managing director. FACILITY: modified thrust stage in a converted gymnasium (capacity 244); black-box (capacity 115). AUDITIONS: New York City in March. STATUS: Equity Guest Artist. ANNUAL BUDGET: $802,000 (1994). ANNUAL ATTENDANCE: 26,000 (1993). FOUNDED: 1963, Paul Barry.

The New Jersey Shakespeare Festival (NJSF) had its beginnings at the historic Cape May Playhouse in the summer of 1963. There, Paul Barry, NJSF founder, presented a season of premodern and modern classics, including Shakespeare's *The Taming of the Shrew*. He repeated the format in 1964, including *Richard III* for a one-week run. In 1965, Barry expanded his program to include two Shakespeare plays presented in repertory for three weeks in the middle of his ten-week Cape May season. That fall, he toured three productions of Shakespeare to Natick and Lynn, Massachusetts, with the support of the *Boston Herald-Traveler* newspaper syndicate.

For three years (1965-67), Barry continued to produce ten plays during the summer at Cape May, including a three-week presentation in repertory of two Shakespeare plays and a contemporary play, followed by a fall tour of three Shakespeare plays or other classics to the Boston area. Although Barry has conceded that this was a demanding schedule, it did help promote the reputation of his Cape May company and the experience was invaluable. In 1965, Ellen Barry (neé Reiss) joined the company and, in 1969, became its long-time producing director.

At the close of the 1968 season, the Cape May Playhouse was razed, and a motel was built on the site. Homeless, the company toured area schools in the autumns of 1968 and 1969 under a federally funded grant. In 1970, the company played another season in Cape May in the ballroom of the old Lafayette Hotel, but safety codes and insurance requirements forced the Lafayette's owner to tear down the building following this season: the NJSF again found itself without a theatre.

In the spring of 1971, however, Barry was invited by the president of Drew University, Robert F. Oxnam, to locate the NJSF there. Oxnam, a former actor, thought the presence of the festival would give the university a new cultural dimension and public visibility. Indeed, he hoped to build a performing arts complex on the Drew campus that would house several resident artistic organizations. Madison is a relatively affluent, mainly academic community. In addition to Drew University, Fairleigh-Dickinson University and the College of Saint Elizabeth are located there. The town, moreover, is surrounded by many other small, bucolic towns and villages in northern New Jersey, and it is only one hour away from New York City by automobile or commuter train . In all, Madison was an ideal location for such a venture. Unfortunately, Oxnam died unexpectedly in 1975, and his dream of a performing arts center was never realized, but the NJSF was nenetheless to flourish in Madison.

Drew University had no real theatre building, but Barry was allowed to convert an old gymnasium into an open thrust-stage theatre and to air condition the building. Other rooms in this and adjacent buildings were turned into administrative offices, rehearsal studios, dressing rooms, and costume and scenery shops. It was a functional conversion but by no means ideal. The NJSF paid for these improvements and for utilities during their season, but the university did not charge any rental fee for the use of the facilities. University housing was made available to company members during the season at the usual student rate. The university, furthermore, provided major assistance with fund raising for the festival for its first few seasons, but the NJSF remained a separately incorporated, autonomous, professional theatre company.

In June 1972, the NJSF opened its first season in Madison, presenting five plays in repertory over an 11-week period. Henry Hewes, the veteran theatre critic of the *Saturday Review* (5 August 1972), undoubtedly reflected the reactions of many playgoers, calling the "migration from Cape May . . . fortuitous in the extreme" and praising the productions of *The Taming of the Shrew* and *Troilus and Cressida*. By 1975, the NJSF had expanded to a 21-week season of eight plays playing to over 89 percent capacity. Following the summer repertory season, three to five productions were then continued for runs of three or four weeks each through the fall. This was to remain the production format for the next 19 seasons.

During the next four years, total attendance and the number of season subscribers steadily grew. In 1979, for example, there was a total attendance of over 35,000 with almost 3,300 season subscribers. Critical reaction also was mainly positive. John Beaufort of the *Christian Science Monitor* (29 June 1973), for example, praised Barry's *Coriolanus*, updated to the World War II era, for generating "tension, dramatic excitement, [and] a sharp sense of psychological conflict". Bruce Chadwick of the New York *Daily News* (8 July 1975) wrote that *Henry IV, Part Two* (staged together with *Part One*) was "enjoyable . . . meaningful . . . [and] in the end superb as a political drama." Joseph Catinella of the *New York Times* (19 July 1981) called *Cymbeline* "fresh, high spirited and well spoken." Noted Shakespearean scholar and director, Bernard Beckerman, in a more reserved assessment of the 1976 Shakespearean productions, wrote that there were some lapses in acting and interpretation, but *Titus Andronicus* in particular "showed ingenuity and boldness of imagination" and that, overall, the festival "proved that it can achieve work of a high order" [*Shakespeare Quarterly* 29 (Spring 1978) 233-34]. Similarly, Carol Rosen, in *Shakespeare Quarterly* (Spring 1980, 202-04), found much to praise in the 1979 productions of *King Lear* and *A Midsummer*

Night's Dream, including Barry's "imaginative," "insightful," and "illuminating," direction and the company's "fine ensemble work."

By the early 1980s, the NJSF had developed a reputation for imaginative, thoughtful stagings of Shakespeare, other modern classics, and contemporary plays. Chadwick (*Daily News,* 26 July 1981) commended the festival for "presenting some of the best regional theatre in America." The festival also began to attract financial support from state arts agencies, private foundations, and corporations. The Barrys were thus encouraged in their artistic mission to maintain a professional, classically oriented theatre company, aiming to do all of Shakespeare's plays, three each season in repertory, and other plays from the world repertory, as Barry has written, "based on their value as compared with Shakespeare."

In 1983, having already presented Shakespeare's most popular plays, as well as many of the less frequently revived works, the Barrys daringly mounted all three parts of *Henry VI* and *Richard III* as *The War of the Roses,* presenting the entire tetralogy in repertory over three performance evenings. Later, in August, *The War of the Roses* cycle was seen on a Saturday in a single marathon performance, running eight and one-half hours (with two meal breaks). With 70 actors and hundreds of costumes and properties, it was a challenging venture for a modest-sized regional theatre. Generally, critics responded favorably to *The War of the Roses.* Chadwick (*Daily News,* 28 August 1983), for example, praised it as "easily the theatre event of the year and one of the great events in the cultural history of New Jersey," while Laura Haywood of the *Princeton Packet* (20 July 1983) wrote that "everything about it works to perfection." For this production, the Barrys also initiated the Colloquium Weekend, an intensive weekend of performances complemented by lectures and panel discussions, featuring members of the company and distinguished theatre artists and Shakespearean scholars. (By 1990, the Colloquium Weekend was attracting over 700 participants.) But, despite good notices and the success of the Colloquium Weekend, *The War of the Roses,* according to Barry, did not attract at the box office he had hoped and ended the season with a substantial deficit. With *The War of the Roses* production, Barry found that he had directed all but six of Shakespeare's plays. He determined to mount these six over the next few seasons. This decision, however, did have certain consequences for the financial stability and management of the NJSF.

Although it peaked in 1979, attendance at the NJSF had remained consistently high through the early 1980s. Moreover, through 1986, only five seasons in Madison had ended with deficits, and these usually were eliminated during the following year. The deficit incurred with *The War of the Roses,* for example, was eliminated by the beginning of the 1985 season. But, in the late 1980s, attendance did decline, perhaps because of some programing choices (to complete the canon, these seasons included critically well received but relatively unpopular productions of *The Two Noble Kinsmen, King John* and *Timon of Athens*). Production expenses and expenditures for much-needed facilities and equipment repairs and improvements, coupled with this decline in attendance, led to a serious financial situation by the end of 1990, when the NJSF debt had grown to almost $250,000.

As the cumulative deficit grew in the late 1980s, the Barrys found themselves, their artistic objectives, and their management style at odds with their trustees, with state arts funding agencies, and with Drew University. Undoubtedly, the economic conditions and the general political climate in the state of New Jersey during this time also contributed significantly to the complex financial and interpersonal tensions within the organization of the NJSF. It should be noted that many other regional theatres were running sizable deficits during these years as well; the NJSF was hardly unique in this respect. At the end of the 1990 season, however, after 19 years that had been artistically and, for the most part, financially successful, the Barrys were informed by the chairman of their board of trustees and the new president of Drew University (former New Jersey governor, Tom Kean) that their contracts would not be renewed.

Ironically, with the production of *King John* in 1990, the NJSF became one of the very few companies worldwide to complete the entire Shakespeare canon, and Barry himself became the first American and one of only two people in this century to have directed all of Shakespeare's plays. In 1992, he was presented a life-time achievement award by the Shakespeare Globe Centre of North America. (The only other recipients of this award to date have been Joseph Papp, founder of the **New York Shakespeare Festival** and director Michael Kahn of the **American Shakespeare Theatre**). Barrys' accomplishment was remarkable: 196 productions in 28 years, including 65 productions of Shakespeare's plays and works by over 100 other playwrights ranging from Sophocles to David Mamet. Moreover, they had offered opportunities for numerous talented actors, directors, designers, composers, and stage managers to work in a classically oriented repertory theatre and for thousands of playgoers to see high-quality theatrical performances.

In 1991, a new team of artistic director Bonnie J. Monte and general manager Michael Stotts assumed the management of the festival. In their first three seasons, they have generally adhered to the original aims of the NJSF, but they did abandon repertory in favor of the limited run. They also dropped the NJSF's LORT-D status for a less expensive Equity guest-artist contract. To date, they have succeeded in maintaining high attendance and in reducing the debt by implementing cost saving and new promotion, marketing, fund-raising and development strategies. Undoubtedly ticket sales were bolstered in their first season by the appearance of Elizabeth McGovern and Edward Hermann, who are both well known from film, television, and the New York stage, as Viola and Malvolio in *Twelfth Night*.

The festival's production of *A Midsummer Night's Dream*, that I attended in 1991 was set on a Caribbean island somewhere in the Bermuda Triangle. According to director Dylan Baker, the island is the home base of the fairy world from where they "go all over the world to achieve their objective . . . to bring harmony to nature and have the world . . . growing abundantly." Oberon, Titania, and Puck were dressed in festive Caribbean carnival costumes, suggesting their connections with the fertility spirits at the roots of this celebration. Calypso music enhanced the association. The mortal characters were costumed from a range of historical periods and locales—all kinds of presumably lost people who had been rescued by the spirit world and brought to the island, a kind of "New Athens." Hippolyta, for example, was dressed like the lost aviatrix, Amelia Earhart; the lovers were supposed to be settlers from the Lost Colony of Roanoke; the mechanicals were a CNN (Cable Network News) television crew lost en route to the 1991 Persian Gulf war, complete with various video and audio equipment. In a reference to classical mythology, an aged, blind Theseus had also been rescued from the sea and brought to the island where he had become the leader.

Without the program note to explain this concept and the "who's who" among the *dramatis personae*, many spectators undoubtedly would have been totally confused by the absurd goings-on, especially young theatregoers unfamiliar with the play. But the production was ultimately rescued from the convoluted concept, at least in part, by the energies and talents of the performers. The lovers were attractive and altogether winning. Oberon and Titania evinced a compelling erotic tension, and Oberon and Puck were united in sparkling boyish mischievousness. The Pyramus and Thisbe scene was riotously funny. Indeed, Marcus Giametti as Pyramus "made the eyes water . . . [with] merry tears," pantomiming with manic vitality myriad methods of suicide, not only by stabbing himself to death, but also by poisoning, hanging, and jumping from a tall building. At the curtain, the production was enthusiastically received, especially by the many teenagers in the audience.

For the future, the new managers aim to eliminate the debt and to explore moving to or building a new facility. Although the campus itself is attractive and accessible, the Bowne Theatre building is, in fact, old, physically deteriorating, and very limiting in terms of its audience capacity and its small, cramped stage space. The workshops, dressing rooms, and offices (located in a trailer adjacent to the theatre building) are also overcrowded, shabby, and altogether inadequate to the needs of a professional regional theatre. At the same time, relocating and especially building a new facility will require a major fund-raising effort.

In 1992, the NJSF celebrated its thirtieth year and expanded from three to four Shakespearean productions and to two modern classics with a larger Equity company and additional artistic, technical, and managerial staff. In 1993, NJSF initiated a second program to mount productions of experimental or avant-garde works. The prospects that it will continue as an important regional festival remain promising.

Production History: 1963 (at Cape May): *Shr.*, *Come Blow Your Horn*, *The Hostage*, *Irma La Douce*, *Period of Adjustment*, *Rashomon*, *Rhinoceros*, *A Shot In the Dark*, *South Pacific*; 1964 (at Cape May): *R3*, *Anna Christie*, *Bus Stop*, *Mister Roberts*, *My Fair Lady*, *Night of the Iguana*, *Show Boat*, *Stop the World . . . I Want To Get Off*, *A Taste of Honey*, *A Thousand Clowns*; 1965 (at Cape May): *Ant.*, *Wiv.*, *The Fantasticks*, *A Funny Thing Happened on the Way to the Forum*, *The King and I*, *Luther*, *Mary, Mary*, *Never Too Late*, *The Rose Tattoo*, *Who's Afraid of Virginia Woolf?*; (at Natick and Lynn, Massachusetts): *H5*, *Mac.*, *Beyond the Fringe*, *Carnival*, *The Devils*, *How to Succeed in Business Without Really Trying*, *Incident at Vichy*, *Oklahoma: The Subject was Roses*, *You Can't Take it With You*; 1966 (at Cambridge and Natick, Massachusetts): *Ham.*, *JC*, *Shr.*; 1967: *JC*, *Ado*, *Any Wednesday*, *Barefoot in the Park*, *Funny Girl*, *Guys and Dolls*, *Inadmissible Evidence*, *Luv*, *Marat/Sade*, *The Sound of Music*; 1967 (at Cambridge and Natick): *Rom.*, *Oedipus Rex*, *The Rivals*; Summer, 1968: *MND*, *Oth.*, *The Apple Tree*, *The Birthday Party*, *Desire Under the Elms*, *Finian's Rainbow*, *The Odd Couple*, *The Owl and the Pussy Cat*, *Star Spangled Girl*, *Sweet Charity*; 1968: *Mac.* (school tour); 1969: *Spoon River Anthology* (*school tour*); 1970 (at Cape May): *Ham.*, *Tmp.*, *I Do, I Do*, *Man of La Mancha*, *Rosencrantz and Guildenstern are Dead*; 1971 (Tour of NJ schools): *The Rivalry*; 1972 (all subsequent seasons at Drew University): *Shr.*, *Tro.*, *Beyond the Fringe*, *The Bourgeois Gentleman*, *The Hostage*; 1973: *AYL*, *Cor.*, *Luther*, *Oh Dad, Poor Dad*, *Summer & Smoke*, *Home Free*, *Krapp's Last Tape*; 1974: *MM*, *R2*, *J.B.*, *Steam Bath*, *Under Milk Wood*, *The Dumbwaiter*, *The Tiger*; 1975: *1H4*, *2H4*, *TGV*, *John Brown's Body*, *The Lady's Not For Burning*, *Sweet Bird of Youth*, *That Championship Season*, *Uncle Vanya*, *Dark Lady of the Sonnets*, *To the Chicago Abyss*; 1976: *H5*, *Tmp.*, *The Best Man*, *The Devil's Disciple*, *Of Mice and Men*, *The Playboy of the Western World*, *Private Lives*, *Stop the World . . . I Want To Get Off*; 1977: *Ado*, *Tit.*, *Cyrano De Bergerac*, *An Enemy of the People*, *The Glass Menagerie*, *The Hot L Baltimore*; 1978: *Ham.*, *LLL*, *Arms and the Man*, *The Country Girl*, *Rosencrantz and Guildenstern are Dead*, *Who's Afraid of Virginia Woolf?*; 1979: *Lr.*, *MND*, *The Importance of Being Earnest*, *Luv*, *A Streetcar Named Desire*, *Travesties*, *Two for the Seesaw*, *Man Without A Country*; 1980: *Err.*, *Mac.*, *The Caretaker*, *A Christmas Carol*, *Knock, Knock*, *Volpone*, *Waltz of the Toreadors*; 1981: *Cym.*, *Rom.*, *DA*, *The Entertainer*, *Tartuffe*, *Vanities*; 1982: *Tim.*, *TN*, *Cat On A Hot Tin Roof*, *Fifth of July*, *Our Town*, *Wild Oats*; 1983: *The War of the Roses* (*1, 2, 3H6* and *R3*),

Beyond the Fringe, Born Yester-
day, Let's Get A Divorce, Mass
Appeal; **1984**: *MV, Oth., All the*
Way Home, The Crucible, School
for Scandal, The Sunshine Boys;
1985: *H8, Wiv., A Lesson From*
Aloes, Light Up The Sky, A Man
For All Seasons, The Plough and
the Stars; **1986**: *Ant., JC, TNK, A*
Child's Christmas in Wales, Hurly-
burly, Noises Off, Terra Nova;
1987: *Cor., Shr., WT, A Christmas*
Carol, The Dairy of Anne Frank,
Present Laughter, A Streetcar
Named Desire, Translations; **1988**:
AWW, Ham., TGV, A Moon For
the Misbegotten, On the Verge,

Rosencrantz and Guildenstern Are
Dead; **1989**: *AYL, Per., Tit., Night*
of the Iguana, Tom Jones, Waiting
for Godot; **1990**: *Jn., MM, Rom.,*
Death of a Salesman, A Life in the
Theatre; **1991**: *Tmp, TN, MND,*
The Skin of Our Teeth, Dark of the
Moon; **1992**: *Mac., 1H4, Ado, Shr.,*
The Importance of Being Earnest,
The Sea Gull; **1993**: *Arms and the*
Man, Ghosts, Shr., Oth., Err.,
MM., Venus and Adonis (a staged
reading); **1994**: *Rom., AYL., Wiv.,*
Electra, The Diary of a Scoundrel,
Man to Man, Goodnight Desde-
mona, Good Morning Juliet.

Research Resources: Paul and Ellen Barry maintain numerous records and documents for the New Jersey Shakespeare Festival at their home, while some other materials—production photographs, reviews and programs—are housed in the NJSF offices on the Drew University campus. I am indebted to the Barrys for information about the history of the NJSF, including Paul Barry's unpublished essay, "New Jersey Shakespeare Festival History: 1963-1990," and copies of reviews and programs. Productions of the NJSF were regularly reviewed in issues of *Shakespeare Quarterly* from the late 1970s to the mid-1980s and in *Shakespeare Bulletin* from 1987 to 1992.

Site visit: 16 July 1991; interviews: 16-17 July, September 1991,
Daniel J. Watermeier

NEW MEXICO

SHAKESPEARE IN SANTA FE. MAIL: P.O. Box 111, Santa Fe, NM 87501. SITE: Meem Library Courtyard at St. John's College. ADMINISTRA-TION/BOX OFFICE: 505/982-2910. ADMISSION: general admission, free; reserved seats, $15. SEASON: 21 performances in July and first half of August; 7:00 p.m., Fri.–Sun. PRINCIPAL STAFF: Rachel Kelly, producing artistic director; Sharon Merrill, managing director, Casey Cline, director of develop-ment. FACILITY: open-air courtyard. ANNUAL BUDGET: $150,000 (1993).

ANNUAL ATTENDANCE: 8,000-10,000 (1993). AUDITIONS: local in February. STATUS: community theatre. FOUNDED: 1987, Rachel Kelly, Steven Schwartz.

Founded in 1987 by Rachel Kelly and Steven Schwartz, Shakespeare in Santa Fe (SSF) was originally named Shakespeare in the Park. Plays were presented for three seasons at the Amelia White Park in Santa Fe, but the need for more space and a better facility led Kelly and Schwartz to look elsewhere. In 1991, SSF moved to the Meem Library Courtyard at St. John's College, where performances still take place, in Kelly's words, "outdoors under the dramatic New Mexico sky." SSF is building a strong partnership with the four-year liberal arts college, which has a tradition of offering a variety of educational and cultural events free to the public.

In keeping with the founders' belief that Shakespeare should be accessible to all people, general admission is free, but a membership program provides for reserved seating at $15 per person. A preshow concert begins one hour before performance, while hot and cold dinner items can be purchased at the Bard's Fare concession stand. SSF is funded in part by the Marshall L. and Perrine D. McCune Charitable Foundation, the Witter Bynner Foundation for Poetry, and the City of Santa Fe Arts Commission, as well as by a 1-percent lodgers' tax.

Schwartz served as producing director until 1992. Besides directing all productions, including the 1993 *Romeo and Juliet,* Schwartz directed the first season of the Shakespeare in the Schools outreach program, which took scenes from *A Midsummer Night's Dream* to over 5,000 students in 1992-93. Kelly, who played Luciana in *The Comedy of Errors*, Celia in *As You Like It*, Puck in *A Midsummer Night's Dream*, and Maria in *Twelfth Night*, became producing artistic director in 1993.

SSF prides itself on reflecting and responding to the local culture. The company letterhead incorporates a bright orange, yellow, and turquoise Pueblo border pattern. The program is filled with drawings by local artists: "We want to flavor every aspect of our company with the rich and colorful heritage that is alive in Santa Fe."

Production History: **1987**: *Err.*; **1988**: *AYL*; **1989**: *MND*; **1990**: dark; **1991**: *TN*; **1992**: dark; **1993**: *Rom.*

Felicia Hardison Londré

NEW YORK

ACTORS SHAKESPEARE COMPANY. MAIL: P.O. Box 85, Albany, NY 12260. SITE: Washington Park Parade Grounds, off Henry Johnson Blvd., in downtown Albany. ADMINISTRATION: 518/783-1971. ADMISSION: free. SEASON: three plays, 11–12 performances each, early July–mid-August; 8:00 p.m., Tues.–Sun. PRINCIPAL STAFF: Peter Greenberg, Jennifer Langsam, John Plummer, artistic directors; Harriet Sobol, managing director. FACILITY: open-air platform; seating on bleachers and blankets. AUDITIONS: Albany and New York City in February and March. STATUS: non-union contract. ANNUAL BUDGET: $95,000 (1991). ANNUAL ATTENDANCE: 6,000. FOUNDED: 1988, Peter Greenberg, John Plummer, Jennifer Langsam.

Actors Shakespeare Company (ASC), founded in 1988 by Peter Greenberg, Jennifer Langsam, and John Plummer, was created out of the desire of those actors to control their own work. A family connection through Langsam brought the three to Albany, New York. Langsam's mother, Harriet Sobol (now ASC's managing director), suggested that Langsam and her friends perform on the grounds of Sobol's new home when her husband was elected state commissioner of eduction. That invitation led to the start of a company. Sobol convinced the trio that Albany needed more theatre. Two productions, *Romeo and Juliet* and *Two Gentlemen of Verona*, were produced at the Sobols' home and on the Washington Park Parade Grounds in downtown Albany. These proved to be popular successes. Through Sobol's connections, the actors met community leader Vivienne Anderson, who introduced them to Mayor Thomas M. Whalen III and to the people at city hall. Those introductions resulted in an invitation to perform on the parade grounds on an ongoing basis. The ASC has received $10,000 from the city each year since 1989, as well as numerous in-kind services like the installation of a power pole and light towers. City workers help the troupe put up its stage every year, and city park rangers provide security.

Washington Park is a 223-acre park built between 1869 and 1880. The company erects a temporary stage on the corner of the eastern side of the park. Four sets of bleachers, plus an open area where people may bring their own blankets and chairs, provide seating for 300 people. Attendance averages 250 per performance. No sound amplification is used for actors' voices. Sets are built on the site, and costume shop space is provided by corporate sponsors. The company's administrative offices are located in the Albany Arts Studios.

The initial $11,500 budget was underwritten by the founders' personal friends and relatives. Sobol laughs: "Everybody who owed anybody anything was asked for a donation." The 1991 budget was $95,000, including a $7,125 grant from Albany's Community Development Block Grant program and $2,000 from the New York State Council on the Arts Decentralization Program. Other major contributors include the City of Albany, Norstar Bank, Key Corporation, Capital Newspapers, Columbia Development Group, NY Telephone, and First American Bank. Sobol stresses that the ASC gets very little big money but lots of smaller contributions. Major in-kind support is provided by Barry, Bette and Led Duke Construction Corporation, which provides rehearsal space and trailers; by the Albany College of Pharmacy, which provides housing for actors; and by the Whitehurst Press, which donates the printing. Sobol stresses that Mayor Whalen's commitment to cultural activities for all the people of Albany has played a major role in the ASC's success.

The permanent staff, in addition to the artistic directors and Sobol, includes associate director Vincent Murphy and associate managing director Caroline Jaczko. Jaczko also coordinates the outreach programs. The board of directors began with three members and, by 1991, had expanded to eleven. The major criterion for being on the board is a genuine support for the company's artistic work and philosophy. Rather than raising money, board members are asked to use their connections to acquire needed items. Sobol does most of the fund raising.

The original company was composed of friends of the three founding artistic directors. Now, besides special invitations to certain actors, the company holds auditions in New York and Albany in the spring. The acting company is composed of ten to fourteen core members who are cast in all the plays, plus additional actors as demanded by the season. The actors are non-Equity and, in 1991, were paid $107 per week for an 11-week contract. Housing and some transportation are also provided.

Albany is located in eastern New York. The major employer in this capital city of 100,000 is the state government. The three-city area of Albany, Schenectady, and Troy includes a potential audience of 300,000. The ASC's audience represents a cross-section of the population. Langsam describes the experience of attending one of their performances as similar to riding a bus in New York: You get all kinds of people sitting side by side. The majority of ASC's audience is between 18 and 35 years old. The downtown location draws inner-city residents. Many of the ASC's audience members had not previously been exposed to Shakespeare in performance. Greenberg was especially heartened by an audience member who wandered by during a dress rehearsal of *Measure for Measure* and stayed for the whole evening, commenting, "I've never been to a play before, but I'm coming back again to see this one." Greenberg adds: "I like to think that happens a lot."

Major marketing is accomplished through the newspapers. The *Times Union*, the *Saratogian*, and the *Daily Gazette* regularly publish preview articles and reviews. The performance schedule is carried in the *New York Times* (Arts and Leisure Guide) and various other publications.

The strengths of the company include the youthful enthusiasm and commitment of the artistic directors, combined with the strong support of the mayor and city hall. The company's commitment to social action through theatre is seen in its extensive outreach programs. Under the Theatre Nights program, sponsored by Norstar Bank of upstate New York, children are bused to performances from inner-city community centers. The company has also taken performances to boys' and girls' clubs, the YMCA, and the AIDS Ward at Albany Medical Center.

Problems include the need for better sound barriers between the performance area and that of another organization in the park that presents musicals to crowds of 2,000. (*My Fair Lady* could be heard throughout the evening at the Shakespeare performance this writer attended.) Additional concerns arise from the increasing administrative demands on the artistic directors' time, as well as the need for adequate compensation for this work. Artistic concerns include the difficulty of finding directors who share the ASC's aesthetic philosophy. (ASC has dismissed two directors in its first four years.) In the future, the company hopes to create a year-round home for itself in Albany and to include Equity guest artist contracts. Management's goals are to make more effective use of the board and volunteers and to place greater emphasis on long-range planning.

The ASC's stated mission is: "to present relevant, alive theatre that will both echo and theatricalize our lives. The company strives to attract a Capitol District audience that cuts across social, economic, and racial boundaries." In practice, this mission translates into actor-driven productions using simple designs. Directorial concepts are secondary to actors' needs. Plummer states: "We want a theatre where the actors are more important that the special effects." The ASC's directors work to make the language very understandable and clear, without demonstrating it or belittling it (Langsam). In order to create productions that are relevant to a contemporary audience, the company is developing an acting style that is physical, visceral, and energetic. The company is ensemble-oriented and frequently interacts with the audience. The ASC does cut the text and change the period—or, more often, makes up an original "historical" period.

Unlike many ASC productions, the 1991 presentation of *All's Well That Ends Well* was a relatively traditional period production. Marred by a lack of directorial vision and guidance (the director was dismissed midway through the rehearsal period), the production lacked a unity of theme and style. Overall, this production was more successful in mining the play's comic elements than in dealing with its serious undertones. Left to their own devices, several actors managed to shine. Most notable was Langsam's intelligent and determined Helena. She performed with urgency, charm, and sincerity. In her physically vibrant performance, she conveyed her love for Bertram, seeing some inherent good in him that was not apparent to the general public. Bertram, as played by Ted McClellan, was a snobbish and immature adolescent. It was easy to become impatient with Bertram for not seeing Helena's goodness. This production did little to answer the basic question of what she sees in him. Character actor David Constable played the clown Lavatch as a dwarf. A natural comic, Constable found the humor and the sexual innuendo, adding a grotesque element to his scenes. Greenberg as Lord Lafew was handsome and eloquent. Other actors were less successful in portraying some of the mature roles; some acting was marred by young actors' stereotypical choices in playing the older roles. The company came into its own with the Parolles taunting scene. Plummer as Parolles was extravagant, selfish, and comfortable with slapstick and force. The ASC's broad, bold, and energetic approach to Shakespeare shone in the latter half of the play. The unit setting, a two-level tavern-like structure, did more to support the battle scenes than to suggest the opulence of the court or the count's estate. The costumes, Victorian-period garments and khaki military uniforms, were serviceable but also did little to enhance the production.

Production History: **1988**: *Rom.*, *TGV*; **1989**: *MM*, *TN*; **1990**: *Mac.*, *AYL*, *AWW* (adaptation), *True West*; **1991**: *Molière's Shorts*, *JC*, *AWW*, *Coyote Ugly*; **1993**: *TGV*, *R3*; **1994**: *Err.*, *Ham.*

Research Resources: The Actors Shakespeare Company archives are informally maintained in its administrative offices. See also Dan Hulbert, "Polished Panic,"*American Theatre* 8 (July/August 1991): 5-6.

Site visit and interviews: 25 July 1991.
Cindy Melby Phaneuf

AMERICAN GLOBE THEATRE. MAIL: 145 West 46th Street, New York, NY 10036. SITE: The Studio, same as mail. ADMINISTRATION/BOX OFFICE: 212/869-9809. ADMISSION: $5–$12 (1993). SEASON: three to four productions presented consecutively for limited run, October through May. PRINCIPAL STAFF: (1993) John Basil, artistic director; Jacqueline Lowry, producing director; Angela Bond, general manager. FACILITIES: The Studio, flexible (capacity 74). AUDITIONS: New York. STATUS. Equity off-off-Broadway. ANNUAL BUDGET: $40,000 (1993). ANNUAL ATTENDANCE: 2,600 (1992). FOUNDED: 1988, John Basil.

The American Globe Theatre (AGT) was founded in the fall of 1988 by John Basil, mainly as a conservatory to train actors in what he calls the "Rough and Ready" method of presenting Shakespeare. Working from facsimiles of the First Folio, the rough and ready approach concentrates on the text as an emotional and musical blueprint, taking cues not only from the words themselves but also from idiosyncrasies of punctuation, spelling, capitalization, syntax, irregularities in meter, use of italics, and explicit or implicit stage directions. Influenced in part by various teachers at the **Royal Shakespeare Company**, especially John Barton and Patrick Tucker, Basil believes the rough and ready method approximates how Shakespeare's actors rehearsed their productions. Basil believes that by focusing on the spoken word in this fashion invigorates performances of Shakespeare, in particular, but also other classical and contemporary drama beyond the style of presentation typically seen on the American stage. (Basil's approach seems similar to that of Jan Powell at the **Tygres Heart Shakespeare Company** and Timothy Holcomb at the **Hampshire Shakespeare Company**.)

In the fall of 1989, Basil had a sufficient number of performers trained in his rough and ready approach to form a small repertory company and to present several productions each year. Generally, an AGT season consists of one or two Shakespearean plays, an American classic, a new American play, and workshops of new works being considered for full production. Actor training is central to the company's mission. On a continuing basis the conservatory offers a series of "Playing Shakespeare" courses, based on the rough and ready approach, as well as courses in voice and speech, stage combat, and audition techniques. By the early 1990s, over 300 individuals had been trained in the Rough and Ready method. The AGT has also offered on a fairly regular basis workshops, demonstrations, and performances of abridged versions of Shakespeare's plays to community groups, schools, churches, camps, and hospitals in the greater metropolitan New York area.

The company's earned income provides about 40 percent of its budget, with the remainder coming from a fairly extensive list of private and business contributions, ranging from $50 or less to over $2,000. In terms of planning, production, and day-to-day operations, the company relies on the shared commitment of a small year-round staff of six, on the members of the company, and on numerous volunteers.

Over the last several years, AGT productions have garnered critical praise for their clear, straightforward style. Writing in *Shakespeare Bulletin* (Fall 1993), Robert Kole, for example, praised Basil's production of *Julius Caesar* for "its straightforward emotions, perfect diction, and fully realized setting." The *mise-en-scène* suggested "a primitive future" with the male characters wearing "necklaces of plastic rings that suggest sado-masochistic rites." The female characters wore loose-flowing outfits and harem costumes. Appropriate to their mode of dress, the actions of Portia and Calpurnia were "overtly sexual" in their scenes with their respective husbands. Calpurnia, for example, wrapped her arms and legs around Caesar, "as if to seduce him away from going to the capitol." The setting consisted mainly of a Mayan-style pyramid, and the battle scenes evoked "the mechanized squealing of laser weapons and guided missiles." Despite the novel *mise-en-scène*, Kole thought the productions more notable for Richard Fay's "virile aggressive Brutus" and for its "violent passion than for its futuristic concept."

Production History: (Shakespeare productions only): **1990**: *AYL*, *Ado*, **1991**: *WT*; **1992-93**: *JC*; **1993-94**: *TN*.

Research Resources: John Basil maintains an informal collection of materials about the American Globe Theatre. This essay draws on materials furnished by him.

Daniel J. Watermeier

ARDEN PARTY. MAIL: 48 East 43rd Street, 7th floor, New York, NY 10017. SITE: Ohio Theatre, 66 Wooster Street, New York City. ADMINI-STRATION: 212/682-4181. ADMISSION: $12. SEASON: two to four productions, each running approximately four weeks. PRINCIPAL STAFF: Karin Coonrod, artistic director; Deborah Gunn, managing director. FACILITY: variable configuration (capacity 90–125). AUDITIONS: announced occasionally to supplement permanent company. STATUS: AEA mini-contract. ANNUAL BUDGET: $60,000 (1994). ANNUAL ATTENDANCE: 3,500 (estimated, 1993). FOUNDED: 1987, Karin Coonrod.

In 1987, after directing a production of *As You Like It*, Karin Coonrod decided to establish a company that would represent the aesthetic she had been exploring. The play itself suggested the company name, Arden Party (AP), which is intended to convey the idea of an expedition into a special world, followed by a return to the city, with a celebration of "new-found secrets." Coonrod describes her aesthetic as taking a "clown" approach while going to the heart of the material to create a theatrical world in brand-new territory. The plays are set in no specific location or time but rather in an imaginative space that is aesthetically highly organized and finds its specificity in truthful moments. Although the repertoire has included both modern and premodern classics, Coonrod claims that "Shakespeare is always in our imagination."

Sixteen members form the permanent company, including a designer, a dramaturg, a composer, and a playwright. Most productions, however, use only five or six actors. *Romeo and Juliet*, for example, had a cast of six, and *King Lear* five. There are exceptions, however, like *Love's Labour's Lost* with a "huge cast" of 17. Company members range in age from 26 to 40, and all can expect to play any type of role, as casting often goes against gender and age. "We are more concerned with meeting the soul of the character," says Coonrod. As a closely knit ensemble, AP members often participate in Saturday morning workshops, that serve as a springboard for production ideas. They think about shows for a long time before mounting them. According to Coonrod, "*King Lear* has been rumbling in our heads since 1988, and now we're finally getting into mounting it."

AP has been using the Ohio Theatre on Wooster Street since 1988. In addition, several summer productions have been mounted in New Jersey. During the summers of 1987, 1988, and 1989, AP used a dilapidated 1930s movie theatre in Sandy Hook, New Jersey, as well as an outdoor site that "looks like Scotland." The Ionesco program in 1990 was presented at the Count Basie Theatre in Red Bank, New Jersey. In 1991, readings of Molière and other authors were presented on the boardwalk in Asbury Park at 10:00 p.m. Ultimately, however, AP defined itself as a New York City company and decided to concentrate its attention and money there. School matinee performances of the last few productions have been quite successful. Eventually, AP plans to take programs into the schools. In 1993, AP was awarded its first major grant from the New York State Council on the Arts.

Production History: **1987**: *Shr.*, *Threepenny Opera*; **1988-1989**: *LLL,*; **1990-1992**: no Shakespeare. **1993**: *Rom.*, *The Beggar's Opera*; **1994**: *Lr.*, *Dr. Faustus*.

Research Resources: Arden Party's archives are maintained by Karin Coonrod. See John Bell, "Arden Party's Lear," *TheaterWeek* (6-12 June 1994): 16-17; Louis Charbonneau, "Off-Off-Broadway or Bust: Arden Party," *TheaterWeek* (4-10 January 1993): 20-23; Pamela Renner, "Romeo and Juliet," *Village Voice* (9 February 1993).

Telephone interview: 12 February 1994.
Felicia Hardison Londré

BLACKFRIARS TRAVELING SHAKESPEARE THEATRE. MAIL: 119 Jayne Avenue, Port Jefferson, NY 11777. SITES: as booked by theatres, libraries, schools, public and private groups. ADMINISTRATION/BOX OFFICE: 516/928-6045. ADMISSION: variable. SEASON: year-round. PRINCIPAL STAFF: Bill Van Horn, artistic director; Rita Schwartz, general manager; John Castiglione and Gene Durney, dramaturgs. FACILITY: no permanent space. STATUS: non-professional. ANNUAL BUDGET: $5,000. ANNUAL ATTENDANCE: 3,000. FOUNDED: 1987, Bill Van Horn, Rita Schwartz, and Robert C. Wheeler.

Theatre on Long Island is predominantly commercial. Nevertheless, local actors addicted to Shakespeare and other classics got in the habit of meeting with director Bill Van Horn to drink some beers and read the plays just so they could have a chance "to say those wonderful words." Contrary to their high school memories, they found that Shakespeare made them laugh and provoked discussion about interpretation. The enthusiasm of these actors led them to create the **Blackfriars Traveling Shakespeare Theatre** as a means of sharing their experience of the plays through performance. Bookings include local theatres, schools, clubs, and assorted performance spaces in New York City.

The company philosophy is that the essence of Shakespeare is "words, actors, and audience." Performances are designed to attract audiences who ordinarily would not attend "serious theatre." They emphasize the timeless plots and characters, and the actors strive to break the fourth wall by having the audience participate in scenes as townsfolk, soldiers, and so on. They use found props, no sets, and simple costuming. Reviewers have praised the avoidance of stilted delivery and the sense of fun that makes the plays accessible. The 1991 *As You Like It*, for example, was given an American Southern accent by setting the family feud in the bayou country around New Orleans. Cajun music, blues, gospel, and folk tunes were used for the script's musical moments, blending seamlessly with Shakespeare's words. *Newsday* cited the production as one of the best of the season on Long Island.

Production History: **1987**: *TN*; **1988**: *TN*; **1989**: *TN*; **1990**: *MND, The School for Scandal*; **1991**: *AYL, Cat Among the Pigeons*; **1992**: *WT; Wiv., Ado, The Good Woman of Setzuan*.

Research Resources: Archives for the Blackfriars Traveling Shakespeare Theatre are maintained by Rita Schwartz.

Felicia Hardison Londré

HOFSTRA UNIVERSITY ANNUAL SHAKESPEARE FESTIVAL. MAIL: Department of Drama and Dance, Hofstra University, Hempstead, NY 11550. SITE: Globe Stage of the John Cranford Adams Playhouse. ADMINISTRA-TION: Fax: 516/563-5444. BOX OFFICE: 516/463-6644. ADMISSION: $5–$6 for performances; lectures and symposia free. SEASON: various dates in March; 8:00 p.m., Thurs.–Sat.; 3:00 p.m., Sun. PRINCIPAL STAFF: Peter Sander, director. FACILITY: a five-sixths life-size replica of the John Cranford Adams model of the Globe playhouse (capacity 1,134). AUDITIONS: on campus for Hofstra students. STATUS: academic production with guest professional. ANNUAL BUDGET: approximately $13,000, plus a portion of faculty/staff salaries, including three full-time Adams playhouse technicians. ANNUAL ATTENDANCE: 7,500. FOUNDED: 1950, Bernard Beckerman, John Cranford Adams.

Every spring for 43 years, the entire campus of Hofstra University has been transformed into the world of William Shakespeare, with performances presented by the drama and music departments at the core of a three-week schedule of guest lectures, symposia, and activities for high school students. The focus of the festival is a five-sixths life-size Globe Stage. This stage is based upon the John Cranford Adams model, which was on display at the Folger Shakespeare Library in Washington D.C. from 1950 to 1984 and is now housed at Hofstra. Adams, who was president of Hofstra from 1944 to 1964, built a 32-inch-high model of the original Globe Playhouse as an outgrowth of his doctoral dissertation research at Cornell University. Its details replicate Tudor prototypes; for example, a central doorframe reproduces one at Ford's Hospital in Coventry, while the door itself duplicates one at Chantmarle in Dorset.

In 1951, Donald H. Swinney, designer-technical director of Hofstra's drama department, supervised the construction of the Globe Stage, which was then erected annually in Calkins Gymnasium for the festivals. Since the 1958 opening of the John Cranford Adams Playhouse, the Globe Stage has been set up there each season, an effort requiring 800 man hours for assembly and 300 hours for disassembly and storage. Among the distinguished artists who have performed with the students in the Shakespeare productions are William Hutt, Ted Kazanoff, and Patrick Duffy. Students who have participated in the festival and gone on to fame include Francis Ford Coppola, Madeline Kahn, Susan Sullivan, Peter Friedman, and Margaret Colin.

Peter Sander became chair of the department of drama in 1989, bringing his vast experience of professional Shakespeare production to the festivals and reinvigorating the tradition by presenting the first *Merchant of Venice*. He also brought in the noted Broadway and regional theatre director Larry Arrick as the first non-faculty director in the festival's history. Although some expressed concern that play's apparently anti-Semitic content could arouse strong feelings, Sander proved justified in his feeling that "the community would be open and not react in a fanatical, bigoted way."

The forty-second Annual Shakespeare Festival offerings, from 7 to 17 March 1991, typified the usual range of events. Seven performances of *Hamlet,* directed by Sander, set the theme. The Hofstra Collegium Musicum, directed by William E. Hettrick, presented *Night and Day,* a program of medieval and renaissance musical selections thematically chosen to reflect the night and day imagery in *Hamlet.* Remy Charlip's *Young Omelet,* a Freudian dramatic offshoot of *Hamlet,* shared the musicale's bill for three performances. Charlip was also that semester's John Cranford Adams Distinguished Visiting Professor. Pre-festival activities included February lectures by W. Thomas MacCary and Steven Urkowitz and the first of two symposia on *Hamlet.* During the festival period, high school dramatic societies presented two programs of scenes from Shakespeare. A tour of the Globe Stage was also available. James J. Kolb prepared an impressive study guide for the department.

Production History: **1950**: *JC*; **1951**: *1H4*; **1952**: *TN*; **1953**: *Mac.*; **1954**: *Ado*; **1955**: *Oth.*; **1956**: *R3*; **1957**: *AYL*; **1958**: *Ham.*; **1959**: *Wiv.*; **1960**: *Rom.*; **1961**: *LLL*; **1962**: *Tmp.*; **1963**: *MND*; **1964**: *JC*; **1965**: *Shr.*; **1966**: *TN*; **1967**: *Rom.*; **1968**: *AYL*; **1969**: *Err., The*

Boys from Syracuse; **1970**: *Ham.*; **1971**: *Wiv.*; **1972**: *R3*; **1973**: *MM*; **1974**: *MND*; **1975**: *LLL*; **1976**: *Ado*; **1977**: *Rom.*; **1978**: *TGV*; **1979**: *WT*; **1980**: *TN*; **1981**: *Mac.*; **1982**: *Shr.*; **1983**: *AYL*; **1984**: *MND*; **1985**: *Tmp.*; **1986**: *Rom.*; **1987**: *Err.*; **1988**: *TN*; **1989**: *MV, It Happened in Venice*; **1990**: *Oth., The Tragedy of Tragedies, or Tom Thumb*; **1991**: *Ham., Young Omelet*; **1992**: *MM*.

Research Resources: John Cranford Adams's model of the Globe is exhibited on the ninth floor of the library in the Hofstra Cultural Center. The festival archives are maintained at the university. See also: Barbara Delatiner, "Hofstra to Offer Offbeat 'Merchant,'" *New York Times* (5 March 1989); Irwin Smith, *Shakespeare's Globe Playhouse* (New York: Charles Scribner's Sons, 1956); which deals with Adams' reconstruction and includes detailed plans.

Felicia Hardison Londré

HUDSON VALLEY SHAKESPEARE FESTIVAL. MAIL: 155 Main Street, Cold Spring-on-Hudson, New York, 10516. SITE: Boscobel Restoration, Garrison-on-Hudson, New York. ADMINISTRATION: 137 Main St., Cold Spring-on-Hudson, NY 10516; 914/264-7858. BOX OFFICE: 914/265-9575. ADMISSION: $14–$22 (1992). SEASON: one production presented for 19 performances, including two previews, from early July to early August; 8:00 p.m., Wed.–Sun. PRINCIPAL STAFF: Melissa Stern, producing director (Susan Landstreet succeeded Stern as producing director in 1993); Terrence O'Brien, artistic director. FACILITY: open stage inside a tent (capacity 300). AUDITIONS: New York City in April. STATUS: Equity SPT. ANNUAL BUDGET: $130,000 (1992). ANNUAL ATTENDANCE: 3,585 (1991). FOUNDED: 1987, Melissa Stern, Terrence O'Brien.

The Hudson Valley Shakespeare Festival (HVSF) was founded in 1987 by Melissa Stern and Terrence O'Brien. They had both studied acting at the American Conservatory Theatre in San Francisco in the late 1970s and then pursued careers on the West Coast and in New York City. In 1986, Stern married and took up residence in her husband's home in Cold Spring-on-Hudson, a village on the east bank of the Hudson River, directly across from West Point, about a one hour drive north of New York City. Asking herself "What am I going to do up here?," she thought she would start her own theatre in which she could continue to act. In 1987, she invited O'Brien to coproduce and direct *A Midsummer Night's Dream* at the Manitoga Nature Center in Garrison with the assistance of the 29th Street Project, Inc., a not-for-profit collective of professional theatre artists working in New York City.

The production was staged in an open meadow. The actors dressed in casual contemporary clothing and colorful high-top canvas sneakers; a simple but clever lighting design, helped by flashlights carried by the actors, illuminated both the performers and highlighted the natural beauty of the performance site. Despite rain and the fact that access to the meadow was via a primitive, candle-lit forest path, several hundred enthusiastic patrons attended five performances in mid-September, often sitting beneath umbrellas. The reviewer for the nearby *Poughkeepsie Journal* (16 September 1987) commended the interpretation, as well as the skill and talent of the performers, noting that Stern and O'Brien had "a good head start" in their ambition to produce an annual Shakespeare festival.

Thus encouraged, they assembled a board of directors and incorporated as The Hudson Valley Shakespeare Festival. They also moved their performance site from the Manitoga Nature Center to a large yellow-and-white tent erected on the spacious lawn of Boscobel, a restored nineteenth-century country mansion that has been acclaimed as an outstanding example of domestic architecture of the Federal period. Opened as a public museum in 1961, the house, with its famous gardens and superb view of the Hudson River Highlands, attracts hundreds of visitors, particularly during the summer months. Indeed, the tent is so situated that the Highlands provide a natural backdrop to the performances, especially impressive at sunset and twilight. Theatre patrons are invited to picnic on the grounds before the performance (the only time when this activity is allowed).

Gradually over the next four years, Stern and O'Brien nurtured their festi-val. Their approach to presenting Shakespeare's plays has remained consistently centered on actors and the text. Unlike many festivals of comparable size, HVSF spends five weeks in rehearsal, much of the time spent focusing on careful text analysis, with the aim, according to Stern, "to tell the story as clearly and understandably and essentially as possible." They eschew the trappings of elaborate production, choosing instead a minimalist approach to costumes, setting, lighting, and properties. In fact, after choosing a production style, usually centered in some decade of the twentieth century, actors are required to find their own costumes by rummaging through local antique and old clothing shops. This activity is viewed as part of the process of developing their characters. (The HVSF then pays a costume rental fee to the actors, in accordance with their Equity contract.) Scenery is confined to essential pieces of furniture, and properties also are kept to the bare minimum.

As Stern and O'Brien honed their production approach, they began to attract attention beyond their immediate locale. The distinguished critic of *The New Yorker*, Mimi Kramer, wrote about the production of *Twelfth Night* (21 August 1989) that it "boasted lively intelligent acting, a lucid, moving reading of the play, and a good deal of directorial panache—all of which created an esprit de corps on both sides of the metaphorical footlights that were not used to witnessing at open-air productions of Shakespeare." She went on to compare favorably the acting by "virtual unknowns" to a performance of *Twelfth Night* running simultaneously at the celebrated **New York Shakespeare Festival** in

Central Park. Indeed, the critic for the Gannett *Westchester* newspaper (26 July 1989) thought that, "as a pure acting job," the HVSF *Twelfth Night* was "far superior to the one in Central Park." Alvin Klein of the *New York Times* called the HVSF production of *Much Ado About Nothing* (14 July 1990) "enchanting." By 1991, the HVSF was playing to a total of over 3,500 patrons at 14 virtually sold-out performances, had a box office gross of over $55,000, and was attracting additional financial support from numerous individuals and the New York State Council on the Arts.

The production of *Romeo and Juliet* that I saw in 1991 evoked the 1950s, with the young men sporting sunglasses, jeans, and T-shirts or wild Hawaiian print shirts and the young women in A-line skirts, ponytail hairdos, and Capezio shoes. Capulet made his first appearance carrying a bag of golf clubs. The incidental music—a doo-wop version of "I Only Have Eyes For You," for example, in the ballroom scene—enhanced the evocation of the milieu. But 1950s gimmickry never overwhelmed the story, the language, or the character relationships. Indeed, the strength of the production remained firmly centered on the acting, which was totally natural, unpretentious, and clear. Each character was individualized, but the company as a whole remained a carefully tuned ensemble. Director O'Brien's staging was simple but frequently imaginative. That Juliet was on a balcony, for example, was indicated by having her stand on a plain wooden step ladder. There was also a considerable amount of surprising but not inappropriate humor. Ultimately, as the Gannett *Westchester* newspaper critic observed (17 July 1991), the HVSF production "delivers the tragic tale of the star-crossed lovers with its emotional power intact." In its own way, in fact, this was one of the most effective productions of *Romeo and Juliet* that I have seen to date. The audience, drawn from all over the Hudson Valley, Westchester County, and New York City and ranging in age from retirees to teenagers, applauded enthusiastically at the curtain call.

With its expansion in performances in 1992, the HVSF added a third year-round employee, a managing director, to its administrative staff, but the festival remains—perhaps astutely so—modest in size and ambitions. In 1993, Stern did announce, however, her intention to expand to two productions in 1994.

Production History: **1987**: *MND*; **1988**: *AYL*; **1989**: *TN*; **1990**: *Ado*; **1991**: *Rom.*; **1992**: *Shr.*; **1993**: *Wiv.*; **1994**: *Mac., Err.*

Research Resources: An informal archive of programs, reviews, photographs, newsletters, and so on is maintained at the Hudson Valley Shakespeare Festival office.

Site visit and interviews: 17-18 July 1991.
Daniel J. Watermeier

KINGS COUNTY SHAKESPEARE COMPANY. MAIL: 155 Henry Street, # 8B, Brooklyn, NY, 11201. SITES: Various locations in Brooklyn and Manhattan. ADMINISTRATION/BOX OFFICE: 718/596-9685. ADMISSION: varies; performances in Prospect Park and other outdoor locations usually free. SEASON: three major productions per year, normally include a summer production the Prospect Park Bandshell in Brooklyn and a winter production in Manhattan. PRINCIPAL STAFF: Deborah Wright Houston, artistic director, producer; Liz Shipman, associate artistic director. FACILITY: no permanent facility. AUDITIONS: open and Equity auditions during the year in Brooklyn and Manhattan. STATUS: Equity LOA. ANNUAL BUDGET: $50,000 (1993). ANNUAL ATTENDANCE: 8,000 (1993). FOUNDED: 1983, Deborah Wright Houston, Liz Shipman.

The genesis of the Kings County Shakespeare Company occurred in 1983 when Deborah Wright Houston and Liz Shipman were invited to produce a program for Shakespeare Day at the Brooklyn Botanic Gardens. The resulting *Shakespeare Sampler*, directed by Houston, was a quick success. The company was incorporated, and the program was repeated in 1984. With support from the New York State Council on the Arts and the Brooklyn Arts and Culture Association, in 1985 the company produced *The Tempest*, directed by Houston, and *As You Like It*, directed by Geoffrey Owens, at various sites in Brooklyn and in Manhattan's Central Park. According to Houston and Shipman, it was the Central Park performances that attracted the attention of Steven L. Zimmer, who joined the company as director-in-residence from 1986 to 1990. Zimmer's 1986 production of *The Winter's Tale* at the Picnic House in Prospect Park marked the beginning of a continuing association with The Fund for the Borough of Brooklyn's "Celebrate Brooklyn" program. The company's first production for "Celebrate Brooklyn" in the 1,000-seat Prospect Park Bandshell was Zimmer's *All's Well That Ends Well* in 1987. In 1988, he restaged *The Winter's Tale* in the band shell in a production that featured Houston as Hermione and Charles Stanley as Leontes. Set in the kingdom of Russia in the Renaissance, this production was critically acclaimed and is regarded by Houston and Shipman as an embodiment of the company's high artistic aspirations and public success. Having remained with the company since *Winter's Tale*, Stanley recently directed *Genet/Hamlet* (1992), which featured an all-male ensemble in a that which evoked the European prison system of the 1930s. The Prospect Park Bandshell production *Much Ado About Nothing* in 1991 was set during the woman suffrage movement and directed by Judy Goldman. The company returned in 1992 with *Romeo and Juliet* directed by Houston. In the face of diminishing financial support from municipal sources, the company finds itself in a transitional phase in which it seeks to diversify and strengthen its financial resources while maintaining ties to the borough of Brooklyn where it is undeniably popular and welcome.

The Kings County Shakespeare Company is informally organized with no permanent administrative or performance space. Various aspects of the operation—everything from mailing lists to costume storage—are maintained by the principal company staff at their residences. A local church has donated rehearsal and storage space, and additional rehearsal space is frequently rented. Though the lack of permanent facilities may be seen as a hindrance to production, Houston and Shipman declare that the advantages far outweigh the difficulties. Most importantly, this situation insures that theirs will always be an actor-centered company. Also, it allows the company to channel all its funds into production and removes the large financial burdens associated with maintaining a facility. The company has always used Equity performers, occasionally assisted by non-Equity personnel, and has always operated with Equity approval. All personnel, including the artistic directors, are paid fees on a show-by-show or task-specific basis. The company is incorporated as a nonprofit organization.

The company's mission is concisely stated in its own promotional materials: "Our mission is to serve our Community by presenting superior and affordable productions of Shakespeare's plays and classic plays of all ages and cultures, to develop an accessible American Classical style of acting, to encourage community participation on all levels, and to establish Brooklyn as the home of a nationally acclaimed theatre company." The first objective has clearly been met, and though the company has not done so on a regular basis, it did go beyond Shakespeare in 1989 with *The Way of the World* and in 1991 with productions of *The Changeling* and *Alice 91* (an adaptation from Lewis Carroll). Its most ambitious and interesting objective is the development of "an accessible American Classical style of acting." According to Houston and Shipman, this goal represents a process, rather than a specific acting style, in which directors and actors seek to integrate their traditional American training, which is oriented toward emotional truthfulness in performance, with work in voice, verse-speaking, and movement. Accessibility within this context refers to emotional, physical, and vocal truth that is readily apparent to audiences. Accessibility also refers to avoiding English accents, or "Shakespearean diction," and to employing staging strategies that support and enhance language. The primary means that the company has to involve its community is to go to its audiences in the parks and in other locations. The company is committed to using members of the community in its productions, both on stage and off, and Houston addresses each audience to invite the playgoers' participation. She looks forward to the eventual establishment of a participatory guild. Additionally, the company draws its board of directors and its principal financial support from Brooklyn.

I observed first-day rehearsals for *Romeo and Juliet*. Houston chose an early Renaissance Veronese setting for the production because she believed that this transitional age reflected the vigor and the idealism of the star-crossed lovers, as well as their unhappy situation. Before the formal, Equity-sanctioned rehearsals, of which this was the first, Houston and Shipman had held a series of process workshops to which the cast was invited on a voluntary basis. The value of these workshops was immediately apparent to me as I watched Shipman choreograph a movement piece for the whole company to perform during the prologue. With driving, strident, medieval music in the background, masked Capulets and Montagues constantly interposed themselves between Romeo and Juliet while they performed an allegorical dance based upon such childhood games as "Red Rover," "Ring Around The Rosey," and "Streets and Alleys." Shipman derived her choreography from games developed during the workshops, and they were instantly recognized by the company. I also watched a session in which Juliet and the Nurse went through an exploration of Act II, scene 5, under the guidance of Houston. Houston discussed objectives and circumstances with both actors and asked them to improvise the scene with a set of objectives, which she provided secretly to each. This trademark technique of company rehearsals stimulates creativity and spontaneity by encouraging actors to improvise, rather than arrange, their responses to each other. Houston explained that the use of these exercises was precisely what she meant when discussing her intention to develop a "classical" acting process for American actors. She believes that Americans should not abandon their tried-and-true methods when faced with Shakespeare or other classical texts.

Production History: **1983**: *A Shakespeare Sampler I*; **1984**: *A Shakespeare Sampler II*; **1985**: *Tmp.*, *AYL*; **1986**: *WT*, *Ado*, *TGV*; **1987**: *TN*, *Shr.*, *AWW*, *AWW*; **1988**: *Rom.*, *Err.*, *WT*; **1989**: *The Way of the World*, *Per.*, *MM*; **1990**: *Mac.*, *AYL*, *MND*; **1991**: *The Changeling*, *Alice 91*, *Ado*; **1992**: *Genet/ Hamlet*, *Rom.*; **1993**: *Oth.*; **1994**: *Tmp.*

Research Resources: Deborah Wright Houston maintains photo albums for most Kings County Shakespeare Company productions. See also the following selected publications:

Kantor, Michael. "Southern-Fried Shakespeare in B'klyn." *Newsday* (26 June 1990): 2:11,13.

Kole, Robert. "*As You Like It* and *A Midsummer Night's Dream*." *Shakespeare Bulletin* (Fall 1990): 28.

Parker, Barbara. "*Much Ado About Nothing*." *Shakespeare Bulletin* (Fall 1991): 43.

Site visit and interviews: 25 July 1992.
Maarten Reilingh

NATIONAL SHAKESPEARE COMPANY. MAIL: 414 West 51st Street, New York, NY 10019. SITES: variable. ADMINISTRATION: 212/265-1340. ADMISSION: varies. SEASON: 8–10 weeks in fall, 14 weeks in spring, 3–4 weeks in summer; about 100 performances. PRINCIPAL STAFF: Elaine Sulka, artistic director; T. Walker Rice, tour director. AUDITIONS: three times a year, in New York City. STATUS: non-Equity. ANNUAL BUDGET: $400,000 (1991). ANNUAL ATTENDANCE: 90,000 (estimated). FOUNDED: 1963, Philip Meister, Elaine Sulka.

The National Shakespeare Company (NSC) was founded by a husband-and-wife team, the late director Philip Meister (1926-1982) and actress Elaine Sulka. Sulka had acted with the now-defunct **American Shakespeare Theatre** and the San Diego National Shakespeare Festival. In 1963, she and Meister founded their own company, Stagecraft Productions, with the mission of taking the classics, primarily Shakespeare, to people and places whose access to them was limited by economics or geography. The first tour of Stagecraft Productions was to New York metropolitan area high schools for six weeks in the spring of 1964. In 1965, the company was incorporated as the NSC, and, by 1966, it was playing at colleges and universities in communities from coast to coast and border to border. Although colleges, universities, and community arts councils became the primary sponsors of the NSC, it continued until 1989 serving secondary schools in Pittsburgh, San Antonio, Chicago, Los Angeles, and Detroit with special 90-minute school matinee versions of Shakespeare plays.

The NSC presents fully mounted productions in straightforward interpretations that emphasize fidelity to the text and clarity of word and action. The period costuming tends to be traditional, although liberties are sometimes taken, especially with the comedies. The simple settings can be put up in an hour by the actors, who are their own crew, along with eight helpers supplied by the sponsor. The self-contained company carries its own light and sound equipment and can perform in almost any type of facility.

The 12-member acting ensemble is non-union. It is currently recruited from the New York market through ads in *Backstage*. Major professional theatre-training programs—for example, New York University's Tisch School of the Arts, Carnegie Mellon, ACT, and the Goodman—are invited to submit talent. The NSC has a long history of interracial, nontraditional casting. Up to 25 percent of the ensemble each season has been composed of minority actors. Dan Snow, an African-American who has toured with the NSC for about ten seasons, has played not only Othello but also Shylock, Petruchio, King Lear, Creon, and Prospero. Among the NSC actors who have gone on to fame are Jeffrey DeMunn, Karen Black, Dana Ivey, Steve Root, Gregory Sierra, Christopher Curry, Sharon Martin, and Gina Bellafonte.

Over the history of the NSC, we have seen a number of their touring productions, which, in the 1970s especially, seemed to adhere to a fairly high level of performance with a company of young but generally skillful actors. In recent years, however, the NSC performances that we have seen have been decidedly uneven. In 1991, for example, NSC's *King Lear* was a clear, well-paced, and altogether competent production, with Dan Snow powerful and compelling in the title role. In contrast, the 1992 production of *Othello,* set in the Edwardian period, unfortunately was rather amateurish. Indeed, the acting of Othello and Iago was often so broad that it provoked inappropriate laughter from the college student audience, many of whom left the performance at intermission. Undoubtedly, there are many factors contributing to this unevenness, but, considering that the NSC is one of the few companies touring Shakespeare productions to college campuses, one might hope that it would strenuously guard against a diminution of it traditionally high artistic standards.

The NSC has also been involved in the operation of the Cubiculo Experimental Arts Center at its New York headquarters. While the NSC's touring company emphasizes the classical and the traditional, the Cubiculo concentrates on presenting new American playwrights, choreographers, composers, and poets. In 1974, the NSC inaugurated the National Shakespeare Conservatory for actor training. The school was accredited in 1977 and became a separate entity in 1983.

Although the NSC is a not-for-profit company, it operates basically on earned income and has never received major outside funding. The NSC's 1994 fees were $4,800 for a single performance during the regular season and $3,500 for the summer. Lower fees are possible under special circumstances. Ticket prices are set by the local sponsor.

Production History: 1963-64: *Shakespeare's World, Shr.*; 1964-65: *Shakespeare's World, Shr., Mac.*; 1965-66: *Ham., Mac., AYL*; 1966-67: *JC, Ham., Ado, Shakespeare's World*; 1967-68: *TN, Rom., Volpone*; 1968-69: *Shr., Oth., Murder in the Cathedral*; 1969-70: *Mac., Tmp., School for Wives*; 1970-71: *Ado, Ham., Oedipus Rex*; 1971-72: *TN, Rom., She Stoops to Conquer*; 1972-73: *MND, Lr., Antigone*; 1973-74: *Saint Joan, AYL, JC*; 1974-75: *TGV, The Miser, MV*; 1975-76: *Ado, Tmp., Mac.*; 1976-77: *Rom.,* *TN, Err.*; 1977-78: *Oth., AYL, WT*; 1978-79: *MND, Ham.*; 1979-80: *Ado, JC*; 1980-81: *Rom., R3, Err.*; 1981-82: *Shr., R2, Tmp.*; 1982-83: *AYL, MND, Lr.*; 1983-84: *TN, Ham., Ado*; 1984-85: *Mac., TGV*; 1985-86: *Err., MV, Oth.*; 1986-87: *Rom., Shr.*; 1987-88: *Tmp., JC, MND, The Importance of Being Earnest*; 1988-89: *AYL, Oedipus Rex, TN*; 1989-90: *Ham., She Stoops to Conquer*; 1990-91: *Lr., Ado*; 1991-92: *Mac., Shr.*; 1992-93: *Oth., Err.*; 1993-94: *Tmp., Rom.*

Research Resources: Archives for the National Shakespeare Company are maintained by the company.

Interview: Kansas City, 23 September 1990.
Felicia Hardison Londré and Daniel J. Watermeier

NEW YORK RENAISSANCE FESTIVAL. MAIL: Creative Faires, Ltd.; 134 Fifth Avenue, New York, NY 10011. SITE: Sterling Forest, Tuxedo, NY. ADMINISTRATION: 212/645-1630 (June-October). BOX OFFICE: 914/351-5171 (June-October). ADMISSION: Festival admission includes all theatre performances: $13.00 adults, $11.00 seniors, $5.00 children. SEASON: August to late September, also Labor Day, Sat., Sun. PRINCIPAL STAFF: Barbara Hope, Donald C. Gatti, creators and executive producers/directors; Sherry Nehmer, artistic director; Gail Winar, managing director. FACILITY: the Globe Stage, an outdoor open stage with architectural facade (capacity 800); six additional outdoor stages are available. AUDITIONS: "Strawhat" and open calls in April in New York City. STATUS: AEA-LOA. ANNUAL BUDGET: $100,000 (1992, estimated Shakespeare-in-the-Forest series only). ANNUAL ATTENDANCE: Faire attracts 155,000–180,000 annually. FOUNDED: 1977, Barbara Hope, Donald C. Gatti.

The annual New York Renaissance Festival (NYRF) offers a "living recreation of a sixteenth-century English country faire, featuring 250 costumed actors, stunt fighters, musicians, folk artists, storytellers and specialty acts plus a bustling Tudor-style marketplace filled with crafts, games, food and drink" (Festival Fact Sheet). Within its busy 65-acre setting is a variety of theatrical presentations, including actual jousting on horseback, the Living Chess Game (in which the chess pieces fight to win their squares), scenes from *The Tales of Robin Hood*, *Christopher Confusion* (in which, with the help of the audience, tales of Christopher Columbus are reinvented), *Instant Shakespeare* (an improvisation show), Richard Wagner's *The Ring* (performed by the Bennington Marionettes), and two Equity productions in 1992: *The Winter's Tale* and Molière's *The Mischievous Machinations of Scapin*.

According to producer Barbara Hope, the NYRF has been, since its inception, a continually evolving event. She and coproducer Donald C. Gatti have always relied upon and welcomed the creative input of both their artistic staff and their audiences. Several years of collaboration with the first artistic director, Richard Klees, led to the formal institution of the Shakespeare-in-the-Forest series in 1981. Klees was artistic director until he left the festival in 1990. He was succeeded by the current artistic director, Sherry Nehmer. The objective of the Shakespeare-in-the-Forest series is to put professional-quality Shakespeare productions in an affordable and accessible context for family audiences. The series succeeds precisely because it presents Shakespeare in the festival setting. As Hope points out, knowing that they can leave the outdoor theatre at any time reduces the fears of typical family audience members. By the time they arrive at the Globe Theatre, audiences have joined a community of participants, and their ears have been tuned to "ye courtly speech." The festival setting, notes Nehmer, also creates some limits for Shakespearean production in style and approach. Though they might not require the strictest historical accuracy, audiences at a Renaissance festival do have some expectation that the production will have a historical look and feel.

I witnessed opening-day performances of *Scapin* and *The Winter's Tale*. Heavy doses of interaction between audiences and performers helped to establish a feeling of community between the two groups. This feeling and a broadly comic style of acting were utilized to great effect by the players of *Scapin* on the Silver Swan Stage, a simple open-air platform surrounded by wooden benches and bleachers. *The Winter's Tale* was presented at the Globe Stage. Its relative distance from other attractions allows for a small measure of subtlety that is not possible in other locations. The production was conventionally staged by Sherry Nehmer in period costumes and a simple Elizabethan-style setting. Adding to the Renaissance ambiance was a small musical ensemble led by music director Grant Herreid. Unburdened by gimmickry, Shakespeare's text and the festival actors overcame the distractions of outdoor presentation and made solid contact with an appreciative audience. Richard P. Gang's Autolycus was most entertaining as he described with great relish and precision how the shepherd's son would be tortured and put to death (Act IV, scene 4). The moving final scene of the unveiling of the "statue" of Hermione was firmly anchored by the sincerity and wonder of Jeffrey Edward Peter's remorseful Leontes, and the authority of Jackie Maruschak's Paulina.

Production History (limited to Shakespeare-in-the-Forest series): **1978-80**: *Scenes from Shakespeare*; **1981**: *Ado*; **1982**: *Shr.*; **1983**: *MND*; **1984**: *TN*; **1985**: *Rom.*; **1986**: AYL; **1987**, *Mac.*; **1988**, TGV; **1989**: AWW; **1990**: *Err.*; **1991**: *Ado*; **1992**: *WT*; **1993**: *MND*; **1994**: *Wiv.*

Research Resources: Archives are informally maintained at the New York Renaissance Festival administrative office.

Site visit: 1 August 1992; interviews: 6 and 19 September 1992.
Maarten Reilingh

NEW YORK SHAKESPEARE FESTIVAL. MAIL: 425 Lafayette St., New York, NY 10003. SITES: Delacorte Theater in Central Park, Joseph Papp Public Theater stages. ADMINISTRATION: 212/598-7100. BOX OFFICE: Public Theater, 212/598-7150; Delacorte Theater, 212/869-7277. ADMISSION: free in Central Park; Public Theater stages, $27.50–$30.00. SEASON: year-round; 8:00 p.m., Tues.–Sun.; 3:00 p.m., Wed.; Delacorte: June–September only, 8:00 p.m. PRINCIPAL STAFF: George C. Wolfe, artistic director; Jason Steven Cohen, producing director; Rosemarie Tichler, associate artistic director; Robert W. Pittman, board chairman. FACILITY:

Newman Theater, proscenium capacity 299); Martinson Hall, flexible (capacity 190); LuEsther Hall, flexible (capacity 150); Little Theater, flexible (capacity 99); Susan Stein Shiva Theater, flexible (capacity 100); Anspacher Theater, 3/4 arena (capacity 275); Delacorte Theater, outdoor thrust (capacity 1,932). AUDITIONS: contact business office. STATUS: AEA, LORT (B), and Off-Broadway contracts. ANNUAL BUDGET: $15,000,000 (1990-91). FOUNDED: 1954, Joseph Papp.

Perhaps no other name in late twentieth-century New York is more closely associated with that of Shakespeare than that of Joseph Papp, and perhaps no other Shakespeare festival in the United States has made free outdoor Shakespeare more a family tradition than the New York Shakespeare Festival (NYSF). Born in Brooklyn in 1921, Joseph Papp began directing Off-Broadway in 1952 and in the same year became a stage manager for the CBS television programs *I've Got a Secret* and *Studio One*. In 1953, he organized the Shakespeare Workshop, later to be renamed the NYSF, at the Emmanuel Presbyterian Church to explore poetic drama and the English classics. In 1954, Papp received a provisional charter from the New York Educational Department to establish a nonprofit theatre to "encourage and cultivate interest in poetic drama with emphasis on the works of William Shakespeare and his Elizabethan contemporaries, and to establish an annual summer Shakespeare Festival." The first production was called "An Evening with Shakespeare and Marlowe," followed by "Shakespeare's Women," *As You Like It, Much Ado About Nothing, Cymbeline,* and *Titus Andronicus,* all in 1955. In 1956, Papp took *Julius Caesar* and *The Taming of the Shrew* outdoors for the first time to the East River Amphitheatre. In 1957, with financial assistance from grant money, Papp purchased a truck and built a 45-foot platform stage to tour the five boroughs of New York City. Ironically, the mobile stage broke down in Central Park, and Papp decided to stay put there and perform. Thus was born America's classic tradition of Shakespeare in the Park. From the beginning, Papp's productions were free. Surviving many battles with the New York parks department in the late 1950s over the issue of charging admission and trampling the grass, Papp attracted many wealthy patrons and grants from foundations to support the NYSF. Papp was a firm believer in federal subsidies for the arts and was joined in his quest for funds by Bernard Gersten, who served as associate producer from 1960 until 1978. In 1961, with funds from the parks department and a gift of $150,000 from publisher George T. Delacorte, the new permanent outdoor theatre in Central Park, named the Delacorte Theater, opened on 18 June 1962 with *The Merchant of Venice,* starring George C. Scott as Shylock. By 1964, the NYSF had expanded its production activity to parks in all five of New York's boroughs, thanks to the acquisition of a mobile theatre consisting of several trailers and a portable stage unfolded from a 40-foot trailer bed. The NYSF inspired both the Metropolitan

Opera and the New York Philharmonic to offer free performances in Central Park.

Papp sought to expand the venue of the NYSF to produce contemporary works. In 1965, he purchased the old Astor Library in the East Village, and, in 1967, the first stage of the new Public Theater opened with the musical *Hair*. There were many financial problems, but, in the end, the city of New York purchased the landmark building for $2.6 million and in return leased the space to the NYSF for one dollar a year. By 1977, the NYSF was operating eight stages: the Newman Theater (proscenium, 299 seats); the Anspacher Theater (three-quarter arena, 275 seats); the Martinson Hall/Cabaret Theatre (flexible, 190 seats); the LuEsther Hall (flexible, 135-150 seats); the Other Stage (flexible, 75-108 seats); the Old Prop Shop Theater (flexible, 55-93 seats); the Delacorte Theater in Central Park (thrust, 1,932 seats); and the Mobile Theater (flexible, capacity 1,500). Over the years, the Public Theater has expanded to include a large exhibition area and now houses five stages (see FACILITIES in main heading). The NYSF's operating budget has expanded from $9,954,419 in 1976-77 to $15,000,000 in 1990-91.

The diversity and richness of the NYSF's 1975-76 season perhaps best illustrates Papp's commitment to Shakespeare, new American playwrights, foreign premieres, and new translations. The season included Shakespeare's *Hamlet* and *The Comedy of Errors*, James Lee's *The Shoeshine Parlor*, David Freeman's *Jesse and the Bandit Queen*, John Guare's *Rich and Famous*, Myrna Lamb's *Apple Pie*, Neil Harris' *So Nice, They Named It Twice*, Thomas Babe's *Rebel Women*, Ntozake Shange's *For Colored Girls. . .*, Arthur Wing Pinero's *Trelawney of the "Wells,"* G. B. Shaw's *Mrs. Warren's Profession*, Bertolt Brecht and Kurt Weill's *The Threepenny Opera* in a new translation, Michael Dorn Moody's *The Shortchanged Review*, David Rabe's *Streamers*, and Dennis Reardon's *The Leaf People*.

Many NYSF productions during the 1970s became so successful at the Public or the Delacorte that they were transfered to Broadway. The list includes *Hair, Much Ado About Nothing, Two Gentlemen of Verona, Sticks and Bones, That Championship Season*, and *A Chorus Line*, Broadway's longest-running production ever. In 1973, Papp signed a lease for the NYSF to become the resident company at the Vivian Beaumont and the smaller Mitzi E. Newhouse theatres at the Lincoln Center for the Performing Arts. The two theatres had been plagued by deficits since their opening in 1965, and even Papp's 90 percent ticket sales could not save this venture from financial disaster. In 1977, Papp left to concentrate on the Public stages and the Delacorte.

In 1980, success was to create another financial crisis for Papp. Revenue from *A Chorus Line* gave the illusion that the NYSF was making plenty of money and the City of New York, suffering from lost revenue, cut the budget for Shakespeare in Central Park to zero. That summer there was no Shakespeare, but, undaunted, Papp mounted one of his most successful productions,

The Pirates of Penzance, with funds from Citibank. New York City's annual funding of Shakespeare in the Park resumed in 1981.

The NYSF has championed new playwrights from diverse cultural and ethnic backgrounds and supported the original work of Ntozake Shange, David Henry Hwang (*F.O.B.*, *The Dance and the Railroad*), Miguel Piñero (*Short Eyes*), Larry Kramer (*The Normal Heart*, a landmark AIDS play), early Sam Shepard, John Guare, and many others. In 1979, the NYSF experimented with a company of black and Hispanic actors and actresses, and, in 1986, a minority acting troupe performed Shakespeare in the city parks for schoolchildren. Perhaps no other company in American theatre has launched as many acting careers and new American playwrights, designers, and technicians as the NYSF. The NYSF has nurtured the careers of such actors as Raul Julia, Kevin Kline, Meryl Streep, George C. Scott, James Earl Jones, Colleen Dewhurst, Martin Sheen, Richard Gere, Douglas Watson, Charles Durning, Julie Harris, and William Hurt. In the design area, Martin Aronstein's lighting designs, Theoni Aldredge's costumes, the stage designs of Santo Loquasto, and the works of Ming Cho Lee have become legendary. Finally, in the context of Shakespeare production, the NYSF has the distinction of having staged all but one of Shakespeare's plays, the lone exception being *Henry VIII*.

Over the years, NYSF activities have been diverse and ambitious. The NYSF has served as host to Richard Foreman, Andrei Serban, Joseph Chaikan, and many other visiting artists and companies. Although Papp was known to favor the production of new American plays, the NYSF frequently offered the American premieres of important foreign works, such as Caryl Churchill's *Top Girls*, Václav Havel's *Memorandum*, David Hare's *Plenty*, and numerous others. In recent years, the NYSF has established a Playwriting in the Schools program, a Festival Latino de Nueva York, a Film Festival at the Delacorte and Public Theater, and, in 1987, it embarked on a six-year marathon of Shakespeare's entire canon. In 1986, the Festival Latino featured more than 400 performers from 31 countries (six musical, four dance, 24 theatrical companies, and 20 films) in 26 days of events at both the Delacorte and the Public.

In the NYSF's first major reorganization, Papp appointed JoAnne Akalaitis, a founding member of the Mabou Mines troupe, to be artistic associate in 1990. He also appointed three playwright directors—George C. Wolfe, David Greenspan, and Michael Greif—to the artistic staff. For the 1989-90 and 1990-91 seasons, Papp served as producer, but finally, in ailing health, he appointed Akalaitis as artistic director of the NYSF in August 1991. In October 1991, Papp died of cancer. He had become an icon of American nonprofit theatre and a champion of free Shakespeare production.

The tickets are much in demand, so either plan ahead or arrive early. The festival is very much a New York experience with all the cultural high points and practical hassle that implies. Although the crowd pressing into the amphitheatre can be a bit overwhelming, being a part of the audience and audience watching are a cultural experience in themselves. The open air, the park, and the anticipation of the event create a festive atmosphere. The sound system is bad, the seats are hard (bring a cushion), and, if it rains, expect a sea of umbrellas and a "Comedy of Errors" singing in the rain. Ruth Leon in *Applause: New York's Guide to the Performing Arts* has described the audience as more like a:

> baseball crowd with the home team winning. . . . Yuppies straight from work in their suits, kids with ice cream and parents in tow, folks who wouldn't be seen dead at Shakespeare but drop in to see what the fuss is about, college students in shorts and bare chests, elderly people on a pension for whom the free tickets are a boon, and everybody cheerful and friendly and out for a good time. Sometimes the performances are incidental to the rush of good humor so rarely seen in a New York Summer.

Joseph Papp, a champion of multicultural theatre, free Shakespeare and new plays with social meaning, built the largest nonprofit subsidized theatre in the United States. Thanks to his legendary leadership and fund-raising ability, the NYSF has become an indelible American tradition. There have been constant deficits, controversy, and logistical problems, but Papp consistently defended the freedom of artistic expression. In 1990, he turned down a grant from the National Endowment for the Arts (NEA) rather than sign an "obscenity clause" added because of Senator Jesse Helms' objection to the Robert Mapplethorpe photographic exhibition. Millions have experienced Shakespeare, many for the first time, in Central Park. And the tradition still continues, deficits and all, under the new leadership of JoAnne Akalaitis.

Production History (Shakespeare only; abbreviations in parentheses refer to performance venues; refer to the key below): **1954**: *An Evening of Shakespeare and Marlowe* (EPC); **1955**: (all EPC) *Shakespeare's Women, Ado, AYL, Rom., Cym., TGV*; **1956**: *JC, Shr.* (both ERA), *Tit.* (EPC); **1957**: *Rom., TGV, Mac.* (all CPB), *R3* (HT); **1958**: *AYL* (HT), *Oth., TN* (both CPB); **1959**: *Ant.* (HT), *JC* (CPB); **1960**: *H5, MM, Shr.* (all CPB); **1961** *Rom.* (HT), *Ado, MND, R2* (all CPW); **1962**: *JC* (HT), *MV, Tmp., Lr.* (all DT), *Ham.* (operatized, Peabody Institute, Baltimore), *Mac.* (HT); **1963**: *Ant., AYL, WT* (all DT), *TN* (HT); **1964**: *Ham.* (DT), *MND* (MT), *Oth.* (DT); **1965**: *LLL* (DT), *H5, Shr.* (both MT), *Cor., Tro.* (both DT), *Rom.* (MT); **1966**: *AWW* (DT), *Mac.* (MT), *MM, R3* (both DT), *Mac.* (MT); **1967**: *Err., Jn., Tit.* (all DT), *Ham.* (PT); **1968**: *1H4* (DT), *2H4* (DT), *Ham.* (MT), *Rom.* (DT); **1969**: *TN* (DT); **1970**: *1H6, 2H6, R3* (all DT); **1971**: *Tim., TGV, Cym.* (all DT); **1972**: *Ham., Ado* (both DT); **1973**: *AYL, Lr.* (both DT), *TGV* (MT), *Tro.* (LCN);

1974: *Tmp.*, *Mac.* (both LCN), *Per.*, *Wiv.* (both DT), *R3* (LCN); **1975**: *MND* (LCN), *Ham.*, *Err.* (both DT), *Ham.* (VB); **1976**: *H5*, *MM* (both DT); **1977**: No Shakespeare, *Threepenny Opera* (DT); **1978**: *AWW*, *Shr.* (both DT); **1979**: *JC* (PT), *Cor.* (PT & DT), *Oth.* (DT); **1980**: No Shakespeare, *Pirates of Penzance* (DT); **1981**: *MND* (PTN), *Tmp.*, *1H4* (both DT); **1982**: *Err.* (Riverside Shake. Company), *MND* (DT), *Ham.* (PT); **1983**: *R3* (DT), *JC* (Front-Page Productions.); **1984**: *Rom.* (MT), *H5* (DT); **1985**: *MM* (DT), *Shr.* (MT); **1986**: *Ham.* (PTN), *TN* (DT); **1987**: *R2*, *TGV*, *1H4* (all DT), *MND* (PT); **1988**: *JC* (PTN), *Rom.* (PT), *Ado*, *Jn.* (both DT), *Cor.* (PT); **1989**: *LLL* (PTN), *WT* (PT), *Cym.* (PTN), *TN*, *Tit.* (both DT), *Mac.* (PT); **1990**: *Ham.* (PT), *Shr.*, *R3* (both DT); **1991**: *1H6*, *2H6*, *Oth.*; **1992**: *AYL*, *Err.* (both DT); **1994**: *Wiv.* (both DT).

Key:
CPB: Central Park/Belvedere Lake
CPW: Central Park/Wollman Memorial Skating Rink
DT: Delacorte Theater
EPC: Emmanuel Presbyterian Church
ERA: East River Amphitheater
HT: Heckscher Theater
LCN: Lincoln Center/Mitzi E. Newhouse Theater
MT: Mobile Theater
PT: Public Theater/Anspacher
PTN: Public Theater/Newman
VB: Vivian Beaumont Theater/Lincoln Center

Research Resources: The papers of Joseph Papp and the NYSF records have been donated to the Billy Rose Theatre Collection, New York Public Library for the Performing Arts at the Lincoln Center. The archives include correspondence, scripts, designs, photographs, clippings, programs, press and publicity materials, and audio- and videotapes. For further information and timetable for processing the materials, see New York Public Library, *Research Library Notes* 5:4 (Fall 1993): 8-9.

Epstein, Helen. *Joe Papp: An American Life*. Boston: Little, Brown, 1994.

Horn, Barbara Lee. *Joseph Papp: A Bio-Bibliography*. New York: Greenwood Press, 1992.

King, Christine E., and Brenda Coven. *Joseph Papp and the New York Shakespeare Festival: An Annotated Bibliography*. New York: Garland Publishing, 1988.

Leon, Ruth. *Applause: New York's Guide to the Performing Arts*. New York: Applause Theatre Book Publishers, 1991.

Loney, Glenn and Patricia MacKay. *The Shakespeare Complex: A Guide to Summer Festivals and Year-Round Repertory in North America.* New York: Drama Book Publishers, 1975.

Samuels, Steven. *Theatre Profiles 10: The Illustrated Reference Guide to America's Nonprofit Professional Theatre.* New York: Theatre Communications Group, 1992.

Site visits: 1985, 1990, 1991, 1992.
Ron Engle

OASIS THEATRE COMPANY. MAIL: Playground Theatre, 230 East 9th Street, New York, NY 10003. SITE: same. ADMINISTRATION/BOX OFFICE: 212/673-3706. ADMISSION: $15 (senior citizen and student discounts available). SEASON: varies; 7:30 p.m., Thurs.–Sat.; 5:00 p.m., Sun. PRINCIPAL STAFF: Brenda Lynn Bynum, founder, producer, artistic director; James Jenner, program director. FACILITY: flexible stage (capacity 55). AUDITIONS: by appointment. STATUS: Equity Tier 2. ANNUAL BUDGET: $65,000 (1993). ANNUAL ATTENDANCE: 3,200 (1993). FOUNDED: 1988, Brenda Lynn Bynum, James Jenner.

After directing John Patrick Shanley's *Welcome to the Moon* in the fall of 1988, Brenda Lynn Bynum decided to find a permanent performance space and form a company. She and founding member James Jenner spent nine months transforming a manufacturing facility into a flexible-stage theatre with red park benches for audience seating. Thus, the Playground Theatre, on East 9th Street between Second and Third Avenues, became the home of the Oasis Theatre Company (OTC), which might be seen as an "oasis" in an urban neighborhood that is otherwise culturally underserved.

The OTC's goal is to make theatre a habit with people, especially those in the local community. To that end, it maintains an active production schedule (averaging seven to eight plays per season) and affordable ticket prices. The OTC has presented eight Shakespeare productions in the last two seasons and plans to produce the entire canon over the next few years. A particularly successful production of *Hamlet*, in which Jenner and Bynum played Hamlet and Ophelia, launched a four-play Shakespeare series (May to October 1993), commemorating the Bard's 429th birthday with a subscription series based on 29-cent stamps. Three subscription levels (Groundlings, Elizabethans, Royalty) all incorporated the figure 29, including the 29-cent stamps on the mailers. Groundlings, for example, could see all four plays for $29. Royalty paid $29 for each opening night ticket, which included a party afterwards.

Everyone in the ten-member ensemble company plays a variety of roles and helps with the administrative work, assisting with the many tasks involved in running a theatre, such as fund raising and audience development. In the intimate space, scenery is kept to a minimum, but good costumes are a point of pride. The OTC approach to Shakespeare puts the emphasis on language, imagination, and illusion. The plays are done with few cuts, no extravagant changes of period, and attention to keeping the story before the audience. A favorite company anecdote recalls a seven-year-old who saw the OTC production of *Cymbeline* and wondered, in effect, why it was so much more understandable than the one in the park.

Among the OTC's other projects are children's theatre productions on Saturdays and Sundays and a late-night cabaret theatre called Midnight at the Oasis. The OTC has also produced a radio series reviving scripts from the Golden Era of Radio.

Production History: 1990: *Welcome to the Moon, Fool for Love, The Good Doctor, Reunion*; 1991: *Canadian Gothic and American Modern, The Diviners, The Water Engine, Richard Corey, Misalliance, The Misanthrope, Hedda Gabler, The Long Christmas Dinner*; 1992: *TN, True West, Uncle Vanya, Rom., The Voice of the Prairie, Three Sisters*; 1993: *A Doll's House, Ham., Shr., Cym., H5, Lr., Candida, WT*; 1994: *Oth.*

Research Resources: Oasis Theatre Company archives are maintained at the Playground Theatre.

Telephone interview: 14 September 1993.
Felicia Hardison Londré

RIVERSIDE SHAKESPEARE COMPANY. MAIL: 316 East 91st Street, New York, NY 10128. SITE: Playhouse 91, 316 East 91st Street; city parks during summer. ADMINISTRATION/BOX OFFICE 212/369-2273. ADMISSION: $20–$30; in city parks, donations. SEASON: 120 performances of four productions, usually three Shakespeare and one classic, October through April; in summer in five borough parks, 15 performances of one production. PRINCIPAL STAFF: Gus Kaikkonen, artistic director. FACILITY: 300 seat indoor proscenium with thrust (capacity 300); outdoor portable stage. AUDITIONS: priority for Riverside Shakespeare Company Academy students. STATUS: AEA special status. ANNUAL BUDGET: $876,000 (1990-91). ANNUAL ATTENDANCE: 16,000 (parks only). FOUNDED: 1977, Stuart McDowell, Gloria Skurski.

Founded in 1977, the Riverside Shakespeare Company (RSC) was created with the goals of illuminating the works of Shakespeare through "understanding of language" and fostering "the growth of modern theatre artists through the exploration of text." The exploration of language is the most important aspect of the RSC's production approach. The RSC features both Shakespeare and contemporary playwrights in their season. The RSC has toured 12 of Shakespeare's plays to parks in all five New York City boroughs. In 1989-90, the company appeared in 16 parks, reaching an audience of over 15,000 people. The RSC provides signed performances for the hearing impaired, priority seating for the physically challenged, and performances in designated low-income and underprivileged areas of the city.

The RSC's complete staff includes an artistic director, an associate artistic director, a director of operations, the academy director (the RSC's acting school), marketing and development directors, a business manager, administrative and development consultants, a press agent, bookkeeper, and a graphic artist. Gus Kaikkonen is artist director, and the associate directors include Linda Masson, Dan Johnson, Robert Mooney, Austin Pendleton, Linus Weiss, Charles Keating, and Stuart Vaughan, a founding artistic director of the New York Shakespeare Company. Earned income from ticket sales and academy tuition represented approximately three-fourths of the total revenue generated in 1991 (roughly $850,000), with the remainder coming from government, corporate, foundation, and individual contributions, as well as benefit performances.

The RSC Professional Acting Academy offers courses in a variety of areas, including verse technique, ensemble scene study, Meisnerr acting technique, acting plays of language, and acting Shakespeare on camera. Academy students may audition on a priority basis for RSC readings, workshops, showcases, and major productions. The Academy students and RSC members present a series of readings and workshops throughout the year. During the summer months, the "Sunday in the Park with Shakespeare" series presents readings of six Shakespeare plays on the steps of the Soldiers and Sailors Monument in Riverside Park. From the readings series, several pieces are selected for workshop presentations, which are open to the public. From the workshop's "work in progress" approach, productions are selected for further development as one of the major productions of the season.

RSC workshops, emphasizing and demonstrating the company's approach to text and language, are available to area high schools and colleges. The workshops are offered alone or in conjunction with special performances. Former artistic director Timothy Oman developed a three-hour workshop in which students are invited to "participate in specially developed 'games' that engage their interest in the investigation of how sound is used to communicate specific thoughts and feelings." Using examples from "modern advertising slogans, students learn to listen for alliteration, assonance, rhythm, and other tools which aid them in interpreting Shakespearean verse."

After 14 years of off-off-Broadway production sites, the RSC moved into Playhouse 91 on East 91st Street in 1990. The intimate theatre seats 300 and has a proscenium with a flexible thrust forestage area. The auditorium is raked, and sight lines are excellent.

For a recent production of *Twelfth Night*, an informal, friendly, and non-commercial atmosphere prevailed at the theatre. The audience was perhaps a bit younger than one normally sees at an off-Broadway theatre and certainly more relaxed and less rushed. Vaughan's production of *Twelfth Night* was straightforward, traditional, and without any contemporary update. The audience was responsive to a production in which clarity of language made the action flow and underscored the sometimes very broad comic antics. The sets and costumes were simple yet festive, and, as Howard Kissel of the *Daily News* commented, the production "had a comfy feel to it, like running into an old friend and having a cozy evening of reminiscence."

The RSC maintains a high level of public support and subsidy, which allows the company to offer classic Shakespearean theatre to audiences at comparatively lower ticket prices than other off-Broadway theatre houses. High schools and colleges may reserve blocks of seats at regularly scheduled performances at up to 60 percent off the normal ticket price. The actors are also available for discussions following performances.

Production History: **1979**: *1H4*; **1982**: *Err., R3, Nicholas Nickleby*; **1983**: *Wiv.*; **1984**: *JC, H5*; **1985**: *Lr., Shr.*; **1986**: *AYL*; **1988**: *Tit.*, **1989**: *R3, Tro., Cyrano de Bergerac, Ham.*; **1990**: *TN*; **1991**: *Rom., Hunchback of Notre Dame, Cinderella*; **1992**: *Candida, Fridays, Iron Bars*.

Research Resources: Informal archives are maintained at the Riverside Shakespeare Company administrative office.

Site visits: November 1991, 1992.
Ron Engle

SHAKESPEARE IN DELAWARE PARK. MAIL: Department of Theatre and Dance, State University of New York (SUNY) Buffalo, Buffalo, NY 14214. SITE: Festival Stage in Delaware Park. ADMINISTRATION: Harriman Hall at SUNY—Buffalo, 716/882-8764. ADMISSION: free. SEASON: late June to mid-August, 18 performances each of two Shakespeare plays; 8:00 p.m., Tues.–Sun. PRINCIPAL STAFF: Saul Elkin, artistic director; Nancy N. Doherty, executive director. FACILITY: outdoor open stage, no fixed seating. AUDITIONS: April, at SUNY–Buffalo Theatre Department. STATUS: Equity SPT. ANNUAL BUDGET: $165,000 (1992). ANNUAL ATTENDANCE: 50,000 (1993). FOUNDED: 1976, Saul Elkin, Gary Gasarella.

Shakespeare in Delaware Park (SDP), or Shakespeare in the Park, as it is called locally, was founded in 1976 by two SUNY—Buffalo faculty members, Saul Elkin and Gary Gasarella. Its original and continuing mission is "to provide free public theatre regardless of ethnic and socio-economic barriers of at least two Shakespeare productions per season." At a more practical level, SDP was also founded to provide a training experience for SUNY—Buffalo theatre students. Through the years, however, student participation appears to have declined, while theatre department alumni participation seems to have increased. In 1976, Elkin and Gasarella mounted one production that was sufficiently successful to encourage them to mount two productions in subsequent seasons. From 1982 through 1985, they toured an additional production to other area parks, but the expense and logistics proved too demanding and the tour was abandoned in 1986.

Since SDP's inception, Elkin has been the main organizing force behind it. Only recently was long-time production manager Nancy Doherty, also a member of the SUNY–Buffalo faculty, promoted to associate artistic director. She and Elkin do most of the planning and organizational work for the festival throughout the year alongside their full-time academic duties. The 1992 company consisted of 15 to 20 full-time and 25 to 30 part-time paid members, plus 13 apprentices. Although Elkin originally used only students, in 1988, he began using Equity actors. The acting company normally consists of students (10 per-cent), and professional actors (90 percent), split between those drawn from the local community and Equity guest artists. The 1992 season production of *Richard III*, for example, employed three Equity actors and two Equity stage managers. The company begins rehearsals three weeks before the opening of the first production. The high school students in the apprenticeship program help construct sets and costumes, run productions, and attend a two-to-three-hour class three days a week. They rehearse and perform a separate show-case production at the end of the season. Entrance to the program is by audition.

SDP takes great pride in the fact that their productions have always been free, and they resist all efforts to induce them to have a box office. The 1992 budget stood at $165,000. Approximately $30,000 is budgeted for sets, lights, and costumes. The remainder of the budget is spent largely on salaries. Since its inception, SDP has been well supported by SUNY–Buffalo and by the governments of the city of Buffalo, and Erie County, and, at times, the state of New York. The degree of public support has diminished over the past few years. For example, in 1992, the city contributed only $5,000, compared to $20,000 the previous year. Similarly, Erie County contributed $18,000 in 1992, compared to $20,000 previously. In 1990, the SUNY–Buffalo subsidy amounted to approximately $45,000, largely in in-kind services consisting of office space, secretarial help, and telephone, and postage costs. At the end of the 1991 season, however, SUNY–Buffalo also reduced its level of financial support. In 1992, SDP incorporated as a not-for-profit organization with its own board of directors, and a major effort is now under way to solicit support from the private rather than the public sector. In 1992, for example, the principal contributor was Marine Midland Bank, whose support amounted to $20,000 in cash and in-kind services of an additional $20,000. A request for contributions is also made before performances and at intermissions. Patron contributions and concession sales amount to approximately 32 percent of the festival's annual budget.

The performance site, a natural amphitheatre in Buffalo's extensive Delaware Park, is across the street from the noted Knox-Albright Art Museum. Theatregoers approach the site on a walkway, passing a small lake with paddle boats on one side and an extensive rose garden on the other. As they pass the "Casino" building on the lake side, they arrive at the top of the rather steep hill that is the natural amphitheatre. At the bottom of the incline is the stage with a view of the lake beyond it. At the entrance, area there are trailers that serve as concession stalls and a control booth. Behind the stage is a large trailer used for dressing rooms.

The stage itself is constructed out of pressure-treated lumber that has been allowed to weather naturally. It is dismantled at the end of each season—the hill is prime sledding territory during the winter—and is then rebuilt, usually with some modifications, each year. In design, it is a variation of the customary Elizabethan thrust. The thrust (48 feet wide) has two levels, and there is an inner below and above with smaller platforms right and left halfway down from the above stage. Steel lighting towers are situated right and left about halfway down the hill. The towers were a gift from a Rolling Stones road tour. In addition, there are two cranked lift devices on which are placed speakers for the sound, which is amplified by microphones placed on the stage floor. Individual body microphones are planned for the 1993 season.

While the goal of having free performances was to make theatre, specifically Shakespeare, available and accessible to a wide socioeconomic spectrum, Doherty has indicated, rather sadly, that the audience through the years has been largely white and middle-class. Although Doherty seemed concerned for the future of the company, the fact that it has been in existence for 17 years testifies to its ability to survive. Moreover, total attendance has been increasing by as much as 5,000 each year for the past several seasons. Still, the need to keep raising money to maintain a free festival means the survival of the organization is always at risk. Looking toward the future (at this writing, the 1993 season), SDP hopes to receive a grant from the New York State Council on the Arts and/or the National Endowment for the Arts to upgrade its sound system. Through the World University Games program to be held in Buffalo, the company plans to bring in a director from Ireland's Abbey Theatre to direct one production.

Upstate Western New York had suffered a long spell of rainy, cold weather that finally cleared on the afternoon of the evening that I attended a performance of *Richard III*. The audience, which began arriving around 7:00 p.m. for the 8:00 p.m. starting time, seemed more than ready to enjoy a pleasant evening out of doors. The arriving audience appeared to be largely couples, mostly white and in their thirties, some with children. Almost everyone was carrying folding chairs, blankets, coolers or picnic baskets. The menu of the group dining *al fresco* near me included French bread, Italian olives, cheese, tins of oysters and sardines, and red wine. Looking at the stage and beyond that to the lake dotted with paddle boats was very pleasant. There seemed to be activity everywhere— joggers running by behind the theatre, actors warming up by throwing a baseball outside their trailer, bicyclers, and children playing on a mound of dirt. About 7:30 p.m., the production's director came on stage and introduced a folk singer who entertained until curtain time. I was impressed by the attentiveness of the audience and its generous applause at the end of each song. Meanwhile, more playgoers continued to arrive and settle down. It was a very relaxed atmosphere.

Promptly at 8:00 p.m., the performance began. Visually, the most remarkable element of the production was the costuming, since the stage was left essentially bare. All the costumes were constructed out of unbleached muslin and were not dyed, sprayed, or otherwise colored. Their design, however, suggested clothing of the fifteenth century and the garments were constructed with considerable detail and attention to pleating and smocking. As dusk deepened and the stage lights began to "read," the whiteness of the costumes became more apparent, almost to the point of distraction.

The actors projected the directorial intent with clarity and remained faithful to the textual interpretation. But, on the negative side, the amplification system tended to distort the vocal work of the actors, making their voices high pitched and unresonated. Considering the range of the performers' background and experiences, the acting quality was remarkably consistent across the company. The vocally and physically strong Richard, played by William Gonta, energized the ensemble. Gonta's Richard was a most efficient character, a quality most unfortunate for anyone interfering with his obsession for power. The actress playing Margaret, whom I have often found a tediously self-pitying character in other productions, made her points positively and earned my sympathy. The roles of the boys, Edward and Richard, were well cast and acted. Edward was played by a boy about 14 years old. When momentarily he became king, the actor seemed to mature and take on a royal aura. The younger Richard appeared to be genuinely fond of his uncle. I found Richard's wooing his nephews to move into the Tower to be particularly well played. Clarence was clearly a thoughtful person, if not an ascetic, and his preparation for death was sensitively expressed and ultimately quite moving.

This was not a production given to pomp and circumstance. There were only a few props and devices as needed, such as the casket and a throne. Hastings, wearing a harness, was hanged from an arm projecting from the upper stage and dispensed into a trap in the stage floor. One of the stronger production values was the music. Synthesized in some manner, it sounded simultaneously historical and modern. Skillfully recorded and amplified, it was technically on cue throughout and always emotionally appropriate for the dramatic moment.

At the intermission, taken at the time of Hastings' death, daylight was gone and the house lights came on. The cast moved quickly and cheerfully through the audience, "passing a hat" for contributions. It had been an attentive and appreciative audience, and the actors paused to greet friends or to have quick conversations with other audience members. SDP is clearly a confident and therefore comfortable operation, bringing pleasure to its audience through honest and simply produced productions.

Production History: **1976**: *WT*; **1977**: *Ham., AYL*; **1978**: *Tmp., Wiv.*; **1979**: *Err., Ado*; **1980**: *MND, R2*; **1981**: *Mac., TN*; **1982**: *Shr., 1H4, Labours of Love* (an adaptation); **1983**: *Lr., R3, Americles* (an adaptation); **1984**: *Ham.,* *MM, TGV*; **1985**: *Rom., Tmp., TN*; **1986**: *LLL, MV*; **1987**: *H5, AWW*; **1988**: *WT, JC*; **1989**: *Lr., Ado*; **1990**: *Wiv., Oth.*; **1991**: *1H4, AYL*; **1992**: *Err., R3*; **1993**: *Rom., MND*; **1994**: *Mac., Shr.*

Research Resources: Informal archival material is housed in the Theatre and Dance Department at SUNY–Buffalo. Materials are more complete from 1982 forward.

Site visit and interview: 24 July 1992
Charles Vicinus

STERLING RENAISSANCE FESTIVAL. MAIL: 15431 Farden Road, Sterling, NY 13156. SITE: same as mail address. ADMINISTRATION: Canterbury Hall at the Farden Road address. BOX OFFICE: 315/947-5783. ADMISSION: $12.99 adults, $5.99 for children six to twelve. SEASON: 4 July to 16 August; 10:00 a.m. to 7:00 p.m. Sat., Sun. (1992). PRINCIPAL STAFF: Gerald and Virginia Young, owner/managers; Gary Izzo, artistic director; Nancy Robbins Izzo, managing director. FACILITY: 35-acre site with two outdoor theatres (capacity approximately 400 seats each). AUDITIONS: Southeastern Theatre Conference (SETC) auditions and other East Coast auditions. STATUS: non-Equity. FOUNDED: 1977, Dennis T. Ouellette.

The Sterling Renaissance Festival (SRF) was founded in 1977 by Dennis T. Ouellette on 35 acres of family owned land north of the small town of Sterling, New York. Ouellette passed away shortly after the festival's opening in 1977. His widow Caroline carried on briefly until the operation was taken over by Ouellette's nephew, Gerald A. Young, and his wife, Virginia. The Youngs now own the festival and lease the 35 acres of land from the Ouellette family.

The festival site is reached via a country road that runs north out of the village of Sterling. There is ample parking immediately outside the festival area. A ticket booth with four windows is just to the side of the entrance. The site itself is surrounded by a wooden fence. Inside, dirt pathways wind their way past some 50 to 60 booths scattered over a heavily wooded sloping area. At the booths one can purchase, among other things, food (for example, roasted turkey legs), drink, and handicrafts, rent a costume, have one's hair braided, or pause to listen to musicians playing on period instruments. The intent is to recreate a semblance of an Elizabethan-era village trade "faire" where Elizabeth I herself has stopped as she "progresses" toward London.

Abbreviated 45-minute versions of Shakespeare's popular comedies are presented in two outdoor theatres, the Wyldwood and the Bankside, each designed to suggest an Elizabethan outdoor theatre. The Wyldwood, for example, has a thrust stage. The scene house contains large, curtained, center openings at stage level and above on a second level. Similarly, on the side arms of the scene house are two smaller entrances, right and left, above and below, with stairs leading down from the upper entrance. The facade of the building is a brown-stained wood, and the curtains are in primary colors. The Bankside is similar in design only smaller. Wooden benches serve for seating in both theatres.

Each year, two Shakespearean comedies are presented along with a comedy by Molière and, with the exception of 1992, two or three *commedia dell'arte* pieces. In 1992, the festival presented *A Midsummer Night's Dream, The Taming of the Shrew*, and Molière's *The Flying Doctor (The Doctor In Spite of Himself)*. They present two different versions of *A Midsummer Night's Dream*. One focuses only on the "Mechanicals" plot, while the other focuses on the lovers' scenes. In a given year, however, the festival will present only one of the versions. One performance of the Shakespeare plays is given each day, and both theatres have a common 2:00 p.m. starting time.

Recently, the performance aspects of the festival were incorporated as the not-for-profit Bless The Mark Players. Nancy Robbins Izzo is managing director and her husband, Gary Izzo, is artistic director. They are in charge of an acting company of about 40, which the Izzos contract out to the festival management. According to the Gary Izzo, who has been with the Festival since 1977, the couple also trains the personnel who staff the booths in "Elizabethan dialects and language"—in actuality, Standard British and Cockney.

Gary Izzo explained that the acting company is trained in what he called "interactive performance," a cross between improvisation and street theatre. The actors essentially work an eight-hour day. During the day, they may appear in one of the plays; the rest of the time, they perform around the village in large improvised playlets. For example, Queen Elizabeth, followed by six or seven courtiers, is seen in various locations around the village in partly scripted and partly improvised ("interactive") scenarios. For example, I saw her at the very popular mud-wrestling site, where she vocally, but not physically, interacted with the wrestlers, her courtiers, and the audience. Gary Izzo indicated that the average age of the performers was about 26. Actors are paid a base salary that starts at $1,300 for an 11-week session and receive housing as well.

The 45-minute *Midsummer Night's Dream* that I observed in the Wyldwood used only nine actors and was the version that focused on the lovers' scenes. Theseus and Hippolyta appeared with Egeus, and the conflict that sends the lovers to the forest was established. There were neither extras nor court retinue. In the forest, along with the lovers, only Oberon and Puck appeared to set up the various chases, wooings, and mistaken identities.

As might be expected, the acting was broad with a lot of physical action. When they wooed, they did so energetically, with the women in particular literally throwing themselves at the men. This is not to imply that Shakespeare's script was parodied in any way, but rather that the action was more "bawdy" and farcical than one might ordinarily expect in a production of *A Midsummer Night's Dream*. The Wyldwood is located in very low ground with the tall rushes of a swamp visible behind the theatre. It had rained for several days and the audience area was very muddy. This did not deter the audience, however, and many people literally sat with their feet in mud, enjoying it as part of an authentic Elizabethan ambience. The actors quickly developed a rapport with the audience and held their attention throughout. Some of the action took the actors into the audience area and consequently into the mud. They did not let this throw them in anyway, but rather they worked with it. The actors obviously enjoyed what they were doing and so did the audience.

The Sterling Renaissance Festival is a very popular "theme park" in Central New York. The management would not release either attendance or budget figures, but, on a typical weekend 10,000 people may attend the "faire."

Production History: **1992**: *MND, Shr.*, *The Flying Doctor* (Molière's *The Doctor In Spite of Himself*); **1993**: *Wiv., Tmp.*; **1994**: *Rom., AYL*, *The Cheats of Scapin.*

Site visit and interview: 25 July 1992
Charles Vicinus

THEATRE FOR A NEW AUDIENCE. MAIL: 154 Christopher Street, Suite 3-D, New York, NY 10014-2839. SITE: St. Clements Church, 423 West 46th Street, New York, NY. ADMINISTRATION: 212/229-2819. BOX OFFICE: 212/279-4200. ADMISSION: $30 with half-price rush tickets. SEASON: three productions, January to April; 8:00 p.m., Thurs.–Sat.; 2:00 p.m., Sat. PRINCIPAL STAFF: Jeffrey Horowitz, artistic/producing director; Peter M. Kindlon, general manager; Jennifer Clarke, development/marketing director; Margaret Salvante, educational director. FACILITY: flexible (capacity 99). AUDITIONS: scheduled through Equity. STATUS: Equity LOA. ANNUAL BUDGET: $1,022,195 (1994). ANNUAL ATTENDANCE: 12,000 (1994). FOUNDED: 1979, Jeffrey Horowitz.

Theatre for a New Audience (TFANA) was founded by Jeffrey Horowitz in 1979. Horowitz had trained at the London Academy of Music and Dramatic Art (LAMDA) from 1968 to 1971. During his training years in London, Horowitz was especially impressed with the organization of the **Royal Shakespeare Company** (RSC) and the Royal National Theatre (RNT), both of which, in contrast to the usual American theatrical practice, employed permanent companies and offered ongoing training and relatively long rehearsal periods. Coming to New York in 1971, Horowitz continued his training with such distinguished acting teachers as Stella Adler, Sanford Meisner, and Lee Strasberg, all of whom had been leaders of the Group Theatre. Like the RSC and the RNT, the Group Theatre also employed a permanent company of actors, rehearsed productions over a fairly long period, and was dedicated to ongoing training and developing a common aesthetic.

Finding few theatres in New York in the mid-1970s that had organizational structures and goals like those of the RSC, the RNT, or the Group Theatre, Horowitz established his own theatre. TFANA had several goals, chief of which was to bring productions of Shakespeare, other classics from the world repertoire, and contemporary plays to a culturally diverse audience of all ages. To this end, Horowitz assembled a multiethnic ensemble of actors to explore new ways of communicating classical texts to a contemporary audience. He was determined to create an hospitable environment not only for his acting ensemble but also for emerging playwrights, directors, designers, and composers, supporting their creativity by providing adequate development and rehearsal time and a program of ongoing training. Although Shakespeare remained central to his mission, Horowitz also aimed to commission the development and production of new plays that both addressed provocative social issues and were compelling in terms of language and theatricality.

Between its founding and 1983, TFANA was mainly a small ensemble of performers who toured public and private schools and colleges in the Northeast with collages of scenes, soliloquies, and songs from Shakespeare. The scenes, however, were directed by Frank Corsaro, a distinguished director of opera and theatre. Julie Taymor, then a gifted, young, emerging theatre artist, created inventive masks, settings and costumes for one of the touring productions. In 1984, Joseph Papp invited TFANA to present its production of *A Midsummer Night's Dream*, adapted for eight actors and reduced to a playing time of about 75 minutes, at the **New York Shakespeare Festival's** Public Theatre. This unusual production was directed by Amy Saltz and incorporated masks, puppetry, and costumes designed by Taymor, multiethnic casting, and a striking musical score composed by Elliot Goldenthal. It quickly established TFANA's reputation in the Off-Broadway theatrical community. Subsequent to its Public Theatre performances, this production was also presented at the Whole Theatre Company in New Jersey in 1985 and at The Lincoln Center Institute in 1989.

In 1985, TFANA did not mount any Shakespeare plays but rather launched a program called New Voices to develop new plays that focused on social issues. Indeed, in the early 1980s, TFANA had presented the premiere of Joyce Carol Oates' *The Changeling*. The first two New Voices productions were James de Jongh's *Do Lord Remember Me*, a play based on first-hand accounts of former slaves, and *I Love You, I Love You Not* by Wendy Kesselman, which focused on the relationship between a teenager and her grandmother, a survivor of the Holocaust. In 1986, however, TFANA for the first time presented a Shakespeare play, *The Tempest*, and a new play, *Home Street Home*, a musical political satire about how young people view homelessness. Directed and designed by Taymor with an original score by Goldenthal, *The Tempest* was a highly innovative production that integrated performance conventions from *commedia dell'arte, bunraku,* Kabuki, and modern realistic theatre. The *New York Times* critic (27 March 1986) wrote that it was "a splendid vehicle to draw in the young audiences the company mostly aims for, and it's hard to imagine an adult who could resist its charm." It was revived the following season and was invited to the **American Shakespeare Theatre** in Stratford, Connecticut.

To date, TFANA has generally followed the pattern set in 1986, producing one or two Shakespeare plays each year and a new play that the company may have commissioned. Maintaining a commitment to bring classical and contemporary theatre to audiences of all ages and of diverse ethnic and economic backgrounds during each week of a production's run, TFANA usually presents three special performances during the day for New York City fifth through twelfth grade public school students in addition to evening and matinee performances for adults.

Over the years, TFANA has gradually earned a reputation for often imaginative and always clear interpretations of Shakespeare. For example, writing in the *New York Times*, Stephen Holden praised the cast of TFANA's *The Taming of the Shrew*, directed by Taymor, for delivering "Shakespeare's verse with a down-to-earth conversational gusto that keeps the momentum at a brisk clip" (16 February 1988). Veteran theatre critic, Clive Barnes, an early champion of TFANA, wrote that the company's *Twelfth Night* was "delivered with an unvarnished elegance that does Shakespeare proud in its couth simplicity" (*New York Post*, 25 March 1987). Barnes called the 1989 production of *Macbeth*, featuring two young actors from the Stratford Festival (**Stratford Festival of Canada**), Joseph Ziegler and Nancy Palk as the Macbeths, "simple, powerful, and direct—Shakespeare at its most unaffectedly effective."

At the end of the 1987 season, Horowitz began negotiations with a number of world-class, experienced Shakespeare directors to direct TFANA productions. In 1990, William Gaskill, a veteran director of London's Royal Court and National Theatre, staged a very well-received *Othello*. Barnes enthused that it was "one of the best New York Shakespeare productions of the past twenty years or so," with Gaskill directing with "unforced invention and a kind of happy virtuosity of movement" (*New York Post*, 19 January 1990). In

1991, the RSC's Bill Alexander staged *Romeo and Juliet* at the Victory Theatre, reclaimed as a legitimate theatre after decades as a West 42nd Street X-rated movie house. Melanie Kirkpatrick in *The Wall Street Journal* praised the direction as "spirited and fast paced" (8 February 1991). Gaskill returned in 1992 to direct an energetic and entertaining *The Comedy of Errors*. In 1993, TFANA mounted two Shakespeare plays: *Henry V*, directed by RSC director Barry Kyle, and *Love's Labour's Lost*, directed by former Guthrie Theatre and Stratford Festival (**Stratford Festival of Canada**) artistic director, Michael Langham. *Henry V*, featuring young Anglo-American actor Mark Rylance in the title role, garnered excellent reviews and a Lucille Lortel Award for the best Off-Broadway revival of the season (in 1994, Rylance won a coveted Olivier Award for his performance as Benedick in his own production of *Much Ado About Nothing*). Langham drew his cast largely from recent graduates of the Juilliard School, where he was head of the drama division, resulting in what Mel Gussow praised as "a salutary choice for a youthful company like the one assembled at St. Clements. There is more than enough orchestrated ardor . . . on this pun-filled and poetic landscape" (*New York Times*, 11 March 1993). For the 1994 season, Rylance returned to TFANA to direct an imaginative, thoughtful *As You Like It*, which received enthusiastic reviews. Taymor staged *Titus Andronicus* in a visually compelling, post-modern style. It mixed costumes and props from various historical eras, an atonal musical score by Goldenthal, and a physically charged acting style. Barnes called it "phantasmagorical" (*New York Post*, 14 March 1994), while Vincent Canby praised it as "good looking, inventive and sometimes witty . . . like a terrible fairy tale from Mars" (*New York Times*, 20 March 1994).

Promoting artistic development is a major activity of TFANA. This is done by working with artists who play a leadership role such as the aforementioned directors, and by providing development opportunities to promising artists. Taymor directed her first Shakespeare at TFANA. Rylance, who has primarily worked as an actor, directed TFANA's 1994 *As You Like It*, making his American directing debut. Numerous young actors who made their debut with the TFANA have gone on to make a strong contribution to American Shakespeare performance. For example, Miriam Healy-Louie played Juliet in TFANA's *Romeo and Juliet* and has since appeared on Broadway, at the **Shakespeare Theatre** (Washington DC) and at the **New York Shakespeare Festival**.

In addition to its Shakespeare productions, TFANA has continued to mount productions of new plays, often by playwrights of color, including *Inside Out* by Willy Holzman, *Evening Star* by Milcha Sanchez-Scott, *Red Sneaks*, a contemporary musical theatre piece by Elizabeth Swados, and *The America Play* by Suzan-Lori Parks. Since its founding, TFANA has also gradually expanded its educational outreach program which is intended to be mutually reinforcing for artists and young people. Students are regularly bussed to TFANA productions. A team of TFANA "teaching artists" goes into each class between five and seventeen times before and after a production to help teachers coordinate classroom performance projects centered around the productions. The New York Board of Education funds between 40 and 50 percent of the outreach program's $600,000 budget, with the remainder coming from various governmental agencies, private foundations, corporations, and individuals. In 1994, 114 schools were involved in the program—46 elementary schools, 33 middle schools, and 35 high schools—representing over 5,000 students. Since 1988, over 45,000 students have participated in the program.

Although a relatively small-sized organization, TFANA has solid financial backing and audience support. It is widely regarded as one of New York's leading Off-Broadway theatre companies, noted especially, in the words of Clive Barnes, for its "consistently excellent" Shakespeare productions. For the future, Horowitz hopes to expand TFANA's financial base and to build a contingency fund to cover the inevitable budgetary emergency. He also plans to establish a core company of actors, increase the salaries paid to actors, and offer workshops with the distinguished voice teacher Cecily Berry.

Production History: 1979-1983: Toured the northeast United States with collages of Shakespeare's scenes, soliloquies, and songs; **1984**: *MND*; **1985**: *Do Lord Remember Me, I Love You, I Love You Not*; **1986**: *Tmp., Home Street Home*; **1987**: *TN, Inside Out*; **1988**: *Shr., Evening Star*; **1989**: *Mac., MND, The Red Sneaks*; **1990**: *Oth., The Red Sneaks*; **1991**: *Rom., The Mud Angel* (Darrah Cloud); **1992**: *Err., The New Americans*; **1993**: *H5, LLL*; **1994**: *AYL, Tit., The American Play*.

Research Resources: An informal archive is maintained at the TFANA administrative office. This essay is based on material furnished by TFANA. See also Simi Horowitz, "Hope for the Future: Theatre for a New Audience integrates theatre and kids' lives," *TheatreWeek* (21-27 February 1994): 36-39.

Daniel J. Watermeier

NORTH CAROLINA

NORTH CAROLINA SHAKESPEARE FESTIVAL. MAIL: P.O. Box 6066, High Point, NC 27262. SITE: High Point Theatre and Exhibition Center, 220 East Commerce Avenue, in downtown High Point. ADMINISTRATION: 919/841-2273. BOX OFFICE: 919/841-6273. ADMISSION: $8–$18. SEASON: 45 performances, late July to early October; 8:00 p.m., Thurs.–Sat.; 2:00 p.m., selected Sat. and Sun. PRINCIPAL STAFF: Pedro M. Silva, producer;

Louis Rackoff, artistic director; Thomas Gaffney, managing director. FACIL-
ITY: proscenium stage (capacity 634). AUDITIONS: open auditions in High
Point; AEA lottery in New York City. STATUS: LORT D; (B for tour).
ANNUAL BUDGET: $1.1 million (1991). ANNUAL ATTENDANCE: 17,500.
FOUNDED: 1977, Mark Woods, Stuart Brooks.

The North Carolina Shakespeare Festival (NCSF) was founded in 1977 by
Mark Woods and Stuart Brooks, "two actors tired of the jaded audiences, dingy
showcase theaters and high production costs of New York plays." Woods and
Brooks met in Greensboro, North Carolina, in 1975. On discovering their
shared goals, they founded the North Carolina Theatre Ensemble, which
produced 18 plays in 18 months. When that venture ran out of operating funds,
they decided to start a not-for-profit theatre, which would allow them to raise
money. Woods, who served as managing director of the NCSF until 1983,
recalled that no one predicted success for the new company, because there was
no perceptible demand for Shakespeare in a small town like High Point and
because the summer months (when the High Point Theatre was available) were
considered vacation time by the locals. By marketing the festival as a statewide
cultural asset, however, the NCSF drew 11,000 people to the 24 performances
of its inaugural season. On a $100,000 budget, the NCSF employed 25
professional actors in three visually splendid productions.

NCSF's current producer Pedro Silva joined the original company as an
actor in response to an invitation from Brooks and Woods. Drawn by the
opportunity to perform a variety of roles in classical plays, he left the off-
Broadway scene and never looked back. In order to create year-round work for
himself with the festival, he began the "Actor in the School" program. In 1983,
Silva replaced Woods as managing director, and, in 1990, he became NCSF's
producer.

Artistic director Louis Rackoff was hired in 1988 and was the first to fill
that position full time. He succeeded Malcolm Morrison, who had been the
part-time artistic director since 1979 while serving full time as dean of drama
at the North Carolina School of the Arts. Rackoff, who had been a production
stage manager for eight years at the **New York Shakespeare Festival** and a
freelance director working out of New York City, expanded the NCSF's
repertoire to include more modern plays. He also began an internship program
offering college credit for students working with the festival and reduced the
number of productions in order to increase rehearsal time. As a native New
Yorker, Rackoff felt a little "like a fish out of water, living in the South," but he
quickly came to appreciate the local attitude toward theatre: "Our audiences
aren't looking for the definitive production; they just want something that's
worth their time and maybe worth the dollars they pay at the box office. There
is an opportunity here to do really innovative, interesting work, and we'll not
be plagued by New York critics who are looking to wipe you out if possible,
because it's good newsprint."

Rackoff and Silva developed the following statement of purpose for the NCSF:

> The Festival is dedicated to producing great plays of social and political relevance in a variety of theatrical forms and styles. We want to present theatre that is entertaining, exciting, passionate and culturally and educationally stimulating. The Festival is committed to non-traditional casting, to developing the strongest ensemble acting company possible, and to complementing the work of our actors with a creative technical and administrative staff working on the highest professional level. We hope that the Festival can grow, along with our audiences and the greater North Carolina community, toward realizing the possibilities of regional theatre as an integral part of our culture.
>
> The festival will serve the audiences and citizens of tomorrow by touring its productions to schools throughout the state and nation, reaching youth in their formative years and broadening their vision and understanding of themselves, the world and the theatre.

The NCSF's primary audience base is "the Triad"—Greensboro, High Point, and Winston-Salem—along with nearby towns like Thomasville and Lexington. A program called "Outreach Tours" takes a major Shakespeare production to colleges and civic centers throughout the Southeast every fall, plus a special production based on Shakespeare's works (*This Wooden O*, 1983-86; *Globeworks*, 1987-93) to high schools around the state in the winter and spring. Other special programs are: "Pre Views," pre-show discussions of the regular season productions; "Hands-On Shakespeare," a three-day teacher workshop; "SchoolFest," mid-morning school matinees; the "Tiny Tim Project," free attendance at *A Christmas Carol* for disadvantaged youth; and the "Pay What You Can Plan," making ticket purchases affordable to everyone. NCSF is also exploring possible "Second Stage" performance spaces in Greensboro or Winston-Salem, where new plays and "fringe classics" can be done in an intimate space. "We are interested in redefining what a regional theatre might be," says Rackoff. "Regional theatre can be the kind of Mecca of art that draws people from 500 miles around as the Guthrie does. But what a regional theatre is really meant to do is serve the people of a given region. And by sometimes taking its work to the people in their localities, regional theatre can serve them best."

The High Point Theatre is a comfortable proscenium theatre with a pleasant lobby area. The exterior of the building, however, is undistinguished, if not downright unattractive. Rackoff dreams of acquiring a small section of the parking lot across the street where he could create a Shakespeare garden. The NCSF's administrative offices are in another building down the street, at the Holt McPherson Center, 305 North Main Street, in High Point. The scene shops and costume shops are located in a city-owned warehouse in High Point. Rehearsals for mainstage productions are held in a large assembly hall rented from the local synagogue. A smaller rehearsal hall located in the same building as the administrative offices is used as a second rehearsal space.

Although Rackoff has expanded the repertoire to include more modern plays, he remains committed to a program that is at least 50 percent Shakespeare. At the box office, the Shakespeare plays consistently do better than the non-Shakespeare plays. When the 1989 season included only one Shakespeare work, subscribers did not hesitate to register their complaints. 1993 will bring an all-Shakespeare season.

The 1990 *Hamlet* was a textbook example of "accessible" and "immediate" Shakespeare. Without imposing any heavy-handed or high-concept interpretation, director Rackoff brought out the play's contemporary resonances. The great speeches sounded fresh, spontaneous, and utterly believable. On a virtually bare stage, modified only by a metal grating in the floor, the actors took focus in their eclectic mix of costumes: modern-dress soldiers, an ever-smiling Claudius in a Nehru jacket with sash and medals, Gertrude in a beautifully draped peach and gray turn-of-the-century gown, Ophelia in a medieval-style gray dress, Polonius in a Disraeli-style frock coat. The intelligent, witty, and surprisingly passionate Hamlet portrayed by Allan Hickle-Edwards looked frumpily academic in his baggy-pants black tweed suit with black sweater vest. Claudius seemed genuinely likable, as long as we saw only his public face; when the private man emerged in all his cunning and ruthlessness in the latter half of the play, one felt like a fool for having been taken in by him. Gertrude, on the other hand, seemed at first like a cold fish, but, by the end, her inscrutability had become integrity—or, at least, dignity in the face of her crumbling personal relationships. Claudius' questioning of Hamlet concerning the whereabouts of Polonius' body was conducted more like an interrogation as Claudius slapped and punched Hamlet so violently that gasps were heard in the audience. In his scenes subsequent to this beating, Hamlet seemed to achieve an equanimity to replace his earlier crisis mentality. It is perhaps indicative of the richness, freshness, and clarity of this production that, having seen it on two consecutive evenings, I found myself wishing I could see it a third time.

Production History: **1977**: *Shr., The Miser, H5*; **1978**: *Ado, A Man for All Seasons, MV, Servant of Two Masters, All My Sons, The Importance of Being Earnest, A Christmas Carol* (revived every season); **1979**: *MND, The Rivals, 1H4, The Adventures of Sherlock Holmes, The Servant of Two Masters, Summer and Smoke, She Stoops to Conquer*; **1980**: *TN, The Imaginary Invalid, Mac., Born Yesterday, The Last Meeting of the Knights of the White Magnolia, The Heiress*; **1981**: *AYL, Hay Fever, Ham., Just a Song at Twilight, Err., Wait Until Dark*; **1982**: *Jn., A Flea in Her Ear, Rom.*; **1983**: *This Wooden O* (high school tour; revived 1984-86), *The Hollow Crown, TGV, Of Mice and Men, Light Up the Sky, Long Day's*

Journey into Night, Oth.; **1984**: *Lr., Treasure Island, A Streetcar Named Desire, Wiv.*; **1985**: *Scapino, R3, Amadeus, Shr.*; **1986**: *Tmp., Tartuffe, And A Nightingale Sang, LLL*; **1987**: *Globeworks* (high school tour, revived 1988–93), *R2, MND, Our Town, Rom.*; **1988**: *Ado, The Hostage, Mac.*; **1989**: *Billy Bishop Goes to War,* *TN, An Enemy of the People, Arms and the Man, Waiting for Godot*; **1990**: *Eleemosynary, Ham., The School for Scandal, The Time of Your Life, Err.*; **1991**: *JC, The Matchmaker, The Dybbuk, AYL*; **1992**: *Wiv., The Front Page, Oedipus Tyrannos, TGV*; **1993**: *Shr., MV, Lr.*; **1994**: *Ado, MM, Tmp.*

Research Resources: Archives are informally maintained in the NCSF production office. See also: Vicki Bridgers, "Versatile Silva Plays His New Role With Authority," *High Point Enterprise* (15 January 1984): 3D; Andy Duncan, "Shakespeare fest's new director doth aim to make Triad a stage," [Greensboro] *News and Record* (24 June 1988): C3; Ramona Jones, "Shakespeare in High Point? It can't work–but it did," *Raleigh Times* (15 August 1981).

Site visit and interviews: 3–4 August 1990.
Felicia Hardison Londré

OHIO

ACTORS' SUMMER THEATRE: SHAKESPEARE IN THE PARK. MAIL: 1000 City Park Avenue, Columbus, OH 43206. SITE: Schiller Park. ADMINISTRATION: 614/444-6888. ADMISSION: Shakespeare plays are free; musicals are $3–$5 for adults; children under 12 years of age are free. SEASON: approximately 30 performances of three plays, two Shakespeare and one musical, from mid-June through late August; 8:00 p.m., Thurs.–Sat.; opening night at 7:30 p.m. PRINCIPAL STAFF: Patricia B. Ellson, artistic director; Robert W. Tolan, producing director; Gary Ellson, dramaturg. FACILITY: outdoor, open stage (capacity 600). AUDITIONS: local in April and May. STATUS: non-Equity. ANNUAL BUDGET: $159,000 (1992). ANNUAL ATTENDANCE: 28,000-30,000 (1991). FOUNDED: 1982, Patricia Ellson.

Patricia Ellson, the founder of **Actors' Summer Theatre** (AST), admits that she was inspired by Joseph Papp's **New York Shakespeare Festival**. Both she and her husband Gary believed that free presentations of Shakespeare would be attractive to Columbus playgoers. Such a program, moreover, would

engage talented local actors who were not working during the summer off-
season. They also realized that a mostly unused natural amphitheatre in
Schiller Park, a small park located in the German Village section of central
Columbus, offered an ideal site for such an operation. They secured permission
to use the amphitheatre from the Columbus Recreation and Parks Department
and, in 1982, presented *A Midsummer Night's Dream.*

This first season proved sufficiently successful that the following season
they presented Shakespeare's *Twelfth Night* and the musical *Oklahoma.* In
1984, they presented two Shakespeare plays, *The Taming of the Shrew* and
Macbeth, plus the musical *South Pacific.* This format of two Shakespeare plays
and one musical has been followed up to the present.

While there are only two year-round full-time staff members in addition to
Patricia Ellson—a producing director and a clerk/secretary—during the season,
AST employs up to 100 performers and production personnel. Although AST is
a non-Equity operation, all key performers and production personnel are paid.
Indeed, 42 percent of AST's budget is expended on personnel. Like many
summer Shakespeare festivals, AST also depends on numerous volunteers to
serve as ushers, stagehands, concessionaires, and so forth.

Ellson's goal as artistic director is to make Shakespeare's plays as accessible as possible to a popular audience. She believes that Shakespeare's plays
were originally intended mainly to entertain and hence should be presented
today in a style that will accomplish this goal. To this end, she frequently sets
the plays in an historical period closer to our own than Shakespeare's era. *The
Comedy of Errors,* for example, was set in an American circus milieu at the
turn of the century, while *As You Like It* was set during the American
Revolutionary War. It should be noted, however, that AST also mounts
productions that are more traditionally set in the Renaissance period. Ellson
also cuts and edits the scripts so that performances will have a running time of
no more than two and one-half hours and will be as clear as possible to her
audiences. She will even modernize some words if she believes such a change
will reinforce audience understanding.

Scenery is generally kept to a minimum. The permanent stone and concrete
amphitheatre stage is covered and expanded with an open wooden platform
stage, and then a different unit setting for each production is designed for this
space. Lighting instruments and audio speakers are fixed to pipes and towers
above and at the sides of the stage. Control boards are situated on a table at the
rear of the amphitheatre. Spectators sit on the hillside in front of the stage on
blankets or beach chairs.

Clearly, her approach has proved successful. Total attendance has increased
from several thousand in the early 1980s to about 30,000 in 1991. Her
audiences are drawn primarily from the surrounding area within a 30-mile
radius with 10 to 15 percent coming from out of state. Like the audiences at
most festivals, AST audiences are relatively affluent and well educated.
According to Ellson, they come because of her approach, because with free

performances they can experience Shakespeare "at no risk," and because of the casual ambience of Schiller Park. AST has also benefited from the rehabilitation and restoration of German Village and the adjacent Brewery District into a charming blend of nineteenth-century homes, restaurants, boutiques, and art galleries. The entire area has become a major tourist attraction, and AST, along with the annual German Village Art Exhibition and the Oktoberfest, is undoubtedly perceived as one of the attractions.

AST earns about 10 percent of its budget through souvenir sales and from program advertisements paid for by various local businesses. In 1992, the company also began charging admission for the musical. With the musical production attracting as many spectators as both Shakespearean productions combined, the Ellsons thought that it could become another income source to support free Shakespeare. (Interestingly, there seems to be a different audience for the musicals than for Shakespeare, with little cross-over from the musical to Shakespeare. The Shakespeare audience, however, does cross-over to the musicals.) Most of AST's annual budget is derived from state and municipal grants, from corporate support, and from contributions from private foundations and individuals. At the end of 1992, AST projected a significant operational deficit, the result mainly of (1) unusually cool and rainy weather that forced the cancelation of some performances and generally affected attendance and (2) reduced support from governmental arts agencies because of a statewide economic recession. The Ellsons, however, remain guardedly optimistic about the long-range development of AST.

Indeed, the production that I attended in 1992 was canceled halfway through the first act because of a light but steady rainfall. A clearly disappointed audience of several hundred spectators would have been willing to sit in the rain. Most were prepared for the weather with umbrellas and rainwear, but the rain posed a threat to unsheltered sound and lighting equipment, while the water-slicked stage was unsafe for the performers. The production, however, handsomely set, with seventeenth-century costumes, began with energy and clearly delineated characters. The *Columbus Post Dispatch* (8 August 1992) reviewer praised the performance he saw for its "verve and brisk pace" and singled out several actors for the strength of their performances.

Production History: **1982**: *MND*; **1983**: *TN, Oklahoma!*; **1984**: *Shr., Mac., South Pacific*; **1985**: *Ado, MV, The Music Man*; **1986**: *Rom., MND, West Side Story*; **1987**: *AYL, Tmp., Guys and Dolls*; **1988**: *Err., JC, Kiss Me Kate*; **1989**: *Oth., Wiv., Bye Bye Birdie*; **1990**: *Shr., Ham., Camelot*; **1991**: *1H4, LLL, The Music Man*; **1992**: *Tmp., TN, 1776*; **1993**: *Lr.*; **1994**: *R3*.

Research Resources: An informal archive is maintained at Actors' Summer Theatre administrative offices.

Site visit and interview: 14 August 1992.
Daniel J. Watermeier

GREAT LAKES THEATER FESTIVAL (formerly Great Lakes Shakespeare Festival). MAIL: 1501 Euclid Avenue, Suite 250, Cleveland, OH 44115. SITE: The Ohio Theatre, Playhouse Square Center, 1511 Euclid Avenue, Cleveland, OH 44115. ADMINISTRATION: 216/241-5490. BOX OFFICE: 216/241-6000. ADMISSION: $12–26 (1994). SEASON: five productions, 15 performances each, October–May. PRINCIPAL STAFF: Gerald Freedman, artistic director; Anne B. DesRosiers, managing director; John Ezell, associate artistic director; Bill Rudman and Victoria Bussert, associate directors. FACILITY: proscenium stage (capacity 1,000). STATUS: LORT-B. ANNUAL BUDGET: $3.3 million (1993-94). ANNUAL ATTENDANCE: 50,000 (1993-94). FOUNDED: 1961, Dorothy Teare.

The 2,000-seat Civic Auditorium of Lakewood, a western suburb of Cleveland, was constructed in 1959 as an addition to Lakewood High School and served as a home for both educational and municipal cultural events during the academic year. Dorothy Teare, president of the school board, was eager to see it put to use during the summer as well. She learned in 1961 that the summer Shakespeare troupe at Antioch College in Yellow Springs, Ohio, needed a new venue. At her urging, Arthur Lithgow (who had initiated the Antioch project and staged all 37 Shakespeare plays there) submitted a proposal, which was accepted by the city council, for professional Shakespeare performances in Lakewood. Most of the preparatory legwork was undertaken by a volunteer women's committee, with strong support from school superintendent William Edwards and *Cleveland Plain Dealer* critic Harlow Hoyt. One of the greatest hurdles was finding housing for the actors from New York, because some locals expressed concern, in those days when crewcuts were the norm, about the presence of the "transients" who had let their hair grow for their roles.

The Great Lakes Shakespeare Festival (GLSF)—renamed **Great Lakes Theater Festival** (GLTF) in 1985—opened its inaugural production, *As You Like It*, on 11 July 1962. The six-play rotating repertory season included several actors who have since achieved renown: Laurence Luckinbill, Donald Moffat, and Lithgow's teenaged son John (who played Dr. Pinch in that summer's *Comedy of Errors*). Teare served from 1962 to 1964 as the first president of the GLSF's board of trustees. Lithgow saw the venture through its first three seasons. After the haphazard business management of the first season, Lakewood banker Carl Dryer joined the board as chairman of finance and spent the next three years nursing GLSF through serious deficits, bringing its operations into the black by the end of the fourth season. In 1965, Lithgow initiated a cooperative venture with the McCarter Theatre of Princeton, New Jersey, whereby the two companies would each create three or four productions to be performed at both theatres. This arrangement also occasioned the introduction of some non-Shakespearean classics into the repertoire.

In 1966, Lithgow left the GLSF to become full-time executive director of the McCarter. He was succeeded by Lawrence Carra, a member of the Carnegie-Mellon theatre faculty, who served as the GLSF's artistic director from 1966 to 1975. Under Carra, a typical GLSF season was composed of a comedy, a tragedy, and a history or problem play by Shakespeare, and two other classics. Carra recognized and further galvanized the community spirit behind the festival. According to Teare, the main thing that kept the volunteers going during the difficult years was "that we could see what we were doing for children and young people." The 1968 *Hamlet* with Jeremiah Sullivan had extraordinary appeal for audiences of high school students. In 1972, the GLSF produced the American premiere of the Marowitz *Hamlet*. The GLSF's all-time greatest hit, however, was the 1971 production of *Godspell*, conceived by one of Carra's students, John-Michael Tebelak. In 1972, Mary Bill became the GLSF's first year-round staff member, hired to develop the educational component. In addition to her nationally recognized program of workshops and school programs, she wrote grant proposals that brought the 1975 budget up to $300,000, almost double what it had been when she joined the staff. In 1982, Bill became managing director, a position she held until her retirement in 1993.

Vincent Dowling took over the artistic directorship in 1976, when it was decided that that function too needed to be a year-round position (Carra being otherwise engaged during the academic year). Dowling, a veteran actor and director of Ireland's Abbey Theatre, was described as "a charismatic promoter who brought great visibility to the Festival at a time when it was needed." Dowling economized by putting a one-person play into the middle of each season; this also maximized rehearsal time for the large-cast shows. Dowling's tenure, 1976-84, saw Shakespeare balanced with modern American classics like *Peg o' My Heart* and the Thornton Wilder plays that served as the showpieces for a national symposium on Wilder in 1984. One of Dowling's discoveries, a young California actor named Tom Hanks, earned his Equity card under Dowling's guidance, acting Shakespeare to critical acclaim from 1977 to 1979 before going on to New York and, eventually, Hollywood.

As early as 1975, the GLSF had virtually outgrown a facility that could not meet professional theatre standards. Some problems were temporarily alleviated by the purchase of a former firehouse for administrative offices and a costume shop. Dowling's vision of a new facility constructed on a cliff overlooking Lake Erie foundered on the shoals of financial reality. Finally, in 1980, the GLSF was able to capitalize on the community's plan to refurbish three contiguous theatres—the State, the Palace, and the Ohio, all built in the 1920s—in downtown Cleveland's Playhouse Square. The GLSF opened its 1982 season at the 1,000-seat, Thomas Lamb-designed Ohio Theatre on 9 July, with *As You Like It*. The season budget jumped from $980,000 to $2.4 million, including

$35,000 a month in rent for the Ohio (as opposed to $12,000 for the entire summer at the Lakewood Civic Auditorium). To this, Dowling added another challenge: mounting the first American production of the eight-hour, 300-character Dickens adaptation, *The Life and Adventures of Nicholas Nickleby*, in 1982 and again in 1983. Requiring 500 rehearsal hours and a cast of 46, the risky venture paid off handsomely in national recognition for the GLSF, which toured the production to Chicago for a successful 12-week run. The transition to a new scale of operations proved financially hazardous, however, and problems persisted despite the sacrifice of GLSF's traditional rotating-repertory format. Dowling resigned in 1984.

Since 1985, artistic director Gerald Freedman has led the festival to ever-increasing recognition. Although the organization remains committed to producing at least one Shakespeare play each season, budgetary considerations and the wealth of other classical drama to be explored led the board to change the company name to the Great Lakes Theater Festival. During Freedman's tenure, the artistic quality of production has soared and the company has become comfortable in its large facility. In May 1987, the GLTF saluted the hundredth birthday of the legendary director-producer-playwright George Abbott by producing two of Abbott's Broadway hits, *Broadway* (1926) and *The Boys from Syracuse* (1938). Abbott himself was brought to Cleveland to direct the revival of his own *Broadway*, which moved to New York's Broadway that June. Among the celebrities who honored Abbott at a "Classic Broadway" weekend symposium in Cleveland were Eddie Albert, Betty Comden, Adolph Green, Sheldon Harnick, Garson Kanin, Harold Prince, Donald Saddler, Oliver Smith, and Nancy Walker. By means of such symposia and an array of community outreach efforts for both students and adults, the GLTF has created a rich educational context for its productions, reaching thousands in the greater Cleveland community, while enhancing the company's national visibility.

Production History: 1962: *AYL, MV, R2, Oth., 1H4, 2H4*; **1963**: *Err., Rom., Wiv., H5, JC, MM*; **1964**: *Ham., Shr., H6, R3, Ant., Ado*; **1965**: *MND, H6, Mac., Cor., The Rivals, The School for Wives, The Marriage Proposal*; **1966**: *TN, Lr., WT, The Importance of Being Earnest, She Stoops to Conquer*; **1967**: *Rom., AWW, LLL, Misalliance, Cyrano de Bergerac*; **1968**: *Tmp., Ham., Cym., Arms and the Man, The Beaux' Stratagem*; **1969**: *AYL, Candida, Tro., The Would-be Gentleman*; **1970**: *MV, R.U.R., JC, Volpone, Err.*; **1971**: *Oth., You Never Can Tell, Shr., Godspell, 1H4*; **1972**: *Wiv., The Beggars' Opera, R3, The Marowitz Hamlet, Electra*; **1973**: *TN, Tartuffe, MND, Ado, The Italian Straw Hat*; **1974**: *Lr., The Playboy of the Western World, MM, Under the Gaslight, Err.*; **1975**: *AYL, The Miser, Our Town, The Frogs, WT*; **1976**: *Tmp., Dear Liar, Ah, Wilderness!, Celebration Mime Theatre, The Devil's Disciple, Rom.*; **1977**: *Ham., Peg* *o' My Heart, In a Fine Frenzy, The Glass Menagerie, The Importance of Being Oscar, Shr.*; **1978**: *Polly, TGV, What Every Woman Knows, Wild Oats, The Nine Days Wonder of Will Kemp, Jn.*; **1979**: *TN, Juno and the Paycock, Clarence, Do Me a Favorite, Blithe Spirit, Oth.*; **1980**: *1H4, Err., Tit., Charley's Aunt, My Lady Luck, Hughie, The Boor*; **1981**: *The Matchmaker, Streetsongs, Lr., A Doll's House, Ado*; **1982**: *AYL, The Playboy of the Western World, Piaf. La vie! L'amour!, The Life and Adventures of Nicholas Nickleby, A Child's Christmas in Wales*; **1983**: *Wiv., Blanco!, Waiting for Godot, H5, The Island, The Dark Lady of the Sonnets, W.S., The Life and Adventures of Nicholas Nickleby, A Child's Christmas in Wales*; **1984**: *Shr., She Stoops to Conquer, Our Town, Alcestis and Apollo, Jeeves Takes Charge, Peg o' My Heart, MND*; **1985**: *TN, The Skin of Our Teeth, Miss Margarida's Way, The Game of Love, Tartuffe, Open Admissions, Take One Step!*; **1986**: *Arsenic and Old Lace, Ghosts, Barbara Cook in Concert, The Show-Off, Mac.*; **1987**: *Broadway, The Boys from Syracuse, Rom., The Regard of Flight, Hedda Gabler, Up from Paradise, Absent Forever*; **1988**: *LLL, Blood Wedding, A Doll's House, Man and Superman, Lady Day at Emerson's Bar and Grill*; **1989**: *Ham., The Threepenny Opera, The Seagull, A Christmas Carol, Grandma Moses: An American Primitive*; **1990**: *Lr., A Delicate Balance, The Lady from Maxim's, La Ronde, Dividing the Estate*; **1991-92**: *Uncle Vanya, Paul Robeson, A Christmas Carol*, **1992-93**: *Ohio State Murders, Mother Courage, Cyrano de Bergerac, Rough Crossing, Shakespeare's Women, Oth., A Christmas Carol*; **1993-94**: *The Cherry Orchard, Noel & Gertie, A Christmas Carol, Shr., Death of a Salesman.*

Research Resources: Margaret Lynch, *The Making of a Theater: The Story of the Great Lakes Theater Festival* (Cleveland: GLTF, 1986); Glenn Loney, and Patricia MacKay, *The Shakespeare Complex* (New York: Drama Book Specialists, 1975): 114-119.

Felicia Hardison Londré

SHAKESPEARE AT STAN HYWET. MAIL: Stan Hywet Hall and Gardens, 714 North Portage Path, Akron, OH 44303-1399. SITE: Stan Hywet Hall and Gardens. ADMINISTRATION/BOX OFFICE 216/836-5533. ADMISSION: $6–$10. SEASON eight performances, third and fourth weekends in July; 7:00 p.m., Fri.–Sun. FOUNDED: 1975.

Stan Hywet Hall and Gardens is a 65-room Tudor revival-style mansion surrounded by 70 acres of landscaped gardens and grounds, located in the northwest suburbs of Akron. The mansion was originally the home of Frank A. Seiberling, cofounder of Goodyear Tire and Rubber Company, and his family. It was the largest private residence in Ohio and one of the more opulent in the United States. Following the death of Seiberling, his estate eventually came to be managed by a private nonprofit trust to insure the mansion's preservation. The mansion is open to the public for tours and for special events, including musicals, madrigal dinners, and antique car exhibitions.

Since 1975, a Shakespeare play has been staged annually at Stan Hywet on weekends in mid-July. The performances are staged outdoors on the expansive raised patio at the rear of the mansion. The Tudor architecture serves as an impressive scenic background and "tiring house." The actors are amateurs drawn from the greater Akron community, often from several universities and colleges in the area. Attendance usually averages about 350 people for each performance. Theatregoers are invited to picnic on the grounds before the performance. In 1994, *The Taming of the Shrew* was presented.

Telephone interview: 24 July 1994.
Daniel J. Watermeier

OKLAHOMA

OKLAHOMA SHAKESPEAREAN FESTIVAL. MAIL: Box 1074, Durant, OK 74702. SITE: Montgomery Auditorium, Southeastern Oklahoma State University. ADMINISTRATION: 405/924-0121, ext. 217. BOX OFFICE: 405/924-0121, ext. 352. ADMISSION: $8.00; $6.00 for seniors and students (1992). SEASON: 22 performances, mid-June to late July; 8:00 p.m., Mon.–Sun.; 2:00 p.m., Sat.–Sun. PRINCIPAL STAFF: Molly Risso, artistic director; Bill Schroeder, managing director; Gary Varner, technical director; Riley Risso, administrative assistant. FACILITY: Montgomery Auditorium, proscenium (capacity 1,200); Theatre Complex Dinner Theatre, cabaret (capacity 250); Fine Arts Theatre, thrust (capacity 250). AUDITIONS: February-March, regional theatre auditions. STATUS: non-Equity professionals and apprentice company. ANNUAL BUDGET: $150,000 (1992). ATTENDANCE: 12,000 (1992). FOUNDED: 1980, Molly Risso.

In the early 1960s, Molly Risso, a young actress from Dallas with credentials at such venerable regional theatres as the Cleveland Playhouse, joined the **Oregon Shakespeare Festival**. Risso spent several summers in the lush Oregon hills, playing such roles as Gertrude in Hamlet, Lady Percy in *Henry*

IV, Part 1 and the Countess of Roussillon in *All's Well That Ends Well*. She recalls that she was astounded that a Shakespearean enterprise could flourish in a nonurban area, "three hundred miles from anywhere." Shortly thereafter, several of Risso's Oregon colleagues journeyed to Cedar City, Utah, to help found the **Utah Shakespearean Festival**. Risso noted that both Ashland and Cedar City had something in common that abetted the success of their respective Shakespeare festivals: each was situated near a major summer tourist area that offered would-be theatregoers daytime diversions.

Risso eventually abandoned her acting career for the security of academe. After several years of teaching in Texas, she accepted a position in 1979 to teach theatre at Southeastern Oklahoma State University in the small (population 16,000), charming hamlet of Durant. "DEWrant" (as locals call it) is situated in one of the most poverty-stricken areas of the country and sustains itself mostly through ranching and peanut farming (it is the home of what is proudly touted as "the world's largest peanut"). Thirteen miles west of downtown Durant is Lake Texoma, a huge body of water that straddles the Oklahoma-Texas border; it is the largest lake in the lower Midwest and annually draws hundreds of thousands of visitors. It is little wonder that Risso's memories of Ashland and Cedar City were revived as she envisioned a "perfect setting" for what would eventually grow into the Oklahoma Shakespearean Festival (OSF).

Given the region's economy, the relatively low educational level of its citizens, and the lures of the Dallas metroplex (roughly 90 miles south of Durant), building a Shakespeare festival has been no easy task for Risso and her artists, but she has persevered and sustained the OSF since 1980. From a modest beginning with (a production of *A Midsummer Night's Dream*, plus a small-scale musical and a children's theatre piece), the OSF has grown into an annual event that now produces two Shakespearean plays (usually a comedy and a tragedy), a full-scale musical, a dinner-theatre comedy, a collage of Shakespearean scenes and set pieces performed by the OSF apprentice company, a teen theatre revue, and a fully mounted children's show. The seven productions are mounted in three different spaces on the SOSU campus by a company of approximately 50 young professionals and academics from the South and lower Midwest. The grueling schedule has been affectionately dubbed "the Shakespearean Boot Camp" by those who endure the OSF's demanding eight-week residency.

Having established the viability of the OSF, Risso continues to dream her ambitious dreams. Eventually she would like to add a third play from the Shakespearean canon so that Oklahoma audiences can see a comedy, a tragedy, and a history each season (which actually happened in 1989). She also envisions a theatre on the shores of Lake Texoma, the better to accommodate the campers and outdoor enthusiasts who converge there.

The two Shakespeare plays and the musical ("a great way to get people in to see Shakespeare," says Risso) are performed in cavernous Montgomery

Auditorium, a 1,200-seat theatre that is, quite rightly, curtained off to create a more intimate audience area of about 300; the capacity can be adjusted upward for more popular shows. Audiences come not only from the immediate area but also from Oklahoma City and Tulsa, and the OSF proudly boasts of regular subscribers from as far away as Santa Fe. What the audiences may lack in big-city sophistication, they more than make up for with small-town enthusiasm and a graciousness toward the artists-in-residence that is enviable. Southeastern Oklahoma State University—known as "the campus of a thousand magnolias"—further adds to the "old South" charm of the OSF.

Shakespeare at the OSF runs the gamut from the highly traditional to the experimental. "We want our audiences to experience the full range of possibilities for Shakespeare," says Risso. "They've certainly become more knowledgeable over the years, and they are now as comfortable with 'treatments' as with conventional approaches." The 1991 season was surely a conventional season for the OSF. Both its *Macbeth* and *As You Like It* were well spoken and highly competent, if not especially daring. Perhaps the 1991 festival's most memorable moment was the killing of Lady Macduff: as he garrotted her, the First Murderer gave the lady a long, lingering kiss as the life went out of her body. The *As You Like It* was a pretty-to-look-at staging that capitalized on that summer's most popular film (*Robin Hood*).

By contrast, 1992 featured two decidedly nontraditional approaches to Shakespeare. Director Buzz Podewell cut 1,000 lines from *Henry V* and inventively restructured the script to effect a Brechtian exploration of the many faces of war. The action was backed by myriad slides illustrating the horrors—and, to be sure, the brotherhood—of war from medieval times through Desert Storm. Similarly, the combatants wore an eclectic mix of soldierly costumes to suggest that Shakespeare's story of Henry's war was about all wars. Young Henry, enveloped in smoke and fog, stood atop an ancient cannon, urging his soldiers to enter once more the breach at Harfleur. Battlefield scenes of low comedy alternated with shocking, almost Artaudian, scenes of gore: Pistol wore a pork-pie hat and gaudy floral shirt while evading the fighting; Bardolph was hanged on stage; the boys of the luggage were savagely slaughtered; and Fluellen, whom Podewell made the spokesman for these warriors for the working day, matter-of-factly emptied his .45 into the heads of the captured French. The battle scenes (staged by OSF technical director Gary Varner) were as exciting and complicated as any seen at the most renowned Shakespeare festivals. John Risso (a graduate student at Ohio State) played Henry as a "psychotic" who violently threw the Dauphin's gift of tennis balls quite literally throughout the theatre; he gradually developed into an assured, respected king of great warmth and good humor. The 1992 *Henry V* was a stunning display of theatrical virtuosity that provided Oklahoma audiences with both a multisensory experience and a provocative exploration of controversial subject matter.

By contrast, *Comedy of Errors* spoke directly to its constituent audience in the local dialect. Set in a 1940s "Hollywoodized" version of the Old West, this *Comedy* relocated the action to Muskogee, Oklahoma. The Antipholi of Muskogee and Corsicana (Texas) wore "twelve-gallon" cowboy hats, heavily fringed Western shirts, and wildly splotched "pony chaps." Their Dromios were younger versions of Gabby Hayes. Adriana cracked a mean bullwhip during the assault on Antipholus of Corsicana (Act II, scene 2), fired a shotgun through the roof of the Phoenix upon hearing that her "husband" had made a pass at Luciana, and dunked Dromio into the town watering trough. Luciana and Antipholus sang a country-Western ballad à la Roy and Dale, while the whole action was backed by a quintet of singers dubbed "The Grandsons of the Pioneers" (who sang "cool, clear water" anytime someone on stage referred to water). Topical jokes were inserted to make the humor instantly accessible to locals: for example, Dromio's raunchy exploration of Luce's "territories" in Act III, scene 2 was filled with funny references to Colorado ("In her breasts . . . all peaks and valleys"), California, and Baja Oklahoma (that is, Texas). Egeon told his sad tale in Act I, scene 1 abetted by an animal skin map sewn into the lining of his well-traveled jacket; Dr. Pinch was a snake-oil salesman whose exorcism of Antipholus in Act IV, scene 4 evolved into an old-fashioned revival meeting; the Courtesan was a Dolly Parton lookalike who slinked from "The Thunderbird" (the local saloon) in a hilarious costume that featured a prominently placed fig leaf and a snake; and the Abbess (who resided in a priory aptly named "St. Plautus") wore cowboy boots under her habit. Certainly no self-respecting cowboy tale can end without a chase, and the OSF *Comedy of Errors* obliged its patrons with a three-minute exercise in comic and Western madness at the beginning of Act V. Naturally, the show concluded with the twin Dromios heading off into the sunset and with the cast singing "Happy Trails to You" as a curtain call. Little wonder the opening night performance received a standing ovation from its happy Oklahoma audience.

Production History (Shakespeare plays only): **1980**: *MND*; **1981**: *Shr.*, *Rom.*; **1982**: *TN*, *Mac.*; **1983**: *AYL*, *MND*; **1984**: *Oth.*, *Ado*; **1985**: *Tmp.*, *MV*; **1986**: *Err.*, *Lr.*; **1987**: *R2*, *TGV*; **1988**: *Ham.*; **1989**: *Shr.*, *Rom.*, *1H4*; **1990**: *LLL*, *MM*; **1991**: *AYL*, *Mac.*; **1992**: *Err.*, *H5*; **1993**: *TGV*, *R3*; **1994**: *Tmp.*, *Ado.*

Research Resources: Archives for the Oklahoma Shakespearean Festival are informally kept in the Department of Theatre at Southeastern Oklahoma State University.

Arbuckle, Leann. "Oklahoma Shakespearean Festival." *Texoma Magazine* 1:10 (June 1990).

"Creative Storm Encompasses Area In Form of Shakespearean Festival." *Durant Daily Democrat* (7 June 1992): 7.

"Faithful Festival-Goers Are Part of Multi-Million Dollar Tourist Business in State." *Durant Daily Democrat* (1 July 1990): 7-A.
"Oklahoma Shakespearean Festival Begins 12th Season." *The Southeastern* (18 June 1991): 3.
"OSF Directors Have Diverse Backgrounds." *The Southeastern* (23 June 1992): 3.

Site visits: 17-18 July 1991; 16-17 July 1992.
Michael L. Greenwald

OKLAHOMA SHAKESPEARE IN THE PARK. MAIL: P.O. Box 1171, Edmond, OK 73083. SITE: E. C. Hafer Park, 9th and Bryant Streets, Edmond. ADMINISTRATION: 405/340-1222. BOX OFFICE/ADMISSION: $5 adults; $4 students; children under 12 free. SEASON: four outdoor productions, last week of May to first week of September; 8:00 p.m., Thurs.–Sun.; "Winter Classics" season varies. PRINCIPAL STAFF: Kathryn Huey O'Meara, artistic director; Sue Ellen Rieman, business manager. FACILITY: outdoor amphitheatre (capacity 1,000). AUDITIONS: local and Southwest Theatre Conference. STATUS: non-Equity. ANNUAL BUDGET: $100,000 (1991). ANNUAL ATTENDANCE: 10,000. FOUNDED: 1985, Jack J. O'Meara, Kathryn Huey.

Oklahoma Shakespeare in the Park (OSP) maintains close identification with Edmond, a bedroom community just north of Oklahoma City, though it draws loyal audience members from several surrounding small towns, some from as far away as Lawton and Stillwater. The operation, begun almost on a whim, has been allowed to grow at its own leisurely pace, with the goal of becoming an Equity company envisioned for around the turn of the century.

Kathryn Huey, a native of Edmond, had gone to New York for her Master of Fine Arts in Theatre. On a return visit home, she met Jack O'Meara, a television promotions director, who shared her enthusiasm for Shakespeare. They realized that the small stage in Hafer Park, which was available for use by various community groups, could also serve for outdoor summer Shakespeare productions. O'Meara and Huey rounded up local actors, generated enthusiasm, and even obtained a $500 grant from the Oklahoma Arts Council, though much of the funds for the first summer's venture came out of their own pockets. In July and August 1985, they presented *Twelfth Night* and *A Midsummer Night's Dream* for five weekends each, a ten-week season that drew 6,000 people. Given so many people willing to endure Oklahoma's summer heat and mosquitoes for Shakespeare, O'Meara and Huey determined to continue what they had begun, and OSP was incorporated in 1986, with O'Meara functioning as a managing director and Huey as artistic director.

Office and costume storage space was rented at the Edmond Community Center, a WPA building that also housed an all-purpose room. There, OSP presented three winter seasons of classic plays, including Shakespeare. These productions, like the summer series, were made available for the Oklahoma Touring Program sponsored by the State Arts Council of Oklahoma. The indoor space had to be shared with dog shows, cotillions, and other rental uses, however, which necessitated striking the set after almost every performance. Finally, they put the "Winter Classics" part of the operation on hold until a more suitable space could be found.

Meanwhile, the summer series thrived, expanding from two to three productions in 1988 and going to a rotating repertory format in 1989. Budget limitations forced a return to stock performances for the four-play, 59-performance season of 1990, but rotating repertory remains a goal for the company. Admission was charged for the first time during the 1988 season, but, even so, attendance hit a record 12,000 for the three shows. In 1989, the City of Edmond and its parks department created a new performance site for the company. One of Huey's goals is to increase the slope of the land in order to avoid introducing the use of body mikes as attendance grows. The parks department mows the site and, in 1991, funded the construction of permanent toilet facilities, but, in 1990, the company built its own semipermanent two-story wooden thrust stage. OSP's 25-member board takes responsibility for two benefits each year, raising between $15,000 and $20,000. By 1991, OSP was starting to get fairly large grants and contributions from companies like Phillips Petroleum and Target Stores.

Before the move to the new location, the cicadas in the nearby trees often buzzed loudly enough to drown out the performers' voices. That problem was remedied by having the costumed actors run under the trees with torches during intermission, thus quieting the creatures without incurring the rancor of environmentalists. In 1989, Mother Nature hit the company with a rainy summer. In addition to 15 full rainouts, daytime rains often made the ground so mucky that all but the hardiest Shakespeare enthusiasts were deterred. One performance was given for an audience of only 15 people, all from a home for retarded adults. "Bless their hearts," Huey recalls, "they're out there, so we'll be out there too."

Demographically, the most striking feature of the OSP audience is its youth. It is composed mostly of college students and young professionals, including many doctors, lawyers, teachers, and people in the oil business. A 1988 demographic survey (3,491 responses) revealed that fully half of the audience learned about OSP by word of mouth and that most rarely attended live theatre apart from OSP. The festival atmosphere—pre-performance music and a young company pre-show, combined with picnicking—appeals to families with small children, but this also means that they like to end the evening by 10:30 p.m. OSP audiences tend to prefer traditional-style Shakespeare, to the extent that the occasional "high-concept" production inevitably brings some calls and letters of protest.

"Traditional," however, does not mean setting every show in the Elizabethan period; the 1991 *Richard III*, for example, was set in the 1480s, the actual historical period. And the company has not shied away from nontraditional casting by race or sex. The 1989 *Hamlet* featured a black Claudius, and that summer's *Taming of the Shrew* was set in the Wild West, with Baptista cast as a woman. Huey recalls that "it created an interesting dynamic among the three women, Bianca, Kate, and their mother Baptista. She was a real tough lady. She ran a bar."

OSP's "house style" is based upon deep respect for directors, coupled with extensive discussion about the text and ways of interpreting it. The school programs provide a stimulus for keeping a kind of rawness and vitality in the work. The company's youth is considered one of its great selling points. OSP's "Winking Willie" logo, in use from the beginning, underscores the sense of fun: Against a starry night sky, a line drawing of an earringed Shakespeare smiles drolly and winks an eye. OSP's mission statement announces that the group aims: "To provide Oklahoma with quality stage productions in unique and exciting theatre environments at a reasonable price and to develop cultural growth in Oklahoma through classical plays, lectures, classes, seminars, television, film and other educational and theatrical projects."

The 1991 production of *Richard III* offered an exuberant and uncomplicated retelling of the story. Jon McClure's Richard was particularly effective in establishing complicity with the audience. The two murderers of Clarence delivered their dialogue as stand-up comedians. Buckingham, as played by Jonathan Freiman, was obtusely overfamiliar with Richard, slapping his back, leaning on his shoulder, playfully punching his arm. The audience could see Buckingham virtually digging his own grave almost from the start of the relationship. Although the fight scenes suffered from the lack of a professional combat director, the stage space was imaginatively used for the sequences set in the opposing encampments and for Richard's troubled dream. Whatever difficulties Nature might have imposed in the past were surely compensated by the full moon and soft breeze enhancing this August night's performance.

Production History: 1985: *TN, MND*; **Classics 85-86**: *Servant of Two Masters, She Stoops to Conquer, Rom.*; **1986**: *Err., Shr.*; **Classics 86-87**: *Tartuffe, David Copperfield, Ado, The Three Musketeers*; **1987**: *Wiv., AYL*; **Classics 87-88**: *The Playboy of the Western World, David Copperfield, MV*; **1988**: *Tmp., MND, Mac.*; **Classics 88-89**: *Ham.*; **1989**: *Shr., TN, On to Oklahoma!, Rom., Ado*; **Classics 89-90**: *The Importance of Being Earnest, MND*; **1990**: *Err., MV, LLL*; **1991**: *Wiv., MM, TGV, R3*; **1992**: *AYL, Tro., MND, H5*; **1993**: *Oth., TN, AWW, She Stoops to Conquer, JC.*; **1994**: *Shr., Ant., Tmp., Cyrano de Bergerac.*

Research Resources: Archives are informally maintained at the Oklahoma Shakespeare in the Park office.

Site visit and interview: 24 August 1991
Felicia Hardison Londré

RENEGADE SHAKESPEARE COMPANY. MAIL: P.O. Box 355, Norman, OK 73070. SITES: Sooner Theatre, 101 East Main St. (winter); Andrews Park (summer). ADMINISTRATION/BOX OFFICE: 405/364-4488. ADMISSION: $7 reserved, $5 general, $3 students and seniors (winter); free (summer). SEASON: one week in January; two weeks in July. PRINCIPAL STAFF: Sandy Taylor, executive director. FACILITIES: historic Sooner Theatre; Andrews Park amphitheatre. AUDITIONS: November and May; call for dates and locations. STATUS: community theatre. ANNUAL BUDGET: $23,000 (1992). ANNUAL ATTENDANCE: 5,000 (1992). FOUNDED: 1991, Sandy Taylor.

The Renegade Shakespeare Company (RSC) is an all-volunteer, nonprofit company founded in February 1991 by Sandy Taylor, who brought to the venture an extensive background in acting, writing, directing, stage managing, technical directing, and lighting design in theatre, film, and touring ice show. She and her company members, known as "The Renegades," began by presenting Shakespearean vignettes and other plays (like her own *Richard the Lionheart's Quest*) at Norman's Medieval Fair, Midsummer Night's Fair, City Arts Week, and Art in the Park. For the Brookhaven Christmas Celebration, they presented a version of *The Fifteen Minute Hamlet*. RSC also coordinates and hosts the **Sooner Shakespeare Festival** in downtown Norman for three days each July. It was for the latter event in 1991 that the RSC offered its first full-length production, *The Tempest*, in the Andrews Park Amphitheatre in downtown Norman.

The second full production, *Much Ado About Nothing,* was presented in January 1992 in the historic Sooner Theatre, a Spanish Gothic-style building designed by Harold Gimeno, one of Oklahoma's earliest architects. Constructed in 1929 expressly for the new talking pictures, it is listed on the National Register for Historic Places. Restored in 1982 as a performing arts facility, the Sooner Theatre hosts a variety of programs guided by a 21-member board in cooperation with the City of Norman Parks and Recreation Department. The southwest corner of the facility houses the RSC administrative office.

The RSC's logo, used as the main design element on its programs and promotional materials, is a shield across which two rampant lions, one serious and one happy reach out to touch claws. A staircase divides the crest diagonally, with a fleur-de-lys in each half. Beneath it appears the motto, "*At Foelix Utentis Applausu* [sic]."

The RSC dedicates itself "to the education, enlightenment and entertainment of the community and surrounding areas." In addition to its production-related activities, it sponsors children's classes. A generous gift from Target Stores has supplied class materials free of charge to the children. Given the limited funding available in Oklahoma, Taylor does just about everything herself. Although upbeat about the volunteer help she has had, she notes that "community spirit is not paying our phone bills." The RSC's first summer was largely underwritten by the Norman Arts and Humanities Council, as was a performance and lecture by Elaine Sulka of the **National Shakespeare Company** for the 1992 **Sooner Shakespeare Festival**. The City of Norman Convention and Tourism Committee underwrote the advertising for the latter event. Finally, in 1993, the RSC will be eligible to apply for state funding.

Production History: **1991**: *Tmp.* (summer); **1992**: *Ado* (winter), *Shr.* (summer); **1993**: *Rom.* (winter), *MND* (summer).

Research Resources: Archives for the Renegade Shakespeare Company are maintained by Sandy Taylor.

Felicia Hardison Londré

SOONER SHAKESPEARE FESTIVAL. See also **Renegade Shakespeare Company**.

The Sooner Shakespeare Festival (SSF) is an annual three-day festival in July of music, lectures, and performances, all coordinated and hosted by the **Renegade Shakespeare Company** (RSC) in downtown Norman, Oklahoma.

The 1991 festival included a concert of Elizabethan music, four lectures, and a film at the Sooner Theatre; two lectures, a workshop, and a discussion at the Santa Fe Depot; a juggling workshop in the Santa Fe Depot Courtyard; an Elizabethan costume display from the University of Oklahoma; and a performance of *The Tempest* by the RSC in Andrews Park Amphitheatre. These attractions were partially subsidized by the Norman Arts and Humanities Council Grants Program, funded by the Norman Transient Guest Room Tax to support the development of cultural events in the community.

In addition to the RSC's free outdoor performance of *The Taming of the Shrew*, the 1992 festival included a discount-priced performance of the University of Oklahoma Drama Department's production of *I Hate Hamlet*. Also on the 1992 SSF program were a concert of "Musica Transalpina: The Italian Style in Elizabethan Music," a stage combat demonstration, and four lectures, including ones by Michael Addison of the **California Shakespeare Festival** and by Elaine Sulka of the **National Shakespeare Company**.

Activities especially oriented to children were scheduled all day and evening on Saturday in Andrews Park; these included a juggling workshop, a magician, storytelling, maypole dancing, making shields and banners, and a poetry reading.

Felicia Hardison Londré

OREGON

OREGON SHAKESPEARE FESTIVAL. MAIL: P.O. Box 158, Ashland, OR 97520. SITES: Ashland: adjacent to Plaza and Lithia Park in downtown Ashland; Portland: Portland Center for the Performing Arts. ADMINISTRA-TION: 503/482-2111. BOX OFFICE: Ashland: 503/482-4331; Portland: 503/274-6588. ADMISSION: Ashland: $8–$36, depending on season (Spring, Summer, or Fall) and theatre; Portland: $8–$28 (1993). SEASON: Ashland: mid-February to end of October; different productions in overlapping repertory; 1:00 or 2:00 p.m. and 8:00 or 8:30 p.m., Tues.–Sun.; Portland: early November to mid-April, five productions presented consecutively; 7:00 or 8:00 p.m., Tues.–Sun.; 2:00 p.m., Sat.–Sun. PRINCIPAL STAFF: Henry Woronicz, artistic director; William W. Patton, executive director; Paul Nicholson, general manager. FACILITIES: Elizabethan Theatre, outdoor (capacity 1,193); Angus Bowmer Theatre, modified thrust (capacity 600); Black Swan, flexible (capacity 140); Intermediate Theatre at the Portland Center for the Performing Arts, proscenium (capacity 860). AUDITIONS: major cities nationwide and in Ashland and Portland. STATUS: special Equity contract based on LORT B status. ANNUAL BUDGET: $12,068,300 (1993). ANNUAL ATTENDANCE: Ashland: 354,708; Portland: 92,020 (1992). FOUNDED: 1935, Angus L. Bowmer.

The Oregon Shakespeare Festival (OSF) is the oldest Shakespearean festival in the United States. It was founded in 1935 by Angus L. Bowmer (1905-1979), a professor at what is now Southern Oregon State College in Ashland. The roots of the festival, however, can be traced back to the Chautauqua societies of the 1890s. Originating in Lake Chautauqua, New York, these societies were designed to promote culture in rural areas, especially during the period between planting and harvesting. Although it is a relatively remote town on the Northern slope of the Siskiyou range separating California from Oregon, Ashland had a longstanding history in the region as a central town, a gathering place, and a vacation site. From its beginnings in 1893, the Ashland Chautauqua drew numerous visitors from the region to hear concert performances and lectures and to engage in literature-and Bible-study groups. A large, wooden-domed auditorium, accommodating about 1,000 people, was built for these activities. It was enlarged in 1905 and then completely rebuilt in 1917 when attendance rose to about 3,000. By the early 1920s, however, the Chautauqua movement had declined in popularity, and the auditorium fell into disrepair. In the late 1920s, the Chautauqua auditorium's wooden dome was razed. All that remained was the circular concrete wall of the building surrounding what soon became a gently sloping open field.

Bowmer had been a student at the University of Washington in the early 1930s. There he had acted in productions of *Love's Labour's Lost* and *Cymbeline* mounted by a guest director at the university, Ben Iden Payne, a celebrated English and Broadway director and proponent of the neo-Elizabethan style of staging Shakespeare pioneered by William Poel. Bowmer "fell in love with Payne's modified Elizabethan staging" of Shakespeare's plays (see Bowmer, *The Ashland Elizabethan Stage*, p. 13). In Ashland, he noted the similarities between the old Chautauqua auditorium's walls and the open-air circular theatres pictured in seventeenth-century panoramic views of London. Bowmer persuaded the leaders of Ashland to build, as a Depression-era Works Progress Administration project, an Elizabethan style stage, modeled after designs for Payne's productions, inside the Chautauqua walls.

Bowmer's stage consisted of a trapezoid platform, slightly recessed behind the old auditorium wall, and overhung by a shallow roof, or "penthouse," as he called it, supported by wooden pillars; at the rear of the platform was a makeshift inner above and inner below. A curtain could be drawn between the wooden pillars, essentially closing off the inner above and below areas from the forestage. Bowmer even utilized "curtain pages" who sat near the pillars throughout the performance to handle the curtains when required. Shed-like structures at the right and left of the stage housed on one side a prompter's booth and on the other the lighting control booth. On the sloping hillside, the former auditorium floor, a series of rough wooden benches and a row or two of folding chairs were arranged parallel to the stage. A small pit orchestra was placed at stage left for overtures and other incidental music.

On this stage, as part of Ashland's Fourth of July celebration, Bowmer presented, in a semblance of Elizabethan dress, one performance of *The Merchant of Venice* and two performances of *Twelfth Night* on 2, 3, and 4 July. The cast was drawn from Bowmer's students from the college and townspeople. The total attendance was about 500, and, at admission prices of $.50 and $1.00, Bowmer cleared enough to cover the loss from what had been planned as a fund-raising Fourth of July boxing match.

Bowmer's first season was sufficiently successful to warrant an annual Shakespeare festival around the Fourth of July holiday. By 1939, the season had expanded to two performances each of four different Shakespeare plays, with total attendance reaching 2,000. That same year, the festival was brought to national attention when it performed at the World's Fair in San Francisco and had a performance of *The Taming of the Shrew* broadcast on the radio nationwide. Unfortunately, in the middle of the 1940 season, a fire broke out in the costume storage area, destroying the costume stock and damaging the stage. This event, coupled with the imminence of World War II, led the festival to discontinue its operation.

In 1947, after the war, Bowmer was persuaded to rebuild the stage and reopen the festival. For the most part, the new stage house followed the configuration of the first stage. The inner above and below were increased in width, however, and moved farther downstage. Sidedoors and windows were added to the facade. Widening the stagehouse and bringing it forward allowed the auditorium to be reconfigured into a series of arched rows of individual seats. This second stage served the festival for over a decade. The 1947 season proved a great success, with nearly 5,000 playgoers attending four performances each of four different productions.

For the next decade, under Bowmer's direction, the OSF gradually increased its number of productions and performances while attendance steadily grew. The quality of the productions also improved, in large part because of the talented people Bowmer recruited from several university theatre programs, principally Stanford University where Bowmer himself had gone for graduate studies in 1947-48 under the G.I. Bill educational program. Among these were Dr. Margery Bailey, a Stanford professor of literature, who was appointed academic adviser to the festival; she also helped organize the Tudor Guild as a volunteer auxilary service for the festival and the Institute of Renaissance Studies, which offered classes and lectures on Shakespeare and Renaissance culture. Bailey helped to further Bowmer's vision of a festival that would both entertain and educate the public. William Patton and Richard Hay, both students at Stanford, also came to Ashland after the war, spending their summers working on lights, acting, and doing whatever needed to be done. In 1953, Patton was appointed to be the festival's first general manager and its first year-round employee, while Hay was appointed festival designer and technical director. (They continue their association with the OSF to the present day.) Directors like James Sandoe, from the University of Colorado, and Robert Loper and Allen Fletcher from Stanford University also contributed to the development of the OSF. Richard Graham, an accomplished professional actor, came to Ashland in 1948 to gain Shakespearean acting experience and remained for 12 seasons playing most of the great roles, including Lear and Othello. Ben Iden Payne himself played Friar Laurence in *Romeo and Juliet* and directed *Cymbeline* in 1956 and *A Midsummer Night's Dream* in 1961. By the 1957 season, OSF had expanded to five productions playing in repertory for over 30 performances, with attendance reaching nearly 25,000. In 1958, with the production of *Troilus* and *Cressida*, the festival became one of the few theatres to have produced the entire Shakespeare canon.

At the end of the 1958 season, a local fire inspector ruled that the stagehouse had become unsafe and had to be replaced. Hay undertook the design of a new theatre, drawing on the models of Elizabethan theatres proposed by scholars C. Walter Hodges and John Cranford Adams. Opening in 1959, the open-air Elizabethan Theatre, as it was called, was a much more elaborate structure than its predecessor. The entire stagehouse facade, half-timbered in the Tudor style, was nearly twice as high as the older structure, and the platform stage thrusted more deeply into the auditorium. There were two doorways at each side of the platform, along with a pair of mullioned, leaded windows that could be opened outwards and a second, curtained balcony or "musicians' gallery." The stage floor contained a series of traps, extending from the inner below to the front of the forestage to allow for appearances of actors and staging pieces from below. Thrusting out from the inner above and two steps down from that level was still another staging area that Bowmer called the "pavilion." The lower floor of this pavilion, furthermore, contained a slip stage that allowed thrones or other pieces of furniture to be setup behind closed curtains and then winched forward to the middle of the stage when needed. The pavilion and slipstage also eliminated the need for curtains between the pillars of the penthouse. The seating area was also expanded so that it had a steeper pitch in the rear half to improve the view of the stage. But because of limitations imposed by the old Chautauqua walls, the auditorium actually continued to resemble the configuration of an ancient Greek theatre rather than an Elizabethan one.

Nevertheless, theatrical practice for over two decades on this outdoor, modified Elizabethan stage contributed significantly to a distinctive OSF style of Shakespearean production. Inspired chiefly by Payne, Bowmer believed that the most effective way to stage Shakespeare's plays was to follow Elizabethan staging conventions as they were known, or as they could be discovered using the festival's Elizabethan Theatre. For Bowmer, this choice meant, first, fidelity to the text, leaving it essentially unchanged and virtually uncut. It also meant utilizing the various stage areas to create continuous, fluid action, with one scene flowing into or overlapping another without the interruption or distraction of scene changes. So confident was he that Shakespeare's plays were intended for continuous, uninterrupted movement that, at least in the early years, there were no intermissions at the OSF. The approach to scenery was utilitarian and minimalist. Scenery consisted of an occasional set piece (a tent, for example), pieces of furniture, and decorative banners. Costumes were in a Tudor or generally Renaissance style. Since the performances were always staged in the evening, however, Bowmer from the start conceded to artificial lighting. With the aid of his Elizabethan Theatre, furthermore, Bowmer coached his actors toward what he called a "story telling tempo," a performance rhythm that was dynamic and expressive, that was essentially realistic, and that emphasized the drama of character and conflict.

The OSF also continued to adhere to a repertory mode of presentation. "See Four Plays in Four Days" was the marketing slogan, and most playgoers did exactly that. Audiences responded positively to the OSF's production style, to its continuing development in artistic quality over the years, and to the repertory system. By 1965, the OSF was presenting 48 performances of five plays, with a total attendance of over 54,000 or 99.9 percent of capacity. The repertoire had also expanded beyond Shakespeare to include productions of John Webster's *The Duchess of Malfi* (1960), Ben Jonson's *The Alchemist* (1961) and *Volpone* (1965) and Francis Beaumont and John Fletcher's *The Knight of the Burning Pestle* (1964). In 1964, furthermore, to celebrate the four-hundredth anniversary of Shakespeare's birth, the OSF accepted an invitation to tour three productions to Stanford University, where 12 performances played to another 25,500 playgoers in the Frost Amphitheatre.

With the season virtually sold out, continued and sustained development of the festival would nevertheless be limited unless the season could be extended beyond the summer months, but such an extension would necessitate an indoor theatre. Moreover, the festival, as a strictly summer affair, continued to draw its actors, directors and production personnel mostly from college and university theatre programs. The OSF, in Bowmer's own words, was essentially "a stepping stone between the academic and professional theatres" (*Time* 31 July 1964), although some Equity actors had joined the company as guest artists as early as 1959. Bowmer seemed to have realized, however, that only by offering a core of experienced professional actors the opportunity for year-round employment could he continue to elevate the artistic quality of OSF productions.

In the winter of 1951, for example, Bowmer, in association with Richard Graham, mounted a season of four contemporary plays in the Lithia Theatre (formerly the Vining Theatre), an unused legitimate theatre in Ashland. Although they reportedly had "encouraging success" (see Brubaker and Brubaker, *Golden Fire*, p. 87), their efforts were cut short when the theatre was destroyed by fire in the middle of their second season. In the early 1960s, Bowmer again tried to mount, with sponsorship from Southern Oregon College, a "second season" in the Varsity Theatre, an Ashland movie house, but "the effort was too expensive to continue." In 1966, however, Bowmer finally succeeded in augmenting festival income, if not extending the season, by mounting matinee performances of ballad operas in the Varsity Theatre. In the same year, a fund drive was initiated to raise money for a new indoor theatre. The drive was helped by a report from the University of Oregon's Graduate School of Business, which documented the festival's fragile financial situation and its significant impact on the economy of the local community. Spurred by this report, the city of Ashland successfully applied for a matching grant from the Economic Development Administration division of the U.S. Department of Commerce, using the proposed theatre as the centerpiece for a series of downtown improvements. On 21 March 1970, the new indoor theatre, named by its chief donor in honor of Angus Bowmer, opened with a spring season of four productions; the Varsity Theatre and the annual ballad operas were abandoned.

With the addition of the Angus Bowmer Theatre, the OSF became a nearly year-round operation. The number of productions doubled, and the number of performances tripled. Attendance soared in one season from about 65,000 in 1969 to almost 127,000 in 1970. Access to Ashland was also enhanced by the completion in 1970 of Interstate Highway 5, the major thoroughfare between San Diego and Seattle that passes immediately to the east of downtown Ashland. By the late 1970s, the OSF's annual attendance exceeded 220,000.

In 1970, Bowmer, after 35 years, stepped down as the festival's producing director. He was succeeded by Jerry Turner who had first come to the Festival in 1957. Under the leadership of Turner and Bill Patton, the OSF continued to flourish in the 1970s and 1980s, with longer seasons and an expanding repertory. While still centered on Shakespeare, the recent repertory has included productions of other great classical and modern dramas, as well as contemporary plays. In 1977, a small black-box theatre, named The Black Swan, was added to the festival's growing facilities. With a flexible seating plan that could accommodate approximately 140 patrons, The Black Swan allowed for experimentation in design, acting, and staging techniques and for the presentation of plays that might not be commercial successes but were worthy of serious production. Working in consort, Turner, Patton, and Hay also recruited a number of talented young actors, directors, designers, and managers to assist them in maintaining the artistic vitality of the festival. And to maintain a firm financial foundation for the festival as it expanded, the Development Office was established in 1978. With Turner's production of *Troilus and Cressida* in 1978, the OSF completed the Shakespeare canon for a second time.

The festival's longstanding commitment to education was enhanced in the 1970s with the appointment of an education coordinator. Working with the festival's Institute of Renaissance Studies, the Information and Education Office developed classroom materials, sent teams of actors to area schools for lectures and demonstrations, and sponsored workshops for teachers and students. By the late 1980s, the Education Office's School Visit Program was sending two- or three-actor teams to hundreds of schools throughout the Western states, including Alaska and Hawaii. It is one of the largest theatre education programs in the United States. In 1992, for example, the School Visit Program traveled to almost 230 educational institutions ranging from elementary schools to universities. Total attendance at the various performances and workshops offered was over 142,000. Among the other outreach activities sponsored by the OSF Education Office are the Summer Seminar for High School Juniors, the Wake Up With Shakespeare summer classes, and the Teachers' Symposia. The festival has also created an Exhibit Center, which is a walk-through history of the festival, where costumes and properties from past productions are displayed and video documentaries on the OSF are continuously projected. There is also a backstage tour where members of the company guide more than a hundred visitors daily through all three theatres, answering questions along the way. Company members perform many such services on a voluntary basis, for additional stipends, throughout the season. The festival has also sponsored the publication of a number of books and monographs, including Bowmer's memoir *As I remember, Adam* (1975), *A Space for Magic: Stage Settings by Richard L. Hay* (1978), and Edward and Mary Brubaker's *Golden Fire: The Anniversary Book of the Oregon Shakespeare Festival* (1985).

The early 1980s were marked by a number of high points for the festival. In 1982, for example, the OSF mounted a very successful two-week tour of *The Comedy of Errors* throughout the state of Washington. In 1983, the festival became the only theatre in the country to win the National Governors' Association award for distinguished service to the arts. Simultaneously, it also won an Antoinette Perry ("Tony") Award for its achievements over the years. In 1984, its production of *The Taming of the Shrew* successfully toured for seven weeks throughout California. The OSF, like many not-for-profit regional theatres, depends on the support of numerous volunteers. There are over 11 different volunteer organizations in Ashland; a core of about 800 members have responsibilities that range from ushering to staffing the Tudor Guild giftshop to constructing costumes. In 1986, festival volunteers received the President's Volunteer Action Award in Washington, D.C.

By 1987, over 5,000,000 playgoers had attended one or more OSF productions. Season attendance was over 320,000, or over 91 percent capacity, with more than half of the 681 performances playing to standing room only. The OSF management decided to expand its operations once again by accepting an offer from the city of Portland to establish a satellite theatre company at the new Portland Center for the Performing Arts. With its own staff, support facilities, and six-month season (November-April) of five productions presented consecutively, the Portland company nevertheless became an integral part of OSF. With the addition of the Portland operation, the OSF became the largest not-for-profit theatre in the United States, mounting 15 to 16 productions each year and employing over 500 theatre professionals recruited from across the United States. Attendance at OSF-Portland steadily increased in its five years of operation, from 28,593 in 1988 to 90,000 in 1992, or about 69 percent capacity. Unlike the Ashland operation, however, which, remarkably, has had only one deficit season, OSF's Portland operation had not yet become financially secure by 1993 and continued to run at a yearly deficit. OSF's board moved to separate the Ashland and Portland operations and to assist Portland in the tranistion toward a completely autonomous organization.

In the late 1980s, the OSF embarked on an ultimately successful campaign to raise $7.5 million to build a new seating area for the Elizabethan Theatre. The resulting structure, called the Allen Pavilion after the Washington state family foundation that made the largest single financial contribution to the project, was completed in time for the opening of the 1992 summer season. The three-story Allen Pavilion wraps around the former seating area. It leaves the

Elizabethan Theatre an open-air performing space, but it creates a new actor-audience intimacy; much more than the former configuration, it somewhat evokes an Elizabethan public theatre, although far larger in size. The pavilion also serves to improve the acoustics within the theatre, shields performances from exterior noises, allows for the use of state-of-the-art sound and lighting technology, and generally enhances the comfort of audience members. As part of this project, new restrooms and concession booths and a new stage for the pre-performance Greenshow were also constructed.

In June 1991, Jerry Turner, after 20 very successful years, stepped down as artistic director and was named artistic director emeritus and consultant. He was succeeded by Henry Woronicz, who had joined the festival as an actor in 1984. Since assuming the artistic directorship, Woronicz has expanded a series of Friday morning readings of new plays, taken steps to integrate more closely the management of the Ashland and Portland operations, hired a vocal coach, and established the "Studio Program" as a continuing, in-house, training program for company members. Woronicz also seems committed to staging not only the standard classics but also the more problematic historical plays and challenging new dramas in a range of production approaches that will continue the artistic development of the OSF.

As the festival approaches its sixtieth anniversary, it certainly must be viewed as one of the most successful American theatre companies of the modern era. Its achievements are notable. In 1992, the OSF Ashland played to over 93 percent capacity. The audience it has developed extends far beyond its immediate location. Over 88 percent of festival patrons travel over 125 miles to Ashland, while 17 percent come from the populous San Francisco Bay Area, over 350 miles distant. A respectable 7 percent come from across the United States and abroad. Over 76 percent of its annual budget comes from earned income. For the remainder, the OSF depends chiefly on individual supporters. In 1992, there were almost 15,000 members of the Oregon Shakespeare Festival Association, representing people in virtually all 50 states as well as Canada and countries abroad. Contributing amounts for membership range from $50 to over $5,000 to support the festival. Numerous regional and national corporations and foundations also contribute to the festival. With such patronage, the OSF rightly views itself not as a regional, but as a national or even international theatre with a high sense of mission and high standards of theatrical presentation.

In the summer of 1990, we visited Ashland for the first time. Although the OSF is the town's major draw, Ashland is also an unusually attractive community. Situated in a narrow valley of remarkable natural beauty, there is a wholesomeness, authenticity, and unpretentiousness about its eclectic mixture of restaurants, boutiques, bakeries, bed-and-breakfasts, and residential neighborhoods. It has none of the tackiness or kitsch that often mars other vacation or tourist attractions. Though it has many features in common with the towns where other major festivals are located (for example, Stratford-upon-

Avon, Stratford, Ontario, or Niagara-on-the-Lake, Ontario, the site of the Shaw Festival), we found Ashland the most attractive of these communities. The festival also has clearly been embraced by the community. Many company members, affectionately called "Shakespeares" by the locals, are permanent residents of Ashland. This sense of community attachment, as the Brubakers have rightly noted, "rubs off on the thousands who . . . come to make Ashland their town for theatre." The sense of welcome, of shared community, and of informality encourages a festive mood. This mood is also enhanced by the pre-performance Greenshow, a mixture of Tudor-style music and dancing. Compared to other major festivals, ticket prices for OSF performances, as well as the ancillary costs of accommodations and meals, are very moderate. Idyllic though it is, the milieu is carefully orchestrated and managed by the festival and the community. The festival reaps community goodwill that results in enthusiastic playgoer attendance and support; the community in turn benefits economically. In the early 1990s, for example, the total economic impact of the festival on the region was over $60 million, a significant sum for a mainly rural area.

We saw productions in all three theatres, a total of seven plays: *The Winter's Tale, Henry V, The Comedy of Errors, The Merry Wives of Windsor, Peer Gynt, God's Country*, a contemporary play centered on the neo-Nazi cults inhabiting communities in the Northwest, and S. N. Behrman's *The Second Man*. All adhered to an exceptionally high standard of theatrical presentation. On the Elizabethan stage, the visually compelling *Winter's Tale*, directed by Libby Appel, drew upon an eclectic mix of images, with its Klimt-patterned gowns, classical Greek-inspired masks, and various Judeo-Christian emblems. Mimi Carr, double-cast as Time and Paulina, functioned as a shamanistic ringmaster, as if to put the focus on a superior female consciousness. For sheer charisma, however, Patrick Page soared in the role of Autolycus. Similarly, Marco Barricelli gave a magnetic and utterly moving performance in the title role of *Henry V*, directed by James Edmondson. In his stirring call to battle at Harfleur, his conscience-stricken remorse over Richard II, and his playful courtship of Katherine, Barricelli embodied all that is implied in the epithet "this star of England." Given a Middle Eastern flavor in its bright costumes and exotic music, *The Comedy of Errors* presented a bloodthirsty populace for whom violence was the way of life. They played ball with severed heads, clamored for more executions, and slapped each other around with abandon, but, with the appearance of the Abbess at the end of the play, Arabian Nights cruelty gave way to Christian redemption. That interpretation aptly demonstrates how the OSF's season is chosen to juxtapose plays that seem to comment on one another. The power of Christian example to promote a kinder, gentler side of humanity contrasted interestingly with a neo-Nazi order's skewed exploitation of Christianity as depicted in *God's Country* in the Angus Bowmer Theatre.

For *The Merry Wives of Windsor*, also in the Bowmer and set in the period immediately following World War I, director Pat Patton and scenic designer Vicki L. Smith filled the stage with a complete English village. From left to right were the facades, all with practical doors and windows, of the Inn of the Garter complete with a red phone booth outside, the Page house, a perspective street, the Ford house, and Mistress Quickly's establishment. Mr. Ford, an uptight, nervous, little businessman in a conservative brown suit with briefcase, seemed to live out a fantasy when he donned a buccaneer's black eyepatch and peg-leg to disguise himself as Brook. The comic mileage wrung from the fake wooden leg was endlessly clever, including Ford's ducking into the phone booth for a quick change into Brook's outfit just before Falstaff spotted him. For the scene in the woods, a greenish light and tree shadows were thrown over the entire set. Among the elaborately costumed "fairies" were two wearing gas masks. Although the OSF has produced *The Merry Wives of Windsor* five times (1940, 1954, 1963, 1973, and 1980), this was the first production to set the action outside the Elizabethan period, an indication perhaps that the festival is open to moving away from its generally conservative production approach. The OSF rigorously eschews "stars" in favor of the ensemble; the acting was uniformly skillful and well balanced with very strong performances in several of the leading roles. Some veteran actors are clearly regarded as "star performers" by festival patrons, however. Before the curtain for *The Winter's Tale*, for example, it was announced that veteran Henry Woronicz would be standing in for the regular Leontes, and the audience burst into enthusiastic applause. Woronicz's skillful performance, far beyond what one expects of an "understudy," warranted the premature ovation. To see his *tour-de-force* performance as Peer Gynt the following evening gave one special insight into the depth of talent in the company. It is also one of the delights of the repertory system to be able to see the same performers in often radically different roles.

The OSF is one of the "treasures" of the contemporary American theatre. With its unusual combination of theatres, milieu, production style, clear sense of mission, financial stability, committed artistic and managerial staff, and strong patronage, it will undoubtedly remain the premier Shakespearean festival in the United States for many decades to come.

Production History (abbreviations in parentheses refer to performance venues; refer to key below): **1935:** *MV, TN;* **1936:** *MV, TN, Rom.;* **1937:** *TN, Shr., Rom.;* **1938:** *Ham., Shr., TN, MV;* **1939:** *Ham., Shr., Err., AYL;* **1940:** *Wiv., Err., Ado, AYL.* **1941–46:** No productions during World War II; **1947:** *Ham.,* *LLL, Mac., MV;* **1948:** *Oth., MV, LLL, Jn.;* **1949:** *Rom., R2, MND, Oth., Shr.;* **1950:** *1H4, AYL, Ant., Err.;* **1951:** *TN, MM, Lr., 2H4,;* **1952:** *Tmp., JC, H5, Ado;* **1953:** *Cor., MV, 1H6, Shr.;* **1954:** *Ham., WT, Wiv., 2H6;* **1955:** *Tim., MND, 3H6, Mac., AWW;* **1956:** *R3, LLL, ' Rom., Cym., Tit.;* **1957:** *AYL, Oth.,*

TGV, H8, Per.; **1958**: Ado, Lr., MV, Tro.; **1959**: TN, The Maske of the New World (an original entertainment to celebrate the Oregon Centennial), Jn., MM, Ant.; **1960**: Shr., JC, Tmp., R2, The Duchess of Malfi; **1961**: AWW, MND, Ham., 1H4, The Alchemist; **1962**: AYL, Err., 2H4, Cor., A Thieves' Ballad; **1963**: Wiv., Rom., LLL, H5; **1964**: MV, Lr., TN, 1H6, The Knight of the Burning Pestle, Lovers Made Men; **1965**: Ado, Mac., WT, 2H6, Volpone; **1966**: (ET): MND, Oth., TGV, 3H6; (VT): The Beggar's Opera; **1967**: (ET): Per., Ant., Shr., R3; (VT): The Maid of the Mill; **1968**: (ET): Cym., Ham., AYL, H8; (VT): Lock Up Your Daughters; **1969**: (ET): Tmp., Rom., TN, Jn.; (VT): Virtue in Danger; **1970**: (BT): You Can't Take It With You, Antigone, The Fantasticks, Rosencrantz and Guildenstern are Dead, MV, The Imaginary Invalid, The Glass Menagerie; (ET): Err., JC, R2; **1971**: (BT): MND, A Man for All Seasons, Arsenic and Old Lace, Under Milkwood, The Glass Menagerie, U.S.A.; (ET): Ado, Mac., 1H4; **1972**: (BT): Room Service, The Crucible, Uncle Vanya, The Playboy of the Western World, Tro., Our Town; (ET): Shr., LLL, 2H4; **1973**: (BT): The Alchemist, Oth, Our Town, The Importance of Being Earnest, Dance of Death, Waiting for Godot; (ET): AYL, Wiv., H5; **1974**: (BT): Waiting for Godot, Hedda Gabler, TGV, The Time of Your Life, A Funny Thing Happened on the Way to the Fo-

rum; (ET): Ham., Tit., TN; **1975**: (BT): WT, Charley's Aunt, Oedipus the King, The Petrified Forest, Long Day's Journey Into Night; (ET): Rom., AWW, 1H6; **1976**: (BT): Err., The Devil's Disciple, The Tavern, Brand, The Little Foxes; (ET): 2H6, Ado, Lr.; **1977**: (BT): MM, Angel Street, The Rivals, A Streetcar Named Desire; (ET): 3H6, Ant., MV; (BS): A Taste of Honey, A Moon for the Misbegotten; **1978**: (BT): Tartuffe, Private Lives, Mother Courage and Her Children, Tim., Miss Julie; (BS): The Effect of Gamma Rays on Man-in-the-Moon Marigolds, Night of the Tribades.; (ET): Shr., R3, Tmp.; **1979**: (BT): Mac., Born Yesterday, The Play's the Thing, Miss Julie, The Wild Duck; (BS): Who's Happy Now?, Root of the Mandrake, Indulgences in a Louisville Harem; (ET): AYL, MND, The Tragical History of Doctor Faustus; **1980**: (BT): Cor., The Philadelphia Story, AYL, Of Mice and Men, Juno and the Paycock, Ring 'Round the Moon; (BS): Seascape, Sizwe Banzi is Dead, Lone Star/Laundry and Bourbon; (ET): Wiv., R2, LLL.; **1981**: (BT): Wild Oats, TN, Death of a Salesman, 'Tis Pity She's a Whore, Oth., TGV; (BS): Artichoke, The Birthday Party, The Island; (ET): TN, TGV, 1H4; **1982**: (BT): Blithe Spirit, Inherit the Wind, Oth., JC, Spokesong, The Matchmaker; (BS): Wings, Hold Me!, The Father; (ET): Err., Rom., H5; **1983**: (BT): Ham., Man and Superman, Ah, Wilderness!: The Matchmaker,

What the Butler Saw, Dracula;
(BS): *The Entertainer, Don Juan
in Hell, Dreamhouse*; (ET): *Ado,
R3, Cym.*; **1984**: (BT): *Tro., Lon-
don Assurance, Dracula, Hay Fe-
ver, Cat on a Hot Tin Roof, The
Revenger's Tragedy*; (BS): *Trans-
lations, Seascape With Sharks and
Dancer*, (ET): *Shr., H8, WT*; **1985**:
(BT): *Lr., Trelawny of the "Wells,"
Light Up the Sky, An Enemy of the
People, Crimes of the Heart;* (BS):
*Strange Snow, The Majestic Kid,
Lizzie Borden in the Late After-
noon*; (ET): *MV, AWW, Jn.;* **1986**:
(BT): *Tit., The Three Penny Op-
era, On the Verge, An Enemy of
the People, Broadway, Three Sis-
ters*; (ET): *Tmp., AYL, MM*; (BS)
*Strange Snow, Sea Marks, Cold
Storage*; **1987**: (BT): *R2, She
Stoops to Conquer, The Hostage,
The Curse of the Starving Class,
The Member of the Wedding*; (BS):
*Taking Steps, "Master Harold". . .
and the boys, Ballerina;* (ET):
*Mac., MND, The Shoemakers
Holiday*; **1988**: (BT): *Rom., Boy
Meets Girl, A Penny for a Song,
Enrico IV (The Emperor), The
Iceman Cometh*; (BS): *The Mar-
riage of Bette and Boo, Ghosts,
Orphans*; (ET): *1H4, LLL, TN*; (I):
*Per., Heartbreak House, Steel
Magnolias, The Miser, Terra
Nova;* **1989**: (BT): *Per., Cyrano de
Bergerac, And a Nightingale Sang.
. ., All My Sons, Breaking the Si-
lence*; (BS): *Hunting Cockroaches,
Not About Heroes, The Road to
Mecca*; (ET): *Ado, TGV, 2H4;* (I):

*The Seagull, Holiday, Burn This,
Six Characters in Search of An
Author, Noises Off,* **1990**: (BT):
*Wiv., Peer Gynt, The House of
Blue Leaves, God's Country, Aris-
tocrats*; (BS): *The Second Man,
The Voice of the Prairie, At Long
Last Leo.*; (ET): *Err., H5, WT*; (I):
*Madame Butterfly, Our Country's
Good, The Recruiting Officer,
Glengarry Glen Ross, Tmp.*; **1991-
92**: (BT): *MV, Major Barbara, Our
Town, Other People's Money*; (BS)
*Two Rooms, Woman in Mind,
Some Americans Abroad*; (ET):
JC, Shr., 2H6; (I): *Fences, Sea-
son's Greetings, The Guardsman,
Betrayal, Lr.*; **1992-93**: (BT):
*AWW, Toys in the Attic, The Play-
boy of the Western World, La Bête,
The Ladies of the Camellias.* (BS):
*Restoration, The Firebugs, Hea-
then Valley*; (ET): *Oth., 2,3H6,
AYL;* (I): *The Glass Menagerie,
The Ladies of the Camellias, TN,
Lips Together, Teeth Apart, Spunk*;
1993: [Ashland only (OSF also
mounted seasons in Portland dur-
ing 1993-1994)] (BT): *R3, A Flea
in Her Ear, Joe Turner's Come and
Gone, Lips Together, Teeth Apart,
The Illusion*; (BS): *Cym., Light in
the Village, The Baltimore Waltz,
Mad Forest*; (ET): *Ant., MND, The
White Devil;* **1994**: [Ashland only]
(BT): *You Can't Take It With You,
The Pool of Bethesda, Ham., The
Fifth of July, The Rehearsal*; (BS):
*Tales of the Lost Formicans,
Oleanna, The Colored Museum*;
(ET): *Tmp., Ado, TNK.*

Key:
BS: Black Swan

BT: Bowmer Theatre
ET: Elizabethan Theatre
I: Intermediate Theatre
VT: Varsity Theatre)

Research Resources: The OSF maintains a well-organized and managed archives in its Administration Building. This essay was based on information from OSF annual reports, programs, attendance records, and production lists, from interviews with William W. Patton, Jerry Turner, and Pat Patton, and from some of the publications listed below. OSF productions were reviewed on a regular basis in *Shakespeare Quarterly* between the late 1970s and the mid-1980s.

Bowmer, Angus L. *As I Remember, Adam: An Autobiography of a Festival.* Ashland: The Oregon Shakespeare Festival Association, 1975.

————. *The Ashland Elizabethan Stage.* Ashland: The Oregon Shakespeare Festival Association, 1978.

Brubaker, Edward, and Mary Brubaker. *Golden Fire: The Anniversary Book of the Oregon Shakespearean Festival.* Ashland: The Oregon Shakespearean Festival Association, 1985.

Oyler, Verne William Jr. "The Festival Story: A History of the Oregon Shakespearean Festival." Ph.D. diss., University of California, Los Angeles, 1971.

Site visits and interviews: 5-6 July, 13-15 July, and 15 August 1990.
Daniel J. Watermeier and Felicia Hardison Londré

TYGRES HEART SHAKESPEARE COMPANY. MAIL: 710 S.W. Madison, Suite 506, Portland, OR 97205. SITE: Portland Center for the Performing Arts. ADMINISTRATION/BOX OFFICE: 503/222-9220. ADMISSION: $15–$20 (1992). SEASON: three productions, October to May. 8:00 p.m., Wed.–Sat.; 2:00 p.m., Sat., Sun. PRINCIPAL STAFF: Jan Powell, artistic director. FACILITY: Dolores Winningstad Theatre (in the Portland Center for the Performing Arts), black-box theatre (capacity 300). AUDITIONS: spring; plays cast from within company in late summer. STATUS: non-Equity. ANNUAL BUDGET: $215,000 (1992). ANNUAL ATTENDANCE: 12,000 (1992). FOUNDED: 1989, Jan Powell.

"Ferociously good Shakespeare in an intimate setting" is the motto of this small company based in Portland, Oregon. The unusual name, "Tygres Heart," is taken from *Henry VI, Part 3:* "Oh Tygres Heart wrapt in Womans Hide," spoken by the Duke of York about Margaret of Anjou. Like its motto, the name encapsulates the central aim of the company: to produce theatrically exciting productions of Shakespeare (as a tiger) with intimacy (as a heart). The spelling, maintained from the Folio text, not only sets the name apart but also reflects the company goal to be as close to the spirit of the original text as is possible after over 400 years.

When the **Oregon Shakespeare Festival** began a company in Portland in 1987, there was an expectation that productions of Shakespeare would be regularly offered to city theatregoers, but OSF-Portland usually presented only one Shakespeare play a season. For local theatregoers, opportunities to see Shakespeare in performance remained limited. Jan Powell was looking for an opportunity to produce a type of Shakespeare about which she was becoming increasingly excited. She combined a British, language-centered approach, learned while attending the certificate program at the Royal Academy of Dramatic Art, with an appreciation for the more visceral American style—which she describes as more "raw" and emotionally spontaneous than British acting. Thus Powell founded Tygres Heart Shakespeare Company (THSC) in November 1989 to provide a regular season of Shakespeare to Portland audiences and to realize her artistic ambitions.

Tygres Heart performs in the Dolores Winningstad Theatre within the Portland Center for the Performing Arts. The theatre, seating no more than 300 and built to suggest an Elizabethan tiered courtyard theatre albeit indoors, provides the company with the intimate setting central to its artistic mission. While the company is not the first to use the space, it is the first to explore its potential fully, utilizing its unique dimensions for productions "in the round" or in "reverse stage settings," to use company terminology. According to Powell, audiences are surprised and delighted with the company's dedication to the unique use of the space.

The first two seasons of the Tygres Heart were well received by Portland critics and audiences alike, evidenced by the company's garnering of several local awards. In 1990, the company opened with *As You Like It*, staged in the round and providing audiences with a fresh relationship to the milieu of this pastoral comedy. With *King John*, the company's second production, audiences were challenged with a strong avant-garde interpretation. Powell set the play in a human-created Hell where characters first appeared as zombie-like figures, were assigned an identity, and then set off to perform the play. Opening soon after the Persian Gulf War, the play's critique of violence seemed especially relevant, and the production was a tremendous success. With *A Midsummer Night's Dream*, the final production of that season, audiences were brought into the sensual world of colonial India. Oberon and Titania appeared as Hindu divinities with Puck a type of monkey-god figure. One of the more unusual aspects of this production included the use of a trapeze from which suspended fairies watched both the performance and the audience watching the performance. The second season saw productions of a somewhat dark *Two Gentlemen of Verona* and an even darker *Macbeth*, both staged by guest directors, and a challenging *Richard II*, which descended into a futuristic world of drug addiction, violence, and sexual abuse. The 1992-93 season continued a mix of traditional and avant-garde productions of Shakespeare including *The Merry Wives of Windsor, 1 Henry IV,* and *Romeo and Juliet.*

The office staff of the Tygres Heart Shakespeare Company consists of artistic director Powell and an office manager. Administrative duties are for the most part shared by an active, voluntary board of directors from the Portland corporate community. The office is located in a small one-bedroom apartment in downtown Portland, across the street from the Portland Center for the Performing Arts where the company performs. Expansion is an ever-present goal, both physically and organizationally, as the young company looks to create more effective management structures and refine an already successful approach to production.

Ensemble work in production is an integral part of the company's mission. Tygres Heart works with an established group of theatre artists in the Portland area, looking to this group for costume, scenic, and lighting design. Edgar Reynolds, a professor of theatre at Lewis and Clark College, functions as the company's resident scholar, active in both season selection and actor training. Even more indicative of the dedication to ensemble work is the creation each season of a single company to perform the plays. Auditions for the company of approximately 25 are held in the spring in Portland. Once selected, company members participate in a summer training session where they learn the special language and character development techniques on which Powell draws during rehearsals. In the process, they develop as a true ensemble. Casting then occurs from within the company at the end of the summer.

As Powell explains it, the company structure is fairly loose. Members can decline a particular role if they wish and are free to work on other shows outside the company should the opportunity arise. New members are brought in when they are needed. Nevertheless, the core company is an important aspect of Tygres Heart performances. The company structure allows a group of actors to share a basic technical language and to develop a unique company personality. It also provides the opportunity for artists to accept challenges and develop skills that may not be properly nurtured outside such a structure.

As artistic director, Powell seeks to establish a particular signature style for the company. This includes a unique approach to the language, a strong physical realization of the character, and finally a challenging use of the theatre. In addition, Powell works to keep open a dialogue with theatre scholars, realizing that the work of textual analysis adds much to the understanding of the drama. Powell maintains that Shakespeare's verse structure is the "heartbeat" of the character. The rhythm of each line becomes connected to the passion expressed within it. In turn, this rhythm becomes the basis for the development of a type of musical line unique to that character. In rehearsal, the operative words are isolated, subjectively chosen by the actors as the word within each line that carries the most weight. Each beat is analyzed for the arc of the thought within it, while the operative words are used as guideposts to carry both actor and audience from the beginning of a thought to its conclusion. Audiences may not understand each word, allusion, or metaphor, but this technique often gives the illusion of complete understanding. According to Powell, audiences thus achieve an appreciation and comprehension that often surprises them pleasantly.

Despite this somewhat conservative approach to Shakespeare's language, Powell is not averse to radical interpretations or significant paring of the texts. Her chief aim is to make the plays verbally and visually understandable to modern audiences. According to a company publication, the actors "emphasize the richness of the verse and traditions of Shakespearean stagecraft, with an honest and open approach to the text. The aim of the company is to spark the imagination and excite the ear through the magic, power, and beauty of the spoken word." Thus, Tygres Heart productions tend to be staged across a broad range of styles, from the traditional to the avant-garde. Powell acknowledges and respects the unique feeling of ownership that audiences tend to have for Shakespeare's plays. This recognition challenges the company to justify its unusual choices and prevents production concepts that can be reduced to gimmick interpretations. The company is dedicated to colorblind casting, signed performances, and presents 90-minute family matinees. Tygres Heart's recent all-female *The Taming of the Shrew* is an example of how the company continually challenges audience expectations at the same time that it fosters a deeper appreciation for the text.

Production History: **1990-91**: *AYL, Jn., MND*; **1991-92**: *TGV, Mac., R2*; **1992-93**: *Wiv., 1H4, Rom.*; **1993-94**: *LLL, 2H4, Shr.*

Site visit and interview: 16 September 1992.
David V. Schulz

PENNSYLVANIA

PENNSYLVANIA SHAKESPEARE FESTIVAL. MAIL: 2755 Station Avenue, Center Valley, PA 18034-9568. SITE: Labuda Center for the Performing Arts, on campus of Allentown College of St. Francis de Sales. ADMINISTRATION: 215/282-WILL. BOX OFFICE: 215/282-3192. ADMISSION: $15–22 (1992). SEASON: three productions for ten weeks, June–July. PRINCIPAL STAFF: Gerard J. Schubert, O.S.F.S., producing artistic director; Roger W. Mullin, Jr., president of the board. FACILITY: Labuda Mainstage, proscenium-thrust (capacity 473); Arena Stage (capacity 225-275). STATUS: LOA. ANNUAL BUDGET: $272,000 (1992). ANNUAL ATTENDANCE: 11,000 (1992 estimate). FOUNDED: 1991, Gerard J. Schubert, O.S.F.S.

The Reverend Gerard Schubert joined the faculty of Allentown College of St. Francis de Sales in 1969 as director of the theatre department. In 1971, he made his first proposal for an outdoor summer Shakespeare festival, but the idea was defeated by summer thunderstorms and mosquitos. With the opening of a new performing arts center in 1982, Schubert began producing indoor Shakespeare during the academic year. During the summer, he brought in Equity guest artists for productions of light musicals and comedies for subscription audiences. A 1991 sabbatical provided an opportunity to visit approximately 20 Shakespeare festivals, where he saw about 35 productions. Armed with ideas garnered from his travels, Schubert incorporated the Pennsylvania Shakespeare Festival (PSF) at Allentown College in July 1991 and began planning the 1992 inaugural season.

A questionnaire distributed to audiences in summer 1991 revealed that 40 percent of the 3,200 who responded had never attended a professional Shakespeare production. Another survey showed that 80 percent of Pennsylvania high school English teachers had never seen a live Shakespeare production. To one who questioned the value of staging Shakespeare, Schubert replied: "You don't hate Shakespeare. You've never met him."

Fund raising began in the fall of 1991 with a goal of $90,000 in contributions. More than 300 individuals and businesses helped to underwrite the first season. Allentown College made an in-kind contribution of $61,000 by allowing rent-free use of the arts center on campus. A poster contest stirred up interest among high school students. More than 100 volunteers joined the PSF Guild.

A core company of professional actors and students performed in the opening season; 14 performances of *The Taming of the Shrew* in June and 14 of *Romeo and Juliet* in July on the main stage were supplemented by 23 matinee performances of *Pinocchio* on the arena stage in the Labuda Center for the Performing Arts. Schubert has also managed to take advantage of the college's picturesque setting by offering an outdoor greenshow—Renaissance dances, poetry, juggling, and madrigals—outside the center, beginning 45 minutes before curtain time. Audience members are encouraged to picnic on the green, while festival members are served free soft drinks in a tent outside the lobby.

The inaugural production of *The Taming of the Shrew*, directed by Schubert, was set in the 1950s on a unit setting of "stairs and elevated walkways, shutters and tubular tiles" evoking a Paduan plaza. Festival attendance has increased and the company hopes to attract even larger audiences from the region.

Production History: 1992: *Shr., Rom., Pinocchio*; **1993**: *TN, Mac.*; **1994**: *MND, MV, Aladdin*.

Research Resources: Geoff Gehman, "The Pennsylvania Shakespeare Festival Makes its Debut," (Fall 1991): 35-36; "A Shakespearean summer at Allentown

College," *The* [Allentown] *Morning Call* (7 June 1992): F1-2; *"The Taming of the Shrew," Shakespeare Bulletin* (Winter 1993): 30-1

Felicia Hardison Londré

PHILADELPHIA SHAKESPEARE IN THE PARK. MAIL: care of Cabrini College Theater, 610 King of Prussia Road, Radnor, PA 19087. SITE: grounds of Cabrini College, behind the Administration Building. ADMINISTRATION: 215/971-8510. BOX OFFICE: 215/242-2483. ADMISSION: free. SEASON: mid-July to mid-August; 8:00 p.m., Wed.–Sat. PRINCIPAL STAFF: Neal Newman, artistic director; Tom McDugall, financial director and chairman of the board. FACILITY: outdoor platform, audience seating on blankets (capacity 200). AUDITIONS: local in March. STATUS: LOA. ANNUAL BUDGET: $50,000 (1992). ANNUAL ATTENDANCE: 11,000 (1992). FOUNDED: 1985, Ellen Taft.

In 1985, the Chestnut Hill Theater began presenting free outdoor Shakespeare in the natural amphitheatre of Pastorius Park in Chestnut Hill's Fairmount Park. Dating its origins to that venture, which was spearheaded by Ellen Taft, Philadelphia Shakespeare in the Park (PSIP) continued to offer performances there until 1992. Performances have also been given on the campus of Spring Garden College in Chestnut Hill/Mount Airy, but the operation is now headquartered at Cabrini College, under the direction of Neal Newman. In 1993, due to the loss of city funding, PSIP relocated its public performances to the Cabrini College campus in the nearby suburb of Radnor. A wide platform stage erected behind the campus administrative center (the former servants' quarters on the estate of the Campbell Soup family) takes advantage of the building's brick and *faux*-Gothic facade as a backdrop for the plays.

PSIP is an independent nonprofit company that is dedicated to bringing the classics to a broad and diverse audience in Philadelphia and surrounding areas. Its major program is "Shakespeare in the Park," the free summer outdoor performances of one Shakespeare production each summer, but there are two additional programs. Chamber theatre productions of shortened versions of Shakespeare's plays are toured to schools and community centers. In 1989, for example, a one-hour "portable musical" version of *Twelfth Night* was presented by five actor-musicians. A second project of PSIP is its classical theatre training program, begun by Newman in 1988 with an eye to nuturing a local talent pool of classically trained actors. Actor John Timmons, for example, moved easily from the training program into the role of Bottom in the 1989 version of *A Midsummer Night's Dream*. He commented: "The biggest thing for me is that Neal is able to demonstrate how everything an actor needs is contained in Shakespeare. Shakespeare gives an actor stage direction, motivation, and characterization in the way the poetry is constructed. The rhythm of the verse and the structure of the speeches generate emotion. That's different from modern theatre."

Each season has brought increased attendance for the outdoor productions as the festival grew to 24 performances for over 11,000 people in 1992. With the move to the Cabrini College campus in 1993, the seating capacity was somewhat reduced, since a stone retaining wall limits the space directly facing the stage and the width of the stage means that people seated very far to either side have difficulty hearing the lines. During the hour before curtain-time, amplified trumpet voluntaries periodically resound, to help theatregoers find the performance site on campus. If funding problems can be resolved, Newman envisions expanding the season to two productions and giving additional performances in different parts of the city. Over the years, Coopers & Lybrand, the accounting firm, has been a bedrock contributor to PSIP.

Reviews of the 1988 *A Midsummer Night's Dream* at Fairmount Park were ecstatic about PSIP's evocation of the magic of the sylvan setting with its rough stone bridges and stream. Newman's direction exploited the trees, bushes, and other natural features, such as the reflecting pool that served as a mirror for Bottom's discovery of his donkey head. Newman also composed musical accompaniment for the action, employing 13 instruments (temple bells and ram's horn included) played by musicians hovering around the action. As if in tribute to the previous season's all-woman *As You Like It*, the "rude mechanicals" were all played by women. Such was the production's success that "the *Dream*" was chosen again for the summer of 1989. Because Fairmount Park had no restrooms, the plays were performed without intermission there. Newman recalls that "our 1990 production of *The Tempest* ran two hours and fifteen minutes, and then the audience cleared out of there *fast*."

For *Henry IV, Part 1* in 1993, Newman incorporated a sequence from *Richard II* at the beginning and ended with the transfer of the crown to Prince Hal from *Henry IV, Part 2*. One side of the wide stage was set as the Boar's Head tavern, and the throne stood at the opposite extreme. A small thrust with a flight of stairs at down center provided an area for ceremonial scenes and fights. Prince Hal was engagingly portrayed by Trevor Davis, contrasting vividly with David Mann's manic Hotspur. After the prince was summoned by his father, he ascended the steps and paused at center, as if torn between turning left (back to the tavern) or right (toward the throne). That was the final image before the intermission in a clear and fast-paced production.

Production History: **1986**: *Shr.*; **1987**: *AYL*; **1988**: *MND*; **1989**: *MND*; **1990**: *Shakespeare's Lovers, Tmp.*; **1991**: *Rom.*; **1992**: *Ham.*; **1993**: *1H4*.

Research Resources: Karla Brandt, "Shakespeare workshop set for September," *Chestnut Hill Local* (24 August 1989): 19; John Corr, "Hark! At dark—it's Shakespeare in the park," *Philadelphia Inquirer* (15 July 1988): 3.

Site visit: 7 August 1993.
Felicia Hardison Londré

THREE RIVERS SHAKESPEARE FESTIVAL. MAIL: 1617 Cathedral of Learning, University of Pittsburgh, Pittsburgh, PA 15260. SITE: Stephen Foster Memorial Theatre at the University of Pittsburgh's Oakland Campus. ADMINISTRATION: 412/624-1953. BOX OFFICE: 412/624-7529. ADMISSION: $5–$22 (1992). SEASON: six productions in two theatres, presented consecutively for about 20 performances each, May–September; 7:00 p.m., Tues.–Thurs.; 8:00 p.m., Fri.–Sat.; 2:00 p.m., Thurs., Sun. (1991). PRINCIPAL STAFF: Laura Ann Worthen, artistic director (1993). FACILITIES: Foster Memorial Theatre, proscenium (capacity 565). AUDITIONS: Pittsburgh. STATUS: Equity LOA/URTA. ANNUAL BUDGET: $668,500 (1990-91). ANNUAL ATTENDANCE: 25,000 (1991 paid admissions only). FOUNDED: 1980, Attilio Favorini.

The Three Rivers Shakespeare Festival (TRSF) was founded in 1980 by Attilio "Buck" Favorini, a professor of theatre at the University of Pittsburgh and a Shakespearean scholar, in part because of a personal and professional interest in producing the plays of Shakespeare, in part to fill a void in classical theatre production in the region, and in part to provide opportunities for theatre students to participate in a classically oriented summer theatre. In an interview with a reporter from the *Pittsburgh Post-Gazette* (27 June 1980), Favorini announced that above all, he wanted to make Shakespeare "accessible" to theatregoers. In comparison to the **Old Globe Theatre** and the **Oregon Shakespeare Festival**, the TRSF aimed to be "definitely Pittsburgh—unpretentious, but not cheap, . . . with a straightforward, clear spoken, accessible performing style." The ideal audience for Favorini "would be made up of half of people who know the plays so well they will catch all the nuances and half of people who have had absolutely no contact with Shakespeare." Staffed primarily by students and volunteers, TRSF presented an inaugural eight-week season of two plays, 20 performances each. Critical reception was very positive. The reviewer for the weekly *Valley News Dispatch* (30 June 1980), for example, called *The Taming of the Shrew* "sheer perfection in every theatrical aspect. Acting, staging, costuming, lighting, set design, properties, music—all were executed with outstanding professionalism." The *Pittsburgh Press* (28 July 1980) reviewer described *Romeo and Juliet* as a "vigorous," and "brilliant," "pulsating" production. Bolstered by such reviews and enthusiastic audiences, Favorini set out to make the TRSF an annual event.

Over the course of a decade, the TRSF gradually expanded its number of productions and performances, while simultaneously elevating its artistic standards and building widespread and solid community support. By 1990,

TRSF was presenting three plays in the Foster Memorial Theatre, for a total of 74 performances. The TRSF had developed, moreover, from an amateur theatre company to virtually a fully professional company, employing seven individuals year round and over 130 people during the height of the season, including 20 Equity performers. Adhering, furthermore, to Favorini's original artistic impulses, the TRSF had built a reputation for clear, energetic, insightful, and often bold interpretations of Shakespeare's plays. For example, Susan Harris Smith, a professor of English at the University of Pittsburgh and a reviewer for the *Pittsburgh Press*, described the 1986 production of *A Midsummer Night's Dream* as "splendid and magical" (5 June 1986). She complimented director W. Stephen Coleman for the way his "physical reading of one of Shakespeare's best-loved works bodies forth its energy, and stresses what the play means to the eye"; she noted that the notions of duality and metamorphosis inherent in the dramatic action were embodied in the fresh and imaginative scenery, modern costumes, and original incidental music, as well as in the doubling not only of Hippolyta/Titania and Theseus/Oberon, but also of the fairies with the mechanicals. In 1988 (*Pittsburgh Press* 28 July 1988), Smith was equally enthusiastic about the TRSF's production of *Julius Caesar*, which she described as "a riveting interpretation" in which "the troubled conspirators are brought to life as timeless composites of Samurai warriors, fighters in the Islamic Jihad, and grunts in Vietnam." Patty S. Derrick, reviewing the entire 1991 season for *Shakespeare Bulletin* (Winter 1991), observed that all three productions were "marked by energy, rapid pacing, and clever scenic designs." The TRSF's artistic success was also reflected in an increasing number of annual Critic's Choice Awards, (sponsored by Pittsburgh's two daily newspapers, the *Pittsburgh Post-Gazette* and the *Pittsburgh Press*, and the arts-oriented weekly *Arts Weekly*).

In 1983, in an effort to bring wider attention to the festival and to broaden its audience, TRSF offered a special performance by well-known actress Claire Bloom, who presented readings of various Shakespearean heroines. The success of this program led to similar one-person recitals by Tammy Grimes and Nicholas Pennell in 1984, by Donal Donnelly in 1985, by Brian Bedford in 1989, and by F. Murray Abraham in 1990.

The 1990 season saw the inauguration of the Young Company, comprised exclusively of University of Pittsburgh students, who presented two additional productions for a total of 20 performances in a small theatre called The Pit (formerly the City Theatre) adjacent to the university's campus. The Young Company provided a showcase for student actors in major roles, as well as a venue for experimental productions, Shakespeare off-shoots, and new plays inspired by the classics. Although a project of the TRSF, virtually all the operations of the Young Company were handled by the students themselves, including theatrical design, direction, and front-of-house management.

As it developed in the early 1980s, the TRSF also initiated a number of community educational and outreach programs. In 1984, for example, the

TRSF started a School Matinee Series, as part of a larger Shakespeare in the Schools (SITS) program, which offered students and teachers from the area around Pittsburgh an opportunity to see special preview performances of TRSF productions at a significantly reduced ticket price—usually $5.00. Attending schools received a packet of various educational materials and were offered post-performances discussions and in-school workshops—all to enhance student understanding and appreciation of the performance. By 1991, over 25,000 students in 93 schools in Pennsylvania, Ohio, West Virginia, and Maryland had participated in the SITS program. In 1989, the TRSF expanded its outreach effort with the Shakespeare on Tour program, which toured a 45-minute version of *The Tempest*, adapted for elementary school students, and *Maids & Blades*, a collection of love and fight scenes from Shakespeare, for high school students. In 1990, the TRSF toured an original play called *Everykid* (based on the medieval play *Everyman*) by Gillette Elvgren to elementary schools and *Shakespeare on Broadway*, a collage of Shakespeare scenes of love and duty, coupled with popular musical numbers based on Shakespeare plays, to middle and high schools. In 1991, an adaptation of *Macbeth* was presented in two different versions for elementary and high schools. Since its inauguration, the Shakespeare on Tour program has played to a total of over 50,000 students. The TRSF also offers at least one signed performance for the hearing impaired, and it coordinates a readers' service for visually impaired theatregoers. Beginning with its inaugural season, the TRSF contracted with the city to distribute free tickets to elderly and economically disadvantaged citizens.

In 1985, the TRSF launched what was to become one of its most important traditions: an annual tour of one of its mainstage productions for a number of post-season, free, outdoor performances in two city parks. Favorini explained that the festival could get away with selling tickets to a show that would later be presented free, because the public announcement of which show will be taken to the park is withheld until well into the run of the third mainstage show for paying audiences. Generously supported by the City of Pittsburgh, the Pittsburgh Department of Parks and Recreation, and the Allegheny Bureau of Cultural Programs, the outdoor performances are presented on Flagstaff Hill in Schenley Park and at Hartwood Acres. Although the clientele for these performances is not markedly different from the paying audiences, they do tend to attract many families with small children. By 1991, TRSF's outdoor Shakespeare performances had been seen by over 35,000 people; over 360,000 people had attended other TRSF performances.

Over the years, the TRSF has employed some imaginative marketing strategies. In order to arouse interest in Shakespeare among those who attended only the non-Shakespeare productions, the TRSF scheduled *Hamlet* and *A Funny Thing Happened on the Way to the Forum* in rotating repertory, with the two shows designed so that they could coexist on the stage. The audience for the musical would initially see the *Hamlet* scenery on the stage. As the lights dimmed, they would hear Shakespearean lines and see a trap door open; then, suddenly, the entire set would be changed in 15 seconds. According to Favorini, the design concept "worked like a dream," but the experiment in expanding the audience's acceptance of other material was "only moderately successful." An unexpected financial success was a black and white poster, dominated by a photograph of a primly dressed, bespectacled woman over the caption: "Did this woman kill Hamlet?" Smaller lettering beneath the picture carried a disclaimer ("With all due respect to the teachers who made us read it, we think one should experience Shakespeare the way he intended") and information about the TRSF season. At $5.00 apiece, the posters sold "like hotcakes." The mail brochure for the 1989 season was an eight-page comic book, "The Amazing Adventures of Super Bard." The cartoon hero, described as "faster than Cleopatra on a date, more powerful than Falstaff's breath, able to run the iambic pentameter in a single bound," overcomes Neil Simonite to save Pittsburgh from the spectre of summer boredom. The back cover included a tear-off ticket order form.

From the outset, the TRSF has operated as a project of the Department of Theatre Arts at the University of Pittsburgh. It has never incorporated as a separate, not-for-profit theatre organization. The university provides extensive in-kind support to the TRSF, in the form of facilities and services, as well as a modest cash contribution for operations. Within the university structure, however, the TRSF is operated as an independent, autonomous organization, with its own budget lines and a separate advisory board comprised of influential Pittsburgh business and community leaders. TRSF has also been able to generate significant private, corporate and governmental support for its programs. In 1990-91, for example, directly contributed income amounted to almost 40 percent of the TRSF's operating budget. In many respects, the organization of the TRSF is similar to that of several other successful university-based festivals, such as the **Colorado Shakespeare Festival**, **Shakespeare Santa Cruz**, and the **Illinois Shakespeare Festival**.

Visiting the TRSF in July 1991, we had an opportunity to see two productions and to attend a rehearsal of a third. In the Foster Theatre, we attended a production of *A Horse of a Different Color*, freely adapted by Ralph Allen from Feydeau's *Chat en poche* (*Cat in a Bag* or *A Pig in a Poke*). The production was skillfully directed by Allen and his associate director Harriet Nichols and was expertly performed by a cast of experienced professional actors. The setting, "an elegant townhouse in Gramercy Park" in the spring of 1911, and the period costumes were also expertly rendered. In all, it was a high-quality, delightfully amusing farce. A production of *Cymbeline* presented by the Young Company at The Pit, was an altogether different experience. It was decidedly postmodern, mixing costumes and properties, as the program noted, from "the present, medieval past and echoes in between," and the production embraced a highly physical, sometimes almost burlesque, acting style. Although the style of the production did not always enhance an understanding of the complex plot or character relationships, the youthful, irreverent spirit and energy of the cast were appealing. The performance was warmly received by the audience, who frequently applauded or laughed uproariously at moments and gave the production a standing ovation at the curtain. We also attended a rehearsal of *The Comedy of Errors,* directed by James L. Christy. A single actor played both Dromios and another single actor both Antipholuses. With the play set in the 1920s, the rehearsal promised an entertaining, lively, and inventive production. Overall, our experience confirmed that the TRSF merited its reputation as a leading summer Shakespeare festival.

Despite its successes, however, the financial stability of the TRSF, like that of many Shakespeare festivals, has remained fragile, easily subject to damage by any number of unexpected events. The 1992 season proved to be a watershed for the development of the TRSF. A prolonged strike by delivery men against Pittsburgh's major newspapers, which began in the spring and lasted throughout the summer, crippled the TRSF's abilities to advertise and market its season effectively. Municipal budgetary cutbacks forced the cancellation of a planned production of *Pericles.* A documentary drama about the history of Pittsburgh called *Steel/City,* originally written by Favorini and by director and playwright Gillette Elvgren to celebrate America's bicentennial in 1976, and revived to coincide with the centennial of the Homestead Steel Strike, proved moderately successful at the box office. Nonetheless, a cross-over of the audience from this production to the Shakespeare plays, which Favorini and his management staff had anticipated, never materialized. Lastly, despite a variety of inventive marketing strategies and direct mail advertising, overall attendance dropped, as did corporate support, perhaps in large part due to a downturn in Pittsburgh's general economic condition. Despite a well-attended *Twelfth Night* put on by the Young Company, the season closed disappointingly, with founding producing director Favorini resigning in frustration. The 1993 season was scaled back to two productions, mounted in the Foster Theatre with a predominantly student company, while the university and the TRSF advisory board regrouped to explore various options and opportunities. The future of the TRSF is by no means certain.

Production History (abbreviations in parentheses refer to special performance circumstances; refer to key below): **1980**: *Shr., Rom,*; **1981**: *Err., WT, AYL*; **1982**: *Ham., Wiv., Tmp.*; **1983**: *1H4, Ado, Oth.,* Claire Bloom in *These are Women: A Portrait of Shakespeare's Heroines*; **1984**: *Mac., MV, LLL,* Tammy Grimes *In Concert* and Nicholas Pennell in *A Variable Passion*; **1985**: *Rom., TN, MM,* Donal Donnelly in *My Astonishing Self*; **1986**: *MND, AWW, Lr.*; **1987**: *TGV, Cyrano de Bergerac, R3*; **1988**: *Shr., Volpone, JC*; **1989**: *Ham., A Funny Thing Happened on the Way to the Forum, Tmp.* (SITS), *Maids & Blades* (SITS), Brian Bedford in *The Lunatic, The Lover and The Poet*; **1990**: *Tmp., R3, AYL, Wiv.* (YC), *Tartuffe*

(YC), *Everykid* (SITS), *Shake-speare on Broadway* (SITS), F. Murray Abraham in *A Gilded Age Gala*; **1991**: *Oth.*, *A Horse of a Different Color*, *Err.*, *Goodnight Desdemona*, (*Good Morning, Juliet*) (YC), *Cym.* (YC), *Mac.* (SITS); **1992**: *TGV*, *Steel/City*, *Ophelia* (YC), *TN* (YC); **1993**: *MND*, *Ado*, *Lr.* (SITS); **1994**: *Shr.*, *MV*, *MM*.

Key:
YC: Young Company
SITS: Shakespeare in the Schools

Research Resources: An informal archive for the Three Rivers Shakespeare Festival is maintained in the Curtis Theatre Collection in the University of Pittsburgh Library.

Site visit and interview: 12-13 July 1991.
Felicia Londré and Daniel J. Watermeier

RHODE ISLAND

THE RHODE ISLAND SHAKESPEARE THEATRE. MAIL: P.O. Box 1126, Newport, RI 02840. SITE: St. George's School, Middleton, Rhode Island. ADMINISTRATION/BOX OFFICE: 401/849-7892. ADMISSION: $10. SEASON: four plays, 14–19 performances each (approximately 70 performances), mid-May to late September; 8:00 p.m., Thurs.–Sun. (1991). PRINCIPAL STAFF: Bob Colonna, artistic director; Michelle Armstrong Roche, managing director; Roger Warburton, treasurer, Eileen Warburton, producer. FACILITY: St. George's School Gymnasium Stage (capacity 100). AUDITIONS: Newport, one week prior to rehearsals for each production. STATUS: non-Equity. ANNUAL BUDGET: $100,000 (1991). ANNUAL ATTENDANCE: 5,500. FOUNDED: 1971, Bob Colonna.

The Rhode Island Shakespeare Theatre (TRIST), founded in 1971 by Bob Colonna, began as a young people's theatre. Colonna, then an actor with Trinity Repertory Company, was asked by a colleague if he wanted to direct a play on a boat. Colonna agreed, thinking the ship would be at sea. As it turned out, the new performance space was an old ferry boat docked in Pawtucket and slated for use as an arts center. Colonna was given one half of the lower deck of the ship, which had formerly been used to park cars, to build a theatre. The space reminded Colonna of an Elizabethan theatre, and he decided to produce *Twelfth Night*. After three successful years as a youth theatre, the group lost

Pawtucket's sponsorship, so, in 1974, Colonna began the Young Rhode Island Shakespeare Theatre, a traveling group of players who performed outside on temporary stages in Providence. The year 1975 marked the first time the group performed two plays, *Henry IV, Part 1* and a musical version of *The Merchant of Venice*. A turning point in the company's history occurred when *Henry IV, Part 1* was performed in a parking lot in an Italian neighborhood. Despite the fact that there were no seats, the audience, many of whom did not speak English, stood and watched the three-hour performance. It was this experience that gave Colonna an appreciation for the Italian and the operatic in Shakespeare, and he realized that his theatre had found an audience.

By 1976, the group had matured, and the players dropped the "young" from their name. For one and one-half years, TRIST performed in an East Street church in Providence, followed by one and a half years in an old warehouse. Nearby government office workers found TRIST's activities suspicious and asked the company to leave.

In 1979, desperate for a permanent home, the company placed a newspaper ad outlining the need for a theatre. The Newport Art Museum responded and showed TRIST an intimate 82-seat theatre with a proscenium stage on the Swanhurst Estates in the heart of the mansion district. Delighted with the company's new prospects, TRIST restaged *Twelfth Night* and added a musical version of *The Alchemist* and *Antony and Cleopatra*. No sooner had TRIST begun making long-term plans for the space, however, than an arson's fire (still unsolved) severely damaged the theatre and destroyed the props and costumes. Shaken but still determined to produce a season, TRIST borrowed costumes from Trinity Repertory and presented *Romeo and Juliet* outdoors while the theatre underwent repairs. A successful decade at Swanhurst unfortunately ended in 1988, as economic conditions forced the museum to sell the property to condominium builders. Losing their "ideal theatre" was a brutal blow. Much of the audience drifted away during TRIST's migrations to temporary spaces in the Newport Armory, a shopping center, Bellecourt Castle, and Salve Regina College. Acquiring the old Quaker Meeting House, courtesy of the Newport Historical Society, for the 1989 and 1990 seasons boosted company morale. The 1991 season was held at St. George's School in Middletown (just beyond the Newport city line). In 1991, the company was once again searching for a permanent home.

The first TRIST company was composed of "at risk" teenagers from Pawtucket and the surrounding area. Through various transformations and name changes, the company now numbers 50, including professionals, semi-professionals, community players, young actors, and technicians-in-training. Bill Rodriguez, reviewer for the *Providence Journal*, noted that Colonna heads the group "like a strutting piper leading an enthusiastic and enchanted troupe here and there since 1971."

Auditions are held one week prior to the start of rehearsals in Newport. The actors are asked to read from the script. Each play is cast separately, rather than as part of a repertory company. For many years, the artistic director, actors, and technicians were unpaid. In 1991, the company members were paid a stipend of approximately $4,150 for the rehearsal and performance period (usually eight weeks), depending upon box office revenues. Rehearsals are held evenings and weekends, since many actors have full-time jobs during the day. Actors in the company constitute three distinct groups. Some actors are training for professional careers, some are community talent who have an avocational interest in the theatre, and others are professionals who just want a place to work.

Summer staff members, in addition to artistic director Colonna, include managing director Michelle Armstrong Roche and producer Eileen Warburton (also on the board of directors). Colonna is the only one on a year-round contract ($100 a week). Colonna makes his living primarily by doing voice-overs for commercials in Boston, and he acts professionally when opportunities arise.

The $100,000 budget is derived from 40 percent ticket sales, 40 percent grants, and 20 percent gifts and the "kindness of strangers." Most of the fund raising is done by Eileen Warburton and an active and enthusiastic board of directors headed by Washington Irving. Major grants have come from the Rhode Island State Council on the Arts ($6,000 in 1991), F. H. Prince Charitable Trusts, New York Times Co. Foundation, New York Community Trust Fund, and the Van Buren Charitable Trust. The company is also grateful to its generous landlord, Rob Robin. Fund-raisers, whether cocktail parties or an evening of murder mystery, net around $3,000 per event. Newport is a very difficult area for fund raising, and the company has not yet found a major patron or received donations from the millionaires who have "summer cottages" in the town.

The performing space used in 1991 was the gymnasium stage of St. George's School, a flexible space that seats approximately 100 people. Administrative offices and rehearsals are held in TRIST's second-floor office space in Newport, which is shared with a dance studio.

Newport is located on the southern tip of Aquidneck Island, an hour south of Providence on Highway 138. One of New England's prime vacation destinations, Newport is known for its "summer cottages" built the Vanderbilts, Astors, and Morgans. It is home to a renowned jazz festival and major Navy and Coast Guard installations. Fifty percent of TRIST's audience is from Newport itself, the rest primarily from Jamestown and Middletown, and a few make the one-hour trek from Providence. A generally well educated yet diversified audience attends according to which play is being presented; *Romeo and Juliet*, cast with high school actors, for example, drew a younger crowd. Some audience members are familiar with Shakespeare, but many are not. Once they come they tend to return. An enthusiastic and involved group of 400 subscribers attend the opening weekend performances, following TRIST loyally from place to place.

Although TRIST has not attracted Newport's millionaires to their theatre, the middle- and working-class segments of the community see the company as a cultural asset. Extensive marketing is still needed to attract an audience. Radio and newspaper ads, as well as public service announcements, begin in March or April. The mailing list for season brochures numbers 10,000. The season is listed in 15 to 20 calendars. The area press (*Newport Daily News, Providence Journal*, etc.) provide feature articles, previews, and reviews.

TRIST seeks a permanent home and has joined other arts and cultural organizations in the area to lobby for an arts center. A permanent heated theatre would allow TRIST to perform year-round, another of the theatre's goals. Additional hopes are to increase revenues in order to pay the artists.

TRIST's stated mission is: "to produce Shakespeare and other classics in original and creative ways that provide immediate, exciting, and entertaining access for contemporary actors, audiences and the community." Colonna directs the majority of the plays himself, searching for means to "blow the play open." He traces his philosophical roots to his ten years of work with Adrian Hall at Trinity Repertory. He cuts the plays freely and often combines characters to gain stronger continuity from beginning to end. Musical adaptations of Shakespeare and other plays have proved to be popular. In addition to Shakespeare, TRIST has produced 25 original musicals and adaptations of classic books.

TRIST's 1991 production of *Mother Courage* was simply staged and thoughtfully designed, making the most of TRIST's limited resources. The production was entertaining and thought-provoking, although the opening scenes were more effective than the closing moments. Brecht's stylistic demands were met with varying degrees of success. For example, the degree of emotional identification with character was inconsistent, some actors presented the story while others realistically enacted it. The quality of acting varied greatly, but the strongest of the actors made bold, clear choices that rendered their performances memorable. Barbara Finelli had a grounded, no-nonsense approach to the title role, effectively anchoring the cast. All of the actors, regardless of their level of experience, brought a strong sense of commitment to their roles.

Music for the production utilized composer Richard Cumming's score, originally developed for Adrian Hall's 1966 production at the Milwaukee Repertory Theatre. An enthusiastic audience of TRIST subscribers attended the opening weekend production.

Production History: **1971**: *TN*; **1972**: *MND*; **1973**: *Tmp.*; **1974**: *TN*; **1975**: *MV* (musical version); **1976**: *Mac.*, *2H4*, *WT*; **1977**: *R2*, *AYL*, *Cor.*; **1978**: *MND*, *Ado*, *Rom.*; **1979**: *TN*, *The Alchemist* (musical version), *Ant.*; **1980**: *Mac.*, *AYL*, *Rom.*; **1981**: *1H4*; **1982**: *Billy Bishop Goes to War*, *Ham.*; **1983**: *The Hound of the Baskervilles*, *Shr.*, *Androcles and the Lion*; **1984**: *Jn.*, *Life on the*

Mississippi, Hobson's Choice; **1985**: *Err., Turn of the Screw*; **1986**: *Medea, MM, Wiv.*, **1987**: *JC, Threepenny Opera, Arms and the Man, WT*; **1988**: *Ado, Great Expectations, The Outcasts of Poker Flat*; **1989**: *Tmp., Treasure Island*; **1990**: *Shr.*; *Ida Lewis, The Prime of Miss Jean Brodie, The Women*; **1991**: *The Lion in Winter, Rom., Mother Courage, R3*; **1992**: *AYL, Faustus.*

Research Resources: Archives for The Rhode Island Shakespeare Theatre are informally maintained in the company's administrative office. See "Celebrating two decades of the Rhode Island Shakespeare Theatre," *Providence Journal-Bulletin* (6 June 1991).

Site visit and interview: 27-28 July 1991.
Cindy Melby Phaneuf

WESTERLY SHAKESPEARE IN THE PARK. MAIL: One Granite Street, Westerly, RI 02891; or John Eisner, 395 Riverside Drive, #12B, New York, NY 10025. SITE: Wilcox Park, near the YMCA adjacent to High Street. ADMINISTRATION: 401/596-0810. ADMISSION: free. SEASON: (1992) 28 performances, 2 July–16 August; 7 30 p.m., Wed.–Sun. PRINCIPAL STAFF: Ezra Barnes, John Eisner, Harlan Meltzer, festival producers. FACILITY: outdoor park, temporary stage (capacity 900, up to 1,500 partial view). AUDITIONS: late spring; New York City, Providence, New Haven, and Westerly. STATUS: Equity SPT (in connection with the Colonial Theatre) and LOA. ANNUAL BUDGET: $60,000 (1991). ANNUAL ATTENDANCE: 9,000 to 10,000 (1991). FOUNDED: 1990, John Eisner, Ezra Barnes, Harlan Meltzer.

Westerly Shakespeare in the Park's (WSP) inaugural season in July 1991 exceeded all expectations. The company produced *A Midsummer Night's Dream* outdoors in Wilcox Park as a special project of the Colonial Theatre. The opening night performance drew 900 people. Actor-producers John Eisner and Ezra Barnes say that the idea for the project grew out of a desire to produce Shakespeare with some freedom. They joined forces with Harlan Meltzer, producing artistic director of the Colonial Theatre, who had begun a similar project five years earlier. At first, Eisner and Barnes thought the idea was far-fetched, but when they quickly (within a week) received favorable responses to their proposals from community leaders, they were encouraged to continue. Producing the festival became a community effort. Two foundations, the state arts council, the city, the public schools, the town library, area businesses, and local arts organizations all became involved.

The producers scaled WSP's original budget of $126,000 down to a far more achievable goal of $45,000, with considerable in-kind contributions making up the difference. They eventually raised $74,567 and spent $59,698, giving them a financial cushion to begin the 1992 season. The total income broke down as follows: $24,400 from foundation grants, $35,942 from private donation, $7,650 from state and city grants, $4,135 from corporations, and $2,400 in concessions and advertising sales.

Administrative responsibilities are shared among the three festival producers. Eisner is in charge of publicity, promotion, and grants; Barnes handles development and public relations, while Meltzer does production organization and serves as community liaison. Artistic decisions are made by all three of them. The theatre's proximity to New York and its Small Professional Theatre (SPT) contract along with an Equity letter of agreement allowed them to attract ten Equity guest artists who were willing to work for $150 per week. For *A Midsummer Night's Dream*, the company also used local amateurs, including what were referred to as the "football fairies from Hell" from Stonington High School. Education Director Jack Cottle provided the pre-show entertainment. Designers were attracted from across the United States, most notably scenic and lighting designer Marcus Abbot. Award-winning Amherst College music professor Lewis Spratlan composed a score for 23 musicians, including ten singers, seven flutes, five trumpets, and percussion.

The professionals who joined the initial company included Christopher Murney as Bottom, a Narragansett (Rhode Island) native who is a founding member of the Actors Theatre of Louisville. Richard Edelman, an artist with international credits, directed. Advisory Board members included such notables as Tony Church, former **Royal Shakespeare Company** member and Dean of the National Theatre Conservatory, as well as Adrian Hall, former artistic director of Trinity Repertory Theatre. WSP also received organizational advice from FEDAPT. The board of trustees of the Colonial Theatre has fiscal responsibility and WSP shares administrative offices and technical shops with the Colonial Theatre. Rehearsals are conducted in the park, weather permitting.

The section of the 12-acre city park chosen for the festival holds about 900 people, although as many as 1,500 have crowded in and braved obstructed views to be a part of the event. Platforms and ramps, together with the natural park terrain, provided the *A Midsummer Night's Dream* setting. A pond in the background, lush trees, and gently rolling terrain were prominently featured. Body mikes were used. Audience members were encouraged to bring their own chairs and blankets. The 20-page glossy program gives company biographies, a financial statement, and opening remarks from arts advocate Anne Utter, actor Earle Hyman, and John Eisner.

Westerly, population 25,000, is a place of historical and natural splendor. Located on the southwestern coast of Rhode Island, an hour west of Newport, Westerly is "blessed by the proximity of the open sea and by the haunting beauty of the free flowing Pawcatuck River" (1991 program). The community is an interesting mix of distinctive Italian and Portuguese groups, corporate executives, and summer tourists. Many of the audience members are newcomers to Shakespeare, and a major purpose of the festival is to create an interest in going to the theatre. According to Eisner, audience surveys of other arts centers in the area indicate that the festival has been effective in creating an interest in theatre. Especially pleasing to Eisner is the response of the children, who have been seen enacting scenes from *A Midsummer Night's Dream* in parks across the city. The most imitated action was Puck's exit, swinging from a rope in Act III, scene 2, yelling "I go."

Marketing depends heavily on public service announcements and publicity in local and regional papers. Generous coverage has been provided by the *Westerly Sun, Stamford Advocate, Boston Globe,* and other local and regional newspapers. Innovative marketing techniques include enlisting the superintendent of the public schools to send flyers home with the children's report cards, encouraging students and their families to attend performances.

Future plans include enlarging the season to two plays in 1992 and expanding the educational programs. Eisner hopes that WSP will become a community resource. In addition, the producers hope to integrate the summer project into the Colonial Theatre season and to include a play-reading series, also free of charge. Practical needs include finding a larger performance space and acquiring rain covers so that WSP can perform in inclement weather. A van is also needed for transporting artistic personnel. Next year's fund-raising drive will seek additional corporate contributions, admittedly a tough task, given New England's recent economic climate.

WSP's mission is to provide a straightforward production of a Shakespeare play that would be appealing to audiences with little or no theatre-going experience as well as to sophisticated theatregoers. The focus is on entertainment with fast-paced action that communicates visually as well as vocally.

Local critics found the inaugural production of *A Midsummer Night's Dream* well adapted for its time and place. Critic William Gale noted that it was "fast moving, funny, mildly bawdy and captured Shakespeare's idea that love can be loony. . . . Actors swung from ropes and ran through greenery, sometimes eliciting laughter from a football field away." Outstanding performers included Willy Conley as Puck, an engaging hearing-impaired actor from the National Theatre for the Deaf, who spoke and signed his lines, and Christopher Murney as a bold and vigorous Bottom.

The 1993 season left WSF with a substantial deficit, which the company hoped to eliminate by charging for reserved seating. Because the Parks Department would not agree to this solution, the 1994 season had to be scaled down to only four performances.

Production History: 1991: *MND*; 1992: *AYL, Tmp.*; 1993: *Ado*; 1994: *Mac.*

Research Resources: Archives for Westerly Shakespeare in the Park are maintained at the Colonial Theatre. See also William Gale, "Perchance, a dream of a play in the park," *Providence Journal-Bulletin* (10 July, 1991).

Interview: 4 September 1991
Cindy Melby Phaneuf

TENNESSEE

NASHVILLE SHAKESPEARE FESTIVAL. MAIL: Darkhorse Theater, Nashville Shakespeare Festival, 4610 Charlotte Ave., Nashville, TN 37209. SITE: Centennial Park Bandshell, 25th and West End Avenues. ADMINISTRATION/BOX OFFICE: 615/297-7113. ADMISSION: free. SEASON: one production, 12 performances, in August; 6:30 p.m., Fri.–Sun. FACILITIES: outdoor amphitheatre (capacity 1,000). PRINCIPAL STAFF: Donald Capparella, president; Melissa Williams, company manager. AUDITIONS: Nashville, early summer. STATUS: non-Equity. ANNUAL BUDGET: $21,000 (1992-93). ANNUAL ATTENDANCE: 8,000 (1993). FOUNDED: 1988, Donald Capparella, Steve Chambers, Jill Jackson, Jane Perry.

The Nashville Shakespeare Festival (NSF) was founded in 1988 as a grassroots effort to provide free performances of Shakespeare's plays to the general public in the Nashville metropolitan area. The NSF is very much a community organization. With only one full-time staff member, it is managed principally by an eight-member volunteer artistic board, which in 1994 still included three of the founding members. Each member of the board has a specific area of responsibility, is occasionally assigned a special project, and is involved in all policy decisions relating to the festival. Jill Jackson, for example, serves as the director of NSF productions. NSF also has an advisory board to offer administrative and artistic guidance. Ann Cook Whalley, for example, professor of English at Vanderbilt University, a prominent Shakespearean scholar, and chairman of the International Shakespeare Association, serves on the advisory board. Performers, technicians, ushers, and so forth are also drawn from the community. Since its inception, NSF productions have been supported by the Nashville Metropolitan Board of Parks and Recreation with in-kind services estimated to be equivalent to about $30,000 per season. Metro Parks, for example, provides the band shell in Centennial Park rent free and the services of its own resident scenic designer and technical director. Metro Parks also absorbs the costs of water, electricity, and other services during rehearsals and performances. Additional income for NSF programs is raised through private and business contributions and various fund-raising events and activities.

In 1991, the NSF launched an educational outreach program called the Shakespeare Sampler. The Sampler program tours the Nashville public schools with a one-hour adaptation of a Shakespeare play performed by four or five actors. The week before the performance, the actors visit the school to hold a preparatory workshop with teachers and students. The NSF also distributes a printed curriculum guide to participating teachers. In 1991, the NSF's Sampler tour of *Macbeth* played to three schools; in 1992, *Hamlet* played to eight schools; and, in 1993, *Romeo and Juliet* played to 13 schools. To date, the NSF has provided this outreach program free to municipal public schools. For a modest fee, it will also offer the program to metropolitan private schools and to public schools outside of the Nashville municipal area.

Prior to 1990, the NSF occasionally presented non-Shakespearean plays in the fall and winter at the Looby Theatre. In 1990, the NSF began producing a regular indoor season of three or four productions of original and contemporary plays at the Darkhorse Theater. Unlike its policy for Shakespeare productions, the NSF does sell tickets for Darkhorse Theater presentations.

NSF Shakespearean productions are often updated to broaden their public appeal and contemporary relevance. The costumes in *The Merry Wives of Windsor,* for example, suggested both Elizabethan and contemporary dress to emphasize that human foibles are unchanging or, as the reviewer of *The Tennessean* noted, "as freshly pertinent now as when Shakespeare wrote it" (2 August 1990). The 1991 production of *Othello* was set futuristically in the year 2012, "to illustrate that jealousy and hatred are not time specific" (*Nashville Banner*, 14 August 1991). *The Comedy of Errors* in 1993 employed "a vaudeville look and feel, a sort of Charlie Chaplin-meet-Laurel and Hardy flavor," complete with bowler hats, baggy pants, and funny shoes (*The Tennessean*, 5 August 1993).

Clearly the NSF's approach has been successful. In 1988, an estimated 1,000 people attended the performances; by 1993, attendance had grown to over 8,000. Building on its successes, the NSF plans eventually to become a fully professional theater mounting two productions annually in Centennial Park and a winter season of plays, including perhaps another Shakespeare production, in the Darkhorse Theater.

Production History (Shakespeare only): **1988**: *AYL*; **1989**: *Per.*; **1990**: *Wiv.*; **1991**: *Oth.*; **1992**: *Ado*; **1993**: *Err.*; **1994**: *MND.*

Research Resources: An informal archive of reviews, programs, and photographs is maintained at the Nashville Shakespeare Festival administrative office. Material for this essay was provided by NSF.

Daniel J. Watermeier

TEXAS

AUSTIN SHAKESPEARE FESTIVAL. MAIL: care of Department of Theatre and Dance, University of Texas at Austin, Austin, TX 78712. SITE: Rock Island, Zilker Park. ADMINISTRATION: 512/454-BARD. ADMISSION: free. SEASON: one to three productions, mid-May to mid-July; 8:00 p.m., Thurs.–Sun. PRINCIPAL STAFF: Jeff Ellinger, artistic director; Rita Diaz, managing director. FACILITY: Festival Theatre at Zilker Park, open-air performance space (capacity 1,000); Zachary Scott Arena Stage. AUDITIONS: late February, local. STATUS: student and community performers. ANNUAL BUDGET: $35,000 (1992). ATTENDANCE: 15,000 (1992). FOUNDED: 1984, Jeff Ellinger.

Given Austin's penchant for outdoor activities, its arts-friendly environment, and its huge university community, a Shakespeare-in-the-Park enterprise would seem a natural for the capital city of Texas. Since 1974, there have been several attempts to create an audience for Shakespeare in Austin, first by Stephen Coleman's Gallimaufry Players, and more recently, in 1984, by Jeff Ellinger's Austin Shakespeare Festival (ASF). And, while the latter has achieved some degree of success, thanks mostly to the perseverance of ASF's founder, Shakespeare has not enjoyed the popularity afforded the Aquafest, the Club Armadillo, or any of the other myriad cultural outlets in this city of a half-million people. Nevertheless, the ASF embodies Ellinger's vision of providing "accessible, essential theatre in a natural setting . . . to those who don't usually go to live theatre."

Ellinger, an employee of Austin's Park and Recreation Department, did not set out to create a Shakespeare festival. Like Malvolio's notion of greatness, it was "thrust upon" him in 1984, when two busloads of San Antonio Shakespeare lovers were disappointed to find that a performance by the Gallimaufry Players had inexplicably been canceled. Himself a veteran of **Shakespeare at Winedale**, Ellinger hastily organized a series of Shakespearean scenes to be played on the bandstand at Woolridge Park so that Austin would not face a summer without Shakespeare. After this initial attempt at producing Shakespeare, Ellinger gathered a band of artists for a "conspiracy meeting" at the Barker History Center where plans were made among diverse groups to launch the ASF. In June 1985, the plans became a reality when *A Midsummer Night's Dream* was performed "on the soccer fields" at Zilker Park, an event that drew some 6,600 spectators.

The following year, the ASF mounted *Twelfth Night* and coproduced the Guare-McDermott-Shakespeare rock musical *Two Gentlemen of Verona* with Southwest Texas State University (from nearby San Marcos); the Tank Players added their production of *All's Well* to this, the ASF's most ambitious season to date. In 1987, the ASF was victimized by its own ambition: Local professional actor Julius Tennon had been engaged to play Othello but withdrew shortly before opening when an attractive film offer came his way. The production was canceled, and Ellinger learned a lesson about the dangers of using professional actors on a minuscule budget. It is hoped that the ASF will evolve into a professional repertory company framed within the context of an academic setting, either through affiliation with the University of Texas (which currently provides the bulk of its talent pool) or by founding its own "Shakespeare Academy," through which teacher-artists can make sufficient money to support themselves while performing in the company.

ASF productions were originally performed on and around a natural rock stage that provided a superb "natural" setting. Though the venue had some attractive qualities for free-spirited Austinites (audiences could come and go unimpeded, picnic blankets could be spread out over the enormous expanse of the Zilker soccer fields, and passers-by could "stumble" onto a cultural experience), there were problems with focus and acoustics. In 1990, the theatre space was better defined through a series of flats (painted to suggest a Tudor village) that enclosed the performance area and enhanced its acoustics. Other innovations included "Bard Blasters," personal amplifiers that allowed actors to be heard in the large space (where actors must compete with traffic noise from a nearby bridge) and a series of bleacher seats encircling the outer rim of the theatre. The actors still do the bulk of their performing atop "the Rock" and on a portable stage donated by Festival co-sponsor Chuy's Restuarante, but they no longer have to push for effect.

Austin has been called "Texas' Berkeley" because it is surely the most liberal-thinking city in this normally conservative state. Not surprisingly, ASF productions consciously—conspicuously—reflect the city's outlook. In 1989, *Much Ado About Nothing* was staged with Hispanics as the romantic leads (with the Watch played by Anglos), and the 1990 *Comedy of Errors* featured African-Americans as the Antipholi, the Duke, and Aegeon in an "Ephesus as pirate port" setting. Ellinger envisions furthering a multicultural approach to Shakespeare; indeed, he had planned a bilingual version of *Romeo and Juliet* for 1992, but casting problems precluded his concept.

The 1992 *Romeo and Juliet* production emerged as among the most conventional of the ASF's offerings. The costumes and setting (multileveled and very efficiently etched into "the Rock") were evocative of the Renaissance but punctuated here and there with reminders of our own century: Romeo wore what looked like combat fatigues under his doublet; Lady Capulet wore a black-sequined "pill-box" hat; Paris looked more the transplanted Scotsman than Italian nobility; and the lesser gentry wore pants most likely culled from personal wardrobes. The eclecticism was less a conceptual statement about the contemporary relevance of this our most cherished love story and much more a by-product of a small budget. The cast did a credible job of defining the major moods and most of the big moments. For example, the Tybalt-Mercutio sword fight, was superbly established as a bit of foolish games-playing that quickly got out of hand; the Romeo-Tybalt clash was restaged as an expressionistic dream sequence as Juliet lay in the tomb waiting for the potion to take effect. But there was little nuance in the speeches, save those by the thoughtful, focused Friar Laurence. What was "cut" grievously undermined an otherwise thoughtful, inventive production. The first encounter between the lovers was so rushed and unfocused that the chemistry between the two was never firmly established. Without a solid emotional core, the love interest was never truly interesting. Still, the audience seemed genuinely moved by the final tableau of Juliet and her Romeo, largely because of the power of Shakespeare's woeful tale and partly because of the ambience created by a warm May evening on the Rock at Zilker Park.

Production History: **1984**: Scenes for "Shakespeare in the Park"; **1985**: *MND*; **1986**: *TN, TGV* (rock musical version), *AWW*; **1987**: *Oth.* (canceled); **1988**: *Wiv., Tmp.*; **1989**: *Ado, LLL*; **1990**: *Err., MND*; **1991**: *AYL*; **1992**: *Rom., MND*; "Wars of the Roses" (scenes from *H6*); **1994**: *Mac.*

Research Resources: Archives for the Austin Shakespeare Festival are informally kept in the Department of Theatre and Dance, University of Texas at Austin and at the Austin Historical Center. See also:

Barnes, Michael. "All the City's a Stage." *Austin American-Statesman* (7 June 1991): 9.

Faires, Robert. "Keeping the Faith: Austin Shakespeare's Jeff Ellinger." [Austin] *Chronicle* (31 May 1991): 26.

Sevcik, Kim. "Festival Draws Diverse Audience." *The Daily Texan* (6 June 1991).

Site visits: 22 June 1991; 23 May 1992.
Michael L. Greenwald

THE GLOBE OF THE GREAT SOUTHWEST. MAIL: 2308 Shakespeare Road, Odessa, TX 79761. SITE: adjacent to Odessa College. ADMINISTRA-TION/BOX OFFICE: 915/332-1586. ADMISSION: $6–$8. SEASON: variable; usually a Shakespeare play one weekend in March, April, May; other shows as available; 8:00 p.m., 2:30 p.m., Sat. or Sun. PRINCIPAL STAFF: Clay Francell, managing director; Carleen Wadley, board president. FACILITY: Globe Theatre (authentic replica of Old Globe; capacity 405, wheelchair access). STATUS: touring professional and university companies; occasional community company. ANNUAL BUDGET: varies. ATTENDANCE: 3,600 (1992). FOUNDED: 1958, Marjorie Morris.

Touchstone's observation about "great reckonings in small rooms" may well find its most notable example in the west Texas oil patch town of Odessa. Standing there on the barren plains is a full-scale replica of Shakespeare's Bankside theatre: the Globe of the Great Southwest, a structure that Allardyce Nicoll has called "the most nearly authentic replica of Shakespeare's own Globe anywhere on earth."

The small room that gave birth to this great reckoning was a classroom in Odessa High School, where, in 1948, a young English teacher named Marjorie Morris responded to a crude miniature of the original Globe that had been constructed by a student as part of the class exploration of *Macbeth*. "Wouldn't it be nice," a student wondered aloud, "if we could have a Globe of our own." "We can," Morris assured her students. Twenty years later, the Globe of the Great Southwest began producing Shakespeare on a permanent basis and has continued its mission "to re-create Shakespeare's plays as he meant them to be given" for a family audience—before thousands of people a year, many of them coming in buses and caravans from Amarillo, El Paso, neighboring New Mexico, and even the tiny, mostly Hispanic town of Sierra Blanca, in the mountains above El Paso.

The evolution of Odessa's Globe of the Great Southwest (GGS) is an extraordinary story of vision, perseverance, and commitment to an ideal. Little wonder that James Michener chose to end his epic *Texas* (1985) with a paean to Mrs. Morris' dream; for Michener, GGS was the quintessential emblem of the frontier "can do" spirit that he celebrated in his saga:

> But what gave the Cobbs renewed hope for Texas every time they saw it was an amazing structure in the roughneck town of Odessa . . . an accurate replica of Shakespeare's Globe Theatre. There it stood in the sandy desert, full scale, and to it came Shakespearean actors from many different theatres and countries to orate the soaring lines of the master. . . . "I'll be sending you a check one of these days," Mrs. Cobb said, for the Globe was kept alive by families like the Cobbs who felt that Shakespeare added a touch of grace to the drylands.

Morris returned to North Texas State University in Denton, where she was born, the daughter of a Nazarene minister and educator, to work on a Master's Degree. To the surprise of no one in West Texas, her thesis was on "The Proposed Globe Theatre at Odessa." The work was illustrated by J. Ellsworth Powell, among the most prominent architectural designers in the Odessa region. Powell, who had never designed a theatre, soon became as obsessed as Morris about recreating the Globe, particularly as he delved into the many books that she provided to him from the Folger and other libraries. Powell finally settled on John Cranford Adams' celebrated conjecture (the basis of a much smaller theatre at Hofstra University, where Adams was president). Powell drew the blueprints for the replica *gratis* and later personally supervised every detail of the two-decade construction project, including the choice of stone work from five different states in the southwest and, most notably, worm-eaten pecky cypress that was imported from England to lend authenticity to the walls of the theatre's interior.

Morris was also aided by other West Texans. Sally Ratliff, on whose ranch oil had been found, offered her the project's first thousand dollars, which was followed by an equal contribution from Mrs. Rich, the Globe's first treasurer. Mary Hurt (Ratliff's daughter) headed the theatre's first patron drive, enlisting the help of such prominent ranching families as the Tom McKnights, the Cal Smiths, the Jay McGees, Bessye Cowden Ward and others. Local companies, banks, and schoolchildren also succumbed to Morris' pleading. There is a much-told story of a local judge who tried to escape her persistent pleas by actually locking himself in the county jail. "I'll wait until he returns," the imperturbable Marjorie Morris informed his clerk; the judge returned, check in hand, when taunts from inmates raised more judicial hackles than the English teacher's pleas for assistance.

Working on initial pledges of $35,000, the GGS founders broke ground in 1958 on a triangular patch of ground adjacent to Odessa Community College, for which Morris now taught English and from which she had secured the donation of a $7,500 gift of land. Walls were put up, but money ran short and construction was stopped, although the theatre had been officially chartered. Work began anew in the early 1960s, and, in April 1966, Paul Baker brought actors from his Dallas Theatre Center to Odessa to inaugurate the theatre with a production of *Julius Caesar*. The interior was not yet finished (Morris then lacked about $53,000 of the project's total of $350,000 needed to complete the theatre), but the audience, who sat on lawn chairs on a concrete floor, did not seem to mind. Among those theatregoers was Howard Taubman, theatre critic for the *New York Times*, who noted that, "curiously enough," this Globe, standing "implausibly and serenely on what was once an old oil field, looks as if it belongs."

Powell, who took time off from his paying job to supervise construction when funds were available, actually used the dimensions of the Fortune Theatre for his replica, which measures 84.5 feet across its octagonal shape. The thrust stage is 1,800 square feet, with a 22-foot-high ceiling. The intimate auditorium contains 410 seats, most of them on the steeply banked ground floor, with the remaining seats in a two-level gallery surrounding the staging area. Powell designed the theatre "to last forever." The open thrust stage, with the six acting areas typical of an Elizabethan public theatre, is built of pine, while the building around it is constructed with eight steel beams that hold up thick walls covered by plaster. As a concession to Odessa's fierce heat and tempestuous spring winds, the theatre is roofed; Powell painted the cupola midnight blue to suggest "the heavens." Both the sightlines and acoustics in Powell's masterpiece are virtually perfect. The original plans called for a miniature Thames moat to surround the theatre, but the idea was discarded. There is, however, a recently opened (1990) replica of the Anne Hathaway Cottage adjacent to the theatre; it is used for assemblies, concerts, and the traditional "victory dinner" that the town hosts for visiting acting companies. In November 1991, the local garden club unveiled in the cottage a life-size portrait, painted by prominent local artist Delores Petersen, of Marjorie Morris—wearing the regalia of Queen Elizabeth I.

A production of G. B. Shaw's *Arms and the Man* officially opened the completed theatre in September 1968, and, in 1969, GGS produced its first full-fledged Shakespeare Festival, with professional actors performing in *A Midsummer Night's Dream* and *The Taming of the Shrew*, directed by Charles David McCally. A Victoria native who had founded the defunct Victoria Shakespeare Festival, Texas' first professional festival and assistant to Paul Baker at the Dallas Theatre Center, McCally was GGS's first artistic director, and it was he who led the enterprise to national prominence during that theatre's salad days in the early 1970s. McCally's best-known GGS production was a revival of *The Taming of the Shrew* in 1972. McCally relocated the play's action to nineteenth-century West Texas. A preshow barbecue from a chuck wagon was served to patrons, among them an emissary from the British consulate in Washington, who judged McCally's *Shrew* "a fun idea, and not really so way out, as it is a good rustic play tied in with the countryside itself." The bullwhip-cracking Petruchio was played by Will (a.k.a. "Mark") McCrary, a professional actor who would later found the **Post Summer Shakespeare Festival**.

McCally's leadership and the unequaled opportunity to work in this extraordinary new space drew talented actors from across the country. Mark Dempsey, a New York actor who played Macbeth in the 1970 season, declared the Odessa Globe as "the best example of positive thinking I have ever seen. It is an actor's theatre with outstanding acoustics." McCally eventually left to pursue other creative interests (he is now a talent agent in Tulsa, after a teaching career at Oral Roberts University), and the professional company was disbanded.

Today, partly as a result of the devastating Texas oil bust of the 1980s, GGS must rely mostly on university and community theatre companies to provide its fare, though the peripatetic **National Shakespeare Company** visits Odessa each March. In 1991, for example, west Texans saw the **National Shakespeare Company**'s *Much Ado About Nothing*, McMurry University of Abilene's *Macbeth*, and Texas A&M's *Merchant of Venice*.

Conceived and devised at their respective home institutions for college audiences, the McMurry *Macbeth* and the A&M *Merchant of Venice* were decidedly postmodern in look and message. Neither, Morris emphasized, reflected GGS's decidedly traditionalist production philosophy, yet she graciously brought them to west Texas to provide area residents with the opportunity to experience experimental Shakespeare. Played largely on metallic scaffolding (which, alas, obscured the Globe's distinctive architecture), the

McMurry *Macbeth* explored the "power as aphrodisiac" theme. The witches seemed to be refugees from an MTV music video, the Macbeths' plotting in Act I, scene 7 was played seductively, and Macbeth's assault on Lady Macbeth after the banquet scene (Act III, scene 2) underscored both his political and sexual power lusts. Most memorable, however, were Banquo and Fleance (who began the play strumming a guitar and singing Elton John's "The King Is Dead"); here they were played by Hispanic brothers whose dress, hair style (including beadwork in the woven strands of hair), and facial characteristics were thoroughly native American. Given the rich multicultural heritage of Texas (which GGS is in a unique position to explore), there was something particularly resonant about this Banquo's ghost stalking an Anglo Macbeth. This casting gave this production of *Macbeth* a contemporary urgency.

Texas A&M's *The Merchant of Venice* also used contemporary popular music to frame the story; the androgynously costumed Salanio and Salerio sang Kinky Friedman's "They Ain't Makin' Jews Like Jesus Any More" after Shylock threatened them with a knife during his famous "Hath not a Jew eyes" speech. The Christians were self-centered grifters who exploited one another, pointedly ignored Jessica, and savaged Shylock at every turn. Shylock, played by a Hispanic actor, was clearly a victim of his environment, returning his animosity more than in kind. Rather than submit to Antonio's edict that he should "presently become a Christian," this Shylock hanged himself in a shocking epilogue. Despite these nontraditional, even iconoclastic renderings of Shakespeare, Odessa audiences awarded the talented actors from both schools standing ovations.

"We prefer our Shakespeare traditional," Marjorie Morris whispered several times during the *Macbeth* production, and there is a stated policy that offensive language and excessive bawdry are forbidden on the Globe stage. "The Globe is dedicated to the good, the true, the beautiful," explains Odessa's *grande dame*. Despite the current hard times that impede the Globe's mission, there is hope that the dream that began in that English class over 40 years ago will not vanish—that the good, the true, and the beautiful will continue to emanate from this magnificent theatre on the West Texas plains.

Production History: **1966**: *JC*; **1968**: *Arms and the Man*; **1969**: *MND, Shr.*; **1970**: *AYL, Mac.*; **1971**: *Mac.*; **1972**: *Shr., Rom., School for Wives*; **1973**: *Tmp., Err., Cyrano de Bergerac*; **1975**: *TN, Ado*; **1977**: *MM, TGV, School for Scandal*; **1978**: *Oth., LLL*; **1979**: *Cym., Ant.*; **1980**: *Ado, JC, MND*; **1981**: *Rom., Wiv., Err.*; **1982**: *Tmp., TN, Mac.*; **1983**: *Lr., Ham., MV, AYL*; **1984**: *Ado, Oth.*; **1985**: *Ham.*; **1986**: *Err., Tmp., MND*; **1987**: *Shr.*; **1988**: *JC, TGV*; **1989**: *AYL, TN, Pirates of Penzance*; **1990**: *Ham., She Stoops to Conquer, Oth., Lr., Shr.*; **1991**: *Ado, Mac., H8, MV*; **1992**: *TN,*

Tmp., Scapin; **1993**: *Rom., Came-lot, Rosencrantz and Guildenstern*   *are Dead, Ham.*; **1994**: *MND*.

Research Resources: Archives for the Globe of the Great Southwest are informally maintained in offices adjacent to the theatre.

Anderson, Godfrey. "Englander Thinks Odessa a Strange Place for Globe." [Odessa] *American* (12 October 1972: 4-B.

Berthelsen, Alice Anne Boggs. "The Globe of the Great Southwest." *Shakespeare Quarterly* 31 (Summer 1980): 248.

Dachslager, Earl L. "Shakespeare at the Globe of the Great Southwest." In Philip C. Kolin, ed., *Shakespeare in the South*. Jackson: University Press of Mississippi, 1983.

Englander, Anne H. "Shakespeare at the Odessa Globe, 1975." *Shakespeare Quarterly* 27 (Winter 1976): 72-76.

Fulton, Robert. "Shakespeare Southern Fried." *Shakespeare Quarterly* 36 (Autumn 1985): 362-64.

"Genesis of the Festivals." *Theatre Crafts* (March-April 1973): 9, 34.

Havens, Neil. "Shakespeare in Texas." *Shakespeare Quarterly* 29 (Spring 1978): 249-51.

Hewes, Henry. "The Theater." *Saturday Review* (10 October 1970): 19.

Loney, Glenn, and Patricia MacKay. *The Shakespeare Complex*. New York: Drama Book Specialists, 1975.

McNeir, Waldo F. "Shakespeare in Texas." *Shakespeare Quarterly* 30 (Spring 1979): 221-25.

Velz, John W. "Shakespeare at the Odessa Globe." *Shakespeare Quarterly* 24 (Autumn 1973): 435-37.

Site visits: 14-15 April, 7-8 June, 31 October-3 November 1991.
Michael L. Greenwald

HOUSTON SHAKESPEARE FESTIVAL. MAIL: School of Theatre, University of Houston, Houston, TX 77204-5071. SITE: Miller Outdoor Theatre, Hermann Park. ADMINISTRATION: 713/743-2930. BOX OFFICE: 713/520-3291. ADMISSION: free. SEASON: ten performances in rotating repertory, late July to mid-August; 8:30 p.m., Thurs.–Sun. PRINCIPAL STAFF: Sidney Berger, producing director; Suzanne Phillips, associate producer; Roxanne Collins, business manager; Jonathan Middents, production manager. FACILITY: stage under open A-frame (1,582 fixed seats with additional seating up to 8,000 on grassy knoll). AUDITIONS: local. STATUS: LORT D-LOA. ANNUAL BUDGET: $250,000 (1991). ANNUAL ATTENDANCE: 50,000 (1991). FOUNDED: 1975, Sidney Berger.

Sidney Berger is the powerhouse behind the long-lived success story of the Houston Shakespeare Festival (HSF) as well as the Shakespeare Theatre Association of America (STAA), which he cofounded in 1990, serving as that national organization's president from 1990 through 1992. His students have been instrumental in the development of other Shakespeare festivals (for example, Kathy Barber at **Texas Shakespeare Festival**), and many recent festival founders have learned that it pays to visit Berger's operation to learn how it should be done. James H. Pickering, senior vice president and provost of the University of Houston (UH), commented in 1992, on the occasion of STAA's annual meeting there: "I have long since stopped being surprised at anything that Sidney Berger does."

Berger's lifelong passion for Shakespeare impelled him, fresh out of college, to seek directing opportunities beyond his experience. He wrote to "every Shakespeare festival in existence" asking to be hired. When that effort brought no results, he created his own opportunity in Houston, where he had joined the UH faculty in 1969. He noted that the city-supported Miller Outdoor Theatre offered free summer performances by the ballet, the symphony, and the opera, but that there was no spoken drama. Meeting with the Miller's advisory council and with university administrators, he proposed a bill of two Shakespeare plays on a $10,000 budget, with in-kind support from the university (office and rehearsal space, production facilities, and personnel). The collaboration between city and university proved successful. "I simply opened the doors and actors came out of the woodwork," marvels Berger. Attendance surpassed all expectations in that trial season. Indeed, the public's hunger for Shakespeare was demonstrated at the opening performance of *The Taming of the Shrew*. A generator went out just before curtain time, but the crowd waited patiently while a replacement generator was located and transported to the site. The second generator blew also, but still the audience waited, and there was no noticeable attrition when the performance finally began around midnight. A standing ovation and cheers from the capacity audience came at the final curtain. Letters of appreciation from the community insured that the Shakespeare festival would become an annual event.

On a separate but slightly overlapping budget, Berger and the university also produce an annual Childrens' Theatre Festival (CTF). After starting his Shakespeare festival, Berger cast about for other vacuums to fill. He recalled his years with USO shows, when he realized that many enlisted personnel had never seen a live performance. "It was like playing to a child audience," he says. "In our culture, few are producing children's theatre very seriously. So I started the Children's Theatre Festival in order to set up the child audience for Shakespeare and adult theatre in general. Child audiences and free outdoor audiences are very much the same: you'll find out if they're not interested. You tell them a lie, and they'll walk out and find something else to do." Indeed, honesty and immediacy are keynotes of HSF productions. The HSF's mission is "to present the works of Shakespeare, free of charge, so that every socioeconomic strata of the population of the city and its environs may perceive the work easily and without pretension and distortion."

In 1982, the HSF and CTF boards of directors were merged to form The Festivals Company. Festival Angels is a volunteer support organization. Funding support from corporations has grown steadily. An important financial boost came in 1978 with the inauguration of a citywide 1 percent for the arts hotel/motel tax, one-twentieth of which is specifically set aside for the Miller Outdoor Theatre. In 1989, the Cullen Trust for the Performing Arts awarded the HSF a special grant, enabling it to join LORT. Shakespeare Outreach is described as "a touring company of young actors performing 35-minute programs designed to break down Shakes-Fear (a delusion rampant among students that Shakespeare is boring, impossible to understand, and irrelevant)." The programs, created in collaboration with the Shakespeare Globe Centre of the Southwest, are offered free of charge to area schools and libraries.

The Miller Outdoor Theatre, in operation for seven decades, is a source of great civic pride in Houston. Over 400,000 people each year attend the free arts programs presented there, within walking distance of Houston's major museums. A well-equipped, if somewhat old-fashioned stagehouse includes a box office, refreshment stand, dressing rooms, and minimal backstage area. Although all events are free, the box office dispenses tickets on the day of the performance for those who wish to reserve places in the fixed seating closest to the stage, under the huge canopy. Besides the 1,582 seats, this area includes spaces for 27 wheelchairs. Due to Houston's heat and humidity (not to mention mosquitoes), however, many elect to sit in the open air on the grassy slope behind the fixed seats. Attendance often reaches up to 8,000 on weekend evenings. The HSF's audiences are among the most ethnically diverse of any Shakespeare festival in the country. African-Americans, Asian-Americans, and Hispanics can all be seen in significant numbers.

The 1990 production of *Troilus and Cressida*, directed by Rutherford Cravens, explored the work's comedic elements to the fullest. Robert Strane as Pandarus elicited gales of laughter with his well-timed line deliveries and clever character touches, including the use of a cane as an extension of his personality. Even the battle scenes began humorously—Diomedes getting his sword point stuck in the stage floor, Agamemnon being unable to unfold his map properly—before finally segueing into horrible brutality. Claude Caux's fight choreography and Robert Nelson's music aided the subtle transition from hilarity to violence.

Berger himself directed a charmingly postmodern *Tempest* in a Dali-esque setting that included elements of Kabuki staging. Ferdinand and Miranda's initial encounter emphasized their strangeness to each other: He spoke slowly, with gestures, as if to a foreigner; they touched as if each were trying to see what the other was made of; when Ferdinand offered his hand to shake, Miranda, not knowing the custom, laid her face on his hand. The innocence of their mutual attraction was interestingly counterpointed by an almost erotic intimacy between Prospero and Ariel. Michael LaGue played a particularly irascible Prospero. Most gratifyingly, the production's magical qualities arose from the blocking and the characterizations more than from visual effects.

Production History: 1975: *MND, Shr.*; 1976: *Tmp., Rom.*; 1977: *Ham., Err.*; 1978: *Wiv., Mac.*; 1979: *TN, Ado*; 1980: *AYL, Lr.*; 1981: *MND, MV*; 1982: *LLL, Tmp.*; 1983: *WT, Err.*; 1984: *Ham., TGV*; 1985: *MM, R3*; 1986: *Oth., AWW*; 1987: *JC, Shr.*; 1988: *R2, TN*; 1989: *Cor., AYL*; 1990: *Tmp., Tro.*; 1991: *MV, Wiv.*; 1992: *Ado, Rom.*; 1993: *H5, MND*; 1994: *LLL, Ham.*

Research Resources: Personal archives for the Houston Shakespeare Festival are maintained by Sidney Berger and Suzanne Phillips.

Site visit and interview: 27-28 July 1990.
Felicia Hardison Londré

POST SUMMER SHAKESPEARE FESTIVAL (Festival operation ceased in 1991, although Garza Theatre remains in operation). MAIL: 226 East Main Street, Post, TX 79356. SITE: Garza Theatre. ADMINISTRATION/BOX OFFICE: 806/495-4005. SEASON: eight to ten performances mid-July. PRINCIPAL STAFF: Jane Prince-Jones, managing director; Lena Johnston, office manager. FACILITY: proscenium theatre (capacity 220). STATUS: community theatre. ANNUAL BUDGET: $1,500 (Shakespeare production only). ATTENDANCE: 800–1,000. FOUNDED: 1986, Will McCrary.

The history of the American theatre is filled with romantic tales of artist-entrepeneurs who brought live drama to frontier outposts. To these must be added the story of Will McCrary, a veteran New York stage, dinner theatre circuit, and Shakespeare festival actor who, in 1986, returned to his home town of Post, Texas (population 3,961) to begin a vibrant, regional theatre enterprise that for four astonishing years hosted the Post Summer Shakespeare Festival (PSSF).

The town of Post was founded in 1907 when C. W. Post, the breakfast cereal magnate (and inventor of a type of suspenders and the bicycle-built-for-two), came to Texas' rugged caprock country, 38 miles south of Lubbock, to build, from the ground up, "a self-sufficient city that would provide everything its townspeople would need." Post's first paid employee was a Mr. McCrary, grandfather of the PSSF founder; Post's own granddaughter is actress Dina Merrill, the festival's most prominent "angel."

After studying theatre at Texas Christian University in Fort Worth, Will McCrary joined the navy and found himself in San Diego in the early 1950s. There he spent his off-duty hours performing small roles for Craig Noel in the now defunct San Diego Shakespeare Festival. After a professional acting and scenic design career of 43 years (including a stint with Walter Matthau in *The Odd Couple*), McCrary returned to Post, partly to found the Garza Theatre, and partly to continue work on a book on John Wilkes Booth.

The Garza Theatre, on Post's appealing turn-of-the-century Main Street, was constructed in 1916 and used first as a vaudeville house, appropriately named "The Palace," and later as a movie house. In 1955, the theatre was closed and remained boarded up for 30 years. In 1986, McCrary opened up the old Palace, refurbished it (particularly the stage area, which had been burned by vandals in 1957), and added lobby, refreshment, and box office space by reworking the adjacent mercantile store. Today, the Garza Theatre, named after the county in which it is located, is a spartan yet very charming, brick-walled theatre, comfortably seating 220 people in a steeply raked auditorium. Pictures of every show staged at the new Garza line the walls, and there is a feeling of community pride that thoroughly permeates every cranny of this venerable theatre.

During an initial season of mostly "pop" community theatre plays, McCrary determined to produce "popular classics of the English language theatre" at the Garza. "It's an opportunity for me to share of my life-long training in every aspect of theatre," said McCrary as he announced the "First Annual Summer Shakespeare Festival," the highlight of which would be a fully mounted production of *The Taming of the Shrew*. Trying to recruit actors who had never seen Shakespeare and who had mostly unpleasant memories of high school encounters with Caesar and Romeo was no easy task. McCrary nonetheless rounded up a cast of would-be Shakespeareans, mostly through impromptu auditions on Main Street. He convinced the local newspaper editor that he would make a fine Baptista, and he persuaded a prominent high school athlete that he could play a handsome young lover. "There are no bad actors, just bad directors," McCrary told Post's citizenry, as well as others from nearby Slaton and similar ranch and oil communities.

McCrary's *The Taming of the Shrew* was set on a cattle ranch in West Texas. The concept was a natural for Post's clientele, particularly since McCrary planned to have the actors arrive via horse-drawn carriages at nearby Algerita Park for a preshow chuck wagon barbecue and small-town variety show. The names of nearby locales were substituted for the Italian ones. Petruchio and his sidekicks arrived astride stick horses to take rooms in the Algerita Hotel. Katerina carried a bull whip. All was played to the rinky-tink sound of a saloon piano.

Bouyed by the success of the first PSSF, McCrary quickly announced that he would revive *Shrew* and add *Richard III* the following year. That notion proved too ambitious even in the "can do" town of Post, so McCrary staged a modest *Midsummer Night's Dream* in which he played Nick Bottom. Again he cajoled town locals (including both the Methodist and Presbyterian ministers!) into becoming part of his "dream." Word of McCrary's work spread to

Lubbock, a 45-minute drive away, and others, including students from Texas Tech, joined the Garza company. In 1989, McCrary hired 16 disadvantaged youths through a government training program to work backstage as well as on stage in his company. McCrary, said one of the ministers with whom he worked, "never saw color" when he cast a show. Thus, his staging of *The Tempest*, in which he also played Prospero in a fanciful sorcerer's costume, featured a multiracial cast of mariners who maneuvered an almost full-sized sailing ship across the Garza stage; later they played sprites and spirits who dove off the Garza stage into a deep orchestra pit. The PSSF's *Tempest* later toured to the **Globe of the Great Southwest** where, according to members of the cast, the playgoers were astounded at the highly professional quality of the performance.

In 1990, McCrary staged *Romeo and Juliet*, a production remembered for its exciting sword play and for its portrayal of the feuding fathers by the two ministers. It was the most conventionally costumed of the PSSF productions, as McCrary, ever the practical man of the theatre, was never hesitant to make Shakespeare as accessible as possible to his West Texas audiences. If there was a "house style" for the PSSF (save the Renaissance *Romeo*), it was decidedly "eclectic Americana."

Although he worked almost exclusively with untrained amateurs, McCrary elicited remarkably credible performances from his casts, particularly in comedy. (McCrary was himself a superb comedian; although I did not observe a Shakespeare play during my visit to Post, I was fortunate to see McCrary act in *The Sunshine Boys*). "He had a standard and you met it," recalls the Reverend Charles Sommervill, a veteran of several Garza Shakespeare productions. An autocratic director, intolerant of debate in the rehearsal process, McCrary pushed actors, regardless of their age, experience, race, or innate ability, to meet his professional expectations. Though his tactics alienated some, those who stuck with him developed what the Reverend James Bell calls "a passion for theatre in their hearts that's still with them." Clearly, McCrary achieved the goals that he had set for himself and his neighbors when he returned to Post. McCrary died suddenly in September 1991. The Garza Theatre and the many actors who played upon its stage under McCrary's tutelage remain Post's most fitting monument to this native son who longed "to bring Shakespeare to those who didn't know him."

Production History: 1987: *Shr.*; **1988**: *MND*; **1989**: *Tmp.*; **1990**: *Rom.*

Research Resources: Archives for the Post Summer Shakespeare Festival are informally kept at the Garza Theatre and at the Post *Dispatch* office. See also articles from the Post *Dispatch*:
"First Shakespeare Festival at Garza July 23." *Dispatch* (1 July 1987): 1.
"Post's Summer Festival Features *The Tempest*." *Dispatch* (19 July 1989): 1.
"*Romeo and Juliet* Delights Garza Audiences." *Dispatch* (25 July 1990): 1.

"Summer Festival Will Spotlight *The Tempest.*" *Dispatch* (6 July 1989): 1.

Welborn, Lonnie. "*A Midsummer Night's Dream* Casts Spell on Garza Theatre Audiences." *Dispatch* (27 July 1988): 1.

"William McCrary." [obituary] [Post] *Dispatch* (2 October 1991).

Site visits and interviews: 8 June 1991; 21 February 1992.
Michael L. Greenwald

SAN ANTONIO SHAKESPEARE FESTIVAL (ceased operation in 1992). SITE: Sunken Garden Theatre, Brackenridge Park. ADMISSION: free. SEASON: 12 performances of one play, last two weeks of June; 8:30 p.m., Tues.–Sun. PRINCIPAL STAFF: Jake Beasley, artistic director; Louisa Kerry-Rubenstein, program director; Susan Gadke, production coordinator. FACILITY: Sunken Garden Theatre, open-air classical amphitheatre (capacity 2,200). AUDITIONS: late March, early April. STATUS: six Equity actors, with community actors. ANNUAL BUDGET: $165,000 (1991). ATTENDANCE: 21,000 (1991). FOUNDED: 1990, Jake Beasley.

Texans thrive on competition, and the San Antonio Shakespeare Festival (SASF) began when a group of San Antonians, led by Jake Beasley, determined that the Alamo City needed a Shakespearean enterprise to match those of Dallas, Fort Worth, and Houston. "Although this is a new idea for San Antonio, it's been going around the country for 35 years. We're just filling in the blanks for San Antonio," said Beasley in preparation for his inaugural season. Although the SASF staff projected a first-year audience of 6,000 (and hoped for 10,000), in 1990 over 18,500 people helped "fill in the blanks" and quickly establish the SASF as a quality festival of considerable promise.

There is much to recommend about the SASF, not the least of which is the city of San Antonio itself, the nation's tenth largest and among its most picturesque. Playing its Shakespeare upon a New Deal-era classically designed open-air stage in Brackenridge Park (a couple of miles north of the famed River Walk), the SASF enjoys an ambience that is difficult to match. The amphitheatre is surrounded by a variety of food vendors, and the smell of *fajitas* wafts across the festival grounds. Audiences reflecting the city's rich multicultural heritage assemble well in advance of curtain time to enjoy the semitropical park and secure good seats in the huge space before the Sunken Garden Theatre.

From the festival's inception, Beasley and the SASF board of directors have been intent on developing a festival that would be distinctly San Antonio. Under the joint sponsorship of the San Antonio Parks Department and food giant H-E-B, the SASF quickly incorporated the city's multiethnic appeal into its premiere production, *A Midsummer Night's Dream*, which received what Beasley termed a "folk baroque" treatment. Specifically, the *mise-en-scène* and music drew upon the Hispanic heritage for which the city is famous. The fairies wore costumes taken from Mayan folk art, especially the colorful *milagros* (tiny metallic religious icons) that shimmered in the stage lighting. Quince and company wore Mexican wedding shirts and multihued blankets as they negotiated Athens' magic forest, represented by a fanciful collection of Central American folk art trees. All was played to the otherworldly sounds of Andes flute music.

Despite the popular and critical success of this initial season, Beasley feels that much more must be done to involve the city's minority talent pool in the SASF. He tells of a conversation with a fine Hispanic actor who declined to audition because "I didn't think you wanted Mexicans . . . and I don't do British accents." Beasley hopes to forge a working relationship with the Guadeloupe Theatre Company, the city's only other professional theatre enterprise. "We are the largest city in America without a major professional theatre company," he laments. Beasley has also convinced SASF sponsors, in principle, that producing a second show at the amphitheatre at Mission San Jose, on the city's almost exclusively Hispanic south side, would do much to broaden the constituency of the SASF. In four to five years, Beasley and his fledgling company hope to produce a variety of professional theatrical offerings year round, while retaining the Shakespeare plays as a "free" festival in the early summer months.

As the SASF builds, it must rely on actors and directors from Houston and Dallas because the professional talent pool is limited in San Antonio. The SASF currently uses six to seven Equity actors plus a stage manager and directors from the Dallas Theatre Center or Houston's Alley Theatre as the foundation of its company; to these are added high-quality community-theatre actors and students from the various colleges and universities in San Antonio. Costumes are constructed at Incarnate Word College, and scenery is designed at Trinity College. This mix of professional, community, and educational theatre sources has proven quite salutary, if the 1991 *Taming of the Shrew* is truly indicative of the calibre of work produced by the SASF.

Drawing his inspiration from the film *1900* (and from parts of *Godfather II*), Allan McCalla, veteran Dallas Theatre Center actor and director, set the battle between Kate and Petruchio in early twentieth-century Padua. The elaborate town square prominently featured the "Banco Goldoni," a thoughtful reminder that Shakespeare was indebted to the *commedia dell'arte* for many elements of this comedy. McCalla cut the Christopher Sly prologue and substituted a colorful dumb show to establish Kate's shrewishness: she terrorized the town, kicking the cane from the grasp of a blind man, shoving a fig in the fruit seller's mouth, and scaring off the poultryman by out-crowing his rooster.

Wearing Indiana Jones boots and a leather safari hat, Petruchio entered to battle Kate more with words than with the physical *shtick* that frequently accrues in the play. The production evinced a consistently thoughtful exploration of the Kate-Petruchio relationship that transcended the purely comical. The interpretation compromised neither Shakespeare's intentions nor a modern audience's sensitivity about the problems faced by women in a male-dominated society. As played by Jennifer Griffin, a Dallas-based actress and accomplished jazz singer, Kate's petulance was both a rebellion against the "man-on-every-corner" world in which she lived and a stultifying indulgence that diminished her ability to be accepted by *any* world. After a well-conceived first encounter, in which he and Kate silently stalked one another in a long, sensual mating dance, Petruchio tamed this shrew through sheer charm and good humor—and a bit of her own medicine: in Act IV, scene 5, Petruchio rolled about on the ground, pounding his fists childishly at "This is a man, old, wrinkled, withered/And not a maiden, as thou say'st she is" (lines 43-44), a hilarious imitation of the tantrum Kate had thrown earlier in the haberdasher's scene.

The Act 5 capitulation speech—or what one post-show observer termed "that politically incorrect speech"—was delivered feistily, yet sincerely, *to the men* at the wedding banquet. For the first 18 lines, Kate, exuding confidence in her new-found "self," circled the banquet area, playfully chucking each of the town fathers on the shoulder or chin. At "Such a duty as the subject owes the prince/Even such a woman oweth her husband," Kate sat triumphantly astride the banquet table. It was an extraordinary visual image that showed that she had indeed become an equal in their domain and thus could—as an equal—give her husband the obedience he sought because he had merely liberated her from her uncomely past.

Production History: 1990: *MND*; **1991**: *Shr*.

Research Resources: Archives are informally maintained at the San Antonio Shakespeare Festival office.

Bennett, Steve. "Culture at Its Finest Graces City This Weekend." *San Antonio Light* (16 June 1991): 7A.

———. "Partake of Shakespeare in the Park." *San Antonio Light* (20 June 1991): G1.

Corning, Blair. "Sponsors Keep Bard on Boards." *San Antonio Express-News* (30 January 1991): 4E.

Londré Felicia. "Shakespeare Sans Sous." *American Theatre* (December 1990): 54-56.

Martin, Harper. "*Ser O No Ser*: Shakespeare Festival Presents a Hispanic Dream." *San Antonio Light* (8 July 1990).

Richelieu, David Anthony. "Beasley Gets Credit Due." *San Antonio Express-News* (9 February 1991).

"San Antonio." *Texas Monthly* (June 1990): 76.

Site visit and interview: 21 June 1991
Michael L. Greenwald

SHAKESPEARE AT WINEDALE. MAIL: P.O. Box 11, Round Top, TX 78954 (tickets); CAL 20, University of Texas, Austin, TX 78712 (administration). SITE: Winedale Historical Center (4 miles from Round Top). ADMINISTRATION/BOX OFFICE: 409/278-3530. ADMISSION: $4. SEASON: four productions in rotating repertory, first three weekends in August; 7:30 p.m., Thurs.–Sun; 2:00 p.m., Sat.–Sun; one play on last Saturday in April, 7:00 p.m. PRINCIPAL STAFF: James B. Ayres, artistic director; Gloria Jaster, managing director of Winedale Historical Center. FACILITY: The Theatre Barn, thrust stage in nineteenth-century barn (capacity 450). AUDITIONS: January through April; interviews in Austin. STATUS: non-Equity, college students only. ANNUAL BUDGET: $30,000 (1991). ATTENDANCE: 6,000 (1991). FOUNDED: 1970, James B. Ayres.

A *grande dame* with the unlikely name of Ima Hogg ("Miss Ima" to several generations of Texas arts patrons) first suggested that Shakespeare should be performed in a nineteenth-century barn atop a hill in some of the most attractive ranch country in Central Texas. In 1970, James B. Ayres, now Regents Professor of Shakespeare at the University of Texas (UT), attended a Hogg Foundation reception at the Winedale Historical Center. The center consists of a coach stop and a collection of German-settler farm buildings (some dating back to the pre-Alamo days of 1831), located on a 195-acre spread that Miss Ima donated to the university as a weekend retreat and study center. Ayres was introduced to Miss Ima, daughter of former Governor James Hogg, as "a Shakespeare professor"; she instructed him to walk up the hill and take a look around the old barn, informally known as "the theatre barn" because locals occasionally performed plays and musical entertainments there. Ayres told his hostess that he was struck by the power of the structure, with its rust-colored clay floor, lofts, and hand-hewn cedar beams, to evoke the ambience of Shakespeare's Bankside theatre. "Well, I want you to come here and do some Shakespeare," Miss Ima replied.

Ayres and a small band of students returned to Winedale six weeks later, dropped their baggage at the old Lauderdale House (which had been converted to a dormitory for UT study groups), and spent a weekend in the barn "doing some Shakespeare," as well as a hastily improvised performance of Dylan Thomas' *Under Milkwood.* Now, for over 20 years, university students, representing almost every state in the country, have been performing Shakespeare (and Thomas Dekker's *Shoemaker's Holiday* in 1989) to large and appreciative audiences willing to endure the infamous heat of August in Texas in exchange for some of the most intelligent and enthusiastic performances of the Bard's plays one will encounter in the United States.

Ayres recalls the transformation "the place" produced among that first group of students at Winedale in November 1970: "It immediately became apparent that the place itself enlivened the group. It isolated them; it helped define their interest in the project as a group." Ayres' first "companies," consisting of students enrolled in his spring Shakespeare course, were modest in scope, performing short scenes from the canon. In the summer of 1971, 11 students stayed a fortnight to produce an evening of "dramatic study of Hamlet through his Shakespearean antecedents"; this project consisted of five scenes performed under the collective title "What a Piece of Work Is a Man." The first true Shakespeare at Winedale Company (SAW), 18 strong, was in residence for four weeks to prepare scenes from *Henry 4, Part 1*. "That was the first time I knew it would work," Ayres recalls. The first complete play, *The Tempest*, was staged in 1973, and Winedale has produced plays each summer since. The most memorable of these may have been a 1975 *Much Ado About Nothing*, which had locals and audience members lining the picturesque road leading to the Barn, shouting welcome and waving flags for Messina's returning soldiers. The practice of presenting three plays in rotating repertory was inaugurated in 1977, and a fourth was added in 1984.

At present, a company of 16 to 20 students, selected through a meticulous interview process (SAW does not "audition"), enrolls in a course entitled: "The Play: Reading, Criticism, and Performance." By design, Ayres does not select traditional theatre students, nor necessarily even English majors. Many of his actors are true neophytes, both to Shakespeare and the stage. "I primarily want people who have a genuine curiosity about Shakespeare and are willing to invest two months of their lives totally immersed in getting to know his plays and language," Ayres insists. "A background in theatre or literature is not a prerequisite." Indeed, the 1991 "class" featured a second-year medical student, a finance major, a couple of French majors, and a Ph.D. candidate in philosophy from UCLA. Among SAW's most memorable alumni is Terry Galloway, now a professional actress. Ayres cast her as Falstaff, a performance that he still calls "definitive." Cross-gender casting is not uncommon at Winedale: a woman has also played Shylock to some acclaim.

The company gathers at Winedale in late June and spends five weeks of nearly fifteen-hour-a-day sessions learning to perform three Shakespearean plays (a separate company mounts a single performance of another play in late April). Prior to arriving at the new dormitory (the Lauderdale House burned in 1981), each actor is assigned a large, medium, and at least one small role in the three plays. Actors arrive with all their lines memorized and a letter from "Doc" Ayres bearing the command: "Confront the words honestly, continually, inviting the struggle. When you arrive at Winedale, you should be able to do *anything* with the words."

Because he believes that most productions of Shakespeare suffer from "systems of preparation and direction that emasculate, control, and fix the play," Ayres steadfastly refuses to "direct" the SAW company in the traditional sense, other than occasionally composing a large group scene. He will tolerate virtually any question from his student-actors except "What do you want me to do here?" Through playing improvisational games and exercises, reading a vast array of critical material about the plays, and mostly immersing themselves in the scripts, the students together shape each play to reflect a collective consensus about its plot, characters, language, and issues. Students themselves suggest any "cuts" in the script as an exercise in understanding the play. Ayres proudly notes that the 1991 ensemble deleted only about 15 lines from *Measure for Measure*, leaving *Love's Labour's Lost* and *A Winter's Tale* intact.. Those not performing in a scene become what Tyrone Guthrie once called "the ideal audience' of one," offering constructive feedback to their colleagues. At other times, these "little eyasses" are busy stitching costumes, focusing lights (which are run in performance by whoever happens to be closest to the board and is not needed on stage), or fashioning simple properties. Though one will not find trendy interpretations, postmodern stagings, or quirky fashion statements at SAW, one can—if the three plays I saw in August 1991 are accurate indicators—be assured of well-told stories, sharply etched characters, and language spoken with authority, intelligence, and (best of all) a genuine sense of discovery. If there is a consistent subtext running through the performances it would be, to paraphrase Miranda: "O brave new world that hath such language in it!"

At the conclusion of the five-week exploratory stage, the SAW students take their final exam—three weekends of public performances in which the stated artistic mission of the company is brought to life: "To share with others what we learn together through play and performance." The "others" come from nearby population centers such as Houston (70 miles), Austin (90 miles), College Station (65 miles), San Antonio (85 miles), and even Dallas-Fort Worth (160 miles), as well as locals from the rich ranch country around Winedale. Nearby Round Top hosts one of the finest classical music festivals in the Southwest, and the area abounds with art and antique stores; thus, a sizable, appreciative clientele is attracted to SAW's productions. Regional newspapers and magazines regularly run feature stories about SAW's new season. There is little advertising *per se*, but the forthcoming festival logo, showing Shakespeare in a bandanna and a well-worn cowboy hat, sucking on a blade of prairie grass, beckons patrons to let their "imaginary forces work" in the Theatre Barn.

Frequent playgoers know to pack a huge picnic basket for a preshow feast on the theatre's attractive, historic grounds. They also know to dress as comfortably as possible, though the recent addition of 16 ceiling fans has made watching Shakespeare in the oppressive summer heat much more pleasant (there is also a large trunk filled with straw fans available at the entrance), as do the generous cups of free, ice-cold lemonade and beer at intermission. Folding chairs and benches surround the small thrust stage, which is backed by a loft that serves admirably as the raised gallery of Globe fame. Save the occasional banner or floral spray, scenery is virtually nonexistent, and settings consist mostly of multifunctional stools, benches, and tables. Still, there is a unified look to the *mise-en-scène*, thanks to the rustic look of the setting and properties. Part of the fun of an SAW weekend is to watch the performers find new ways to use the space and its trappings efficiently and imaginatively. Costumes are either pulled from stock or made by the students themselves, with the generous help of "The Sewing Elves" (local women who assist the festival). The look is invariably Renaissance, though there is little attempt at detail. Like so many other elements of the SAW experience, evocation takes precedence over replication.

Though the students are amateurs in the best sense of the work (that is, those who "love" what they do), their performances are surprisingly good. While these neophytes may saw the air with their hands too much and occasionally tear a passion to tatters, they nonetheless speak the language with an intensity and clarity that many of the professionals performing across the state might envy. Of the eight Shakespeare festivals I attended in Texas and Oklahoma in 1991, no company consistently told its stories as clearly and with such a sense of discovery as the SAW students. Unencumbered by a trunk full of actors' tricks, which they have not yet accumulated, nor by the subtleties of modern psychological acting, for which they have had no formal training, the young actors focused on playing each scene for its inherent dramatic values and on creating vivid, broadly drawn characters, to remind us of the engaging plots Shakespeare devised. The great themes and cosmic issues ultimately take care of themselves, and one leaves Winedale thinking, "This is what the Children of St. Paul's or—closer to our own time—William Poel's company must have been like."

In 1991, SAW performed *Love's Labour's Lost*, *Measure for Measure*, and *The Winter's Tale*. Any discernible thematic insights came largely through the casting. In *Love's Labour's Lost*, Berowne (Biron), whose slightly hammy acting made his hypocrisy all the funnier, proclaimed an enthusiasm for "women's eyes" that had the same joy of discovery that Costard finds in the famous "remuneration" speech. There was, as is so trendy in many current productions, no underlying cynicism in this Berowne, and the youthful exuberance of the quartet of lovers made this satire on academe all the more immediate. The troubles encountered in the rustics' pageant of the Nine Worthies also had an air of authenticity that more experienced actors frequently lose. Similarly, SAW's *Measure for Measure* offered an Isabella whose own youth and innocence made her progress from naive maiden to knowing woman all the more believable, a Froth who literally frothed at the mouth throughout his scene, and, best of all, a Lucio played by a young woman in a huge mustache, whose "send-up" of that fantastic's macho posturing absolutely underscored the boorishness of his jibes and gambols. A heavy-set young man played Mistress Overdone "straight" and very funny. *The Winter's Tale* featured a Hispanic Polixenes whose foreignness in Sicilia was especially well defined. One wishes, however, that this Autolycus had foregone the British accent to effect his roguery; there are rustic accents aplenty in the Texas Midlands that would have served him better. The trial scene was splendid for its unabashed passion, nowhere more tellingly than in Leontes' cathartic cry that "I have too much believed mine own suspicion." These young actors were playing for very high stakes indeed, and this "sad tale" was the better for it. Bohemia's rites of spring were spirited and colorful in one of SAW's most effective uses of color and accessories. Hermione's awakening in the last act could not quite overcome the Theatre Barn's other notable drawback: During afternoon performances, it is impossible to darken the stage, and, without a true discovery space, the actress had simply to enter and assume her statue position, thus diminishing the effect of Shakespeare's magical moment.

Perhaps the finest testimonies to SAW's appeal for participants and observers alike come from former student-actors themselves. Joy Howard, who spent the summers of 1979 and 1982 in the Theatre Barn, said it best: "Every time I think of Winedale, I think of those lines of *Hamlet*: 'You would play upon me, you would sound me from my lowest note to the top of my compass . . . and there is much music, excellent voice in this little organ.' Winedale is a sounding of the self. If anything in my life has worked me from one end to the other, it's Winedale. You really have to dig deep out there."

Production History: 1971: *What a Piece of Work Is a Man;* 1972: *Fools, Madmen, and Monsters* (scenes from nine plays), and *The Illusions of Play, Dream, Life* (scenes from six plays); 1973: *Tmp.;* 1974: *MND;* 1975: *Ado;* 1976: *AYL;* 1977: *Err., Shr., MV;* 1978: *MND, Rom., LLL;* 1979: *AYL, Ado;* 1980: *Err., TN, Lr.;* 1981: *TGV, MM, WT;* 1982: *MND,* *Wiv., Mac.;* 1983: *MV, Tmp., Ham., TN;* 1984: *Shr., Ado, AYL, TN;* 1985: *Err., Wiv., Ham., Shr.;* 1986: *LLL, WT, Rom.;* 1987: *MND, TN, Lr., R3;* 1988: *AYL, MND, Ham., Shr.;* 1989: *WT, TGV, MV, Shoemaker's Holiday;* 1990: *TN, 1H4, Ado, AYL, Err.;* 1991: *LLL, MM, WT, Shr.;* 1992: *MND, Per., Lr.;* 1993: *TN, AWW, Ham.;* 1994: *Rom., Cym., Wiv.*

Research Resources: Archives for SAW are informally maintained at Winedale and at the University of Texas at Austin.

Carlson, Lavonne. "The Play Is the Thing at Winedale" *Daily Texan* (8 August 1985).

Stokes, John. "The Bard Lives Again for Texas Students." *Houston Post* (4 August 1985): 1F.

Sowers, Leslie. "The Bard in a Barn." *Houston Chronicle* (4 August 1989): D1.

Stromberger, Clayton. "Much Ado About Something." *Alcalde* (July/August 1990): 6-9.

——. "Shakespeare at Winedale." *Texas Libraries* (Summer 1986): 35-40.

————. "Winedale: Shakespeare Comes Alive in a Country Barn." *Texas Country (August* 1985): 14-17.

Site visit and interviews: 3-4 August 1991.
Michael L. Greenwald

SHAKESPEARE–BY–THE–BOOK. MAIL: 1727 Marshall, Houston, TX 77098. SITE: George Memorial Library, 1001 Gulfton, Richmond, TX. ADMINISTRATION: 713/630-7264. ADMISSION: free. SEASON: rotating repertory, two weekends in July; 8:00 p.m., Fri.–Sun. PRINCIPAL STAFF: Kate Pogue, artistic director; Joyce Claypool, managing director. FACILITY: amphitheatre (capacity 700). AUDITIONS: local, announced in March. STATUS: town and gown. ANNUAL BUDGET: $5,500 (1991). ANNUAL ATTENDANCE: 4,000. FOUNDED: 1988.

A 1988 production of *Much Ado About Nothing* by the Encore Players in the amphitheatre of the George Memorial Library in Richmond (north of Houston on highway 90A) demonstrated that there were enthusiastic audiences for Shakespeare in Fort Bend County. The following summer, the library joined forces with Houston Community College (HCC) for a production of *Twelfth Night* in the amphitheatre, and a pattern was established. HCC provided the theatrical expertise for a Shakespeare event hosted by the library. The library's sponsorship suggested the name Shakespeare–by–the–Book (SBB).

In 1990, Kate Pogue of the fine arts department at HCC directed *A Midsummer Night's Dream* set in Athens, Georgia, during the Civil War. The quality of this production brought a wave of support from businesses in the Fort Bend County area. The 1991 festival was expanded to two Shakespeare productions plus an Elizabethan market square festival on the days of performances. Among the attractions at the latter have been morris dancers, madrigals, puppet shows, Scottish dancers, mummers, and a green show. The 24-page program booklet for *Macbeth* and *Comedy of Errors* abounds with advertising from Rosenberg, Katy, Simonton, and Sugarland—a clear indication of local suppport for SBB.

The company's approach to Shakespeare is somewhat determined by budget constraints, the use of student performers, and "a new (but very eager) audience of families with young children in a small town." Thus, SBB presents the most familiar plays, which are cut to keep the running time under two hours. With its two-play seasons, SBB has adopted the practice of presenting one work traditionally costumed in the period in which the play is set, and one work with a contemporary slant. According to Pogue, "Our goal is to give new young performers and an eager but inexperienced audience an exciting and intensely pleasurable introduction to Shakespeare. Luckily this 'introduction' is balanced by the **Houston Shakespeare Festival** nearby, which is able to present the full range of the literature, professionally and inventively."

For the 1993 season, an opening weekend of performances is planned at the Heinen Theatre of HCC Central. The Heinen Theatre is a lovely proscenium house in a building that once served as a synagogue for congregation Beth Isreal, the oldest Jewish congregation in the state of Texas. The decorative elements of the Temple were skillfully incorporated into the 302-seat theatre. The HCC Central campus is located at 1300 Holman in Houston.

Production History: **1988**: *Ado*; **1989**: *TN*; **1990**: *MND*; **1991**: *Err.*, *Mac.*; **1992**: *AYL*, *R3*; **1993**: *Rom.*, *Shr.*; **1994**: *MV*, *Oth.*

Felicia Hardison Londré

SHAKESPEARE FESTIVAL OF DALLAS. MAIL: Sammons Center for the Arts, 3630 Harry Hines Boulevard, Suite 306, Dallas, TX 75219. SITE: Samuell Grand Park (East Grand Avenue at Tenison Parkway). ADMINISTRATION: 214/559-2778; Fax: 214/559-2782. ADMISSION: free ($3 donation suggested). SEASON: second week of June through end of July (may vary slightly). PRINCIPAL STAFF: Reynolds B."Cliff" Redd, Jr., executive producer; Carl G. Hamm, development director; Jeanie Parrent, production manager; Diann McCallum, executive assistant. FACILITY: natural outdoor amphitheatre. AUDITIONS: local; regional auditions by appointment only. STATUS: LORT D. ANNUAL BUDGET: $455,000 (1993). ANNUAL ATTENDANCE: 50,000 (approximately, for summer productions), plus 30,000 students on annual Shakespeare-in-the-Schools tour. FOUNDED: 1972, Robert Glenn.

A single performance of readings from Shakespeare by actor Peter Donat on a balmy summer night, 16 July 1972, attracted 1,800 people and launched the longest-running admission-free Shakespeare festival in the Southwest. Bob Glenn founded the Shakespeare Festival of Dallas (SFD) with a mission of "producing FREE Shakespeare that is entertaining, accessible, and enlightening." For 17 seasons, SFD presented summer Shakespeare in the 3,800-seat Fair Park Band Shell, reaching over 650,000 people. Among the artists who performed with SFD during this period were Sigourney Weaver in *As You Like It* (1981), Morgan Freeman in *Othello* (1982), and Earle Hyman in *King Lear* (1987). The 1985 *Shogun Macbeth* went on to a successful run at the Pan Asian Repertory Theatre in New York. Other innovative stagings included an Old West version of *The Taming of the Shrew* (1980), *Much Ado About Nothing* (1985) as a 1930s shipboard romance, and *The Merry Wives of Windsor* (1993), directed by Charles Marowitz and set in the "Roaring Twenties."

With Glenn's retirement, Dale AJ Rose assumed the artistic directorship in 1986. As a faculty member in the professional theatre-training program at Southern Methodist University, Rose had been directing for the SFD since 1982. In 1989, Dejon Austin Malley joined the staff as managing director, just in time to face a major crisis. In the summer of 1988, a new Starplex Amphitheatre opened at Fair Park, built by the city to accommodate PACE Entertainment, producers of rock concerts. During the Starplex's inaugural summer, the concert schedule was light enough that conflicts with SFD performance dates could be avoided, but it was clear that in subsequent summers the Shakespearean dialogue would be drowned out by the high-decibel music. Limited parking space posed a further problem. SFD optimistically announced its 1989 season and held auditions without knowing where the festival would be located. The festival staff investigated such options as building baffles around the Band Shell, moving to City Hall Plaza, or accepting one of seven invitations to relocate to a suburb of greater Dallas. Most of the city parks in Dallas had to be rejected because they were under flight paths from Love Field. Even after SFD personnel decided on Samuell Grand Park, municipal leaders delayed granting approval of the site. Meanwhile, SFD's apparent homelessness cost the festival an estimated $70,000 in contributions.

Because of the funding shortfall, the SFD canceled one of its planned productions (*Macbeth*) but extended the run of the other (*Two Gentlemen of Verona*). Once matters were settled, the city helped out with grading the hillside, installing lighting towers, and constructing a paved entrance with lighted walkways. In fact, the park site was leased to the SFD for only a dollar a year. "And they still haven't billed me for it," Malley has noted, while commenting on the public outcry over the city's less than admirable treatment of the festival. She has used the city's "guilt" to win concessions, recognizing that, with each passing year, "the guilt is not as readily available as it was before." Over the next four years, however, the SFD and the park department developed a long-term contract securing the Samuell Grand amphitheatre as the permanent performance site for the festival through the year 2013. The plan also addressed the need to develop the amphitheatre into an integrated, multi-user, performance complex.

The popularity of the SFD's rockabilly version of *Two Gentlemen of Verona* proved to be an important enticement in getting the public to follow the festival to its new location. As directed by Rose, the action began in the small town of Verona, Texas, in the 1950s and took the two gents to the bright lights of Havana, Cuba. The play was transformed into a musical, with original songs composed by Johnny Reno of the Fort Worth Sax Maniacs and by songwriter Willy Welch. Reno himself (with saxophone) played one of the bandits who were costumed as early Castro-led revolutionaries. According to reviewer Jerome Weeks (*Dallas Morning News*, 16 June 1989), "the show is very broad, and it uses a down-home Texas setting that allows its hammy roughness to approach, if not a virtue, at least a hayseed charm."

Things were looking up for the SFD, as the production drew large crowds and generous contributions to the "Bard Buckets" during the show's run. Then, on 2 July, at the final performance, disaster struck. A sudden, severe thunderstorm, with winds up to 95 miles per hour, struck Dallas and hit the festival site shortly before curtain time. Indeed, the entire contents of the preshow Bard Buckets (estimated at $1,000 in dollar bills and small change contributed by the 1,300 audience members) were gone with the wind. Amazingly, despite the collapse of the stage and light towers (causing losses estimated at $500,000), nobody was injured at the festival site, thanks especially to production manager John Scott, who spotted the approach of the destructive green cloud and led many to safety, even after the rains brought zero visibility. Difficulties in getting wheelchair-bound patrons to safety demonstrated to the city the need to pave the upper terrace for handicapped access.

Reynolds B. "Cliff" Redd became artistic director of the SFD in 1991. For his directorial debut that summer, he brought back Earle Hyman to play Prospero in a production of *The Tempest* that emphasized magic and spectacle, complete with glitter-studded props, fireworks displays, and so on.

In 1992, SFD mounted a major fund-raising event with the International Shakespeare Globe Centre. The project, spearheaded by Sam Wanamaker, Cedric Messina, and Redd, culminated in August, with Messina directing a special evening of Shakespeare readings in the Morton H. Meyerson Symphony Center. The evening included such luminaries as Rosemary Harris and Janet Suzman, and it netted over $80,000 for the two companies.

Local support for the SFD has been demonstrated in many ways besides financial growth. In-kind donations over the years have included rehearsal space valued at $10,000, luxury apartments for out-of-town actors, complete furnishings for six apartments, and American Airlines travel vouchers. A core base of individual donors numbers about 2,000. Despite the board's trepidation about doing a little-known play like *Pericles* in 1990, every performance attracted corporate sponsorship. Malley has spoken with particular enthusiasm about what Shakespeare can do for the community:

> Part of our mission is to educate. We educate people without their knowing it. We realize our role in the community, and it's more than just presenting Shakespeare. We're here to help cultural awareness along. We have a culturally diverse audience. We get people who don't want to put on a tie or jacket—or can't afford them—and they bring their children and watch something that feels good. They can go home feeling better about themselves.

The SFD also runs an ambitious school program, sending five actors out each spring to about 175 junior and senior high schools. One of their more successful programs involved scenes from *Romeo and Juliet*. For the first sequence, the actors wore eclectic clothing and performed in a rap style;

successive scenes added more and more period clothing along with an increasingly Elizabethan manner of speaking. Over 150,000 students saw the program, and this may partially account for the younger audiences attending the festival in recent years, along with increasing numbers of African-Americans and Hispanics. Furthermore, the program includes a plot summary of each play in Spanish.

Major administrative changes occurred in 1992. The SFD consolidated the positions of its managing and artistic directors to hire Redd as executive producer. The administrative staff was rearranged to include a development director and to expand the responsibilities of the production manager. In a step intended to lead toward a winter season for the SFD, the festival coproduced *Macbeth* with the Undermain Theater, an experimental company, in the fall of 1993.

For the 30 June 1990 performance of *Pericles* that I saw, guild members (individual donors) and employees of corporate sponsors were admitted to the grounds at 7:00 p.m.; gates opened to the general public at 7:30. Employees wearing first name badges graciously helped people to find blanket space in the central area, while directing those with lawn chairs to the sides. The performance began promptly at 8:15. The setting incorporated ramps and scaffolding in a pattern of curves and swirls, predominantly in turquoise blue with touches of pink and yellow. The brightly colored and highly fanciful costumes, the broad acting style, the mystico-magical sound effects, and music ranging from carnival to Oriental all created what someone described as "a comic book of a show." Even the weather cooperated, providing pink and purple clouds at twilight and an extra brisk breeze to stir up the stage fog during the storm at sea. Strong performances were given in multiple roles by Jerome Butler, Spike McClure, and Ted Shonka.

Production History: 1972: *An Evening of Shakespeare*; **1973**: *Oth.*; **1974**: *Rom., Shr.*; **1975**: *Ham., Wiv.*; **1976**: *R3, TN*; **1977**: *Mac., Ado*; **1978**: *Tmp., Err.*; **1979**: *MND, 1H4*; **1980**: *MV, Shr.*; **1981**: *AYL, Rom., Kemp's Jig*; **1982**: *AWW, Oth.*; **1983**: *Tmp.*, *LLL*; **1984**: *TN, H5*; **1985**: *Ado, Shogun Macbeth*; **1986**: *Ham., MND*; **1987**: *Err., Lr.*; **1988**: *Shr., JC*; **1989**: *TGV*; **1990**: *Per., TN*; **1991**: *Ado, Tmp.*; **1992**: *Rom., Err.*; **1993**: *Wiv., R3*; **1994**: *Mac., Shakespeare for My Father, Shr., Lr.*

Research Resources: Records for the Shakespeare Festival of Dallas are incomplete before 1990, when an archive was set up at the Dallas Public Library. Michael L. Greenwald, "*The Tempest*," *Theatre Journal* (March 1992): 113-16.

Site visit and interview: 30 June-1 July 1990.
Felicia Hardison Londré

SHAKESPEARE IN THE PARK. MAIL: Suite 310, 3113 South University, Fort Worth, TX 76109. SITE: Trinity Park Playhouse, 7th Street in Trinity Park, Fort Worth. ADMINISTRATION/BOX OFFICE: 817/923-6698. ADMISSION: free. SEASON: three weeks, mid-June to early July; 8:30 p.m., Tues.–Sun. PRINCIPAL STAFF: Michael Muller, producing director. FACILITY: open-air stage with band shelter, seating on the grass (capacity 3,000). AUDITIONS: local and University of Washington. STATUS: LORT D, LOA. ANNUAL BUDGET: $493,000 (1990). ANNUAL ATTENDANCE: 40,000. FOUNDED: 1977, Sharon Benge.

Trinity Park lies alongside the Trinity River, not far from downtown Fort Worth. Its WPA-built Shelter House serves as the stagehouse facing a grassy amphitheatre-like slope formed by the curve of the levee. To Sharon Benge, a journalist and producer, the spot seemed natural for outdoor Shakespeare production, and she decided to present free performances there in the summer. Beginning in 1977 with *A Midsummer Night's Dream*, performed for six weekends to 5,000 spectators, Benge directed annual Shakespeare in the Park (SIP) productions for ten years. Zach Ward served as interim director for the 1987 summer season, and Michael Muller began his tenure as producing director with the 1988 season.

Perhaps SIP's greatest strength has been the degree of community involvement it has generated over the years. Over 600 volunteers each year contribute their time and effort to the festival. They organize jumble sales, give rides to actors and help them find apartments, and run the elaborate concessions area at the festival site. About six booths open at 6:30 p.m., selling souvenirs, corn on the cob, chicken on a stick, sandwiches, frozen yogurt, lemonade, beer, and wine. Volunteers deal directly with vendors and do their own bookkeeping on these efforts. The 1990 season offered a particularly vivid demonstration of community support. In early June, Muller and the SIP's board of trustees faced a $50,000 shortfall and determined that SIP would not be able to make it through the summer. A hastily organized five-day "Keep Shakespeare in the Park" campaign involved intensive soliciting of corporations and foundations, while public service radio announcements invited individual donations. In response to a call for drive-by contributions, long lines of cars drove through the park while volunteers stood by the road with sacks to collect the dollars handed through car windows. "Of course, you can only do that once," says producing director Muller, "but it saved us."

Muller speaks ecstatically about SIP's excellent relationship with the city's parks department. The director of parks serves on the SIP board, and the department's in-kind services are invaluable. They hook up the trailers and do all kinds of other work for SIP. It seems only appropriate that one of the most distinctive features of SIP focuses attention on the park environment. That is the annual (since 1981) poster and program cover, based on an award-winning concept by Scott Turner. Each season brings a new illustration of the Bard dressed in contemporary sports gear and engaged in some characteristic park activity; for example, picnicking (1983), picking up litter (1984), bicycling (1988), dunking a basketball (1990), pitching a softball (1991), or rollerblading (1992).

The gates to the Shelter House area are opened at 6:30 p.m., allowing plenty of time for picnicking before the performance begins. Indeed, the grounds appear to reach capacity as early as 7:15. The picnics may not be as elegant as those seen at **Shakespeare Festival of Dallas** (about 30 miles away), but the Fort Worth audience is generally younger and more ethnically mixed. The area nearest the stage is reserved for blankets, while lawn chairs are kept to the sides and further back. Seating is first come, first served, apart from space reserved for the corporate sponsor of the evening's performance.

In recent years, SIP has sponsored December performances of a national touring company's production of *A Christmas Carol* as a fund-raising event. Muller begins his fund raising for the following summer as soon as he has his current season up and running. His immediate goal is to "continue to do good work and keep it free. Keeping it free is real important." Due to continuing budgetary difficulties, however, a compromise was initiated in 1992; in order to continue to offer free performances three nights a week, a $3.00 admission fee is charged three nights a week on the weekends. In addition, a limited number of reserved seats are available for $5.00 each night. While the immediate goal is to maintain the quality of production, the dream is that someday Shakespeare in Fort Worth will be a year-round operation. Apart from *A Christmas Carol*, SIP has only twice produced works other than Shakespeare's. The first was *Diamond Studs* for the 1986 Texas sesquicentennial; *Blood Wedding* was the second.

The production of Federico García Lorca's *Blood Wedding* in 1990, funded by a special projects grant, marked SIP's first bilingual undertaking and was the first professional bilingual production in the state of Texas. Three performances in English alternated with two performances in Spanish by the bilingual actor-singers who also formed the casts for the two Shakespeare plays of that summer: *Romeo and Juliet* (set in 1820s Texas, emphasizing Tex-Mex conflicts) and *As You Like It* (in 1830s Texas Western style). The season was conceived in recognition of the Hispanics who make up about 15 to 20 percent of the local population, percentages that appear to be reflected in attendance at the Shakespeare festival. African Americans also attend in significant numbers at least partly in response to a longstanding policy of multiracial casting. In fact, attendance in general has always been good at SIP. "There is no marketing problem," says Muller. "People love it, and they're amazingly attentive."

SIP also offers a bilingual school program. In 1990, the 45-minute session designed for sixth through twelfth grades was based on a scene from *Romeo and Juliet*. Actors performed the scene three ways: in a contemporary American style, in Spanish translation, and in Elizabethan style. The Spanish sequence made an especially powerful impression on students who had never seen a live performance in their mother tongue.

As You Like It, directed by Patrick Kelly, offered something for everyone: corny touches like the black cowboy hat on the villainous Oliver and the chuck wagon in the exiled duke's forest encampment; subtleties like the choreography of the Orlando-Charles wrestling match, designed to show the triumph of brains over brawn; excellent musical numbers; and a Touchstone (Chris Welch) whose lazzi spoke as eloquently and hilariously as any dialogue. Duke Senior and Duke Frederick were played by the same actor (Lynn Mathis). Orlando (Henry Godinez) played his scenes with "Ganymede" as though he secretly recognized his Rosalind from the first. Looking for signs of lovesickness in Orlando, Rosalind checked him over as one would a horse: teeth, neck, and then stroking his face. Soon the two could scarcely keep their hands off each other. Elizabeth Rouse's Phebe, wearing an outrageous low-cut pink shepherdess costume and speaking in a little-girl voice, came off as a cross between an eighteenth-century porcelain figurine and Marilyn Monroe. Rosalind (Joyce O'Connor) acted so convincingly when tempted to reveal her identity to Orlando that, for a moment, I thought they had rewritten the script. On her line "Believe then, if you please, that I—," she was about to pull off her cap and shake down her hair; but she thought better of it and finished the sentence, "can do strange things." The wedding celebration combined square dancing, a Mexican singer, and a burst of twinkling lights.

Production History: 1977: *MND*; 1978: *Rom., Shr.*; 1979: *Ham., Tmp.*; 1980: *Lr., TN*; 1981: *Ado, Oth.*; 1982: *Mac., MND*; 1983: *Err., MM*; 1984: *R3, AYL*; 1985: *LLL, Rom.*; 1986: *Ham., WT, Diamond Studs*; 1987: *TGV, Shr.*; 1988: *Oth., Tmp.*; 1989: *Mac., Ado*; 1990: *Rom., AYL, Bodas de sangre/Blood Wedding*; 1991: *Wiv., 1H4, 2H4*; 1992: *Ham.Q1*; *Shr.*; 1993: *MND, MM*; 1994: *Rom., Err., JC* (presented by the Anglican Open Air Shakespeare Company).

Research Resources: Archives for Shakespeare in the Park are maintained at the company offices.

Site visit and interview: 1 July 1990.
Felicia Hardison Londré

TEXAS SHAKESPEARE FESTIVAL at Kilgore College. MAIL: 1100 Broadway, Kilgore, TX 75662. SITE: Anne Dean Turk Fine Arts Center. ADMINISTRATION: 903/983-8118. BOX OFFICE: 903/983-8601. ADMISSION: $6–$12. SEASON: 24 performances, rotating repertory, late June–mid-July; 8:00 p.m., Tues.–Sat.; 2:30 p.m., Sat.–Sun. PRINCIPAL STAFF: Raymond Caldwell, artistic director; Kathy Barber, associate artistic director; John Dodd, company manager. FACILITY: Van Cliburn Auditorium, proscenium stage (capacity 250). AUDITIONS: January through March; six sites in 1991, including Dallas, Kilgore, Los Angeles, Irvine, Seattle, New York City. STATUS: non-union contract. ANNUAL BUDGET: $195,000 (1991). ANNUAL ATTENDANCE: 4,950 (1991). FOUNDED: 1986, Raymond Caldwell.

The Texas Shakespeare Festival (TSF), founded in 1986 by Raymond Caldwell, owes its existence to the colorful local history of the town of Kilgore (population, 11,000) in the "Piney Woods" area of East Texas. In 1984, when Kilgore College administrators called for ideas about what the college might contribute to the upcoming Texas Sesquicentennial, Caldwell, who is chair of theatre there, came up with the winning proposal. He suggested commissioning a play based on James Anthony Clark's *The Last Boom*, about the discovery of what was once the world's largest oil field and about the effect of that discovery on the dirt-poor local farmers during the Great Depression. Stewart McLaurin, then president of the college, agreed to fund a professional summer production. During the following year, while Gifford W. Wingate was writing the play, Caldwell realized that it would be easier to attract professional directors, designers, and actors to Kilgore in the summer if the local history play could be incorporated into a larger festival—a Shakespeare festival. McLaurin not only supported Caldwell's expanded proposal but also offered to fund it for two years because he did not think anything should be given only one year to succeed.

Naming his project the Texas Shakespeare Festival was "a bit of a brash move," Caldwell admits. He rejected ideas like East Texas Shakespeare Company or Boom Town Theatre Festival as not likely to attract the professional artists with whom he wanted to work. He knew about the Shakespeare festivals in Dallas, Fort Worth, Houston, and Odessa, but did not know if the name might have been taken by some other group. A call to the Texas Commission on the Arts gave him assurance that the name was available. He was particularly motivated by the idea of using the Texas flag in the festival logo. The copyrighted red, white, blue, and black design, in which Shakespeare's head is framed by the Lone Star, has appeared from the beginning on mailers, programs, T-shirts, and mugs.

The inaugural season of 1986 drew capacity audiences to the 250-seat Van Cliburn Auditorium for all 15 performances of *Twelfth Night*, *A Midsummer Night's Dream*, and *The Daisy Bradford 3*. The local history play's title refers to the gusher that launched Kilgore's oil boom. It was the third hole drilled on

Daisy Bradford's farm by Dad Joiner, a 70-year-old wildcatter, following the advice of Doc Lloyd. The first two holes had turned out to be dusters, but the third blew in on 3 October 1930. Although Kilgore's overnight transformation from a peaceful farm community to a hotbed of unscrupulous opportunism spawned a long parade of villains and heroes in countless real-life dramas, the play focuses narrowly on the travail and faith of Joiner, Lloyd, and Bradford. "It's like a combination of *Our Town* and *The Waltons*. It's a rags-to-riches story, and it's absolutely true," marvels Caldwell. Brought back each summer by popular demand, *The Daisy Bradford 3* has been reshaped by each of its directors in turn. The 1990 edition, directed by David Kaye, was the first to include musical numbers. Kaye, who wrote the lyrics, played the narrator in the original production. He recalls: "Never before had I experienced such a communion with the audience. It then struck me: this wasn't just any story; this story belonged to every single person sitting in that auditorium. It was a story about who they were, who they are, and perhaps even who they were going to be."

While *The Daisy Bradford 3* draws repeat attendance by the local audience every summer, the two accompanying Shakespeare plays each season have created an audience for Shakespeare where none had existed previously. During the 1990 season, an audience member told Caldwell that she was proud to say she had now seen ten Shakespeare plays in her life, the ten that had been mounted by the TSF. In its third year, the festival expanded to three weeks and added a fourth offering, a non-Shakespearean classic. The festival also produces an annual children's play, performed on three consecutive days at the end of the four-production repertory season.

The first TSF company was composed largely of graduate students from Southern Methodist University and other young people from the East Texas area. By 1992, the festival could boast of a company of professionals and theatre students from 23 states and three foreign countries. The full company now numbers about 75 people, bringing their experience from Broadway, Off Broadway, regional theatre, opera, and educational theatre. Auditions are held from mid-January to early March at various sites, including the annual Southwest and Southeast Theatre Conferences. The audition consists of two contrasting monologues—one Shakespearean verse and one contemporary selection—of two minutes each. Technicians are asked to bring a resumé portfolio, and letter(s) of recommendation to their interviews. The actors are hired on non-Equity contracts, with stipends ranging from $500 to $1,200 for the eight-week rehearsal and performance period. All company members receive free housing in an air-conditioned Kilgore College dormitory and 17 meals a week at the college cafeteria. Other meals are provided through the Company Dinner and Adopt-An-Artist Dinner programs, which provide an opportunity for community residents to get to know company members.

In addition to artistic director Caldwell, the permanent staff members are associate artistic director Kathy Barber, technical director Michael Atkins, and company manager John Dodd. Caldwell, Barber, and Atkins are all on the Kilgore College theatre faculty; Dodd is the only one on a year-round festival contract. The summer staff also includes a director of educational programs and a production coordinator. Among the outstanding professionals who have worked with the festival are directors Keith Fowler, Stephen Hollis, Brian Nelson, Scott Shattuck, and Tom Whitaker, costume designers Paul D. Reinhardt and Stephanie Siemens, set designers Larry Kaushansky, Mike Windelman, and Jimmy Humphries, lighting designers Tim Poertner, Karen S. Spahn, and Brackley Frayer, and combat director Claude Caux.

Kilgore College's generous funding of about 85 percent of the $195,000 annual budget has long spared Caldwell and Barber the burden of the year-round fund raising that saps the energies of so many directors of summer Shakespeare festivals, nor has the college encouraged fund raising, since it owns the festival and wants to maintain fiscal control. (There has never been any attempt at artistic control.) A four-year grant from the Rosa Mae Griffin Foundation helped to carry the festival through its first seasons. By the fifth season, however, it became apparent that additional funding was needed, and Barber took on the task of writing grant proposals and working with college development officers and members of the board of advisers. Above and beyond the $195,000 budget, the college provides in-kind contributions of rehearsal space, utilities, support staff, and so on. There is some inevitable overlapping of materials used by the theatre department and by the festival, but separate budgets are maintained. Salaries for Caldwell, Barber, and Atkins are paid directly by the college under two separate contracts for each of them—one for their academic duties and another for what they do in the summer. Dodd's salary is specified in the festival budget. There is some concern about maintaining a distinct identity for the festival, so that the public will not confuse the professional operation with the academic productions. For that reason, all printed materials feature the words "Texas Shakespeare Festival" in a distinctive graphic style, with "at Kilgore College" in small letters beneath. "Of course, the school wants its name attached," says Caldwell, "because they're funding the festival. It's only fair. But I think it's agreed now that just having people know that the Texas Shakespeare Festival is located on campus at Kilgore College is repayment enough. And I think it already has repaid them."

The intimate Van Cliburn Auditorium was built in 1966 and remodeled in 1989. It has a seating capacity of 250. Seats are comfortable, sightlines are good, and the house staff is friendly. The 40-page, glossy-paper program includes a wealth of black-and-white photos, biographies for the entire company, director's notes, and a synopsis for each of the four shows. The well-equipped open-proscenium theatre is located in the Anne Dean Turk Fine Arts Center, which also houses the box office, theatre department offices, dressing rooms, and production facilities. The glass-fronted lobby and main entrance to the building open onto a patio adorned by a fountain that shoots up water in the shape of a gusher. (Company members have jokingly challenged Dodd to add black food coloring to the fountain on *Daisy Bradford* performance dates.) The location is heralded by a banner stretched above Highway 259. There Shakespeare smiles genially from the familiar logo. Just across the highway is the East Texas Oil Museum, which documents the human tale told in the festival's centerpiece play.

Kilgore is located just off Interstate 20, 70 miles west of Shreveport, Louisiana, and 120 miles east of Dallas. The 1930s boom town is still dotted with working pump jacks and nearly 1,200 derricks within the city limits. The people of Kilgore and the 13 counties within a 100-mile radius—that is, a potential audience pool of about 250,000—are the festival's target audience. Longview (population, 72,000) is only ten miles away, and Tyler (population, 76,000) is 25 miles west on highway 31. A significant number come from Austin, Dallas, and Houston, especially friends and relatives of company members from those cities. Nonetheless, the area people who make up the bulk of the audience are not particularly familiar with Shakespeare. Caldwell worked out a plan to lead them gently into the Shakespeare canon, choosing two attractive comedies for his first season: *A Midsummer Night's Dream* and *Twelfth Night*. The second year eased in a mature comedy, *Much Ado About Nothing*, alongside the familiar-from-high school *Romeo and Juliet*. By the fourth season, audiences were judged ready for *Hamlet*, and it was a sell-out. Indeed, Caldwell now sees very little difference in attendance patterns between the Shakespeare and the non-Shakespeare plays. The more significant factor is the day of the week. In the fourth season, when the festival expanded from Thursday-through-Sunday performances to Tuesday through Sunday, it was discovered that attendance would drop on Wednesday, which is a church night in the area. Still, the Tuesday, Wednesday, and Thursday evening performances attended by this reviewer appeared to be sold out.

"People see the festival as a real cultural asset to the area," Caldwell comments. "They can go to a stock car race or football game or other sporting event just about any night of the year. And people come in for the rodeo in Gladewater. But a Shakespeare festival is something completely different for most of them, and they really appreciate it. Last Sunday, for example, after the performance a woman came up to me with tears in her eyes and said, 'Thank you for bringing this to our area.'"

A variety of marketing tools are used, beginning in January with newspaper and radio announcements of the coming season. There is a heavy reliance upon public service announcements. The mailing list for brochures numbers about 13,000. The festival is listed in the travel calendars of *Texas Highways*, *Texas Monthly*, and *Southern Living*. Reviewers from all the major Texas newspapers are invited; the *Dallas Morning News* and the *Austin Statesman* have provided good coverage.

Asked what is distinctive about the TSF, both Caldwell and Barber are quick to agree that it is the hospitality of the local community. "Actors want to come back every summer," says Caldwell. "They tell us they've never had more fun. They say the community is so loving, gracious, and accepting that they feel as if they've become part of the family." Indeed, actor Jon Drahos' nostalgic recollection of his 1989 summer is typical: "They treated us like gods!" On Mondays, local citizens host barbecues, swimming parties, horseback rides, or lake outings for the company. In 1990, the Fourth of July party at the home of two local doctors, tucked away in the Piney Woods, featured a swimming-pool volleyball game as well as a gargantuan feast. Barber notes also that the festival's impact on the young people of the area is beginning to be apparent, as students come into the college with an awareness of Shakespeare that previous freshmen had not had. Some junior high school students have sought involvement with the festival and have been welcomed as "unofficial apprentices"; they put up posters, look for props, and help out with other odd jobs.

The main outreach program has been a project created with the Region 7 Education Service Center, which is headquartered in Kilgore and serves several counties, providing a variety of services for public school teachers at all levels. Under the outreach program, about 40 junior high or high school English and drama teachers come to Kilgore for a weekend workshop during the three-week performance period. They discuss the plays in seminar sessions, talk with the directors and actors, and attend two performances. There has never been any direct outreach into area classrooms, since the TSF is not operational during the school year.

The festival has grown so rapidly that Caldwell and Barber have found it making more and more demands on their time during the regular academic year. As full-time teachers, they have little opportunity to pause and assess the ways in which the TSF might develop. Since both are working to capacity and since the college can provide no budget increase in the foreseeable future, the TSF has probably hit a plateau for a few years; that is, there will be no increase in the number of performances, the size of company, or the amount paid to company members. Thus, Caldwell's two immediate goals are to maintain or improve the existing quality of production and to become more organized in such areas as time management and maintaining archives.

The TSF's stated mission is to develop a professional summer theatre that will appeal to professional theatre artists, to employ high calibre-actors, designers, and directors, and to offer professionals and theatre students the luxury of working on plays from the world's storehouse of dramatic literary masterpieces. Caldwell allows his directors free rein in their production interpretation of the Shakespeare plays. Some judicious cutting of the text is usually done, but there is no rewriting of lines or other alteration in the language. There are no restrictions on changing the period of a play. Since the four plays are done in rotating repertory, stage settings tend to be minimal (indeed, by 1992, a unit set had been adopted), but costumes are lavish and often fanciful. The 1989 *Hamlet* and the 1990 *Merchant of Venice* could be called postmodern. Caldwell is also eager to practice nontraditional casting. Although Hispanics and African-Americans form only a small percentage of the population in east Texas, there has been an effort to hire ethnic minorities in all areas of the company. An African-American actress played Lady Macbeth in 1988. The 1990 acting company included one Asian-American and two African-Americans, and minorities were also represented on the technical staff. "But I must tell you the truth," says Caldwell. "We're seeing very few minority actors at auditions. Very few. It's sad, but it's true."

On the basis of the three 1990 productions that I attended, I would rate the TSF's work well above average for a non-Equity company. Certainly, the costumes were worthy of any fully professional theatre: the fullness and elegance of seventeenth-century laces and brocades in *Cyrano de Bergerac*, the sophisticated, modern, high-fashion look of *The Merchant of Venice* in shades of gray, and for *Othello*, a dominant note of glittering gold, set off by maroons, olive greens, and mustard yellows. Fight sequences choreographed by Claude Caux were another strength in both *Cyrano* and *Othello*. The quality of the acting varied considerably. On the whole, director Brian Nelson elicited the strongest performances in *Cyrano de Bergerac*, benefiting especially from the casting of tall, deep-voiced Mark Mineart in the title role. Mineart's graceful gestures and subtle play of expression over a virtually perpetual smile made him a charismatic figure. The production was marred only by the caricatured portrayal of the Duenna and by the unfortunate choice of music from the wrong period (Satie's *Gymnopédies*) under Cyrano's death scene. *Othello*, directed by Linda De Vries, belonged largely to Iago and Emilia. Jan Russell as Emilia could wring poignancy from a word or a look. Stephen D. Wilson cut a fine figure as Iago in his gray velvet coat with long taupe boots. The suave villain was always calculating, always mentally appraising his own work, and very believable in his direct addresses to the audience. Steven Matt and Annalisa Hill looked wonderful as Othello and Desdemona, even if they did not always get full emotional value from their lines. The petite blonde with a porcelain-doll complexion and sweet features moved with consummate grace in her opulent golden gown and in her swirling white nightdress.

The Merchant of Venice was the "high concept" production. Suspended metal frames against black drapes suggested Venetian architecture. The only set props were a ladder and a table with two chairs. The ladder functioned as a balcony for Jessica's elopement and as a lofty perch for the judge in the trial scene. Paul D. Reinhardt's costumes made important character statements. Antonio wore an elegant gray three-piece suit, with white tie and white carnation in his lapel. Bassanio sported a trendy black shirt and white unstructured jacket with pushed-up sleeves. The portly Shylock looked appropriately businesslike with his small, neatly trimmed beard, gold-rim spectacles, skullcap, and well-tailored dark gray suit. Launcelot wore skin-tight bicycle pants with a belt pouch. At his entrance in Act 5, wearing a Walkman headset, he brought down the house with his rap delivery of "my master will be here ere morning." Shylock and Antonio, skillfully portrayed by Larry Martin and Stephen D. Wilson, gave a sense of stability and balance as the only two characters who maintained their dignity throughout, while everyone else exhibited self-indulgent selfishness or childishness. A cynical Brooklynite Lorenzo, for example, found Jessica's fortune to be her chief attraction. No sooner had she descended the ladder in boy's garb than he, Gratiano, Salerio, and Solanio—all carrying flashlights yet wearing sunglasses—appropriated her jewel box to examine its contents by flashlight. Nuances of sound and lighting further enhanced the production, as when the soft clicking of the courtroom stenotypists underscored the rhythms of the "quality of mercy" speech.

As a 1992 postscript to my report, Caldwell comments: "It is easily the most successful (artistically) season so far. A gorgeous unit set and costumes beyond belief. The acting company has great depth (and age range) and talent. All three classics are beautifully acted and a delight to behold! Am I excited?"

Production History: **1986**: *TN, MND, The Daisy Bradford 3*; **1987**: *Ado, Rom., The Daisy Bradford 3*; **1988**: *Mac., Shr., Importance of Being Earnest*; **1989**: *AYL, Ham., Tartuffe, The Daisy Bradford 3*; **1990**: *MV, Oth., Cyrano de Bergerac, The Daisy Bradford 3*; **1991**: *JC, Err., The Misanthrope, The Daisy Bradford 3*; **1992**: *R3, TGV, She Stoops to Conquer, The Daisy Bradford 3*; **1993**: *Tmp., MM, The Learned Ladies, The Last Titan* (a world premiere by Gifford Wingate); **1994**: *Lr., LLL, Man of La Mancha, The Last Titan*.

Research Resources: Archives are informally maintained in the Texas Shakespeare Festival administrative office. See also Felicia Londré, "Shakespeare and Oil are a Heady Mix in Kilgore, Texas," *TheaterWeek* 4 (27 August 1990): 39-41.

Site visit and interview: 3-5 July 1990.
Felicia Hardison Londré

UTAH

UTAH SHAKESPEAREAN FESTIVAL. MAIL: 351 West Center St., Cedar City, UT 84720-2498. SITES: Adams Memorial Shakespeare Theatre on Southern Utah University Campus, and Randall L. Jones Theatre. ADMINISTRATION: 801/586-7884; Fax: 801/586-1944. BOX OFFICE: 801/586-7878. ADMISSION: $14–$24. SEASON: ten weeks, 191 performances, rotating repertory, July–early September; 2:00 p.m., 8:30 p.m.,

Mon.–Sat. (1991 season). PRINCIPAL STAFF: Fred C. Adams, founder and executive producer; Douglas N. Cook and Cameron Harvey, producing artistic directors; R. Scott Phillips, managing director. FACILITIES: Adams Memorial Shakespearean Theatre, thrust (capacity 817); Randall L. Jones Theatre (capacity 769); University Main Stage, proscenium (capacity 988). AUDITIONS: January and February; 12 sites in 1991. STATUS: non-union and Equity guest artist contract. ANNUAL BUDGET: $2.4 million (1992). ANNUAL ATTENDANCE: 125,000 (projected, 1992). FOUNDED: 1961, Fred C. Adams.

The Utah Shakespearean Festival (USF), founded in 1961 by Fred Adams, presented its first season in 1962. Adams, then a young faculty member at the College of Southern Utah (now Southern Utah University), saw a potential audience for a summer festival in the region's 150,000 tourists visiting seven national parks. Shakespeare seemed the ideal choice. Historically, the people of southern Utah had demonstrated a love for the works of William Shakespeare. Early Mormon settlers presented *The Merchant of Venice* within two weeks of their arrival. After visiting all the major festivals in existence at the time, Adams saw strong similarities between Cedar City, Utah, and Ashland, Oregon. Both were small towns in areas of scenic splendor. Both had small colleges with supportive administrations and easy access to larger metropolitan areas.

The Taming of the Shrew, Hamlet, and *The Merchant of Venice* were presented by a company of 20 college students and townspeople. An outdoor platform, backed by a partial replica of an Elizabethan tiring-house, served as a theatre. That initial two-week season played to 3,276 audience members, netting a $1,000 profit on which to build a second season.

In 1991, 109,313 ticket holders viewed 191 performances in two theatres over a ten-week season. The USF is now a year-round operation with a full-time staff of 21 and a budget exceeding $2.4 million. In the early years, the USF depended on coaxing people from the parks to come and spend an evening at the festival, but now Adams proudly claims that people come primarily to the festival, and time permitting, spend a few hours at the parks. In addition to the plays, there is an extensive greenshow beginning an hour before the stage performance, consisting of dancers, madrigal singers, musicians, puppeteers and other specialty performers, including a professional falconer. An orientation precedes each performance, and literary and production seminars are held each morning. A hundred volunteers sell tarts and Elizabethan candies. A Royal Feaste and an afternoon tea are also popular festival events. Outreach programs include a touring costume cavalcade and a high school Shakespeare play competition. The festival's history, characterized by steady growth, shows no signs of slowing down.

The USF's management structure is unique, and, although consultants have advised change, Adams says that the current organization works for them. Fred

Adams is the founder and executive producer and is responsible for the festival's overall vision and fund raising. He also hires directors. The producing artistic directors are Douglas N. Cook and Cameron Harvey. Cook is responsible for all visual components of the festival, including design elements and graphics, while Harvey assures efficient production planning and organization. R. Scott Phillips, managing director, works with Adams on fund raising and supervises administrative details. Additional staff members include Fern Hunter, box office supervisor; Jyl Shuler, development director; Jay Decker, box office manager; Rick Van Noy, associate casting and operations; Roger Becker, director of marketing and public relations; Michelle Livermore, art director; plus approximately one dozen other individuals.

Three boards comprise the governing structure of the USF. Southern Utah University's board of trustees establishes policy and maintains fiscal responsibility for the festival. The members of a board of governors lend their names and status to enhance and publicize the festival as well as raise funds each season. Finally a working board, the Utah Shakespearean Festival Council, represents the needs and concerns of Southern Utah University, the Cedar City Chamber of Commerce and the Cedar City community

The strong support of the university's president, Dr. Royden C. Braithwaite, was a major factor in the USF's early establishment and subsequent growth. Braithwaite fought for the festival in the legislature and believed in Adams' vision. Another factor contributing to its success is that the USF has always been fiscally conservative. Growth is based on predictable audience demand, and 80 percent of the budget is earned income. The Adams Memorial Theatre plays to approximately 96 percent capacity. The newly opened Randall Theatre plays to 59 percent capacity. The 1992 production company consisted of 309 individuals. They presented six plays in classic repertory. The acting company is composed primarily of non-Equity actors hired from selected conservatory training programs and by invitation at regional auditions. Non-Equity actors were paid $1,800 (approximately $112 per week) in 1992, plus a housing and travel allowance. Equity actors earned $550 per week. Nonperforming personnel were paid similarly, according to the position and level of experience. Directors receive $5,500 for their six-week commitment. Designers are paid between $4,000 and $5,000 and are in residence during the building period. Efforts are made to create a strong company spirit, stressing the importance of all members of the production team. The festival has attracted a number of outstanding professionals during its over 30-year history, including directors Howard Jensen, Sanford Robbins, and John Neville-Andrews. Notable designers include Kent Dorsey, Gene Chesley, Rosemary Inglman, and John Iacovelli. Recognizable actors include Henry Woronicz, Harold Gould, Michelle Farr, Patricia Kelembar, Bradley Whitford, William Leach, and Sam Tsoutsouvas.

The $473,000 Adams Memorial Shakespearean Theatre, dedicated in 1977, was designed by Douglas N. Cook along with Max Anderson of the Utah State

Building Board. Experts say that it is one of the few theatres that comes close to the design of the Globe Theatre. It seats 781, plus 40 Lord's gallery seats and 60 standing-room places. After an international search, the British Broadcasting Corporation (BBC) chose to use the Adams for a film series in 1981. The Adams was built in stages and was designed to be taken apart and moved. In case of rain, the performances are moved indoors to the university mainstage, which is also used for festival orientations. The $5.5 million Randall L. Jones Theatre, dedicated in 1989, is a 769-seat modern indoor facility, designed to produce classic plays in repertory. The modified thrust stage has state-of-the-art technology, including three wagons that house complete sets for easy change-overs. Designed by the architectural firm of Fowler, Ferguson, Kingston and Ruben of Salt Lake City, with theatrical design by Cameron Harvey and the California firm of Landry and Bogan, it was featured in the August 1990 edition of *Architecture* magazine. Major funding for this theatre came from the family and descendants of Randall L. Jones. Fully equipped scenic and costume shops are part of each theatre's design.

Cedar City, now called the " Festival City," is located on Interstate 15, three hours north of Las Vegas and five hours south of Salt Lake City. The city is accessible by Skywest Airlines as well as by Greyhound buses. The city's population of 20,000 welcomes the USF as one of its major industries. Extensive volunteer support is provided by the community.

Audience demographics in 1988 showed a strong Southwestern appeal: 43 percent of the playgoers come from Utah, 38 percent from southern Nevada, 12 percent from Arizona and the remaining 7 percent from throughout the country. Families from all walks of life make up the bulk of the audience. Plays that students study in school have proven the most popular at the box office.

The USF uses a variety of marketing techniques throughout the year to attract audiences, including a mailing list of 33,000. Fall, winter, and spring newsletters promote the season and provide educational information. The annual season brochure is mailed each fall. A preseason flyer provides brief season information a year in advance, while an elaborate souvenir program provides detailed production information and multiple color photographs. A study guide is distributed free to high school teachers of English and drama and is available for sale at the festival gift shop. The *Salt Lake Tribune, Deseret News, Las Vegas Sun*, and *Las Vegas Review Journal* all provide regular coverage. The *Phoenix Gazette* and selected California papers provide occasional coverage.

Festival strengths include the passion and clear vision of founding producer Fred Adams, the excellent geographical location, and the relatively healthy economy of Utah and especially Las Vegas, Nevada (3,000 to 4,000 people a month currently move to Las Vegas). Problems include having outgrown the USF's current home on the university campus.

These problems and strengths have led the organization to its most ambitious dream to date: the Utah Shakespearean Festival Center for the

Performing Arts. Completion is planned for 1997 to coincide with the centennial celebration of Southern Utah University and the sesquicentennial of the early pioneers entering the Salt Lake valley. The projected center will feature Renaissance-style buildings surrounding a brick-paved central plaza and a bronze sculpture featuring some of Shakespeare's characters. Adams elaborates:

> The center will include the Randall Theatre, the Adams Theatre, and one additional small performance facility, as well as a bookstore, an ale house, new costume and scene shops, office and storage space, and a Renaissance Study Centre, where scholars and the general public will find resource material to further the world's understanding of Shakespeare and his times.

The estimated cost for this center is approximately $18 to $20 million. In 1991, the fund raising was in its initial stages, and $500,000 had been raised. The festival's short-term goals include improving the pay and quality of the acting company as well as forming a separate nonprofit organization for the festival.

The USF's new mission statement reads:

> By producing Shakespeare's plays along with the distinguished work of other great playwrights and new plays which have the potential for future greatness, the Utah Shakespearean Festival presents its classic repertoire to entertain and enrich our audiences through dramatic themes and resonances which continue to affect contemporary lives. The commitment of our company of seasoned professionals, interns and apprentices is to provide the highest standard of production, organization, collaboration and dramatic achievement.

The festival aesthetic emphasizes historical accuracy. Plays presented in the Adams Theatre are set in Jacobean or earlier periods, so as not to clash with the architecture of the theatre. The Randall Theatre, with its more contemporary design, is open to any period. Adams says he is not a purist and does not mind cutting plays. Adams' future artistic goals include year-round production and designing a third theatre that will inspire writers. "If I were a writer I would want a space of unlimited possibilities, where the audience can be in any relation to the audience and the space is completely hydraulic." Adams sees this experimental theatre being underwritten by presenting Gilbert and Sullivan operettas on the University Mainstage.

The six plays produced in the 1991 season were *Hamlet*, *Twelfth Night*, and *Volpone*, in the Adams Memorial Shakespearean Theatre, and *The Taming of the Shrew*, *Misalliance*, and *Death of a Salesman* in the Randall Jones Theatre. Of these six productions, I found *Misalliance* and *Death of a Salesman* the most effective.

Misalliance by George Bernard Shaw is billed as a "riotous 1910 send-up of the unmannerly nouveau riche." Director John Neville-Andrews focused on family relationships in this charming and traditional production of the play.

The set, designed by Richard M. Isackes, was an impressive high-ceilinged glass pavilion, lovingly filled with period furnishings including umbrella racks, victrola, candy-striped swing, plants, and a Turkish bath. Lighting designer Pat Simmons and costume designer James Berton Harris combined forces to give the production a bright and sunny look.

The acting ensemble was up to the challenge of creating Shaw's eccentric characters. Among the stand-outs were William Leach as John Tarleton, a womanizing but lovable father to Hypatia, played by Jody Barrett as a fickle young woman bursting with life. Michael Boudewyns as Bentley Summerhays filled his performance with physical bits revealing both his awkwardness and immaturity. Susan Sweeney was a loving and knowing Mrs. Tarleton, effectively holding together this flamboyant household. David Cheaney gave a richly dimensional performance as Joseph Percival, while Elisabeth Ritson used her unusual and intriguing looks to full advantage as the Polish daredevil acrobat, Lina. Outstanding moments included John Tarleton's "thinker" monologue that built steadily to "meditating on my destiny" and his attempted seduction of Lina. Overall, inventive comic bits, intriguing characters, and impressive and detailed visual elements combined to create a witty and captivating experience.

Director Eli Simon saw *Death of a Salesman* as "a love story between a father and his son." In this production, Willy Loman's broken dreams were painfully clear for everyone to see—everyone except Willy himself, sensitively played by William Leach. Leach's glazed stare, slumped shoulders, and cracking voice revealed a man whose dreams were shattered beyond repair. Leach never gained tragic stature but aroused pity and fear as one who suffered more than he deserved. The focus was on Willy's precarious and vulnerable mental state. Biff's confrontation with his father was convincingly played by Paul Sandberg. David Cheaney was especially effective as Bernard the boy and the caring and successful young attorney.

Images of loss, isolation, and loneliness permeated the landscape, with shadows used as an integral part of the lighting design. The blue-gray world was warmed only briefly by Willy's memories. A haunting, lonely flute melody drifted in and out of the action. The set design, a dreamscape of Willy's tortured mind, took its cue from Miller's original title, "The Inside of His Head." Designer Isackes created a steely gray world without walls where Willy's mind could wander at will. Weathered doors served as metaphors for the lost opportunities in Willy's life. An old sink, table, wooden chairs, bunk beds, a bulletnose grill from a 1950 or 1951 Studebaker, a water heater, and empty seed envelopes suggested images of Willy's past and future choices. This production was rich in images of missed connections between father and son, brother and brother, employee and boss, husband and wife, and, finally, a man and his dreams.

Production History: 1962: *Shr.*, *Ham.*, *MV*; **1963**: *Oth.*, *AYL*, *Ant.*; **1964**: *TN*, *Mac.*, *MND*; **1965**: *Wiv.*, *Ado*, *Lr.*; **1966**: *Shr.*, *JC*, *TGV*; **1967**: *Err.*, *Ham.*, *Tmp.*; **1968**: *MV*, *AYL*, *Rom.*; **1969**: *MND*, *Oth.*, *LLL*; **1970**: *R3*, *Wiv*, *TN*; **1971**: *Shr.*, *1H*4, *Tmp.*; **1972**: *Err.*, *Lr.*, *WT*; **1973**: *MND*, *Mac.*, *Ado*; **1974**: *AYL*, *Ham.*, *H8*; **1975**: *MV*, *R2*, *TGV*; **1976**: *Tmp.*, *LLL*, *JC*; **1977**: *Shr.*, *Cor.*, *Rom.*, *The Mikado*; **1978**: *TN*, *Oth.*, *MND*, *Scandals*; **1979**: *Wiv.*, *Lr.*, *AWW*; **1980**: *Err.*, *Mac.*, *MM*; **1981**: *Ado*, *Ham.*, *1H*4, *The Guardsman*; **1982**: *AYL*, *Rom.*, *2H*4; **1983**: *TGV*, *H5*, *MV*; **1984**: *Shr.*, *Tmp.*, *Tro.*; **1985**: *Ant.*, *TN*, *Wiv.*; **1986**: *MND*, *JC*, *LLL*; **1987**: *Err.*, *R3*, *Ado*; **1988**: *AYL*, *Oth.*, *Cym.*; **1989**: *Tmp.*, *Mac.*, *WT*, *The Glass Menagerie*, *The Imaginary Invalid*, *Nothing Like the Sun*; **1990**: *Rom.*, *Tit.*, *TGV*, *Ghosts*, *Waiting for Godot*, *The Importance of Being Earnest*; **1991**: *Ham.*, *Shr.*, *TN*, *Death of a Salesman*, *Misalliance*, *Volpone*; **1992**: *JC*, *Lr.*, *MV*, *Wiv.*, *Blithe Spirit*, *Cyrano de Bergerac*; **1993**: *MND*, *R2*, *Tim.*, *Our Town*, *Tartuffe*, *The Royal Family*; **1994**: *LLL*, *AYL*, *R3*, *A Flea in Her Ear*, *The Shoemaker's Holiday*.

Research Resources: Archives are maintained in the USF administrative offices. See also: Terral Sam Lewis, "The Utah Shakespearean Festival: Twenty Five Years in Retrospect," Ph.D., Texas Tech University, 1991; Glenn Loney, and Patricia MacKay, *The Shakespeare Complex* (New York: Drama Book Specialists, 1975).

Site visit and interview with Fred C. Adams and R. Scott Phillips: 24 August 1991.

Cindy Melby Phaneuf

VERMONT

CHAMPLAIN SHAKESPEARE FESTIVAL. (Ceased operation after 1989 season.) SITE: Royall Tyler Theatre, University of Vermont, Burlington, VT. SEASON: approximately 40 performances, rotating repertory, early July to mid-August. PRINCIPAL STAFF: Greg Falls, 1959-62, founding producing director; Edward J. Feidner, 1962-80, producing artistic director; William Schenk, 1980-89 general manager. FACILITIES: 1959–73, arena theatre (capacity 150–200); 1975–89, Royall Tyler Theatre, flexible thrust (capacity 300–350). AUDITIONS: Burlington and New York. STATUS: Equity LORT D for ten years from 1966–1975, then non-union. ANNUAL BUDGET: $150,000 at its peak, $100,000 in 1989. ANNUAL ATTENDANCE: 11,000–13,000 at its peak, 8,000–9,000 in later years. FOUNDED: 1959, Greg Falls.

Champlain Shakespeare Festival (CSF) was founded by Greg Falls in 1959 as part of the 350th anniversary celebration of the discovery of Lake Champlain. The first fully professional theatre in Vermont, its mission was "to provide young American actors experience in playing major classical roles." In its 31-year history, the CSF produced three plays per season in repertory and completed the entire canon.

Greg Falls became the first director of drama at the University of Vermont in 1952. In 1958, Ed Feidner became the second member of the theatre faculty as a stage and technical director. Together, they approached Ray Phillips, director (later dean) of continuing education with their vision for a summer Shakespeare festival. A Shakespeare fan and a skillful administrator, Phillips gained the support of the president of the university and found the funding to make the festival a reality. In its first season, the festival won an award from the New England Theatre Conference.

Falls left for Seattle in 1962, where he became head of the School of Theatre at the University of Washington and artistic director of A Contemporary Theatre, which he founded. The festival was left in the capable hands of Feidner as producer and artistic director. For 19 years, Feidner ran the festival and often directed two of the three plays. In 1965, the CSF became an Equity LORT D theatre, hiring 10 to 12 Equity members to perform alongside students. In the peak years, the budget grew to $150,000, and houses were filled to 98 percent capacity, with audiences from all over New England and Canada. Outstanding outreach programs included the Institute on Elizabethan Arts and Literature (1965-1969), supported in part by the National Endowment for the Humanities. This five-week, high-powered, and highly successful institute brought world-renowned Shakespeare scholars such as Morris Carnovsky, Phillip Burton, Sir Roy Strong, and Richard Dyer-Bennett together with students and teachers to study Shakespeare's plays. In 1980, Feidner resigned after more than two decades of fruitful association with the CSF. Feidner reflects, "I got tired of fighting the same battles, but I'd had a great time for over 20 years." After a year of transition, the next major figure in CSF's history was William Schenk, who was general manager during the last decade of the festival. A change in the university's administrative priorities meant a realignment in the administrative structure of the festival. A new provost moved the festival's funding from the dean of continuing studies to the dean of arts and sciences. The higher administration began to run the university as a business, including greater fiscal accountability for the festival. Pressure was exerted to produce popular fare (such as *Man of La Mancha* and *Charley's Aunt* in CSF's 1985 season) rather than all classic plays. Season selection became subject to the approval of the dean of arts and sciences. With smaller university subsidy, production budgets declined and audiences dwindled. Frustrated that they were no longer able to offer salaries that were competitive, the faculty decided to discontinue the festival after its 1989 season. Current theatre chairman Martin Thaler looks forward to a summer theatre program but doubts that it will be Shakespeare because of the financial demands, as well as uncertainty about whether a Shakespeare festival meets university and community needs.

Champlain Shakespeare Festival was produced by the University of Vermont; 50 percent of its $100,000 to $150,000 annual budget came from the university and 50 percent came from box office receipts. The major artistic and administrative staff positions were filled by the theatre faculty. The leadership was provided by a producing director or general manager who was aided by an administrative director. Throughout its history, the festival attracted outstanding young actors from across the country. In its Equity years (1966-1975), the company was comprised of 10 to 12 Equity actors and an Equity stage manager under the LORT D contract. The remainder of the company included promising young actors and students who were beginning their professional careers. Some of the CSF's outstanding actors include Randall Duk Kim, who played the title roles in *Titus Andronicus* and *Richard III* at CSF and later went on to become artistic director of the **American Players Theatre** in Spring Green, Wisconsin. Jason Miller, author of *That Championship Season*, acted at the CSF, as did Carole Demas, later praised for her work on Broadway in *Grease*. Other notable artists include Ralf Bode, the cinematographer of *Saturday Night Fever* and *Coal Miner's Daughter*.

In its early years, the festival took place in the tiny Arena Theatre, located in the "nether reaches of the Robert Hull Fleming Museum, not dissimilar in shape and ambience from Shakespeare's 'wooden O.'" Despite that theatre's technical limitations, artists and audience members enjoyed its intimacy and warmth. In March 1974, the Royall Tyler Theatre became the festival's new home. "Like the Old Arena, however, the Tyler was built into a pre-existing structure. This time it was the old gym-auditorium, a handsome brick and masonry building dating back from 1901" (Loney and MacKay, *The Shakespeare Complex*, p. 107). It seated up to 350 around its flexible thrust stage (33 by 30 feet). Costumes, sets, and props were built on site, using university facilities.

Burlington is an impressive New England city with lovely old churches and stately Victorian mansions. Its major industries include I.B.M., G.E., and the university. Burlington County has a population base of 150,000 and the state of Vermont 500,000. Vermont's lush green mountains attract tourists from across the country. In its heyday, the CSF attracted a widely diversified audience from 48 states, including tourists who made the rounds of festivals. Feidner is proud that the festival was popular with a diverse audience, saying: "My housekeeper never missed a production and university custodians still ask, 'when is the festival coming back?'"

At its peak, the CSF played to 98 percent capacity houses. Regular coverage was provided by the *Montreal Star*, *Boston Herald*, and *Boston Globe*, as well as local papers. From 1965 to the early 1980s, the CSF was regularly reviewed by *Shakespeare Quarterly*. According to Feidner, despite this extensive regional attention, CSF was unable to "crack New York." In later years, the CSF played to 70 percent houses. The organization needed but could not afford a marketing director. The mission of the CSF was "to provide the best possible Shakespearean stagings, given the time, budget, playing space, and talent available" (Loney and MacKay, *Shakespeare Complex*, p. 104). Because the festival was designed to give young actors more experience in classical theatre, actors were hired for only two or three seasons; then they were encouraged to move along. Feidner did not want the CSF to become a "home or womb to return to," but rather a launching pad for the young actors' professional careers. The season was most often composed of a comedy, tragedy, and history play by Shakespeare. Occasionally CSF would branch out to include other classical plays, such as *The Miser*, *Edward II*, or *She Stoops to Conquer*.

Both traditional and nontraditional approaches were taken. *The Comedy of Errors* was once presented in Elizabethan garb and at another time as a circus troupe under the big top, with the Dromios in clown white and the Antipholi in harlequin masks. A modern-dress *Julius Caesar* evoked images of "Kent State," and a "mod version" of *Love's Labour's Lost* capitalized on Edwardian images reminiscent of the Beatles. Randall Duk Kim played Richard III with the vision of this king as a black widow spider, effectively taking the audience "inside his head." Tight budgets for everything demanded that the CSF be truthful and honest with the play. Feidner elaborates: "I am not interested in directors 'doing their thing' with Shakespeare, it must fit the play well." The CSF prided itself on its strong design elements. Periods were often changed, and the text was usually cut, although the language was never altered. Feidner's overall governing principle was "to trust Shakespeare," believing "if you play around too much you do him a disservice."

Production History: **1959**: *TN, MND, The Miser*; **1960**: *Shr.*; **1961**: *Ado, Ham., H5*; **1962**: *Tmp., JC, R3*; **1963**: *Wiv., Oth., R3*; **1964**: *AYL, Rom., Jn.*; **1965**: *MV, Ant., H8*; **1966**: *Err., Ham., 1H4*; **1967**: *LLL, 1H4, Lr.*; **1968**: *AWW, Mac., 2H4*; **1969**: *Oth., WT, R3*; **1970**: *TN, Tro., Edward II*; **1971**: *Shr., JC*; **1972**: *Wiv., AYL, Tit.*; **1973**: *MND, R3, Rom.*; **1974**: *Tmp., Cym., Ham*; **1975**: *Our Town, Ado, Tim.*; **1976**: *Err., Lr., R2*; **1977**: *TGV, Mac., 1H4*; **1978**: *TN, Oth.*; **1979**: *Shr., MM, She Stoops to Conquer*; **1980**: *AYL, MND, Per.*; **1981**: *Rom., Wiv., Rosencrantz and Guildenstern are Dead; Ado, Hay Fever, Cor.*; **1982**: dark; **1983**: *Tmp., LLL, 2H6/3H6*; **1984**: *Err., R3, The Importance of Being Earnest*; **1985**: *Man of La Mancha, Charley's Aunt*; **1986**: *Shr., The Miracle Worker, The Three Musketeers*; **1987**: *Rom., A Man For All Seasons; The Glass Menagerie*; **1988**: *MND, Streetcar Named Desire*.

Research Resources: Archives for the Champlain Shakespeare Festival dating from 1959 are maintained at the University of Vermont Special Collections. See Glenn Loney and Patricia MacKay, *The Shakespeare Complex* (New York: Drama Book Specialists, 1975).

Interviews with Ed Feidner, Greg Falls, Martin Thaler, and William Schenk: 3 and 4 September 1991.
Cindy Melby Phaneuf

VIRGINIA

SHAKESPEARE AT THE RUINS. MAIL: P.O. Box 1, Barboursville, VA 22923. SITE: at the ruins of Governor Barbour's mansion on the grounds of Barboursville Vineyards, on State Route 678. ADMINISTRATION: 703/832-5355. BOX OFFICE: 800/768-4172. ADMISSION: $3–$10. SEASON: 12 performances, first three weekends in August; 8:00 p.m., Thurs.–Sat.; 5:00 p.m., Sun. PRINCIPAL STAFF: Sara M. Smith, president of the board and artistic director. FACILITIES: outdoor platforms; in case of rain, indoors at Community Center theatre (capacity 250). AUDITIONS: local, evenings in June. STATUS: community theatre. ANNUAL BUDGET: $8,000. ANNUAL ATTENDANCE: 2,500. FOUNDED: 1990.

"Shakespeare is an anomaly for the Four County Players," states Sara M. Smith, artistic director of Shakespeare at the Ruins (SATR). According to Smith, this is because Four County Players (FCP) was founded in 1975, but a Shakespeare play was not produced by the Barboursville community theatre group until 1990. FCP's success with modern plays and musicals as once-a-year moneymakers misled the board of directors into thinking that Shakespeare would be too difficult for amateur actors and loyal audiences, and therefore would cause the loss of both audiences and income. The impetus for undertaking Shakespeare productions was an agreement reached with winemaker Luca Paschina. He would allow FCP's use of the grounds of the ruins of Governor Barbour's mansion, located within the Barboursville Vineyards, as the site for a stage and parking for an outdoor Shakespeare production. FCP presented nine performances of *A Midsummer Night's Dream* at the ruins in 1990. Enthusiastic responses from the actors (all amateurs) and the audience (composed almost equally of local residents and tourists) led to the expansion of the season to 12 performances of *The Taming of the Shrew* in 1991 and 12 of *Twelfth Night* in 1992.

Unlike the plays produced during the regular season at FCP's indoor proscenium-arch theatre at Barboursville's Community Center, the SATR production is performed on an outdoor platform stage erected before the west front of the former mansion, which is now a registered Virginia Historical Landmark. Designed by Thomas Jefferson for his friend James Barbour (who served as governor of Virginia, U.S. senator, secretary of war, and ambassador to the court of St. James), the mansion was built in 1822 and destroyed by fire on Christmas Day 1884. Once the most elaborate plantation in the county, Barboursville is now a 50-acre commercial vineyard.

SATR playgoers bring lawn chairs to place within an area framed on three sides by immense boxwood trees, fragrant in the twilight. Behind the audience and hidden by the trees are a gentle swale planted with grapevines and, beyond that, the winery itself. The sounds of cattle, ducks, and other farm animals float on the air. Many playgoers bring their own picnics and sample the prize-winning wines that the vineyard makes available for purchase. Others call in advance (703/832-3485) to book the dinner buffet served on the site by the Toliver House Restaurant of Gordonsville. For *The Taming of the Shrew*, the Toliver House presented an Italian buffet featuring dishes that might have been served at Kate the shrew's wedding feast: antipasto salad, torta rustica, lemon garlic pasta, zucchini with mint, focaccia, and assorted desserts. Live musicians stroll the grounds during the dinner hour.

The support of Barboursville Vineyards is crucial to the success of SATR, but the financial benefits of the formal written agreement have been mutual. The vineyard not only wins customers for its premium wine list but also gets a percentage of the box office receipts. The annual budget for Shakespeare is about $8,000, with about 30 percent of that amount coming from ticket sales. Prices are $10 for adults, $8 for senior citizens and children over age 12, and $3 for children under 12. Attendance is limited to 250 per performance because that is the number of seats in the indoor theatre, which is used in case of rain; a duplicate setting on the stage at the Community Center is constructed to prepare for that eventuality. Because many performances are sold out, advance ticket purchase is required. The occasional benefit evening generates money for local nonprofit social agencies. Smith proudly claims that *The Taming of the Shrew* netted $12,200, double the amount formerly earned by FCP musicals.

Barboursville's location—only 22 miles from Charlottesville and the University of Virginia, 69 miles from Richmond, and 98 miles from Washington, D.C.—makes it accessible to both urban and rural populations. For those who would stay overnight in the area, information about nearby inns and bed-and-breakfasts can be obtained from the Orange County Visitors Bureau (703/672-1653). The bureau will also supply a map showing local historical sites, like the Wilderness Battlefield and Montpelier, home of President James Madison.

FCP is governed by a board of directors, for which Smith served as president in 1991 and 1992. She has directed all three SATR productions, casting by audition. The actors have come from eight counties. The part-time office/theatre manager and the production manager are paid positions; all other participants are volunteers. Disclaiming the title "artistic director," Smith comments: "I don't know what I am. I do everything. We all do." A resident of nearby Rapidan and a Ph.D. candidate in English at the University of Virginia, Smith has a clear-sighted attitude toward Shakespeare as presented at the Ruins. "We all have respect and enthusiasm for Shakespeare's plays. We believe that ordinary people, with lots of hard work and doing their best, can bring his plays alive." Smith's aim is "authenticity," which she defines as having the look of Shakespeare's own time while communicating meaningfully to today's audiences. As an example of her attention to authentic detail, she points out that the women's costumes for *The Taming of the Shrew* are dated to the 1570s, rather than the 1590s, because the gigantic sleeves worn during the later decade restricted movement overmuch. The stage at the Ruins may resemble the boards set up in an innyard by Elizabethan traveling players.

The plays are presented with few cuts. For example, the induction was performed with *The Taming of the Shrew*. Smith admits to cutting no more than eight lines of *Twelfth Night*. In rehearsal, she pays special attention to character. For *The Taming of the Shrew*, she asked the actors to write papers about their characters. The result was performances about which reviewer Christopher Brasted commented: "the characters'. . . body language, their facial expression, were identification enough." Amateur acting is often looked down upon, but the amateurs performing *Twelfth Night* at SATR's 1992 opening night achieved a high standard of performance without falling from grace or, as Jonathan Miller has put it, having to be "merely endured." The words of the text were obviously understood and their meanings conveyed.

The dark side of *Twelfth Night*—Feste's melancholy and the cruelty in the treatment of Malvolio—was slighted, as Smith felt that such an emphasis would be inappropriate to the youth and skill of the actors. Indeed, the performance was charming. Among the actors were Steve West (Orsino), a carpenter with a college degree in sociology; Stuart Wilson (Andrew Aguecheek), a waste management specialist; Mark McLendon (Malvolio), a graduate student in English; Michelle Wiehr (Maria) and Heather Ward (Viola), high school students; and Joanne Hutchison (Olivia), a housewife of English parentage, who had never acted before. Smith had trained all of them well. Music was provided by a guitarist, a flautist, and a tamborinist who also sang. Costumes were designed by Cheryl Barnes and lighting was designed by Brent Cerves in consultation with Robert Brand, a theatre lighting professional engaged through a grant from the Virginia Arts Council. Although the actors may sometimes have gestured over enthusiastically and ineffectively, their clarity was beyond reproach.

Production History: **1990**: *MND*; **1991**: *Shr.*; **1992**: *TN.*; **1993**: *Ado*; **1994**: *AYL*.

Research Resources: Archives for Shakespeare at the Ruins are informally maintained by Sara M. Smith. See Christopher Brasted, "The Bard Getting Better at Ruins," *Orange County Review* (8 Aug. 1991): 3; Jonathan Miller, *Subsequent Performances* (New York: Viking, 1986): 22.

Site visits and interviews: 17 February and 14-15 August 1992.
Hassell B. Sledd

SHAKESPEARE BY THE SEA FESTIVAL. (ceased production in 1988.) SITE: 1977-1981, Kempsville Playhouse, also called Recreation Center Theatre, of Virginia Beach Department of Parks and Recreation; 1982-1988, Pavilion Theatre of Performing Arts of the Virginia Beach Convention Center. SEASON: 10-12 performances of two plays in rotating repertory, in July or August 1982-1987; final season, 31 performances of three plays in rotating repertory, 6 July–11 August 1988. PRINCIPAL STAFF: Henry deShields, director; Joyce Murtland, publicist and assistant to director; Tom Magee, production manager. FACILITY: Pavilion Theatre of Performing Arts (capacity 1,000). STATUS: non-union contract. FOUNDED: 1977, Henry deShields.

In 1975, Henry deShields set aside his professional acting career and returned to the Virginia Tidewater area to develop a summer Shakespeare program that in 1982 became the Shakespeare by the Sea Festival (SSF). Beginning in 1977, a single play was performed each summer through 1981 in the 175-seat Kempsville Playhouse (also called the Recreation Center Theatre), one of the facilities of the Virginia Beach Department of Parks and Recreation, which sponsored the event. As the SSF, the company expanded to two productions and moved to the 1,000-seat Pavilion Theatre of the Performing Arts of the Virginia Beach Convention Center.

Through 1986, the SSF continued presenting two plays each summer for a total of ten or twelve performances in the Pavilion. The festival charged relatively low ticket prices: $3.50-$5 for a single performance, $7–8 for a season ticket. In 1987, the Department of Parks and Recreation began to share sponsorship and funding with the newly formed Festival Foundation. Three plays were presented, each with a guest star: Rita Moreno as Katharina in *The Taming of the Shrew*, John Wesley Shipp as Mark Antony in *Julius Caesar*, and Michael Greer as Theseus and Oberon in *A Midsummer Night's Dream*.

The 1988 season brought a broadened interpretation of "Shakespeare" with the presentation of the musical version of *The Taming of the Shrew*: Cole Porter's *Kiss Me, Kate*. *Edmond Ironside* and *Romeo and Juliet* completed the season. An admission-free debate on the authorship of *Edmond Ironside* was offered on 11 July, with Eric Sams upholding Shakespeare as the author, Donald Foster speaking in opposition, and O. B. Hardison moderating. The opening on 6 July was advertised as the American premiere of *Edmund Ironside*, but that claim was challenged by others including Robert F. Fleissner and Mimi Mekler. Indeed, Daniel J. Watermeier presented a performance of *Edmund Ironside* followed by a post performance discussion as part of the Ohio Shakespeare Conference held at the University of Toledo in March, 1987. In 1988, *Edmund Ironside* was also staged at the Globe Playhouse of Los Angeles.

In addition to its summer performances, the SSF toured one production each season to schools and parks in the Virginia Beach area. More than 5,000 students saw the SSF's *Macbeth* in 1984. The SSF also occasionally played in the Center Theatre in Norfolk and the Chrysler Museum Theatre. Despite strong support by local audiences, the SSF did not attain the national visibility that would have allowed it to sustain low ticket prices and an expensive star system. Financial pressures forced the SSF to cease production after the 1988 season. Although near retirement age, the energetic deShields has remained devoted to the task of making Shakespeare available to the people of his community. In June 1992, for example, he organized a group tour to see Ian McKellan in *Richard III* in Washington D.C.

Production History: **1977**: *Shr.*; **1978**: *TN*; **1979**: *MV*; **1980**: *MND*; **1981**: *Wiv.*; **1982**: *Rom.*, *Shr.*; **1983**: *AYL*, *MM*; **1984**: *Err.*, *Mac.*; **1985**: *TN*, *R3*; **1986**: *Ado*, *TGV*; **1987**: *JC*, *Shr.*, *MND*; **1988**: *Rom.*, *Edmund Ironside*, *Kiss Me, Kate*.

Research Resources: Robert F. Fleissner, "Letter to the Editor," *Shakespeare Quarterly* 40 (Summer 1989): 254; Mimi Mekler, Mario Romano, and Alec Stockwell [directors], "Emund Ironside," *Shakespeare Quarterly* 41 (Fall 1990): 628; Eric Sams, ed., *Shakespeare's Lost Play: Edmund Ironside* (New York: St. Martin's Press, 1986).

Interview: 20 February 1992.
Hassell B. Sledd

SHENANDOAH SHAKESPEARE EXPRESS. MAIL: P.O. Box 944, Dayton, VA 22821. SITE: variable. ADMINISTRATION: 703/434-3366 or 800/SAY-PUCK. ADMISSION: varies; determined by sponsoring organization. SEASON: year-around. PRINCIPAL STAFF: Ralph Alan Cohen, executive director; Terry Flynn, general manager; Celia Alexander, business manager; Paul Menzer, director of development; Jim Warren, managing director. FACILITY: as provided by sponsor. AUDITIONS: Harrisonburg in September. STATUS: non-Equity. ANNUAL BUDGET: $120,000 (1992). ANNUAL ATTENDANCE: 20,000 (1992). FOUNDED: 1988, Ralph Alan Cohen, Jim Warren; incorporated August 1990.

As a professor of English at James Madison University (JMU) in Harrisonburg, Virginia, Dr. Ralph Cohen discovered that he could best illustrate his lecture material on Shakespeare by taking his students to London to see the **Royal Shakespeare Company** (RSC) productions. He organized the university's Studies Abroad program in the 1970s and over the years conducted "hundreds" of American students on theatregoing trips there. After Trevor Nunn left the RSC, however, that company seemed to offer more large-scale productions, complete with lavish sets and costumes, but less to satisfy Cohen's students. Cohen began taking his charges to see fringe productions of Shakespeare and noticed that small, low-budget companies like **Cheek by Jowl** were more successful at capturing the students' imaginations.

At JMU in the fall semester 1987, Cohen organized a senior seminar on *Henry V*, devoted to a close study of the text and to Elizabethan principles of staging. Cohen quickly realized that the smaller London fringe companies were applying exactly those principles. Cohen and his students decided to produce *Henry V* in the same manner. The JMU theatre department welcomed the English department's use of the black-box Experimental Theatre, and, in April 1988, the "JMU Shakespeare Company" performed *Henry V* with 15 actors playing 47 roles. Its success led Cohen and Jim Warren, a graduating senior, to form an independent, professional traveling troupe. Another student actor, Bill Gordon, who served as business manager, proposed several names, including "Volkspeare: Shakespeare for the People," but the group soon settled on another of Gordon's suggestions: Shenandoah Shakespeare Express (SSE).

Richard III, directed by Warren and cast entirely with college-age actors, opened in December 1988 at Trinity Presbyterian Church in Harrisonburg and went on to a 14-performance state tour. The following May, Warren directed a production of *The Taming of the Shrew* that tripled the previous number of bookings and toured to New England, including performances at Dartmouth College, and to the off-Broadway John Houseman Theatre in New York. Then Warren moved to Los Angeles, leaving Cohen to run the company. Cohen mounted *Julius Caesar* and was invited to bring it to Philadelphia for presentation at the Shakespeare Association of America's annual meeting in March 1990. That experience is seen as a turning point for the SSE, since it led to the formation of an advisory board with such stellar names as David Bevington, Dame Judi Dench, Michael Goldman, Bernice Kliman, Sam Wanamaker, and Jerry Zaks. It also marked SSE's move to a repertory format. *A Midsummer Night's Dream* opened in April, and thenceforth the company has offered at least two shows back to back.

In September 1990, Warren returned to manage the company, which was gradually moving away from employing college students. That season saw SEE's first fund-raising gala, its first Southern tour, its first summer season at a new "home" (the Dayton Learning Center), and one-week runs in Philadelphia and Washington, D.C. The latter residency included a performance at the Folger Shakespeare Library Teacher's Institute. Bugle Boy,

Inc., began donating the sportswear that is worn as a basic garment in productions. 1991 also brought SSE's first grant, for a teacher seminar on Shakespeare, funded by the Virginia Foundation for Humanities and Public Policy.

To date, SSE has operated entirely on earned income. This has been possible because the company's overhead is low. SSE requires only 15 by 20 feet of floor space, with the audience on three sides and some general lighting. As stated in the company brochure, "no one in the audience should be more than 45 feet from the actors (the furthest distance from the stage at the Globe)." There are never more than 15 in the constantly changing troupe of actors, who are mostly in their twenties.

Eighty-five percent of SSE's budget comes from performance fees, and the remainder is earned through the fund-raising gala. The standard fee at colleges and universities is $1,200 for one performance and $1,500 for two. High schools get the lowest rates: $700/$1,000. There is an additional charge for workshops. A package "SSE Week" for $8,500 includes five public performances with discussions afterward and classroom workshops. For longer runs, the company will work out a partnership, perhaps splitting advertising costs and sharing the take, with 70 percent for SSE, 30 percent for the sponsor. Sponsors have charged up to $15 per ticket, but when SSE performs at its home space in Dayton, ticket prices are $7.00 for adults and $5.00 for students. The actors' pay was largely on a per diem basis in the 1991–92 season, but it was expected that actors engaged for the 1993 calendar year would be paid salaries ($100 per week for 50 weeks), with housing for eight provided in a new rental space where the office will also be located.

High school and college audiences are targeted during the academic year, but, in summer, SSE operates more like a commercial fringe company. While the company maintains its office and rehearsal space in Harrisonburg, its summer base at the Dayton Learning Center, two miles away, is a performance space in the gym area of a former elementary school. Given the space in exchange for helping to remodel the building for use as an adult education center, SSE put in sound baffling and built a thrust stage. There they offer a four-week summer season for audiences of up to 200.

In 1992, the company traveled over 30,000 miles to give 250 performances for over 30,000 people. Standing-room-only crowds greeted the company for a two-week run in Washington on the Folger Library's Elizabethan stage. The company went west for the first time, with shows presented from Albuquerque to Walla Walla. In SSE's first venture across the Atlantic, it enjoyed two-week runs at the Shakespeare Globe Museum in London and at the Edinburgh Fringe Festival.

The National Endowment for the Arts (NEA) gave SSE a grant toward its 1993 season. From February to December, the company performed *Antony and Cleopatra, Romeo and Juliet,* and *A Midsummer Night's Dream* in repertory. Appearances in 1993 also included performances at the Piccolo Spoleto

Festival's theatre fringe festival, a tour of the Pacific Northwest, and a return to the Folger Library for three weeks in the summer.

The SSE logo expresses its youthful spirit: a prop crown perches jauntily on a pair of hightop tennis shoes emblazoned with Shakespeare portraits, all surmounted by the motto, "The Unroyal Shakespeare Company." The company brochure spells out the principles to which SSE adheres: performances last no more than two hours; the same general lighting is used for audience and actors; the text is spoken as natural language; humor and action are stressed. The by-laws also specify that no more than 20 words may be changed in any given play.

"We want people to think Shakespeare is as immediate to them as rock and roll," says Warren. "If kids think of Shakespeare as 'culture,' they're turned off and assume 'this isn't about me.' But we think Shakespeare is about those kids. We're into opening those kids up to the humanity that's in those plays. We're trying to take the works off the cultural pedestal and put them back into real life." The immediacy of the plays is enhanced, Warren thinks, by the company's policy of nontraditional casting. Women often play male roles. Julius Caesar was played by a black actor; his murder by a gang of white men helped the black high school students to see contemporary meaning in the play. SSE's *Merchant of Venice*, directed by Cohen, has stimulated post-performance discussions of bigotry.

A performance of *The Merchant of Venice* at the 1992 annual meeting of the Shakespeare Association of American typified SSE's production style. The attractive, youthful actors kept up a lively pace on the simple platform in a hotel ballroom. The only set props were black wooden rehearsal blocks with handholes and hinged tops. Although the 12 identical blocks were constantly being rearranged, the actors were unerring in opening the one that would yield just the right prop or costume piece. The cast of 12 entered as an ensemble, all dressed in black Bugle Boy jeans, white shirts, gray jackets, and black and white canvas hightop sneakers. A change of posture or the addition of a costume accessory enabled them to play more than one role each, which they did with remarkable clarity.

Production History: **1988**: *R3*; **1989**: *Shr.*; **1990**: *JC, MND*; **1991**: *MM, TN, MND*; **1992**: *MV, Mac., Err.*; **1993**: *Ant., Rom., MND*; **1994**: *Ado, Oth., Shr.*

Research Resources: Archives are informally maintained at the Shenandoah Shakespeare Express office in Harrisonburg.

Interview: 18 April 1992.
Felicia Hardison Londré and Daniel J. Watermeier

VIRGINIA SHAKESPEARE FESTIVAL. MAIL: College of William and Mary, Williamsburg, VA 23187. SITE: Phi Beta Kappa Memorial Hall, Jamestown Road, Williamsburg. ADMINISTRATION: 804/221-2659; Fax: 804/221-1773. BOX OFFICE: 804/221-2660. ADMISSION: $10/seat; $17/season of two plays. SEASON: 20 performances in July; 8:00 p.m., Tues.–Sat.; 2:00 p.m., Sun. PRINCIPAL STAFF: Jerry H. Bledsoe, executive director. FACILITY: proscenium theatre (capacity 800). AUDITIONS: January–March local, SETC, ECTC. STATUS: Equity Guest Artists. ANNUAL BUDGET: $85,278 (1992). ANNUAL ATTENDANCE: 6,316 (1991). FOUNDED: 1978, Jerry H. Bledsoe, Bruce McConachie, Christopher J. Boll, Patrick Micken.

The Virgina Shakespeare Festival (VSF) was founded in 1978, when four young faculty members of the College of William and Mary, Jerry Bledsoe, Patrick Micken, Christopher Boll, and Bruce McConachie, started a Shakespeare festival to fill the void in summer theatre in Williamsburg, Virginia, left by the demise in 1977 of *The Common Glory*, a patriotic outdoor pageant about Thomas Jefferson. *The Common Glory* had been directed since 1946 by Howard Scammon, a long-time member of the college faculty. During summer runs of the pageant, Scammon had also directed Sunday evening performances of Shakespeare plays at the pageant's outdoor theatre. According to the 1983 festival program, his purpose had been to "challenge" the actors and "get them to realize there were other things they could do and that they could stretch and improve themselves." One of the Sunday night performances in the 1960s included Goldie Hawn as Juliet, and another, in the 1970s, offered Glenn Close as Rosalind. Scammon's involvement with Shakespeare had begun at least as early as 1932 undergraduate production of *As You Like It*, a photograph of which is reproduced in the program and shows Scammon as Touchstone.

These roots may go even deeper, however, through generations of student productions about which the records are "sketchy," back to what the distinguished theatre historian Charles Shattuck has called the first professional performances of Shakespeare in America. The date was 1752, the play was *The Merchant of Venice*, and it was acted in a building especially constructed as a theatre in Williamsburg, according to Shattuck. In Virginia, where the longer the tradition the greater its prestige, the long and academic tradition of the VSF expresses the worth of the festival to citizens of the Old Dominion, indicates its connections, and suggests its limits.

By 1988, the VSF had become a fully professional, regional summer theatre under the artistic direction of G. Leslie Muchmore. Twenty-five of the plays in the Shakespeare canon had been brought to life in the air-conditioned theatre in Phi Beta Kappa (PBK) Memorial Hall. (Since the 1960s, air conditioning has come to be considered more or less a necessity in Williamsburg, where the summers are both fiercely hot and drenchingly humid.) The festival put on a lengthy fall tour and had an elaborate support system, involving volunteers, private donors, corporations, the College, and state and local arts commissions. VSF's expenses, however, were budgeted on the basis of expected income rather than money in hand, according to Bledsoe, the present executive director of the festival and now himself a long-time member of the college faculty. Financial records reveal deficits for several years in the 1980s. Whether due to the deficits alone or to other difficulties as well, plans for 1989 were abruptly canceled early in the year.

A season was planned for 1990, but a new difficulty arose. This time, asbestos was found in PBK Hall. The theatre was closed until the dangerous substance could be removed, and the season was again cancelled and advertising withdrawn. Nonetheless, the summer interns—young people, some of whom were undergraduates and were given tuition and free housing for the period of the festival—were kept on. With them, Bledsoe and director Keith Fowler of the University of California–Irvine mounted seven performances of *The Comedy of Errors* in a 150-seat concert hall in Ewell Hall, a music building. The hat was passed at the door and about $8,000 was collected. Clearly there was still audience interest in the Virginia Shakespeare Festival.

The support system, though interrupted, was still largely intact, and the college continued its in-kind support of the air-conditioned theatre, workshop space, utilities, and so on. The records of the 1991 festival show a total of 20 performances of two plays on a budget of $55,500. The actual expenses were considerably less. Total income was more than $100,000, of which about $58,000 came from box office sales, more than $38,000 from gifts, and the remainder from concessions and other activities. With that surplus, the 1992 season could be budgeted from money in hand. The 1991 records shows that the VSF was, as Bledsoe says, in an "austerity mode" more importantly, however, it reveals the generous and continuing support enjoyed by the VSF.

The VSF is governed under a mission statement that declares that its purposes are: first, to provide experience in theatre study to "students, faculty, townspeople, and selected artists and craftsmen"; and, second, to offer "high quality productions" to residents of the area, students of the college, and visitors. The players are to be non-Equity, although provision is made for the engagement of Equity personnel from time to time. This statement gives the VSF room to grow in several directions—for example, in the number of productions and the inclusion of plays by authors other than Shakespeare, but it simultaneously limits VSF's autonomy. It declares that the administration of the VSF is to be entrusted to an executive director chosen from the theatre faculty, and it names the VSF's "official function" as "a second major-production program of the department," the first presumably being productions during the academic year. While in some respects limiting, the VSF's academic connection has provided the personnel, material, and continuity necessary for artistically satisfying productions of the plays. It also has provided a conduit for private contributions.

Bledsoe writes that he has "long been pondering the basic questions of how useful innovation in Shakespearean staging really is." Bledsoe continues: "I think [innovation] probably *is* useful in particular cases and mean to make a place for it [at VSF] when it becomes viable and when I perceive an artist with a truly important idea." In the meantime, Bledsoe mounts "strong traditional shows . . . as opposed to imitations of innovative approaches elsewhere."

PBK Memorial Hall is located on Jamestown Road, a few blocks from "Confusion Corner," where five heavily traveled streets cross at the juncture of the campus of the College of William and Mary and the restored area of Colonial Williamsburg. The restoration, accomplished at a cost of more than $90 million since 1927, paid for mainly by the Rockefeller family and foundations, includes several hundred restored or reconstructed buildings. In the restored areas, colonial life is reproduced by craftsmen, housewives, merchants and others going about their daily business in colonial dress. Only 50 miles from Richmond and 150 miles from Washington, D.C., Williamsburg is a prime tourist center, especially in the summer when the festival is on; therefore, reservations for rooms and meals, always wise, are almost necessary, especially in the facilities operated by the Colonial Williamsburg Foundation. At the performances I attended, however, I did not notice many obvious tourists. According to Bledsoe, most members of the audience are retirees, academics, and business and professional people who come from Williamsburg or nearby towns purposely to see the plays.

The VSF's strategies for selling tickets are mainly print oriented, with both advertising and editorial material being used, the former as newspaper ads, fliers, posters, and direct mail, the latter as press releases and arts events calendars; radio and TV public service announcements are also used. Support from volunteers and donors is sought through direct mail, invitations to meetings, and the promotion of membership in the Lord Chamberlain Society (LCS), which is a perquisite for contributors to the festival. Membership brings with it "advance season brochures, news of productions, invitations to company receptions, and notices of LCS social functions—all the judicious coddling we can manage," stated Bledsoe in a 1991 brochure appealing for funds. Support in 1992 was about the same as in 1991, according to Bledsoe.

PBK Memorial Hall, a large building dedicated in 1957, houses a box office, the Dodge Room (a parlor for contributors and dignitaries that houses concessions during the festival run), an 800-seat proscenium theatre, a costume repository and workshop, a set workshop, an archives room, and the offices and classrooms of the theatre and speech department. The building is named after the first Greek-letter fraternity in the United States, founded in 1776 and now a scholastic honorary society. The first play presented in PBK Hall was *Romeo and Juliet*, with Juliet played by Linda Lavin, then an undergraduate and now well known on television and in the theatre.

The operating budget for 1992 included a considerable amount for "scenery" with which to make the set look new. By far the largest portion of the budget was for personnel, with the second largest for housing, and the third for advertising. There festival has a total of 41 salaried positions, including: an executive director/teacher, a guest director/teacher, a costume designer/teacher, two lighting designers and scenic artists, a technical director/production manager/teacher, a production stage manager, two box office and house managers, a guest actor, eight technical assistants, a promotion manager, an administrative office assistant, and 21 acting and technical interns.

Bledsoe's artistic philosophy emerges well in a letter he wrote to me:

> I expect you will find our operation to be fairly grass-roots in nature, compared to some . . . , but you could characterize us as in a retrenchment posture [in 1992], at this point in our fifteenth year. As you know, we believe our current austerity mode to be temporary, and we intend to be back among the best of them. Meanwhile, we are determined to be as good as we can be.

For the 1992 VSF season, a unit set, designed in 1972 and rebuilt in 1978, was used. It provides several levels, stairs, windows, and so on and is reminiscent, in a nonrepresentative way, of post World-War II reconstructions of Shakespeare's Globe Theatre. The set is handsome but definitely a part of the "austerity mode" admitted to by Bledsoe.

Of the two productions of the 1992 season, *Macbeth* was less impressive than *The Two Gentlemen of Verona*. *Macbeth* was directed by J. H. Crouch, founding director of **Colorado Shakespeare Festival**, in a somewhat static style. Still, by focusing attention on the words and action of the play, the performance had considerable power. William D. Michie, a VSF veteran and one of two Equity members in the cast, played Macbeth as an ambitious soldier in a performance that was particularly strong. Henry Lopez, a young but talented actor, with a handsome presence and a musical voice of exceptional range, was an effective Macduff. Rebecca Lenkiewicz, a pretty young woman with large eyes and a melodious voice, played Lady Macbeth as a pretty young woman in love with her husband and eager for his advancement. When she greeted him upon his return from the wars, she giggled with delight and rushed to kiss him. She was intense when she upbraided him for his waffling about the murder of Duncan. In the sleep-walking scene, she played with a sufficient change of manner, but she failed to capture Lady Macbeth's guilt.

The deaths of Banquo, Lady Macduff, and her sons were quickly accomplished on stage, without groans or gore. Banquo's ghost was quite bloody, however, provoking inappropriate laughter. Minor cutting of the text included the English Doctor, the Hecate scene, and some lines in Act IV, scene 1. This follows Bledsoe's opinion that the text should be played virtually "as is."

The unit set worked efficiently. Its upper level was used for Lady Macbeth's entrance in the sleep-walking scene and for the apparition of the kings of Scotland, as well as for other scenes. The inner below at stage level was effectively used to stage the murder of Lady Macduff and her two sons. A nice touch with the inner below was placing the empty thrones of Macbeth and Lady Macbeth there and having Banquo gaze at them for a moment as he began, "thou hast it now: King, Cawdor, Glamis, all." The three witches with their cauldron rose on a lift at center stage. The lift worked flawlessly, but the witches seemed to provoke almost no reaction from Macbeth or Banquo.

In line with the "austerity mode" of the festival, the program for *Macbeth* was only four pages long and gave only a title page, a few remarks by the director, and the names of the cast of characters, the 1992 Festival Staff, and the members of the Lord Chamberlain Society. I regretted the absence of biographical information on several people, including Richard Luken, who was credited with lighting design (successful because unobtrusive); David H. Dudley, who was listed as being responsible for technical direction/production management and was said by Bledsoe in an interview to be "the kingpin of our operation" (and the man who made the lift work); and Patricia Wesp, whose responsibility was given as production management but who apparently also designed the successful, because unobtrusive, costumes for *Macbeth*.

The Two Gentlemen of Verona has been called an apprentice work, a "limping forerunner" to Shakespeare's later comedies. It was none of these at the VSF. The production was a delight from beginning to end. This delight was achieved by performing the text without lengthy cuts, without patronizing it, and without gimmicks. Bledsoe, as director, remarked to me: "The words and action are funny as they are; you don't need to exaggerate them. Just say the words as they are written and the play will be funny." His players performed straightforwardly, without archness or exaggeration, and they were funny. Props, such as the cords by which Valentine plans to climb to Silvia's bedroom, received their just due, but no more.

Francis J. Gercke made Valentine's shift from laughing at love to falling in love a pleasure to watch. Robert A. Goddard III made Valentine's faithless friend Proteus equally amusing. Jennifer Johnson's voice and slender delicacy were well suited to both Julia and Sebastian. Early in the play she found just the right blend of young lady and hoyden when clowning with Lucetta, a part vigorously played by Beth Harre. Rebecca Lenkiewicz used intensity well as Silvia, a smaller part than that of Julia and one that can easily be overplayed, especially toward the end of the play. Chan Casey as Speed, Valentine's witty servant, acted with sufficient restraint to let the wit shine. John Goodlin capably enacted Silvia's father. Crab, Launce's dog, was not an actor in a dog suit but a real dog, that scratched, yawned, grinned, and attempted to wander. James Luse as Launce had enough strength to demand and get the attention of the audience as he spoke of his affection for Crab. Launce's words form a crucial commentary on the silliness of the young lovers. Luse, dramaturg and reader of new plays for the Long Wharf Theatre, gave them full value. Overall, *The Two Gentlemen of Verona* was brought to graceful life in a production that was altogether artistically satisfying. It was a pleasure to find that the play need not limp; in this production, it danced.

Production History: 1978: *Shr., Rom., TN*; **1979:** *MND, Ado, Mac.*; **1980:** *Err., MV, AYL*; **1981:** *TGV, JC, Tmp.*; **1982** *R3, Wiv., AWW*; **1983:** *TN, Oth., WT*; **1984:** *MND, Ham., MM*; **1985:** *Shr., R2, Cym., The Miser*; **1986:** *LLL, 1H6, Rom.,* *The Gebbar's Opera*; **1987:** *H5, Ado, Ant., Wild Oats*; **1988:** *Lr., Per., Tmp., The Pirates of Penzance*; **1989:** dark; **1990:** *Err.*; **1991:** *AYL, MV*; **1992:** *Mac., TGV*; **1993:** *JC, AWW.*; **1994:** *Oth., MND.*

Research Resources: An extensive informal archive of programs, posters, financial documents, and photographs of the Virginia Shakespeare Festival is housed in the Department of Theatre at William and Mary. See also:

Christopher, Georgia B. "Shakespeare in Virginia." *Shakespeare Quarterly* 31 (1980): 211-12; 33 (1982): 233-34.

Fehrenbach, Robert J. "Virginia Shakespeare Festival." *Shakespeare Quarterly* 30 (1979): 197-200.

Fulton, R. C. "Shakespeare in the Southeast." *Shakespeare Quarterly* 34 (1983): 219-23.

Knapp, Jeanette M. "Virginia Shakespeare Festival." *Shakespeare Quarterly* 35 (1984): 471-74.

Shattuck, Charles. *Shakespeare on the American Stage*. Washington, D.C.: Folger Shakespeare Library, 1976.

Winston, Mathew. "Virginia Shakespeare Festival." *Shakespeare Quarterly* 32 (1981): 211-13.

Site visits and interviews: 19 February and 25-27 July 1992.
Hassell B. Sledd

WASHINGTON

SEATTLE SHAKESPEARE FESTIVAL. MAIL: 1904 Third Avenue, Suite 327, Seattle, WA 98101-1183. SITE: The Playhouse Theatre (formerly the Glenn Hughes Playhouse) in the University District of Seattle just off the campus of the University of Washington. ADMINISTRATION/BOX OFFICE: 206/467-6283. ADMISSION: $12–$15 (1992). SEASON: (1993) two productions in rotating repertory, August through early September; 8:00 p.m., Wed.–Sat.; 7:00 p.m., Sun; 2:00 p.m., Sat.–Sun. PRINCIPAL STAFF: Paul T. Mitri and Terry Edward Moore, co-artistic directors FACILITY: indoor, thrust stage (capacity 250). AUDITIONS: Seattle, late spring. STATUS: Equity SPT 3. ANNUAL BUDGET: $98,000 (1993). ANNUAL ATTENDANCE:

1,500–2,000 (1993). FOUNDED: 1991, Cornelia Duryèe, Jay Johnson, Paul T. Mitri, Terry Edward Moore, Lorre Myers, Doyle Myers, Susan Riddiford.

The first stirrings of a Shakespeare company in Seattle began in the summer of 1989 when Paul Mitri, having completed his M.F.A. degree at the University of Washington, independently produced a modern-dress, ethnically diverse *Romeo and Juliet*. Friends from the community and the university participated in this first production, which ran for eight performances and just broke even. The following summer (1990), Mitri decided to produce *Cymbeline*, borrowing money from friends and using a similar core group of theatre talent by now calling itself "Shakespeare in Seattle." Eventually this project proved too much work for Mitri alone. He gathered six of his friends in the Seattle theatre community, and, after a series of discussions, they together founded the Seattle Shakespeare Festival (SSF) in March 1991.

The founding members, referred to by Mitri as "the gang of seven," included actor/director Terry Edward Moore, actor/director/fight choreographer Mitri, actor/choreographer Cornelia Duryèe, actor Susan Riddiford, designer Jay Johnson, Lorre Myers, and composer Doyle Myers. Together they sought to provide Seattle with a permanent home for Shakespeare, and, in the process, to provide for themselves an opportunity to work with classic English texts and a language-based acting style. *Richard III* (1991), featuring Mitri in the title role, was the inaugural production. *Othello* and two non-Shakespearean productions, *Billy Bishop Goes to War* (a one-man musical comedy featuring Moore) and *When Love Speaks* (a two-hour romantic comedy adapted from Elizabethan love poetry) formed the company's second season in 1992.

Unique to the SSF is its commitment to management by an artistic committee. The commitment was made at the formation of the company (largely at the instigation of Moore) as a type of experiment in non hierarchical management and as a statement of dedication to collaboration and actor empowerment, since several of the committee members are actors. Mitri, who has compared the committee to a marriage, agrees with the basic premise that a more collaborative administration fosters greater collaboration in production. He points out that while committee members do not always agree with every decision, the commitment to consensus has forced committee members not only to see different points of view but also to incorporate divergent opinions within their own artistic philosophical framework. Their commitment to genuine collaboration and consensus has kept their work vital.

The SSF performs in space rented from the University of Washington School of Drama. The Playhouse Theatre, formerly the Glenn Hughes Playhouse, is a 250-seat thrust theatre located in the commercial district near the university campus in the heart of Seattle. The intimacy of the space, which places the actor close to the audience, fosters an immediacy of communication that actors and audience members alike find appealing. The Playhouse is especially effective for productions of Shakespeare, since the thrust approximates the stage configuration of the Elizabethan theatre, focusing on the actor and the language. For the SSF, this has proven a happy coincidence, since language and the actor are the primary focus of their artistic work.

The SSF continues to carve out a niche for itself in a city with a fair number of theatres. Larger theatres like the Seattle Repertory and Intiman, produce Shakespeare plays perhaps once every other season, while the smaller Bathhouse Theatre has proven more consistent, producing at least one Shakespeare play a season. Nonetheless, until the SSF formed, Seattle remained one of the few large metropolitan areas without a Shakespeare festival or company. The SSF hopes that, as the city's only permanent company principally dedicated to producing Shakespeare's plays, it will become the home of Shakespeare in Seattle.

Competition for theatre audiences in Seattle is often keen, and the summer, when the SSF produces its season, is especially competitive. Summer is the only dry season in rainy Seattle. Potential theatregoers are drawn not to the theatre but to outdoor activities. Theatres thus compete not only with each other but with nature as well. In addition, the **Oregon Shakespeare Festival** (OSF) in Ashland, a nine-hour drive away, remains the major destination festival for dedicated Shakespeare playgoers in the Northwest. The SSF, however, has chosen not to compete with the OSF (recognizing perhaps the futility of their "David" going against that "Goliath") but rather offers the Seattle community a "smaller," alternative Shakespeare in a more intimate though urban setting.

The production philosophy of the SSF varies slightly depending on which artistic committee member is asked. The mission statement, however, provides the core philosophy: "to use the power of the spoken word to communicate the great stories of the theatre in accessible productions that are both theatrically innovative and faithful to the text." Seeing two dangerous extremes in an overly precise emphasis on beautiful recitation and in an emotionally indulgent "method" approach, Moore and Duryèe emphasize that their approach lies somewhere between those poles. Textual analysis is always in service to the actor. For example, Moore begins with facsimiles of the published folios, examining aspects such as punctuation, spelling, and capitalization for more suggestive indications of spoken emphasis than modern editions contain. Reading "WARRE," Moore explains, gives an actor more clues to the weight of the word in the text than the modernized "war." (See **Hampshire Shakespeare Company** and **Tygres Heart Shakespeare Company**.)

With slightly different emphases, Mitri hopes to produce Shakespeare for contemporary appreciation. Mitri's approach emphasizes a "stripping away" of layers of acting technique and language to reveal a core of human passion in the characters and in their interactions. In contrast to Moore, whose production style may be called "traditional," Mitri looks to produce experimental productions, challenging audiences with theatrically innovative performances. To date, however, the SSF has been dedicated to producing Shakespeare that features an artistically empowered actor in the text. The SSF hopes to balance its method training with textual scholarship, producing a language-rich theatre that reaches audiences on a personal level. On this the committee finds consensus.

To that end, the SSF's 1992 production of *Othello* combined a keen sense of the language among all company members with a depth of emotion stirred by the intimacy of the tragedy. With an opening dumb show that represented Brabantio's prophetic dream of Desdemona's elopement, the tragedy was framed at the beginning and at the end by bedroom scenes, emphasizing the human intimacy of the drama. Anthony Lee as Othello was perhaps slightly lacking when called on to portray the public figure, but he achieved a powerful sensuality when presenting the private man. Mitri as Iago portrayed a man who, as he put it, could be anyone's best friend. Passing over an interpretation that would more obviously display the conniving soldier, Mitri's Iago was a solid, rather blunt individual, more reminiscent of a favorite dog gone rabid than a spidery figure weaving a complex web. Riddiford, like Mitri, a member of the artistic committee, played a Desdemona who matched the sensuality of Lee's Othello. Riddiford gave Desdemona an unusual strength and independence, creating the implication that her strong will provided a greater threat to Othello than did the rumors of infidelity. With the exception of the opening moments, the production proved faithful to the text, which was, in the spirit of the company philosophy, featured to advantage.

The scenery consisted of a small unit set of platforms and beams fashioned together to offer a complex variety of levels and interior spaces. Controlled by the actors, who rotated it for scene changes, the set provided a space on, around, and in which the actors could perform. In addition, by moving the set themselves, the actors actively controlled the space of the performance. Challenged to convey the sense of historical time and space, since the scenery was minimal, Sherry Lyon designed costumes that gave a strong sense of Elizabethan fashion without losing the contemporary actor underneath. The SSF as a producing organization fits well into the theatrical topography of Seattle. The group's dedication to the actor and the text provides Seattle audiences with a place to see and hear Shakespeare performed as language-rich human drama.

Production History: 1991: *R3*; **1992**: *Oth., Billy Bishop Goes to War, When Love Speaks*; **1993**: *Ado, MM*; **1994**: *Shr., When Loves Speaks*.

Research Resources: Records are informally maintained by the Seattle Shakespeare Festival directors.

Site visit and interviews: Terry Moore and Cornelia Duryèe, 27 August 1992, and Paul Mitri, 5 September 1992.
David V. Schultz

WASHINGTON SHAKESPEARE FESTIVAL (Puget Sound Theatre Ensemble). MAIL: Puget Sound Theatre Ensemble, P.O. Box 1501, Olympia, WA 98507. SITE: Washington Center for the Performing Arts, Olympia. ADMINISTRATION OFFICE: 206/943-9492. ADMISSION: (1994) $10–$12. SEASON: two productions in alternating repertory, three weeks in August; 8:00 p.m., Tues.–Sat.; 2:00 p.m.. PRINCIPAL STAFF: James A. Van Leishout, artistic director. FACILITY: flexible space (capacity 125). AUDITIONS: Olympia, mid-May. STATUS: non-Equity. BUDGET: $45,000 (1994). ANNUAL ATTENDANCE: 2,000 (1994). FOUNDED: 1985, Capitol Repertory Theatre.

The first Washington Shakespeare Festival (WSF) originated in 1985 with an Olympia theatre group, the Capitol Repertory Theatre. James A. Van Leishout was hired to direct the first production, *Twelfth Night*, and was appointed artistic director of the company. Capitol Repertory experienced administrative difficulties that first year, however, and the company folded. A new organization, Capitol Playhouse 24, took over the festival in 1986 and produced the second season. Under the management of Capitol Playhouse 24, many of the ancillary festival programs initiated by Capitol Repertory were dropped, so that, by 1988, the festival consisted solely of one Shakespeare production—*Macbeth*. In the fall of 1988, Capitol Playhouse 24 announced that it would drop the festival from its production schedule. A new theatre company promptly organized to continue it. Calling itself the Puget Sound Theatre Ensemble, this group, which included Van Leishout, produced the Shakespeare festival in the summer and a separate season of productions during the rest of the year. In 1989, the ensemble gradually expanded the ancillary festival programs. In 1990, for example, the festival began what has proven to be one of its most popular programs, the Renaissance Fair. Concomitantly organized with the Society for Creative Anachronism, the fair is a single-day event held in a nearby city park in downtown Olympia. In 1991, a sonnet-writing contest was conceived for regional poets, and, in 1992, a second play was added to the season. In addition, the festival arranges with the Olympia Film Society to present a Shakespeare film series complementing the staged productions. In 1992, Orson Welles' *Othello* and *Macbeth* and Derek Jarman's *The Tempest* and *Angelic Conversations* were featured. The festival is becoming a significant event in the cultural life of Olympia.

Van Leishout works with approximately 50 volunteers who are organized into various committees that run the many components of the festival. These include the fair, the productions, and various educational events. The committee heads form the Shakespeare committee, which oversees the administrative duties. The non-professional company members come largely from local colleges around western Washington and the Puget Sound region. All the members of the organization, with the exception of Van Leishout, volunteer their services, attesting to the support the festival receives from the community. While the WSF remains primarily a local event for the residents of Olympia and nearby towns, artistic director Van Leishout hopes to increase the festival's reach and size, making the festival attractive to tourists visiting the Pacific Northwest.

The principal goal of the WSF is to make the plays understandable and enjoyable to the broadest possible audience. Van Leishout tries to approach the plays from the freshest possible perspective, attempting to treat each play as if it had never been produced before, although he realizes that this is an impossible ideal. The plays are selected to maximize their popular appeal, and cutting is executed for the sake of clarity of language and story. Van Leishout prefers scenic minimalism, using a virtually bare stage on which the language paints the specific setting or locale. While he is occasionally willing to offer conceptual productions, such as a version of *The Taming of the Shrew* staged as a Russian fairy tale, his chief interests as a director lie in emphasizing dramatic structure and language.

In 1992, the WSF featured productions of *A Midsummer Night's Dream* and *Romeo and Juliet*. Performed in the Washington Center for the Performing Arts, a 1,000-seat road house (an impressive but oversized facility for WSF), *Midsummer Night's Dream* proved a lively, if somewhat unsophisticated, production. Director Eve Hilgenberg, mounting her first noncollege production, chose to discover an "elemental" aspect to the comedy, offering Celtic shadings in the music and in her interpretation of the fairies. The set consisted of a series of stone archways (which doubled as the basic architectural feature of *Romeo and Juliet* with a few modifications), enhanced by groups of branches in front to suggest a woodsy or forest environment. Behind the arches, the stage sloped rather steeply, offering a greater use of the floor space as well as emphasizing the theatricality of the performance. The stage was washed in bold colors such as fuchsia and green to create an eerie, unearthly glow throughout. Costumes were vaguely Elizabethan for the mortals, while the fairies were dressed in body suits of various colors (peach, blue, or black) with lightweight fabric capes that flowed as the fairies moved expressively.

The acting of the young cast was occasionally uneven, mostly due to the actors' lack of experience rather than ability. Most, however, had a decent grasp of the language. Van Leishout gave a rollicking performance as Bottom, especially as the self-important mechanical ass, spouting his text with gusto at center stage. The fairies were an ever-present element as they mingled with the other characters, sometimes providing background forest noises, and at other times functioning as mysterious scenic elements, presumably trees, rocks, shrubs, and so on. On occasion, the fairies' movement about the stage had the unfortunate effect of crowding the space and distracting from the main focus. The WSF provides an excellent training ground for the first-time performer or director of Shakespeare; while enjoyable, however, the performances may as a consequence show signs of inexperience.

Production History: **1985**: *TN*; **1986**: *MND*; **1987**: *Rom., Shr.*; **1988**: *Mac.*; **1989**: *Tmp.*; **1990**: *Oth.*; **1991**: *Shr.*; **1992**: *MND, Rom.*; **1993**: *AYL, Lr.*; **1994**: *Wiv., Mac.*

Research Resources: Archives for the Washington Shakespeare Festival are informally maintained at the Puget Sound Theatre Ensemble administrative office.

Site visit and interview: 22 August, 1992.
David V. Schulz

WISCONSIN

AMERICAN PLAYERS THEATRE. MAIL: P.O. BOX 819, Spring Green, WI 53588. SITE: between Spring Green and Taliesin/House on the Rock. ADMINISTRATION: 608/588-7401. BOX OFFICE: 608/588-2361. ADMISSION: $1–$24. SEASON: four productions in rotating repertory, late June to early October; 7:30 p.m., Tues.–Thurs.; 8:00 p.m., Fri.–Sat.; 3:00 p.m., Sat.; 6:00 p.m., Sun. PRINCIPAL STAFF: David Frank, artistic director: Kay Long, associate artistic director. FACILITY: outdoor stage and amphitheatre (capacity 900). ANNUAL BUDGET: $1.8 million (1993). ANNUAL ATTENDANCE: 70,000 + (1993). FOUNDED: 1979, Randall Duk Kim, Anne Occhiogrosso, Charles J. Bright.

Abandoning successful theatre careers in New York and Washington, three friends decided in 1977 to dedicate themselves to producing the classics in a natural setting somewhere else in America. Over the next two years, they considered approximately 200 locations and finally chose an abandoned 71-acre dairy farm in the hills above the Wisconsin River, near the small Wisconsin farming community of Spring Green (population, 1,200). Located less than a mile from Frank Lloyd Wright's Taliesin home, American Players Theatre (APT) presented its first season in 1980, drawing theatregoers from Chicago (over a three-hour drive), Milwaukee (two hours), and Madison (45 minutes). The presence of the architects at Taliesin was a factor in the site selection. APT founder Randall Duk Kim reminisced in 1987 that "this area set Frank Lloyd Wright's standard for what is beautiful. The hills and woods are so tranquil here. And the presence of the Taliesin architects stimulates us. The kinship with them has been comforting, because the struggle has been very difficult."

The renowned Hawaiian actor Randall Duk Kim had been performing professionally since 1960 in New York and regional theatres; he served as APT's artistic director until 1991. Cofounder Anne Occhiogrosso became literary manager, as well as acting and directing for the company. Charles J.

Bright, former director of sales and promotion at the John F. Kennedy Center and the National Theatre in Washington, D.C., joined the Wisconsin venture as cofounder and managing director. In preparation for APT's opening season, Kim toured a one-man show around the Midwest. With 6,300 hours of volunteer labor, the facilities were readied; the farmhouse was converted into administrative offices and the barn into rehearsal and workshop space, while a 700-seat amphitheatre complete with control booth and dressing rooms, was built in a natural bowl on a hilltop. The Elizabethan-style thrust stage nestles idyllically before an endless vista of foliage. Additional seating installed in 1992 brought the theatre's capacity to 900.

After arriving at APT by chartered bus or car (one sometimes sees tractors in the parking lot also), the theatregoer must climb a winding uphill footpath through the trees to arrive at the amphitheatre on the other side of the hill. "People tend to think that art happens only in cities," says Kim. "But why can't it come from where the beauty is? To me, poetry and nature go hand in hand." Although the locals initially appeared skeptical about the prospect of Shakespeare in their backyard, the first season won them over and, reportedly, the favored Christmas gifts that year were editions of Shakespeare. After a performance of *Comedy of Errors* in 1987, a burly, plaid-shirted gentleman was overheard to remark; "It's funny every time we see it."

APT grew steadily over its first six seasons. The souvenir programs were beautifully produced, glossy, 48-page booklets full of color photographs and substantial text, including an essay on the area's wildflowers. Kim established a policy of producing only uncut versions of the plays in the all-classic repertoire. He has commented: "In order to know the plays, I want to be able to play the music whole. I don't want to miss a note of it. I want to know where the transitions are, how a character goes from one moment to the next. With a cut script, I wouldn't get close enough to what the playwright had in mind." After several seasons devoted exclusively to Shakespeare, Kim began to explore Chekhov's plays, beginning with a bill of one-acts and moving to full-length plays in subsequent seasons. The seasonal staff of over 100 professional artists has included such exceptional actors as Theodore Swetz, Stephen Hemming, and Lee E. Ernst. Performances are further enhanced by live musicians performing original music.

Although APT reaped a Tony nomination in 1985, it was facing a $700,000 debt that threatened to cancel the 1987 season. Governor Anthony Earl called a meeting of business and government leaders, which resulted in the offer of a $750,000 low-interest loan from the state, provided that the theatre could raise matching funds. The immediate community and all of southern Wisconsin pitched in to save the festival. The 18-week season proceeded as scheduled. Indeed, it was in 1987 that APT brought in its first guest directors, Phoebe Brand and Morris Carnovsky, to stage the full-length *Ivanov*. Kim had seen Carnovsky play Shylock and Malvolio in the early 1960s at the **American Shakespeare Theatre** in Stratford, Connecticut, and recalled that "the truth and beauty he brought to Shylock was like a light at the end of a tunnel. The memory of his Shylock guided me in all the Shakespearean roles I've done, to try to find the feelings, and what's genuine, what's real, the passions as well as the thought, the action, the story." Carnovsky and Brand returned in 1989 to direct *King Lear*.

The financial worries took a toll on Kim, however. "I know there's a cutoff time for me. I long for Mother Ocean," he told Jacob Stockinger, referring to his native Hawaii. Nonetheless, he stayed with APT long enough to see it well stabilized before going to join the Honolulu Youth Theatre. In 1991, the board of directors announced that, after an extensive national search, David Frank had been hired as artistic director.

Five productions that I attended during the 1987 season provided a representative sampling of APT's strengths: verbal clarity, sumptuous costuming, and a company skilled at playing a range of styles. Sandra Riegel-Ernst and Fred Ollerman directed *Twelfth Night* for uncluttered story values. In the absence of physical comedy (even the below-stairs drinking party seemed terribly sober), the verbal comedy scored well, and the responsive audience found often overlooked humor in the spoken lines. *The Comedy of Errors*, a perennial favorite with APT audiences, was full of clever stage business and hilarious horseplay to match the wildly stylized costumes and masks; Ted Swetz was the inventive director of the fast-paced action. *The School for Scandal*, directed by Jewell Walker, brilliantly captured the visual and verbal period style in the exchanges of civilities, the handling of wigs and props, and even the scene changes. The production blended opulent design elements and comedy to perfection. In *Ivanov*, Kim played the title role as one vitiated by life, and yet he held the stage amidst the energy and bustle of the others. The production abounded with inventive details evoking the vulgarity and pretentiousness of the characters.

A matinee performance of *Hamlet* on 1 August elicited laughs early in the play with lines like "Tis bitter cold" and "I am too much in the sun," but the audience remained rapt throughout the four-hour performance under a cloudless sky. With the temperature over 100° F on stage, a precurtain announcement explained that the actors would not be wearing as many layers of costume as usual. Kim delivered Hamlet's soliloquies from center stage, without blocking or gestural embellishment, but giving full value to every word. The character had become quite overwrought by the time he was sent to England, but, on his return, he had pulled himself together to start afresh; the "readiness" was apparent. Hamlet died sitting up in Gertrude's throne, delivering his last line with his head back, looking up at the sky. Although the scene was set inside the palace, the attitude seemed to unify the story and the outdoor setting, as if one were in the presence of a soul rising to heaven.

Production History: 1980: *MND, Tit.*; **1981**: *Jn., Err., TGV, MND,* *Tit.*; **1982**: *Rom., Tit., Err.*; **1983**: *Shr., TGV, MND*; **1984**: *Rom.,*

Tamburlaine the Great, Part I, LLL, Shr., MND, The Twin Menaechmi; **1985**: *Err., JC, MV, Wiv.*, 3 Chekhov one-acts; **1986**: *Ham.*, 3 Chekhov one-acts, *MV, Wiv., Err.*, 3 Chekhov one-acts (different bill); **1987**: *Ham., Wiv., Err., TN, The School for Scandal, Ivanov*; **1988**: *MND, Tmp., TN, The Seagull*; **1989**: *MND, Lr.*,

Oedipus Rex, The Comedy of Asses; **1990**: *Mac., Tmp., The Proposal, Et Cetera!, An Enemy of the People*; **1991**: *Tartuffe, WT, An Enemy of the People, Err., MND*; **1992**: *MND, Oth., Ado, Our Town*; **1993**: *MV, Shr., 1H4*; **1994**: *Ham., AYL, The Learned Ladies, The Beaux' Stratagem.*

Research Resources:

Kimbrough, Robert. "Shakespeare in Wisconsin." *Shakespeare Quarterly* (1985): 349-53.

Londré, Felicia. "Kim Champions Classics in Nature's Setting." *American Theatre* (November 1987): 45-46.

Slack, Steve. "Zounds! Shakespeare Wows 'em in the Wisconsin Woods." *Midwest Living* (August 1987): 42-45.

Stockinger, Jacob. "Kim ponders past, future; sets stage to leave APT." [Madison] *Capital Times* (15 May 1987): 35-36.

Vukelich, George . "Theater in the Wild." *Milwaukee* (June 1986): 25-28.

Site visits: 31 July, 1–2, 8 August 1987; interview: 2 August 1987.
Felicia Hardison Londré

WISCONSIN SHAKESPEARE FESTIVAL. MAIL: University of Wisconsin–Platteville, 1 University Plaza, Platteville, WI 53818-3099. SITE: Center for the Arts, UW–Platteville. BOX OFFICE: 608/342-1298. ADMISSION: individual tickets, $7–$15; subscriptions, $18–$42. SEASON: approximately 40 performances, rotating repertory, early July–mid-August; 8:00 p.m.; 2:00 p.m., Wed. and Sun. PRINCIPAL STAFF: Thomas P. Collins, artistic director; Thomas S. Goltry, associate director; Wendy W. Collins, costume designer. FACILITY: thrust stage (capacity 242). AUDITIONS: local and at selected universities, January–March. STATUS: non-Equity. ANNUAL BUDGET: $118,000. ANNUAL ATTENDANCE: 7,000. FOUNDED: 1976, Thomas P. Collins, Thomas S. Goltry.

The Wisconsin Shakespeare Festival (WSF) presented its initial season in 1977, making it the oldest professional Shakespeare festival in the Midwest. The origins of the festival can be traced to the Summer Love Repertory Theatre, a professional theatre company associated with the University of Wisconsin–Platteville, which for several years in the early 1970s included in its repertory one Shakespeare comedy each season. Cofounder and current artistic director

Tom Collins marveled at the positive response by patrons to the Shakespeare offering. Therefore, along with his wife, Wendy, and fellow theatre professor and director at the university, Tom Goltry, he began in the early 1970s to explore ways to start a summer Shakespeare festival in Platteville, similar in scope and design to the **Oregon Shakespeare Festival** in Ashland. Thanks to the encouragement of UW-Platteville's chancellor, the organizers drew up a budget and began incorporation in 1976.

Plays for the first year included *As You Like It* and *A Midsummer Night's Dream*, produced in the present format of three plays in repertory performed over about a six-week period in mid-summer. The budget for the first year was approximately $25,000, and actors were hired from graduate and undergraduate university theatre programs throughout the country as well as locally. Although no Equity actors were hired initially, all performers were paid. Performances were held in the university auditorium on a traditional proscenium stage on which was constructed a semblance of the original Globe Theatre, including inner-below and upper-above playing areas. According to Collins, "the first season was a risk, with no assurance of audience acceptance, but response was overwhelmingly positive even without the comforts of air-conditioning." It was clear to cofounders Collins and Goltry that there was an audience for a summer season of Shakespeare in the southeastern Wisconsin area.

In 1983, the WSF received a new home on the Platteville campus. Due in part to the success of the festival, a new center for the performing arts was built, complete with a small 254-seat studio theatre where the festival plays are currently performed. The stage is a rectangular thrust jutting out about 30 feet to the first row of seats with a balcony on either side. The audience on the ground level sits entirely in front of the action. In past years, an upper-above playing area has been incorporated onto the basic thrust in a typical Elizabethan format. For 1991, the stage was one level with a tapestry design on the back wall. According to Collins, future goals include the duplication of an Elizabethan theatre similar in scope and design to the New Swan Theatre in Stratford-upon-Avon, with elaborate woodwork, balconies, and railings.

Since its inception in 1977, the WSF has not maintained strict adherence to the Shakespeare canon. Interestingly, productions of *The School for Scandal* in 1983, *Ah, Wilderness!* in 1984, and *Tartuffe* in 1985 proved less popular with theatergoers than any of Shakespeare's plays. Thus, since 1985, only Shakespeare's plays have been produced.

The organizational structure of the WSF is simple. The University of Wisconsin-Platteville is the controlling body for the festival. The artistic director, answerable to the vice-chancellor of the university, is the driving force behind the festival and is in charge of all administrative duties as well as artistic decisions. There is no business manager or administrative director. The board of advisers meets twice a year and is strictly an advisory board, consulting on matters such as public relations, fund-raising, and marketing.

Tom Collins, who is the festival's first and only artistic director, has directed at least one play each season. Associate director Tom Goltry has directed 14 plays since the festival's inception in 1977, and Wendy Collins has costumed all but three of the productions. In 1979, a guest director position was created.

Since the festival is a function of the university, the school provides the salaries for the resident staff of three as well as building costs, maintenance, and utilities. The WSF operates on an annual budget of from $103,000 to $118,000, depending on the size and complexity of the season. Approximately 53 percent of the budget is covered by box office receipts. A Christmas mailing campaign soliciting contributions brings in another 20 percent. A student activity fee and the interest from an endowment fund are responsible for another 12 to 13 percent of the budget revenues. Sales of souvenir programs, receipts from a university theatre organization, program sales, and gifts and grants from local businesses round out the remaining sources of income. State grants have supplied small amounts of funding through the years but are not a significant factor in the overall budgetary picture.

The WSF attracts the majority of its audience from the southern half of Wisconsin, the eastern one-third of Iowa, and the northwestern one-third of Illinois. Approximately 33 to 37 percent of patrons are from Platteville, 12 percent from Dubuque, Iowa, and 5 percent travel the 60 miles from Madison, Wisconsin. The festival's average patron is over 40 years of age, a statistic that concerns Collins. Attendance has averaged between 80 to 85 percent of capacity. The WSF usually presents two comedies and a tragedy in a season. Only three history plays have been produced: *Richard II*, *Richard III*, and *Henry IV, Part 1*.

The acting company for the WSF consists primarily of young actors currently enrolled or recently graduated from professional actor-training programs. In recent years, Collins has recruited heavily for his company (which numbers 20 to 25 actors) from M.F.A. training programs at the University of Delaware, the University of Seattle, and the North Carolina School of the Arts. The festival does send out an audition notice to many theatre programs, and auditions can be informally arranged in Platteville. Collins employs one or two actors on Equity Guest Artist contracts each year.

Actors are paid for the nine-week season, at rates ranging from $2,000 for major roles, $1,500 for supporting roles, and $1,400 for what Collins calls the apprentice level—those who are cast in smaller roles and assist in various technical capacities. With few exceptions, most roles are distributed after the company is assembled. Housing is not provided, but low-cost housing is available nearby. Travel expenses are the responsibility of the actor. The company rehearses six days a week in two, four, and one-half hour sessions with Mondays off. The first production opens at the end of the fourth week. In the middle of the fifth week, the second play enters production, and, by the end of the fifth week, the third play joins the repertory.

Although plays were more traditionally produced in the early years of the festival, Collins experimented in 1986 with a modern-dress version of *Hamlet*. Spurred by its success, he now encourages diversity in production concepts. "If people are coming to see the festival, then we ought treat them with visual variety." Collins admits that the texts are cut to keep the productions at a length that will be enjoyable to the audience.

The WSF is a nonprofit organization that, according to Collins, has as its primary purpose "to keep Shakespeare alive to audiences, to make it meaningful to our time, to provide excellent professional entertainment, but also to serve an educational function as well." Besides his dream of a theatre structure modeled after Stratford's New Swan, Collins would like to consider the potential for educational outreach programs in conjunction with the festival.

In viewing the 1991 repertory of *Hamlet, As You Like It,* and *Measure for Measure,* I found that the WSF places less emphasis on spectacle and overall grandeur than many festivals. The theatre is small (capacity 242), and set design is usually limited to a tapestry or backdrop on the back wall, with one or two facades to suggest locale or atmosphere. This is, as Peter Brook would say, indeed an "empty space." The productions were well cast and the performances uniformly strong, so that one left the small studio theatre with a sense of satisfaction at a good evening's entertainment.

Hamlet, directed by Michael Duncan, had few "bells and whistles," and Equity guest artist, Lee Ernst, was definitely not a Hamlet who suffered from lack of motivation or concerns about his own inadequacies. He totally controlled Ophelia as well as his adversarial peers, Rosencrantz and Guildenstern. Hamlet was so sure of himself that one lost any sense of indecisiveness. The result was a production that was exciting on one basic level—that of a revenge tragedy.

As You Like It, directed by Tom Collins, opened with a scene set in London in the 1850s, with street beggars hovering around a pot warmer on a cold, snowy evening. The montage was effective in introducing the opening scene between Orlando, played convincingly by Robert Tyree, and old Adam. It also provided a dynamic contrast to the forest scenes. The costumes by Wendy Collins and an interesting facade that rotated 180 degrees to transport the audience from the back streets of city life to the forest of Arden were instrumental in making this well-paced production a delightful interpretation of *As You Like It.*

Thomas Goltry's concept for *Measure for Measure* was a "rehearsal" interpretation, with actors garbed in suggestive contemporary costumes and with stage scaffolding providing various set pieces such as Claudio's cell. Often actors sat on bare metal chairs and viewed the production along with the audience. Lee Ernst was sincere in his portrayal of the self-deceived Angelo, and Elizabeth Heflin portrayed an honest and compassionate Isabella. Cynthia Hood's "hooker" interpretation of Mistress Overdone and Tom Laughlin's

Pompey provided much-needed relief from the rhetorical dialogue that accentuated much of this unembellished production.

Production History: 1977: *AYL, Ham., MND*; **1978**: *Mac., Shr., MV*; **1979**: *R3, Wiv.*; **1980**: *Ado, MM, Rom.*; **1981**: *Oth., Err., LLL*; **1982**: *AWW, MV, Tmp.*; **1983**: *The School for Scandal, Lr., MND*; **1984**: *TGV, R2, Ah Wilderness!*; **1985**: *Tartuffe, Ham., Shr.*; **1986**: *TN, AYL, Mac.*; **1987**: *WT, Wiv., Ado*, **1988**: *MND, Rom., Ant.*; **1989**: *JC, Err., 1H4*; **1990**: *LLL, MND, Oth.*, **1991**: *Ham., AYL, MM*; **1994**: *The Three Musketeers, H5, Ado.*

Research Resources: Archives for the Wisconsin Shakespeare Festival are informally maintained at the university office.

Site visit and interview: early August 1991.
Alan Klem

1. Monica Bell and Ray Chambers in the 1990 Alabama Shakespeare Festival production of *Twelfth Night*. Photo by Scarsbrook/ASF.

2. Demolition of the original 1935 Old Globe Theatre, San Diego, destroyed by arson in 1978. Photo courtesy Old Globe Theatre.

3. Current Old Globe Theatre, San Diego. Photo courtesy Old Globe Theatre.

4. Auditorium, Old Globe Theatre, San Diego. Photo courtesy Old Globe Theatre.

5. Rehearsal of *Romeo and Juliet*, 1980, Festival Stage, Old Globe Theatre, San Diego. Photo courtesy Old Globe Theatre.

6. Reduced Shakespeare Company, Los Angeles. Publicity photo courtesy Reduced Shakespeare Company.

7. André Braugher as Iago and Avery Brooks as Othello, 1991, Shakespeare Theatre, Washington, D.C. Photo courtesy Shakespeare Theatre.

8. Tom Hulce as Hamlet, directed by Michael Kahn, 1993, Shakespeare Theatre, Washington, D.C. Photo by Joan Marcus, courtesy Shakespeare Theatre.

9. Carter Barron Amphitheater in Rock Creek Park, Shakespeare Theatre, Washington, D.C. Photo courtesy The Shakespeare Theatre.

10. Orlando Shakespeare Festival's 1992 production of *A Midsummer Night's Dream*, directed by Robert Hall, featured modern-day lovers and a semi-surrealistic, live-action forest. Photo by Michael Glantz, courtesy Orlando Shakespeare Festival.

11. John Ammerman and Masked Revelers in *The Comedy of Errors,* 1989–90, Georgia Shakespeare Festival. Photo by Helen DeRamus, courtesy Georgia Shakespeare Festival.

12. Triney Sandoval as Romeo and Mhari Sandoval as Juliet, 1992, Idaho Shakespeare Festival. Photo by David Bogie, courtesy Idaho Shakespeare Festival.

13. A scene from A *Midsummer Night's Dream*, Oak Park Festival Theatre, Oak Park, Illinois. Photo courtesy Oak Park Festival Theatre.

14. Timothy Thilleman as Dogberry and watch members (from left: Mick Cain, Christopher Miller, and Ashley Hugen) in *Much Ado About Nothing*, 1993, Shakespeare on the Green, Lake Forest, Illinois. Photo courtesy Shakespeare on the Green.

15. *Much Ado About Nothing*, with (from left) Jonathan F. McClain, Thomas Patrick, Seth Jacobs, and Michael Drennan, 1993, Shakespeare on the Green, Lake Forest, Illinois. Photo courtesy Shakespeare on the Green.

16. Greg Allen Williams, Jeanette Schwaba, and Bruce A. Young in Shakespeare Repertory's 1987 production of *Troilus and Cressida*, Chicago, Illinois. Photo by Jennifer Girard, courtesy Shakespeare Repertory.

17. *Taming of the Shrew*, directed by Curt L. Toffeland, 1990, Kentucky Shakespeare Festival, Louisville. Photo courtesy Kentucky Shakespeare Festival.

18. Theatre at Monmouth, Monmouth, Maine. Photo courtesy Theatre at Monmouth.

19. Christopher J. Guilmet as Lorenzo and Cate Damon as Jessica in *The Merchant of Venice*, 1990, Theatre at Monmouth, Monmouth, Maine. Photo by Maura Smith, courtesy Theatre at Monmouth.

20. *Romeo and Juliet*, Shakespeare on Wheels, 1986, Baltimore, Maryland. Photo courtesy Shakespeare on Wheels.

21. Jonathan Croy as Sir Andrew Aguecheek, Julie Nelson as Fabian, Malcolm Ingram as Sir Toby Belch, and Karen MacDonald as Maria in *Twelfth Night*, 1991, Shakespeare & Company. The Mount, Lenox, Massachusetts. Photo by Richard Bambery, courtesy Shakespeare & Company.

22. *Macbeth*, directed by Cindy Phaneuf, set by Steve Wheeldon, 1990, Nebraska Shakespeare Festival, Omaha, Nebraska. Photo courtesy Nebraska Shakespeare Festival.

23. Charles Carroll as Falstaff and Douglas Paterson as Bardolph in *Merry Wives of Windsor*, directed by Alan Klem, costumes by Kathleen Gossman, set by Steve Wheeldon, 1990, Nebraska Shakespeare Festival, Omaha, Nebraska. Photo courtesy Nebraska Shakespeare Festival.

24. Christina Haag as Princess of France, Enid Graham as Lady Maria, and Melissa Bowen as Lady Rosaline in *Love's Labour's Lost*, 1993, Theatre for a New Audience, New York. Photo by Gerry Goodstein, courtesy Theatre for a New Audience.

25. The 1,200-seat Allen pavilion of the Elizabethan Theatre, shown during a performance of *Othello*, 1992, Oregon Shakespeare Festival, Ashland. Photo by Christopher Briscoe, courtesy Oregon Shakespeare Festival.

26. The courtyard of the Oregon Shakespeare Festival in Ashland Oregon. Pictured are the Allen Pavilion of the Elizabethan Theatre (left) and the Angus Bowmer Theatre (right). The courtyard, fondly referred to as "the bricks," is a gathering place for theatregoers, Ashland visitors, and the local community. Photo by Christopher Briscoe, courtesy Oregon Shakespeare Festival.

27. Mark Woollett as King John and Sean T. Parker as Philip, the Bastard, in *King John*, 1991, Tygres Heart Shakespeare Company, Portland, Oregon. Photo courtesy Tygres Heart Shakespeare Company.

28. Robert Martini as Antipholus and Ellen Newmann as Adriana in *Comedy of Errors*, directed by James Christy, 1991, Three Rivers Shakespeare Festival, Pittsburgh, Pennsylvania. Photo courtesy Three Rivers Shakespeare Festival.

29. William Conley as Puck in *A Midsummer Night's Dream*, 1991, Westerly Shakespeare in the Park, Newport, Rhode Island. Photo courtesy Westerly Shakespeare in the Park.

30. Melissa Chalsma as Olivia and Melanie van Betten as Viola in *Twelfth Night*, directed by David Hammond, scenic design by John Iacovelli, costume design by McKay Coble, 1991, Utah Shakespearean Festival, at Cedar City. Photo courtesy Utah Shakespearean Festival.

31. Adams Memorial Shakespearean Theatre, dedicated 1977, Utah Shakespearean Festival, Cedar City, Utah. Photo courtesy Utah Shakespearean Festival.

32. Stuart Hughes as Lord Talbot, surrounded by members of the company, in *Henry 06*, directed by Peter Hinton, set and costume design by John Ferguson, choreography by Denise Clarke, 1992, Dream in High Park, Toronto, Canada. Photo courtesy The Canadian Stage Company.

33. Cara Kelly, Sarah-Jane Fenton, Daniel Flynn, and Ben Miles in *The Winter's Tale*, directed by David Thacker, 1991, The Young Vic, London, England. Photo by Gordon Rainsford, courtesy The Young Vic.

34. From left: Thomas Sarbacher as Margaret Page, Norbert Kentrup as Sir John Falstaff, Renato Günig as Quickly, Erik Rossbander as Anne Page, and Christian Dieterle as Alice Fluth [Ford] in an all-male *The Merry Wives of Windsor*, 1991, Bremer Shakespeare Company, Bremen, Germany. Photo by Bärbel Emde, courtesy Bremer Shakespeare Company.

35. Actors Redl and Schäfer in Michael Bogdanov's *Hamlet*, 1989, Deutsches Schauspielhaus, Hamburg. Photo courtesy Deutsches Schauspielhaus, Hamburg, Germany.

International Companies and Festivals

AUSTRALIA

BELL SHAKESPEARE COMPANY. MAIL: P.O. Box 10, Miller's Point, Sydney, Australia. SITE: varies (touring company). ADMINISTRATION: 61-2-241-2722; Fax: 61-2-241-4643. ADMISSION: varies with venue. SEASON: irregular, rehearsals and touring occupy approximately nine months per year. PRINCIPAL STAFF: John Bell, artistic director; Virginia Henderson, board chairperson; Craig Hassall, general manager; Jane Tavener, administrative coordinator. FACILITY: no permanent facility (began performing in a circus tent for 1991, now use standard end-stage theatres). AUDITIONS: by arrangement. STATUS: professional. ANNUAL BUDGET: $2.5 million Australian (1993). ANNUAL ATTENDANCE: 70,000 (1992). FOUNDED: 1990, John Bell, Tony Gilbert.

The Bell Shakespeare Company (BSC) was founded by and is based around John Bell, one of Australia's best-known classical actors and directors. After a period in England with the **Royal Shakespeare Company** in the mid-1960s, Bell returned to Australia where he cofounded the Nimrod Theatre in Sydney in 1970. His work at the Nimrod included a number of highly popular Shakespeare plays that were directed and performed in a distinctively Australian style. During much of the 1970s, the Nimrod was arguably the most influential and innovative theatre in Australia. It closed in 1987, two years after Bell's departure.

In 1990, Bell and Tony Gilbert founded the BSC with the express goal of creating a repertory, touring, ensemble company of predominantly young actors, aiming at "the re-interpretation at the highest possible standard of the Shakespeare for Australian audiences." The company was established under the aegis of the Australian Elizabethan Theatre Trust.

One of the reasons for choosing a repertory structure was to give the company of younger actors the chance to deepen their craft through repeated performances of Shakespeare's plays over a long period. Whenever a production is revived for a new tour, it is thoroughly re-rehearsed, giving the actors the opportunity to explore and reinvent their performances further. Touring is important in a country with a relatively small population like Australia, if a theatre company is to operate for a sufficient part of the year to give the actors financial security and continuity. The ensemble nature of the company is of particular importance to Bell who, from the period of the Nimrod Theatre onward, has shown a preference for this approach to directing.

The BSC's first two productions, both in 1991, were *Hamlet*, directed by John Bell, and *The Merchant of Venice*, with Bell as Shylock in a company of 12 full-time actors. These plays were performed in-the-round in a circus tent in Sydney, Canberra, and Melbourne, but the tour was aborted because of the financial collapse of the BSC's umbrella funding organization, the Australian Elizabethan Theatre Trust. BSC disbanded temporarily and regrouped in 1992.

Abandoning the idea of the tent theatre in favor of a more conventional proscenium-arch stage, the company revived and reworked the two earlier productions, the company having been expanded to 16 actors, and added *Richard III* with Bell directing and playing the title role. The 1992 season opened in the Lyric Theatre in Brisbane and toured Newcastle, Sydney, Canberra, and Melbourne. For the 1993 season, *The Merchant of Venice* was dropped from the repertoire and a new production of *Romeo and Juliet* was added. The production opened in the Theatre Royal, Sydney, the three productions toured to Melbourne, Adelaide, and Canberra during 1993. The 1994 season toured productions of *Macbeth* and *The Taming of the Shrew*.

Production History: **1991**: *Ham., MV*; **1992**: *Ham., MV, R3*; **1993**: *Ham., R3, Rom.*; **1994**: *Mac., Shr.*

Research Resources: Records are informally maintained at the Bell Shakespeare Company administration site. Adrian Kiernander is preparing a biography of John Bell.

Adrian Kiernander

GRIN AND TONIC THEATRE TROUPE. MAIL: 146 Bonney Avenue, Clayfield, Queensland, 4011 Australia. SITE: touring, various. ADMINISTRATION: 61-07-262-8537 PRINCIPAL STAFF: Bryan Nason, artistic director; Scott Maidment, administrator. AUDITIONS: local, as needed. STATUS: professional. ANNUAL BUDGET: n/a. ANNUAL ATTENDANCE: n/a. FOUNDED: 1974, Bryan Nason.

The **Grin and Tonic Theatre Troupe** (GTT) is a small, professional company specializing in producing Shakespeare for Australian schools. The

GTT had its origins in a more ambitious semiprofessional group called the College Players, also founded by Bryan Nason, which staged his productions of Shakespeare beginning with *The Tempest* in 1965 and including a remarkable *Hamlet* in a boxing ring at a rock-music centre in 1967. The College Players undertook an ambitious pattern of barnstorming train tours along the Queensland coast, combining public performances with a commitment to audience development in schools, and they established a far-flung support group, particularly in the far north Cairns to Townsville region.

That company disbanded at the end of 1969 when it was marginalized by a larger and better-funded state company. Working from his north Queensland base, Nason founded a new, smaller group, Grin and Tonic, which has defiantly continued to work outside the state-subsidized live theatre industry, supporting itself for over 20 years principally by performing scenes from Shakespeare in secondary schools. The core company is supplemented for occasional larger-scale productions that often explore atmospherically appropriate stage locations, such as a cathedral for *Macbeth* in 1992.

Influenced by the illustrative-gesture rhetorical acting style advocated by B. L. Joseph, Nason directs Shakespeare with careful attention to language and has succeeded in developing a method of theatrical communication highly popular with younger audiences.

Production History: 1992: *Mac.*

Research Resources: No formally maintained records are available.

Richard Fotheringham

AUSTRIA
(See GERMAN-LANGUAGE SHAKESPEARE)

CANADA

BRITISH COLUMBIA

BARD ON THE BEACH. MAIL: 7 East 7th Ave., Vancouver, B.C., Canada V5T 1M4. SITE: Vanier Park, at the south end of the Burrard Street Bridge, overlooking English Bay. ADMINISTRATION: 604/875-1533; Fax: 604/875-1534. BOX OFFICE: 604/739-0559. ADMISSION: $15. SEASON: late June–early September; 8:00 p.m., Mon.–Sun. (7:00 p.m. after 5 September).

PRINCIPAL STAFF: Christopher Gaze, artistic director/general manager; Ronald Fedoruk, scenographer. FACILITY: tent (450 capacity). AUDITIONS: local, late November. STATUS: Equity. ANNUAL BUDGET: $357,000 Canadian (1993). ANNUAL ATTENDANCE: 26,000 (1993). FOUNDED: 1990, Christopher Gaze.

Founded in 1990, Bard on the Beach (BOB) rapidly moved to Equity status and purchased its own facility in time for the 1992 season. Its success and rapid growth vindicated founder Christopher Gaze's belief that Vancouver was ripe for regular doses of summer Shakespeare produced in an "affordable and accessible" manner. As an added ingredient, the action is set against a spectacular scenic vista. "Our theatre is a custom-made tent which opens onto a glorious backdrop of city, sea, and mountains," Gaze says, "perfectly complementing Shakespeare's effective use of nature in his plays."

Typically, the shows begin with the hoisting of the rear flap of the tent to exploit what Gaze calls "one of the most beautiful spots in the world for a theatre." The sky over English Bay and the mountains beyond still glows with sunset colors, which deepen to blackness as theatregoers are seduced into the story. On rainy nights, the tent flap remains closed, but the show goes on.

The inaugural season, which was supported by a Canada Council Explorations grant and some intensive fund raising, drew 6,000 people to 34 performances of *A Midsummer Night's Dream* in a rented, 275-seat tent. The second season brought a more lavishly mounted production of *A Midsummer Night's Dream*, a second production, *As You Like It*, and a season expanded to 47 performances; attendance increased to 10,000. BOB was an Equity cooperative company for its first two seasons, when the cast could be promised "nothing but a percentage of whatever the box office yielded."

In 1992, BOB became an Equity company and acquired its own tent with seating capacity increased to 450. Attendance increased correspondingly, to 22,300, for the 60 performances of *Twelfth Night* and *The Tempest*. Directed by Douglas Campbell, *Twelfth Night* had a continuous run throughout July and then was performed in rotating repertory with *The Tempest* in August and early September. For that season, BOB employed 17 Equity artists (13 actors, two directors, a production stage manager, and a choreographer) as well as eight non-Equity actors, three designers, two assistant stage managers, and about 25 additional technical and administrative staff members. Gaze finally put himself on the payroll as well, as artistic director and general manager. In addition, 115 volunteers support the festival by carrying out nightly duties on the site.

The company's success might be attributed not only to the beauty of the setting but also to Gaze's proclivity for large casts and elaborate costuming: what he calls "the visual impact of large-scale Shakespearean theatre." Gaze's enthusiasm is infectious. He has worked hard to develop a rapport with the local community, and he makes a point of talking informally from the stage before each performance. During intermission, the costumed actors mingle with audience members. BOB's 1992 production of *The Tempest* was given a northwest Canadian flavor. Ariel, for example, was a Nanabush (Native American archetypal trickster). In 1994, due to heavy demand for tickets, BOB expanded its season to 13 weeks.

Production History: **1990**: *MND*; **1991**: *AYL, MND*; **1992**: *TN, Tmp.*; **1993**: *Rom., Shr.*; **1994**: *Wiv., Lr.*

Research Resources: Lloyd Dykk, "Bard hits the beach for a third summer," *Vancouver Sun* (3 July 1992): C5.

Felicia Hardison Londré

MANITOBA

SHAKESPEARE IN THE PARK, ASSINIBOINE THEATRE. MAIL: 918 Grosvenor Ave., Winnipeg, Manitoba, R3M 0N4 Canada. SITE: Assiniboine Park at the Lily Pond behind a pavilion. ADMINISTRATION/BOX OFFICE: 204/453-6657. ADMISSION: silver collection (free, donantions welcome). SEASON: one production, 18 performances, first two weeks in July, 7:00 p.m., weekdays; 2:00 p.m., 7:00 p.m., Sat.–Sun. PRINCIPAL STAFF: Daphne Korol, artistic director. FACILITY: open-air grassy area (capacity approximately 300). AUDITIONS: open, in April. STATUS: non-Equity. ANNUAL BUDGET: $10,000. ANNUAL ATTENDANCE: 6,000. FOUNDED: 1986, Daphne Korol.

Daphne Korol, a Winnipeg native and director of its performing arts school, the Assiniboine Theatre, founded Shakespeare in the Park (SP) in 1986 to provide Winnipeg, the capital of Manitoba, with the opportunity to experience Shakespeare performances during the summer months. Korol chose a compilation of scenes from Shakespeare for SP's first season in 1986. Her desire to provide an opportunity for local Winnipeg artists to participate in and experience a professionally directed Shakespeare production was greeted with great enthusiasm, and, by 1988, the audience had doubled to over 5,000 spectators. Her artistic mission was simply to provide an "enjoyable and understandable experience with Shakespeare." Korol notes that, for many audience members, SP is their "first exposure to live theatre and is painlessly educational." With the motto "New York has it, Toronto has it, now Winnipeg has it," the annual event has developed into a major tourist attraction.

The setting for the performances is located behind a large pavilion, an imposing Tudor-style structure, in the center of the lush English gardens of

Winnipeg's Assiniboine Park. The 152-hectare Assiniboine Park, located west of the city center along the Assiniboine River, is a major retreat area in the summer with its many activities, large zoo, conservatory, and pavilion. Facing the back of the pavilion structure, a large U-shaped arbor with a boardwalk and vine-draped pillars forms the setting for the SP performances. A grassy area in the center of the arbor slopes down to a large lily pond. Wooden platforms approximately 25 feet across are erected over a portion of the lily pond and provide the acting area for the performances. Surrounded on two sides by water, the Winnipeg SP may be the only "floating" Shakespeare festival in the world. The ever present possibility that an actor could fall into the lilly pond provided an additional layer of comic potential for antics in SP's recent productions of *Twelfth Night* and *Midsummer Night's Dream*; the love juice in the eye inspired a "walk on water." Actors make their entrances from all sides of the arbor. The arbor walkway and grassy area accommodate approximately 300 spectators with blankets and lawn chairs, as well as dogs and chipmunks. An occasional airplane approaching the nearby international airport prompts actors to improvise as the roar passes overhead. "Move the airport!" an audience member has cried. The actors diligently pass the hat after performances, and, following a *Twelfth Night* production, for an extra donation, audience members received a copy of the "letter" Malvolio reads, all rolled up in parchment paper with a ribbon tied around it.

Korol prefers a traditional style of production and has no plans to set Shakespeare's plays in the twentieth century. She enjoys using children in her productions and would like to increase the number of Equity actors used, but she notes that the present budget is limited. To cut costs, the SP buys used costumes from the Manitoba Theatre Centre. Of the $10,000 budget, $2,000 is provided by the City of Winnipeg, approximately $2,500 comes from the provincial lottery, and the remainder derives from donations. Korol is optimistic about the future of SP and has received support from area arts groups throughout Manitoba.

Production History: 1986: Scenes from Shakespeare; **1987**: *TGV*; **1988**: *MND*; **1989**: *Tmp.*; **1990**: *Rom.*; **1991**: *TN*; **1992**: *Shr.*; **1993**: *AYL*; **1994**: *Ham.*

Research Resources: Informal archives for Shakespeare in the Park are maintained at the administrative office.

Site visits: July 1991, 1992, 1993, 1994.
Ron Engle

ONTARIO

DREAM IN HIGH PARK. MAIL: Canadian Stage Company, 26 Berkeley Street, Toronto, Ontario, M5A 2W3, Canada. SITE: High Park. ADMINISTRATION: 416/367-8243; Dream Hotline, 416/368-3110. ADMISSION: free ($5 voluntary donation per person is encouraged at entrance to performance site). SEASON: (1992) 8-week run, from end of June to end of August; 8:30 p.m., Tues.–Sun. PRINCIPAL STAFF: Bob Baker, artistic director; Martin Bragg, general manager. FACILITY: outdoor amphitheatre, open stage (capacity approximately 2,000). AUDITIONS: Toronto, in April. STATUS: Canadian Equity. ANNUAL BUDGET: $600,000 (1992). ANNUAL ATTENDANCE: 65,000 (1992). FOUNDED: 1983, Guy Sprung.

The Dream in High Park (DHP) began in 1983 when Guy Sprung, artistic director of the Toronto Free Theatre, mounted a production of *A Midsummer Night's Dream* in the open-air amphitheatre in High Park, a large municipal park in central Toronto. With financial sponsorship from numerous individuals, corporations, private foundations, and government agencies, including the Ontario and Toronto arts councils, the production was presented free of charge for a four-week run (Wednesdays through Sundays) from mid-July to mid-August. Experienced actors were cast in the major roles, but the supporting roles were cast, after a nationwide selection process, with young aspiring professionals, mostly drawn from Canadian actor-training programs. In fact, Michael Mawson, the production's director, was a teacher at the National Theatre School in Ottawa. During rehearsals and performances, training continued, with coaching by several of Canada's leading classical directors and performers. Indeed, providing a strong and supportive training ground for young theatre professionals became a commitment of the DHP. Sprung was also committed to presenting Shakespeare's plays in a manner that would make them accessible to a wider and more diverse audience than is usually the case—hence, the motivation for free performances. Toronto in general and the area around High Park in particular have a highly multiethnic population with numerous new emigré groups from Eastern Europe, Latin America, India, Pakistan, China, and the Caribbean. Sprung wanted the DHP to be a genuinely populist theatre that would bring this audience to performances of Shakespeare.

With such a diverse population in mind, Mawson's production of *A Midsummer Night's Dream* drew heavily on pop culture icons, particularly the *Star Wars* films and other movies of that genre. The costuming and makeup of the fairies, for example, were designed to suggest extraterrestrials rather than a traditional Victorian image of fairies as epitomized in the works of illustrator Arthur Rackham. The production was also very physical, with actors rappelling down trees, bounding off trampolines, and engaged in various knockabout comic routines and pratfalls. (Two Canadian champion gymnasts served as coaches for this stage business.) John Mills-Cockell, a musician known for his work with the Canadian rock band Syrinx, created synthesized pop-rock incidental music that, as one critic wrote, created an ambience of "an electrified hobbitland." Although the production style may have, as even director Mawson conceded, "cut down on the poetic quality of the play" (*Toronto Globe and Mail*, 9 July 1983), it was dynamic, fun, and very popular. The production ultimately played to over 40,000 spectators and was revived for another run in the summer of 1984.

Encouraged by this public reception and support, the DHP thus became an annual venture of the Toronto Free Theatre with the productions generally adhering to the populist approach of *A Midsummer Night's Dream*. The 1985–86 *Romeo and Juliet*, for example, tended to emphasize the conflict between the older and younger generations, which High Park's audiences might find more relevant than the romance of the star-crossed lovers. The production was visually impressive, physically exciting, and very energetic. The massive setting, three stories in height, evoked a Veronese piazza, complete with dimly lit, narrow alleys. The critic for the *Toronto Star* (15 July 1985) described the opening sequence of fist fights, with fire belching from the upper stories of the set and buckets of water thrown from the balconies onto the brawlers below, as "a circus-like, free wheeling melee." During the party scene when Romeo and Juliet meet, an actual fireworks display of skyrockets and flares exploded in the background. To reach Juliet's balcony, Romeo climbed a High Park tree and, hanging nearly upside-down, stretched out an arm to graze Juliet's fingers. Such effects and moments undoubtedly succeeded in maintaining the interest of High Park audiences, but the *Toronto Star's* critic noted that director Sprung was as much "interested in the text as in . . . pageantry." On balance, the critic thought that the production successfully integrated text and *mise-en-scène*. The 1989–90 *Comedy of Errors* was updated to the modern era and located in some trendy beach resort on the Aegean coast. The setting included 50 tons of sand and a working swimming pool in which Esther Williams-style mermaids cavorted from time to time. The Dromios reminded the reviewer for *Toronto Tonight* (27 July-10 August 1989) of "Barnum and Bailey clowns with a dash of the Marx Brothers" as they engaged in numerous farcical pratfalls and business.

In 1989, the Toronto Free Theatre and another principal Toronto theatre company, Centerstage, which was based at the St. Lawrence Centre for the Arts, merged to form the Canadian Stage Company (CSC), with production venues at the St. Lawrence Centre and at a theatre complex on Berkeley Street, the former home of the Toronto Free Theatre. This company became the largest nonprofit theatre company in Toronto and one of the more important arts organizations in Canada. With the merger, the CSC also assumed the responsibility for mounting the annual free Shakespeare in High Park presentation.

To celebrate the tenth anniversary of the DHP in 1992, the CSC mounted an ambitious presentation of *The Wars of the Roses* cycle, comprised of *Henry VI Parts 1, 2*, and *3* and *Richard III*. The *Henry* plays were presented in High Park in two separate productions as *Henry 06, his death* and *The rise of Edward 04*, using the same company of 24 actors—12 seasoned professionals and 12 journeymen or apprentices. Later in the fall, *Richard III* was presented indoors at the St. Lawrence Centre for the Arts. This production was followed in November by a production of a new play entitled *The Queens*, in which Quebec playwright Normand Chaurette reimagined *Richard III* from the perspective of six women from Shakespeare's history cycle.

In August 1992, I was able to attend a performance of *The rise of Edward 06*. High Park is on the immediate northwestern side of downtown Toronto, surrounded by mainly residential neighborhoods and easily accessible by subway or bus. There is also ample parking for automobiles. The park is one of the largest in central Toronto and heavily used for a variety of outdoor recreational activities. The "Dream Site," as the amphitheatre is called, is located in a natural glen almost in the center of the park. The grassy hillside has been contoured into a number of level terraces where patrons can spread blankets or set up folding chairs. The glen is ringed with ancient, massive oaks and other hardwood trees.

For the 1992 season, a semipermanent, impressive constructivistic setting of steel and treated lumber was erected at the bottom of the glen. It was a large, multileveled affair, three-stories high, with a series of staircases connecting the various levels and the broad, open, thrust stage. A series of steel towers encircling the glen supported lighting instruments and speakers. (The setting was later to be transported to the St. Lawrence Centre for the production of *Richard III* and to the Berkeley Street facility for *The Queens*.)

Although the performance was not scheduled to begin until 8:30 p.m., all the choice places on the hillside were occupied by 7:30. As with so many outdoor Shakespearean performances, the audience was in a relaxed festive mood, and most spectators had brought picnic suppers. A food kiosk near the entrance to the glen also sold a variety of soft drinks, juices, coffee, ice cream, cookies, and other light refreshments. At another kiosk, were souvenir T-shirts, sweatshirts, and posters. The composition of the audience was diverse, although mostly on the youngish side, with many of Toronto's various ethnic communities represented. Many spectators came with groups of friends or in families. A number of children capered about; a few people had even brought their dogs. Although it was a weeknight, there were undoubtedly over 1,000 spectators sitting on the hillside by the start of the performance.

The performance began with Jack Cade's rebellion (*Henry VI, Part 2*, Act IV, scene 2). The rebels entered boisterously from a path in the woods behind the setting. A rousing musical march—a complex percussive synthesis, partly

New Age rock and partly medieval—accompanied them. Dressed in a mixture of contemporary clothes (leather motorcycle jackets, motorcycle boots, T-shirts, tennis shoes), they had the look of a vicious mob, a group of thugs. When Dick the Butcher, brandishing a cleaver, snarled, "The first thing we do, let's kill all the lawyers," the audience broke into laughter and applause.

The Lancastrians were dressed in red sweat suits, with black gloves and shoes; the Yorkists were dressed completely in black sweat suits, while the French were blue. The armor was a mixture of hockey and football helmets and padding. Indeed, the numerous pitched battles and duels, fought with black quarterstaves and short, Japanese-style wooden swords, evoked the hockey rink and football field as much as they did medieval warfare.

The entire performance was marked, in fact, by a highly energetic and bold acting style. As the red and black costume scheme signaled, this was not intended to be a subtle interpretation. (Outdoor Shakespeare generally does not lend itself to subtle presentation styles.) The direction by Peter Hinton and Bob Baker, however, skillfully maintained a fast-paced, clear narrative line, which is not an easy task with these plays. Audience members were also aided by a program that contained plot synopses and genealogies of the houses of Lancaster and York, with portrait photographs of the actors attached to the various roles they played. Moreover, it was a visually and kinetically arresting presentation with many often surprising moments of ironic humor. While this was an ensemble production, there were several strong individual performances. Some critics, like Liam Lacey of *Toronto Globe and Mail* (30 June 1992), complained about the production's anachronistic, even silly, "visual affectations" and about performances in which "actors surf on the text without any evidence of real engagement." The audience, however, clearly enjoyed the presentation and applauded enthusiastically at the curtain call. Clearly the "Creative Team," as they called themselves, headed by Hinton and Baker, succeeded in blowing some cobwebs off Shakespeare, demonstrating that even these seldom-staged history plays can be exciting, popular theatre.

Plagued by an usually cool, rainy summer, almost one-third of the 48 scheduled performances of *Henry 06, his death* and *The rise of Edward 04* were rained out. Nonetheless, overall attendance in 1992 still reached a peak for DHP. Undoubtedly, the program will continue to provide high-quality, free performances of Shakespeare to the Toronto community. For 1993, a production of *Twelfth Night* was scheduled to be directed by Jeanette Lambermont.

Production History: **1983**: *MND*; **1984**: *MND*; **1985**: *Rom.*; **1986**: *Rom.*; **1987**: *Tmp.*; **1988**: *Blood Brothers*; **1989**: *Err.*; **1990**: *Err.*; **1991**: *AYL*; **1992**: *Henry 06, his death* and *The rise of Edward 04* (*1, 2, 3, H6*).

Research Resources: An informal archive for the Dream in High Park is maintained at the CSC administrative offices.

Site visit and interviews: 20 August 1992.
Daniel J. Watermeier

STRATFORD FESTIVAL OF CANADA. MAIL: P.O. Box 520, Stratford, Ontario, N5A 6V2 Canada. SITE: Stratford. ADMINISTRATION: 519/271-4040. BOX OFFICE: 519/273-1600. ADMISSION: $18.74–$49.50, Canadian (1993). SEASON: 11 to 16 productions in rotating repertory, 28 weeks from early May to mid-November; 8:00 p.m., Tues.–Sun.; 2:00 p.m., Wed., Sat., Sun. PRINCIPAL STAFF: Richard Monette, artistic director (1994-1996); Gary Thomas, general manager; Colleen Blake, producer. FACILITIES: Festival Theatre, thrust stage (capacity 2,276); Avon Theatre, proscenium stage (capacity 1,107); Tom Patterson Theatre, thrust stage (capacity 494). AUDITIONS: Stratford, Toronto, and other Canadian cities. STATUS: Canadian Equity/PACT. ANNUAL BUDGET: $24,711,000 (1991). ANNUAL ATTENDANCE: 500,000 (1991). FOUNDED: 1952, Tom Patterson.

The Stratford Festival (SF) was the inspiration of Tom Patterson, a professional journalist and a Stratford native, who, as John Pettigrew and Jamie Portman have written, "when still in his teens [in the 1930s] . . . first thought of using the city's name to advantage by having Shakespeare's plays presented there"; in the process, he posed "a possible answer to the crushing impact of the Depression" on his rural home town. Not until the early 1950s, however, was Patterson able to realize his adolescent dream.

Although Patterson is rightly credited with conceiving the festival, he was assisted in his efforts by a number of forceful personalities, among them Tyrone Guthrie, Robertson Davies, Mavor Moore, and Dora Mavor Moore. Guthrie, for example, convinced the festival's organizers to build an innovative, open, platform stage, designed by his long-time collaborator Tanya Moiseiwitsch and initially housed in a large circus-like tent. Guthrie also set an early standard for the festival as a professional, classical repertory theatre, aspiring to rate with the best theatres in the world.

After two years of intensive organizing, planning, fund raising, and building, on the evening of 3 July 1953, the Stratford Shakespearean Festival of Canada, as it was initially called, was inaugurated with a performance of *Richard III*. The production was directed by Guthrie, designed by Moiseiwitsch, and featured Alec Guinness in the title role. On the following evening, a production of *All's Well That Ends Well* opened, again directed and designed by Guthrie and Moiseiwitsch, respectively, with Guinness as the King of France and Irene Worth as Helena. Both productions then played in rotating repertory for over 20 performances each until 22 August. Because of the heavy demand for tickets, both productions were extended for a week. As one observer enthused on the opening night of the festival, it "was the most exciting night in the history of the Canadian theatre." During its six-week season, the 1,500-seat tent theatre played to 98 percent capacity. There were no doubts on the part of the organizers that the festival could become an annual event.

Although Guthrie took a sabbatical from his duties as artistic director during part of the 1954 season (these responsibilities were assumed by his long-time associate Cecil Clarke), he successfully led the SF for its first three seminal seasons. During his tenure, he mounted several notable productions, including *The Taming of the Shrew* (1954), *Oedipus Rex* (1954; revived as *King Oedipus* in 1955), and *The Merchant of Venice* (1955). He succeeded in bringing international attention to Stratford and in laying a strong foundation for its future development. Perhaps more interested in founding theatres than in running them, however, Guthrie left the SF after the 1955 season to pursue his directing interests and, in the early 1960s, to found the Guthrie Theatre in Minneapolis. He did return, however, in subsequent years to direct *Twelfth Night* (1957) and celebrated productions of *H.M.S. Pinafore* (1960) and *The Pirates of Penzance* (1962). In the 40 years since its founding, despite a few financial and artistic setbacks, the SF, as Guthrie envisioned, has steadily grown into a world-class, classical repertory theatre under a succession of artistic directors.

Guthrie was succeeded in 1956 by Michael Langham, a young English director who had made his festival directorial debut in 1955 with a well-received production of *Julius Caesar*. Langham started his tenure auspiciously with a bicultural production of *Henry V* featuring a young Montreal actor, Christopher Plummer, in the title role. The French roles were played by Francophone actors from Montreal's Théâtre du Nouveau Monde, while the English roles were played by Anglo-Canadians. Over the next ten seasons (1956-67), Langham, building on Guthrie's foundation, led the festival to a position of importance in North American theatre.

Under Langham, the original tent theatre was replaced in 1957 with a permanent building, designed by Toronto architect Robert Fairfield. Built on the same site as the tent theatre and using virtually the same stage, the new building, called the Festival Theatre, housed not only the theatre itself, but administrative offices, dressing rooms, scenic and costume shops, storage areas, and rehearsal halls. The theatre's seating area sweeps almost three-quarters of the way around the stage (220 degrees) and holds 2,276 people (1,418 in the orchestra and 858 in the balcony); no spectator is more than 65 feet from the stage. As J. A. B. Somerset has pointed out, the Festival Theatre served as a model for the Guthrie Theatre in Minneapolis and the Crucible Theatre in Sheffield, England. It also influenced the design of the Chichester Festival stage, the Vivian Beaumont Theatre at Lincoln Center in New York, the National Arts Center in Ottawa, and the Royal National Theatre's Olivier Theatre. Over the years, the theatre and stage have been modified, adjusted, and improved, but the basic configuration has remained essentially unchanged.

It has proven to be remarkably adaptable and effective for staging a range of plays, including musical comedies and operettas, in a variety of styles.

Langham also laid the foundations for a second SF performance space. In 1963, the SF purchased the Avon Theatre, a former vaudeville theatre turned cinema, located in the commercial center of Stratford, principally as a venue for non-Shakespearean productions better suited to a proscenium stage. In fact, the Avon Theatre had been rented by the SF since 1956 for its ancillary music and film festivals. *Three Farces* by Molière, directed by Jean Gascon, was staged there in 1956, as was *The Beggar's Opera* in 1958 and Guthrie's productions of *H.M.S. Pinafore*, and *The Pirates of Penzance*. The Avon Theatre has been refurbished twice, first in 1963-67 and then in 1984-86, when backstage dressing rooms, rehearsal studios, and administrative offices were added.

During his tenure, Langham developed a strong acting company, often enhanced with such notable English and American stars as Zoë Caldwell, Jason Robards, Jr., Alan Bates, Julie Harris, and Tammy Grimes. A number of Canadian actors also rose to prominence under Langham, including not only Plummer, but also William Hutt, Douglas Rain, Frances Hyland, Leo Ciceri, Martha Henry, and Bruno Gerussi. The number of productions and performances expanded significantly. In addition, Langham encouraged productions of new Canadian plays through a competition sponsored by the *Toronto Globe and Mail*. He further extended the festival's national and international reputation by touring and televising festival productions. In April 1964, to celebrate Shakespeare's quatercentenary, the SF toured three productions to the Chichester Festival. Langham initiated a school performances program and promoted Stratford's International Film Festival and a celebrated series of musical performances, including operas. (The International Film Festival was mounted annually from 1956 through 1961. After a ten-year hiatus, it was revived from 1971 through 1976. The music festival operated until 1975.)

In 1967, the SF's board of governors approved Langham's recommendation that Jean Gascon, one of the founders of the Théâtre du Nouveau Monde and its artistic director, and John Hirsch, artistic director of the Manitoba Theatre Center, take over the artistic directorship of the festival, as executive director and associate artistic director, respectively. At a time of heightened tensions between Canada's two major cultures—French and English—tensions that increasingly affected Canadian arts and arts organizations, this joint appointment undoubtedly seemed politic. But, as Ross Stuart has noted, "the two men . . . were artistically and temperamentally dissimilar." Hirsch, according to Portman and Pettigrew, found it difficult to "play second fiddle" to Gascon and was "sharply critical . . . both of the Festival and of its leadership." Moreover, his 1969 productions of *Hamlet* and his controversial adaptation of Petronius' *Satyricon*, were judged artistic failures by the leading critics, although they did well at the box office. At the end of 1969 season, Hirsch resigned.

Gascon remained artistic director until 1974. He expanded the repertoire to include productions of Molière, Jonson, Webster, Shakespeare's less frequently produced plays (such as *Cymbeline* and *Pericles)*, and modern European plays by Ibsen, Strindberg, Feydeau, Brecht, and others. In 1971, Gascon opened the Third Stage in a community building on Lakeside Drive, as a venue for new and experimental Canadian plays and operas; the space had been used from 1955 to 1958 for the SF's various musical activities. Gascon, like his predecessor, promoted the talents of a number of Canadian actors, including Hutt, Rain, Henry, Nicholas Pennell, and Pat Galloway who became the core of his company. Under Gascon's leadership, the festival company also toured to the United States in 1969, to Holland, Denmark, Poland, and the Soviet Union in 1973, and to Australia in 1974. For two winter seasons in 1968 and in 1969, the SF was also in residence at the new National Arts Centre in Ottawa.

With nationalist sentiments running high in the 1970s, the appointment of young English director Robin Phillips to succeed Gascon sparked protests from the Canadian theatrical community. Phillips' tenure remained haunted by the controversy of his appointment, but he proved to be an astute and imaginative artistic director. He founded the Young Company, as part of a long-range plan to develop a resident Canadian classical theatre company at Stratford. He expanded the season at the Avon Theatre, giving it parity with the Festival Theatre. Like Gascon, Phillips relied on a number of Stratford veterans for the core of his company, and the company as a whole was largely Canadian. He was not averse, however, to supplementing this company with visiting foreign stars, notably Maggie Smith, Hume Cronyn (Canadian by birth), Jessica Tandy, Max Helpmann, Brian Bedford, and Peter Ustinov. Generally, however, these visitors were incorporated into the company and cast in several roles in the season's repertoire. With a season gradually expanding to 14 productions in repertory in three theatres over 22 weeks, Phillips invited both foreign and Canadian directors to Stratford, including even those who had been critical of his appointment, like John Hirsch and Bill Glassco. He featured young Canadian actors in major roles in classical and modern plays. Thus, for example, Nicholas Pennell and Richard Monette alternated as Hamlet in a 1976 production codirected by Phillips and Hutt. Phillips also promoted Canadian theatrical designers. Perhaps his most important contribution, however, consisted of the dozens of imaginative, inventive productions that he staged at Stratford during his tenure, including *A Midsummer Night's Dream* (1976-77), *Richard III* (1977), *The Winter's Tale* (1978), and *King Lear* (1979).

Portman and Pettigrew have documented, furthermore, that the Phillips regime was "fiscally responsible." Despite significant economic pressures, including years of increasing inflation and declines in governmental grants, the SF "was able to sustain a period of unparalleled growth from 1978 to 1980," with total attendance exceeding 500,000. It was a remarkable achievement for both Phillips and the management of the SF. Burned out, however, by the strain of his gradually increasing artistic and managerial duties—Phillips had also assumed the duties of general manager in 1977—Phillips resigned in 1979, effective at the end of the 1980 season.

Despite Phillips' early resignation, the SF board, for a variety of complicated reasons, both personal and political, failed to recruit a successor even after a prolonged search. Instead, an "artistic directorate," comprised of four Stratford veterans (Urjo Kareda, festival literary adviser; actress Martha Henry; and directors Peter Moss and Pam Brighton), was initially appointed to plan and execute the 1981 season. This committee was summarily dismissed when the board learned that English director John Dexter was keenly interested in the artistic directorship. The often embarrassing public debacle that resulted from the board's undoubtedly well-intentioned but controversial actions was partially resolved when John Hirsch agreed to serve as artistic director for a five-year term, although it would take another decade to recover fully from this 1980-81 crisis.

Hirsch, building on Phillips' initiatives, developed the Young Company at the Third Stage as a new theatre-training program. He succeeded in renewing contacts with the Canadian Broadcasting Corporation (CBC) for recording and televising several SF productions. (Hirsch had served as head of CBC Television Drama in the 1970s.) During his tenure, both the Avon and Festival theatres were renovated, adding rehearsal spaces and shops. The Avon Theatre became noted as the home of Brian Macdonald's skillfully staged productions of Gilbert and Sullivan operettas. Hirsch also recruited a number of distinguished designers, directors, and actors to Stratford, including Ming Cho Lee, John Neville, Michael Langham, Michael Bogdanov, Ronald Eyre, Douglas Campbell, Len Cariou, Alan Scarfe, Peter Donat, and Sada Thompson. Despite his successes, the overall artistic quality of the festival was generally judged uneven. Some thought that the repertoire relied too heavily on Shakespeare's popular comedies. At the same time, Bogdanov's risky and risqué, and inventive staging of *Measure for Measure* proved too controversial for the tastes of conservative festival audience members and critics. Moreover, mounting debt continued to dog the festival. By the end of Hirsch's last season, the accumulated deficit was over $3 million.

When John Neville assumed the artistic directorship in 1986, his goal was "to restore both financial and artistic footing securely," according to Neville's biographer, Robert Gaines. Over the next four seasons, he accomplished both goals brilliantly. Although his decision was not altogether popular, he abandoned the annual Gilbert and Sullivan operettas staged at the Avon, deciding instead to mount a popular American musical in the larger Festival Theatre. The Avon was returned to classical theatre. Neville's programing choices were often astute. In 1986, for example, he mounted productions of *Hamlet, Rosencrantz and Guildenstern are Dead, Henry VIII*, and *A Man for All Seasons*. Not only did these plays complement each other thematically, but, since they could utilize the same settings and many of the same costumes, Neville could also reduce production costs. He mended fences with several former Stratford veterans who had been disaffected by the board's actions in 1980-81. William Hutt, for example, returned in 1987 to play Leonato in *Much Ado About Nothing* and, in 1988, his second *King Lear* for the SF, supported by the Young Company at the Third Stage. Robin Phillips was invited back to direct a number of productions over three seasons (1986-88), including a memorable *Cymbeline* and several scaled-down but imaginatively staged productions with the Young Company. When Neville turned the reins over to David William in 1990, the SF was not only debt-free, but, artistically, it had recovered much of the former glory that had been tarnished by the 1980-81 crisis and the controversies and criticisms of the Hirsch years.

William generally maintained the direction set by Neville, although he staged more Canadian (including French Canadian) and more contemporary plays than his predecessor. William brought back Brian Macdonald, the director of the popular Gilbert and Sullivan operettas in the 1980s, to stage the annual musical, including reprises of *H.M.S. Pinafore* and *The Mikado* in 1992 and 1993. Langham returned in 1992 to direct a skillfully realized ensemble production of *Measure for Measure*; while Robin Phillips returned in 1993 to direct an insightfully staged *King John*. William's own productions of *Hamlet* (1991) and *The Tempest* (1992) were of a very high order. Like his predecessors, William has relied for the core of his company on a number of Stratford veterans, many of whom have been with the festival since its inception, but he has supplemented this core with visiting artists, such as Alan Scarfe, William Hutt, Brian Bedford, and Kate Reid, all of whom, however, have had past relationships with the festival. William has also given a new focus to the Third Stage, renamed the Tom Patterson Theatre in 1991, as a home for new Canadian plays, experimental pieces, productions of Shakespeare's less popular plays, and the Young Company's annual production. With a renovated air-conditioning system, newer lobby facilities, and a new reserve seating policy (formerly only general seating was available), the Tom Patterson Theatre has been more fully integrated with the festival's other theatres and the season repertoire. Under William's leadership, the overall quality of festival productions remained exceptionally high, while programing became more diverse. In 1993, the SF board of governors announced that Richard Monette would succeed William as artistic director in 1994. After Jean Gascon, Monette becomes only the second native-born Canadian to serve as artistic director.

With its dramatic growth and development over four decades, the SF has become keenly aware of its international standing. As its 1989 mission statement noted, the SF "seeks to be an international cultural resource—one that serves as a repository of the finest theatrical achievements of our civilization, preserves and increases appreciation of the English language, and performs plays which facilitate an understanding of the human condition." While the plays of Shakespeare remain at the heart of its repertoire, the SF aims to present the very best of world drama, both classical and contemporary. The SF also remains committed to the repertory system as an artistic ideal and to the training not only of actors but of all the members of the artistic and administrative staff. Like most companies with an international focus and reputation, however, the SF also operates within the context and pressures of its own national culture. While it aims "to hire the best personnel without regard to their origin or current location," it gives preference to Canadian citizens or long-time residents of Canada. It has, furthermore, an understandable special interest in developing and promoting Canadian theatrical talent. Thus, while the SF regularly employs guest artists "to enhance the quality of productions and to exchange artistic expertise with members of the company," it seeks to develop its "own 'stars' in all facets of the festival organization."

The SF is the largest nonprofit performing arts organization in North America. Over the course of a season, it employs over 800 people, including several hundred actors, actresses, and production personnel, and a full panoply of administrative, educational, managerial, and training staff. In 1992, the SF mounted 548 performances of 11 productions in its three theatres. Total attendance regularly runs over 500,000 or about 60 percent of its 823,000 seat capacity. (It should be noted that the Festival Theatre, with its almost 2,300 seats, is a very large theatre. Thus, for the SF, total attendance is a more significant figure perhaps than percent of capacity. The **Oregon Shakespeare Festival**, for example, plays to over 90 percent capacity in its three Ashland theatres, but annual attendance there is about 350,000.) The SF draws about 60 percent of its audience from the greater Toronto metropolitan area and from other cities and towns in southwestern Ontario; about 35 percent come from the United States, mostly from the states contiguous to Ontario, while the remaining 5 percent come from Quebec, western Canada, and abroad. Perhaps as much as 50 percent of the audience consists of patrons who return regularly every year, while another 20 percent is represented by patrons who come frequently but not every year. As part of its outreach efforts, the SF offers a number of "school performances" with significantly discounted tickets for school groups on weekdays during the spring and fall portions of its season. Students, however, probably comprise less than 20 percent of the total SF audience. The SF audience, like audiences for professional theatre elsewhere in North America, is mostly older (50 years of age and up), affluent, and well educated.

In 1993, over 74 percent of the SF's total budget of almost $24 million, came from box office receipts. This amounted to over $18,308,000. About 10 percent of its income comes from national and provincial grants. For the remainder, the SF depends chiefly on individual and corporate donors. In 1993, there were almost 15,000 individual donor members of the SF, representing all the Canadian provinces, 45 American states, and a number of countries abroad. Contributions for membership range from $50 to $1,000 or more. Furthermore, numerous regional and national corporations, as well as private foundations, contribute to the support of the SF. It is estimated that the total economic impact of the festival on Stratford and the surrounding community is over $100 million, a very significant sum for a city of only 28,000 in a basically rural area. The SF also estimates that it generates over $25 million in taxes for the provincial and national governments.

The overall operation of the SF has been capably managed in the last decade or so, especially under general manager Gary Thomas, who has held various SF administrative positions since 1975 and became general manager in 1986. The operating base budget of the SF has been fairly stable in recent years, but heavy dependency on box office revenues means that the budget is not risk free. To reduce the risk as much as possible, the SF has made major efforts to increase overall attendance and especially the percentage of patrons who are annual returnees. Through a range of discounts, the SF has tried to increase attendance among both younger and older (senior citizen) audience members. It continues as well to develop its level of private and corporate support. Undoubtedly, the SF's development efforts have been enhanced by the composition of its board of governors. Although originally comprised mainly of Stratfordians, the board now consists of leaders in the arts, professions, and business world from across Canada and the United States.

The SF from its founding has considered education to be central to its cultural mission. The SF started its school matinee program in 1958. Since then, millions of secondary school students from across Canada have attended these special performances. With the appointment of an education coordinator in 1977, the SF has undertaken a range of educational programs, in addition to the student matinees, aimed at both student audiences and the general public. The SF education department, for example, circulates study guides on productions and publishes the *Stratford for Students* newsletter. It coordinates annual seminars of the Teacher-Festival Liaison Council which explores new ways to present Shakespeare and theatre in the classroom and assists a number of educational institutions with seminars and workshops held in Stratford. The education department also organizes an annual series of forums, panel discussions, lectures, and backstage tours of the Festival Theatre and the Festival Warehouse of costumes and properties. In partnership with The Gallery/Stratford, the SF regularly mounts theatrical exhibitions.

I visited Stratford for the first time in 1985. The city itself provides a very attractive ambience for a summer theatre festival. The Festival and Tom Patterson Theatres, for example, are immediately adjacent to a small lake created by a dam on the Avon River, which flows through Stratford. The lake is the centerpiece of a series of island parks and walking paths. Swans, Canadian geese, and ducks patrol the lake, and theatre patrons can usually be found strolling or picnicking along its banks. As one might expect, the downtown area mixes commercial businesses with an eclectic range of restaurants, antique shops, and boutiques. There are a number of centrally located hotels and motels, but many patrons lodge at one of the dozens of bed-and-breakfast inns located in the neighborhoods on both sides of the lake. On the weekends, there are usually *al fresco* exhibitions of local art and crafts in the lakeside park area.

There is ample parking for cars in the areas surrounding the theatre, and many patrons walk from their lodgings to the theatres and around the downtown area. It is a relaxed, informal, leisurely atmosphere, an idyllic retreat from the hustle and bustle of more metropolitan urban areas.

Since my first visit, I have been an annual visitor to the festival, usually attending most, if not all, of the productions offered each season—certainly too many productions to review or summarize briefly in the manner of other essays in this book. In light of the publications listed below under Research Resources, moreover, such a summary is undoubtedly unnecessary. Nevertheless, I would cite several SF productions that were, in my view, by world standards of theatrical production—Shakespearean production, in particular—especially outstanding. Among these were: *Measure for Measure* (1985), directed by Michael Bogdanov; *The Government Inspector* (1985), directed by Ronald Eyre; *Pericles* (1986), directed by Richard Ouzounian; *Cymbeline* (1986), directed by Robin Phillips; *Troilus and Cressida* (1987), directed by David William; *Much Ado About Nothing* (1987), directed by Peter Moss; *The Taming of the Shrew* (1988), directed by Richard Monette; *The Merchant of Venice* (1989), directed by Langham; *As You Like It* (1990), directed by Monette; *Timon of Athens* (1991), directed by Langham; *World of Wonders* (1992), directed by Richard Rose; and *Measure for Measure* (1992), directed by Langham. I have also been enthralled by numerous outstanding performances over the years including, to cite but a few, Brian Bedford's Shylock, Timon, and Vincentio, Alan Scarfe's Vincentio and Vanya, William Hutt's and Douglas Campbell's very different interpretations of Lear, and by Goldie Semple, Lucy Peacock, Nicholas Pennell, and Colm Feore in a dozen widely divergent roles, both Shakespearean and non-Shakespearean. One of the particular strengths of SF productions, furthermore, is the quality of performance in supporting and even minor roles. Veteran performers, many of whom have been continuing members of the company for a decade or more, such as Edward Atienza, Mervyn Blake, Douglas Chamberlain, Peter Donaldson, William Needles, the late Kate Reid, Mary Blendick, and Barbara Byrne, regularly have brought a special depth and skill to their finely etched character portrayals. Very few Shakespearean festival companies can match the SF in this respect. In addition, SF productions have often been notable for their visually spectacular scenery, properties, and costumes, as well as for their sophisticated sound effects and original incidental music. Indeed, the extravagant visual aspects of some productions have sometimes been the subject of criticism, but audiences seem to find spectacle an especially attractive and expected element of SF presentations.

On balance, considering its physical facilities, budget, overall organization and management, patronage, and the general excellence of its artistic presentations and various outreach programs, the SF ranks as one of the world's outstanding classical repertory theatres. With continuing effective leadership and financial support, it is likely to maintain this position for many years to come.

Production History (abbreviations in parentheses refer to performance venues; refer to the key below): Somerset provides a detailed and inclusive chronological list of all SF productions from 1953 through 1990. **1991**: (FT) *Ham.*, *Ado*, *Carousel*, *Treasure Island*; (AT) *Our Town*, *TN*, *Les Belles Soeurs*, *The School for Wives*, *An Enemy of the People*; (TPT) *Tim.*, *Homeward Bound*, *The Rules of the Game*, *The Knight of the Burning Pestle*, *Love Letters*; **1992**: (FT) *Tmp.*, *Rom.*, *LLL*, *MM*; (AT) *World of Wonders*, *H.M.S. Pinafore*, *Entertaining Mr. Sloane*; (TPT) *The Wingfield Trilogy*, *Uncle Vanya*, *Bonjour*, *là Bonjour*, *Shirley Valentine*, *TGV*; **1993**: (FT) *Ant.*, *MND*, *Gypsy*, *The Imaginary Invalid*; (AT) *The Mikado*, *The Importance of Being Earnest*; (TPT) *Jn.*, *The Wingfield Trilogy*, *Bacchae*, *Fair Liberty's Call*, *The Illusion*; **1994**: (FT) *TN*, *Pirates of Penzance*, *Cyrano*, *The School for Husbands*, *The Imaginary Cuckold*; (AT) *Oth.*, *Alice Through the Looking Glass*; (TPT) *Ham.*, *In the Ring*, *Err.*, *Long Day's Journey Into Night*.

Key:
AT: Avon Theatre
FT: Festival Theatre
TPT: Tom Patterson Theatre.

Research Resources: The SF maintains a well-organized, well-managed, and extensive archives housed in a separate building at 363 Burritt St., in Stratford. The archivist is Lisa Brant. The archives are not open to the general public, but they are open to scholars with research interests in its holdings. A fee is charged for access and/or assistance. The archives currently holds about 1,500 shelf-feet of records documenting every aspect of the Stratford Festival's history. For further information about the archives, write to Stratford Festival Archives, P.O. Box 520, Stratford, Ontario N5A 6V2 or phone 519/271-4040, extension 278. J. A. B. Somerset's *The Stratford Festival Story* provides a description and general index to the archives. SF productions have been reviewed by major newspapers and journals in Ontario, as well as by several major U.S. newspapers and journals. Somerset's list includes bibliographical references to selected reviews through 1989. SF productions have also been reviewed in issues of *Shakespeare Quarterly* and *Shakespeare Survey*. This essay was based on information derived from the publications listed below, from various SF publications, from interviews with Gary Thomas and David William, and on my personal experience as an SF patron.

Gaines, Robert A. *John Neville Takes Command*. Stratford: William Street Press, 1987.

Guthrie, Tyrone, and Robertson Davies. *Renown at Stratford: A Record of the Shakespeare Festival in Canada, 1953*. Toronto: Clarke, Irwin & Company, 1953;

————. *Twice Have The Trumpets Sounded: A Record of the Stratford Shakespearean Festival in Canada, 1954*. Toronto: Clarke, Irvin & Company, 1954.

Guthrie, Tyrone, Robertson Davies, Tanya Moiseiwitsch, and Boyd Neel. *Thrice the Brinded Cat Hath Mew'd: A Record of the Stratford Shakespearean Festival in Canada, 1955*. Toronto: Clarke, Irvin & Company, 1954.

Patterson, Tom. *First Stage: The Making of the Stratford Festival*. Toronto: McClelland and Stewart, 1987.

Pettigrew, John, and Jamie Portman. *Stratford: The First Thirty Years*. Vol. 1 (*1953-67*), Vol. 2 (*1968-82*). Toronto: Macmillian of Canada, 1985.

Somerset, J. Alan B. *The Stratford Festival Story: A Catalogue-index to the Stratford, Ontario, Festival 1953-1990*. New York: Greenwood Press, 1991.

Stuart, Ross. "The Stratford Festival." In *The Oxford Companion to the Canadian Theatre*, ed. Eugene Benson and L. W. Conolly. New York: Oxford University Press, 1989.

Watermeier, Daniel J. "Shakespeare in Canada: The 1987 Stratford Festival." *Shakespeare Quarterly* 39 (Summer 1988): 226-32.

————. "Shakespeare in Canada: The 1988 Stratford Season." *Shakespeare Quarterly* 40 (Summer 1989): 212-17.

Site visits, 1985-1994; interviews 19-20 September 1990.
Daniel J. Watermeier

SASKATCHEWAN

SHAKESPEARE ON THE SASKATCHEWAN FESTIVAL. MAIL: Nightcap Productions, Box 1646, Saskatoon, Saskatchewan, S7K 3R8, Canada. SITE: Saskatoon near South Saskatchewan River. ADMINISTRATION: 306/653-2300; Fax: 306/653-2357. BOX OFFICE: 306/652-9100. ADMISSION: varies, discount for students, seniors, matinees, and groups of ten or more. SEASON: July to mid August; 8:00 p.m., Tues.–Sun.; 2:00 p.m., Sun. PRINCIPAL STAFF: Henry Woolf, artistic director; David Hennessey, general manager. FACILITY: large red and white striped festival tent. AUDITIONS: contact business office. STATUS: Canadian AEA. FOUNDED: 1985, Gordon McCall.

The Shakespeare on the Saskatchewan Festival (SSF) was founded in 1985 by Gordon McCall in Saskatoon in the Canadian province of Saskatchewan. The SSF has gained an international reputation with its unique approach to Shakespeare production. The SSF has focused on multicultural approaches to the plays of Shakespeare and has produced a bilingual production. In 1990, in the SSF's *Romeo and Juliette*, a French Canadian Juliette and her family speak French, while Romeo and his family speak English. Situating the dramatic action within the political and social context of contemporary Canada, noted Canadian avant garde director Robert Lepage's *mise-en-scène* was imaginative and compelling. Capulets and Montagues were not noble citizens of Verona but typical, modern-day Canadians, living in the prairie provinces of Saskatchewan or Manitoba. Costuming, for example, was entirely contemporized. Inside the tent theatre, the setting consisted of a concrete road running between two sets of spectator bleachers. Loose sand and gravel provided a shoulder on either side of the road. An abandoned truck and a weathered telephone pole added to the ambience. The setting evoked the bareness and harshness of the prairie and the importance of highways and automobiles to the culture. Country-western music blared over the loud-speakers. For the opening scene melee, two older model sedans were driven on from opposite ends of the concrete road. Stopping near the center, young Capulets and Montagues emerged, taunting each other in French and English. A gang-style fight ensued. The ball of Act I, scene 4 was staged as a prairie barbecue. The balcony scene was played in the back of a blue pickup truck. For Act II, scene 4 and Act III, scene 2, a bed with a brass headboard was rolled on. In Act III, scene 1, Mercutio arrived on a Suzuki motorcycle. Even Juliette's burial ceremony, along the highway, illuminated by emergency road flares, proved, in the context of the entire production, appropriately mysterious and moving. With a strong cast of both Francophone and Anglophone actors performing in an often intensely physical, highly emotional, but essentially realistic style, this was one of the more affecting productions of *Romeo and Juliet* that I have witnessed in recent years,

The production received considerable attention in the Canadian press and subsequently toured to a number of Canadian towns and cities, including a two-week run at the **Stratford Festival**. Others multicultural approaches have included a Ukrainian interpretation of *Twelfth Night* and a Native actor playing the lead role in *Othello*.

As stated in its program, the SSF's artistic policy has been to "develop a multi-faceted ensemble company that illuminates Shakespeare and other works for contemporary audiences." The SSF was nominated for the Spirit of Saskatchewan Tourism Award and has attracted visitors from across Canada and the United States. The performances take place in a large red and white striped festival tent on the banks of the South Saskatchewan River along the Meewasin Valley Trail in central Saskatoon. Most performances play to capacity audiences.

Production History: **1990**: *Rom.*; **1991**: *TN*; **1992**: *Oth.*; **1993**: *Ado*; **1994**: *Ham.*

Research Resources: Informal archives for the Shakespeare on the Saskatchewan Festival are maintained at the administrative office.

Touring site visit in Stratford: 1990.
Ron Engle and Daniel J. Watermeier

CHINA

CHINA SHAKESPEARE FESTIVAL. Shanghai and Beijing, China, 1986. Second festival scheduled for 1994.

Interest in staging Shakespeare in China can be traced back as far as a 1913 production of *The Merchant of Venice* (retitled *The Flesh Coupon*); it was adapted from a 1903 Chinese translation of Charles and Mary Lamb's prose version in *Tales from Shakespeare* (1807), a work intended for parents to read aloud to their children. Throughout the first half of the twentieth century, the number of Shakespeare productions increased in number and sophistication. Plays were translated into Chinese directly from standard English texts, and the productions, like their counterparts in Europe and North America, reflected different styles of presentation, sometimes combining traditional Chinese theatrical conventions with Western approaches. In 1930, for example, a production of *The Merchant of Venice* was staged in Shanghai, the first Chinese spoken drama of a Shakespeare play. This was followed by a number of other notable professional productions, including *Romeo and Juliet* (1937, Shanghai), *Othello* (1938, Chongqing), and *Hamlet* (1942, Jian An).

The social and political upheaval of World War II and its aftermath, combined with widespread anti-foreign sentiments, impeded the continuing development of Shakespearean studies and performance throughout the 1940s. With the establishment of the People's Republic of China in 1949, however, there was a renewed interest in Shakespeare, in part because his plays were viewed as thematically proto-Marxist. New translations and critical studies were published. Hundreds of state-owned professional theatre companies were established, and spoken drama especially was promoted. Performances of Shakespeare's plays became acceptable practice. In the mid-1950s, there were several outstanding productions, including a *Romeo and Juliet* (1956, Central Academy of Drama) and a *Much Ado About Nothing* (1957, Shanghai Academy of Theatre). Film versions of *Hamlet, Twelfth Night,* and *Othello* were viewed by millions all over China. But these promising developments were soon to be interrupted.

In 1964, an ambitious project to celebrate the 400th anniversary of Shakespeare's birth was curtailed by the government. Productions of *The Merchant of Venice* by the Shanghai Academy of Theatre and of *King Lear* by the Liaoning People's Art Theatre were canceled. Theatre artists and scholars involved in the project were severely criticized. During the decade of the Cultural Revolution (1966-76), "Shakespeare's plays were removed from libraries and bookstores, translated film and stage versions were banned . . . even Shakespeare's name vanished from the lips of a population of nine hundred million people" (He, "China's Shakespeare," 155).

With the end of the Cultural Revolution, a Chinese renaissance in Shakespearean scholarship and performance began to develop. A major event in this recovery of Shakespeare was the November 1979 visit of the **Old Vic** Company to Shanghai and Beijing where *Hamlet* was presented with simultaneous Chinese translation. This visit stimulated a series of Shakespeare productions in the 1980s, including a *Measure for Measure* translated by the distinguished actor Yin Ruocheng, who also directed in association with the British director Toby Robertson. (This performance was reviewed in *Shakespeare Quarterly* 33 [1982], 499-502.)

Shakespeare studies and productions of Shakespeare's plays in China were further promoted with the establishment toward the end of 1984 of the Shakespeare Society of China (SSC). Hu Qiaomu, then secretary of the Central Committee of the Communist Party of China, accepted the position of honorary chairman; Cao Yu, a distinguished playwright, Shakespeare translator, and chairman of the Chinese Theatre Association, was elected chairman of the SSC. With such prestigious leadership, the SSC was immediately recognized as a major academic and theatrical organization in China, and Shakespeare was officially approved as a significant Western dramatist. As one of its first official acts, the SSC resolved to hold a China Shakespeare Festival in Shanghai between the end of April and the end of May once every four years, with the first festival occurring in 1986. Such a festival was intended to promote Shakespeare in China by integrating Shakespeare research with contemporary performance practice. The festival would include a range of approaches to presenting Shakespeare's plays, including productions in both Western style and traditional Chinese theatrical styles. The theatre companies of Shanghai and eastern China were to form the main participating body of the festival, but companies from Beijing and other regions of China were also to be invited to participate. The Shanghai Academy of Theatre was designated as the principal venue. A committee of Shakespearean scholars and theatre artists was established to award prizes in the areas of acting, direction, design, and overall performance. To raise funding for the festival and for the operation of the SSC, the China Shakespeare Foundation was created. Ba Jin, the noted Chinese writer, was named honorary chairman of the foundation, and Chen Gongming, the president of the Shanghai Academy of Theatre, was elected chairman of its board of directors.

The Secretariat of the SSC was given responsibility for the preparatory organization of the festival. In April 1985, Jiang Junfeng, secretary-general of the SSC and vice-president of the Shanghai Academy of Theatre, went to Beijing to report on the preparations to date and to solicit recognition of the festival from various national academic and theatrical organizations, including the Chinese Theatre Association, the Central Academy of Drama, the China Youth Art Theatre, and the Beijing People's Art Theatre. The organizers were heartened by the enthusiastic endorsement of these key organizations, whose support was essential if the festival was to be successfully realized. In August, the SSC invited the heads of leading theatre companies from various cities and provinces in China to an organizational meeting in Shanghai. The meeting resulted in agreement on various issues, including the number of productions that would be part of the festival, on complementary academic activities, and on a strategy to finance the festival.

A memorandum summarizing this meeting was then forwarded to the Press and Culture section of the Central Committee of the Communist Party of China, the Central Ministry of Culture, the National Association of Literature and Arts, the Chinese Theatre Association, and the various municipal and provincial cultural bureaus to which the participating theatre companies belonged. Monies for the festival were duly appropriated by the central government to the local cultural bureaus, which then in turn allocated portions of their budgets to the theatre companies participating in the festival. The SSC provided scholars and theatre specialists as consultants to participating companies. The festival was budgeted at 200,000 yuan, with the Central Ministry of Culture allocating 10,000 yuan and the Shanghai municipal government 40,000 yuan against this total sum. For the remainder of the budget, the organizers relied on various local governmental, academic, and theatrical organizations. In Shanghai, for example, in addition to funds from the Cultural Bureau, the Academy of Theatre, and the Shanghai branch of the Chinese Theatre Association, several daily newspapers, radio and television stations, and a publishing agency also contributed financial support for the festival. As plans for the festival continued, a decision was reached that, for logistical and financial reasons, the festival would be held in both Shanghai and Beijing between 10 and 23 April.

After months of preparation, the first China Shakespeare Festival opened simultaneously in Shanghai and Beijing on 10 April. Over the course of the next two weeks 18 different productions were presented in Shanghai by 16 companies, for a total of 60 performances. In Beijing, 11 companies staged 12 different productions, for a total of 34 performances. (See the Production History below.) I was unable to see every production of the festival. Indeed, with two venues, hundreds of miles apart, it was physically impossible to do so. But I did see every production in Shanghai. The following summary highlights some of the most notable productions there. Drawing on the reports of others, or productions which subsequently toured from Beijing and production videotapes, I also touch on several Beijing productions.

The Shanghai portion of the festival began with a visually splendid production of *Titus Andronicus*, presented by the Research Institute of the Academy of Theatre in its Experimental Theatre. The production was designed in part to take advantage of the theatre, one of the largest and best equipped in China. It featured, for example, a monumental setting, consisting mainly of columned platforms and steps that suggested ancient Rome but that also contributed to dynamic movement patterns. A strongly expressionistic style of lighting reinforced the dramatic mood. The director (Xu Qiping) began the performance with a striking visual prologue. As the curtain rose, the bodies of numerous dead soldiers were discovered littering the entire stage (Over 180 actors were used for this production). Battle instruments were scattered everywhere, and the whole stage was flooded with thick white smoke; a beam of intense red light suggested a path of blood. Titus knelt in front of his dead son, while his other four sons slowly carried corpses off the stage. Titus soon followed them as an off-stage voice read the dialogue between Titus and Marcus about killing a fly (Act III, scene 2, lines 52-67). A church bell tolled, and a long mourning procession passed across the stage. This prologue served as a pre-text for a production that emphasized the bloodiness of war and the ruthlessness of human revenge. To bring the production—and the dramatic action—full circle, Xu also cut Act V, scene 3 after Lucius kills Saturnius (lines 66-199). With the corpses of Lavinia, Tamora, Titus, and Saturnius on stage, Lucius knelt before the body of Titus and then faced the audience. To the sound of a continuous, slow, funereal drumming, one heard again from off stage the same lines from Act III, scene 2 that were used in the prologue. A spotlight focused on Lucius' face for a moment and then gradually dimmed.

Two productions of *The Taming of the Shrew* were presented in Shanghai. The more interesting of the two was the Shanghai People's Art Theatre production, staged by visiting British director Bernard Goss. (This production was supported in part by a grant from Mobil Oil of Hong Kong.) In what has become a cliché in modern approaches to staging *Shrew*, the performance started with what appeared to be the rehearsal of a play. An actor dressed in T-shirt and blue jeans entered from the audience, interrupting the rehearsal. After some discussion, the assembled actors proceeded to discard their rehearsal clothes and donned period costumes and manners to enact *Shrew*, with the disruptive, T-shirted actor assuming the role of Petruchio. Although the production concept explored the relationship between life and theatre, the focus was mainly on Katherina's and Petruchio's respective journeys towards self-discovery. As Goss wrote in a program note: "This is a play about the self; it reflects the self viewed through the eyes of the other." A series of large mirrors placed upstage as part of the setting reinforced this idea. The Goss interpretation aimed not so much at taming Katherina as at creating a harmonious relationship between Katherina and Petruchio through the taming process.

Three different productions of *King Lear* were presented: one in Shanghai and two in Beijing. The Liaoning Provincial People's Art Theatre production at the Experimental Theatre of the Shanghai Academy of Theatre featured the celebrated actor Li Moran in the title role. Although the production was presented in an essentially Western style, Li succeeded in integrating certain Beijing opera conventions into his performance, thus making Lear more familiar and acceptable to a Chinese audience. The scenic design was also interesting; the setting suggested a huge crown that gradually deteriorated with each scene until it collapsed at the end of the play. The Tienjing People's Art Theatre production in Beijing was also performed in a translation close to Shakespeare's text and in a traditional and generally realistic Western style. The Central Drama Academy of Beijing, however, presented an adaptation by the Chinese Shakespeare scholar Sun Jiaxiu, entitled *Li Ya Wang* (literally, *King of the Li Kingdom*). The opening scenes, for example, were presented in a setting that suggested the Empress' theatre at the Imperial Summer Palace. All the characters took Chinese names and wore historical Chinese costumes, and the performance style was more Chinese than Western. Indeed, the characterizations and production as a whole recalled a typical Chinese story as much as Shakespeare's play.

Other essentially Western-style productions also successfully incorporated elements of traditional Chinese theatre. In the Wuhan Spoken Drama Troupe's production of *The Merry Wives of Windsor*, for example, the noted actor Hu Qinshu incorporated Beijing opera movement conventions into his portrayal of Falstaff. The scenery likewise echoed the traditional setting of Chinese opera. In contrast, the Central Experimental Theatre's production in Beijing was, as J. Philip Brockbank noted, "an English experience, with a half-timbered set and Elizabethan costumes." The China Youth Art Theatre's production of *The Merchant of Venice*, a somewhat revised revival of a celebrated 1980 production, adapted the conventions of the Beijing opera to pantomime effectively , in the absence of any semblance of a real canal or real water, a gliding gondola in the opening scene. As Brockbank recalled, "gondolier and courtiers bobbed, swayed, and flourished on what became an almost audibly lapping canal."

The most acclaimed festival productions, however, were those that adapted Shakespeare's plays almost completely into the various traditional Chinese opera styles. A production of *Twelfth Night* by the Shanghai *Yueju* Opera House kept Shakespeare's play nearly intact within *yueju* (also called *Shaoxing*) opera's musical and performance conventions, although there were some interesting adaptations and compromises. The costumes, for example, were more Elizabethan than Chinese. Indeed, as Peide Zha and Jia Tian commented, the costumes made the production look like "a play in which foreigners sang *Shaoxing* opera tunes." The musical accompaniment was even bolder than in traditional *yueju* and included Western instruments such as the cello and harp. The singing did not follow one particular school of *yueju* opera, which is the usual practice, but rather the performers drew on various Chinese opera styles and folksongs, as well as on Western opera styles. As Zha and Tian observed; "Their goal was not to play the schools of singing but to play Shakespeare's roles." This eclectic approach to performance was perhaps most effectively exemplified in Shi Jihua's Malvolio. In the course of his performance, he appeared in several different *yueju* opera role categories. For example in most scenes, he appeared in the dignified *jing* (painted-face) role; when reading the love letter, however, he assumed the *xiao sheng* (scholar-lover) role; in the yellow-stockings scene, he appeared as the *chou* (clown) character. In this latter character, he was especially well received by the audience. Although purist *yueju* opera fans were displeased with this eclectic interpretation, theatre professionals and Shakespeare scholars were enthusiastic. Later in the year, the production won several prizes in the third annual Shanghai Theatre Festival.

The production of *The Winter's Tale* by the No. 1 Troupe of Hangzhou *Yueju* Opera House followed the conventions of the style much more closely than the Shanghai company did in *Twelfth Night*. Shakespeare's plot, for example, was arranged into six scenes with a prologue and an epilogue. Each scene had a title similar to those in traditional *yueju* operas, which tend to be romantic love stories with tragicomic overtones, much like *The Winter's Tale* itself. Unlike *Twelfth Night*, which used both actors and actresses, *The Winter's Tale,* adhering to *yueju* opera tradition, was performed entirely by actresses. All of the characters, moreover, were given Chinese names. The whole production had a strong folk-theatre flavor typical of Zhejiang province. Autolycus, for example, played very effectively by Zhou Lili, was turned into a typical Chinese folk-theatre traveling peddler. Time's soliloquy in Act IV, scene 1 was omitted, and, instead, Autolycus (or Jiao Gouzi, as he was called) sang a folk ballad describing seasonal farming activities to suggest "my swift passage that I slide/O'er sixteen years." Overall, the local audience seemed to appreciate this adaptation more than *Twelfth Night*.

Much Ado About Nothing was adapted to the *huangmeixi* opera style by the Anhui *Hungmeixi* Opera Troupe. Shakespeare's play was set among an unidentified, generalized ethnic minority group in a border region of ancient China with no identification of the historical dynasty. All of the characters were given Chinese names, which nonetheless suggested the sound of the originals, and were dressed in historical Chinese costumes. A number of *huangmei* performance conventions were integrated into the play's actions. For example, on the first meeting of Li Hailuo (Hero) and Lou Diao (Claudio), they looked into each other's eyes from across the stage. Li Bicui (Beatrice) pantomimed drawing from their eyes an imaginary ribbon or string which she then knotted in the center. Using this string, she led the couple around the stage in a stylized movement accompanied by lyrical music, until she finally broke the string, resulting in Li Hailuo and Lou Diao nearly falling down. Li Bicui and Bai Lidi

(Benedick) also effectively adapted the "water sleeve" conventions—techniques using the long, wide sleeves of traditional Chinese opera costumes—to express their inner feelings during their bickering duets. This production proved very popular with the audience; subsequently, in September, this production was presented for a two-week run in Beijing.

Macbeth, retitled *Bloody Hands*, was adapted into *kunju* opera, the oldest of the existing Chinese opera styles, by the Shanghai *Kunju* Opera Troupe. Shakespeare's play was rearranged into nine scenes, and, as in *Much Ado* and *The Winter's Tale*, the names of the characters were sinocized: Macbeth became Mapei, King Duncan became King Zheng, and so on. The costumes were traditional, and the actors observed the manners of the Chinese royal court. Generally, characters in *kunju* opera conform to a single stereotype. Ji Zhenghua, a well-known *kunju* opera actor, however, adapted three male role-categories to capture Mapei's character. These were the dignified, middle-aged, bearded *laosheng* character, the *wusheng* or military man, specializing in acrobatics and fighting techniques, and the *wenshen* or older civilian man, specializing in singing and diction. Ji also used typical techniques like "beard stroking," "beard flicking," and "hair throwing" to express Mapei's inner turmoil, according to Zha and Tian. Zhang Jinglan played Lady Macbeth basically in the *dan* role traditions, but she also incorporated elements of the *huadan* (flowery woman), or woman of questionable character, and the *pishadan* (fighting woman), or cruel and severe woman, specializing in physically difficult movements. The actors portraying the weird sisters combined the *caidan* (woman clown) and *xiao gui* (elf) roles and walked in the *aizi bu* (dwarf gait).

The adaptation also added some business to Shakespeare's play. For example, immediately after the murder of Duncan, a green puppet parrot (the symbol of gossip in Chinese mythology) that was part of the castle setting, echoed the word "murder." Lady Macbeth grabbed it and viciously tore its head and body apart to visualize her earlier lines, "I would . . . /Have plucked my nipple from his boneless gums/and dashed the brains out" (Act I, scene 7, lines 56-58). In the sleepwalking scene, the ghosts of Duncan, Banquo, Lady McDuff, and the parrot appeared and spat fire, a traditional business for ghosts in *chvanju* opera. *Bloody Hands* was considered a highlight of the festival and one of the more effective adaptations of Shakespeare into traditional Chinese opera styles. The production subsequently toured to the Edinburgh International Theatre Festival and has been frequently revived by the Shanghai *Kunju* Opera Troupe.

Other highlights of the festival included a production of *Othello* staged by the Mongolian students in their third year at the Shanghai Academy of Theatre. This was the first Shakespeare production ever done in Mongolian. Several English language productions were also presented by student theatre groups in both Beijing and Shanghai. Students of the Arts Academy of the Chinese People's Liberation Army produced a *Merchant of Venice* in English, while students at the Second Foreign Languages Institute of Beijing presented *Timon of Athens*. In Shanghai, the WAIWEN Drama Club of Fudan University presented in English acts 1 and 5 of *Much Ado About Nothing* in their entirety, summarizing the other acts with a combination of pantomimic action and narration.

In addition to the many performances, the festival included a number of scholarly lectures, symposia, and exhibitions. For example, symposia were held on stage design, acting, and directing, Shakespeare's sinolization, and Shakespeare in traditional operatic styles. Seven numbers of a Festival Newsletter and three numbers of a Festival Journal were issued during the festival by the Festival Office in Shanghai. An exhibition, "Contemporary Shakespeare Performance in England," organized by the British Council, was displayed in the Experimental Theatre at the Shanghai Academy of Theatre.

With a total attendance of almost 100,000 at the various performances and complementary events in both Beijing and Shanghai, the first China Shakespeare Festival was considered a resounding success. The Shakespeare scholar, Philip Brockbank, who as a guest of the SSC, had seen many of the festival productions, proposed that the SSC mount an international Shakespeare festival in Shanghai in 1990. The SSC responded positively to this proposal and began to lay a foundation for such a festival to include as well the second China Shakespeare Festival. By the end of 1989, however, it was clear that funding for such an enterprise was inadequate, and the festival was postponed until 1991. Subsequently, the festival was postponed a second time, but, in the spring issue of the International Shakespeare Association Newsletter, a second Chinese Festival was announced for the fall of 1994.

Production History: China Shakespeare Festival, 1986: A List of Productions. (Date indicates first festival production.)

Shanghai

Titus Andronicus. 10 April, Research Institute of the Shanghai Academy of Theatre, Experimental Theatre; Shanghai Academy of Theatre; Director: Xu Qiping.

The Taming of the Shrew. 12 April, Shanghai People's Art Theatre, Shanghai Art Theatre; Director; Bernard Goss.

The Merry Wives of Windsor. 13 April, Wuhan Spoken Drama House, Experimental Theatre; Shanghai Academy of Theatre; Director: Hu Dao.

Love's Labour's Lost. 15 April, Jiangsu Provincial Spoken Drama, Shanghai Literature and Art Hall; Director: Xiong Guodong.

Alls Well The Ends Well. 17 April, Xian Spoken Drama House, Chang Jiang Theatre; Director: Yang Huizhen.

King Lear. 18 April, Liaoning Provincial People's Art Theatre, Experimental Theatre, Shanghai Academy of Theatre; Director: Ding Ni.

Twelfth Night. 11 April, adapted into *yueju* opera by the Shanghai *Yueju* Opera House, Chang Jiang Theatre; Director: Hu Weiming.

The Winter's Tale. 20 April, adapted into *yueju* opera by the No. 1 Troupe of Hangzhou *Yueju* Opera House, China Theatre; Director: Wang Fuming.

Much Ado About Nothing. 20 April, adapted into *huangmeixi* opera by the Anhui *Huangmeixi* Opera Troupe Ruijin Theatre; Director: Jiang Weiguo.

Macbeth (Bloody Hands). 10 April, adapted into *kunju* opera by the Shanghai *Kunju* Opera Troupe. Children's Art Theatre; Director: Li Jiayao.

Twelfth Night. (The Twin Brother and Sister). 20 April, a puppet theatre production by the Shanghai Puppet Theatre Company, Fenglei Theatre; Director: Yao Jinshi.

Othello. 19 April, Mongolian Class of the Shanghai Academy of Theatre, Children's Art Theatre; Director: Liu Jiangping.

The Taming of the Shrew. 21 April, Shaanxi People's Art Theatre, Chang Jiang Theatre; Director: Xuan Ying.

Much Ado About Nothing (in English). 20 April, WAIWEN Drama Club of Fudan University, Fudan University Hall; Director: Olivia Lillich and Yan Bin.

Antony and Cleopatra. 11 April, Shanghai Youth Spoken Drama Troupe, Chang Jiang Theatre; Director: Hu Weimin.

Merchant of Venice. 23 April, China Youth Arts Theatre, Experimental Theatre, Shanghai Academy of Theatre; Director: Zhang Qihong.

Beijing

The Merchant of Venice (in English). 19 April, Arts Academy of the Chinese People's Liberation Army, Small Theatre of Central Academy of Drama;. Director: He You.

Timon of Athens (in English). 19 April, Beijing Second Foreign Languages Institute, Small Theatre of Central Academy of Drama; Directors: Wen Pulin and Zheng Ziru.

Twelfth Night (all women). 17 April, North China Drama Society of Beijing Teachers's University, Capital Theatre; Directors: Li Zibai and Chang Yuling.

Timon of Athens. 19 April, North China Drama Society of Beijing Teachers's University, Capital Theatre; Director: Cai Xiang.

King Lear. 18 April, Tienjing People's Art Theatre, National Palace; Director: Sha Wei.

King Lear. (Li Ya Wang) 17 April, Central Academy of Drama, Small Theatre of Central Academy of Drama; Directors: Ran Jie, Liu Mudao, Li Zibai.

Othello. 14 April, adapted into Beijing Opera by the Beijing Experimental Beijing Opera Troupe, National Palace; Director: Cheng Bi-xian.

Othello. 18 April, TIELU (China Railways) Spoken Drama Troupe, 2.7. Theatre; Director: Chen Ping.

Richard III. 10 April, China Children's Art Theatre, Capital Theatre; Directors: Zhou Lai and Huang Yilin.

The Merry Wives of Windsor. 13 April, Central Experimental Spoken Drama House, Capital Theatre; Director: Yang Zongjing.

A Midsummer Night's Dream. 12 April, MEIKUANG (China Coal Miners') Spoken Drama Troupe, Small Theatre of Central Academy of Drama; Director: Xiong Yuanwei.

Merchant of Venice. 11 April, China Youth Art Theatre; Director: Zhang Qihong; Artistic Adviser; Cao Yu.

Research Resources: Archives are informally maintained at the festival administrative office of the Shakespeare Society of China.

See also the following selected publications:

Brockbank, J. Philip. "Shakespeare Renaissance in China." *Shakespeare Quarterly* (Summer 1988): 195-204.

Cao, Shujun; Sun, Fuliang. *Shakespeare on the Chinese Stage (Shashibiya zai zhongguo wutaishang).* Harbin Publishing House, 1989.

Daconte, Eduardo Marceles. "Shakespeare en China." *Magazin Dominical* 174 (27 July 1986): 5-9.

Fan, Shen. "Shakespeare in China: The Merchant of Venice." *Asian Theatre Journal* (Spring 1988): 23-37.

He, Qixin. "China's Shakespeare." *Shakespeare Quarterly* (Summer 1986): 149-159.

Kynge, James. "Shakespeare in China." *Play and Players* (July 1986): 16-17.

Li, Ruru. "Chinese Traditional Theatre and Shakespeare." *Asian Theatre Journal* (Spring 1988): 38-48.

Lin, Yang. "China Makes Much Ado About the Bard." *Beijing Review* (26 May 1986): 30-31.

Office of the 1st China Shakespeare Festival. *"Newsletter of the 1st China Shakespeare Festival"* (*Shoujie zhongguo shashibiya xijujie jianbao)*, Nos. 1–7. Publishing House of Shanghai Culture & Art Weekly, 1986.

Shakespeare Society of China. *"Shakespeare in China"* (*Shashibiya zai zhongguo).* Shanghai Literature & Art Publishing House, 1987.

Tsai, Chin. "Teaching and Directing in China: Chinese Theatre Revisited." *Asian Theatre Journal* (Spring 1986): 118-131.

Weiss, Alfred. "The Edinburgh Festival, 1987." *Shakespeare Quarterly* (Spring 1988): 79-89 [on the *kunju Macbeth*].

Yang, Daniel S. P. "Theatre in post Cultural Revolution China: A Report Based on Field Research in the Fall and Winter of 1981." *Asian Theatre Journal* (Spring 1984): 90-103.

Yeh, Chen Chun. "A hit, palpable hit in China," *The Times* [London] (2January 1982): 6.

Yu, Weijie. "Topicality and Typicality: The Acceptance of Shakespeare in China." In *The Dramatic Touch of difference: theatre, own and foreign,* ed. by Erika Fischer-Lichte, Tübingen: Gunter Narr Verlag, 1990.

Zha, Peide; Tian, Jia. "Shakespeare in Traditional Chinese Operas." *Shakespeare Quarterly* (Summer 1988): 204-211.

Zhang, Yike. "Traditional Opera: Challenge and Response." *China Reconstructs* (September 1987): 19-23.

Zhu, Zhenglian. "Local opera jumps on Shakespeare theme." *China Daily* (25 February 1986): 5.

Victor Weijie Yu

FRANCE

LES AMIS DU JARDIN SHAKESPEARE DU PRÉ CATELAN. MAIL: Marie-Louise Hemphill, présidente, 1 Place de Wagram, 75017 Paris, France. SITE: Jardin Shakespeare du Pré Catelan, Bois de Boulogne, Paris, France. ADMINISTRATION: 42-27-39-54. BOX OFFICE: tickets may be purchased at the site one hour before performance. ADMISSION: 50–70 francs ($10–$14 in 1992); free for children under 15. SEASON: seven to ten performances, usually in May or September; 12:00 noon, Mon.–Sun. PRINCIPAL STAFF: Marie-Louise Hemphill, présidente-foundatrice (chairperson). FACILITY: natural open-air theatre in Jardin Shakespeare (capacity 500). ANNUAL BUDGET: $20,000 (1992). ANNUAL ATTENDANCE: 1,500. FOUNDED: 1982, Marie-Louise Hemphill.

Les Amis du Jardin Shakespeare du Pré Catelan (AJSP) was founded in 1982 by Marie-Louise Hemphill to promote the unique and exquisite Shakespeare garden in Paris. The organization brings in groups of actors and musicians to perform in this garden. Under Hemphill's dedicated leadership, this Anglo-French venture shares English culture and language with the people of France, combining the two cultures' mutual love of gardens and poetry. The organization stands as a tribute to British culture and the long-standing friendship between the two countries.

The garden itself has an interesting history. In 1888, an impressive statue of William Shakespeare, much admired by Parisians, was erected in the 8th arrondissement in Paris. It stood in the middle of the roundabout at the junction of Avenue de Missine and Boulevard Haussmann, not very far from the Parc Monceau. Designed by Paul Fournier and owned by William Knight, it was a tribute to the playwright and to the English people. Unfortunately, this memorial disappeared during World War II. Rather than commission another statue, a prominent Parisian citizen, André de Fouquières, suggested a living memorial—a Shakespeare garden. Robert Joffet, then director of the Paris Parks and Gardens, began to look for a suitable site. In the Bois de Boulogne he discovered an abandoned and rundown area that had a rudimentary amphitheatre. The garden project was begun in October 1952 and completed in June 1953. Joffet and his staff chose five Shakespeare plays to create the garden. They wanted the garden to reflect the comedies and tragedies, as well as two distinct regions, northern and southern Europe. *As You Like It*, *Macbeth*, and *Hamlet* were chosen to represent countries bordered by the North Sea: England, Scotland, and Denmark. *A Midsummer Night's Dream* and *The Tempest* were chosen to represent countries bordered by the Mediterranean: Greece and Italy. Trees, plants, and flowers mentioned in these plays, augmented by French plants, went into the design. Cypress trees, Ophelia's willow growing aslant near a brook, Macbeth's heath, Titania's flowers, and the forest of Arden are all represented. Each play has its own area, accompanied by appropriate quotations from Shakespeare. Opening ceremonies on 29 June 1953, conducted by Frédéric Dupont, president of the Municipal Council of Paris, honored Joffet by saying, "Vous êtes bien le technicien du miracle." Charles Russell (the Mayor of Westminster), Lady Harvey (British ambassador to France), and actor Maurice Chevalier all attended the opening dedication ceremonies and marveled at the garden's beauty. In honor of the occasion, students of the Oxford Dramatic Society performed *Troilus and Cressida*. On the second day of the performance, it rained, dampening people's enthusiasm for outdoor play production. "Obviously, they had not been to England to know that rain does not stop anything, not even the coronation of the queen," laughs Hemphill. Nonetheless, plays were performed there for the next 30 years.

The Shakespeare garden might have remained dormant if it had not been for the vision and determination of Marie-Louise Hemphill. Upon returning to France after living for a number of years in England, Hemphill was shocked and disappointed to discover that the performance space was unused. She wrote an article, suggesting the formation of the AJSP, that attracted the attention of some influential people, including Lady Hibbert, wife of the British ambassador to France. On 27 June 1981, Lady Hibbert was introduced to the garden by Hemphill. Marks and Spenser donated sherry to celebrate the occasion. Once again, rain poured, but it failed to dampen their enthusiasm. Encouraged by Lady Hibbert's support, Hemphill announced the creation of AJSP on 22 January 1982. The organization received 5,000 francs from Jack Lang, the French Minister of Culture. In June of 1982, the AJSP invited the Bristol Old Vic Theatre School to present five performances of *As You Like It*, bringing to life the garden that had been silent for 30 years.

In 1983, the tradition continued with a bilingual production of *Le Songe d'une nuit d'été* (*A Midsummer Night's Dream*) by le Théâtre de Juillet. The fairies spoke French while the human world of the court and the mechanicals spoke English. *The Comedy of Errors* was also presented that same year by the English television channel. *Twelfth Night*, directed by Graham Bushnell and *Love's Labour's Lost* by the Sherman Arena Company (Cardiff University, Wales) comprised the 1984 season. The year 1985 was dark, but, in 1986,

Cruel Love, a series of Shakespeare scenes directed by Ruth Handlen with her company, Théâtre et Anglais, was presented in the garden. In 1987, Handlen's company mounted *Very Midsummer Madness*. The Wilde Players performed *Hamlet* in 1988, and, in 1989, the AJSP presented *Hommage à Lord Olivier*, a compilation of scenes from *Hamlet*, *Henry V*, *Henry VI*, and *Romeo and Juliet*, and *Richard III* was performed by the Capital Theatre Company. The Westminster School boys performed *The Tempest* in 1990, using costumes from the **Royal Shakespeare Company**. *The Taming of the Shrew*, in French, was given by Christ's College, Cambridge, in 1991, and the 1992 season featured *The Merry Wives of Windsor* by the Tower Theatre Islington. *Macbeth* is the only play represented in the garden that has not had a complete presentation there.

The AJSP books primarily amateur groups that tour. The success of the venture depends on cooperation between the AJSP, the producing organization, and the Paris Parks and Gardens department. The AJSP's 1,000 members, divided into committees, provide housing, publicity, and front-of-house operations. The producing group provides its own transportation, food, costumes, and props. The city provides the upkeep on the Shakespeare garden. Profits, if any, are shared following the final performance. The AJSP's costs for *The Merry Wives of Windsor* came to £10,000. Donations from patrons and membership dues (150 francs per year), along with various fund-raising events such as dinners and lectures held throughout the year, help to supplement box office income.

An open space embraced by mature trees, flowers, walking trails, and lily-covered ponds, provides an idyllic environment in which to view Shakespeare. A gently raked green allows up to 500 spectators, on temporary seats, to have an unobstructed view of the stage. The stage itself is a flat green area, approximately 40 feet wide by 20 feet deep. An orchestra pit, hidden by hedges, lies at the front of the stage. The natural backdrop consists of a variety of vegetation, including cypress trees and a waterfall stage right whose gently tumbling waters can be heard during performances. An upstage tunnel made of natural rock provides a space for actors to make entrances as well as cross over backstage without being seen by the audience.

Performances are held in the afternoon, and the space is intimate enough that no sound amplification is necessary. Dressing rooms and makeup rooms are housed in rented trailers. The program provides a plot synopsis in French, cast information, and facts about the producing company as well as information on the AJSP. Although the AJSP's season is limited (usually two weeks in either May or September), the garden is open year-round. Admission is three francs (approximately 60¢ at 1994 exchange rate) and is well worth the visit. David Conville, former director of the **Open Air Theatre** in London's Regent's Park, called it "the most beautiful garden and open-air theatre in the world."

Parisians, unfortunately, are mostly unacquainted with the Shakespeare garden. So are the 50,000 British and American families living in the city. Limited publicity and an "out of the mainstream" location in the Bois de Boulogne combine to keep attendance much lower than it deserves to be. Hemphill also notes that the nationalism of the French people sometimes limits their interest in English and in Shakespeare's plays. The audience consists primarily of AJSP members and friends, as well as schoolchildren who are brought in for the performances. The Shakespeare garden is located in the center of the Bois de Boulogne on the west side of the city. From the Bagatelle/Pré Catelan bus stop, it is a five-minute walk to the garden.

Beginning several months before the performance, various marketing tools are used to reach the 9 million people living in Paris and its surrounding region. There is a mailing list of 1,000 and a newsletter is produced twice a year. The organization tries to get coverage in local newspapers and reviewers from the major newspapers are invited to the performances. *Le Figaro* provides good coverage. Hemphill herself is a tireless promoter. On the day we walked to the garden, she took every opportunity to tell people in the park and on the bus about the Shakespeare garden and her organization.

At age 84, Marie-Louise Hemphill says her primary goal is simply to "carry on." She wants to make sure that English plays are presented in the Shakespeare garden and that it is not allowed to become only an open-air theatre that ignores its origins as a *Shakespeare* garden. She has no objections to presenting plays other than Shakespeare as well but wants to see a permanent commitment to Shakespeare production at least once a year. The new director of the garden is inclined to produce French plays and leave out the name of Shakespeare in his advertising of the garden—a great concern to the AJSP. The organization's major problem will be replacing the infectiously enthusiastic and indefatigable Marie-Louise Hemphill. Hemphill notes that her replacement must be a French person with a love and knowledge of both Shakespeare and gardens. Ties to aristocracy and wealth (Hemphill is the great-niece of Louis Pasteur) are also helpful qualifications for the position.

The AJSP usually hosts producing organizations that take a simple, straightforward, and relatively traditional approach to Shakespeare. Plays are generally in English and uncut. Focus is on the language, well spoken. Hemphill does not believe in translating because "one wants to hear the melody." The other aesthetic consideration is that the staging must be sensitive to the environment and not harm the garden. The AJSP would welcome a producing organization from America.

Production History: **1982**: *AYL*; **1983**: *Le Songe d'une nuit d'été* (*MND*, bilingual); *Err.*; **1984**: *TN*, *LLL*; **1985**: no production; **1986**: *Cruel Love*; **1987**: *Very Mid-summer Madness*; **1988**: *Ham.*, **1989**: *Hommage à Lord Olivier*; 1990: *Tmp.*, **1991**: *Shr.* (in French); **1992**: *Wiv.*

Research Resources: Archives are informally maintained at the home of Marie-Louise Hemphill. See Marie-Louise Hemphill, *À l'Ombre du Jardin Shakespeare du Pré Catelan* (Paris: Imprimeries Reunies de Bourg, 1990).

Site visit and interview with Marie-Louise Hemphill: 29 July 1992.
Cindy Melby Phaneuf

FOOTSBARN TRAVELLING THEATRE COMPANY. MAIL: "La Chaussé," Herisson, France. SITE: varies. ADMINISTRATION: (33) 70-06-84-84; Fax: (33) 70-06-84-71. ADMISSION: varies. PRINCIPAL STAFF: John Kilby and Béatrice Beaucaire, administrators. FACILITY: tent (capacity 500); rehearsal rooms, offices, etc., on a farm in Herisson. FOUNDED: 1971, Oliver Foot, John Paul Cook.

Footsbarn Travelling Theatre Company (FTTC) was founded in 1971 when six actors and six musicians began performing material based on local lore in the streets, markets, pubs, fairs, and schools of villages in Cornwall, where the troupe was based. The company name derived from the idea of taking theatre to people who had never seen it, as pioneered in the eighteenth century by Sir Isaac Foot and his Barn stormers (performing in barns in an era before England's provincial cities had permanent theatres). The shows were collectively created through improvisation and exploration of techniques of puppetry, mask-work, mime, and dance.

By 1975, the FTTC had acquired a tent and trucks, which allowed increased independence and mobility. A "short history" provided by the company describes its status in that transitional phase as

> known throughout the South West [of England] as a theatre adept in creating fantasy, pathos, and bawdy comedy which was a delight to many but for some it bordered on something akin to Anarchy. Funding was an ever increasing problem, especially as local authorities formed the opinion that it was like giving money to pirates! With many of the group members trying to support families, it was decided to accept the increasing number of invitations that were coming from abroad, where people had a more open handed policy to support unusual theatre.

The feasibility of becoming an internationally itinerant company seemed assured after the FTTC's *Hamlet* was presented successfully in the Netherlands, Germany, and Denmark.

The FTTC abandoned its Cornish base in 1981 and performed that year in France, Holland, West Germany, Spain, and Portugal, as well as at various sites in England, Wales, and Ireland. The next five years brought performances in

11 different countries and at 24 international festivals. From temporary bases in Portugal, Italy, and France, the FTTC created five new productions, including a *King Lear* (in Italy, 1983), forged from severely limited resources after the company lost much of its equipment and nearly disbanded. A 1984 grant from the European Community's (EC) Cultural Commission provided for the purchase of a new tent and travel to six different countries with *Chinese Puzzle*, a show designed for non-English-speaking audiences. A Mercedes bus accompanied the FTTC and functioned as a school complete with two full-time, qualified teachers. Thus it could be claimed that "the Footsbarn children have attended the same school in 17 different countries."

Beginning in 1988, the FTTC was regularly invited by Les Fédérés of Montluçon to perform there in the geographical center of France. Company members fell in love with the area and decided to make it their permanent headquarters. In 1990, FTTC bought a farm in Hérisson, named it La Chaussée, and began a two-year development project to create rehearsal rooms, workshops, offices, a music studio, garage, and canteen. The company still includes four of the original founding members, as well as performers, designers, and technicians from Canada, the United States, Australia, Algeria, France, the Netherlands, Poland, and Russia.

Perhaps the fact that Shakespeare's plays are in themselves an international language justifies their centrality in the FTTC repertoire. The 1992 production of *Romeo and Juliet* was conceived as a street spectacle for rural audiences. Challenged by the idea of translating Shakespeare's poetry into a more visual theatrical language, the FTTC marshalled all the skills it had been developing over the years: music, puppets, ritual combat, clowns, and conjuring effects.

Production History: **1971**: *Next Time I'll Sing to You, Endgame, Jeu gratuit, The Lesson, The Bald Primadonna, The Gump St Just, Tregeagle, Perran Cherry Beam, The Woodcut*; **1972**: *Crow 10, Tristan, A Resounding Tinkle, The Bear, Giant, Zoo Story, Punch and Judy Show.* **1973**: *Master Patalan, His Farce, Streetshow, The Adventures of John Tom*; **1974**: *Greta's Follies, Pot of Gold, The Scarecrow and the Cornspirit, Incident at the Crazy Cowpoke Saloon, Jack and the Beanstalk*; **1975**: *Underwater World, Legend, Beauty and the Beast, This is Your Life, The Stranger*; **1976**: *Midsummer Madness* (a version of *MND*), *Peter Pan*; **1977**: *The Scarecrow, The Dancing Bear, The Circus Tosov, Robin Hood*; **1978**: *Tmp., The Circus Tosov, Jungle Fever*; **1979**: *Arthur, The Golden Fleece*; **1980**: *Ham., Tall Stories*; **1981**: *Arthur*; **1982**: *The Rockin Tossers, O Diabo, O Doutour e o Louco*; **1983**: *Lr.*; **1984**: *The Chinese Puzzle*; **1986**: *Mac.*; **1987**: *Babylone*; **1988**: *The Circus Tosov*; **1989**: *The Pearl*; **1990**: *MND*; **1991-1992**: *Rom.*

Research Resources: Archives maintained by the Footsbarn company. Geraldine Cousin, "Shakespeare from Scratch: the Footsbarn 'Hamlet' and 'King Lear,'" *Theatre Quarterly* (February 1985): 105-125; Geraldine Cousin, "Footsbarn: from a Tribal 'Macbeth' to an Intercultural 'Dream,'" *Theatre Quarterly* 33 (February 1993): 16-30.

Felicia Hardison Londré

SHAKESPEARE EN AVIGNON. MAIL: 68, rue Vieille du Temple, 75003, Paris, France. SITE: Fort Saint-André, Villeneuve-les-Avignon. ADMINISTRATION: (33) 1-42-77-70-25. BOX OFFICE: (33) 90-25-66-05. ADMISSION: 60–80 francs. SEASON: seven to ten performances in July and August. PRINCIPAL STAFF: Eve Brennan, director; Ada Brown Mather, master teacher. FACILITY: fourteenth-century tower rooms and an eighteenth-century house inside Fort Saint-André. AUDITIONS: write for application form. STATUS: professional training. ANNUAL BUDGET: 120,000 francs (1991). ANNUAL ATTENDANCE: 1,500 (1991). FOUNDED: 1989, Eve Brennan.

Given her cross-cultural heritage (an American father and a French mother), Eve Brennan has naturally maintained an international outlook. After training as an opera singer at the Manhattan School of Music and studying acting under Ada Brown Mather, Brennan returned to France in January 1989 and conceived the idea of an international academy that would combine life in a culturally lively French locale with work on Shakespearean texts in English. Because her classes under the renowned British director Mather had been so remarkably stimulating, Brennan also wanted a project that would allow her to continue that association. In less than four months, Brennan had laid a solid enough foundation that she was able to invite Mather's participation and to announce a program for that summer. She chose Avignon, a historic city in south central France, because its annual summer festival was already well established as a key event in French theatre. Brennan therefore named the project **Shakespeare en Avignon** (SEA).

Brennan haunted the local tourism offices and gained the support of the director of the Festival d'Avignon. Eventually she also obtained subsidies from the French government and the British Council. "The first year was difficult," Brennan recalls, "because in France nothing is decided orally. Without a file, a dossier, you don't exist. So I had to create a dossier out of absolutely nothing." Much of her preparatory work was done from Paris, but she made an initial ten-day visit to Avignon to scout out workshop and performance spaces as well as lodgings for the participants.

Across the Rhône from Avignon is the smaller town of Villeneuve-lez-Avignon, built around the hilltop on which the monumental Fort Saint-André is perched. The fourteenth-century ramparts enclose the remains of an eleventh-century church and former village, as well as an elegant eighteenth-century house with terraces affording a stunning view of the Rhône valley. The house, located about half a block down the street on the right as one enters the fort, now serves as the summer headquarters and workshop space for SEA. Performances are given in a vaulted room inside one of the massive twin towers flanking the entrance to the fort. Thus, the participants in SEA have easy access by foot or by bus to the hundreds of theatrical events going on during the Avignon festival, but their workshops and rehearsals are conducted in the quiet atmosphere of a relatively isolated historical setting.

Because SEA is not actually produced by the Festival d'Avignon, it is not listed in the official program, but there is nevertheless a linkage, in that SEA offers, in addition to its workshops and productions, a master class for actors from the festival. Thus, SEA is the only nonfestival event listed in the daily press bulletin published by the Institut de la Communication d'Avignon. The master class draws about 60 actors. Audiences for the SEA productions are composed of festival-goers; the average attendance is 120 to 150 at each performance. Because most members of the audience are French-speaking, the English-language performance is given an introduction in French. "We try to link our Englishness to their Frenchness," says Mather. For the 1990 production of *Richard III*, for example, they incorporated a French chorus to comment on events.

Participants are admitted to SEA on the basis of applications that include recommendations from acting teachers. Approximately 12 students are admitted for each two- or four-week session; usually there is a mix of nationalities, including American, British, Canadian, Danish, Dutch, French, and Norwegian. "To have actors coming from different countries into this unusual environment, this neutral territory where theatre is happening around us, really makes them jump to another level," says Brennan. "Coming here is a kind of upheaval, and people from different backgrounds bring different energies, but they all work on Shakespeare in English and bring out unsuspected possibilities in each other." Classes meet five days a week from 9:30 to 12:30; afternoons are given over to rehearsals. Tuition fees in 1992 were 5,000 French francs for the two-week session, and 9,000 francs for four weeks. After acceptance into the program, the deadline for full payment is May 1.

Ada Brown Mather has taught acting and directing at the Royal Academy of Dramatic Art, the Juilliard School, New York University, and South Coast Repertory Conservatory, and she now runs her own studios in New York, Los Angeles, and London. She conducts the SEA training program and directs the productions. Asked to describe her way of working with actors, Mather says:

I'm a great preparer, but I'm very much a person who works on the instinct of the moment. It depends on what you see happening with the individual. I work a lot on rhythm and breathing. It's thrilling to help people release the sensibilities they have within their beings. And it's almost always accompanied by some kind of breath effort.

In a *New York Times* interview, André Serban said of Mather: "She guides actors in making the text part of their being, as if they had lived through it yesterday, slept through it last night and wakened with it this morning. With her, Shakespeare becomes what he should be: an extraordinary contemporary author writing about things that concern us today."

Brennan credits Mather with cofounding SEA, "because it wouldn't have happened without her." The two work harmoniously together, one often finishing the other's sentences. Brennan handles the administrative work and also performs. Mather teaches and directs. The productions, shaped to fit the needs of those enrolled in each session, often relate to a theme developed by the group, so that process and product go hand in hand.

"The important thing is that we're dealing with Shakespeare from an actor's point of view, and what it's about is creating true actors—actors who are creating the event of the play in reality and not in a display of some technique of speaking words. That's our thrust," says Mather, summing up SEA's artistic mission.

Production History: **1989**: *Come unto these yellow sands* (based on *Tmp.*, *MND*, *WT*); **1990**: *R3*, *Scenes, monologues, and sonnets by Shakespeare*; **1991**: *Shakespeare's Women: Love and Power*, *My business is circumference* (poems and letters of Emily Dickinson); *D. H. Lawrence* (poems), *Scenes, monologues, and sonnets by Shakespeare*; **1992**: *Un filet d'or. . .* (based on *Ado*); Shakespeare: *Monologues, Scenes, and Sonnets.*

Research Resources: Archives for Shakespeare en Avignon are maintained by Eve Brennan in Paris.

Site visit and interview: 4 July 1991.
Felicia Hardison Londré

GERMAN-LANGUAGE SHAKESPEARE: AUSTRIA, GERMANY, SWITZERLAND

Shakespeare is one of the most produced playwrights in the German theatre and has become a tradition in the repertory of German-language theatres. Translations in the late eighteenth and early nineteenth centuries by A.W.

Schlegel, Ludwig Tieck, and Graf Baudissin established a performance tradition that has been continued in this century by Hans Rothe, Erich Fried, Heiner Müller in his controversial translations, and a recent proliferation of translations and adaptations by individual artists. In the 1988-89 theatre season, there were 103 new productions of 30 Shakespeare plays; in the 1990-91 season, 104 productions of 23 of his plays were presented in 1,985 performances. Important productions by the most celebrated and often controversial directors of our time have occurred on the German stage in the last 30 years. Directors such as Peter Zadek, Claus Peymann, Peter Stein, Klaus Michael Grüber, Arie Zinger, Heiner Müller, Hans Hollmann, Eric Vos, Leopold Lindtberg, Hansgünther Heyme, and others have produced unusual and often provocative productions. Some of these productions are discussed by **Andreas Höfele** in the accompanying essay.

Among the distinguished foreign directors recently engaged by a German theatre has been Michael Bogdanov, the artistic director of the **English Shakespeare Company**, who served from 1989 to 1991 as Indendant of the **Deutsches Schauspielhaus** (DS) in Hamburg. In a 1991 interview with Bogdanov before his departure from the DS, he commented on Shakespeare and the German theatre. Bogdanov praised the German actor as the best in the world and commended the extraordinary versatility in their command of voice, especially in classical verse, and their ability to combine vocal quality with the physical characteristics of their role. Bogdanov also praised the ability of German actors to take risks in their work. Bogdanov's Shakespeare productions of *Romeo and Juliet, Hamlet*, and *The Tempest* played to near capacity audiences. Previously, Bogdanov had guest-directed a production of *Julius Caesar* at the DS in 1986 and most recently has been a guest director at the Cologne Schauspielhaus.

In recent years, the Deutsche Shakespeare-Gesellschaft in Weimar and the Deutsche Shakespeare-Gesellschaft West in Bochum, have invited German companies to perform at their annual conferences. In 1991, the **Bremer Shakespeare Company** performed in both Weimar and Bochum. Following reunification, the two societies, which had been one group before 1964, held a joint conference in 1990 and announced in 1993 their plans to reunite. The Deutsche Shakespeare-Gesellschaft was founded in Weimar on the 300th anniversary of the birth of Shakespeare in 1864. The society met in Weimar for its annual meeting until 1927, when for the first time, the members met in Bochum because of a major Shakespeare project conceived by Saladin Schmitt—the performance of all the "King" plays performed in the course of a week, from three in the afternoon until two in the morning, on a daily basis. Schmitt became president of the society, but the executive committee remained in Weimar. Following the Second World War, both Weimar in the German Democratic Republic, and Bochum in the Federal Republic retained the same president and a joint executive committee. Arguments arose between the two groups and the Bochum group established an independent Shakespeare-

Gesellschaft West; since 1964, it has also published its own *Jahrbuch* (yearbook), an important publication that provides detailed production records for each year, in addition to essays, critical reviews, and so forth. Both societies have approximately 2,000 members each, and their separate conferences average about 400 in Bochum and 600 in Weimar. Headquarters for the new DSG will be in Weimar, and the "West" group will be dissolved by 1996. The 1994 "Shakespeare-Tage" will be a joint conference in Bochum. A joint yearbook is planned for 1995.

The following entries include the **Bremer Shakespeare Company**, which is the only theatre in Germany devoted exclusively to the works of Shakespeare, and a selection of theatres where Shakespeare is frequently produced or where significant or important productions have occurred in the postwar years. While the Bremer Shakespeare Company is the only company devoted to Shakespeare, it is difficult to limit the entries because of the frequent appearance of Shakespeare in German theatre repertories. Many theatres mount a new Shakespeare production each year, some two or three. An attempt has therefore been made to include the most representative of these theatres.

The numbers in parentheses are the area codes for the various locations. The "0" in front of the area code should not be dialed when calling from the United States; it is to be used only within a given country (Federal Republic of Germany, Austria, or Switzerland). Many theatres have an Indendant and separate artistic directors for drama and for opera. Since many German theatres have more than one dramaturg (some may have as many as eight), the "chief" or head dramaturg is listed with "et al." meaning "and others." It should also be noted that the central union for all German theatre workers is the Genossenschaft Deutscher Bühnen-Angehörigen, founded in 1889. Unless otherwise noted, theatres are normally open from September through June or July. August is traditionally dark. The national weekly newspaper *Die Zeit* [Hamburg], published each Thursday, provides a useful schedule of performances ("Programme deutsch-sprachiger Bühnen") of many German-language theatres in Germany, Austria, and Switzerland for the following week. Information is for 1993 and includes the new German zip code numbers.

BREMER SHAKESPEARE COMPANY. MAIL: Theater am Leibnizplatz, Leibnizplatz, Postfach 10 66 65, D-28066 Bremen, Germany. SITE: Leibnizplatz. ADMINISTRATION: (0421)-50-02-22. BOX OFFICE: (0421)-50-03-33; Fax: (0421)-50-33-72. ADMISSION: 23,-DM; 12,-DM for students, unemployed, handicapped. SEASON: year-round. PRINCIPAL STAFF: actors; Norbert Kentrup and Renate Heitmann, contact persons. FACILITY: proscenium (capacity 350); studio (capacity 70). AUDITIONS: advertised as necessary. STATUS: Genossenschaft Deutscher Bühnen-Angehörigen. ANNUAL BUDGET: 800,000,-DM (1994). ANNUAL ATTENDANCE:

80,000 (1993). FOUNDED: 1984, Chris Alexander, Gabriele Blum, Hille Darjes, Renato Grünig, Rainer Iwersen, Norbert Kentrup, Dagmar Papula.

German theatre companies regularly include at least one Shakespeare production in their repertories, but only the Bremer Shakespeare Company (BSC) has established Shakespeare's works as the core of its repertory. Founded in 1983, the BSC is dedicated to the production of Shakespeare's work as a collective ensemble in which no single concept or star performer overshadows the overall ensemble. In addition to producing Shakespeare, the BSC also strives to create a workshop environment where the artists can develop their own new works as individuals or as an ensemble through improvisation. The BSC founders include Chris Alexander, Gabriele Blum, Hille Darjes, Renato Grünig, Rainer Iwersen, Norbert Kentrup, and Dagmar Papula, all dedicated to a free, self-governed, unsubsidized theatre ensemble. The original company members, who came from both established theatres and small freelance groups throughout Germany, were dissatisfied with the traditional organizational structure and bureaucracy of German theatres. The BSC was established to serve as a "model" of a new theatre organization in Germany, and it now includes a total of 32 members. In keeping with the "theatre collective" approach, all BSC members receive the same wages and benefits. Rainer Iwersen, a company member and organization contact person, has explained that there is no single artistic director or company director and that the company as a whole, "actors and actresses," is listed as the "artistic director" in theatre directories. Although individual directors are responsible for particular productions, the group works with a *Volkstheater* approach in the development of artistic works. The company also produces new plays, either written by individual company members or developed as a group, and continually explores works in progress.

The BSC rented a Bremen theatre, the Kammerspiele in der Böttcherstrasse, for the company's first season in 1984. Although the founding BSC members scorned subsidy, so successful was their venture that the senate of the City of Bremen agreed to build the BSC a permanent theatre in a former Gymnasium (German high school) auditorium, now called officially the Theater am Leibnizplatz. The stage is a proscenium with a thrust forestage area approximately 12 meters wide and 17 meters deep. The BSC uses minimal sets, with full emphasis placed on presentational theatre. There is no attempt to give the illusion that the action on stage is taking place without spectators present.

The BSC views itself as a Shakespeare repertory company whose artistic work is dedicated to the exploration of the "power of imagination" and of poetic reality, with the hope of providing the audience with the joy of "thinking, crying, laughing, judging, and contradicting." All of the BSC Shakespeare productions utilize new translations made by Chris Alexander, Maik Hamburger, and Rainer Iwersen. Iwersen has explained that the new translations are necessary because of the growth and development of the

German language since the period when the most often used translations were originally made. As is the custom in German theatres, the play text and translation used by the theatre may be purchased by audience members as they enter the theatre. While Shakespeare is the primary focus of the BSC, Iwersen has stressed that the working environment of the company enables the members to use the inspiration of Shakespeare in their own theatre pieces. In a series of new scripts for the stage, the BSC produces several new (contemporary) works each season.

The BSC's *Volkstheater* approach embraces the tradition of a collective work that is generated through the artistic process and that establishes a closer bond and intimacy between the spectator and performer. What makes the BSC unique in Germany are structures and policies contrary to German tradition. In some ways, the innovations of the BSC are more closely akin to the traditions of American summer theatre and of many American Shakespeare festivals. For example, the BSC emphasizes contact between the audience and the actors throughout the theatrical experience. When one calls to reserve a ticket, one speaks with an actor; the actors greet audience members as they enter the theatre; the coat check is operated by actors, and the program texts are sold by actors. Iwersen has explained how the actors break the barrier between the actor and the audience in an attempt to change the traditional "class and professional artistic barrier" that exists in most German theatres. The actors meet the audience members and show them to their seats as well as hand out the programs. Indeed, when one enters the Leibnizplatz theatre, one is warmly greeted by BSC members as in no other professional German theatre. During the performance, the lights remain on in the auditorium so that the audience is aware that theatre is taking place and that they are a part of that process. Following the performance, the actors mingle with the playgoers as they leave the theatre. German audiences, known to be complacent at times and often reserved in expressing emotion, seem to lighten up and respond to this interaction between actors and audience members.

The BSC has now (1994) produced 21 of Shakespeare's works, all in new translations, in addition to premiering many new contemporary works developed through improvisation by the BSC members in their workshop environment. The BSC tours to many cities throughout Germany; for example, in 1991, there were guest engagements in Gütersloh, Marburg, Siegen, Wolfsburg, Syke, Magdeburg, Bad Pyrmont, and over 60 other communities, including Villach in Austria. The BSC has performed in Poland, Belgium, Switzerland, England, and other countries, and both the German Shakespeare societies, the Deutsche Shakespeare Gesellschaft in Weimar, and the Deutsche Shakespeare Gesellschaft-West in Bochum, have invited the BSC to perform at their annual conferences. In 1989, a BSC performance of *Shrew* was broadcast live on German television and beamed by satellite throughout Europe. Meanwhile there have been seven TV-productions. The BSC has received several distinguished awards, among them an award for developing the performing arts (Förderpreis Darstellende Kunst) by the Academy of Arts in Berlin and an award from the Land Bremen for the development and encouragement of new play scripts for the BSC's production of *Wo Ich die Welt Anseh, Möcht Ich sie Umdrehen* by Dagmar Papula.

The all-male cast of the BSC's 1991 production of *The Merry Wives of Windsor* proved to be one of the season's most popular offerings and has had over 100 performances. Norbert Kentrup's Sir John Falstaff was praised for his earthy character and the comic business created by the ensemble provoked outbursts of laughter from the audience that at times seemed neverending. Not only were the timing and interaction of the actors with the audience spontaneous and creative, but the performances were genuine and true to the *Volkstheater* philosophy of the BSC. No pretense was made that the audience was part of a theatrical performance. To be more precise, the audience members "had fun" and enjoyed themselves; moreover, the atmosphere was more like a cabaret than a theatre. The virtuosity of the ensemble was apparent throughout the performance.

The BSC encourages parties from schools and other interested groups to attend open rehearsals and other functions by the company. Not only does the BSC actively encourage and foster an interest in theatre and Shakespeare in young people, but company members take time to work with students in the schools, present workshops for them in the Leibnizplatz theatre facility, and welcome visitors from around the world. The BSC has established a policy of open rehearsals for students, special groups, and anyone interested in theatre, followed by discussions with the ensemble. In 1993, there were approximately 200 open rehearsals scheduled.

The BSC performed in 1991 in the German model of "The Globe," originally built in the Westphalia town of Rheda-Wiedenbrück in 1988 and then moved to Neuss, near Düsseldorf. BSC member Norbert Kentrup has told stories of acting on the apron of the German "Globe" stage. "It is a crazy experience, because you suddenly understand how to speak verse." In 1993, *The Merry Wives of Windsor* was the opening production for Shakespeare's Globe in London. Directed by Pit Holzwarth, the production has been one of the BSC's most popular productions.

As an expression of the cooperation with the International Shakespeare Globe Centre in London, the German International Shakespeare Globe Centre was founded in 1993 in Bremen. The Centre aims to support and to establish cooperation between German theatres, universities, and schools, and also provide financial assistance for the building of Sam Wanamaker's reconstruction of the Globe on the "Bankside" of the Thames in London.

In addition to opening its 1993-94 season in the open-air theatre in the Bremer Bürgerpark am Hollersee in September, the BSC celebrated its tenth anniversary by sponsoring an international Shakespeare festival called "Shakespeare & Companies." In the fall of 1993, four companies performed seven Shakespeare productions for a total of 26 performances in Bremen. The

Annette Leday/Keli-Company from India performed a "Kathakali" version of *King Lear*, directed by Annette Leday and David McRuvie. The Canadian Théâtre Repère presented *Macbeth*, *Coriolanus*, and *The Tempest* directed by Robert Lepage (see **Shakespeare on the Saskatchewan**), the Chilian company Gran Circo Teatro presented *Richard II* and *Twelfth Night*, directed by Andrés Pérez Araya, and, from Italy, the ensemble of the Teatro Due di Parma performed *Henry IV*. In early 1994, the Festival will continue with a series of lectures by directors, actors, and theatre scholars from the United Kingdom, the United States, and Australia. Other events include a film series, an exhibition of stage designs, a concert series of Elizabethan music, and a special "Hamlet-Projekt" with participation of English, Danish, and German schools. Finally, open-air productions are scheduled for the summer by the ensembles of the **Footsbarn Traveling Theatre Company** from France, and the Ornitorrinco from Brazil.

The BSC has established itself as a major German theatre company and has surprised many of the traditionalists in Germany's highly structured theatre hierarchy. The artists of the BSC view themselves as a model for a working collective dedicated to the unity of performance and organization. The ensemble for the 1994-1995 season included Robert Brandt, Christian Dieterle, Pit Holzwarth, Christian Kaiser, Norbert Kentrup, Barbara Kratz, Peter Lüchinger, Dagmar Papula, Erik Rossbander, Ariela Ruchti, Thomas Sarbacher, Birge Schade, and Petra Schmid. The BSC consistently performs Shakespeare to near sell-out crowds (92 percent capacity in 1992). But most important for the ensemble of the BSC, the public has been highly receptive to the Volkstheater model created by the BSC.

Production History: 1985: *Lr.*, *Oth.*, *Err.*, *Ich*, *Paula*, *Paula Becker*, *Paula Becker-Modersohn*, *Sie Können ganz besorgt in die Zukunft Blicken*, *Kopfkrieg*, *Es war Einmal*, *Die Mäuse von Konstantinopel*; **1986**: *1H4*, *H5*; **1987**: *TN*, *WT*, *Rochade—Ein Zug und Nichts ist, wie es war*, *Neugier*; **1988**: *Shr.*, *Tro.*, *Mensch Herrmann*, *Wo ich die Welt anseh*, *möcht ich sie umdrehen*; **1989**: *Mac.*, *Und was Du hast ist Atem zu holen*, *Götterspeise*, *Die Erfindung der Freiheit oder Kann denn Fliegen Sünde sein*; **1990**: *Ant.*, *Was brennt länger oder warum schreit Ihr Kind so*; **1991**: *Wiv.*, *Tmp.*, *Unter dem Glück*, *Bruderbande*; **1992**: *MND*, *Tit.*; **1993**: *AYL*, *R2*, *Milena. Wie ich Dich fand ist kein Wunder*; **1994**: *TGV*, *Ich*, *die Fliege*, *Lust ist Tod—Shakespeares Sonette*; **1995**: *Per.*, *Cym.*, *Ham.*

Research Resources: Informal archives are maintained at the Bremer Shakespeare Company administrative office at Leibnizplatz.

Site visit and interviews: June 1991, June 1992.
Ron Engle

The following are selected German language companies noted either for their Shakespeare production schedules or the quality of their Shakespeare performance. See essay above and essay on "Trends in German Shakespeare Production" by Andreas Höfele following the entries.

AUSTRIA

VIENNA
BURGTHEATER. MAIL: Dr.-Karl-Lueger-Ring 2, A-1014 Vienna I, Austria. SITE: Burgtheater. BOX OFFICE: (1) 5 14 44-22 18 (located at Goethegasse 1). ADMINISTRATION: (1) 5 14 44-0; Fax (1) 5 14 44-21 20. PRINCIPAL STAFF: Hermann Beil, Claus Peymann, Sylvia Stauber, Gerhard Blasche (Direktion); Hermann Beil, Michael Eberth, dramaturg, et al. FACILITY: proscenium (1314 seats, 109 standing places, 2 wheelchair places). FOUNDED: 1776, original structure completed 1888; rebuilt 1955.

GERMANY

BERLIN
SCHILLER THEATER (Staatliche Schauspielbühne Berlin). MAIL: Bismarckstrasse 110, 10625 Berlin, Germany. SITE: Schiller Theater. ADMINISTRATION: (030) 31 95 1; Fax: (030) 31 95 2 00. BOX OFFICE: (030) 3 12 65 05. PRINCIPAL STAFF: Alfred Kirchner, director, et al; Alexander Lang, artistic director; Frank Busch, dramaturg, et al. FACILITY: proscenium (capacity 1,004); workshop (capacity 96). FOUNDED: 1908.

DEUTSCHES THEATER / Kammerspiele. MAIL: Schumannstrasse 13a, 10117 Berlin, Germany. SITE: Deutsches Theater. ADMINISTRATION/BOX OFFICE: (030) 2 87 10; Fax: (02) 2 82 41 17. PRINCIPAL STAFF: Thomas Langhoff, Intendant; Michael Eberth, dramaturg, et al. FACILITY: proscenium (capacity 612); Kammerspiele, proscenium (capacity 420). FOUNDED: 1850, named Deutsches Theater in 1883.

VOLKSBÜHNE. MAIL: Rosa-Luxemburg-Platz, 10178 Berlin, Germany. SITE: Volksbühne. ADMINISTRATION/BOX OFFICE: (030) 2 80 51 03.

PRINCIPAL STAFF: Frank Castorf, Intendant; Matthias Lilienthal, dramaturg. FACILITY: proscenium (capacity 803); 3 studios, flexible (capacity 70–100). FOUNDED: 1913, rebuilt 1954.

BOCHUM
SCHAUSPIELHAUS BOCHUM. MAIL: Königsallee 15, 44789 Bochum, Germany. SITE: Schauspielhaus. ADMINISTRATION/BOX OFFICE: (0234) 33 33 0; Fax: (0234) 33 22 32. PRINCIPAL STAFF: Gabriele Groenewold, artistic director; Gabriele Groenewold, Andreas Nattermann, dramaturg, et al. FACILITY: proscenium (capacity 836); Kammerspiele, proscenium/open thrust (capacity 409 seats). FOUNDED: 1915; new structure 1953; Kammerspiele built 1966.

BRAUNSCHWEIG
STAATSTHEATER. MAIL: Am Theater, Postfach 45 39, 38100 Braunschweig, Germany. SITE: Staatstheater. ADMINISTRATION/BOX OFFICE: (0531) 4 84-27 00. PRINCIPAL STAFF: Jürgen Flügge, Indendant; Eva Johanna Heldrich, dramaturg. FACILITY: proscenium (capacity 900); "Kleines Haus" at Grünewaldstrasse (capacity 210). FOUNDED: 1861; rebuilt 1948; "Kleines Haus," 1949.

BREMEN. See **BREMER SHAKESPEARE COMPANY**

DARMSTADT
STAATSTHEATER. MAIL: Marienplatz 2, 64283 Darmstadt, Germany. SITE: Staatstheater. ADMINISTRATION: (06151) 28 11-3 16. BOX OFFICE: (06151) 28 11-2 11; Fax (06151) 28 11-2 26. PRINCIPAL STAFF: Dr. Peter Girth, Indendant; Barbara Suthoff, dramaturg, et al. FACILITY: proscenium (capacity 956); "Kleines Haus," proscenium (capacity 482); workshop, flexible (capacity 150). FOUNDED: 1819; present structure 1972.

DRESDEN
STAATSSCHAUSPIEL (SCHAUSPIELHAUS). MAIL: Theaterstrasse 2, 01067 Dresden, Germany. SITE: Schauspielhaus. ADMINISTRATION/BOX OFFICE: (0351) 48 42-0, Kleines Haus (0351) 5 26 31. PRINCIPAL STAFF: Dr. Dieter Görne, Intendant; Karla Kochta, dramaturg, et al. FACILITY: proscenium (capacity 909); Kleines Haus (capacity 375). FOUNDED: Schauspielhaus, 1913; Kleines Haus, 1945, rebuilt, 1987/88.

DÜSSELDORF
DÜSSELDORFER SCHAUSPIELHAUS. MAIL: Gustaf-Gründgens-Platz 1, 40211 Düsseldorf, Germany. SITE: Schauspielhaus. ADMINISTRATION/BOX OFFICE: (0211) 36 87-0; Fax (0211) 36 27 22. PRINCIPAL STAFF: Dr. Volker Canaris, Indendant and artistic director; Joachim Lux,

dramaturg, et al. FACILITY: main house, proscenium (capacity 968); "Kleines Haus" (experimental/workshops), flexible arena/proscenium (capacity 250-300). FOUNDED: present structure, 1970.

ESSLINGEN
WÜRTTEMBERGISCHE LANDESBÜHNE. MAIL: Ritterstrasse 11, 73728 Esslingen, Germany. SITE: Stadttheater located at Strohstrasse 1; Studio at Blarerplatz 4. ADMINISTRATION: (0711) 35 12-30 50; Fax: (0711) 35 12-30 80. BOX OFFICE: (0711) 35 12-30 44. PRINCIPAL STAFF: Jürgen Flügge, Indendant (until 1993); Tristan Berger, dramaturg, et al. FACILITY: proscenium (capacity 460). FOUNDED: present structure, 1982.

FEUCHTWANGEN
KREUZGANGSPIELE (Annual summer festival often includes Shakespeare productions by guest companies). MAIL: Kultur- und Verkehrsamt, 91555 Feuchtwangen, Germany. SITE: Ruins of a former Benedictine monastery. ADMINISTRATION/BOX OFFICE: (09852) 9 04-44; Fax: (09852) 9 04 32. PRINCIPAL STAFF: Imo Moszkowicz, Indendant. SEASON: June through August. FACILITY: proscenium (capacity 585). FOUNDED: 1948, by Otto Kindler.

HAMBURG
DEUTSCHES SCHAUSPIELHAUS. MAIL: Kirchenallee 39, 20099 Hamburg, Germany. SITE: Deutsches Schauspielhaus. ADMINISTRA-TION/BOX OFFICE: (040) 2 48 71-0; Fax: (040) 2 80 33 73. PRINCIPAL STAFF: Frank Baumbauer, Intendant; Michael Propfel, dramaturg, et al. FACILITY: proscenium (capacity 1,397); Studio, fexible (capacity 300). FOUNDED: 1899-1900, Alfred Freiherr von Berger.

THALIA THEATER. MAIL: Alstertor, 20095 Hamburg, Germany. SITE: Thalia Theater. ADMINISTRATION: (040) 3 28 14-0; Fax: (040) 3 28 14-2 01. BOX OFFICE: (040) 32 26 66. PRINCIPAL STAFF: Jürgen Flimm, Intendant; Niklaus Helbling, dramaturg. FACILITY: proscenium (capacity 900); Thalia in der Kunsthalle, proscenium/thrust (capacity 304). FOUNDED: 1843; present structure 1960; Kunsthalle, 1972.

HANNOVER
LANDESBÜHNE HANNOVER. MAIL: Bultstrasse 7-9, 30159 Hannover, Germany. SITE: Landesbühne Hannover; also Studio in der Bultstrasse, Gartentheater, and Orangeriegebäude at Herrenhausen Park. ADMINISTRA-TION: Fax: (0511) 28 10 43. BOX OFFICE: (0511) 28 10 23-26. PRINCIPAL STAFF: Reinhold Rüdiger, Indendant; Kurt-Achim Köweker, dramaturg. FACILITY: Proscenium (capacity 489); Studio (capacity 150); open air proscenium Gartentheater (capacity 904); Orangeriegebäude (capacity 642).

FOUNDED: Gartentheater, 1690; Orangeriegebäude, 1720; studio, 1976; new structure, 1987.

HEIDELBERG

THEATER DER STADT. MAIL: Friedrichstrasse 5, 69117 Heidelberg, Germany. SITE: Theater der Stadt. ADMINISTRATION: (06221) 58 35 02; Fax: (06221) 58 35 99. BOX OFFICE: (06221) 58-35 20. PRINCIPAL STAFF: Prof. Dr. Peter Stoltzenberg, Indendant; Barbara Christ, dramaturg. FACILITY: proscenium (capacity 619); Studio, flexible (capacity 198). FOUNDED: 1853; present structure remodeled 1978; Studio built 1982.

KASSEL

STAATSTHEATER KASSEL (SCHAUSPIELHAUS). MAIL: Friedrichsplatz 15, 34117 Kassel, Germany. SITE: Schauspielhaus. ADMINISTRATION: (0561) 10 94-0; Fax: (0561) 10 94-2 04. BOX OFFICE: (0561) 1 58 52 PRINCIPAL STAFF: Michael Leinert, Intendant; Karl Gabriel v. Karais, dramaturg, et al. FACILITY: proscenium (capacity 540-580). FOUNDED: present structure, 1959.

KÖLN (COLOGNE)

SCHAUSPIELHAUS. MAIL: Offenbachplatz (Postfach 18 02 41), 50767 Köln, Germany. SITE: Schauspielhaus. ADMINISTRATION/BOX OFFICE: (0221) 2 21-0; Fax: (0221) 2 21-82 10. PRINCIPAL STAFF: Günter Krämer, Intendant; Ursala Rühle, dramaturg, et al. FACILITY: proscenium (capacity 918). FOUNDED: present structure built 1962.

LEIPZIG

SCHAUSPIELHAUS. MAIL: Bosestrasse 1, 04109 Leipzig, Germany. SITE: Schauspielhaus. ADMINISTRATION: Fax: (0341) 29 11 65. BOX OFFICE: (0341) 79 22-0. PRINCIPAL STAFF: Wolfgang Hauswald, Intendant; Dr. Wolfgang Kröplin, dramaturg, et al. FACILITY: proscenium (capacity 748). FOUNDED: present structure 1956.

MÜNCHEN (MUNICH)

BAYERISCHES STAATSSCHAUSPIEL (Neues Residenztheater). MAIL: Maximilianstrasse 15/IV (also Postfach 10 01 55), 80539 Munich 1, Germany. SITE: Max-Joseph-Platz 1. ADMINISTRATION: (089) 2 18 51. BOX OFFICE: (089) 22 57 54, located at Max-Joseph-Platz 1. PRINCIPAL STAFF: Günther Beelitz, Intendant, artistic director; Gerd Jäger, dramaturg, et al. FACILITY: Residenztheater, proscenium (capacity 903). FOUNDED: Altes Residenztheatre (Cuvilliés-Theater) built 1751-1753; Neues Residenztheater, built 1951, renovated 1991.

MÜNCHNER KAMMERSPIELE. MAIL: Maximilianstrasse 26-28, 80539 Munich, Germany. SITE: Kammerspiele. ADMINISTRATION/BOX OFFICE: (089) 2 37 21-0; Fax: (089) 2 37 21-2 68. PRINCIPAL STAFF: Dieter Dorn, Intendant, artistic director; Dr. Hans-Joachim Ruckhäberle, dramaturg, et al. FACILITY: proscenium (capacity 720); Workshop studio (located at Herrnstrasse 54), flexible (capacity 299). FOUNDED: 1900, renovated 1970; studio built 1957.

MÜNSTER
STÄDTISCHE BÜHNEN. MAIL: Neubrückenstrasse 63, 48143 Münster, Germany. SITE: same. BOX OFFICE: (0251) 59 09-1 00. ADMINISTRATION: (0251) 59 09-0; Fax: (0251) 5 90 92 02. PRINCIPAL STAFF: Achim Thorwald, Intendant; Wilfried Harlaandt, dramaturg. FACILITY: proscenium (capacity 955 seats; studio, flexible (capacity 321 seats max. FOUNDED: present structure 1954; studio 1969.

SCHWERIN
MECKLENBURGISCHES STAATSTHEATER. MAIL: Alter Garten, 19055 Schwerin, Germany. SITE: Staatstheater. ADMINISTRATION/BOX OFFICE: (0385) 88 20. PRINCIPAL STAFF: Joachim Kümmritz, Intendant; Andrea Koschwitz, dramaturg, et al. FACILITY: proscenium (capacity 640); studio (capacity 220). FOUNDED: 1886.

WEIMAR
DEUTSCHES NATIONALTHEATER. MAIL: Theaterplatz 2, 99423 Weimar, Germany SITE: Deutsches Nationaltheater. ADMINISTRATION/BOX OFFICE: (03643) 75 50. PRINCIPAL STAFF: Fritz Wendrich, Intendant; Gisela Kahl, dramaturg, et al. FACILITY: proscenium (capacity 859). FOUNDED: 1779 as Komödienhaus; Goethe as Indendant, 1791-1817, present structure, 1908; latest renovation of interior commensurate with 1,000 year celebration of city of Weimar, 1975, rededicated with performance of Goethe's *Faust I.*

WIESBADEN
HESSISCHES STAATSTHEATER. MAIL: Christian-Zais-Strasse 3-5 (Postfach 3247), 65189 Wiesbaden, Germany. SITE: Hessisches Staatstheater. ADMINISTRATION: (0611) 1 32-1; Fax: (0611) 13 23 37. BOX OFFICE: (0611) 1 32-3 25; PRINCIPAL STAFF: Claus Leininger, Intendant; Dr. Gunter Selling, dramaturg, et al. FACILITY: proscenium (capacity 1041); "Kleines Haus," proscenium (capacity 328); studio (capacity 89). FOUNDED: 1894; Kleines Haus, 1950; studio, 1963; all spaces renovated 1978.

SWITZERLAND

ZÜRICH

SCHAUSPIELHAUS (Schauspielhaus am Pfauen). MAIL: Rämistrasse 34, 8001 Zürich, Switzerland. SITE: Schauspielhaus. ADMINISTRATION: (01) 2 65 57 57; Fax: (01) 2 65 58 00. BOX OFFICE: (01) 2 51 11 11, also (01) 2 65 58 58. PRINCIPAL STAFF: Gerd Leo Kuck, artistic director; Dr. Reinhard Palm, dramaturg, et al. FACILITY: proscenium (capacity 823). FOUNDED: present structure rebuilt 1978.

Ron Engle

TRENDS IN GERMAN SHAKESPEARE PRODUCTION SINCE 1960

In *Pravda,* a comedy by Howard Brenton and David Hare, set in the contemporary London newspaper world, there is a scene in which a reporter returns to the editorial office cursing and swearing—not, as it turns out, because he has just discovered another political scandal, but because he has spent an evening at the opera:

> I have been to see *Don Giovanni* at Covent Garden. Can you believe it? Directed by some stone-faced East German. I can only tell you: Donna Elvira wore pebble glasses. *Della Sua Pace* was sung from the barrel of a tank.

Maybe the British authors were thinking of Matthias Langhoff, who murdered their play in its first and only German production (Hamburg, 1986), or perhaps of Jürgen Gosch, another East German director working in the West, of whom more will be said later. Nonetheless, "West German" would have done equally well for this send-up of cranky stage experimentalism, for nowhere has the director—historically speaking, still a relative newcomer to the history of the theatre—gained a more central position than in the German-speaking countries. And nowhere has this led to more conspicuously unconventional productions of the classics.

Edward Gordon Craig's call for a new type of theatre artist whose job it would be to create a genuinely theatrical synthesis out of the separate contributions of the dramatist, stage designer, music composer, and actor was first fully realized in the early years of this century by Max Reinhardt. Following Reinhardt, directors like Karl Heinz Martin, Jürgen Fehling, Leopold Jessner, and Erwin Piscator gave the theatre of the Weimar Republic its avant-garde profile during the 1920s and early 1930s. Frequently and deliberately, these directors offended conservative notions of how the classical texts should be presented on stage. "Klassikertod" (classics killing) became a conservative battle cry in the heated public debate on the limits of the theatre director's artistic license.

This debate was reopened 30 years later in the early 1960s when a new generation of directors launched fresh attacks on the sterile academicism of their predecessors. This was a style of presentation very much in keeping with the cultural climate of the 1950s—devoid of any reference to politics or the reality of everyday life, a cold declamatory classicism of little physical vitality. Moreover, this academic style's leading practitioners had been seriously compromised by their involvement in the theatre of the Third Reich. The young directors of the 1960s—who still, to a large extent, shape the German theatre today—were disciples or admirers of Fritz Kortner, Erwin Piscator, and Bertolt Brecht, three eminent figures of the theatre of the 1920s who returned to Germany from political exile after the war but did not fit into the conservative restoration of the 1950s.

The young directors' most conspicuous contribution to the stage of the 1960s was their irreverent (indeed, to many outraged critics, audiences, and city councillors, nothing short of scandalous) treatment of the classics: Goethe, Schiller, and, of course, Shakespeare. In retrospect, one can see how the upheaval in the theatre was part of the general cultural and political reorientation that manifested itself most flamboyantly in radical student movements. Like the students, the theatre directors rebelled against a status quo based on a tacit understanding that all reminders of Germany's Nazi past were taboo. While the fathers had suppressed their guilty involvement in Hitler's genocidal regime and gotten on with the business of rebuilding the economy, the sons and daughters vehemently questioned the values of a society that they felt was built on a lie.

Since the eighteenth century, the theatre in Germany has been regarded not just as a place of entertainment but also, to use Schiller's famous phrase, as a "moral institute" and therefore the most dignified of all cultural arenas. Since this view of the theatre as a secular "temple to the Muses" had proved easily adaptable to Nazi ideology and then just as easily to the Christian humanism of the postwar decade, it was highly suspect to the generation that began to shape the German theatre in the 1960s. Almost as suspect as the "temple" itself were its "holy" texts, the classics, which had not resisted the ideological take-over either. Shakespeare was not exempt from this "critical review of the cultural heritage" (Hortmann, "Changing Modes," p. 221). His influence on German intellectual history and the German theatre can hardly be overestimated. It would be no exaggeration to say that German literature began to break out of its provincial limitations when Gotthold Ephraim Lessing in the 1750s rejected the rules of French classicism and instead hailed Shakespeare as the universal genius upon whose work a new national drama ought to be modeled. Not only did "Goethe, Schiller, Kleist, Grillparzer, Hebbel and Büchner, in fact, all the major dramatists in the German language up to the end of the nineteenth century, acknowledge . . . their debt to Shakespeare" (Patterson, *Peter Stein*, p.

123), but his works, translated by the two Romantic writers A. W. Schlegel and Ludwig Tieck, became an integral part of German literature. Numerous quotes from the Schlegel-Tieck translation have gained proverbial status. While generations of melancholic young Germans have cultivated a Hamlet complex, the poet Ferdinand Freiligrath, writing in the 1840s, identified the politically paralyzed, disunited country as a whole with the hesitant prince (Pfister, "Germany is Hamlet," pp. 106-126). A century later, the Nazis gave this idea a grotesque turn by claiming that Shakespeare, the "Nordic" genius, by right belonged to Germany much more than to his native England, the despised "nation of shopkeepers" (Habicht, "Shakespeare in the Third Reich," pp. 194-204). Shakespeare has dominated the German stage since the early nineteenth century. He regularly tops the annual charts as most frequently performed dramatist.

Bearing all this in mind, one can understand why some of the most radically experimental productions of the 1960s and 1970s took Shakespeare as their subject or, as some critics would say, their target. It was not only the traditional way of presenting the plays but very often the plays themselves that, as Wilhelm Hortmann puts it, "were made to stand in the dock."

> Had they not, in the harmonizing endings of their fifth acts, dispensed a spurious justice in the service of the status quo? Had they not lent their powerful authority to support a repressive value-system and thus weakened the utopian hope that it might be altered? Traditional reception, it was felt, had harmonized the plays into icons of ultimate reconciliation. "But take away this constraint towards affirmation and immediately the classical play will show what it is made of: glaring oppositions and negations, disruptive egoisms, murderous passions in the grip of an incomprehensible, absurd disorder." This was how Jan Kott interpreted Shakespeare as "Our Contemporary" (German edition 1964), and the theatrical avant-garde in Germany soon "outkotted" Kott. In the course of this process they arrogated unheard-of formal freedoms in speaking, acting, costume, music, stage design; they tested new aesthetics of ugliness, violence, absurdity; they made a bonfire of all the old rulebooks and thoroughly thwarted the theater-goer's expectations in sight, sound, logic and sense. (Hortmann, p. 221)

In Peter Palitzsch's 1967 production of *Wars of the Roses,* a substantially altered two-part version of Shakespeare's trilogy *Henry VI,* the influence of both Kott and Brecht, with whom Palitzsch had worked before moving to West Germany, was more than obvious. History itself, seen à la Kott as the relentless grinding of the "great mechanism," determined the course of events, reducing Shakespeare's feudal lords in their cut-throat struggle for power to expendable puppets. A grotesque, deliberately de-psychologized ritual of killing and being killed took place on a brightly lit stage whose whole width was spanned by a frieze consisting of charred timbers, skulls, hacked-off limbs, and skeletons. This was a parable of Brechtian clarity in which a much grimmer view of history prevailed than in John Barton's and Peter Hall's *Wars of the Roses* of 1963-64 or Giorgio Strehler's *Das Spiel der Machtigen,* another adaptation of *Henry VI* staged in Salzburg in 1973. Three years before Palitzsch's *Henry VI,* Peter Zadek had staged an irreverently anti-heroic version of *Henry V,* ironically entitled *Held Henry (Harry, the Hero).* Shakespeare's homage to the ideal soldier-king was turned into a travesty of militarism, pointing to the message "that patriotism is *made* and that the hero is a *product* of a cult and of manipulation. A screen at the back showed Hitler's troops marching into Paris and 'Harry' taking the salute; a backdrop showed fifty portraits of kings and queens, some of them changing into the heads of Hitler, Stalin, Billy Graham, football stars, and so on" (Hortmann, p. 221).

While this scenic collage remained fairly close to Shakespeare's text, Zadek's 1967 production of *Measure for Measure* became the much-quoted epitome of the debunking, iconoclastic treatment of Shakespeare in the 1960s, "a total smashing up of the play" to some, a genuinely pioneering venture to others. Wilfried Minks, who had also created the striking stage designs for Palitzsch's *Wars of the Roses* and Zadek's *Harry, the Hero,* provided a vast empty acting space framed by countless light bulbs. A programme note warned the audience that any expectations raised by either the name of the author, Shakespeare, or the title of the play, *Measure for Measure,* would not be fulfilled. This proved to be absolutely true. "Let's not be so fainthearted," Zadek wrote, "We're timid enough in everyday life."

There was certainly nothing timid about this production. A new and deliberately roughed up German text was provided by the neo-naturalist playwright Martin Sperr. "If I hop into bed with Angelo, you're free, Claudyboy. You make me vomit, you're a beast, utter dirt," ran a much-quoted line from Sperr's version. This very free adaptation was complemented by what one critic hailed as "the discovery of a body language" (Rischbieter, *Theater Heute,* p. 26). In developing it, Zadek followed the example of The Living Theatre without, however, adopting any of its messianic aspirations. The result was a brutally truthful act of creative violence, laying bare not so much the essence of Shakespeare's play as that essence that Shakespeare, after having confronted his audience with the potential danger and nastiness of the situation, took good care to cover up again in a happy ending.

Zadek's actors gave a performance of unprecedented violence, loudness, and physical impact. No well-meaning duke guaranteed that good would prevail in the end. The plotting ruler had, instead, become a malevolent voyeur, secretly enjoying the psycho-torture inflicted on Isabella, Claudio, and Mariana. Claudio and Angelo are both beheaded, and the duke himself is killed and replaced by the procuress Mistress Overdone (bluntly renamed Frau Meier) who, in turn, kills Mariana. This mercilessly "despoiled" Shakespeare, however, did not just caricature the play. By letting the physical urges behind all rhetorical pretense dominate the stage action, Zadek attacked the audience with moments of overwhelming intensity. These included the scene where

Isabella passionately embraces Angelo while trying to wring a reprieve for her brother from him and, later on, when Claudio's increasing panic is pitted against Isabella's hardening resolve not to sacrifice her virginity for his life in a sequence of fierce physical interaction, half wrestling match, half embrace. The production was hailed, or condemned, as a relentless attack on middle-class sexual morality.

Five years later, Zadek returned to Shakespeare with a production of *The Merchant of Venice*. Ulrich Wildgruber, the protagonist of Zadek's subsequent productions of *Lear* (1974), *Othello* (1976), and *Hamlet* (1977), appeared as a Lancelot Gobbo who was turned from a very minor character into an omnipresent clownish commentator, thereby, according to one of the country's leading theatre critics, totally disrupting the play (Kaiser, "Shakespeare," p. 18). It would, however, be a crass oversimplification to say that Zadek's *Merchant of Venice* and his productions of the three great tragedies amounted to no more than a debunking of Shakespeare. Iconoclasm was certainly an element in all of them but hardly the main thrust of the director's intent. Wildgruber's highly idiosyncratic Lear, Othello, and, especially, Hamlet certainly "thwarted the theater-goer's expectations in sight" as well as sound (a standard objection to his acting being that he mumbled his lines). Nevertheless, if this negative effect alone had determined Zadek's choice, he would surely not have tried to achieve it three times and then yet again, when he cast Wildgruber for the part of Leontes in *The Winter's Tale*. Throughout his career, Zadek has aimed for the vitality of the theatrical event, not for the perfection of a finished artifact, preferring living chaos to dead classicism. Ruptures, tensions, contradictions, a mixing of tragedy and the grotesque, of high art and kitsch, a preference for the cabaret and the circus, a strongly erotic brand of curiosity, an insistent probing of the physical potential of a situation—these distinguishing traits of Zadek's work correspond ideally with his protagonist's readiness to experiment, to explore even the most outrageous variations on a theme, to blend sensitivity with silliness, emotional depth with the vanity of a poseur, and never to allow his role to settle into a fixed shape.

This fluidity became the aesthetic principle of Zadek's *Hamlet* of 1977. "My Hamlet," Zadek wrote, "lives in a chaotic world, a world of illusion, and he plays parts while observing others playing parts, too. He questions the world, which never stands still long enough to give convincing answers." This open-ended process of questioning communicated itself to the audience by way of *dramatis personae* who constantly changed not only their costumes but their personalities as well. The performance took place in an empty factory hall sparsely furnished with only a few seemingly arbitrary props matching the arbitrariness of the costumes. The acting area occupied most of the available space and was covered with ordinary black gym mats. The audience (about 300 people) was seated along the walls so that whatever happened in the play was always seen against a backdrop of onlookers. This was only one of several strategies intended to ensure a constant awareness of the play as play, of the ever-present tension between actors and action, momentary physical reality and the historicity of fiction. Virtually every part was cast against type. Hamlet was considerably older than his mother; the ghost (who later doubled as Fortinbras), Polonius, and Rosenkrantz were all played by women; Laertes was not an agile youth but a thick-set, middle-aged man. Zadek never allowed a character to assume fixed contours; he orchestrated a constant changing of register, from shrill, deliberate ham-acting to most subtle nuances. He took his company on a journey of discovery that in turn became the audience's journey of discovery. The linearity of story was discarded in favor of a network of correlated situations, a multilayered "scenic text" constantly opening up references to other possible texts. In obliterating the canonized distinctions between tragedy and comedy, Zadek played a game of intertextuality, full of sexual innuendo and Grand Guignol horrors, such as the cutting up of Polonius' corpse or the mad Ophelia's vision of a world full of pigs.

The same season saw another notable Shakespearean venture: *As You Like It* performed by the ensemble of the Berlin Schaubühne under the direction of Peter Stein. Like the Zadek *Hamlet*, this production was not housed in a normal theatre building but in a huge film studio at Berlin-Spandau, over an hour's bus ride away from the city centre. Apart from their unconventional locations, however, the two productions were almost diametrically opposed in their approach to Shakespeare. Zadek and Stein have often been described as the two opposite poles of the German theatre, Zadek's anarchic, disorderly, erotic, carnivalesque vitality contrasting sharply with Stein's rationalism and sophistication, his drive for aesthetic perfection, his much more subtle (and sometimes self-consciously academic) ways of confronting the historical with the topical. Whereas Zadek has derided Stein's productions as "Shakespeare for high school teachers," Stein has accused Zadek of presenting "Shakespeare with his trousers down." Stein's perfectionism, his keenness on exploring the historical dimensions of the text, is underscored by the fact that he first approached Shakespeare by means of an extensive, highly elaborate research project leading to the staging of *Shakespeare's Memory* (1976), a nine-hour collage of simultaneous scenic displays presenting various aspects of Elizabethan art, thought, and society—an inventory of Shakespeare's world, a kind of "Living Programme." There was a "masked procession, morris dancing, fencing, acrobatics, musical contributions and folk drama. . . . The audience of some 360 . . . remained standing . . . , moving around to view the different acts, many of which were performed simultaneously in spaces cleared in their midst by the actors." Then:

> banquet tables were rolled out, and the audience were invited to sit for food and drink, while the show continued in the aisle between the tables. Pageant wagons were pulled in, one at first bearing personifications of grammar, rhetoric and dialectics, and then academicians in debate. Another wagon carried a "cage of

fools" who dismounted to perform . . . a piece of folk drama incorporating a dance with swords. . . .

The final item of the first evening was entitled "The Museum." It was here that the ensemble displayed its erudition about astronomy, using models, instruments and a planetarium. This developed into presentations of astrological theory . . . and concluded with a visit to the adjacent "Garden of Sympathies," where intersecting passages displayed exhibits about the Renaissance conception of humours and correspondences, and to the "Cabinet of Utopians" containing life-size models of various utopian beings: the hermaphrodite, the androgynous man, the hermit, the embryo, the zodiac man and the man of humours. (Patterson, p. 125)

The second evening included demonstrations of the arts of perspective and of rhetoric, an extract from Burton's *Anatomy of Melancholy* performed "in a circular theatre based on a design by Leonardo da Vinci," various speeches by Queen Elizabeth I, and a scene from Tourneur's *The Revenger's Tragedy*. From "a huge cross-section of a ship . . . accounts of voyages into the New World and of the effects of colonization" were delivered. Finally, a series of highlights from Shakespeare's plays was "performed on an 'island' of tables, wagons and rostra." This part, which was to have provided the grand finale to the marathon show, was generally felt to be rather disappointing. Had this first-rate ensemble's efforts at total immersion in Shakespeare's world added up to nothing more than conventional, on the whole second-rate, performances? The highly ambitious project had ended, in the words of one critic, "in an exhibition of outmoded theatre styles, in Christmas-card schmaltz, repertory theatre emotionalism, and mannered intensity" (Henrichs in *Die Zeit*).

As *Shakespeare's Memory* was only a first, experimental foray into the Shakespeare universe, expectations were extremely high when Stein, almost universally acknowledged to be the leading German theatre director of the decade, tackled *As You Like It*, a proper Shakespearean play. The result was a production of outstanding visual quality whose splendid and monumental sets, however, seemed at times to overwhelm both the action and the actors. Stein's stage designer, Karl-Ernst Herrmann, had built two worlds: the court and the forest. The cold, oppressive formality of Frederick's court impressed itself strangely on the audience, who for the first part of the performance had to stand crammed in a long, high-ceilinged hall gleaming with an unreal, glacier-like, pale blue brightness. The actors hovered on elevated walks and platforms along the walls, all clad in sumptuous Elizabethan costumes whose formality was reinforced by the chokingly tight high collars—so immobile at first "that they seemed like waxworks." The acting was irritatingly but deliberately stilted, a necessary strategy in order to build up a feeling of discomfort in the audience, a wish to escape. After a wrestling match of impeccable ritualistic perfection, for which Stein had signed up a well-known professional as Orlando's opponent, release came when the audience was invited to follow Orlando into the Forest of Arden. "This meant a fifteen-minute, single-file walk on a dark, narrow, thorny, and labyrinthine path obstructed with (artificial) briars and puddles, through gusts of wind and patches of blinding light, and past such surprises as a wild bear and a sleeping hermaphrodite" (Habicht, *Shakespeare Quarterly*, p. 299).

The symbolism of this passage from one world to another was palpable: an experience of being born anew, "a metaphorical journey through the uterine canal" (Patterson, 138). Awaiting the traveler at the end was a magnificent woodland setting, containing, among other splendors, a genuine beech tree transplanted into the hall. The actors, no longer in period costume, now performed in a much less formal and more relaxed style, using various parts of the vast set for a sometimes simultaneous presentation of scenes—a practice reminiscent of *Shakespeare's Memory*. Although the inventiveness and aesthetic perfection of the production found due recognition, a certain lack of vitality was also noted. Stein himself also felt that he had somehow failed, that Shakespeare's "infinite variety" had proved unmanageable for him. Not until 12 years later did he try his hand at Shakespeare again, directing *Titus Andronicus* in Rome. In Stein's work with the Schaubühne, *As You Like It* marks a stage at which the dangers of a tendency toward the statuesque and the monumental began to show.

It was Klaus Michael Grüber, not Peter Stein, who directed the next major Shakespeare production at the Schaubühne. For many critics, his *Hamlet* of 1982 marked no less than the beginning of a new era. Those who had deplored the liberties that directors like Peter Zadek had taken in staging the classics hailed this new *Hamlet* as a return to reason. Boisterous iconoclasm, they said, had given way to reverence for the integrity of the author's work. Partisans of theatrical shock therapy, on the other hand, saw Grüber's work as a sure sign that the theatre was lapsing into that same neo-conservatism that was overtaking the country as a whole under its new Christian-Democratic government. Both views were wide of the mark, for, in spite of the fact that Grüber had his actors speak the whole, uncut Shakespearean text—thereby blowing up the duration of the performance to an unprecedented six hours—the result was not a return to the familiar but something quite different. The production became something like a slow-motion replay of the splendors of a tradition now irrevocably lost. Grüber, the visionary of the German theatre, celebrated *Hamlet* as an elegy for a cultural heritage whose treasures can now be seen only behind glass, as in a museum. Everything was steeped in beauty and sadness. Bruno Ganz as Hamlet wore the doublet that another famous Hamlet had worn on stage before him: Joseph Kainz, the late nineteenth-century virtuoso, mad King Ludwig's favorite actor. His movements and gestures, like those of the other actors, were exquisitely graceful. Many a precious pose put the audience in mind of medieval or Renaissance paintings or of old *Hamlet* illustrations. The actors' magnificent period costumes were in striking contrast to the bare concrete walls of the vast, empty, semicircular apsis of the Schaubühne's new home, at Lehniner Platz in downtown West

Berlin. The human figures and their problems were reduced to insignificance by the sheer expanse of this stage, which, like Shakespeare's Globe, had a "heavens," a canopy of countless little lamps—stars that symbolized man's loneliness in an empty universe. No action, only gestures. No hope, no real conflict, only resignation. Where Zadek had cheerfully deconstructed *Hamlet*, Grüber presented a world in a state of terminal paralysis: entropy, posthistoire. Hamlet's inability to act was shown to be not just his personal problem but a condition he shared with the whole of mankind.

This exhaustive and, in the end, exhausting production of *Hamlet* has become something of a landmark in recent German theatre history. Although it constituted far too strange an experience to be labeled simply a return to the old ways, its creation of an exceptionally beautiful artifact, paradoxically coupled with the message that life is futile and all action pointless, may serve as an emblem of the state of the theatre in the 1980s. The satirical energy that fired the breaking of traditional forms was fed by the assumption that (political) change was possible and that the theatre had a part to play in effecting it.

Many practitioners and critics feel that the theatre of the 1980s has lost its function as a "subsidized opposition"—a paradoxical phrase coined by Hansgünther Heyme, one of the politically committed directors of the Zadek/Stein generation—and has lapsed back into the ivory tower of *l'art pour l'art* while still paying lip-service to the anti-establishment ideology of 1968. "The tasteful, the aesthetically safe, a sumptuously decorated mediocrity" (Becker, "Brodelts oder blubberts," p. 9) have been diagnosed as the characteristics of the present German stage by the editor of the country's leading theatre journal.

Jürgen Gosch's 1987 *Midsummer Night's Dream* had obvious affinities with Grüber's *Hamlet* except that Gosch was even more rigorous in his search for stylization. All traces of the traditional, romantic conception of the play were eliminated. So were all causes for mirth. This *Midsummer Night's Dream* was no Comedy. While Peter Brook's famous production of 1970 had also been done without the conventional stage forest and had presented the dynamic essence of the play in an empty white box, Gosch's production took its extremely slow course on a totally black stage. The "set" consisted of a single, upright, rectangular canvas frame that divided the circular revolving stage into two halves. In the forest scenes, the set was kept in continual slow rotation, an effect that at first created a dreamlike atmosphere and then became simply tedious. "Dream" was indeed the keyword of the whole production. The actors moved and talked with a somnambulant slowness and monotony, Puck's magic flower having the effect of a strong sedative. The strangeness of it all was reinforced by the actors' voices, which were delocalized through the use of body microphones and amplifiers. The Athenian court appeared in flowing classical Greek garments. The pale, bloodless fairies, with their blackened eye sockets, looked like melancholic vampires from an expressionist movie. They wore black leotards and huge hang-glider-like wings of transparent plastic. With these contraptions, there was naturally very little room for movement, let alone touching, but Gosch's ascetic concept did not allow any erotic tension to develop anyway. Love, sex, and their unsettling, potentially dangerous consequences were clearly not part of the director's intention. But what was his intention? The solemn, slow-motion ritual rendered no answer. It constituted an aesthetic world of its own, hermetically closed off from any recognizable form of lived experience, past or present. When Gosch brought this relentless minimalism to bear on *Macbeth* the following season, the critics had a field day. The stranglehold of uncompromising stylization drained all life out of the play. "With great gesture," one critic wrote, "Gosch simulates a style and yet has nothing to say" (Iden in *Frankfurter Rundschau*).

The same accusation—that the director has nothing to say—has sometimes been leveled at Dieter Dorn, director of the Munich Chamber Playhouse (Kammerspiele) since 1976, whose productions of *Midsummer Night's Dream* (1978), *Twelfth Night* (1980), and *Troilus and Cressida* (1986) have earned him the reputation of one of the leading Shakespeare directors in the country. Dorn himself would emphatically deny that his work is noncommittal. He is suspicious, though, of a subjectivism that will always impose its own personal obsessions on any given play. The text, he says, always comes first for him. It is "the driving force behind all his work." He disapproves of what he calls "editorial" productions—productions, in other words, that force a prefabricated interpretation on the audience. Instead, he wishes to free the spectators to see and evaluate for themselves. This is worthy democratic principle, no doubt, yet one that can make it easy for an audience to escape any real confrontation with the play. While Dorn himself has often declared his commitment to a theatre of ideas, his critics have occasionally drawn unflattering parallels between his opulent productions and the expensive boutiques that lie next door to his theatre in Munich's fashionable Maximilianstrasse.

Troilus and Cressida, the production that found nationwide acclaim in 1986, shows both the strengths and shortcomings of Dorn's treatment of Shakespeare. The impeccable professionalism that Dorn brought to the task showed itself not only in every detail of the production itself but also in the excellent new translation of the play by Michael Wachsmann, Dorn's codirector at the Kammerspiele. Dorn located Shakespeare's Trojan War on an abstract stage enclosed with white canvas walls; these bore seemingly random paint strokes, suggestive of chaos and destruction, but nevertheless formed an elegantly balanced abstract picture. Through sliding doors, the Trojans raced on stage: warriors from an exotic world, part American Indian, part African, part Oriental, propelled—or so it seemed—by the beat of a live percussion band. The ritual had begun. Speed and movement, so often missing from the German stage, abounded in this production, which made extensive use of diagonal long entrances and exits. Dorn directed his large and brilliant cast with the precision of a choreographer. He created numerous striking images and managed to hold a delicate balance between the tragic and the ludicrous, an ambivalence most fitting for Shakespeare's "problem play." No psychological depths were sounded; the audience was not enticed into any deep involvement with the *dramatis personae*, who were deliberately presented as types or even caricatures. From predominantly comical beginnings, the production descended into the grimness of the final slaughter, which was shown in a series of short scenes divided by blackouts. The business of plotting and killing was executed by men of very doubtful courage—prejudiced, petty, vain and finally dehumanized into faceless war machines. The climax of cruelty was reached when Hector was murdered by the henchmen of the treacherous Achilles. And yet, in spite of all the bloodshed, the killing was never allowed to become really ugly. The same aesthetic perfection that characterized the whole production prevailed to the bitter end. War remained a ritual. Style overruled emotion. Dorn, true to his principles, allowed his audience to remain at a safe distance, enjoying the thrill of it all. A splendid piece of theatrical art, yet one that left the spectators curiously unmoved.

The moral of these observations seems clear enough. With the erosion of the political and aesthetic tenets that inspired two decades of often rather willfully modernistic experimentation, there has been a return to a more empathetic and reverent treatment of the classics. The integrity of the cultural heritage has, to some extent, been restored, but at the same time we seem to have lost some of the emotional intensity generated by the theatre of the 1960s and 1970s. Those who condemned the more radical experiments as pure destructiveness were blind to the fact that the energy behind all this derived from the belief that whatever happened on stage was of vital importance for the life of society outside the theatre. Today, the theatre is safely back within its traditional boundaries, the autonomous realm of art.

Paul Feyerabend's well-worn slogan "Anything goes" provides an apt enough label for the present situation. Anything does, indeed, seem to go. While uncompromisingly anti-conventional stagings of the old Shakespearean texts are no longer the norm, they nevertheless still occur. For example, Frank Castorf's prankish *Hamlet* (Cologne, 1989) and Werner Schroeter's sexually exhibitionistic *King Lear* (Düsseldorf, 1990) triggered public scandals reminiscent of those caused by Peter Zadek in the 1960s. While the kind of scenic fossilization we have found in Grüber's *Hamlet* and Gosch's *Midsummer Night's Dream* and *Macbeth* also prevails in Robert Wilson's *Lear* (Frankfurt) and in Heiner Müller's seven-and-a-half-hour marathon *Hamlet* (East Berlin)—creating, as I have tried to show elsewhere, monumental tableaus of posthistoric stagnation (Höfele, "A Theatre of Exhaustion?," pp. 80-86)—other productions rely with regained confidence on rather traditional means of presentation conveying rather traditional meanings.

Dieter Dorn's 1992 *King Lear* is a case in point. After a whole year in rehearsal, the play emerges as a solid, very well acted, carefully organized production with a wealth of clever detail, but it drags somewhat in its overall rhythm and suffers from a conspicuous lack of any major new findings about

Lear's world or our own. Much the same may be said of Claus Peymann's *Macbeth* (Vienna, 1992), which, like Dorn's *Lear,* was presented to the public after one whole year of rehearsals. Meticulous direction, aesthetically impeccable as well as ingeniously functional sets, and a highly professional cast—produced an overall result that never carried us beyond the familiar world of "our" Shakespeare.

The one pervasive trend discernible in this pluralistic diffuseness is the diminishing role of dramaturgical analysis. Thematic concepts, heterodox messages read into the canonized texts, the whole idea of a new reading recasting the old textual mold—these hallmarks of German Shakespeare productions during the 1960s and 1970s have virtually disappeared. Thus, it is difficult, if not impossible, to say what Dorn's, Peymann's, Gosch's, or Castorf's recent productions "are about." Today's productions refrain from committing themselves to a recognizable, coherent interpretation. Whatever Dorn and Peymann may have done during the long months of rehearsals, it cannot have been discussing the relevance of Shakespeare's play to the contemporary world. In neither case, at least, does the finished product suggest such a debate. In this respect, Frank Castorf's playful deconstruction of *Hamlet,* although in some ways reminiscent of the early Zadek, differs substantially from the latter's 1967 *Measure for Measure.* While Zadek's disrupting of the conventional Shakespearean spectacle led to the forced coherence of a grim new reading, Castorf's *Hamlet* remains playfully indeterminate. It incorporates the iconoclastic stance without adopting it. Shakespeare's *Hamlet* is mutilated, hacked to pieces, garnished with scraps of contemporary popular culture like a Laurel and Hardy act involving Hamlet *père et fils* and a battered refrigerator, but none of this as much as hints at an overall program or concept—not even that of an *Anti-Hamlet.*

Yet, there are always exceptions and surprises. The arguably most exciting recent Shakespeare production in German, 76-year-old George Tabori's *Othello* (Vienna, Akademietheater, 1990), steered clear of the pitfalls of both safe traditionalism and facile experimentation and certainly had nothing stagnant about it. If we had to look for a label to classify it, something like "essentialism" might do. Tabori, a Hungarian Jew, who, after having worked in England and the United States, began his career in the German theatre in the early 1970s, has done much of his experimental work outside the established civic repertory system. His *Hamlet* of 1978, for instance, was performed by the Bremen Theatre Laboratory. This version acted out the Freudian nightmare of a literally father-ridden son, very appropriately, on a stage whose single prop was a bed in which most of the action took place. This Hamlet wrestled with a father who would not remain dead, and this emotional and physical intensity has been a distinguishing trait of Tabori's best work up to the present. It was most evident in his 1984 production of *Waiting for Godot* (Munich, Kammerspiele) as well as in *Othello.* Under Tabori's direction, the latter play retained its integrity while simultaneously radiating a rare sense of immediacy.

Concentration was the key to this achievement. The square acting space, tipped to one side toward the audience, was enclosed with iron railings and therefore resembled a wrestling ring, sloping ominously downward. Nothing in this production was allowed to distract from the story which, as one critic put it, unfolded with the inevitability of an American movie; it was the story of two men, Iago and Othello, whose fatal entanglement resulted from deep-seated feelings of self-hate and sexual inferiority. To Ignaz Kirchner's twitching, sweating, at once nervously active and worn-out Iago, the happiness of his proud, strong, newly wedded general was simply unbearable. Othello was and had all that Iago was not and had not. Iago's hate became indistinguishable from his admiration; it was tinged with more than passing hints of a homoerotic infatuation. "Honest Iago"—usually an obvious irony—seemed an almost true description of a man who loved his victim almost as much as he hated him.

The centerpiece of the production was the scene in which Iago aroused Othello's jealousy, an almost painfully intense dissection of the moor's identity but also an act of seduction, of courtship. Iago, the ruthless cringing hunter, was threatened, grabbed, and pushed around by his prey, Othello, magnificently played by Gert Voss, whose civilized superiority gave way to outbursts of raging pain and jealousy. Iago had to toil like Hemingway's old man of the sea to land this capital animal, and, like the old fisherman, he left the battlefield destroyed, beaten, besmeared with the black paint from Othello's very skin. The moor's color rubbed off on everybody and everything he touched: Desdemona, Iago, the walls he scraped against in his futile attempts to break free from the hunter's net. In the end, after the killing of the innocent, the seducer and his victim were handcuffed together, and Iago was forced to reproduce Othello's last gestures like a puppet. In its hyperreal clarity, its relentless stripping bare of the characters' emotions, the production achieved a physical impact well beyond the reaches of conventional psychological realism. Whether this *Othello* will remain a strikingly singular achievement or become the paradigm of a new trend in German Shakespeare production remains to be seen.

Andreas Höfele

Research Resources:

Becker, Peter von. "Brodelts oder blubberts: Erste Stichworte im neuen Jahrzehnt." *Theater Heute*, 3 [March] 1990.

Brenton, Howard, and David Hare. *Pravda*. London, New York: Methuen, 1985.

Habicht, Werner. "Shakespeare in 19th-Century Germany: The Making of a Myth." In *19th-Century Germany*, eds. M. Eksteins, and H. Hammerschidt. Tübingen, 1983.

―――. "Shakespeare in the Third-Reich." In *Anglistentag 1984 Passau: Vorträge*, ed. Manfred Pfister. Giessen, 1985.

————. "Shakespeare in West Germany." *Shakespeare Quarterly* 29 (1978).
Henrichs, Benjamin. *Die Zeit*, 31 December 1976.
Höfele, Andreas. "A Theatre of Exhaustion? 'Posthistoire' in Recent German Shakespeare Productions." *Shakespeare Quarterly* 43 (1992).
Hortmann, Wilhelm. "Changing Modes in *Hamlet* Production: Rediscovering Shakespeare after the Iconoclasts." In *Images of Shakespeare: Proceedings of the Third Congress of the International Shakespeare Association, 1986*, eds. W. Habicht, D. J. Palmer, and R. Pringle. Newark, London, Toronto, 1988.
Iden, Peter. *Frankfurter Rundschau*, 21 November 1988.
Kaiser, Joachim. "Shakespeare, unzumutbar und allzu zumutbar." *Theater Heute*, 6 [June] 1973.
Patterson, Michael. *Peter Stein: Germany's Leading Director*. Cambridge: Cambridge University Press, 1981.
Pfister, Manfred. "Germany is Hamlet: The History of a Political Interpretation." *New Comparison* 2 (Autumn 1986).
Rischbieter, Henning. *Theater Heute* 10 [October] 1967.

GREAT BRITAIN

ABBEY SHAKESPEARE PLAYERS. MAIL: Y Felin, St. Dogmaels, Cardigan, Dyfed, Wales, SA43 3DY. ADMISSION: £4.00, profits to charity. SEASON: the first week in August, four performances of one play. FACILITY: open air (approximate capacity 400). STATUS: nonprofit. ANNUAL ATTENDANCE: 750-1,000. FOUNDED: 1987, Mike Hall, Ian Wood.

The ruined twelfth-century abbey of St. Dogmaels forms a perfect setting for the performance of a Shakespeare play in the first week of August each year. The ruined dormitory range of the abbey (by Shakespeare's day converted into a house) provides a stage, raised above the cloister, where the audience sits. The abbey itself is the central feature of a village that nestles in a natural amphitheatre of hills, overlooking the Teifi valley.

St. Dogmaels is a large village on the west coast of Wales, set in the peaceful and beautiful countryside of northern Pembrokeshire. The town of Cardigan lies one mile to the east of St. Dogmaels and is a busy market town and popular holiday destination. A few miles east of Cardigan is Cilgerran Castle, one of the most picturesquely sited monuments in Wales.

The Abbey Shakespeare Players (ASP) is a group of amateur and professional players who gather in St. Dogmaels each year. The group was founded in 1987, reviving a tradition instituted in 1973. Company members have come from the universities of Sheffield, Leeds, Oxford, and Cambridge, at the instigation of Ian Wood, a long-time local resident. Profits go to charity. Proceeds from the 1992 production of *The Winter's Tale* were donated to the Royal National Lifeboot Institution.

Since performances of Shakespeare re-started in 1987, there has been an increasing number of people booking their vacation to coincide with the play. There has been a tendency of late for people to bring a hamper of food and drink to enjoy a pre-show picnic on the grounds of St. Dogmaels Abbey. The natural beauty of the "pastoral bowl of open fields divided by a small stream which comes tumbling down from a steep and narrow valley" into the estuary of the Teifi river, continues to attract visitors and friends of Shakespeare.

The 1994 production of *Macbeth,* marked the first Shakespearean tragedy to be produced by the company. The ruins of St. Dogmaels Abbey provided an ideal setting for the magical elements of the play that were given emphasis in the production.

Production History: 1973: *Tmp.*; **1974**: *MND*; **1987**: *TN*; **1988**: *MV*; **1989**: *MND*; **1990**: *Wiv.*; **1991**: *AWW*; **1992**: *WT*; **1993**: *Shr.*; **1994**: *Mac.*

Information supplied by ASP.
Ron Engle

CHEEK BY JOWL. MAIL: Alford House, Aveline Street, London SE11 5DQ, England. SITE: varies. ADMINISTRATION: same. BOX OFFICE: varies. ADMISSION: varies. SEASON: varies. PRINCIPAL STAFF: Declan Donnellan, Nick Ormerod, artistic directors; Barbara Matthews, administrative director. FACILITY: varies. STATUS: professional, not-for-profit. ANNUAL BUDGET: varies. ANNUAL ATTENDANCE: worldwide attendance unknown. FOUNDED: 1981, Declan Donnellan, Nick Ormerod.

Cheek by Jowl (CBJ) was founded in 1981 by director Declan Donnellan and designer Nick Ormerod. The London-based company quickly began winning awards in England and abroad (it toured to 37 countries in its first decade). Among these were a Fringe First at Edinburgh (1983), an Olivier best director award (1987), and an Olivier best designer award (1988). In 1991, Donnellan was appointed an associate director at the National Theatre, where he staged acclaimed productions of *Fuente Ovejuna* and *Peer Gynt* with members of his own production team, which includes administrator Barbara Matthews, music director Paddy Cunneen, and movement director Jane Gibson.

The company name comes from Demetrius' line in *A Midsummer Night's Dream* (Act III, scene 2): "Follow? Nay, I'll go with thee, cheek by jowl." CBJ's production values, as quoted by Harry Carlson, are: "a simple but evocative setting; an emphasis on intimate, physical, ensemble playing; a subtle, expressive use of music; a choreographic elegance in movement; and a dedication to developing a particular style for each production that somehow seems both persuasively authentic in period feeling, and yet vibrantly modern and relevant." According to writer Simon Reade, "there's something physical about Cheek by Jowl: grunting and sweating, rough and ready, brazen and exuberant. Yet there's a sensitivity in the muscularity . . . refined, graceful, considerate and astute, disciplined in their intricacy. . . . Their productions reek of vulgarity and have an aroma as holy as the mass."

For CBJ's tenth anniversary, Donnellan staged an all-male *As You Like It* that proved neither gimmicky nor campy. According to Gerard Raymond, "The men playing women (and in Rosalind's case playing a man again) give completely unselfconscious performances, and the production joyously celebrates the endless possibilities of crossing back and forth between the sexes. . . . The cast also doubles as musicians, and the glee club of Forest of Arden courtiers is a delightful bonus." For Ian Christensen, it was "a wonderfully warm and surprisingly straight production of the play in which the men playing women are so convincing in the subtleties and nuances of gesture and tone that it comes almost as a shock when the artifice is finally broken." The production was, claimed David Johnston, "the undisputed highlight" of the 29th Belfast festival.

Production History: **1981**: *The Country Wife*; **1982**: *Gotcha, Rack Abbey, Oth.*; **1983**: *Vanity Fair*; **1984**: *Per., Andromache*; **1985**: *MND, The Man of Mode*; **1986**: *The Cid, TN*; **1987**: *Mac.*; **1988**: *A Family Affair, Tmp., Philoctetes*; **1989**: *The Doctor of Honor, Lady Betty*; **1990**: *Sara, Ham.*; **1991**: *AYL*; **1992**: no new production; **1993**: *Don't Fool with Love, The Blind Me*; **1994**: *AYL* (all male cast).

Research Resources:

Carlson, Harry G. "Interview with Declan Donnellan." *Western European Stages* 4 (Spring 1992): 44-48.

Christensen, Ian. "As They Like It." *Plays International* (December 1991): 7.

Johnston, David. "At the 1991 Belfast Festival." *Plays International*.

Raymond, Gerard. "Letter from London." *TheaterWeek* (13 January 1992): 29-31.

———. "Drag *Sans* Camp: The All-Male *As You Like It*." *TheaterWeek* (3 October 1994): 13-16.

Reade, Simon. *Cheek by Jowl: Ten Years of Celebration*. London: Absolute Classics, 1991.

Felicia Hardison Londré

THE CHILTERN SHAKESPEARE COMPANY. MAIL: Bramble Tor, 6 Upper Drive, Beaconsfield, Buckinghamshire HP9 2AG. SITE: The Open Air Theatre, Hall Barn, Beaconsfield. BOX OFFICE: (0494) 673292 (day), 680178 (evening); Fax: (0494) 680178. ADMISSION: £8–12. SEASON: ten performances, mid-July. PRINCIPAL STAFF: Dr. Aviva Wiseman, artistic director; Michael Wiseman, company director; Sue Thorndike, production manager. FACILITY: open air location on private grounds (capacity 600). ANNUAL ATTENDANCE: approximately 4,000. FOUNDED: 1986, Michael, Aviva Wiseman.

As reported in the 1991 program of the Chiltern Shakespeare Company (CSC), Michael Wiseman's inspiration for presenting an annual Shakespeare production in the Chilterns came to him in 1985 during his annual apple-picking holiday in Galilee. The inaugural production, *As You Like It*, directed by Sue Thorndike, was rehearsed at High March School and performed in Harvard Hall at Oakdene School. After three successful indoor seasons, CSC ventured outdoors, thanks to an invitation from Lord and Lady Burnham, to use the grounds of Hall Barn; the first open air production was *A Midsummer Night's Dream*. In 1989, CSC began donating its profits to charity; the British Heart Foundation was given a check for £8,000. Since then, the attendance, the number of charities, and the size of the check have steadily increased.

The outdoor performances are fully amplified and will go on, rain or shine. In 1992, the site was enhanced by covered raked seating for audiences of up to 600. The gardens by the lakeside are open two hours before each performance. Theatregoers are invited to bring their own picnics or to order a "Festival Picnic" for £6.95 from a local catering firm; the 1992 menu was cottage cheese and pickled peach, seasonal salads, chunky chicken in creamy mayonnaise with almonds and apricots, roll and butter, exotic fresh fruit tartlet.

CSC's only mission is "to amuse our audiences and ourselves as Mr. William Shakespeare intended. It is all great fun!"

Production History: **1986**: *AYL*; **1987**: *Women in Shakespeare* (a collage of scenes); **1988**: *Mac.*; **1989**: *MND*; **1990**: *Ado.*; **1991**: *TN*; **1992**: *Wiv.*

Felicia Hardison Londré

D. P. PRODUCTIONS. MAIL: 10 Bracebridge Drive, Bilborough, Nottingham NG8 4PY. ADMINISTRATION: (0602) 29582. PRINCIPAL STAFF: Ian Dickens, managing director. FOUNDED: 1990, Ian Dickens.

D. P. Productions is dedicated to professional touring of Shakespeare in England. In its first two years, the company gave 380 performances on 60 different stages. Operating without government or commercial subsidy, the company is limited to 15 actors and a small crew, with only four rehearsal weeks per production. The company offers a free Shakespeare workshop for children at each venue on its tour itinerary; these have been conducted for up to a 1,000 children at one time. Toby Jones describes Dickens' philosophy as "a no-nonsense, non-ideological approach to the Bard with an emphasis on telling the story."

Production History (partial): **1990**: *MV*; **1991**: *TN*; **1992**: *Mac.*; **1993**: *JC*, *Rom.*

Research Resources:
Jones, Toby. "Shakespeare Tours." *Plays International* (May 1992): 7.

Felicia Hardison Londré

ENGLISH SHAKESPEARE COMPANY. MAIL: 38 Bedford Square, London WC1B 3EG. SITE: varies. ADMINISTRATION: 071/580-6505; Fax: 071/580-6479. BOX OFFICE: varies. ADMISSION: varies by venue. SEASON: varies; 75 weeks (two companies) in 1991-92. PRINCIPAL STAFF: Michael Bogdanov, Michael Pennington, artistic directors; Prudence Skene, executive director; Carole Winter, director of education. FACILITY: varies. AUDITIONS: occasional, through agents; STATUS: professional. ANNUAL BUDGET: £360,000 (1986). ANNUAL ATTENDANCE: 250,000 (1991). FOUNDED: 1985, Michael Bogdanov, Michael Pennington.

In their coauthored memoir of the origins of the English Shakespeare Company (ESC), Michael Bogdanov and Michael Pennington recall that their "lofty motives" sprang at least partially from disappointing experiences with the **Royal Shakespeare Company** (RSC) and the National Theatre. The two Michaels had worked together twice—on *Shadow of a Gunman* at the RSC and on *Strider* at the National—before they discovered a mutual interest in doing "something independent of the two big institutions." One of their lofty motives was the desire to take theatre to the badly underserved regional audiences. In September 1985, they formed a company of two called Mole Productions (because they were still in the dark) and approached the Touring Department of the Arts Council with the idea of producing a two-character play for touring. They learned that other companies (including **Cheek by Jowl**) were already touring small-scale shows and that the real need was for big productions conceived in the grand old tradition of taking the classics on the road, specifically to theatres with 1,000 or more seats in cities like Manchester and Aberdeen.

Given that impetus to think big, Bogdanov and Pennington conferred over coffee and returned to the Arts Council with a proposal to do a three-play Shakespearean history sequence, *Henry IV, Parts 1* and *2* and *Henry V*, using an acting company of about 25, with Bogdanov directing and Pennington playing Prince Hal and Henry V. For each engagement, the plays would be performed on consecutive evenings, with Saturdays devoted to morning, afternoon, and evening presentations of the entire trilogy. On 17 January 1986, the Arts Council awarded them £100,000, with the proviso that the venture would include ten weeks of touring in the United Kingdom with all funding needs guaranteed beforehand. The original capitalization of £360,000 was underwritten by Canadians Ed and David Mirvish (£125,000), Allied Irish Bank (£75,000), the British government's Business Sponsorship Incentive Scheme (£25,000), and in-kind support (£35,000) from the Plymouth Theatre Royal, where the *Henry* trilogy had its premiere engagement, 3-15 November 1986. With the funding in place, Bogdanov and Pennington finally settled on the company's name. The rather stodgy-looking octagonal logo soon followed (and has proved to be a bane to the marketing department).

From November 1986 to June 1987, the *Henry* trilogy played 14 weeks in the United Kingdom, plus an additional six in London, six in Canada, and two on the continent (Pfalzbau, Cologne, Hamburg, Paris). While garnering several awards, the ESC found itself with a budget shortfall of £50,000. It became clear to Bogdanov and Pennington that the key to survival lay in lucrative international touring, to offset the inevitable losses that would be incurred from the requisite performances in English theatres, which offered guarantees far below the ESC's operating costs. The two men determined to take the risk of mounting the remainder of Shakespeare's history cycle from *Richard II* to *Richard III*. Together, Bogdanov and Pennington adapted the texts of the three parts of *Henry VI* to create two parts, which they called *House of Lancaster* (ending with Act IV, scene 1 of the original Part 2) and *House of York*. They had to cope with a dauntingly short rehearsal period for the four new productions, plus other difficulties, including the untimely death of John Price only six weeks before opening (John Castle was recruited to take over Price's eight roles in the seven plays). Nevertheless, *The Wars of the Roses* opened as scheduled in December 1987 at the Theatre Royal in Bath.

The 23-hour *Wars of the Roses* was on the road 14 months. By the end of the tour in April 1989, the ESC had performed another 19 weeks throughout the UK, plus an additional seven in London, eight on the continent (Germany and the Netherlands), three in Japan, and four in the United States. To the 235 performances of the *Henry* trilogy were added 71 performances of *Richard II*, 56 of *Henry IV, Part 1*, 53 of *Henry IV, Part 2*, 54 of *Henry V*, 50 apiece for the two parts of *Henry VI*, and 80 of *Richard III*, for a three-year total of 649 performances. The tour ended with a £50,000 surplus. Among the ESC's numerous major awards was the *Chicago Tribune* Award for the Outstanding Production of the Decade (1988).

In 1989, Bogdanov became Intendant of the Deutsches Schauspielhaus in Hamburg, a position he held until 1991 (see section of this book on German Language Shakespeare). Nonetheless, he and Pennington recognized that the need persisted for their brand of big, popular, touring Shakespeare productions in England. They had filled the largest theatres on the British regional circuit, and those audiences had trebled from the ESC's first to second visit. "People say they have never heard language spoken so clearly and yet so true to the text," Bogdanov told Simon Reade. "The texts are picked over very carefully in rehearsal with the actors, individually and collectively, for meaning and nuance and for rhythm, to try to tell the most clear and exciting and direct story." He noted further that the ESC's commitment to putting Shakespeare "into the context of the modern world" enhances the clarity of the plays. Peter Lewis has quoted Michael Pennington on the ESC approach to Shakespeare's plays: "Once you free them from Elizabethan dress, you can go anywhere—and Bogdanov is a great opportunist. But our joint decisions about putting in modernisms are very careful. We don't put in anything just for the fun of it." The ESC's aim is to bring out "the vulgarity and the grace" of the works. Sally Homer, ESC publicist, defined the "house style" as "accessible, populist Shakespeare that widens the net of theatregoers to include those who wouldn't normally go to see a classic play."

Arts Council funding for the ESC continued for several seasons on a per-project basis. In 1990, the ESC produced *The Comedy of Errors*, directed by Glen Walford. It played 100 performances to 65,000 playgoers during 14 weeks in the United Kingdom and on tour to Kiev, Moscow, and Jerusalem. Three separate new projects were launched in 1991. A large company (23 actors) took *Coriolanus* and *The Winter's Tale*, both directed by Bogdanov and with Pennington in the featured roles, on tour to the large theatres, 12 weeks in the United Kingdom, six weeks in London, and 14 weeks abroad (Japan, Europe, India, Australia). A second company (15 actors) toured *The Merchant of Venice* and *Volpone*, both directed by Tim Luscombe, to small and medium-sized theatres, playing 20 weeks in the United Kingdom, an additional four weeks in London, and two weeks in Japan. The third project was the organization of an Education Department, which offers practical workshops for student groups before they attend a production, two-day Teachers' Development courses, and a small (five actors) touring company. The first production of the Education Department was *God Say Amen*, based upon themes from *The Wars of the Roses*. A second production, *Enemy to the People: Shakespeare and Revolution*, based upon the Roman plays, hit the road in 1991.

The 1991-92 season brought *Twelfth Night*, directed by Pennington; *Macbeth*, directed by Bogdanov, with Pennington in the title role; and a change in the company's Arts Council status from project client to revenue client, which brought a higher level of funding and greater stability to the ESC. Bogdanov ended 1992 with his fifth production of *The Tempest*. For the foreseeable future, the ESC plans to continue sending out two companies, one large and one smaller, as well as to keep up its education programs.

Seeing the seven plays of *The Wars of the Roses* in chronological order in three days at Chicago's Auditorium Theatre, 13-15 May 1988, was a high point in a lifetime of theatregoing. The eclectically costumed cycle progressed through historical periods ranging from the early nineteenth century in *Richard II* to a contemporary *Richard III*. In *Richard II*, Pennington characterized the king as effetely self-possessed, ever the Regency snob playing roles for his own amusement. Much of his blocking had him at the extremes of power or submission, either on a high level up center or on his knees at center. John Castle's Bolingbroke gave the impression of a gentleman gangster, but his Henry IV was a dignified graybeard in a black suit or a navy-blue uniform with gold trim. The costumes in *Henry IV, Part 1* underscored the tension between him and his son, Prince Hal (Pennington), who wore a denim jacket and jeans. Low comedy enlivened the early Hotspur scenes, and the Gadshill ambush was led by a punk with a Mohawk. Barry Stanton's Falstaff supplemented—or commented on—his text with wonderfully inventive pantomimic business and even, in *Henry IV, Part 2*, a couple of gestures acute enough to serve as curtain lines. In *Henry V*, the fatigue-clad English army sailed for France under a banner proclaiming "Fuck the Frogs," while the French court, in elegant pale blue and white uniforms, sat in a refined drawing room looking at slides of England, until the enraged Dauphin smashed his fist through the screen. The two parts of *Henry VI*, with costumes and sandbags evocative of World War I, contained what was perhaps the emotional peak of the cycle up to that point: the molehill scene. *Richard III* opened with a 1930s cocktail party prologue in which the main characters were introduced. Andrew Jarvis as Richard managed to be thoroughly evil and hilariously funny at the same time. In one of Bogdanov's most brilliant directorial touches, the fight between Richard and Richmond—the culmination of 23 hours of theatre depicting centuries of struggle for the English throne—had the two in medieval suits of armor, doing battle with huge, heavy broadswords to dirge-like musical accompaniment, underscoring humanity's seeming inability to break from age-old patterns of ambition, greed, and stupidity. The audience's final standing ovation must have lasted nearly 15 minutes. Clearly, we had experienced one of the landmark events in twentieth-century theatre, a production that remains sharply vivid in memory five years later.

Production History: **1986**: *1H4, 2H4, H5*; **1987**: *R2*, H6 (*House of Lancaster*), H6 (*House of York*), *R3*; **1990**: *Err.*; **1991**: *Cor., WT, MV, Volpone*; **1992**: *Mac., TN, Tmp.*; **1993**: *Rom.*

Research Resources:

Bogdanov, Michael, and Michael Pennington. *The English Shakespeare Company: The Story of the Wars of the Roses, 1986-1989*. London: Nick Hern Books, 1990.
Jays, David. "Bard Fatigue?" *Plays International* (December 1992): 12-3.
Khan, Naseem. "The Bard speaks out to Europe." *The Sunday Correspondent* (28 October 1990): 38.

Lewis, Peter. "A theatrical tour de force." *The Sunday Times* (11 November 1990).

Pennington, Michael. "Bard on the run." *The Independent* (3 April 1991).

Reade, Simon. "Making the ESC International." *Plays International* (February 1989): 16-17.

The ESC's version of *The Wars of the Roses* is available on seven video-cassettes from Films for the Humanities, P.O. Box 2053, Princeton, NJ 08543-2053

Londré interview: London, 20 June 1991; Engle interview: Hamburg, May 1991.

Felicia Hardison Londré and Ron Engle

LUDLOW FESTIVAL. MAIL: Festival Office, Castle Square, Ludlow, Shropshire SY8 1AY, England. SITE: the grounds of Ludlow Castle. ADMINISTRATION:, 0584/875070; Fax: 0584/8776730. BOX OFFICE: 0584/872150 (open May–July). ADMISSION: £2–12 ($4–$24). SEASON: 17 performances, late June to early July; 8:30 p.m., Mon.–Sat.; 2:30 p.m. matinees as advertised. PRINCIPAL STAFF: Anthony Baynon, festival administrator; Ray Sykes, business manager; Alan Cohen, artistic director. FACILITY: open-air theatre on grounds of Ludlow Castle, in the inner bailey of the castle in front of the Great Hall (capacity 1,200). AUDITIONS: early spring in London. STATUS: British Equity provincial theatre contract. ANNUAL BUDGET: £90,000 (1992). ANNUAL ATTENDANCE: 18,000. FOUNDED: 1960, St. Laurence's Parish Church Restoration Committee.

"Ludlow Festival, founded in 1960, is the only festival in the world started by a death-watch beetle," claims festival administrator Anthony Baynon. He elaborates: "The church roof was rotting away from an infestation of beetles, and money was needed for repairs. What better way to raise funds than concerts and plays?" So, in 1953, the St. Laurence Parish Church Restoration Committee sponsored a revival of John Milton's *Comus*, staged by David William, later artistic director of the **Stratford Festival** in Canada. William, then a young Oxford college graduate, recruited Oxford colleagues John Westbrook, William Gaskill, and other now notable artists to play *Comus* . The event was a huge success both artistically and financially, netting a profit of over £1,000. The reviewer in the *Manchester Guardian* noted that the return of *Comus* to Ludlow Castle, a masque originally commissioned for the castle 350 years earlier, "lays so powerful a hold on the imagination that half its battle is won before a word is spoken or a note played." The fine production and beautiful weather added to that enthusiasm. Additional arts festivals were held in 1955, 1956, 1958 and 1959, raising a total of £2,000 for the Church Restoration project. With the fund raising completed, many Ludlovians felt disappointed that the plays and concerts would not continue and urged the creation of an ongoing annual summer festival. On 7 June 1960, an executive committee called the Ludlow Festival Society was formed, composed of Erskine Barrett, Samuel Burgess, Hal Edgehill, Arthur Reynolds, Bob Rose, Jock Slater, Bill Summers, and John Patton as auditor and financial adviser.

The idea for the festival cannot be attributed to one person, but many acknowledge the personal initiative of Arthur Reynolds, the first chairman of the Ludlow Festival Society, as instrumental in getting Ludlow Festival (LF) off the ground. Reynolds' untimely death in 1960 resulted in Samuel Burgess' assuming the chairmanship, a position he held for years. David William was appointed as LF's first artistic director, and *A Midsummer Night's Dream* was staged in 1960.

The early festivals consisted of a play in the castle and a concert in the parish church. Today, LF consists of a Shakespeare play staged in the inner bailey of Ludlow Castle plus 30 additional events outside the castle, including country house and church concerts, jazz and pop recitals, art exhibits, prose and poetry readings, film festivals, excursions, and children's events.

The Festival Council, comprised of 15 elected and ten appointed members, is the governing body of LF. Everyone on the council undertakes some organizational responsibility, dividing into various committees including events, publicity, and house management. LF depends heavily upon its 300 dedicated and experienced volunteers. Ninety stewards (ushers), 30 hostesses, and many others give freely of their time and expertise during the festival fortnight. Without the volunteers, LF could not exist. In the early years, the festival was run entirely by volunteers, but, since 1984, the festival has hired a full-time administrator, Anthony Baynon. Additional part-time staff positions include a secretary/typist, a treasurer, and publicity, sponsorship, and publications officers.

The Festival Council hires a professional artistic director on a year-by-year contract, for a maximum of three years. Advertisements for this position are placed in *The Guardian*. In 1990, 36 people applied and six were interviewed. Many of the artistic directors have been educated at Oxford or Cambridge and have extensive professional credits at such places as the National Theatre or the **Royal Shakespeare Company**. The Festival Council, in collaboration with the artistic director, chooses the play. The artistic director then chooses his or her design staff and the actors. Twenty Equity actors are hired under a Provincial Theatre Contract and are paid £170—£400 per week, plus a subsistence allowance of £55. Fees for the artistic director are negotiated. The play production budget for the 1992 *As You Like It* was £90,000; £60,000 was spent on salaries, £20,000 on design and technical elements, and £10,000 on programs and publicity. The elaborate 52-page full-color program gives company biographies and information on all of the arts events that comprise LF. The program also includes dramaturgical information, plot synopsis, production photographs, and set and costume designs for the Shakespeare play.

LF relies entirely on its festival fortnight for its fund raising, and the festival not only pays for itself but makes a profit. In early years, the Arts Council guaranteed to cover three-quarters of any losses sustained by the festival, supplemented by a one-quarter loss guarantee by the District Council. But, in 1980, the Arts Council declared that LF no longer needed its support. At the time, the festival organizers were devastated, but advertisements in the program and sponsorship have more than made up for any loss from the Arts Council. In fact, LF has £40,000 in reserve in the bank, which gives it an income every year. Nightly sponsors (£1,500) range from major national companies, such as British Gas, Esso Petroleum, and Midland Bank, to local firms and even individual donors. Alternately, groups or individuals can sponsor an actor or musician for £500. Another source of revenue is membership in the Friends of Ludlow Festival, which 1,552 people paid £7 each to join in 1992. The castle, owned by The Earl of Powis, is leased to the festival for a mere £350 each year.

The inner bailey of Ludlow Castle, with its splendid architectural elements and clear and haunting acoustics, is LF's prime asset. The medieval castle was built in the twelfth and thirteenth centuries as a means of keeping out the Welsh. Considered the finest range of domestic buildings of this period in England, the ruins of the castle, built from local Silurian limestone and Old Red sandstone, provide an idyllic setting for many of Shakespeare's plays. When properly lit, the stonework can become "a living beauty of a dozen shaded greys," "blooded red," or "lichened pink." The acoustics have been praised; one critic noted "The walls of Ludlow Castle made a fine sounding board for rhetoric and for quite intimate speaking." The *Financial Times* reviewer in 1974 wrote that "voices bounce off the rugged walls . . . like balls from a squash court."

The stage is created in front of the Great Hall. Light and sound are controlled from the "Judges Lodging" at the back of the house. The 1,200 seats for the audience are set up between the twelfth-century nave of the chapel at St. Mary Magdalen on house right and the ruins of the thirteenth-century great kitchen on house left. Dressing rooms are created out of tents in various other rooms in the castle, and the mud floors are covered by wooden walkways. Fred Reeves, The *Shropshire Magazine* reviewer in 1970, noted: "Here Shakespeare's characters appear so natural, so much in their own world, that it is the audience itself, not the players, which comes to feel curiously costumed and out of time" (Lloyd, King, and Sykes, *Ludlow Festival*, 35).

Ludlow is a bustling country market town of 8,500 people. A pleasant two-hour drive west from Stratford-upon-Avon down winding country roads takes playgoers to this Welsh border town. Many early retirees from London have chosen Ludlow for their home, bringing with them a taste for cultural events. The festival enjoys widespread support from a cross-section of the population who enjoy the festival for its own merits. People come year after year. Business manager Ray Sykes says it is common for people to call in their reservations and then ask, "By the way, what is the play?" Forty-nine percent of the house is sold before the box office officially opens in May; 15 percent come from Ludlow and 85 percent come from 30 miles or more away. The festival's producers are proud to point out that groups from Detroit, Michigan, and Ontario, Canada, studying in England for the summer, attend every year. Over the past two years, the production has played to 95 percent capacity. Sykes, who is also house manager, notes the community's pride and determination: "People will tell me that this is their fifteenth season and it has never rained on them once." In fact, only three performances have been canceled due to weather over the past 33 years. Sound and lights are protected, and the audience comes prepared for the weather. Sykes elaborates: "It is part of the British spirit. They'll bring plastic bags to keep their feet dry and warm as well as sleeping bags and all sorts of things. The people who leave when it rains are mostly Americans. They don't like sitting in the rain."

Ludlow Festival receives wide publicity. The festival is a member of the British Arts Festival Association (BAFA), which sends 28,000 brochures throughout the country to publicize the festival. Advertisements are placed in national newspapers, including *The Guardian* and *The Telegraph*. Local and regional newspapers provide excellent coverage. The *Financial Times, The Guardian, The Telegraph*, as well as *The Birmingham Post* and *The Stage* (the actors' newspaper), review the productions.

Its concentration on a Shakespeare play as the centerpiece of the event makes Ludlow unique among the top 40 professional BAFA festivals in Great Britain. Its success is due to several strengths: high-quality professional productions; the lovely and unique castle setting; satisfied loyal customers; incredible community pride and support, including 300 dedicated volunteers (professional people, plumbers, teachers, etc., who run the concessions, usher, and sell programs); and careful, conservative financial management. Baynon, with his attention to logistical detail and human resource management skills, and Sykes, an accountant by trade, whose financial management has produced an admirable surplus, make a formidable management team.

Currently, the problems are few and the strengths many. There are no plans to lengthen the festival beyond its two-week run, because the 300 volunteers, most of whom work full time, could not afford to give another week. The goals are simply to keep the standards high and to raise the quality a little bit year by year while maintaining the community goodwill and enthusiasm.

LF's mission is "to bring high quality professional entertainment to a thinly populated region." The festival produces the more popular plays from the canon and repeats them after ten years or so. The producers try to alternate a history, a tragedy, and a comedy in a three-year cycle. Plays are cut freely in order to finish by about 11:15 p.m. (after 11:30 p.m., overtime begins, and the budget will not accommodate that). Most of the concepts for the plays are fairly traditional, although some deviations have proved popular. Sykes recalls a production of *A Midsummer Night's Dream* with punk rockers as the fairies that was a hit with Ludlow's conservative audiences. Throughout the years, LF has enjoyed good to excellent reviews for its productions, especially when the castle's natural beauty was used to full advantage. Critics were united in their praise for David King as Lear in 1972 and Edward Woodward's King Richard III in 1982. Artistic director Colin George, following his 1966 production of *Much Ado About Nothing*, described working in the space as follows: "There can be few open-air auditoria that combine such perfect acoustics with such a visual grandeur."

Production History: 1960: *MND*; 1961: *Mac.*; 1962: *TN*; 1963: *R2*; 1964: *MV*; 1965: *Ham.*; 1966: *Ado*; 1967: *MM*; 1968: *R3*; 1969: *Rom.*; 1970: *1H4*; 1971: *MND*; 1972: *Lr.*; 1973: *WT*; 1974: *Oth.*; 1975: *TN*; 1976: *Ham.*; 1977: *H5*; 1978: *Shr.*; 1979: *LLL*; 1980: *Mac.*; 1981: *AYL*; 1982: *R3*; 1983: *Ant.*; 1984: *MND*; 1985: *Tmp.*; 1986: *Rom.*; 1987: *R2*; 1988: *TN*; 1989: *JC*; 1990: *MV*; 1991: *Mac.*; 1992: *AYL*; 1993: *Oth.*

Research Resources: David Lloyd, Rosemary King, and Maureen Sykes. *Ludlow Festival: The First Twenty-Five Years 1960-1984*. This work was published by the Ludlow Festival Society in June 1984 to mark the Festival's silver jubilee and the 350th anniversary of the first performance of *Comus* at Ludlow Castle. Archives for Ludlow Castle are maintained by Maureen Sykes at her home in Ludlow.

Cindy Melby Phaneuf
Site visit and interview with Anthony Baynon and Ray Sykes: 24 July 1992.

MINACK OPEN-AIR THEATRE. MAIL: Rusmar, Red Lane, Rosudgeon, Porthcurno, Penzance, Cornwall. SEASON: late May to early September. FACILITY: amphitheatre (capacity 500). ANNUAL ATTENDANCE: 20,000. FOUNDED: 1930, Rowena Cade.

Minack is a massive outcropping of rock among the Porthcurno cliffs on the coast of Cornwall. There, with the sea at their backs, actors compete to make Shakespeare's words heard above the wind and the seagulls. Theatergoers sit on a rocky slope, often braving the cold and wet weather, to watch plays presented by semi-professional companies invited to perform at the Minack Open-Air Theatre (MOT).

In 1931, after several years of amateur performances of Shakespeare at sites near Porthcurno, Rowena Cade took the initiative to hew a performance space out of the granite boulders on the cliff behind her home. Cade, Charles Thomas Angove, and William Rawlings cut stone and hauled rock to create a terrace stage with turfed tiers of seats. The Minack Open-Air Theatre opened in

August 1932 with an amateur production of *The Tempest*, which was reviewed in *The Times*. The following summer's production of *Twelfth Night* featured two professional actors in the cast.

World War II brought a halt to production, while an anti-aircraft gun post was installed on the site. Cade and Rawlings reopened the theatre in July 1949, and continued making improvements over the years. By the mid-1950s, theatre groups from all over England were applying to be booked for "a week at the Minack." In those days, audience members had to park their cars a mile and a half from the performance site. Not until the 1960s, were safety wires and adequate electric lighting installed to minimize the actors' risk of falling from the stage area at the edge of the cliff—70 feet into the sea below. Professional directors, like Frank Bechhofer, returned to MOT season after season. Today, the Minack productions are a major tourist attraction for Cornwall.

Production History (Shakespeare only, 1932-1968): **1932**: *Tmp.*; **1933**: *TN*; **1934**: (dark); **1937**: *Ant.*; **1952**: *Tmp.*; **1953**: *Lr.*; **1954**: *MND*; **1955**: *Mac.* **1956**: *JC*; **1957**: *TN*; **1958**: *Shr.*, *R2*; **1959**: *Ant.*, *1H4*, *Oth.*; **1960**: *Lr.*, *WT*, *Shr.*; **1961**: *MM*, *LLL*; **1962**: *Ham.*, *AYL*; **1963**: *Rom.*, *Tmp.*, *MND*, *Cym.*; **1964**: *Lr.*, *TN*, *MV*, *Ado*, *WT*, *Mac.*; **1965**: *AYL*, *Cor.*, *MND*, *Lr.*, *Shr.*; **1966**: *R2*, *1H4*, **1967**: *TN*, *MM*, *MV*,; **1968**: *R2*.

Research Resources: Averil Demuth, ed., *The Minack Open-Air Theatre* (n.p.: David and Charles, 1968.

Felicia Hardison Londré

OPEN AIR THEATRE, REGENT'S PARK / NEW SHAKESPEARE COMPANY. MAIL: Inner Circle, Regent's Park, London, NW1 4NP, England. SITE: Inner Circle, Regent's Park. ADMINISTRATION: 071/935-5756. BOX OFFICE: 071/486-2431. SEASON: approximately 125 performances, late May to early September; 8:00 p.m., Mon.–Sat.; 2:30 p.m., Wed., Thurs., Sat. PRINCIPAL STAFF: Ian Talbot, artistic and managing director; Robert Noble, administrator; Sheila Benjamin, sponsorship and marketing director. FACILITY: outdoor amphitheatre (capacity 1,187). STATUS: non-profit, professional. ANNUAL BUDGET: £700,000 (1991). ANNUAL ATTENDANCE: 100,000 (1992). FOUNDED: 1932, Open Air Theatre; 1962, New Shakespeare Company, David Conville.

With its lovely curving walks, profusion of flowers, and swan-inhabited waters, London's Regent's Park has been a favorite site for outdoor concerts and dramatic performances since the turn of the century, when it was called the

Royal Botanical Gardens. There, Sir Ben Greet began a tradition of presenting minimally staged, open-air Shakespeare on the lawn. In 1932, impresario Sidney Carroll teamed up with director Robert Atkins and won permission from the Ministry of Works to take to the park four matinee performances of Atkins' production of *Twelfth Night*, which had been running at the New Theatre (today's Albery). Carroll lost £560 on the project but nonetheless supported construction of a permanent theatre facility in a quiet corner of the park. Tennis courts were taken out, an 80-foot-wide, grass-carpeted stage demarcated between clumps of bushes, and deck chairs set up on a slope facing the playing area, which lay beyond a 12-foot-deep orchestra pit that turned into a moat when it rained. The first full season (summer 1933) of the Open Air Theatre (OAT) opened to an audience of 3,000 to 4,000 people for a revival of *Twelfth Night*. "Greensward" was Carroll's term for the stage. As Master of the Greensward, the 76-year-old Sir Ben Greet would appear, according to J. C. Trewin, "superfluously but avuncularly, before every play to welcome the audience and say something about the weather."

Atkins founded a company called the Bankside Players, which performed under his direction at the OAT until 1960. Atkins is still remembered as one of the most colorful figures in twentieth-century British theatre. Actor Hubert Gregg never saw him defer to anyone except Bernard Shaw, who wrote his one-act *The Six of Calais* for the company's 1934 season and attended the rehearsals. Over the years, Shaw has emerged as the second most frequently performed playwright in the OAT. The first 16 of Atkins' 28 years at the helm saw only two fair-weather opening performances. Despite appearances by star performers like Anna Neagle in 1934, Vivien Leigh in 1936, Gladys Cooper in 1937, and Cathleen Nesbitt in 1938, the operation continued to lose money. Carroll terminated his involvement in 1939, but Atkins soldiered on. During the war years, when the blackout necessitated a curfew, matinee performances only were offered. For two seasons, between 1944 and 1946, Atkins was director of productions at the Shakespeare Memorial Theatre in Stratford-upon-Avon; then he returned to the park.

Money problems plagued the operation in the 1950s, so that the 1953 season had to be cut short by six weeks; the theatre remained dark throughout the 1954 and 1957 seasons. An erosion of standards led to a decline in attendance. David Conville later recalled that Atkins had lost his youthful energy, and "the Park started getting a slightly tatty image." Fortunately, a successful production of *The Tempest*, directed by David William marked Atkins's twenty-third season in Regent's Park in 1955, and 1956 brought an invitation to take two productions to the Baalbeck Festival in Lebanon, where Atkins was awarded the Order of the Cedar. Bad weather ended the 1960 season in July, and there was no 1961 season. At that point, the Department of the Environment (formerly the Ministry of Works) considered reconverting the site to parkland. David William learned of the threat to the OAT and contacted David Conville, whom he knew only slightly. Together, the two walked across the park in a winter snow to look at the theatre. They decided to try their hands at running it.

In February 1962, David Conville Productions, Ltd., signed a contract for a three-month summer season. Conville, as managing director, and William, as artistic director, subsequently raised £4,000, redesigned the stage area to reduce its unwieldy size and remove a concrete prompter's box, and created a new, nonprofit company, the New Shakespeare Company (NSC). Atkins' only advice to Conville was: "Mind you don't get a crick in your neck, old son, looking up at the bloody weather." Twenty years later, Conville was to note that the NSC had "lost only 7 percent of all performances while 75 percent of all perform-ances are played in fine weather."

Richard Digby Day succeeded William as artistic director in 1968, but Conville remained at his post until 1986, when he became chairman of the NSC. By 1969, the annual attendance had reached 75,000. The 1970s brought some experimentation with production styles, a 1974 tour to India and Ceylon (sponsored by the Arts Council and the British Council), and more illustrious names added to the roster of performers: Felicity Kendal, Edward Fox, Jeremy Irons, Zoë Wanamaker, Rula Lenska, and others. Most significant was the construction of a new auditorium in 1974-75. At a cost of £120,000, an invitingly intimate atmosphere was achieved through the construction of a steeply raked, fan-shaped auditorium seating 1,200 people, with no seat more than 80 feet from the stage. The complex also includes a box office, facilities for catered meals (in addition to a separate area for picnickers), dressing rooms, and a small administration building.

In 1986, Ian Talbot succeeded Conville as artistic and managing director of the NSC. The lease on the OAT requires that each season include at least two Shakespeare plays. Beyond that, Talbot's policy has been to present a relatively neglected musical comedy and a production for children. The perennial favorite, *A Midsummer Night's Dream*, has often been revived from one season to the next and is newly produced at least every four years. Because it works so well in the outdoor setting, it has become a kind of signature piece for the OAT. Its midsummer-night performance, which always sells out far in advance, is followed by special festivities, including a late-night cabaret artist. Because there are any number of Shakespeare productions running in London at all times, the NSC does not attempt to compete with the **Royal Shakespeare Company** but concentrates on exploiting its own special atmosphere to best advantage. "The house style is very much dictated by the surroundings," says marketing director Sheila Benjamin. "We try as much as possible to incorporate the trees into the stage set and use the open atmosphere. But on the whole we are best known for rather traditional productions." NSC does, however, adapt to an indoor performance mode for its tours before and after the outdoor season.

Over 2,000 actors submit applications each season; perhaps 200 of them win auditions, and only a handful are hired. The audience is composed mainly of Londoners, including many young professionals and schoolchildren.

Attendance at school matinees averages 11,000 each season. The NSC management is quite content to have only 10 percent of its audience composed of overseas tourists; thus, NSC is less affected than are many other theatres when fluctuations in currency exchange rates or world events cause a drop in tourism.

Box office receipts account for approximately 70 percent of NSC's income, while 26 or 27 percent comes from corporate donations; the remainder is underwritten by the City of Westminster. A great variety of sponsorship packages is available. A major sponsor like British Petroleum, which until recently sponsored the education program as well as one production, will get in return not only acknowledgment in all publicity materials but also complimentary tickets, display advertising, and the opportunity to use the OAT for corporate hospitality.

In a sixtieth-anniversary retrospective publication, Ian Talbot noted:

> The Open Air Theatre is now established as a national institution and is the only fully professional, permanent open air theatre in the British Isles. With both banks full it can seat over 1,200 people, making it one of the largest theatres in London. Over the past three decades the NSC has presented 90 major productions in Regent's Park, 24 national tours, and 13 overseas tours. Since 1962, we have employed over 2,500 actors and staff while 3,000,000 people have watched the plays.

A matinee performance of *A Midsummer Night's Dream* served as a good example of the NSC's characteristic way with Shakespeare: straightforward handling of the text, lots of comic moments, opulent costumes, and exploitation of the natural greenery surrounding the stage. Indeed, the mossy green stage floor, a fallen tree trunk, and a rocky ledge blended so seamlessly with the real bushes and trees that it was impossible to distinguish between nature and artifice. The fairies took much of the focus. Puck and the First Fairy seemed fairly made of cobwebs, and their opalescent wings had a magical quality even in broad daylight. Oberon moved like an insect; his turquoise-blue double wings could spread or drop to good effect. The fairies' lullaby over Titania culminated in their hanging a cobweb canopy over her and covering her with a grassy blanket to camouflage her place of rest. One running gag had Oberon causing a recurring buzz in the First Fairy's head, which almost drove her crazy. The "Pyramus and Thisbe" sequence was very elaborately costumed; Wall, for example, entered encased in a rectangular box painted like bricks. Bottom, as Pyramus, wore a short Roman-style skirt, two funnels as a breastplate, and a colander on his head. Roy Hudd enhanced the role with a wealth of fresh tricks.

Production History: **1932**: *TN*; **1933**: *TN, MND, Tmp*; **1934**: *Err.*   *Comus, AYL, TN, Tmp., R3, MND, Rom., The Six of Calais/Androcles* *and the Lion*; **1935**: *Chloridia, TN, MND, LLL*; **1936**: *H8, AYL, MND, LLL*; **1937**: *Wiv., JC, WT, TN, AYL, MND*; **1938**: *AYL, MND, TN, Lysistrata*; **1939**: *Per., Tobias and the Angel, TN, MND*; **1940**: *MND*; **1941**: *H5*; **1942**: *TN, MV*; **1943**: *Tmp., AYL, Tobias and the Angel*; **1944**: *WT, TN*; **1945**: *AYL, MV*; **1946**: *AYL, MND, Tro.*; **1947**: *TN, MND*; **1948**: *Jn., MND, AYL*; **1949**: *Err., TGV, Ado, Faust*; **1950**: *WT, MV, Shr.*; **1951**: *MND*; **1952**: *Cym., The Boy with a Cart, AYL*; **1953**: *TN, LLL*; **1954**: no productions; **1955**: *Tmp., MND*; **1956**: *Ham., TN, AYL, The Romanticks*; **1957**: no productions; **1958**: *Ado, Shr.*; **1959**: *TN, MND, Tmp.*; **1960**: *Tmp.*; **1961**: no productions; **1962**: *MND, TN, LLL*; **1963**: *Ado, MND*; **1964**: *H5, Shr., TN, R3, Tmp.*; **1965**: *AYL*; **1966**: *MND, Of Eros and of Dust*; **1967**: *MND, Cyrano de Bergerac*; **1968**: *Wiv., TGV*; **1969**: *MV, TGV*; **1970**: *MND, Ado, The Lord Byron Show*; **1971**: *Rom., MND*; **1972**: *Tmp., TN*; **1973**: *TN, AYL*; **1974**: *MND, TNK, Ham., Rosencrantz and Guildenstern Are Dead, Old Times*; **1975**: *Shr., MND, Zoo Story, Sweet Mr Shakespeare*; **1976**: *Oth., LLL*; **1977**: *LLL, H5*; **1978**: *MND, Mac.,* Shaw one-acts; **1979**: *JC, MND, TN,* Shaw one-acts; **1980**: *Ado, MND, Androcles and the Lion*; **1981**: *Ado, Err.*; **1982**: *Shr., MND,* Shaw one-acts; **1983**: *Ham., AYL, MND, Bashville*; **1984**: *Wiv., MND, Bashville*; **1985**: *TN, MND, Ring Round the Moon*; **1986**: *MND, Rom., Arms and the Man*; **1987**: *TGV, MND, Bartholomew Fair, All on a Summer's Day*; **1988**: *WT, MND, Babes in Arms*; **1989**: *MND, TN, The Swaggerer, East of the Elephant*; **1990**: *Ado, JC, The Fantasticks, Big Trouble at Little Happening*; **1991**: *MND, Mac., The Boys from Syracuse, All on a Summer's Day*; **1992**: *MND, AYL, Lady Be Good, The Curse of the Egyptian Mummy*; **1993**: *Shr., Rom., A Connecticut Yankee, The Mona Lisa Mystery.*

Research Resources: *Fifty Years of The Open Air Theatre Regent's Park* (London: The Abbey Press, 1982) contains essays by David Conville, Richard Digby Day, Benny Green, Hubert Gregg, Evan Jones, Ian Talbot, J.C. Trewin, Margaret Wolfit, David William, and others. See also Simon Reade, *Open Air Theatre, Regent's Park: A Celebration of 60 Years* (Abingdon: The Abbey Press, 1992); "Progress in the Park," *Plays International* (June 1992): 10-12.

Site visits: 22 June 1988 and 22 June 1991; interview: 21 June 1991.
Felicia Hardison Londré

THE OLD VIC. MAIL: Waterloo Road, London SE1 8NB, England. SITE: The Old Vic Theatre. ADMINISTRATION: 071/928-2651; Fax: 071/261-9161.

BOX OFFICE: 071/928-7616. ADMISSION: £10.50–£30. SEASON: long runs; 7:45 p.m., Mon.–Sat.; 3:00 p.m., Wed. and Sat. PRINCIPAL STAFF: David Mirvish, producer; Andrew Leigh, general manager; Ed Mirvish, chairman. FACILITY: proscenium stage (capacity 1,078). AUDITIONS: Equity auditions. STATUS: British Actors' Equity. ANNUAL BUDGET: varies by production. FOUNDED: 1818, as the Royal Coburg; 1833, renamed the Royal Victoria Theatre; 1914, as a repertory company, Lilian Baylis.

Shakespeare is an integral part of the Old Vic's long and colorful history. Its association with the plays of William Shakespeare helped establish the theatre's international reputation for great English acting. Notable artists include a "who's who" of internationally acclaimed actors and directors. Twice in its history, the Old Vic has completed the entire canon of the first Folio. For 13 years, it was the "temporary home" of the National Theatre, where the tradition of Shakespeare continued and the reputation of the theatre flourished. In addition to laying the groundwork for a national theatre, the Old Vic's colorful and "religiously devoted" manager Lilian Baylis established the foundation for England's national opera and ballet. For these and many other notable achievements, the Old Vic has a special place in the hearts of London's theatrical community.

The Old Vic opened in 1818 as the Royal Coburg Theatre in honor of Prince Leopold of Saxe Coburg. It was built on reclaimed marshland that had been made accessible to the city by the completion of Waterloo Bridge in 1817. For the first 60 years, the repertoire consisted primarily of melodrama and farce, and the theatre's reputation grew steadily as an uncouth and even dangerous place to visit. In 1833, the theatre was renamed the Royal Victoria (later nicknamed the Old Vic). Despite such royal patronage and the appearance of great eighteenth-century actors such as Edmund Kean, Grimaldi, and others, most Londoners avoided this rough and unsavory neighborhood.

In 1879, the theatre was dark for most of the year. Then Miss Emma Cons took over the management and transformed it from "a rat trap gin palace" to "a cheap and decent place of entertainment along strict temperance lines." She also renamed the theatre the Royal Victoria Coffee Music Hall. Her aim was to put on good drama productions at popular prices. Nineteen years later, in 1898, Lilian Baylis left South Africa to assist her aunt at the theatre. Trained as a musician and knowing little about theatre management, she was to become "the single most important figure" in the Old Vic's history. After she had worked with her aunt for 12 years, the management passed to her in 1912, and in 1914, despite World War I, she formed the Old Vic Shakespeare Company which was subsidized at first by the opera that played there. Over the following nine years, the complete canon of Shakespeare was performed for the first time in any theatre. During the war years, Sybil Thorndike played male as well as female leads. After the war, Robert Atkins was named as director, developing and launching great actors like John Gielgud, Laurence Olivier, Michael Redgrave,

Ralph Richardson, Peggy Ashcroft, and numerous others. The Old Vic's critical acclaim was at an all-time high both in England and abroad.

The 26-year period from 1937-1963 was marked by a series of significant changes in the Old Vic management. In addition, world events, namely World War II, had a direct impact on the theatre. The year 1937 ushered in a new era in artistic leadership, as Tyrone Guthrie was appointed director of the Old Vic. For the first time, a university-educated director who was not an actor provided the guiding vision—a subject of some controversy at the time. After serving one year, he was dismissed and then later rehired. The year 1937 also marked the death of Baylis, ending her productive 40-year association with the theatre. A promising start by Guthrie was cut short by an enemy bomb that hit the theatre in 1941, causing the Old Vic to close and to remain dark for nearly a decade. The theatre reopened in 1950 with *Twelfth Night*, beginning a 13-year series of annual seasons by the Old Vic Company. The second complete canon series began in 1953 with Richard Burton's *Hamlet*, ending five years later with John Gielgud and Edith Evans in *Henry VIII*. A production of *Measure for Measure* on 15 June 1963 officially brought down the curtain on 49 seasons by the Old Vic Company—seasons that had included some of the most notable Shakespeare productions in world history—and ushered in the National Theatre.

The Old Vic housed the National Theatre, under the artistic direction of Laurence Olivier, from 1963-1977. The theatre that had helped to launch Olivier as a classical actor was once again to include Shakespeare as a significant part of its repertoire. Peter O'Toole as Hamlet, directed by Olivier himself, launched the new season. The temporary home for the National Theatre lasted for 13 years, as its permanent theatre complex on the South Bank of the Thames met numerous obstacles on the road to completion. Significant productions included Jonathan Miller's *Merchant of Venice* with Olivier as Shylock. The Old Vic's fruitful association with the National Theatre ended in 1976 with *Hamlet*, just as it had begun, this time featuring Albert Finney in the title role. Many people saw the National Theatre and the Old Vic as inextricably linked, and there was some discussion of retaining the Old Vic as the National Theatre's proscenium stage. Instead, the National Theatre moved to its £20 million, three-theatre complex on the South Bank, and, in 1977, the Prospect Theatre moved into the Old Vic. A successful season led to a "marriage" with the Old Vic, an arrangement that lasted until 1981 when the Prospect Theatre was forced into liquidation.

The latest chapter in the Old Vic's history began in 1982 when the governors, feeling that they could no longer manage the theatre, received permission from the Charity Commissioners to sell the theatre to the highest bidder. Two legitimate offers were received, one from Andrew Lloyd Webber for £500,000, and one from Canadian businessman Ed Mirvish for £550,000. On 5 August 1982, "Honest Ed" bought the theatre, sight unseen, and began a nine-month, £2 million restoration project. "The exterior was restored by architects Renton

Howard Wood Levin to a design close to its 1818 appearance," with a stone and stucco classical facade and arched side wall. The interior was remodeled by Clare Ferraby, inspired by the auditorium design of the 1880s. "Once a maze of stairs and corridors, the foyer was opened up and the stage extended to three times its original size" (Old Vic program). Period wallpaper, fresh paint, new upholstery, and air conditioning completed the project. The Old Vic reopened on 31 October 1983 with Tim Rice's new musical *Blondel*. A series of plays and companies have since occupied the theatre, including the **English Shakespeare Company** in Michael Bogdanov's controversial production of *The Henrys* (*Henry IV, parts 1* and *2*, and *Henry V*) and the **Royal Shakespeare Company** with *Kiss Me Kate*. In January 1988, Jonathan Miller was named artistic director. His mission was to produce lesser-known English classics as well as the neglected European repertoire. The 1988 season included *Andromache, The Tutor, One Way Pendulum, Too Clever by Half, Bussy D'Ambois, The Tempest* with Max von Sydow, and *Candide*. The 1989 season featured *King Lear* with Eric Porter, *As You Like It, A Flea in Her Ear,* and *The Liar*. Disappointed by the size of the audiences, Miller ended his tenure of two and one-half years as artistic director in June 1990 after producing *The Illusion* and *Marya*. Miller reflects: "Ed Mirvish had lost a great deal of money and it was clear that it was not possible to have a commercially viable classical theatre—it needs subsidy." The Old Vic is now a commercial house that books in companies for long runs. The American musical *Carmen Jones* with book and lyrics by Oscar Hammerstein and music by George Bizet opened 27 March 1991.

Production History: 1914-15: *MV, Tmp., Wiv., Shr., King Rene's Daughter, Err., TN, MND, She Stoops to Conquer, AYL, WT, The School for Scandal, Oth., Ham., Mac., JC*; **1915-16**: *AYL, MV, H5, The Rivals, Tmp., Oth., R3, MND, JC, WT, She Stoops to Conquer, The Star of Bethlehem, Rom., Ham., Ado, Mac., Shr., TN, Everyman, The School for Scandal*; **1916-17**: *The School for Scandal, The Rivals, H8, Err., AYL, MV, JC, Tmp., Oth., R2, TGV, King Rene's Daughter, She Stoops to Conquer, The Star of Bethlehem, A Christmas Carol, TN, Shr., Mac., H5, St. Patrick's Day, The Critic, Ado, The Lady of Lyons, Wiv., Ham.*;

1917-18: *Jn., MV, R2, AYL, 2H4, JC, Tmp., Shr., A Christmas Carol, Seaman's Pie, The Star of Bethlehem, The School for Scandal, She Stoops to Conquer, MND, WT, Rom., Lr., Cym., H8, Wiv., H5, TN, Everyman, R3, Masks and Faces, Ham.*; **1918-19**: *MV, Ham., MM, Ado, Mac., TN, Tmp., H5, AYL, LLL, The Coventry Nativity Play, Shr., MND, WT, JC, Everyman, 1H4*; **1919-20**: *Wiv., Tmp., R2, AYL, H5, Mac., She Stoops to Conquer, The Hope of the World, A Christmas Carol, Shr., MV, JC, MND, Ham., Everyman, The Rivals, Oth., Cor., 1, 2H4, The Land of Heart's Desire, The Proposal, Michael, Gallant*

Cassian; **1920-21**: *WT, The School for Scandal, AYL, TN, Jn., Shr., The Hope of the World, Err., Pantaloon, MV, JC, MND, Rom., Everyman, Tmp., Ham., R3, Warrior's Day, Lr., Per.*; **1921-22**: *Ado, R2, AYL, Mac., H5, AWW, Advent, MV, Oth., TN, Peer Gynt, Lr., Everyman, Love is the Best Doctor, Err., Ham., Tim., She Stoops to Conquer, Vic Vicissitudes*; **1922-23**: *Wiv., Shr., 1, 2H4, JC, A New Way to Pay Old Debts, Britain's Daugher, Ant., The Hope of the World, The Cricket on the Hearth, MV, R3, 1, 2, 3H6, King Arthur, Everyman, TN, Ham., MND*; **1923-24**: *LLL, Tit., H5, Tro., TGV, AYL, The Play of the Shepherds, A Chrismas Carol, The School for Scandal, H8, Tmp., Faust, The Rivals, Cor., MV, Everyman, Ham., TN*; **1924-25**: *Oth., MND, Hannele, The Play of the Shepherds, She Stoops to Conquer, R2, Ado, WT, Mac., Everyman, Ham., TN, Trelawny of the Wells*; **1925-26**: *MV, R3, Shr., MM, Ant., The Child in Flanders, Harlequin Jack Horner, Wiv., She Stoops to Conquer, JC, AYL, The Shoemaker's Holiday, Everyman, Rom., Ado*; **1926-27**: *Jn., MND, H5, Tmp., Mac., The Play of the Shepherds, Christmas Eve, TN, R3, WT, Oth., Everyman, St. Patrick's Day, Err., Ham., The Two Shepherds*; **1927-28**: *Shr., MV, Ado, H5, Rom., TNK, The School for Scandal, Everyman, Ham., Lr.*; **1928-29**: *LLL, The Vikings, AYL, TN, Adam's Opera, Mac., Caste, Wiv., Mary Magdalene, H8, The*

Rivals, Ham.; **1929-30**: *Rom., MV, The Imaginary Invalid, R2, MND, JC, AYL, The Dark Lady of the Sonnets, Androcles and the Lion, Mac., Ham.*; **1930-31**: *1H4, Tmp., The Jealous Wife, R2, Ant., TN, Arms and the Man, Ado, Lr.*; **1931-32**: *Jn., Shr., MND, H5, The Knight of the Burning Pestle, JC, Abraham Lincoln, Oth., TN, Ham.*; **1932-33**: *Caesar and Cleopatra, Cym., AYL, Mac., MV, She Stoops to Conquer, WT, Mary Stuart, The Admirable Bashville, Rom., The School for Scandal, Tmp.*; **1933-34**: *TN, The Cherry Orchard, H8, MM, Tmp., The Importance of Being Earnest, Mac.*; **1934-35**: *Ant., R2, Ado, St. Joan, Shr., Oth., The Two Shepherds, Hippolytus, Major Barbara, 2H4, Ham.*; **1935-36**: *Peer Gynt, JC, The Three Sisters, Mac., St. Helena, The School for Scandal, R3, WT, Lr.*; **1936-37**: *LLL, The Country Wife, AYL, The Witch of Edmonton, Ham., TN, H5*; **1937-38**: *Pygmalion, MM, R3, Mac., MND, Oth., The King of Nowhere, Cor.*; **1938-39**: *Trelawny of the Wells, Ham., Man and Superman, The Rivals, MND, She Stoops to Conquer, An Enemy of the People, Shr.*; **1940**: *Lr., Tmp.*; **1941** (At the New Theatre, London): *Jn., The Cherry Orchard*; **1942** (At the New Theatre, London): *Oth., Wiv.*; **1943** (At the New Theatre, London): *MV, Abraham Lincoln, The Russians, Blow Your Own Trumpet*; **1944**: (At the Lyric Theatre, Hammersmith): *Guilty* (At the New Theatre, London) *Ham.*;

1944-45 (New Theatre): *Peer Gynt, Arms and the Man, R3, Uncle Vanya*; **1945-46** (New Theatre): *1H4, 2H4, Oedipus, The Critic, Arms and the Man, Uncle Vanya*; **1946-47** (New Theatre): *Lr., An Inspector Calls, Cyrano de Bergerac, The Alchemist, R2*; **1947-48** (New Theatre): *Shr., R2, St. Joan, The Government Inspector, Cor.*; **1948-49** (New Theatre): *TN, Dr. Faustus, The Way of the World, The Cherry Orchard, The School for Scandal, R3, The Proposal, Antigone*; **1950-51**: *Bartholomew Fair, Captain Brassbound's Conversion, Electra, The Wedding, H5, Wiv., TN*; **1951-52**: *Tamburlaine the Great, Oth., The Clandestine Marriage, MND, TGV, Lr., The Other Heart, Tim.*; **1952-53**: *Rom., The Italian Straw Hat, MV, JC, Murder in the Cathedral, H8*; **1953-54**: *AWW, Cor., Ham., Jn., Tmp., TN*; **1954-55**: *AYL, 1H4, LLL, Mac., R2, Shr.*; **1955-56**: *H5, JC, Mac., Wiv., Oth., R2, Rom., Tro., WT, Major Barbara, Caesar and Cleopatra*; **1956-57**: *Ant., Err., Cym., MV, Ado, R3, Tim., Tit., TGV*; **1957-58**: *Ham., 3H6, H8, Lr., MM, MND*; **1958-59**: *The Cenci, Ghosts, JC, Mac., The Magistrate, Mary Stuart, Tartuffe, Sganarelle, Tmp.*; **1959-60**: *AYL, The Double Dealer, H5, The Importance of Being Earnest, Wiv., R2, Saint Joan, What Every Woman Knows*; **1960-61**: *1H4, Mary Stuart, MV, MND, Rom., The Seagull, She Stoops to Conquer, TN*; **1961-62**: *Dr. Faustus, JC, Jn., Mac., Mourning Becomes Electra, The Oresteia, R3, Tmp., TN*; **1962-63**: *The Alchemist, MM, MV, Oth., Peer Gynt, The Shoemaker's Holiday, Three Sisters*; **1963**: *Ham., Saint Joan, Uncle Vanya, The Recruiting Officer*; **1964**: *Hobson's Choice, Andorra, Play, Philoctetes, Oth., The Master Builder, LLL, H5, Ham., The Dutch Courtesan, Hay Fever, The Royal Hunt of the Sun*; **1965**: *The Crucible, Ado, Mother Courage and Her Children, The Resistible Rise of Arturo Ui, Cor., The Threepenny Opera, The Days of the Commune, Ant., Tro., L'Ecole Des Femmes, Klondyke, Armstrong's Last Goodnight, Love for Love, Trelawny of the "Wells"*; **1966**: *A Flea in Her Ear, Miss Julie, Black Comedy, Juno and the Paycock, A Bond Honoured, Black Comedy, Performance in Aid of the George Devine Fund, The Storm, Tons of Money*; **1967**: *The Dance of Death, Rosencrantz and Guildenstern are Dead, Three Sisters, AYL, Tartuffe*; **1968**: *Volpone, Oedipus, Edward II, Triple Bill—The Covent Garden Tragedy, A Most Unwarrantable Intrusion, In His Own Write, The Advertisement, Home and Beauty, LLL*; **1969**: *Macrune's Guevara, An Evasion of Women, 'H' or Monologues at Front of Burning Cities, Scrabble, Poems of Love and Hate, The Way of the World,* Double Bill—*Macrune's Guevara* and *Rites, Back to Methuselah, Ant., Tro., Rabelais, The National Health, The White Devil, The Travails of Sancho Panza*; **1970**:

The Alchemist, Lr., The Beaux' Stratagem, MV, A Shorter Back to Methuselah, Hedda Gabler, The Idiot, The Dandy Dolls, The Well of the Saints, A Yard of Sun, Cyrano, Hedda Gabler, Mrs. Warren's Profession; **1971**: *The Architect and the Emperor of Assyria, Cyrano, The Captain of Kopenick, A Woman Killed With Kindness, The Rules of the Game, Amphitryon 38, Tyger, Danton's Death, The Father, The Last Sweet Days of Isaac, Pantagleize, The Seventh Commandment: "Thou shalt steal . . . a bit less!", The Good-Natured Man, Long Day's Journey Into Night*; **1972**: *Jumpers, R2, 'Tis Pity She's a Whore, The School for Scandal, The Front Page, Long Day's Journey Into Night, Mac.*; **1973**: *TN, The Misanthrope, The Cherry Orchard, Equus, The Bacchae, Saturday, Sunday, Monday, The Party*; **1974**: *MM, Tmp., Eden End, Next of Kin, Spring Awakening, The Marriage of Figaro, Rom., Equus, The Freeway, Grand Manoeuvres, The Party*; **1975**: *John Gabriel Borkman, Heart-break House, Happy Days, No Man's Land, The Misanthrope, Crossing Niagara,* *All Good Men, Engaged, Nicholas Tomalin Reporting, Judgement, Phaedra Britannica, Comedians, Playboy of the Western World, Ham., Judgement*; **1976**: *Plunder, Watch it Come Down, Tribute to the Lady*; **1976-83**: no records; **1983**: *Blondel*; **1984**: *Master Class, The Mikado, Saturday Night at the Palace, Sergeant Musgrave's Dance, The Boyfriend, Marcel Marceau, Big in Brazil, Phedra, Great Expectations*; **1985**: *The Lonely Road, After the Ball is Over, The Corn is Green, Seven Brides for Seven Brothers, The Cradle Will Rock, Light up the Sky, Same Time Next Year, Beauty and the Beast*; **1986**: *Pride and Prejudice, After Aida, H.M.S. Pinafore, Ross, The Women*; **1987**: *Holiday, The Henrys, Kiss Me Kate*; **1988**: *Andromache, The Tutor, One Way Pendulum, Too Clever by Half, Bussy D'Ambois, Tmp., Candide*; **1989**: *The Wars of the Roses, Lr., AYL, The Government Inspector, Three Sisters, A Flea in Her Ear, Ham.*; **1989-90**: *The Liar, Marya, The Illusion, Kean, Time and the Conways*; **1990-91**: *Into the Woods*; **1991-92**: *Carmen Jones.*

Research Resources: When Ed Mirvish bought the theatre in 1981, the archives were sent to: The University of Bristol Theatre Collection, 29 Park Row, Bristol, BS1 5LT, England; phone: 0272/303218; contact person, Christopher Robinson. There is also some material at the Theatre Museum in London, 071/836-7891. See also:

Findlater, Richard. *Lilian Baylis—the Lady of the Old Vic*. London: Allen Lane, 1975.

Chesire, D. F., Sean McCarthy, and Hillary Norris. *The Old Vic Refurbished*, London: The Old Vic Limited, 1983.

Roberts, Peter. *The Old Vic Story—A Nation's Theatre 1818-1976*. London: W. H. Allen, 1976.
Rowell, George. *The Old Vic Theatre: A History*. New York: CUP, 1993.

Site visit and interview: 24 July 1992; telephone interview with Jonathan Miller: 10 September 1992.
Cindy Melby Phaneuf

RENAISSANCE THEATRE COMPANY. MAIL: 83 Berwick Street, London, WIV 3PJ, England. SITE: varies. ADMINISTRATION: 071/287-6672; Fax: 071/287-5372. SEASON: varies. PRINCIPAL STAFF: Kenneth Branagh, artistic director; David Parfitt, managing director; Stephen Evans, director (fund raising); Iona Price, administrator; Tamar Thomas, assistant to the artistic director. STATUS: British Equity. ANNUAL BUDGET: £250,000 (1988). FOUNDED: 1987, Kenneth Branagh and David Parfitt.

The Renaissance Theatre Company (RTC), founded in 1987 by Kenneth Branagh and David Parfitt, owes its existence to actors' desire to control their own work. The original impulse came from Branagh's rapid rise to fame and his concurrent discontent with his professional situation. At 23, he was the youngest actor ever to play Henry V at the **Royal Shakespeare Company** (RSC), yet the institutional structure of the large organization left him dissatisfied and restless. He fantasized about starting his own semipermanent company, modeled after the earlier RSC, with actors at the center of the organization. Branagh explains:

> I wanted to form a company which tapped the imagination and energy of the actors involved, a company which placed actors in a central position. If the actors wanted to direct or write, then they would be encouraged to do this, and it need not be at the expense of full-time writers and directors. It would be a practical re-alignment of the collaborative process between writer, actor, and director that would step-up the contribution of the performer. I wanted to work on Shakespeare, but I wanted it to be accessible. There *was* an audience for Shakespeare—whether it was Newcastle, Belfast or Reading, and not just for people who knew about RSC.

Branagh left the RSC in September 1985, intent upon acting and directing in a production of *Romeo and Juliet* with a company of his own choosing. While filming *High Season* with Jacqueline Bisset in 1986, Branagh planned his production. He admits: "I knew the play I wanted to do. I had the energy and I had the passion, but what I didn't have was the money or the courage." Despite difficulties in locating a venue and mixed reviews, the project confirmed his desire to have a company of his own. Fellow RSC actor David Parfitt proved a dynamic and effective partner in the pilot project formed to start the company. The word Renaissance was chosen as part of the company's name because "it seemed to reflect our youthfulness and express some sense of rebirth that was going on in the British theatre." Excitement built when Prince Charles agreed to be the company's patron.

The 1987 season began with Branagh's first full-length play *Public Enemy*, in which he also played the leading role. The second production, *Napoleon*, was a one-man show featuring John Sessions, directed by Branagh. *Twelfth Night*, with Richard Briers as Malvolio and Branagh as director, completed the season. Funding for the £250,000 budget was raised privately. RTC started with friends and relatives and then broadened its appeal from that base; 30 to 40 angels, mainly actors and writers, invested sums ranging from £100 to £500 in the production. Branagh invested £25,000 of his own money into the first season. Robin Thornber of *The Guardian* reported: "According to David Parfitt, it was a bumpy start with *Public Enemy*, 'not critically, but it just didn't pull the audiences in. The investors lost their money.' The John Sessions show did well, although it didn't go into profit and *Twelfth Night* did very well. 'It was quite nice to be a hot ticket.'" Thames Television even filmed it. The first season also attracted the attention of stockbroker Stephen Evans, who proved invaluable in the area of raising capital for future projects.

RTC's second season in 1989 brought new ideas to the company's developing aesthetic. It featured a three-month season of Shakespeare, followed by the company's first national tour. The goals were to develop new talent, reach a regional audience with popular art, and fill a gap in the main touring circuit that was "crying out" for a quality product.

The season was launched from the Birmingham Repertory Company's 150-seat studio theatre. In a special arrangement with this regional theatre, space and facilities were given to RTC in exchange for a share of the box office. The plan was to use established actors to direct young actors in classical roles. Away from the intense scrutiny of London, the company would have a chance to develop. Branagh explained: "I wanted to do this in the regions because the audience is different. What we are trying to do is new and raw and I think it will go down very well there. My experience last year was that there was an element of the London audience that thought what we were doing was a little unsophisticated."

Three prominent actors agreed to direct, utilizing different directorial approaches to achieve their results. Judi Dench directed *Much Ado About Nothing* with Branagh as Benedick and Samantha Bond as Beatrice. A "swift and breezy atmosphere in rehearsal" created a production praised for its "freshness, wit and lack of pretension." Geraldine McEwan directed *As You Like It* with Branagh as Touchstone. A "slower and more methodical" process led to a "delicate and beautiful discourse on love." Derek Jacobi directed a "dramatic and highly theatrical" *Hamlet* with Branagh in the title role. This production proved an enormous success beginning with an "electric opening," including multiple curtain calls, and culminating in a standing ovation.

The money was once again raised privately, without government support. Each of the 15 actors was paid £200 a week, around the Equity minimum, and the roles were fairly evenly distributed. Even with sold-out houses, the company began its national tour with a deficit of £80,000, but the larger theatres and popular success of the tour recouped the losses and made it seem that anything was possible.

Branagh was looking for a way to share intimate acting in Shakespeare with "lots of people." He decided to make a film version of *Henry V*, with himself as the lead actor and director. Financier Stephen Evans located the £4.5 million needed for the project. Many of the members of the 1988 Shakespeare season were utilized in the film, and Branagh's international reputation was established.

The following year, the RTC produced a tour of *A Midsummer Night's Dream* and *King Lear* that participated in the Chicago International Theatre Festival in May 1989. The staff spent the summer and fall of 1992, working for its sister company, Renaissance Films, on a film version of *Much Ado About Nothing*, shot on location in Tuscany, Italy.

The RTC operates with a small staff that includes Branagh as artistic director, David Parfitt as managing director, Stephen Evans as director (fund raising), Iona Price as administrator, and Tamar Thomas as assistant to the artistic director. Sales of Branagh's autobiography, *Beginning*, allowed the company to move out of Branagh's home and into an office in Soho. Although the RTC is able to operate as a privately funded company, Branagh "hates" what he calls the "enforced Thatcherism" of it. He is pro-subsidy because he believes "in the value of the arts, in the value of theatre." At the press conference announcing the formation of the RTC, Branagh was asked if he was trying to provide something for everyone. As he recalls in his autobiography, "The answer was yes—the appeal was intended to be very broad. We wanted to present popular art. Not poor art or thin art or even 'arty art,' but popular art that would expand the mind and senses and really entertain." RTC's artistic philosophy has been described by Robin Thornber of *The Guardian* as follows: "Renaissance, while it is an actor-oriented company, isn't anti-director, and it certainly isn't any kind of workers' cooperative. . . . Its ethos is *mainstream* and *classical* rather than *fringe* or *experimental*."

Branagh uses his acclaimed theatre, film, and television career to help finance the company's projects and draw public attention to the RTC. He attempts to maintain a balance between managing the company and pursuing his successful freelance career. With many other professional options open to him, Branagh still needs the RTC. He has explained: "The purpose, the raison d'être, of the company is to do with the way in which one works as much as with what one does. . . . It is concerned with control and involvement and providing a framework on a scale that is conducive to good work. . . . I wished not to be distanced from the work. I wished not just to be a jobbing actor."

Production History: **1987**: *Public Enemy, Napoleon, TN*; **1988**: *Ado, AYL, Ham., H5* (film); **1989**: *MND, Lr.*; **1992**: *Ado* (film).

Research Resources: Archives for the Renaissance Theatre Company are maintained at its administrative offices, but access is extremely limited due to the small administrative staff. The Theatre Museum in Covent Garden has some newspaper clippings. See also: Kenneth Branagh, *Beginning* (London: Chatto & Windus, 1989); John Davison, "Directing a Regional Renaissance," *Sunday Times*, 5 July 1987; Robin Thornber, "Fortunes of Fame," *The Guardian*, 7 March 1988.

Cindy Melby Phaneuf

ROYAL SHAKESPEARE COMPANY. MAIL: Stratford-upon-Avon, Warwickshire CV37 6BB, England. SITES: Royal Shakespeare Theatre, Swan Theatre, and The Other Place, in Stratford; The Barbican Theatre and The Pit, in London. ADMINISTRATION: In Stratford, 44-789-29-6655. BOX OFFICE: in Stratford, 44-789-29-5623; in London, 44-71-638-8891. ADMISSION: varies (average price £13.11 in 1991-92). SEASON: 28 productions, 1,801 performances (1991-92, all theatres except West End transfers and international tours). PRINCIPAL STAFF: Adrian Noble, artistic director; Michael Attenborough, executive producer; David Brierley, general manager. FACILITIES: Royal Shakespeare Theatre, The Swan, and The Other Place in Stratford; Barbican Theatre (capacity 1,160 seats) and The Pit, flexible staging (capacity 200) in London. AUDITIONS: contact business office. STATUS: British Actors' Equity. ANNUAL BUDGET: £23.13 million (1991-92). ANNUAL ATTENDANCE: 1,117,046 (1991-92). FOUNDED: 1879, as Shakespeare Memorial Theatre; renamed Royal Shakespeare Company in 1961.

The Royal Shakespeare Company (RSC), the oldest and most famous Shakespeare company in the world, has its origins in the Shakespeare Jubilee organized by the famous eighteenth-century actor and manager of the Drury Lane Theatre, David Garrick. For three days in September of 1769, Garrick's Shakespeare Jubilee at Stratford became a festival of fireworks, processions, banquets, orations, and a colorful costume ball on the banks of the Avon. Oddly enough, the only event that did not occur at the celebration was the staging of a play by Shakespeare. The festivals continued in a lesser fashion for six years and then ceased, until the Stratford Shakespeare Club organized a festival celebration in 1827 and laid the foundation stone in New Place gardens for a theatre. In 1830, Charles Kean, performing in the new theatre in the title role of *Richard III*, marked the first festival at Stratford to include a performance. The 1864 tercentenary of Shakespeare's birth aroused interest in a festival that would include the production of several Shakespeare plays. The railroad line reached Stratford, 110 miles from London, in 1860, and the town soon realized the potential for tourism. And indeed, Londoners came to Stratford to view Shakespeare's birthplace. The mayor, Edward Flower, and his son, Charles Flower, became the chief organizers of what was to be ten days of celebration and performances. They invited leading actors of the day, including Benjamin Webster, Samuel Phelps, Charles Fechter, and Helen Faucit to appear in various roles. This was to be a stellar engagement of famous actors that would surely attract all of London. The actors all accepted Stratford's invitation, until, that is, each one, beginning with Phelps, heard which roles the others would play. Professional jealousy spoiled the project, and, in the end, all the actors declined to appear. Nevertheless, the manager of London's Princess' Theatre saved the day and agreed to bring his company and the French actress Stella Colas to perform in Stratford. Six plays—*Twelfth Night, The Comedy of Errors, Romeo and Juliet, As You Like It, Much Ado about Nothing, Othello*, and the trial scene from *The Merchant of Venice* were presented in a pavilion theatre. Unfortunately, the festival lost money, and the town failed to raise the funds it had hoped to build a memorial statue of Shakespeare.

The idea of a festival with the performance of plays was criticized by some. Undaunted, Charles Flower set out in 1874 to lay the groundwork for the founding of the Shakespeare Memorial Theatre, dedicated to the performance of Shakespeare's plays. The foundation stone was laid in April 1877, and the theatre was finished for the opening of the festival on 23 April 1879 when *Much Ado about Nothing* was performed. The festivals continued as an annual event, but there was neither an endowment nor a permanent company. From 1886 until 1919, Frank Benson brought his company to Stratford and eventually became the organizer of the annual festival. Benson provided some continuity in the history of the theatre, but it was Charles Flower's grandson, Archibald, who was to rule the Memorial Theatre with an iron hand until his retirement in 1944.

Archibald Flower involved himself in all aspects of the Stratford Theatre, from financial decisions to all artistic ones as well. He stifled artistic creativity but succeeded in fund raising, thereby providing financial stability to the organization; he thus balanced Benson's lack of financial aptitude. Between 1907 and 1911, Benson invited leading actors, such as Lewis Waller, Johnston Forbes-Robertson, Herbert Tree, and many others from London, to make guest appearances in Stratford to bolster the prestige of the theatre. Unfortunately, this policy of featuring star appearances reduced the function of Benson and his acting group to playing supporting roles. In 1911, Benson's financial problems prompted Archibald Flower to remove Benson's control over the company, creating a syndicate called The Stratford-upon-Avon Players. In 1912, no stars were imported and in 1913, Flower decided that the Players should tour to the United States and Canada, with Benson heading the company; and another smaller company would tour to South Africa. Although the eight-month tour was not financially successful, a second tour was planned for 1914, this time without Benson. The tour was canceled when war was declared in August of 1914. The theatre remained closed in 1917 and 1918, reopening in the spring of 1919 when the Benson era finally came to an end following Nigel Playfair's "unconventional" *As You Like It* production at the Memorial Theatre. Unamused by the performance and by Benson's tired productions generally, Archibald Flower secured the support of the Shakespeare Memorial National Theatre Committee (SMNT) and requested the money it had built up over the years since the committee's formation in 1908. William Archer, Granville-Barker, and Bernard Shaw, original members of the committee, were dedicated to building a national theatre. William Bridges-Adams believed that a national theatre would be easier to fund after the establishment of a Shakespeare Company. Archibald Flower convinced them that Stratford was the best place to begin such a project, and, in 1919, a resident company, the New Shakespeare Company (NSC), headed by Bridges-Adams, became a reality.

Bridges-Adams restored many cuts and alterations that had been made previously in performing Shakespeare and offered the plays with only one intermission. The SMNT committee sought to lessen its grant amount to the NSC, and Bridges-Adams realized that the road to becoming self-supporting meant a touring season and a London residency. He also realized that, to create a strong ensemble, he needed proper rehearsal periods and not just quick revivals. In 1924, eight revivals (rehearsed in seven weeks) and two new productions were added in the summer, but the tour before the spring festival was dropped.

On 6 March 1926, the Memorial Theatre, including sets and costumes in storage, burned down. Within six weeks, the only cinema house in Stratford was converted into a stage theatre, and it housed the NSC for the next six years. Benefit performances in London and fund-raising events for the construction of a new theatre began almost immediately. Archibald Flower traveled to the United States and received promises of large donations from John D. Rockefeller, Daniel Guggenheim, J. P. Morgan, Edward Harkness, and Archer Huntington. The money was divided into an American fund and a British fund; some last minute stipulations were to be met by the American Trust from Thomas Lamont.

The new Memorial Theatre, essentially the same building as is used today, without crimson plush, seated 1,000 spectators. The proscenium was 30 feet wide and 21 feet high, with a stage depth of over 40 feet. Sally Beauman in her history of the RSC aptly described the interior:

> It was decorated with wood-panelling that distracted the eye, and flanked by what looked like two odd art deco cupboards, lower than the top of the proscenium, which were assemblies, or side entrances, to the fore-stage. The fore-stage itself was too shallow - little more than a shelf perched above the orchestra pit. Beyond the pit lay the fan-shaped curve of the stalls, modeled on the opera

house at Bayreuth. There were no side balconies or boxes (as there are now), so that the circle was cut off from the stage by an expanse of cold, cream-painted wall, ornamented by more fussy wood-panelling. The effect was to isolate the audience from the stage, and to create a tunnel effect.

The opening was held on Shakespeare's birthday, 23 April 1932, with a matinee performance of *Henry IV, Part I*, and *Part II* presented that evening. The performance was a disaster and critics responded accordingly, some willing to hedge their criticism because of the occasion. Before Bridges-Adams resigned in 1934, Theodore Komisarjevsky was invited by Archibald Flower to direct a production of *The Merchant of Venice*. Flower selected Ben Iden Payne, who had been working and teaching as a visiting professor of drama at the Carnegie Institute of Technology in America for 20 years, as Bridges-Adams' successor. Payne's first company consisted of traditional actors, some from the Benson era. They resisted innovation, but Payne seemed satisfied and erected an Elizabethan stage on the proscenium stage, with inner stages and an upper above, which became standard for all his productions. It provided continuous action but did little to inspire designers. Only Komisarjevsky as a guest director, who relied on lighting effects and a bare stage, along with Randle Ayrton in a notable production of *King Lear* (1936) and Donald Wolfit, continued as box office attractions in the late 1930s. In 1942, Iden Payne resigned, and, in 1944, Fordham Flower succeeded his father, Archibald. In 1946, Sir Barry Jackson was appointed artistic director, brought with him a young actor from the Birmingham Repertory Company named Paul Scofield, and built a company of new young actors. That same year, Peter Brook was invited to direct *Love's Labour's Lost*. Gone was the old guard, but Fordham Flower sensed a lack of "leadership" in Jackson. When Jackson resigned in 1948, Fordham immediately appointed Anthony Quayle to succeed him.

The Memorial Theatre had become self-supporting, but, under Quayle, the size of the company increased, stars from London appeared frequently, and the theatre building was renovated. Quayle revived the company's touring program, not only internationally, to Germany, Australia, Canada, and the United States, but to London as well. Guests included John Gielgud, Peggy Ashcroft, Charles Laughton, Laurence Harvey, Michael Redgrave, among many others; in 1955, Peter Brook's *Titus Andronicus* featured Laurence Olivier and Vivien Leigh. Stratford had achieved world recognition. Glen Byam Shaw worked as a codirector with Quayle from 1953 to 1956 when Quayle resigned. Shaw continued through the 1959 season. On 1 January 1960, a new era was ushered in with the appointment of 29-year-old Peter Hall as artistic director of the Memorial Theatre. Since 1956, Hall had directed three impressively fresh productions at Stratford: *Love's Labour's Lost*, *Cymbeline*, and *Twelfth Night*.

Hall sought to raise the stature of the Stratford company from a mere "shrine" filled with stars to an ensemble company of high quality that would attract outstanding talent in all areas of artistic endeavor. He initiated significant changes in artistic and managerial policies. As an enticement, Hall provided an unprecedented three-year contract to actors, giving them security and guaranteed work. The Stratford stage was redesigned with a rake, a false proscenium, and an apron extending out into the auditorium. He also leased the 1,100-seat Aldwych Theatre in London to provide a space for Stratford productions and to give the company visibility in the major capital of English-speaking theatre. The London season would moreover provide significant exposure and experience for new playwrights and actors. Hall commissioned many new playwrights to write works especially for the Aldwych, including Robert Bolt, Peter Shaffer, and John Arden. Finally, in 1961, the somewhat "musty" "Memorial Theatre" designation was dropped from the company's name, and it became the Royal Shakespeare Company.

Hall encouraged actor training and emphasized a style of delivery that became unique to the RSC. John Barton was appointed an assistant director and helped develop a style of acting that was based more on conveying textual meaning than on projecting emotion. Hall's formula for producing Shakespeare was, according to Alan Sinfield, "Shakespeare-plus-relevance." This approach focused the productions on contemporary social and political issues of the 1960s, and it attracted a younger audience. For the 1961-62 seasons, the Stratford and London companies mounted 12 productions, ranging from Shakespeare to Chekhov. In 1962, Hall invited Peter Brook to become an RSC director, specifically to assist in managing the 350-seat Arts Theatre, which was dedicated to the production of experimental works. Although the Arts Theatre was short-lived, the RSC's commitment to experimental theatre attracted talented actors and directors, as well as the attention of London critics. The RSC was committed to regional tours and later embarked on many full-company tours abroad.

The transition from a company supported financially by private funds to one based on state-subsidized money was far from easy. Although audiences increased during the Hall years, the annual deficits grew. Brook's Brechtian *King Lear* with Paul Scofield brought enormous critical attention to the work of the RSC. In 1963, the RSC received its first annual subsidy from the Arts Council. That same year the company showcased *The War of the Roses*, an adaptation by John Barton, in three parts, of Shakespeare's *Henry VI* plays and *Richard III*. The playing text, a compilation of just over half of the lines in the original four plays, with 1,400 lines written by Barton, created a controversy among critics and scholars, but the unity of concept and execution, with its attention to visual detail showcased Hall's attempt to create a distinct RSC style of acting and staging.

Influenced by the works of Antonin Artaud, the French theatre practitioner, playwright, and poet (who spent the last years of his life in asylums), Brook continued his experimental work in a "theatre of cruelty" workshop presented at the LAMDA studio theatre. In 1964, Brook received international attention with his production of Peter Weiss' *Marat/Sade*. In the same year, Hall established a World Theatre Season at the Aldwych in London, at which seven world-class theatre companies, including the Moscow Art Theatre and the Abbey Theatre, performed. The RSC had gained worldwide recognition as an innovative and provocative company. Along with fame, audience attendance increased from 384,000 in 1959-60 to over 1,000,000 in 1968-69.

After hiring Trevor Nunn as an RSC director, Hall replaced the three-year actor contract with an Associate Artist system. This essentially established a "gentlemen's agreement" that actors notify the RSC of offers from elsewhere, giving the RSC the opportunity to respond appropriately. This helped the RSC maintain a pool of loyal actors who shared the same training, RSC style, and name. Prominent RSC members during the 1960s included Paul Scofield, Diana Rigg, Peggy Ashcroft, Glenda Jackson, David Warner, Ian Holm, Judi Dench, Patrick Magee, Hugh Griffith, and Eric Porter.

Deficits loomed on the horizon, and Hall sought a new subsidized home in London. In 1965, the City of London Court of Common Council approved a plan to build a new theatre in the Barbican development that would be leased to the RSC. Progress was slow, however, and the theatre did not open until 1982. Meanwhile, by 1966, many, including Brook, felt that the RSC's artistic productivity had peaked with so many successes. Although the deficit was being created by the Aldwych, not the Stratford theatre, Hall increased the number of London productions. But there was new competition; the newly formed National Theatre, under the leadership of Laurence Olivier, had established itself as a rival. With the delay in the opening of the Barbican and the death of Fordham Flower in 1966, Hall decided to leave the RSC.

At age 28, Trevor Nunn became the RSC's artistic director in 1968, to be joined by Terry Hands in 1978. During this period, the RSC expanded its venue of new and experimental productions, encouraged company-sponsored workshops with teachers, students, and artists, and expanded its regional touring program. Studio productions were established at The Place (1971) and Donmar Warehouse (1977) in London, and at The Other Place in Stratford (1974). In 1977, in addition to establishing a six-week season at Newcastle-upon-Tyne, the RSC offered eight productions at Stratford, 11 at Aldwych, five at The Other Place, and nine at the Warehouse. From 1970 to 1978, the RSC mounted 291 productions, of which approximately 250 were new stagings. Among the highlights were Peter Brook's *A Midsummer Night's Dream* (1970), Trevor Nunn's staging of the Roman plays in 1972, John Barton's *Richard II*, and Terry Hands' *Romeo and Juliet* and the *Henry VI* cycle in 1977.

In 1982, the RSC moved into its new home, the Barbican Theatre, a part of the giant Barbican Centre, an arts complex incorporating an art gallery, cinema, concert hall, and more. The auditorium, with its 1,160 seats, has two upper tiers of seats that cantilever inwards, providing intimacy and good sightlines. The studio theatre, The Pit, has flexible seating for up to 200 people.

The RSC opened at the Barbican with performances of both parts of *Henry IV*, the same play that had opened the Shakespeare Memorial Theatre in 1932.

In 1986, the same year that Terry Hands assumed the leadership of the RSC as its artistic director and chief executive, the RSC opened a new theatre, the Swan, built as a Jacobean-style playhouse and utilizing part of the shell of the Memorial Theatre that had survived the 1926 fire. The Swan is dedicated primarily to the production of works by playwrights who lived between 1570-1750, most recently a series of Restoration plays, to be followed by the works of Jonson and Marlowe. The Swan's architect, Michael Reardon, also redesigned the Other Place, the RSC's Stratford studio theatre, which was rebuilt and opened in 1991.

In 1991, Adrian Noble, who became an associate director of the RSC in 1982, succeeded Terry Hands as artistic director. Formerly an associate director at the Bristol Old Vic (1976-79), Noble's productions of *King Lear* in 1982 and *Henry V* in 1985 gained him a reputation as an imaginative and original director. Michael Attenborough serves as executive producer and David Brierley as general manager.

In 1993, a support group called RSC Education worked with 5,000 youngsters in 36 locations throughout the United Kingdom. The RSC's extensive outreach program includes an annual regional tour that visits schools and community centers, as well as touring large-scale productions to regional theatres. Recent ambitious tours include productions of *Nicholas Nickleby*, *Much Ado About Nothing*, and *Cyrano de Bergerac* in America, *Richard III* in Australia, and both *The Comedy of Errors* and *Les Liaisons Dangereuses* in Europe and the Far East.

In a 1993 program, the RSC defined its artistic philosophy:

> The RSC is formed around a core of associate actors and actresses with the aim that their skills should continue, over the years, to produce a distinctive approach to theatre, both classical and modern. And, despite its growth from Festival Theatre to international stature, the aims of the RSC are in essence much the same as those expressed by Frank Benson in 1905: "to train a company, every member of which would be an essential part of a homogeneous whole consecrated to the practice of the dramatic arts and especially to the representation of the plays of Shakespeare."

The RSC has the largest budget (£23.13 million) of any Shakespeare company in the world. In fact, the RSC is by far the largest publicly funded theatre company in England, according to the Arts Council. The RSC generates 59 percent of its required income through box office receipts, transfers (that is, successful RSC productions that are transferred to commercial theatres for separate runs), films, television, and sponsorship. The RSC's public subsidy (from the Arts Council) provides 41 percent of its annual costs, equal to a subsidy of £10.16 on each ticket sold; public subsidy was £9.73 million, with a total of £6.82 million returned to the Exchequer in the form of Value Added Tax, employers' and employees' National Insurance contributions, and income tax payments. The Arts Council has noted that "In the scale of its operations, the RSC dwarfs its comparators. It provides 7 percent of the productions, 15 percent of the performances, 21 percent of the attendances and 33 percent of the box office income of all the subsidized building based drama companies in England."

The 1993-94 season will consist of continuous performances in the five RSC theatres, including a tour of *The Two Gentlemen of Verona* to 19 towns and cities throughout the United Kingdom; a 16-week tour of the RSC "mobile auditorium" to sites without access to live theatre; a 13-week tour of *Les Liaisons Dangereuses*; and the annual five-week Newcastle residency. The RSC will also perform in Japan, New Zealand, Australia, and nine cities in Europe, and plans are being made for a 20-week coast-to-coast tour of the United States in 1994.

Production History: A complete listing and a calendar of RSC productions are available in Michael Mullin's standard reference work, *Theatre at Stratford-upon-Avon*. The following list indicates recent trends in RSC productions. **1993-94**: (Royal Shakespeare Theatre) *Lr.*, *MV*, *Tmp.*, *LLL*; (Swan Theatre) *Murder in the Cathedral*, *The Venetian Twins*, *The Country Wife*, *Elgar's Rondo*; (The Other Place) *Ghosts*, *JC*, *Moby Dick*; (Barbican Theatre) *AYL*, *Ant.*, *WT*, *Shr.*, *TGV*, *Tamburlaine the Great*; (The Pit) *A Jovial Crew*, *The Changeling*, *The Odyssey*, *Misha's Party*, *Wallenstein*, *AWW*; (on tour) *WT*, *Les Liaisons Dangereuses*, *JC*, *TGV*; (Transfers) *Les Miserables* (Palace Theatre), *The Gift of the Gordon* (Wyndham's Theatre); 1994: (Royal Shakespeare Theatre) *H5*, *TN*, *MND*, *MM*; (Swan Theatre) *Cor.*, *The Wives Excuse*, *The Broken Heart*; (The Other Place) *H6*; (Barbican Theatre) *MV*, *LLL*, *Lr.*, *Tmp.*

Research Resources: The Royal Shakespeare Company deposits archival material, such as promptbooks, photographs, and clippings, in the Shakespeare Centre Library. The RSC Collection is a permanent display of paintings and sculptures, along with temporary exhibitions of costumes, props, and other theatre material in Stratford. The RSC Collection is housed in the Stratford-upon-Avon Theatre Gallery.

Addenbrooke, David. *The Royal Shakespeare Company, 1960-1972*. London: William Kimber, 1974.

Beauman, Sally. *The Royal Shakespeare Company: A History of Ten Decades*. Oxford: Oxford University Press, 1982.

Chambers, Colin. *Other Spaces: New Theatre and the RSC*. London: Eyre Methuen, 1980.

Day, Muriel C., and J. C. Trewin. *The Shakespeare Memorial Theatre*. London: J. M. Dent & Sons, 1932.

Deelman, Christian. *The Great Shakespeare Jubilee*. New York: Viking, 1964.

Ellis, Ruth. *The Shakespeare Memorial Theatre*. London: Winchester, 1948.

Goodwin, John, Ed. *Peter Hall's Diaries*. New York: Harper & Row, 1983.

Greenwald, Michael L. *Directions by Indirections: John Barton of the Royal Shakespeare Company*. Newark: University of Delaware Press, 1985.

Hayman, Ronald. *British Theatre since 1955*. Oxford: Oxford University Press, 1979.

Kemp, T. C., and J. C. Trewin. *The Stratford Festival*. London, 1953.

Lambert, J. W. *Drama in Britain: 1964-1973*. Essex: Longman Group, 1974.

Liebenstein-Kurtz, Ruth, Freifrau von. *Das subventionierte englische Theater: Produktionsbedingungen und Auswirkungen auf das moderne englische Drama (1956-1976): dargestellt am Beispiel der Royal Shakespeare Company, des National Theatre und der English Stage Company*. Tübingen: Narr, 1981.

Mullin, Michael, ed. *Theatre at Stratford-upon-Avon: A Catalogue-Index to Productions of the Shakespeare Memorial/Royal Shakespeare Theatre, 1879-1978*, 2 vols. Westport, CT: Greenwood, 1980. (Note: Vol. 3, 1979-1990, is currently in press.)

Priestley, Clive. *The Financial Affairs and Financial Prospects of the Royal Opera House, Covent Garden Ltd., and the Royal Shakespeare Company: Report to the Earl of Gowie*. London: H.M.S.O., 1983.

Royal Shakespeare Company. *Program*, 1993-94 season.

Wells, Stanley W. *Royal Shakespeare*. Manchester: Manchester University Press, 1977.

Ron Engle

SHAKESPEARE AT SHELDON. MAIL: The White Cottage, Allington, Chippenham, Wiltshire, England. SITE: Sheldon Manor, Chippenham, Wiltshire. PRINCIPAL STAFF: Elizabeth Anne Gradwell, director.

Shakespeare at Sheldon was a ten-year project, which earned over £20,000 for charities. Inspired by the idyllic water garden setting at Sheldon Manor, Elizabeth Gradwell obtained permission from the Gibbs family to use the site. The inaugural production, *Romeo and Juliet* in 1979, featured John and Elizabeth Gradwell's daughter Charmian (now a professional actress) as Juliet. Eventually, grandchildren of Major and Mrs Gibbs—and Mrs Gibbs herself—found themselves cast. Occasionally, the manor dogs made an "unscheduled appearance." The pool often served the action, as when Tybalt died in the water, or when Falstaff was dunked there, or when a boat sailed in for *Comedy of Errors*. Up to 480 people could be seated under the canopy, so the audience remained dry on rainy evenings even if the actors did not. Mrs Gradwell recalls that "we never canceled a performance, though we sometimes got very wet." Low ticket prices helped to sell out every performance, and low production costs (all services were donated) meant that substantial sums could be raised to benefit a different charity each year.

Production History (partial): **1979**: *Rom.*; **1980**: *WT*; **1981**: *TN*; **1982**: *Mac.*; **1983**: *Err.*; **1984**: *MND*; **1985**: *TGV*; **1986**: *JC*; **1987**: *Wiv.*; **1988**: *Tmp.*

Felicia Hardison Londré

STAMFORD SHAKESPEARE COMPANY. MAIL: Rutland Theatre, Tolethorpe Hall, Little Casterton, Stamford, Lincolnshire PE9 4BH, England. SITE: grounds of Tolethorpe Hall, outside Stamford. ADMINISTRATIVE OFFICE: (0789) 54381. BOX OFFICE: (0780) 56133. ADMISSION: £6.50–£7.50, Mon.–Thurs.; £8.50–£9.50, Fri.–Sat.; £10–£12, gala night. SEASON: three productions, early June to late August; 8:00 p.m., Mon.–Thurs.; 8:30 p.m., Fri.–Sat. PRINCIPAL STAFF: Mrs. Jean Harley, artistic director; Derek Harrison, general manager; Margaret Walker, financial director; Jean Gurr, house manager. FACILITY: open-air stage (capacity 600 under a canopy). AUDITIONS: local, in September and October. STATUS: nonprofit, community theatre. ANNUAL BUDGET: £120,000 (1993). ANNUAL ATTENDANCE: 32,000 (1993). FOUNDED: 1971, Jean Harley.

Beginning with a 1968 production of *A Midsummer Night's Dream*, Shakespeare plays have been performed as part of the town of Stamford's annual summer festival, sponsored by the Stamford Arts Centre Committee. Jean Harley, a professionally trained actress and director, was asked to stage the play, as it had not escaped notice that pupils from her speech and drama studio were winning all the local speech and drama prizes. The Monastery Garden of the fourteenth-century George Hotel on the banks of the Welland River in the center of town made a charming setting for the open-air productions. After four successful seasons (one play running for two weeks each summer), Harley formalized the project by founding the Stamford Shakespeare Company (SSC). When it was announced in 1976 that the garden was to be converted into a car park, the SSC found a new performance site at the derelict Tolethorpe Hall about two miles from Stamford and across the county line. (Stamford is in Lincolnshire, while Tolethorpe Hall is in the former tiny county of Rutland, which was subsumed into Leicestershire in the 1970s.)

Tolethorpe's history can be traced back to Toli the Dane's little Thorp in the pre-Domesday era. The estate of Tolethorpe passed through seven generations of Norman landlords and then to the Burton family in 1316. The Burtons lived at Tolethorpe for 189 years (eight generations), but only an archway remains of their medieval house remains. The Browne family bought the estate in 1503 and retained it until 1840. The main part of the present house was rebuilt during the Jacobean period on the plan of an earlier Elizabethan construction. Two bay windows and the east wing were added around 1865. Tolethorpe Hall has always been described as late Elizabethan. As parcels of the estate were rented out or sold off in the twentieth century, the hall was allowed to fall into disrepair. Taken over by the bank when the last owner went bankrupt, the house stood empty for nine years while wind and dirt swept through the doorless hall with the roofless west wing.

In 1977, the SSC had only £78 to put toward the purchase of this Jacobean landmark, but the bank was eager to get rid of it and worked out terms that made it possible. Thus began for SSC members a continuous process of renovation. Everybody associated with the SSC did the gardening, repairs, and decorating. In order to be licensed by the local council as safe for the public, the road had to be widened to be able to admit fire trucks, at a cost of £15,000. "The first year was a desperate struggle," Harley has recalled. "It was all done in ten weeks. We didn't get our licence to perform until the opening day, and then the caterers walked out." After three years and the accumulation of £150,000 in bills, the bank granted the SSC a loan, which has since been repaid in full. Each season brings improvements to the building and the grounds, as profits are ploughed back into the property.

The SSC is the longest-running amateur theatre organization in England and possibly in the world. With an annual attendance of 32,000, it probably also has the largest attendance of any amateur theatre in the English-speaking world. Only the general manager holds a paid position (he is responsible for both arts administration and estate management). All others, from the artistic director to the designers, stage managers, cast, and crew, volunteer their time. Some volunteers come from as far as 30 or 40 miles away to work each night at the souvenir stand or as dressers or in other capacities. The company is organized as a charity, which means that all earnings are ploughed back into running the theatre and maintaining the house and grounds. The SSC does have to pay a government tax on each theatre seat, which amounts to 17.55 percent of the earnings (or about £29,000), each season.

Before the show, theatergoers may enjoy music while picnicking on the vast green lawn with the view of Little Casterton's church steeple in the distance. It is also possible to book in advance a pre-performance cold buffet in the restaurant located in one of the hall's restored rooms; it has an excellent wine cellar. Another ground-floor room is used as a bar for intermission drinks; its walls are decorated with artifacts relating the house's history. A winding stair, many of the window casements, and other features are original from the late Elizabethan/Jacobean period. Upstairs are a makeup room and wig room; in addition, each of the three productions is assigned its own dressing room.

The performance space, called the Rutland Open Air Theatre, was created in a natural amphitheatre immediately adjacent to and down the steps from the west wing of Tolethorpe Hall. The stage is situated in an enchanting glade, open to the sky, while the audience sits under a canopy in comfortable chairs on the terraced hillside. The SSC's guarantee that "no performance is ever cancelled because of rain" means that only the actors get wet. There is no shortage of people who want to perform with the company. The small children who play fairies in *A Midsummer Night's Dream* (which is staged every fourth season by popular demand) are rigorously disciplined so that not so much as a footfall is heard as they make their way through the grass from the hall to the stage. Many of them have returned to perform for five or six consecutive seasons.

SSC productions emphasize opulent period costuming. Only modern-dress interpretations are avoided, because they "wouldn't look right" next to a 400-year-old building. "We're famous for our costumes," declares house manager Jean Gurr. "They have to stand up to the rain. They're all lined and interlined, and when the actors move about on stage you can tell it's not flimsy material. Those skirts have a sweep to them; they fill the stage."

The text is generally trimmed, as all performances must be kept under three hours, including a 20-minute interval. This restriction is because Friday and Saturday night performances begin late, and English law prohibits perform-ances before midday on Sunday—that is, after midnight on Saturday. The late-curtain weekend performances are popular with Londoners, who like more time to get to the theatre; they also enjoy the full effect of the theatrical lighting when the show starts after dark.

Although the season has been expanded to the practical maximum (12 weeks), the SSC plays to near capacity audiences, including about 3,000 schoolchildren each season. The SSC has also attracted a surprising number of international theatregoers, especially Germans and Japanese, who say they prefer the SSC's more traditional approach to Shakespeare, as opposed to the highly conceptualized productions available in London or Stratford. Many not only book their tickets during the winter for the following summer, but also write to the SSC personnel and send them Christmas cards. As a tourist attraction, Stamford also offers Burghley House, the home of William Cecil, Lord Burghley, Queen Elizabeth's Lord High Treasurer. Burghley was the guardian of Edward DeVere, 17th Earl of Oxford, whom many believe to have been the real author of the Shakespeare plays and sonnets. Burghley enriched himself at his ward's expense, and his estate in Stamford is the largest and grandest from the Elizabethan period in England today. Also in Stamford, a few blocks from the historic George Hotel, is one of the oldest surviving English provincial theatres, opened in 1768.

In 1983, BBC television made a full-length documentary about the SSC. Since 1985, general manager Derek Harrison has spearheaded a marketing campaign that increased audiences by 440 percent and revenue by 600 percent in eight years. He also devised a new type of open-air stage construction, adapting an acrylic tennis court surface, and he recommended a high-tensile fabric, installed in 1993, as the first permanent theatre roof structure of its kind in the United Kingdom. Both of these innovations proved highly successful.

The 1991 production of *Much Ado About Nothing* was a romantic feast for the eyes, performed with gusto. The basic scenic units were two wagons carrying matching trellises and garden benches, which could be rolled into various configurations. Most effective, however, were the entrances made through the natural greenery up center. In the moonlight, with a light mist in the air, the effect of the hand-carried lanterns was beautiful. Benedick and Hero were especially well interpreted, but the popular favorite was Dogberry, whose "character" bits won the favor of a remarkably responsive audience.

Production History: **1968**: *MND*; **1969**: *Tmp.*; **1970**: *Rom.*; **1971**: *Shr.*; **1972**: *R3*; **1973**: *Wiv.*; **1974**: *MND*; **1975**: *Ham.*; **1976**: *H5*; **1977**: *Mac., Shr.*; **1978**: *MND, Oth., TN*; **1979**: *Ham., Wiv., Tmp.*; **1980**: *Lr., AYL*; **1981**: *MND, MV*; **1982**: *Rom., TN*; **1983**: *R2, LLL*; **1984**: *MND, Shr.*; **1985**: *Tmp., Wiv.*; **1986**: *Oth., Ado, AYL*; **1987**: *Mac., WT, TN*; **1988**: *MND, MM, Err.*; **1989**: *Rom., MV, Shr.*; **1990**: *Ham., AWW, Wiv.*; **1991**: *H5, TN, Ado*; **1992**: *LLL, JC, MND.*

Research Resources: Archives for the Stamford Shakespeare Company are maintained by Jean Harley.

Site visit and interview: 20 June 1991.
Felicia Hardison Londré

THEATRE SET-UP, LTD. MAIL: 12 Fairlawn Close, Southgate, London N14 4JX, England. SITES: castles, abbeys, stately houses, gardens, other historic sites. ADMINISTRATION: (081) 886-9572. Fax: (081) 886-9572. PRINCIPAL STAFF: Wendy Macphee, artistic director; Lyndsey Brandolese, Lindsay Royan, directors. SEASON: June through September. ANNUAL ATTENDANCE: 20,000 (1991). FOUNDED: 1976, Wendy Macphee.

Theatre Set-Up (TSU) was founded in 1976 by Wendy Macphee with the aim of touring throughout Great Britain and performing with all the simplicity of Shakespeare's own company; that is, eschewing scenery in favor of economy of "set-up." The company prides itself on "making theatres of beautiful buildings and gardens." The sites listed for the 1992 tour of *The Merchant of Venice*, for example, are: Forty Hall, Enfield; Lacock Abbey and Stourhead in Wiltshire; Dunster Castle, Somerset; Fountain Garden at the University of Birmingham; Kenilworth Castle; Wallington, Northumberland; The Rookery,

Rose Court, Fenton House Garden, Temple Amphitheatre Chiswick House Garden, and Millfield Theatre in London; Kirby Muxloe Castle, Wollaton Hall; Kedlestone Hall, Derby; Tatton Park Old Hall, Cheshire; Peel Castle, Isle of Man; Fountains Abbey, North Yorkshire; Kentwell Hall, Suffolk; Mottisfont Abbey; Carisbrooke Castle, Isle of Wright; Killerton House Garden, Devon; Mount Edgecumbe Country Park, Cornwall; Chaplaincy Gardens, Isles of Falmouth; Penshurst Place, Kent. According to the programs, "performances continue regardless of weather."

Because TSU is a registered charity, the three professional directors receive no pay for their services. However, eight members of British Equity are employed; seven actors and one company manager cover all the roles as well as providing musical accompaniment. Box office returns and donations have sustained TSU throughout its existence. The programs testify to the extensive research done for each annual production. The play analyses often include charts illustrating philosophical concepts relevant to the play, in addition to historical background information and textual analyses.

TSU's goal is "to perform the plays of Shakespeare in a way which is accessible to wide range of people, in the touring/private performance style of Shakespeare's own company, 'The King's Men,' in beautiful and historic sites, making use of natural backdrops, and with the minimum of fuss, cost, and accoutrements. Further, to research and present the secret meanings of the plays."

Production History: **1976**: *Ham.*, *Shr.*; **1977**: *Rom.*; **1978**: *MND*; **1979**: *TN*; **1980**: *AYL*; **1981**: *Ado*; **1982**: *Tmp.*; **1983**: *MND*; **1984**: *LLL*; **1985**: *Wiv.*; **1986**: *Err.*; **1987**: *TGV*; **1988**: *WT*; **1989**; *Cym.*; **1990**: *AWW*; **1991**: *MM*; **1992**: *MV*;

Felicia Hardison Londré

YOUNG VIC COMPANY. MAIL: 66 The Cut, London SE1 8LZ, England. SITE: Young Vic Theatre, near Waterloo Station. ADMINISTRATION: (071) 633-0133; Fax: (071) 928-1585. BOX OFFICE: (071) 928-6363. ADMISSION: £3–£14. SEASON: five plays per year, each running eight to ten weeks depending on the box office; 7:30 p.m., Mon.–Sat. PRINCIPAL STAFF: David Thacker, director; Philip Bernays, administrative director; Brian McLaughlin, development director; Janet Waddington, finance director; Richard Howey, production manager; Karen Stephens, youth and education unit director. FACILITY: Young Vic Theatre, large, square, flexible space, enclosed by tiered wooden benches (capacity 500 in the round, 430 thrust), studio theatre (capacity 110). AUDITIONS: held in London preceding each play. STATUS: British Equity/Theatrical Management Association contract. ANNUAL

BUDGET: £1.3 million (1992). ANNUAL ATTENDANCE: 75,000. FOUNDED: 1970, Frank Dunlop.

Young Vic Company (YVC) was founded in 1970 by Frank Dunlop as a young people's theatre and studio for the National Theatre. Dunlop, then a director at the National, which was housed at the **Old Vic**, convinced his artistic director, Laurence Olivier, and the board of the need for a young people's theatre. Olivier in turn presented the idea to the Arts Council, describing "a theatre which would form a centre for work of a national standard to be accessible to everybody, but particularly to students and young people whose incomes or inclination make existing theatres expensive or forbidding. The theatre's program would include the classics, new plays, experimental theatre and educational work" (Young Vic program). A £30,000 grant from the Arts Council was matched by a £30,000 operational surplus from the National Theatre, giving birth to the Young Vic Company on 12 August 1970.

Founder Frank Dunlop directed the YVC from 1970-1978. His first production, *Scapino*, a popularized version of Molière's *Les Fourberies de Scapin*, featured Jim Dale in the title role. The farcical comedy attracted a new young audience and won over the press, which acclaimed the theatre: "Not just alive—electric!" *The Taming of the Shrew* drew on pantomime and used Cockney interpolations to "hook" its audience. *Waiting for Godot* and Sophocles' *Oedipus* in W. B. Yeats' translation rounded out the season. Within a year, the company was touring European festivals and winning awards. Young Vic's national and international reputation continued to grow. The plays ranged from Beckett to Sophocles, Shakespeare to John Lennon and included the world premiere of *Joseph and the Amazing Technicolor Dreamcoat* in 1972.

Michael Bogdanov, now codirector of The **English Shakespeare Company**, took over as director from 1978 to 1980. During these years, the company's repertory included *The Action Man Trilogy* at the Young Vic and the Old Vic, as well as a new rock version of *Faust*. In 1980, Dunlop returned and continued to build the company until he was succeeded by David Thacker in 1984.

Thacker (artistic director from 1984 to the present) chose *Othello* for his opening production, "with the first black actor to play the lead in a major London Theatre for over 20 years" (Young Vic program). Thacker's accomplishments include several transfers to commercial London theatres, joint productions with regional theatres such as Bristol Old Vic, and a productive working relationship with Arthur Miller. Thacker has continued to produce Shakespeare at the YVC as well as direct at the **Royal Shakespeare Company** (RSC). Thacker's reputation has attracted well-known actors such as Judi Dench (*The Plough and the Stars*, 1991), David Suchet (*Timon of Athens*, 1991), and Vanessa Redgrave as Mrs. Alving in Ibsen's *Ghosts* (1986). Directors have included Trevor Nunn (*Timon of Athens*, 1991) and Sam Mendes (*The Plough and the Stars*, 1991). "As much as any previous Young

Vic Director," said the *Times,* "David Thacker has taken advantage of this theatre's young, unjaded audience to present well-worn classics as if they were brand new plays" (Young Vic program).

Alongside the Young Vic's professional and touring productions, it has also produced successful family plays such as *No Worries, The Small Poppies,* and *A Christmas Carol.* Throughout its history, the theatre has developed participatory and educational programs for young people. The Young Vic Youth Theatre, founded in 1988, produces three or four fully mounted productions per year with amateur casts whose members are 25-years-old and under. In 1991, the Young Vic established the youth and education unit.

Early Young Vic productions were cast with younger National Theatre company members. Today, auditions are held prior to each rehearsal period, and England's most accomplished classical actors work at the Young Vic alongside lesser-known actors in an ensemble atmosphere. The Equity Theatrical Management Association contract's pay is modest compared with West End, National, or RSC contracts.

The Young Vic's £1.3 million budget supports 30 permanent staff members. Thacker, as director of the Young Vic, is responsible for supervising all artistic activities and directs half of the plays for the season. Philip Bernays is administrative director and supervises operational details. Additional staff include Sue Hibberd as box office manager, Brian McLaughlin as development director, Janet Waddington as finance director, and Lorraine Selby as house director. Taylors handles the press and marketing department, and Karen Stephens is director of the youth and education unit. In 1992, the Young Vic invested £50,000 in its development department, hoping to raise £100,000. According to Bernays, raising money privately is still in its infancy at the Young Vic and in England generally. Arts organizations are not accustomed to raising money privately and corporations are not used to giving it. A membership campaign raises £12,500 per year. For a £7–£30 fee, members buy tickets for half price. Annual attendance is 75,000, which averages 61 percent of house capacity. The Young Vic's 13-member Board of Management is primarily responsible for protecting the charitable aims of the YVC.

In 1990, the Young Vic encountered a financial crisis brought on by a collapsing building. The company launched a "Save The Young Vic Campaign," which raised £350,000 to do urgent building work and clear the deficit. In the company's 21st season, a "coming of age" program urged "a recognition of the unique and valuable place that Young Vic occupies in British Theatre and a complete reassessment of the funding needs of the organization." Many people gave large amounts of their time and money to save the Young Vic. Unfortunately, the theatre cannot guarantee that such a crisis will not occur again as it is still underfunded.

The Young Vic Theatre was built very quickly as a temporary facility on the concrete slabs of the bombed houses that had once stood there. It is located a block east of the Old Vic, behind a butcher's shop whose white tile decor became the unusual foyer of the Young Vic. A new coffee bar is attached. The intimate, large, square, flexible space is enclosed by tiered wooden benches holding 500 people in the round and 430 with a thrust stage. A simple studio theatre seats 110. Makeup and dressing rooms are modest but serviceable. Sets are generally simple for performances in-the-round and are built on site. Costumes are constructed at the theatre. The 32-page glossy program includes handsomely designed graphics, black-and-white photos, company biographies, costume sketches, and background information on the play and the company.

The YVC serves "young people—and those who are young in spirit." It prides itself on its friendly and welcoming atmosphere that makes theatregoing attractive to people of all ages. Audience surveys have estimated that 5 percent of the audience comes from the theatre's South London community. Immediate neighbors, who live in nearby flats, are given free tickets to the performances in exchange for their patience with the inconvenience of having a theatre as a neighbor. A significant number of people come from outside London (31 percent) and outside of England (4 percent). Many people experience theatre for the first time at the Young Vic. The company has also won the hearts of the artistic community. David Suchet called performing with the YVC one of the "highlights" of his career. Arthur Miller wrote of his experience as follows:

> I have found something else that is attractive, it is the spirit of the place. . . . After a few days of rehearsal one knows that only the most intense and truthful work will be good enough . . . from leading actors to the young assistants they are all utterly devoted to an ideal. There being so little idealism about in these times, one comes to appreciate its appearance all the more.

Reaching the 75,000 audience members who annually attend Young Vic productions is part of a large marketing campaign to raise awareness about each play. Post, television, and newspaper ads blanket the city. The mailing list numbers 15,000. Memberships are growing, but—according to Bernays—the company is not in a situation where the plays are well sold before they have opened. He continues: "We all have our favorite marketing theories, but I believe it's word of mouth in the end. It takes quite a long time for the audience to grow over the length of a run—which is very frustrating. In the last fortnight, you can't get a ticket for love or money, but in the first fortnight there are plenty of empty seats." The theatre averages 61 percent capacity for its mainstage productions and 85 percent for the Christmas shows. Thirty or more newspapers review YVC productions on a regular basis.

The major strength of the Young Vic is its consistently high quality, which Bernays credits to the theatre's history of outstanding artistic directors: Frank Dunlop, Michael Bogdanov, and David Thacker. "They have all been able to create an identity and importance . . . for the Young Vic. The current talented and dedicated staff is directly attributable to Thacker's personal and professional strengths." Bernays' greatest concern is replacing Thacker with someone of equal calibre, should he decide to leave. Goals and dreams for the theatre include larger Arts Council support and perhaps a new theatre. Costs for a new building are estimated at £12 million, says Bernays, so perhaps the more realistic goal is a completely refurbished theatre.

The YVC's stated purpose is "to present classical and contemporary plays of great artistic merit and to express these plays in productions that are accessible and comprehensible." It is the artistic imperative of the company to satisfy the 16 to 25 year olds, and this group is used as "the litmus test to judge the quality of our work as we seek to reach the widest possible audience for our plays."

The YVC's policy is to do great plays with uncompromising honesty. Its five-play season, with each play running for eight to ten weeks, usually includes one Shakespeare, one newly commissioned play, and one family play. The company would like to play in repertory, but budgets will not allow it. Productions tend to be straightforward presentations that value clarity rather than "production trickery." The YVC does not have a policy of star casting, but it uses recognized names when available because, the company aims for "performers of the highest possible quality." Bernays also notes that he is aware of stars commercial appeal. The intimate acting space and in-the-round performance space keep the focus on the actor and the play. "The central aim of the Young Vic's work is that classic plays should appear like brand-new works and that productions of contemporary plays should be governed by the same values and aspire to the same standards."

Production History: 1970: *Scapino, Oedipus, The Soldiers Tale, Waiting for the Godot, Timesneeze, Shr., The Wakefield Nativity Plays, The King Stag, Byron–The Naked Peacock, Endgame, MM, Happy Days, Little Malcolm and His Struggle Against the Eunuchs, Happy Days*; 1971-72: *Err., Oedipus, The Painters, Cato Street, The Man Who . . ., Sylvester and the Dragon, Rom., St. Patrick's Day, Sweet Mr. Shakespeare, She Stoops to Conquer, The Chairs Plus, The Fantastic Fairground*; 1972-73: *The Maids/Death Watch, The Alchemist, Shadow of a Gunman, The Dwarfs/The Wound, JC, Bible One* (Tour), *Endgame, The Sensation Seekers, Epitaph for George Dillon, Look Back in Anger, Bible One, Hobson's Choice, The Fantastic Fairground, A Taste of Honey, Joseph and the Amazing Technicolour Dreamcoat, Rosencrantz and Guildenstern are Dead, The Incredible Vanishing!, Beckett Shorts, French Without Tears*; 1974-75: *Ado, The Caretaker, Hambledog and The Happy Clogs, The Statues in Room 13, The Spellbound Squire, Tommy Thumb, Roots, French Without Tears*; 1975-76: *The Englishman Amused, The Tragedy of Tragedies: or the Life and Death of Tom Thumb the Great, Crete and Sergeant Pepper, TGV, Mac., Grandson of Oblomov, Charley's Aunt, The Architect and the Emperor of Assyria, That Time*

*of Year, All Walks of Leg, Oth.,
AYL, Stamp and Deliver, Dream
People*; **1976-77**: *A Man for All
Seasons, Ant., If You're Glad. I'll
Be Frank, The Real Inspector
Hound, Tobias and the Angel*;
1978 to 1984: *The Action Man
Trilogy, Bartholomew Fair, The
Canterbury Tales, Hiawatha, The
Hunchback of Notre Dame, The
Ancient Mariner, Rom., Faust*
(rock version), *Rosencrantz and
Guildenstern are Dead, Rom.,
After Margueritte/The Real In-
spector Hound, Lr., Gloo Joo,
Dracula, Pygmalion, R2, Godspell,
Childe Byron, WT, John Morti-
mer's Casebook, Masque-rade,
Rom., Waiting for Godot, Ham,
Oth., MV, Robin Hood, Ant., John
Paul George Ringo and Bert, TN,
The Caretaker, The Duenna, Swan
Esther*; **1984 to 1989**: *Oth., Jail
Diary of Albie Sachs, Flashpoint,
One Day in Lambeth, Lr., Jack and
the Beanstalk, No Pasaran, Some
Kind of Hero, A View From the
Bridge, Mac., Ham., MM, The
Enemies Within, Rom., JC, MND,
Stags and Hens, The Crucible,*

*Owners, Ghosts, Who's Afraid of
Virginia Woolf? Comedians, A
Touch of the Poet, Doctor Faustus,
Solomon and the Big Cat, An
Enemy of the People, Jail Diary of
Albie Sachs, A Christmas Carol*;
1989: *Two-Way Mirror, Solomon
and the Big Cat, Young. Free and
Single, MM, Cor., The Pleasure
Principle, Outbreak of God in
Area 9, Grease, Can't Pay. Won't
Pay, William, Vicious Circles,
Heroes and Sheroes the Birds, Le
Grand Meaulnes, From the Miss-
issippi Delta, A Christmas Carol*;
1990: *The Price, West Side Story,
Anna Christie, Wesker's Women,
The Man Who Had All the Luck,
Grease, Le Grand Meaulnes, Jude,
The Threepenny Opera*; **1991**: *To,
Judging Billy Jones, Tokens of
Affection, Tim., The Plough and
the Stars, Sex Please. We're
Italian, WT. The Snow Queen*;
1992: *All My Sons, The Crucible,
The Caucasian Chalk Circle, In
the Midnight Hour, Guys and
Dolls, Rosmersholm, The Snow
Queen.*

Research Resources: Archives are maintained in the administrative offices at Young Vic.

Site visit and interview with Philip Bernays: 20 July 1992.
Cindy Melby Phaneuf

JAPAN

SHAKESPEARE THEATRE. MAIL: 2-21-4 Sun Plaza Building, Koenji-kita, Suginami-ku, Tokyo 166 Japan. SITE: various theatres in Tokyo and on

tour. ADMINISTRATION: (03) 3337-8665. BOX OFFICE: varies. ADMIS-
SION: 3,500 yen. SEASON: varies. PRINCIPAL STAFF: Norio Deguchi,
artistic director; Ken Yoshizawa, business manager. FACILITY: rehearsal
room/studio theatre in Sun Plaza (capacity 100); public performances booked
into various theatres. ANNUAL BUDGET: 50,000,000 yen. ANNUAL
ATTENDANCE: 5,000 (plus 30,000 students at school programs). FOUNDED:
1975, Norio Deguchi.

After graduation from the University of Tokyo, Norio Deguchi began his
theatre career as a director at the Bungakuza Theatre. Feeling that the large
size of that company stifled his own creativity, he left it to mount his own
productions of Japanese plays. But it was a "big failure," he recalls amid peals
of laughter. "I have nothing! I lose everything!" He then gathered some
students and young "drop-out actors" to form a study group. He spent a year
training them how to speak and act Shakespeare. In 1975, he began directing
Shakespeare and has not stopped since. Indeed, the title of his 1988 book,
Shakespeare wa tomaranai, might be translated as "Shakespeare Never Stops."
By 1981, Deguchi was the only director in Japan to have staged the entire
canon of Shakespeare plays.

The Shakespeare Theatre (ST) originally held its study sessions in the room
that now serves as the company headquarters, on the third floor of the Sun
Plaza Building, a five-minute walk from Koenji JR Station. Eventually, the ST
acquired a space on the second floor of the building, which is used for training,
rehearsals, and occasional (perhaps once a year) presentations for intimate
audiences.

Because Deguchi had "no money" when he founded his company, the actors
were costumed in jeans and T-shirts. "Blue jeans Shakespeare" became his
signature style in contrast to the usual opulent or overproduced Shakespeare of
the 1970s. Making a virtue of necessity, Deguchi demonstrated the power of
Shakespeare-on-a-budget. For example, the banquet scene in *Macbeth* was lit
entirely by "corpse candles" (used for lighting the dead until the funeral; these
were cheaper than Western-style candles). In *Love's Labour's Lost*, to satirize
noblemen who renounce love to devote themselves to study, Deguchi had the
actors sit in old elementary-school desks and chairs that he had bought at a
street market.

In 1993, the ST was still operating 100 percent on earned income. Apart
from ticket sales, the only additional source of revenue is the souvenir program
that sells for 800 yen (about $8). "Ten years ago we sold T-shirts, but it was a
failure. No good!" Deguchi recalls laughingly. The ST cannot pay its actors
adequately, so they have to work at part-time jobs after the nine-to-five
rehearsal day. In 1993, the ST was about to launch its first subscription sales
campaign. Demographic surveys of ST audiences show that Deguchi is
gradually achieving his goal of reaching a broad spectrum of people. It is easy
to get young audiences, he notes, but older people in Japan think of

Shakespeare as academic and hard to understand; he is pleased to see growing numbers of middle-aged people at ST performances. Deguchi's immediate goal is to keep the company going financially, while his dream is to tour to the United States and other foreign countries.

The company logo (which does not appear on the flyers or programs) is an eye framed by a triangle with the words "Shakespeare Theatre" in English at the base of the triangle. The eye was chosen because of Shakespeare's abundant eye imagery and metaphorical references to "seeing." Certainly, eyes are prominently featured in the bold, brightly colored face that adorned the programs and flyers for the spring 1993 season: the pupil of one eye showed a sinking ship (for *Comedy of Errors*) and the other a forest (for *A Midsummer Night's Dream*).

As if demonstrating the truth of Lafcadio Hearn's claim that the genius of the Japanese is "impermanence," Deguchi keeps no records. He maintains no archive of promptbooks, photographs, or clippings, and he files no copies of programs or press releases. His only concession to the hsitorical record is a random selection of videotapes of a few productions. Business manager Ken Yoshizawa has saved some company-related materials in a personal collection.

Training remains an important focus of the youthful company. One of their exercises involves reading lines from a newspaper without emotion and then reading again with feeling. "Nobody doubts that speech in a play must be spoken with emotion," Deguchi says; "but emotion is conveyed in words. We start by listening to what the words themselves speak to us."

Deguchi's approach to Shakespeare is to attempt to bridge the culture gap while remaining faithful to Shakespeare's originality. Using the Yushi Odashima translations, he does little or no cutting or adapting of the text. He acknowledges that a translation in itself removes the audience one step from the original, and cultural differences present another barrier. He cannot hope to convey the concept of "midsummer's eve" to a Japanese audience, for example, but he can compensate by emphasizing aspects of the play that do communicate directly across cultures.

The two productions of the spring 1993 season were fast-paced and brimming with physical action. Coincidentally, both productions had the actors wearing very expressively molded, pastel-colored half-masks; none of his previous productions had used masks. Deguchi has cited several reasons for the masks, beginning with the strong impression made upon him in childhood by the masked dancers at a shrine. (Deguchi was born and raised in Shimane prefecture, where Lafcadio Hearn lived for some time.) For *Comedy of Errors*, Deguchi felt that the masks would help to force a *commedia dell'arte* style of performing. Of course, the use of masks also underscored the confusion of identities among the two sets of twins. In *A Midsummer Night's Dream*, the masks helped to distinguish among the three groups of characters—the artisans (who wore no masks), the Athenians, and the fairies—and allowed the double casting of Hippolyta/Titania and Theseus/Oberon.

Titania emerged as the focal character in *A Midsummer Night's Dream*. Compellingly portrayed by Kiri Yoshizawa, both Titania and Hippolyta were capable, broad-minded women, able to see the big picture but saddled with unreasonable men. Surrounded by her chorus of nine fairies in fanciful black and silver costumes, Titania commanded the stage, never becoming ridiculous, even in her scenes with Bottom-as-ass. Touched by her generosity of spirit, Oberon was the one who learned a lesson and was made foolish by the cruel trick he had played on her. Puck, an athletic young actor wielding a twig broom, kept things stirred up on the three-quarters arena stage. The young lovers' scuffles intensified to extremes of vocal and physical violence. The "rude mechanicals" were directed to respond in unison to Bottom's posturing; somehow they were funnier than Bottom himself, who tended to substitute vocal volume for comic nuance. The "Pyramus and Thisbe" sequence brought some wonderfully inventive business with props and costumes into the minimalist production.

The Comedy of Errors successfully integrated Italian Renaissance and Japanese elements of costuming, gesture, and manners. The physical action seemed more choreographed, more appropriate to the scale of the production, than that in the *Dream*, and consequently, it was funnier. Indeed, the matinee audience presented a vista of broad grins throughout the performance. They laughed spontaneously and heartily at the antics of the two Dromios and at the mistaken-identity plot twists, clearly discovering the play through this production. In this minimalist interpretation, a white ball (about the size of a basketball) served as an objective correlative for anything that is inexplicable or surpasses understanding in human affairs. With almost religious reverence, Egeon addressed his sad tale to it in the opening sequence, while the Duke stood behind him to listen. The ball became the purse that went astray. When tossed back and forth during dialogue between an Antiphilus and a Dromio, it reified their talking at cross-purposes. The recognition scene began with everyone on stage bowing to the Abbess. As they came up from the bow, they did a double take in unison, except for Egeon, who was still weeping over his son's rejection of him. In a very moving moment, the Abbess crossed to her long-lost husband, knelt, and removed his mask. Then everyone else removed their masks, which were left on the stage floor, surrounding the white ball, after the characters' final exit.

Production History: 1975: *TN, Ado, Rom., Err., Ham., MND, MM*; 1976: *TN, Ham., Ado, JC, AYL, Shr., MND, MM, R3, MV*; 1977: *R3, MND, Wiv., MV, Oth., Wiv.*; 1978: *TN, Lr., Oth., Ham., Tit., Tro., MND, MV, LLL, Wiv., Mac., Per.*; 1979: *Wiv., Tit., Shr.,* *1H4, 2H4, Ado, Rom., Mac., H5, Per., Tmp., R2*; 1980: *Lr., Cym., Jn., Rom., Ado, TGV, TN, MND, AWW, Tim.*; 1981: *Rom., H8, 1H6, 2H6, 3H6, Ant., TN, Ado, MND, Lr., LLL, JC, Mac.*; 1982: *LLL, 1H6, 2H6, 3H6, Shr., TN, MND*; 1983: *Err., Per., Lr., 1H4, 2H4,*

JC, TN; **1984**: *MND, Ado*; **1985**:
Shr., MND, TN, LLL; **1986**: *LLL,*
MND; **1987**: *R3, Err., Mac.*; **1988**:

Err., TN; **1989**: *Err., Shr., LLL*;
1990: *Err.*; **1991**: *Per., WT*; **1992**:
Err.; **1993**: *MND, Err., Jn., H8.*

Research Resources: Norio Deguchi, *Shakespeare wa tomaranai* (Tokyo: Kodansha, 1988).

Site visit and interview: 8 June 1993. Productions attended: 26 and 29 May 1993.
Osamu Hirokawa and Felicia Hardison Londré

TOKYO PANASONIC GLOBE. MAIL: 1-2 Hyakunincho 3-chome, Shinjuku-ku, Tokyo, 169 Japan. SITE: a six-minute walk from Shin-Okubo station (JR Yamanote line). ADMINISTRATION: (03) 3360-1121; Fax: (03) 3360-3336. BOX OFFICE: (03) 3360-3336. ADMISSION: 2,000–6,000 yen. SEASON: approximately 30 productions, year-round. PRINCIPAL STAFF: Seiya Tamura, senior managing director (Shinjuku-Nishitoyama Development Co., Ltd.); Mariko Inaba, planning and marketing. FACILITY: thrust stage (movable, partitionable, and height adjustable; capacity 640-700). ANNUAL BUDGET: 5 million yen (1993). ANNUAL ATTENDANCE: 100,000 (1993). FOUNDED: 1988; Shinjuku-Nishitoyama Development Co., Ltd.

Founded by a development company, the Tokyo Globe opened in 1988 after five years of planning. In 1983, the Shinjuku-Nishitoyama Development Company initiated the redevelopment of a site near Shin-Okubo train station. The company's board wanted to include some kind of arts facility along with the apartment buildings, but the area was not considered prime for culture. In discussions with architect Arata Isozaki, the board decided that the most viable operation would be a theatre for some specialized audience. Senior managing director Seiya Tamura recalls the reasoning that led them to settle on a Shakespeare theatre: "If you ask anybody in Japan, they can easily name six or seven plays by Shakespeare; but if you mention any Japanese playwright, they can rarely name even one. Shakespeare is clearly the most popular dramatist in Japan." The investors' faith in Shakespeare has proven to be well founded, as the profit-making operation continues to thrive, especially as Panasonic has begun contributing half of its budget.

Besides the marketability of Shakespeare, Tamura cites the fact that there was no existing theatre with a thrust stage in Japan. Influenced by the ideas in Frances Yates' *Theatre of the World*, which had been translated into Japanese by Minoru Fujita, the company decided to build a "creative reconstruction" of London's original Globe. The relationship that Yates demonstrates between the circular and the rectangular inspired Isozaki's design for a round building—roofed, but clearly evoking the theatres on Hollar's map of London—to contain the stagehouse and auditorium. At ground level, a rectangular courtyard and foyer welcome the theatregoer into the theatrical space. The administrative offices are located on a lower level, as are the dressing rooms and three 109-square-meter rehearsal studios.

The foyer allows access from either of the parallel streets between which the complex is situated. Drinks and snacks are sold at a bar in the attractively furnished lobby, but there is no coat-check facility. Inside the taupe and olive-grey auditorium, the orchestra seating is encircled by three galleries. Maximum capacity is 700 without the thrust stage. When the height-adjustable thrust is used, 650 can be seated. A six-meter deep inner stage can be used for proscenium-style productions; the removable thrust is 8.1 meters deep by 12.7 meters wide. The auditorium floor was originally flat, but, when Ingmar Bergman brought his production of *Hamlet* during the theatre's first season, the floor was rebuilt on a rake to his specifications and has remained that way ever since.

Three kinds of productions fill the Globe's year-round season: those produced by the Globe, those coproduced by the Globe and some other company, and independent productions that rent the space. The average run is eight to ten performances. For the Globe's original productions, there are about ten actors who form what might be called a core company, appearing fairly regularly in Shakespeare but also free lancing elsewhere. The business arrangements for the other two categories vary considerably with each situation. For coproductions, the theatre is often used free of charge, while the box office earnings are split, perhaps 70 to 30 percent. Many of the independent productions booked at the Globe are foreign companies, like the **Royal Shakespeare Company** (RSC), **Cheek by Jowl**, the **English Shakespeare Company**, and the Compass Theatre, all of which are from England and return almost every season. Because the information network among foreigners in Tokyo is very strong, little advertising needs to be done for productions in languages other than Japanese. Otherwise, no distinction is made in the marketing of the three categories of production. Thus, the public might see a student production at the Globe and assume that it is the house company.

The five productions I saw at the Globe are probably a representative cross-section of its offerings. The **English Shakespeare Company**'s multiethnic *The Tempest* used a junkyard setting that seemed to have been designed for a wider stage, as the set itself caused an obstructed view of various playing areas from different parts of the house. RSC actor Gerard Murphy directed Japanese actors in a fast-paced, metatheatrical *Merchant of Venice* on the thrust stage. The 11 youthful actors wore rehearsal clothes and sat on folding chairs to observe the action until cued to enter the action; characterization was achieved through posture, vocal manner, and perhaps a costume accessory. *Richard III* combined live actors, marionettes, colorful slide projections, a jazz combo, and a samisen interlude. With a little tightening and the elimination of some of the show-off effects, it might have been a powerful production. For example, when the talented actress playing Lady Anne began to succumb to Richard, she sank to the floor and lay there, face up, as the marionette Richard crept slowly and sensuously onto her body to lie on her breast and then kiss her lips; the effect was chilling. Operating a marionette that looked exactly like the famous portrait of *Richard III* was a talented actor, who took over the role himself from the coronation scene until Richard began his downhill slide, at which point the marionette again became the character. A shockingly pornographic *Midsummer Night's Dream*, complicated by cross-gender casting, was performed in a circus-like setting by a women's company called Romantica. Hermia and Lysander were played by women, while Helena and Demetrius were both played by men, so that, metatheatrically, the weddings at the end united two same-sex couples. Charles Gounod's opera *Roméo et Juliette* was sung to the accompaniment of a full-scale orchestra in front of the stage; it combined gorgeous voices and a lovely romantic setting.

Production History (abbreviations in parentheses refer to visiting theatre companies; refer to the key below): **1988**: *The Wars of the Roses* (ESC), *Unnatural and Unkind* (RSC), *Falstaff Ossia Le Tre Burle*, *Cym.* (NT), *WT* (NT), *Tmp.* (NT), *Ham.* (RDTC), *Miss Julie* (RDTC), *AYL* (OUDS); **1989**: *Lr.*, *Ado*, *Err.*, *JC*, *Caesar and Cleopatra*, *Opera Otello*, *Opera Hamlet*, *Directions to Servants*, *The Country Wife* (OUDS), *Restoration* (OUDS), *The Fairy Queen*, *Opera Hamlet*, *Ham.* (NT); **1990**: *Markisinnan de Sade* (RDTC), *Lr.* (RTC), *MND* (RTC), *Mac.*, *AYL*, *MV*, *Jew of Malta*, *Ham.*, *Lr.*, *MV* (CTC), *The Alchemist* (CTC), *TN* (OUDS), *Find Me* (OUDS), *R3* (NT), *Lr.* (NT), *Ham.* (Cheek by Jowl), *Cor.* (ESC), *WT* (ESC); **1991**: *Les Liaisons Dangereuses* (RSC), *Opera Hamlet*, *Directions to Servants*, *Shr.* (RSC), *Tro.* (Emballage Theatre, France), *MV* (ESC), *Oth.*, *Lr.*, *Falstaff* (Kyogen version), *MM* (CTC), *Experimental King Lear*, *Ham.* (Kabuki version), *Don Giovanni*, *Die Entführung aus dem Serail*, *MND* (musical), *Waiting for Godot* (CTC), *Krapp's Last Tape* (CTC), *TN* (opera), *Hamlet's Time* (opera), *Tartuffe* (NT), *Tmp.* (OUDS), *Per.*, *TGV*, *JC*, *Ant.*, *Dah-Dah-Sko-Dah-Dah*, *Broken Romeo and Juliet*; **1992**: *AYL* (Cheek by Jowl), *Tmp.* (Bunraku version), *TN* (ESC), *Mac.* (ESC), *Shr.*, *Ado*, *Tit.* (National Theatre of Craiova, Romania), *Prospero's Book*, *MND*, *Rom.*, *The Complete Brandenburg Concerto* (NY Symphonic Ensemble), *Le Nozze di Figaro*, *Ham.* (CTC), *Lr.* (CTC), *Don Giovanni*, *Otello* (opera), *Miss Julie*, *Broken Macbeth*, *Mac.* (Watermill Theatre Company), *TN*, *Ado* (OUDS), *Ham.*, *Wiv.*; **1993**: *Broken Hamlet*, *Heer Ranjha* (the Indian *Rom.*, Tara Arts), *R3* (RSC), *Tmp.* (RSC), *MV*, *R3*, *MND* (ballet), *In Dickicht der Städte*,

MND, Roméo et Juliette (opera),   *Cym.* (CTC), *TN.*
MND, Jn., Hedda Gabler (CTC),

Key:
ESC: English Shakespeare Company
RSC: Royal Shakespeare Company
NT: National Theatre
RDTC: Royal Dramatic Theatre Company (Sweden)
OUDS: Oxford University Dramatic Society
RTC: Renaissance Theatre Company
CTC: Compass Theatre Company

Research Resources: Minoru Fujita and Arata Isozaki, *The Globe: A Shakespearean scholar talks with the architect of the Tokyo Globe* (Tokyo: Shinjuku-Nishitoyama Development Co., Ltd., 1988).

Site visits: 10 April, 21 April, 20 May, 24 June, 1 July 1993; interview: 9 July 1993.
Felicia Hardison Londré

NEW ZEALAND

OUTDOOR SUMMER SHAKESPEARE. MAIL: Theatre Workshop, c/o Auckland University Students Association, Auckland University, Private Bag, Auckland, New Zealand. SITE: Old Arts Quad, behind the bell tower on the Auckland University campus. ADMINISTRATION: 64 (09) 309-0789. BOX OFFICE: 64 (09) 303-3206. ADMISSION: $10–$17.50. SEASON: mid-February to mid-March; 8:00 p.m., Tues.–Sun. FACILITY: open courtyard (stage configuration varies with production; capacity 250-300). AUDITIONS: early November at Theatre Workshop. STATUS: non-union contract. ANNUAL BUDGET: $35,000 (1990). ANNUAL ATTENDANCE; 7,000. FOUNDED: 1962.

The 1991 production of the Outdoor Summer Shakespeare (OSS) festival marked its 28th anniversary season. Beyond the fact that one Shakespeare play has been produced out-of-doors on the Auckland University campus each summer, little is known about the history of this tradition. The name of the founder has been lost. What is known is that the OSS has been produced by Theatre Workshop, the drama club at Auckland University, under the auspices of the Auckland University Students Association since 1962.

Theatre Workshop is a student-run organization with no on-going university faculty or administrative staff involvement. The group membership changes completely every three to four years, so neither history nor planning beyond the yearly season is a primary concern. While Theatre Workshop is officially an Auckland University student drama club, some members are graduates, and a few from the community have an interest in some aspect of theatre and use Theatre Workshop to gain experience.

The mission of the OSS is twofold: first, to provide Auckland audiences (university students, secondary school students and the general public) with an original, innovative Shakespearean production of high quality; second, to make enough money to subsidize the other five Theatre Workshop productions in the season. The mission of Theatre Workshop, while certainly compatible with OSS, is a bit different. Theatre Workshop was formed as a drama club for several purposes; to involve students in theatre; to enrich students' experience by offering workshops in theatre craft; to present a range of dramatic literature, including new plays; and to offer a production experience with a substantial budget, broad profile, and wide audience through the OSS. Including the summer Shakespearean production, Theatre Workshop mounts six productions each year.

The production of a Shakespeare play, which corresponds to the beginning of the academic year, opens the season. Practically, a production effort of this scope is demanding and most easily prepared during the summer vacation when students are not busy with classes. The production also serves as a showcase for the activities of Theatre Workshop and provides a recruitment opportunity for prospective members. Finally, performances occur at the beginning of the term for both secondary and tertiary students well before academic demands might be a deterrent to spending an evening in the theatre.

The organization of the OSS and its operating procedures are determined by Theatre Workshop through its seven-member executive board. The board is comprised of the president of Theatre Workshop and six of its members. It is this group that makes the artistic decisions and is financially liable for the OSS. The selection of the Shakespeare play and its director is made by the board. An open call for play suggestions and production concepts is made. Guided by the goal of presenting innovative and original Shakespeare, the board then selects the play and concept that the members find most provocative. The director who had submitted the proposal is then hired, and it becomes his/her responsibility to gather the designers, technicians and actors for the production. The director and the production manager are the only people involved with the OSS who are paid.

The approach taken by a director is often an attempt to engage the audience in a particular way. In the case of the 1991 production of *The Tempest*, the play's island setting was placed in the South Pacific in order to provide a more vital connection for New Zealand audiences. Director Geoff Clendon, a 1976 graduate of the National Institute of Dramatic Art in Sydney who later returned to his native Auckland, presented the situation in the play as parallel to England's colonization of New Zealand. He cast a Maori, New Zealand's indigenous people, in the role of Caliban and costumed him in Maori attire.

The playing space is the Old Arts Quad, a green on the Auckland University campus. There are buildings on three sides. One of them houses the bell tower, which must be silenced during performances. The setting for the play determines the placement of scenery, backstage space, and audience. There is no standardized format. The audience is seated on bleachers erected on the lawn. The green area has no covering so rain-outs do occur. The opening performance of *The Tempest* was canceled due to the "tempest" on the green.

The green, a multipurpose storage area on campus, and a cubicle provided by the Students Association and housing a desk and telephone used by the president of Theatre Workshop comprise the facilities of the OSS. Sets are built outside on the site, and costumes are constructed wherever the enterprising costume designer can find sewing machines and space. The space and desk allotted to the president of Theatre Workshop serve as the administrative area.

For Auckland, New Zealand's largest city, the OSS provides consistent production of Shakespeare. The cultural and educational contribution is acknowledged by consistently sold-out houses. The three-week season of six performances per week has usually sold out so early in the promotion that an additional week, also sold-out, has been added for the past several years.

The OSS also provides the artists involved with a rich opportunity for experience that is not available elsewhere in the country. For young performers, it is a chance to perform a run more akin to a professional experience. For professionals, such as John Givens, the New Zealand actor/director in film, television, and professional theatre who played Prospero in the 1991 production of *The Tempest*, it is a chance to hone skills in a repertory format and perform roles seldom offered in the commercial theatre. The combination of community support and continued initiative by the Theatre Workshop bode well for the continued success of the OSS.

Production History: **1989**: *Lr.*, **1990**: *MND*, **1991**: *Tmp.*

Interview:10 June 1991.
Jennifer K. Martin

STRATFORD SHAKESPEARE FESTIVAL (Stratford, New Zealand). MAIL: 22 R. D. Stratford, Taranaki, New Zealand. SITE: Upstairs Gallery on Broadway St. in Stratford, Taranaki.ADMINISTRATION/BOX OFFICE: 64 (0663) 27-802. ADMISSION: free–$5. SEASON: one week, biannually, beginning May 1990 and continuing in November 1992. PRINCIPAL STAFF: Marie Walter, president, Stratford Shakespeare Society; Isabel Walter, secretary. FACILITY: an open room (flexible staging). STATUS: non-union contract. ANNUAL BUDGET: $12,229 (1990). ANNUAL ATTENDANCE: 3,000. FOUNDED: 1990, Marie Walter.

The town of Stratford in New Zealand received its name in 1877 when the site was still covered by a dense forest of native trees and bush that bore little resemblance to the English forests of Arden, nor was the Patea River, site of canoe battles in the recently fought Maori wars, like the gentle Avon. Nevertheless, the town was named Stratford and, in its early years, was known as Stratford-on-Patea. As city planning began, it was decided that all streets and boundaries should bear the names of Shakespearean characters. Naming was gradually expanded to include historic places mentioned in the plays and sonnets. A Shakespeare Society was formed in 1899. The following year, when a coat-of-arms emblem was designed for the borough, it included the gold spear against a black background like that found in the coat-of-arms awarded in 1596 to John Shakespeare, father of William.

The first Shakespeare festival in Stratford was held in 1964, marking the four-hundredth anniversary of the Bard's birth. Mrs. H. E. Young, former headmistress of St. Mary's School for Girls in Stratford, organized a month-long festival that included a School Festival of Shakespeare for the secondary schools, a performance of *The Taming of the Shrew*, an anniversary worship service, and a costumed Elizabethan banquet offering a "sturdily satisfying bill of fare." The events were received so enthusiastically that future festivals were anticipated, but, apart from an Elizabethan Shakespeare banquet in 1972, the Shakespeare Society continued mainly as a literary group. Using notes from the 1964 festival, a more ambitious festival was organized by Isabel Walter in 1990. The initial purpose was to commemorate the signing of the Treaty of Waitangi, which is regarded as the birth of New Zealand.

The 1990 Shakespeare festival was produced by the Festival Committee, a 12-member group comprised of Shakespeare Society members plus supporters from the community who assisted in the planning. A chairperson, secretary, and treasurer were elected. Each member of the Festival Committee headed or served on the subcommittees responsible for the different festival events. With the 1992 festival, the Stratford Shakespeare Society will have completed the process of incorporation. The Shakespeare festival in November and the teachers' workshop held during the May school vacation will be organized by an elected committee headed by a chairperson.

New Zealanders are proud of what is often called "Kiwi ingenuity." The festival at Stratford certainly is a wonderful example of that ingenuity. Having no space of its own, the Festival Committee mobilized resources from the community and used the Upstairs Gallery, a large room that was formerly a library, the Stratford High School Assembly Hall, and the Stratford War Memorial Hall for their performance spaces. Costumes and props were rented from local theatre groups. Homes of the members of the Festival Committee served as administrative offices, and the Stratford Information Office became the box office.

In every respect, the Stratford Shakespeare Festival (SSF) remains a community venture. It is supported through grants from local businesses and individuals so that some events can be free of charge. The organization and nearly all performances are done by people within the Taranaki district where the city of Stratford is located. The combination of indoor and outdoor events involves several locales in the town. Settings range from informal street performances to more conventional concert and theatre programing. The variety of activities is designed to interest the widest possible range of people within the community. Elizabethan crafts are sold, along with a wide range of Elizabethan foods and beverages. Lunches and dinners are available by reservation before and after performances. A different pre-show each day usually features singers, instrumentalists, and dancers.

The philosophy that guides the festival grows out of the Stratford community itself. The mission is: to promote the connection that Stratford has with the life, times, and works of Shakespeare; to encourage the production of Shakespeare's plays; and to foster interest in and appreciation of the works of Shakespeare. In addition to the many other activities, the first festival performances of Shakespeare were excerpts from some of his most famous plays. The 1992 festival will include two full-length plays produced by theatre professionals with members of local theatre groups being invited to participate as well. Because the Shakespeare productions are in the context of an Elizabethan festival, a historical framework and textual integrity will be maintained.

Production History: 1990: *Ham., TN, AYL, JC, MND, Mac.* (excerpts).

Research Resources: Archives for the Stratford Shakespeare Festival are located at the Shakespeare Globe Centre in Stratford.

Interview: June 1991.
Jennifer K. Martin

VICTORIA UNIVERSITY OF WELLINGTON SUMMER SHAKE-SPEARE. MAIL: Department of Theatre and Film, P.O. Box 600, Wellington, New Zealand. SITE: The Dell, a clearing in the city of Wellington's Botanical Gardens. ADMINISTRATION/BOX OFFICE: 64 (04) 715-359; Fax: 64 (04) 712-070. ADMISSION: $6–$14. SEASON: two weeks, late February. PRINCIPAL STAFF: faculty of the Department of Theatre and Film at Victoria University. FACILITY: varies; currently Wellington Botanical Gardens. AUDITIONS: September, for Victoria University students. STATUS: academic production. ANNUAL BUDGET: $35,000 (1991). ANNUAL ATTENDANCE: 3,500. FOUNDED: 1983, Adrian Kiernander.

The capital city of Wellington is located on the southern coastline of New Zealand's North Island. A hilly city prone to minor earthquakes, Wellington faces Cook Strait, where the currents of the Pacific Ocean and the Tasman Sea churn up some spectacular winds on a daily basis—and, occasionally, some spectacular stories. Victoria University perches in a beautiful setting high on the bluffs overlooking the city. It is not surprising then that the first site chosen for the Victoria University of Wellington Summer Shakespeare (VUWSS) was a campus spot that offers at least some shelter from the elements.

VUWSS was founded in 1983 by Adrian Kiernander. The idea for a summer Shakespeare festival in Wellington was based on the long-established **Outdoor Summer Shakespeare** on the campus of Auckland University. Initially, the goal of VUWSS was to present an annual student production of a Shakespeare play. This was a very ambitious undertaking for the Drama Club, so a Summer Shakespeare Trust was created to help manage the enterprise. In 1991, the secretary of the trust was David Carnegie.

Despite the volatile weather, an outdoor site was chosen for the first production: a covered area that usually served as a carpark. As a setting for *A Midsummer Night's Dream*, the ugly concrete became an Athens of gray, dehumanized bureaucracy. The bright costumes of the punk fairies, accompanied by a rock band, contrasted sharply with their setting. For the following season's *Macbeth*, the site became a post-Holocaust wasteland. The roofing, however, caused such appalling acoustical problems that the outdoor space was abandoned for the university's proscenium theatre. The indoor seasons were characterized by a wide range of production styles, including a clownish *King Lear*. The move indoors was ultimately deemed "a dull sojourn," however, and another outdoor space was sought.

To regain the festival atmosphere and to widen attendance beyond the university and secondary school students (who remain the primary target audience), the festival was moved off campus. The site chosen was The Dell, a clearing in the city's Botanical Gardens. An association was formed with Wellington's Summer City program. The 1991 production, quite appropriately, was *A Midsummer Night's Dream*.

Faculty members of Victoria University's Department of Theatre and Film provide the organizational core, working with the Drama Club. The Summer Shakespeare Trust provides some fiscal guidance, although 90 percent of the budget is earned income. As with most student theatre, this undertaking has directors essentially creating a new acting and production company from scratch each season. The artistic approach is determined by the director. Directorial freedom has resulted in a wide range of production styles. Administrative and box office tasks are handled through the university.

Production History: 1983-1990: *MND*, *Mac.*, *AYL*, *Ado*, *Lr.*; **1991**: *MND*.

Research Resources: Archives for the Victoria University of Wellington Summer Shakespeare are maintained by the university.

Telephone interview: May 1991.
Jennifer K. Martin

SOUTH AFRICA

PORT ELIZABETH SHAKESPEAREAN FESTIVAL. MAIL: 6 Kloof Villas, Jutland Crescent, 6001 Port Elizabeth, South Africa. SITE: Mannville open-air theatre in Saint George's Park, Port Elizabeth. ADMINSTRATION: 55-2890; Fax: 55-2890. BOX OFFICE: 56-2256. ADMISSION: 5 rands. SEASON: 20 performances in February; 8:00 p.m., Mon.–Sat. PRINCIPAL STAFF: Helen Mann, director; Bruce Mann, president; Helen Wilkins, secretary; Yvonne Howell, treasurer; Edith Porter, wardrobe. FACILITY: Mannville open-air theatre (capacity 500). AUDITIONS: by invitation. STATUS: amateur, with occasional professional guest performers and directors. ANNUAL BUDGET: 30,000 rands. ANNUAL ATTENDANCE: 10,000. FOUNDED: 1960, André Huguenet.

The Port Elizabeth Shakespearean Festival (PESF) is a dedicated amateur group that presents Shakespeare in the Mannville open-air theatre in St. George's Park, as well as musicals and modern drama in the 100-year-old Port Elizabeth Opera House. The PESF owes its existence to five key figures: professional actor/director Will Jamieson, who set the stage for the festival; founding father André Huguenet, who proposed the idea; Leslie French, who brought his expertise in open-air theatre; and Bruce and Helen Mann, who share a love for theatre and have provided managerial and artistic leadership since the festival's inception. In a curtain speech on 10 May 1960, following his acclaimed performance in the title role in *King Lear*, the well-known Afrikaans actor André Huguenet expressed his desire for continuing Shakespeare in the community: "I look forward to the time when Port Elizabeth will be known as Stratford-on-Baakens." That vision has led to the production of over 70 plays performed in a variety of venues and organizational structures. The history of Shakespeare in Port Elizabeth, however, goes back much further than 1960.

In 1799, in Fort Frederick, on a hill overlooking the Baakens River, a performance of *Hamlet* was given by bored British officers of the garrison. Waiting for a Napoleonic attack that never came, they saw a perfect Elsinore

Castle in their mist-covered fort. This was the forerunner of open-air theatre in Port Elizabeth. The next recorded event came in 1938 with *A Midsummer Night's Dream*, featuring South Africa's "First Lady of the Theatre," Taubie Kushlik. This was performed next to the swimming bath (pool) in St. George's park and included Helen Baynes (later Helen Mann) as one of the fairies.

A 1950 production of *Twelfth Night* marked the start of the Will Jamieson era and the beginning of a permanent presence of Shakespeare in Port Elizabeth. Jamieson, a native of Algoa Bay, had trained at the Royal Academy of Dramatic Arts in London and returned to his hometown, Port Elizabeth, to apply his talents. The production brought together Helen Baynes and Bruce Mann, who later married. They were instrumental in forming the Amateur Theatre Guild in 1951, paving the way for the Port Elizabeth Theatre Guild in 1958; this organization, in turn, gave birth to the Shakespearean festival in 1960. Jamieson effectively raised the standards of amateur theatre to the point that his friend André Huguenet, a professional actor, enthusiastically accepted Jamieson's invitation to play Lear. Unfortunately, Lear was Huguenet's last major role, as he died two years later at age 56. His idea, however, lived on, and Shakespeare flourished in Port Elizabeth with Jamieson as the pace-setting director. After Jamieson moved away in 1965, various directors were used, including Helen Mann who demonstrated a talent for directing Shakespeare, beginning with *Romeo and Juliet* in 1969. Schoolgirl Alice Krige played Juliet, later achieving success on the stages of London and New York, as well as in the film *Chariots of Fire*.

In 1970, professional actor/director Leslie French agreed to direct *Twelfth Night* and to play Feste to celebrate the sesquicentennial of the arrival of the British settlers. He brought experience in open-air theatre that he had gained at Maynardville in Cape Town and at the **Open-Air Theatre**, **Regent's Park** in London. Realizing that PESF needed but could not afford its own theatre, French suggested the idea of an outdoor amphitheatre. A 1971 production of *The Merchant of Venice* at Happy Valley, with French as Shylock, drew thousands of people, despite unfavorable weather and unsuitable conditions. A more suitable site was found in 1972 at St. George's Park, which has been PESF's home ever since. That year French directed *A Midsummer Night's Dream*, attracting 6,000 people to the Mannville open-air theatre.

In 1975, French returned to England, and the ongoing directorial responsibilities fell upon Helen Mann. She has impressed audiences with her imaginative exploitation of the open-air setting. She has also played such major roles as Goneril, Viola, Portia, and Lady Macbeth. The PESF's 25th anniversary was marked by a performance of *King Lear* with John Hussey. From 1975 to 1985, the PESF attracted 100,000 theatergoers of all population groups, including busloads of schoolchildren. Bruce Mann, long-time president and executive director of the PESF, says that "a strong nucleus of amateur actors and a large measure of enthusiasm account for continued productions." Volunteers take care of lighting, sound, and other technical matters with the help of the Cape Performing Arts Board. "Tickets have not gone up in price since the early days, but finances are sound, thanks to prudent administration and the good will of sponsors."

The Mannville open-air theatre is named after Bruce and Helen Mann. Laurence Wright and Lin Gubb have described the location: "The choice of site in St. George's was an inspired one. Its natural beauty and seclusion, dominated by two proud Norfolk pines, shroud a raked and terraced auditorium for some five hundred people. Masked by shrubs and trees, the lighting and sound control centres are unobtrusively housed, as is the stone-clad and ample dressing-room block." The entrance to the theatre is equally lovely. A path, bordered by flower beds, lush shrubs, and trees, leads to a statuette of Ariel atop a large boulder, keeping watch over the flowers. Dreaming of the future, Wright and Gubb have proposed a 1999 revival of *Hamlet* at Fort Frederick to bring 200 years of Shakespeare in Port Elizabeth full circle.

Production History: 1960: *Lr., Rope, Our Town*; 1961: *The Lark, Tea and Sympathy*; 1962: *Five Finger Exercise, Rape of the Belt, Death of a Salesman*; 1963: *The Queen and the Rebels, Ham.*; 1964: *Shr., Who's Afraid of Virginia Woolf?*; 1965: *Ado*; 1966: *The Mikado*; 1967: *Oklahoma, The King and I*; 1968: *Brigadoon, Ali Baba and the Forty Thieves*; 1969: *The Student Prince, Rom.*; 1970: *The Desert Song, TN*; 1971: *MV, Oliver!*; 1972: *Everyman, MND, The Sound of Music*; 1973: *AYL, Carmen, Me and My Girl, Tinker's Curse*; 1974: *Tmp., The Lark*; 1975: *Mac., Children of the Wolf, No, No, Nanette, The Queen and the Rebels, The Zeal of Thy House*; 1976: *Shr., Antigone, Veronica's Room*; 1977: *Ham., Sorry, Wrong Number, Our Town, A Phoenix Too Frequent/All Roads Lead to Rome*; 1978: *Oth., Point of Departure, The Crucible*; 1979: *Ado, Night Must Fall*; 1980: *Rom., The Effect of Gamma Rays on Man-in-the-Moon Marigolds*; 1981: *TN, Bosoms and Neglect*; 1982: *MND, A Voyage Round My Father*; 1983: *AYL, Shrivings*; 1984: *Tmp., The Gingerbread Lady*; 1985: *Lr., Our Town* (bi-lingual); 1986: *Mac., Old World, Monday After the Miracle*; 1987: *Ham., Torch Song Trilogy*; 1988: *R3, I'm Not Rappaport*; 1989: *Shr., Passion*; 1990: *MV, The Lark*; 1991: *Rom.*; 1992: *MND*; 1993: *TN*.

Research Resources: Archives for the Port Elizabeth Shakespeare Festival are maintained by Bruce Mann.

Goosen, Helena. "The Bard of the Baakens." *South African Panorama* (September 1985): 18-23.

Hamber, John. *The Port Elizabeth Shakespearean Festival: An Appreciation and a Tribute*. Published privately, 1981.

Jackson, George. "The Port Elizabeth Shakespearean Festival: 25th Anniversary." *Scenario* 50 (March 1985): 28-33.
Wright, Laurence, and Lin Gubb. "A Tribute to 'Stratford-on-Baakens': Thirty Years of the Port Elizabeth Shakespearean Festival." *Shakespeare in Southern Africa*, vol. 3 (1989): 1-8.

Cindy Melby Phaneuf

SPAIN

COMPAÑÍA SHAKESPEARE DE ESPAÑA. MAIL: Colegiata 11, 28012 Madrid, Spain. SITE: varies. ADMINISTRATION: 91/369-27-80. BOX OFFICE: varies. ADMISSION: varies. SEASON: summer touring. PRINCIPAL STAFF: Eusebio Lázaro, producing artistic director; Marina Saura, associate director. FACILITY: varies. STATUS: professional. ANNUAL BUDGET: 1.5 million pesetas (average). ANNUAL ATTENDANCE: 20,000 (average tour). FOUNDED: 1978, Eusebio Lázaro.

The origins of Spain's only professional Shakespeare company can be traced back to 1978, when Eusebio Lázaro, a well-known Madrid actor who had studied in London, first put together a symposium on Shakespeare with some professors and directors from England. The event was open to about 25 young professional actors who spent approximately two weeks studying a Shakespeare play and working on scenes from it. Over the years since then, Lázaro has created several more such symposia *cum* workshops.

Lázaro's next step was to translate some Shakespeare sequences into Spanish to create a dramatic collage called *Power and Villainy*, the production that launched his **Compañía Shakespeare de España** (CSE). A similar project in 1989, *La Rueda de fuego* (*Wheel of Fire*) was directed by Clifford Williams and toured to the Roman theatre in Mérida, among other places. The latter collage drew upon six plays: *Julius Caesar, Richard II, Richard III, Macbeth, Hamlet*, and *Othello*. Lázaro has described the production this way:

I found three scenes from *Julius Caesar* in which Cassius is plotting against Caesar. Those scenes give us the play's through-line about power. After Caesar's death, we have a narrator take us to Richard II's deposition scene. It's a jump to the middle ages, but the problem is the same. After Richard II loses his crown, a narrator and music take us to the world of Richard III, then to a different kind of ambition in *Hamlet*, and yet another aspect in *Macbeth*. We do it all with seven actors and a musician.

For his full-scale productions of *Richard III* in 1983 and *Coriolanus* in 1986, Lázaro himself did the translations, which he tried to make as faithful as possible to the original, and he played the title roles as well. He negotiated to bring in English directors, Clifford Williams for *Richard III* and Toby Robertson for *Coriolanus*. *Richard III* played to packed houses in Madrid for a month and was seen by 18,000 people. *Coriolanus* played to a capacity audience of 3,000 in the Roman theatre in Mérida, then toured to Málaga, Barcelona, and Greece.

Lázaro has summarized his approach to Shakespeare as finding a metaphor for the play and then concentrating on telling the story with a sense of rhythm equivalent to the original English. Each play makes its own production demands, but Lázaro admits to a predilection for natural materials like real wood and primitive fabrics. He sees a huge demand for Shakespeare among Madrid audiences, and yet Shakespeare plays are not commercially viable because the size of the casts means that even sell-out houses will not cover production expenses. That is why he has concentrated on summer touring to the large outdoor amphitheatres. Between productions, Lázaro keeps only an office staff of three. For the future, he hopes to open a theatre production centre where Shakespeare can be more frequently performed in the symposium format.

Production History: **1980**: *Power and Villainy*; **1983**: *R3*; **1986**: *Cor.*; **1989**: *La Rueda de fuego*.

Research Resources: Rosana Torres, "El más moderno Shakespeare," *El País* (Madrid, 4 July 1986): 12; also (11 July 1986): 25.

Interview: 8 July 1991.
Felicia Hardison Londré

SWITZERLAND
(See GERMAN-LANGUAGE SHAKESPEARE)

Appendix A

List of Abbreviations

Abbreviations for Shakespeare's Plays

Ado	*Much Ado About Nothing*
Ant.	*Antony and Cleopatra*
AWW	*All's Well That Ends Well*
AYL	*As You Like It*
Cor.	*Coriolanus*
Cym.	*Cymbeline*
Err.	*The Comedy of Errors*
Ham.	*Hamlet*
1H4	*Henry IV, Part 1*
2H4	*Henry IV, Part 2*
H5	*Henry V*
1H6	*Henry VI, Part 1*
2H6	*Henry VI, Part 2*
3H6	*Henry VI, Part 3*
H8	*Henry VIII*
JC	*Julius Ceasar*
Jn.	*King John*
LLL	*Love's Labour's Lost*
Lr.	*King Lear*
Mac.	*Macbeth*
MM	*Measure for Measure*
MND	*Midsummer Night's Dream*
MV	*The Merchant of Venice*
Oth.	*Othello*
Per.	*Pericles*
R2	*Richard II*
R3	*Richard III*

Rom.	*Romeo and Juliet*
Shr.	*The Taming of the Shrew*
TGV	*The Two Gentlemen of Verona*
Tim.	*Timon of Athens*
Tit.	*Titus Andronicus*
Tmp.	*The Tempest*
TN	*Twelfth Night*
TNK	*The Two Noble Kinsmen*
Tro.	*Troilus and Cressida*
Wiv.	*The Merry Wives of Windsor*
WT	*The Winter's Tale*

Unions/Contract Abbreviations

AEA	Actors' Equity Association
ATPAM	Association of Theatrical Press Agents and Managers
BAT	Bay Area Theatre contract
CAT	Chicago Area Theatre contract
COST	Council on Stock Theatre contract
CORST	Council on Resident Stock Theatre contract
IATSE	International Alliance of Theatrical Stage Employees
LOA	Letter of Agreement
LORT	League of Resident Theatres contract
SPT	Small Professional Theatre contract
SSDC	Society of Stage Directors and Choreographers
TYA	Theatre for Young Audiences contract
U/RTA	University/Resident Theatre Association contract
USA	United Scenic Artists

Organizations and Associations

ATHE	Association for Theatre in Higher Education
BAFA	British Arts Festival Association
ECTC	Eastern Central Theatre Conference
FEDAPT	Foundation for the Extension and Development of the American Professional Theatre
MATC	Mid-America Theatre Conference
NEA	National Endowment for the Arts
NEH	National Endowment for the Humanities
PACT	Professional Association of Canadian Theatre
SETC	Southeastern Theatre Conference
TCG	Theatre Communications Group
USITT	United States Institute for Theatre Technology

List of Companies and Festivals by Geographical Location

United States of America

Alabama
Alabama Shakespeare Festival (Montgomery)
Daphne Renaissance Festival (Daphne)

Arizona
Southwest Shakespeare Festival (Phoenix)

California
ACTER (A Center for Theatre, Education and Research) (Santa Barbara)
California Shakespeare Festival (Berkeley)
Carmel Shake-speare Festival (Carmel)
Globe Playhouse of Los Angeles/ Shakespeare Society of America (Los Angeles)
Grove Shakespeare Festival (Garden Grove)
Los Angeles Shakespeare Company (Van Nuys)
Marin Shakespeare Company (San Rafael)
New Shakespeare Company (San Francisco)
Ojai Shakespeare Festival Theatre Company (Ojai)
Old Globe Theatre (San Diego)
Reduced Shakespeare Company (Los Angeles)
San Francisco Shakespeare Festival (San Francisco)
Shakespeare at Benbow Lake (Garberville)
Shakespeare Festival/LA (Los Angeles)
Shakespeare in the Park (Chico)
Shakespeare Orange County (Orange)
Shakespeare Santa Cruz (Santa Cruz)
Shakespeare Theatre Arts Repertory (Campbell)
Sonoma Valley Shakespeare Festival (Sonoma)
Sonoma Vintage Theatre (Sonoma)

Sunnyvale Summer Repertory (Sunnyvale)
Will Geer Theatricum Botanicum (Topanga)

Colorado
Colorado Shakespeare Festival (Boulder)
Lake Dillon Shakespeare Festival (Dillon)
Theatreworks Shakespeare Festival (Colorado Springs)

Connecticut
American Shakespeare Theatre (Stratford)

District Of Columbia
The Shakespeare Theatre (Washington)

Florida
American Stage in the Park (St. Petersburg)
Florida Shakespeare Festival (Coral Gables)
New River Shakespeare Festival (Fort Lauderdale)
Orlando–UCF Shakespeare Festival (Orlando)
Palm Beach Shakespeare Festival (Jupiter/Palm Beach)

Georgia
Atlanta Shakespeare Company (Atlanta)
Georgia Shakespeare Festival (Atlanta)

Hawaii
Hilo Shakespeare Festival (Hilo)

Idaho
Idaho Shakespeare Festival (Boise)

Illinois
Illinois Shakespeare Festival (Normal)
Oak Park Festival Theatre (Oak Park)
Shakespeare on the Green (Lake Forest)
Shakespeare Repertory (Chicago)

Iowa
Iowa Shakespeare Project (West Des Moines)

Kentucky
Devou Park Summer Classics Theatre (Covington)
Kentucky Shakespeare Festival (Louisville)
Lexington Shakespeare Festival (Lexington)

Maine
Camden Shakespeare Company (Camden)
Theatre at Monmouth (Monmouth)

Maryland
Shakespeare on Wheels (Baltimore)
Travelling Shakespeare Company (St. Mary's City)

Massachusetts
The Company of Women (Boston)
Ever Theater (Somerville)
Hampshire Shakespeare Company (Amherst)
Publick Theatre (Boston)
Roxbury Outreach Shakespeare Experience (ROSE) (Boston)
Shakespeare & Company (Lenox)
Vineyard Playhouse (Vineyard Haven)

Minnesota
Minnesota Shakespeare Company (Minneapolis)

Missouri
Heart of America Festival of Greater Kansas City (Kansas City)
St. Louis Shakespeare Company (St. Louis)

Montana
Montana Shakespeare in the Parks (Bozeman)

Nebraska
Nebraska Shakespeare Festival (Omaha)

Nevada
Shakespeare at Sand Harbor (Incline Village, NV)

New Jersey
Haworth Shakespeare Festival (Haworth)
New Jersey Shakespeare Festival (Madison)

New Mexico
Shakespeare in Santa Fe (Santa Fe)

New York
Actors Shakespeare Company (Albany)
American Globe Theatre (New York City)

Arden Party (New York City)
Blackfriars Traveling Shakespeare Theatre (Port Jefferson)
Hofstra University Annual Shakespeare Festival (Hempstead)
Hudson Valley Shakespeare Festival (Cold Spring-on-Hudson)
King's County Shakespeare Company (Brooklyn)
National Shakespeare Company (New York City)
New York Renaissance Festival (Tuxedo)
New York Shakespeare Festival (New York City)
Oasis Theatre Company (New York City)
Riverside Shakespeare Company (New York City)
Shakespeare in Delaware Park (Buffalo)
Sterling Renaissance Festival (Sterling)
Theatre for a New Audience (New York City)

North Carolina
North Carolina Shakespeare Festival (High Point)

Ohio
Actors' Summer Theatre (Columbus)
Great Lakes Theatre Festival (Cleveland)
Shakespeare at Stan Hywet (Akron)

Oklahoma
Oklahoma Shakespearean Festival (Durant)
Oklahoma Shakespeare in the Park (Edmond)
Renegade Shakespeare Company (Norman)
Sooner Shakespeare Festival (Norman)

Oregon
Oregon Shakespeare Festival (Ashland)
Tygres Heart Shakespeare Company (Portland)

Pennsylvania
Pennsylvania Shakespeare Festival (Center Valley)
Philadelphia Shakespeare in the Park (Philadelphia)
Three Rivers Shakespeare Festival (Pittsburgh)

Rhode Island
The Rhode Island Shakespeare Theatre (Newport)
Westerly Shakespeare in the Park (Westerly)

Tennessee
Nashville Shakespeare Festival (Nashville)

Texas
Austin Shakespeare Festival (Austin)
Globe of the Great Southwest (Odessa)
Houston Shakespeare Festival (Houston)
Post Summer Shakespeare Festival (Garza Theatre) (Post)
San Antonio Shakespeare Festival (San Antonio)
Shakespeare at Winedale (Winedale)
Shakespeare-by-the-Book Festival (Houston)
Shakespeare Festival of Dallas (Dallas)
Shakespeare in the Park (Fort Worth)
Texas Shakespeare Festival (Kilgore)

Utah
Utah Shakespearean Festival (Cedar City)

Vermont
Champlain Shakespeare Festival (Burlington)

Virginia
Shakespeare at the Ruins (Barboursville)
Shakespeare by the Sea (Virginia Beach)
Shenadoah Shakespeare Express (Dayton)
Virginia Shakespeare Festival (Williamsburg)

Washington
Seattle Shakespeare Festival (Seattle)
Washington Shakespeare Festival (Olympia)

Wisconsin
American Players Theatre (Sping Green)
Wisconsin Shakespeare Festival (Platteville)

International

Australia
Bell Shakespeare Company (Sydney)
Grin and Tonic Theatre Troupe (Clayfield)

Austria
(See German-Language Shakespeare)

Canada
British Columbia
Bard on the Beach (Vancouver)

Manitoba
Shakespeare in the Park, Assiniboine Theatre (Winnipeg, Manitoba)

Ontario
Dream in High Park (Toronto)
Stratford Festival of Canada (Stratford, Ontario)

Saskatchewan
Shakespeare on the Saskatchewan Festival (Saskatoon)

China
China Shakespeare Festival (Shanghai and Beijing)

France
Amis Du Jardin Shakespeare Du Pré Catelan, Les (Paris)
Footsbarn Travelling Theatre Company (Hérisson)
Shakespeare en Avignon (Villeneuve-les-Avignon)

German-Language Shakespeare
Bremer Shakespeare Company (Bremen, Germany)
(Very brief listings of several Austrian, German, and Swiss companies follow entry on
Bremer Shakespeare Company, alaphabetically by city under respective countries.)

Great Britain
Abbey Shakespeare Players (Dyfed, Wales)
Cheek by Jowl (London)
Chiltern Shakespeare Company (Buckinghamshire)
D. P. Productions (Nottingham)
English Shakespeare Company (London)
Ludlow Festival (Ludow)
Minack Open-Air Theatre (Penzance, Cornwall)
Open Air Theatre / New Shakespeare Company (London)
Old Vic (London)
Renaissance Theatre Company (London)
Royal Shakespeare Company (Stratford-Upon-Avon)
Shakespeare at Sheldon (Chippenham, Wiltshire)
Stamford Shakespeare Company (Little Casterton, Stamford)
Theatre Set-up, Ltd. (London)
Young Vic Company (London)

Japan
Shakespeare Theatre(Tokyo)
Tokyo Panasonic Globe (Tokyo)

New Zealand
Outdoor Summer Shakespeare (Auckland)
Stratford Shakespeare Festival (Stratford)
Victoria University of Wellington Summer Shakespeare (Wellington)

South Africa
Port Elizabeth Shakespeare Festival (Port Elizabeth)

Spain
Compañía Shakespeare De España (Madrid)

Switzerland
(See German-Language Shakespeare)

Appendix C

List of Companies and Festivals in Alphabetical Order

Abbey Shakespeare Players (Dyfed, Wales, GB)
ACTER -A Center for Theatre, Education & Research (Santa Barbara, CA)
Actors Shakespeare Company (Albany, NY)
Actors' Summer Theatre (Columbus, OH)
Alabama Shakespeare Festival (Montgomery, AL)
American Globe Theatre (New York, NY)
American Players Theatre (Spring Green, WI)
American Shakespeare Theatre (Stratford, CT)
American Stage in the Company (St. Petersburg, FL)
Amis du Jardin Shakespeare du Pré Catelan, Les (Paris, France)
Arden Party (New York City, NY)
Atlanta Shakespeare Company (Atlanta, GA)
Austin Shakespeare Festival (Austin, TX)
Bard on the Beach (Vancouver, British Columbia, Canada)
Bell Shakespeare Company (Sydney, Australia)
Blackfriars Traveling Shakespeare Theatre (Port Jefferson, NY)
Bremer Shakespeare Company (Bremen, Germany)
California Shakespeare Festival (Berkeley, CA)
Camden Shakespeare Company (Camden, ME)
Carmel Shake-speare Festival (Carmel, CA)
Champlain Shakespeare Festival (Burlington, VT)
Cheek by Jowl (London, England)
Chiltern Shakespeare Company (Buckinghamshire, GB)
China Shakespeare Festival (Shanghai and Beijing)
Colorado Shakespeare Festival (Boulder, CO)

Company of Women (Boston, MA)
Compañía Shakespeare de España (Madrid, Spain)
D. P. Productions (Nottingham, GB)
Daphne Renaissance Festival (Daphne, AL)
Devou Park Summer Classics Theatre (Covington, KY)
Dream in High Park (Toronto, Ontario, Canada)
English Shakespeare Company (London, England)
Ever Theater (Somerville, MA)
Florida Shakespeare Festival (Coral Gables, FL)
Footsbarn Travelling Theatre Company (Hérisson, France)
Georgia Shakespeare Festival (Atlanta, GA)
Globe of the Great Southwest (Odessa TX)
Globe Playhouse of Los Angeles / Shakespeare Society of America (Los Angeles, CA)
Great Lakes Theatre Festival (Cleveland,OH)
Grin and Tonic Theatre Troupe (Clayfield, Australia)
Grove Shakespeare Festival (Garden Grove, CA)
Hampshire Shakespeare Company (Amherst, MA)
Haworth Shakespeare Festival (Haworth, NJ)
Heart of America Festival of Greater Kansas City (Kansas City, MO)
Hilo Shakespeare Festival (Hilo, HI)
Hofstra University Annual Shakespeare Festival (Hempstead, NY)
Houston Shakespeare Festival (Houston, TX)
Hudson Valley Shakespeare Festival (Cold Spring-on-Hudson, NY)
Idaho Shakespeare Festival (Boise, ID)
Illinois Shakespeare Festival (Normal,IL)
Iowa Shakespeare Project (West Des Moines, IA)
Kentucky Shakespeare Festival (Louisville, KY)
King's County Shakespeare Company (Brooklyn, NY)
Lake Dillon Shakespeare Festival (Dillon, CO)
Lexington Shakespeare Festival (Lexington, KY)
Los Angeles Shakespeare Company (Van Nuys, CA)
Ludlow Festival (Ludlow, Shropshire, England)
Marin Shakespeare Company (San Rafael, CA)
Minack Open-Air Theatre (Penzance, Cornwall, England)
Minnesota Shakespeare Company (Minneapolis, MN)
Montana Shakespeare in The Parks (Bozeman, MT)
Nashville Shakespeare Festival (Nashville, TN)
National Shakespeare Company (New York, NY)
Nebraska Shakespeare Festival (Omaha, NE)
New Jersey Shakespeare Festival (Madison, NJ)
New River Shakespeare Festival (Fort Lauderdale, FL)
New Shakespeare Company (San Francisco, CA)
New York Renaissance Festival (Tuxedo, NY)
New York Shakespeare Festival (New York, NY)

North Carolina Shakespeare Festival (High Point, NC)
Oak Park Festival Theatre (Oak Park, IL)
Oasis Theatre Company (New York, NY)
Ojai Festival Theatre Company (Ojai, CA)
Oklahoma Shakespeare in the Park (Edmond, OK)
Oklahoma Shakespearean Festival (Durant, OK)
Old Globe Theatre (San Diego, CA)
Old Vic Theatre (London, England)
Open Air Theatre, New Shakespeare Company (London, England)
Oregon Shakespeare Festival (Ashland, OR)
Orlando - UCF Shakespeare Festival (Orlando, FL)
Outdoor Summer Shakespeare (Auckland, New Zealand)
Palm Beach Shakespeare Festival (Jupiter/Palm Beach, FL)
Pennsylvania Shakespeare Festival (Center Valley, PA)
Philadelphia Shakespeare in the Park (Philadelphia, PA)
Port Elizabeth Shakespeare Festival (Port Elizabeth, South Africa)
Post Summer Shakespeare Festival (Garza Theatre) (Post, TX)
Publick Theatre (Boston, MA)
Reduced Shakespeare Company (Los Angeles, CA)
Renaissance Theatre Company (London, England)
Renegade Shakespeare Company (Norman, OK)
Rhode Island Shakespearean Theatre (Newport, RI)
Riverside Shakespeare Company (New York, NY)
Roxbury Outreach Shakespeare Experience (ROSE) (Boston, MA)
Royal Shakespeare Company (Stratford-Upon-Avon, England)
San Antonio Shakespeare Festival (San Antonio, TX)
San Francisco Shakespeare Festival (San Francisco, CA)
Seattle Shakespeare Festival (Seattle, WA)
Shakespeare and Company (Lenox, MA)
Shakespeare at Benbow Lake (Garberville, CA)
Shakespeare at Sand Harbor (Incline Village, NV)
Shakespeare at Sheldon (Chippenham, Wiltshire, GB)
Shakespeare at Stan Hywet (Akron, OH)
Shakespeare at the Ruins (Barboursville, VA)
Shakespeare at Winedale (Winedale, TX)
Shakespeare-by-the-Book Festival (Houston, TX)
Shakespeare-by-the-Sea (Virginia Beach, VA)
Shakespeare en Avignon (Avignon, France)
Shakespeare Festival of Dallas (Dallas, TX)
Shakespeare Festival/LA (Los Angeles, CA)
Shakespeare in Delaware Park (Buffalo, NY)
Shakespeare in Santa Fe (Santa Fe, NM)
Shakespeare in the Park, Assiniboine Theatre (Winnipeg, Manitoba, Canada)
Shakespeare in the Park (Chico, CA)

Shakespeare in the Park (Fort Worth, TX)
Shakespeare on the Green (Lake Forest, IL)
Shakespeare on the Saskatchewan Festival (Saskatoon, Saskatchewan, Canada)
Shakespeare on Wheels (Baltimore, MD)
Shakespeare Orange County (Orange, CA)
Shakespeare Repertory (Chicago, IL)
Shakespeare Santa Cruz (Santa Cruz, CA)
Shakespeare Theatre (Tokyo, Japan)
Shakespeare Theatre (Washington, DC)
Shakespeare Theatre Arts Repertory (Campbell, CA)
Shenadoah Shakespeare Express (Dayton, VA)
Sonoma Valley Shakespeare Festival (Sonoma, CA)
Sonoma Vintage Theatre (Sonoma,CA)
Sooner Shakespeare Festival (Norman, OK)
Southwest Shakespeare Festival (Phoenix, AZ)
St. Louis Shakespeare Company (St. Louis, MO)
Stamford Shakespeare Company (Little Casterton, Stamford, Lincolnshire, England)
Sterling Renaissance Festival (Sterling, NY)
Stratford Festival of Canada (Stratford, Ontario, Canada)
Stratford Shakespeare Festival (Stratford, New Zealand)
Sunnyvale Summer Repertory (Sunnyvale, CA)
Texas Shakespeare Festival (Kilgore, TX)
Theatre at Monmouth (Monmouth, ME)
Theatre for a New Audience (New York, NY)
Theatre Set-Up, Ltd. (London, England)
Theatreworks Shakespeare Festival (Colorado Springs, CO)
Three Rivers Shakespeare Festival (Pittsburgh, PA)
Tokyo Panasonic Globe (Tokyo, Japan)
Travelling Shakespeare Company (St. Mary's City, MD)
Tygres Heart Shakespeare Company (Portland, OK)
Utah Shakespearean Festival (Cedar City, UT)
Victoria University of Wellington Summer Shakespeare (Wellington, New Zealand)
Vineyard Playhouse (Vineyard Haven, MA)
Virginia Shakespeare Festival (Williamsburg, VA)
Washington Shakespeare Festival (Olympia, WA)
Westerly Shakespeare in the Park (Westerly, RI)
Will Geer Theatricum Botanicum (Topanga, CA)
Wisconsin Shakespeare Festival (Platteville, WI)
Young Vic Company (London, England)

Selected Bibliography

Information on the location of archival material and citations for important reference works are provided under Research Resources at the end of each essay entry. Much of the material is archival, and books and other printed materials do not exist for many entries. With few exceptions, the essay entries were based on personally interviewing key company or festival personnel, touring the physical plants, observing audiences, examining publicity materials, programs, and annual reports, and reviewing productions first hand. Relevant bibliographies have been included, but, in the case of established companies and festivals with long production histories, such as the Royal Shakespeare Company, the New York Shakespeare Festival, or the Stratford Festival of Canada, we have included basic reference works only.

In some cases, reviews that appeared in local newspapers have been cited from clippings pasted in scrapbooks that are located in the business office of the company or festival or are in the possession or private collection of the artistic director or founder. We have made an effort to list the location of such materials. Some productions have been reviewed in periodicals that cover the larger established Shakespeare companies and festivals, like the Stratford Festival or the Oregon Shakespeare Festival. These important sources are available in most libraries and include *Shakespeare Bulletin, Shakespeare Quarterly*, published by the Shakespeare Association of America, *The Shakespeare Newsletter, Shakespeare Survey, Theatre Journal,* and *American Theatre*. Others include: *TheatreWeek; Callboard; Theatre Survey; Western European Stages; Asian Theatre; Plays and Players; Plays International; Theatre Research International; Theatre History Studies; Slavic and East European Performance; Studies in American Drama, 1945-Present; Theatre Research in Canada/Recherches Théâtrales au Canada;* the Colorado

Shakespeare Festival's *On-Stage Studies*; *Australian Drama Studies* (Australia and New Zealand); *Canadian Theatre Review* (Canada); *Theater Heute*; *Theater der Zeit* (Germany); and the *Jahrbuch der Deutschen Shakespeare-Gesellschaft* (Weimar), *Shakespeare Studies*, published by the Shakespeare Society of Japan (501 Kenkyusha Building, 2-9 Surugadai, Kanda, Chiyoda-ku, Tokyo 101), and *Shakespeare News from Japan*, published by the Komazawa University Shakespeare Institute in Tokyo: *Estreno: Cuadernos del Teatro Español contemporáneo* (Spain), and *Latin American Theatre Review*.

The following selected bibliography includes books and a few selected articles from periodicals that may be of interest for further reading and research on the subject of Shakespeare companies and festivals, as well as a few books with historical backgound information on the subject in English and other languages. The reader should refer to the Research Resources for the individual company or festival for detailed information on the location of archival material. *Shakespeare Quarterly* publishes a comprehensive "Bibliography" issue (number 5) each year; this contains 4,000 to 5,000 entries in all areas of Shakespeare studies, including reviews of performances.

AFRICA

Al-Shetawi, Mahmoud F. "Shakespeare in Arabic: An Overview." *New Comparison* 8 (Autumn 1989): 114-26

Goosen, Helena. "The Bard of the Baakens." *South African Panorama* (September 1985): 18-23.

Hamber, John. *The Port Elizabeth Shakespearean Festival: An Appreciation and a Tribute*. Published privately, 1981.

Jackson, George. "The Port Elizabeth Shakespearean Festival: 25th Anniversary." *Scenario* 50 (March 1985): 28-33.

Leiter, Samuel L., ed. *Shakespeare Around the Globe: A Guide to Notable Postwar Revivals*. New York: Greenwood Press, 1986.

Lindfors, Bernth. "Shakespeare and Nigerian Drama." *Proceedings of the 6th Congress of the International Comparative Literature Association*. Stuttgart: Bieber, 1975.

Wright, Laurence, and Lin Gubb. "A Tribute to 'Stratford-on-Baakens': Thirty Years of the Port Elizabeth Shakespearean Festival." *Shakespeare in Southern Africa*, vol. 3 (1989): 1-8.

ASIA–SOUTH PACIFIC

Brockbank, J. Philip. "Shakespeare Renaisance in China." *Shakespeare Quarterly* 39 (Summer 1988): 195-204.

Cao, Shujun, and Sun Fuliang. *Shakespeare on the Chinese Stage (Shashibiya zai zhongguo wutaishang)*. Harbin Publishing House, 1989.

Chira, Susan. "Shakespeare Plays the Globe Theater, in Tokyo." *New York Times* (31 May 1988): C15, C18.

Daconte, Eduardo Marceles. "Shakespeare en China." *Magazin Dominical* 174 (27 July 1986): 5-9.

Deguchi Norio, *Shakespeare wa tomaranai*. Tokyo: Kodansha, 1988.

Fan, Shen. "Shakespeare in China: The Merchant of Venice." *Asian Theatre Journal* (Spring 1988): 23-37.

Fujita, Minoru, and Arata Isozaki. *The Globe: A Shakespearean scholar talks with the architect of the Tokyo Globe*. Tokyo: Shinjuku-Nishitoyama Development Co., 1988.

Kennedy, Dennis, ed. *Foreign Shakespeare: Contemporary Performance*. Cambridge: Cambridge University Press, 1993.

Kynge, James. "Shakespeare in China." *Plays and Players* (July 1986): 16-17.

Leiter, Samuel, ed. *Shakespeare Around the Globe: A Guide to Notable Postwar Revivals*. New York: Greenwood Press, 1986.

Li, Ruru. "Chinese Traditional Theatre and Shakespeare." *Asian Theatre Journal* (Spring 1988): 38-48.

Lin, Yang. "China Makes Much Ado About the Bard." *Beijing Review* (26 May 1986): 30-31.

Office of the 1st China Shakespeare Festival. *Newsletter of the 1st China Shakespeare Festival* (*Shoujie zhongguo shashibiya xijujie jianbao*), No. 1-7. Shanghai: The Publishing House of Shanghai Culture & Art Weekly, 1986.

Shakespeare Society of China. *Shakespeare in China* (*Shashibiya zai zhongguo*). Shanghai: Shanghai Literature & Art Publishing House, 1987.

Sisson, C. J. *Shakespeare in India: Popular Adaptations on the Bombay Stage*. London: The Shakespeare Association, 1926.

Tsai, Chin. "Teaching and Directing in China: Chinese Theatre Revisited." *Asian Theatre Journal* (Spring 1986): 118-31.

Weiss, Afred. "The Edinburgh Festival, 1987." *Shakespeare Quarterly* (Spring 1988): 79-89 [on the *kunju Macbeth*].

Yang, Daniel S. P. "Theatre in Post-Cultural Revolution China: A Report Based on Field Research in the Fall and Winter of 1981." *Asian Theatre Journal* (Spring 1984): 90-103.

Yeh, Chen Chun. "A hit, palpable hit in China." [London] *The Times* (2 January 1982): 6.

Yu, Weijie. "Topicality and Typicality: The Acceptance of Shakespeare in China." In *The Dramatic Touch of Difference: Theatre, Own and Foreign*, ed. Erika Fischer-Lichte. Tübingen: Gunter Narr Verlag, 1990.

Zha, Peide, and Tian, Jia. "Shakespeare in Traditional Chinese Operas." *Shakespeare Quarterly* (Summer 1988): 204-211.

Zhang, Yike. "Traditional Opera: Challenge and Response." *China Reconstructs* (September 1987): 19-23.

Zhu, Zhenglian. "Local opera jumps on Shakespeare theme." *China Daily* (25 February 1986): 5.

EUROPE

Addenbrooke, David. *The Royal Shakespeare Company, 1960-1972.* London: William Kimber, 1974.

Ahrens, Rüdiger. "The Critical Reception of Shakespeare's Tragedies in Twentieth-Century Germany." *Shakespeare: Text, Subtext and Context,* ed. Ronald Dotterer. Selinsgrove, PA: Susquehanna University Press, 1989.

And, Metin. "Shakespeare in Turkey." *Theatre Research/Recherches Théâtrales* 6:2 (1964): 75-84.

Beauman, Sally. *The Royal Shakespeare Company: A History of Ten Decades.* Oxford: Oxford University Press, 1982.

Berry, Ralph. *On Directing Shakespeare: Interviews with Contemporary Directors.* 2nd ed. London: Croom Helm, 1989.

Berry, Ralph, and Christian Jauslin. *Shakespeare Inszenieren.* Basel, 1978.

Bogdanov, Michael and Michael Pennington. *The English Shakespeare Company: The Story of the Wars of the Roses, 1986-1989.* London: Nick Hern Books, 1990. (*The Wars of the Roses* is available on seven videocassettes from Films for the Humanities, P.O. Box 2053, Princeton, NJ 08543-2053.)

Bragaglia, Leonardo. *Shakespeare in Italia: Personaggi ed interpreti: vita scenica del teatro di Guglielmo Shakespeare in Italia (1792-1973).* Roma: Trevi, 1973.

Branagh, Kenneth. *Beginning.* London: Chatto & Windus, 1989.

Brock, Susan, and Marian J. Pringle. *The Shakespeare Memorial Theatre, 1919-1945.* Cambridge: 1984.

Chambers, Colin. *Other Spaces: New Theatre and the RSC.* London: Eyre Methuen, 1980.

Chatenet, Jean. *Shakespeare sur la scène francaise depuis 1940.* Paris: Les Lettres modernes, 1962.

Chesire, D. F., Sean McCarthy and Hillary Norris. *The Old Vic Refurbished.* London: The Old Vic Limited, 1983.

Day, Muriel C., and J. C. Trewin. *The Shakespeare Memorial Theatre.* London: J. M. Dent & Sons, 1932.

Deelman, Christian. *The Great Shakespeare Jubilee.* New York: Viking, 1964.

Dutu, Alexander. *Shakespeare in Rumania.* Bucharest: Meridiane, 1964.

Ellis, Ruth. *The Shakespeare Memorial Theatre.* London: Winchester, 1948.

Fifty Years of The Open Air Theatre, Regent's Park [Essays by David Conville, Richard Digby Day, Benny Green, Hubert Gregg, Evan Jones, Ian Talbot, J. C. Trewin, Margaret Wolfit, David William, et al.] London: Abbey Press, 1982.

Findlater, Richard. *Lilian Baylis—the Lady of the Old Vic*. London: Allen Lane, 1975.

Forgách, András. "The Kalap of Voltrinand: A palicsi Shakespeare–fesztivál." [An overview (in Hungarian) of Shakespeare festival in Palic near Subotica in 1986.] *Szinház* 20 (January 1987): 43-48.

Fridén, Ann. *Macbeth in the Swedish Theatre, 1838-1986*. Göteborg: Liber Förlag, 1986.

Gerold, László. "Sekszpiriáde–Palicson." [Shakespeare festival held in Palic in 1986.] *Szinház* 20 (January 1987): 38-42.

Goodwin, John, ed. *Peter Hall's Diaries*. New York: Harper & Row, 1983.

———, ed. *Royal Shakespeare Theatre Company*. London: 1963.

Greenwald, Michael L. *Directions by Indirections: John Barton of the Royal Shakespeare Company*. Newark: University of Delaware Press, 1985.

Gussow, Mel. "Soviet Georgians' Essential 'Lear.'" *New York Times* (4 April 1990): B4.

Habicht, Werner. "Shakespeare in 19th-Century Germany: The Making of a Myth." *19th-Century Germany*, ed. M. Eksteins and H. Hammerschidt. Tübingen: 1983.

Habicht, Werner. "Shakespeare in the Third-Reich." *Anglistentag 1984 Passau: Vorträge*, ed. Manfred Pfister. Giessen: 1985.

Hale, Lionel. *The Old Vic 1949-1950*. London: 1950.

Hayman, Ronald. *British Theatre since 1955*. Oxford: Oxford University Press, 1979.

———. *Thr First Thrust: The Chichester Festival Theatre*. London: 1975.

Hemphill, Marie-Louise. *À l'Ombre du Jardin Shakespeare du Pré Catelan*. Paris: Imprimeries Réunies de Bourg, 1990.

Hortmann, Wilhelm. "Changing Modes in *Hamlet* Production: Rediscovering Shakespeare after the Iconoclasts." *Images of Shakespeare: Proceedings of the Third Congress of the International Shakespeare Association, 1986*. ed. W. Habicht, D. J. Palmer, and R. Pringle. Newark: 1988.

———. *Shakespeare on the German Stage. vol.2: 1915-90*. Cambridge: Cambridge University Press, forthcoming.

Jacquot, Jean. "Vers un théâtre du peuple: Shakespeare en France après Copeau et le Cartel des Quatre." *Etudes anglaises* 13: 2 (1960): 216-47.

———. *Shakespeare en France: mises en scène d'hier et d'aujourd'hui*. Paris: Le Tempe, 1964.

Karpinski, Maciej. "Andrzej Wajda's Second Shakespeare." *The Theatre in Poland* 5 (September-October 1990): 14-15.

Kask, Karin. *Shakespeare eesti teatrie*. Tallinn, Estonia: Eesti Riiklik Kirjastus, 1964 [268-72 in English].

Kemp, T. C., and J. C. Trewin. *The Stratford Festival*. London: 1953.

Kennedy, Dennis. *Looking at Shakespeare: A Visual History of Twentieth-Century Performance*. Cambridge: Cambridge University Press, 1993.

―――. ed. *Foreign Shakespeare: Contemporary Performance*. Cambridge: Cambridge University Press, 1993.

Klajn, Hugo. "Shakespeare in Yugoslavia." *Shakespeare Quarterly* 5 (1954): 41-45.

Lambert, J. W. *Drama in Britain: 1964-1973*. Essex: Longman Group, 1974.

Leiter, Samuel, ed. *Shakespeare Around the Globe: A Guide to Notable Postwar Revivals*. New York: Greenwood Press, 1986.

Liebenstein-Kurtz, Ruth, Freifrau von. *Das subventionierte englische Theater: Produktionsbedingungen und Auswirkungen auf das moderne englische Drama (1956-1976): dargestellt am Beispiel der Royal Shakespeare Company, des National Theatre und der English Stage Company*. Tübingen: Narr, 1981.

Lloyd, David, Rosemary King, and Maureen Sykes. *Ludlow Festival: The First Twenty-Five Years, 1960-1984*. Published by Ludlow Festival Society, 1984.

Mullin, Michael, ed. *Theatre at Stratford-upon-Avon: A Catalogue-Index to Productions of the Shakespeare Memorial/Royal Shakespeare Theatre, 1879-1978*. 2 vols. Westport, CT: Greenwood, 1980. (Note: Volume 3, 1979-1990, is currently in press.)

Pokorny, Jaroslav. *Shakespeare in Czechoslovakia*. Prague: Orbis, 1955.

Priestley, Clive. *The Financial Affairs and Financial Prospects of the Royal Opera House, Covent Garden Ltd., and the Royal Shakespeare Company: Report to the Earl of Gowie*. London: H.M.S.O., 1983.

Reade, Simon. *Cheek by Jowl: Ten Years of Celebration*. London: Absolute Classics, 1991.

―――. *Open Air Theatre, Regent's Park: A Celebration of 60 Years*. Abingdon: Abbey Press, 1992.

Roberts, Peter. *The Old Vic Story—A Nation's Theatre 1818-1976*. London: W. H. Allen, 1976.

Rowell, George. *The Old Vic Theatre: A History*. New York: CUP, 1993.

Samarin, Roman, and Alexander Nikolyukin, eds. *Shakespeare in the Soviet Union*, trans. by Avril Pyman. Moscow: Progress Publishers, 1966.

Shapiro, James. "Konnichiwa Shakespeare-san." *TheaterWeek* (22-28 October 1990): 21-23.

Sideris, Joannis. "Shakespeare in Greece." *Theatre Research/Recherches Théâtrales* 6:2 (1964): 85-99.

Taylor, Gary. *Reinventing Shakespeare: A Cultural History, from the Restoration to the Present*. New York: Weidenfield and Nicholson, 1989.

Trewin, J. C. *Shakespeare on the English Stage: 1900-1964*. London: 1964.

―――. *Going to Shakespeare*. London: 1978.

Wells, Stanley W. *Royal Shakespeare*. Manchester: Manchester University Press, 1977.

Williams, Simon. *Shakespeare on the German Stage*. vol. 1: *1586-1914*. Cambridge: Cambridge University Press, 1990.

Williamson, Audrey. *Old Vic Drama, 1*. London: 1950.

Wood, Roger, and Mary Clarke. *Shakespeare at the Old Vic.* 5 vols. London: 1954-1959.

Zarian, Rouben. *Shakespeare and the Armenians.* Yerevan: Armenian Society for Friendship and Cultural Relations with Foreign Countries, 1969.

Zelechova, Nina. Delovaja pojezdka na prazdnik Teatra. *Teat'r* 48 (November 1985): 46-61.

NORTH AMERICA

Berry, Ralph. *On Directing Shakespeare: Interviews with Contemporary Directors.* 2nd ed. London: Croom Helm, 1989.

Bowmer, Angus L. *As I Remember, Adam: An Autobiography of a Festival.* Ashland: Oregon Shakespeare Festival, 1975.

Bowmer, Angus L. *The Ashland Elizabethan Stage.* Ashland: Oregon Shakespeare Festival, 1978.

Brubaker, Edward, and Mary Brubaker. *Golden Fire: The Anniversary Book of the Oregon Shakespearean Festival.* Ashland: Oregon Shakespearean Festival, 1985.

Champion, Larry S. "'Bold to Play?': Shakespeare in North Carolina." In *Shakespeare in the South*, ed. Philip C. Kolin. Jackson: University Press of Mississippi, 1983.

Cole, Wendell. "Myth Makers and the Early Years of the Carmel Forest Theatre." In *Theatre West: Image and Impact*, ed. Dunbar H. Ogden. Amsterdam: Rodopi B.V., 1990.

Cooper, Roberta Krensky. *The American Shakespeare Theatre: Stratford, 1955-1985.* Washington, DC: Folger Shakespeare Library, 1986.

Cousin, Geraldine. "Shakespeare from Scratch: The Footsbarn 'Hamlet' and 'King Lear,'" *New Theatre Quarterly* 1 (February 1985): 105-27.

Dachslager, Earl L. "Shakespeare at the Globe of the Great Southwest." In *Shakespeare in the South*, ed. Philip C. Kolin. (Jackson: University Press of Mississippi, 1983), 264-77.

Epstein, Helen. *The Companies She Keeps: Tina Packer Builds a Theater.* Cambridge, MA: Plunkett Lake Press, 1985.

Gaines, Robert A. *John Neville Takes Command.* Stratford: William Street Press, 1987.

Glassberg, David. *American Historical Pageantry: The Uses of Tradition in the Early Twentieth Century.* Chapel Hill: University of North Carolina Press, 1990.

Gold, Sylvanie. "Shakespeare: The American Summer Habit." *Theatre Crafts* 18 (May 1984): 16, 52-53.

Guthrie, Tyrone, and Robertson Davies. *Renown at Stratford: A Record of the Shakespeare Festival in Canada, 1953.* Toronto: Clarke, Irwin, 1953;

———. *Twice Have The Trumpets Sounded: A Record of the Stratford Shakespearean Festival in Canada, 1954.* Toronto: Clarke, Irwin, 1954.

Guthrie, Tyrone, Robertson Davies, Tanya Moiseiwitsch, and Boyd Neel. *Thrice the Brinded Cat Hath Mew'd: A Record of the Stratford Shakespearean Festival in Canada.* 1955.

Henry, William A., III. "Midsummer Night's Spectacle." *Time*, 24 August 1992: 60-61.

Horn, Barbara Lee. *Joseph Papp: A Bio-Bibliography.* New York: Greenwood Press, 1992.

Houseman, John, and Jack Landau. *The American Shakespeare Festival: The Birth of a Theatre.* New York: Simon and Schuster, 1959.

Kay, Carol McGinius. "The Alabama Shakespeare Festival." In *Shakespeare in the South*, ed. Philip C. Kolin, Jackson: University Press of Mississippi, 1983.

King, Christine E., and Brenda Coven. *Joseph Papp and the New York Shakespeare Festival: An Annotated Bibliography.* New York: Garland, 1988.

Kennedy, Dennis. *Looking at Shakespeare: A Visual History of Twentieth-Century Performance.* Cambridge: Cambridge University Press, 1993.

Kolin, Philip C., ed. *Shakespeare in the South: Essays on Performance.* Jackson: University Press of Mississippi, 1983.

Laroque, François. *Shakespeare's Festive World.* Cambridge: Cambridge University Press, 1993.

Leiter, Samuel, ed. *Shakespeare Around the Globe: A Guide to Notable Postwar Revivals.* New York: Greenwood Press, 1986.

Leon, Ruth. *Applause: New York's Guide to the Performing Arts.* New York: Applause Theatre Book Publishers, 1991.

Lewis, Terral Sam. "The Utah Shakespearean Festival: Twenty-Five Years in Retrospect." Ph.D. diss., Texas Tech University, 1991.

Little, Stuart W. *Enter Joseph Papp: In Search of a New American Theatre.* New York: Coward, McCann and Geoghegan, 1974.

Loney, Glenn, ed. *Staging Shakespeare: Seminars on Production Problems.* New York: Garland, 1990.

Loney, Glenn, and Patricia MacKay. *The Shakespeare Complex: A Guide to Summer Festivals and Year-Round Repertory in North America.* New York: Drama Book Publishers, 1975.

Lynch, Margaret. *The Making of a Theater: The Story of the Great Lakes Theater Festival.* Cleveland: GLTF, 1986.

Macpherson, Rod. "Shakespeare on the Saskatchewan." *Canadian Theatre Review* 54 (Spring 1988): 29-33.

Oyler, Verne William, Jr. "The Festival Story: A History of the Oregon Shakespearean Festival." Ph.D. diss., University of California, Los Angeles, 1971.

Patterson, Tom. *First Stage: The Making of the Stratford Festival.* Toronto: McClelland and Stewart, 1987.

Pettigrew, John, and Jamie Portman, *Stratford: The First Thirty Years.* vol. 1: *(1953-67)*; vol. 2: *(1968-82).* Toronto: Macmillian of Canada, 1985.

Samuels, Steven. *Theatre Profiles 10: The Illustrated Reference Guide to America's Nonprofit Professional Theatre.* New York: Theatre Communications Group, 1992.

"Shakespeare in Canada" [special issue] *Canadian Theatre Review* 54 (Spring 1988).

Shattuck, Charles H. *Shakespeare on the American Stage: From Booth and Barrett to Sothern and Marlowe.* Cranbury, NJ: Associated University Presses, 1987.

Smith, Irwin. *Shakespeare's Globe Playhouse.* New York: Charles Scribner's Sons, 1956.

Somerset, J. Alan B. *The Stratford Festival Story: A Catalogue-index to the Stratford, Ontario, Festival 1953-1990.* New York: Greenwood Press, 1991.

Stuart, Ross. "The Stratford Festival." In *The Oxford Companion to the Canadian Theatre*, ed. Eugene Benson and L. W. Conolly. New York: Oxford University Press, 1989.

Taylor, Gary. *Reinventing Shakespeare: A Cultural History, from the Restoration to the Present.* New York: Weidenfield and Nicholson, 1989.

Tolaydo, Michael. "Three Dimensional Shakespeare." In *Shakespeare Set Free*, ed. Peggy O'Brien. New York: Washington Square Press, 1993.

Twigg, Alan. "Nanaimo: Leon Pownall at Shakespeare Plus." *Canadian Theatre Review* 12 (Spring 1985): 130-32.

Volz, Jim. *Shakespeare Never Slept Here: The Making of a Regional Theatre; A History of the Alabama Shakespeare Festival.* Atlanta: Cherokee, 1986.

Whittaker, Herbert. *The Stratford Festival, 1953-1957.* Toronto: 1958.

Index of Names

The index includes proper names, company and festival names, and places of performance. See Appendix C for a seperate listing of the companies and festivals in alphabetical order and Appendix B for a listing by geographical location.

Aaron, Jules, 34, 36
Abbey Shakespeare Players (Dyfed, Wales, Great Britain), 446–47
Abbey Theatre, 247, 263, 478
Abbott, George, 264
Abbott, Marcus, 195, 304
Abraham, F. Murray, 295
Academy of Theatre (Shanghai), 406
ACTER -A Center for Theatre, Education & Research (Santa Barbara, CA), 12–22
Actors Shakespeare Company (Albany, NY), 218–21
Actors' Summer Theatre (Columbus, OH), 259–62
Actors Theatre of Louisville, 154, 304
Adams, Fred C., 344–46
Adams, John Cranford, 225–26, 278, 311
Adams Memorial Shakespeare Theatre, 343, 345, 347
Addison, Michael, 22, 25, 274
Adler, Stella, 252
Afro-American Cultural Center (Yale University), 208
Akademietheater (Vienna), 444

Akalaitis, JoAnne, xix, 239–40
Alabama Shakespeare Festival (Montgomery, AL), 1–9
Albee, Edward, 47, 125
Albert, Eddie, 264
Albery Theatre, 460
Aldredge, Theoni, 239
Aldwych Theatre, 477–78
Alexander, Bill, 254
Alexander, Bruce, 19, 21
Alexander, Celia, 357
Alexander, Chris, 424
Allen, Ralph, 297
Allen, Shelia, 17–19
Allen Pavilion, 281
Alley Theatre, 322
Alliance Theatre, 129
Amelia White Park, 217
American Arts Alliance, 116
American Conservatory Theatre, 24, 227, 131
American Globe Theatre (New York, NY), 221–23
American Players Theatre (Spring Green, WI), 372–75
American Repertory Theatre, 106

American Shakespeare Theatre
(Stratford, CT), xvi, 100–7
American Stage in the Park (St.
Petersburg, FL), 115–17
Amis du Jardin Shakespeare du Pré
Catelan, Les (Paris, France),
413–17
Ammerman, John, 133
Anderson, Harold, 203
Anderson, Lane, 130–31
Anderson, Marian, 203
Anderson, Max, 345
Anderson, Vivienne, 218
Andrew W. Mellon Foundation, 103
Andrews, Jessica L., 111
Andrews, Park, 275
Andrews, Sharon, 97
Andrews, Whit, 97
Andrews Park Amphitheatre, 273
Angell, Gene, 26
Angelo, Susan, 85
Angove, Charles Thomas, 458
Angus Bowmer Theatre, 275, 280, 283
Anhui Hungmeixi Opera Troupe, 408
Anhui Huangmeixi Opera Troupe
Ruijin Theatre, 411
Ann Norton Sculpture Gardens, 125
Anne Dean Turk Fine Arts Center,
337, 339
Anne Hathaway Cottage, xiii
Annette Leday/Keli-Company, 427
Anouilh, Jean, 47
Anspacher Theater, 237–38, 241
Antalosky, Charles, 2
APA-Phoenix, 85
Appel, Libby, 283
Arabian Nights, 283
Arbuzov, Alexei, 48
Archer, William, 475
Arden, Jane, 21
Arden, John, 477
Arden Party (New York City, NY),
223–24
Arena Stage, 109–10
Aristophanes, 82
Armstrong, Will Steven, 102
Armstrong, Gareth, 21
Arnest, Mark, 100
Aronstein, Martin, 239

Art Reach of Ohio, 152
Artaud, Antonin, 477
Arts Academy of the Chinese People's
Liberation Army, 411
Arts Council (Great Britain), 479–80,
487, 490
Arts Theatre, 477
Arts Theatre (London), 55
Arundell, Clive, 21
Asbury Park, 224
Ashcroft, Peggy, 465, 476, 478
Assiniboine Park (Winnipeg), 385–386
Assiniboine Theatre (Winnipeg), 385
Astor Library, 238
Atienza, Edward, 399
Atkins, Michael, 338–339
Atkins, Robert, 460, 464
Atlanta Shakespeare Company
(Atlanta, GA), 126–30
Atlanta Shakespeare Tavern, 126,
128–129
Atlanta Stage Company, 130
Attenborough, Michael, 473, 479
Auditorium Theatre (Chicago), 452
Augé II, Roger, 151
Austin, Mary, 29
Austin Gardens, 144
Austin Shakespeare Festival (Austin,
TX), 308–10
Australian Elizabethan Theatre Trust,
381–82
Avon Theatre (Stratford, Canada), 391,
393–95
Aykroyd, Juliet, 17
Ayres, James B., 324–26
Ayrton, Randle, 476

B. Eaton, William, 49
Baalbeck Festival (Lebanon), 460
Babe, Thomas, 238
Backer, Paul, 44–45
Bailey, Margery, 277
Baker, Bob, 387, 390
Baker, David A., 74
Baker, Dylan, 213
Baker, Jordan, 113
Baker, Paul, 129, 312–13
Balboa Park, xv, 46–47
Ball, Stephen D., 185, 187

Banks, Howard M., 90
Bankside Theatre (ND), xv
Bannerman, Celia, 21
Barber, C. L., 70
Barber, Kathy, 316, 337–41
Barbican Theatre, 473, 478
Barbour, James, 354
Barboursville Vineyards, 353–54
Bard on the Beach (Vancouver, British
    Columbia, Canada), 383–85
Barnes, Cheryl, 355
Barnes, Clive, 253, 255
Barnes, Ezra, 303–4
Barratt, Kevin, 205
Barrett, Erskine, 455
Barricelli, Marco, 27, 283
Barroso, Luis Q., 132
Barry, B. H., 186
Barry, Ellen, 210, 216
Barry, Paul, 210–13, 216
Barthoshevitch, Alexei, xiv
Barton, John, 222, 436, 477
Basil, John, 221–22
Bates, Alan, 393
Bathhouse Theatre, 368
Battis, Emery, 112
Baudissin, Graf, 422
Bauer, Beaver, 61
Baumbauer, Frank, 430
Baxter, Keith, 114
Baxter, Lynsey, 19
Baxter, Trevor, 19, 21
Bayerisches Staatsschauspiel
    (Munich, Germany), 431
Bayfront Park Amphitheater, 117–18
Baylis, Lilian, 464–65
Baynes, Helen (Mann), 505
Baynon, Anthony, 454–55, 457
Bearsley, Charles, 82
Bearsley Jr., Conger, 197
Beasley, Jake, 321–22
Beatles, The, 352
Beatty, Ned, 154
Beaucaire, Béatrice, 417
Beaufort, John, 211
Beaumarchais, Pierre-Augustin
    Caron de, 60
Beaumont, Francis, 279
Bechhofer, Frank, 459

Beck, Ellen, 117–18
Becker, Roger, 345
Beckerman, Bernard, 211, 225
Beckett, Samuel, 109, 176, 487
Bedford, Brian, 394–96, 399
Beelitz, Günther, 431
Beethoven, Ludwig von, 148
Beevers, Geoffrey, 21
Behn, Aphra, 111
Behrman, S. N., 283
Beijing Opera, 407
Beijing People's Art Theatre, 405
Beil, Hermann, 428
Bell, James, 320
Bell, John, 381–82
Bell, Monica, 8
Bell Shakespeare Company (Sydney,
    Australia), 381–2
Bellafonte, Gina, 233
Benbow Lake State Park, 62–63
Benedetti, Robert, 91
Benge, Sharon, 334
Ben Greet Players (see also Greet,
    Ben), xv
Bening, Annette, 93
Benjamin, Sheila, 459, 461
Bennington Marionettes, 235
Benson, Frank, 474–480
Berger, Alfred Freiherr von, 430
Berger, Sidney, 315, 318
Berger, Tisrtan, 430
Berglund, John, 116
Bergman, Ingmar, 496
Berkeley Repertory Theatre, 26
Bernays, Philip, 486, 488–91
Berry, Cecily, 255
Berstmann, Ingrid, 61
Best, Martin, 17
Betti, Ugo, 48
Bevington, David, 358
Bidwell Park, 68
Bigelow, Dennis, 61
Bill, Mary, 263
Bill Kinnaman Umpire School, 55
Bingham, Sr., Barry, 154
Birdman, Jerome M., 105
Birdsall, Jim, 196
Birmingham Repertory Company,
    471, 476

Bisset, Jacqueline, 470
Bizet, George, 466
Black, Karen, 233
Blackfriars, 108
Blackfriars Traveling Shakespeare
    Theatre (Port Jefferson, NY),
    224–25
Black Swan, 275, 280
Blackwood, Russell, 59
Blake, Colleen, 391
Blake, Mervyn, 399
Bland, Marjorie, 19
Blasche, Gerhard, 428
Bledsoe, Jerry H., 361–63, 365
Blendick, Mary, 399
Bloom, Claire, 295
Blount, Carolyn, 2
Blount, Tom, 3
Blount, Winton M., 2
Blum, Gabriele, 424
Blumenthal, David, 182
Blythe, Domini, 18–20
Bode, Ralf, 351
Bodge, Jim, 166
Bogdanov, Michael, 73, 114, 395, 399,
    422, 450–52, 466, 487, 489
Bok Amphitheatre, 161, 163
Boll, Christopher J., 361
Bologna, Fratelli, 60
Bolt, Robert, 477
Bond, Angela, 221
Bond, Samantha, 471
Booth, John Wilkes, 319
Booth, Stephen, 23
Borgeson, Jess, 53, 57
Bosco, Philip, 102
Boudewyns, Michael, 348
Bowmer, Angus L., xvi, 275–77, 279,
    281, 284
Bowne Theatre, 210, 214
Boyle, Charles, 178–79
Brackenridge Park, 321
Bradac, Thomas F., 35–36, 69
Bradbury, Ray, 125
Bragg, Martin, 387
Braithwaite, Royden C., 345
Branagh, Kenneth, 470–72
Brand, Phoebe, 373
Brand, Robert, 355

Brandolese, Lyndsey, 485
Brandt, Robert, 427
Brant, Lisa, 400
Brasted, Christopher, 355
Braugher, André, 113–14
Braunmuller, A. R., 32, 86
Brebner, Ann, 40–41
Brecht, Bertolt, 42, 48, 60, 114, 238,
    268, 302, 394, 434–35, 477
Breed, Breed, 68
Breghy, Donna, 164
Bregy, Terry, 162
Bremer Bürgerpark am Hollersee, 426
Bremer Shakespeare Company
    (Bremen, Germany), xiv, 423–28
Brennan, Eve, 419, 421
Brenton, Howard, 433
Breslauer, Jan, 87
Breyer, Stoney, 198
Bridges-Adams, William, 475
Brierley, David, 473
Briers, Richard, 471
Bright, Charles J., 372–73
Brightman, Stacy, 65
Brighton, Pam, 395
Bringham, Judith, 154
Bristol Old Vic, 479, 487
British Arts Festival Association, 457
British Broadcasting Corporation, 346
British Council, 410, 419, 461
British Heart Foundation, 449
Brockbank, Philip, 407
Bronson, Virginia, xv
Brook, Peter, 378, 441, 476–77
Brooklyn Arts and Culture
    Association, 230
Brooks, Avery, 113
Brooks, Jacqueline, 51
Brooks, Mel, 180
Brooks, Phyllis, 25
Brooks, Stuart, 256
Broome, John, 186
Broward Center for the Performing
    Arts, 119
Broward County Main Library
    Theatre, 118–19
Brown, Anne Menelaus, 166
Brown, Lewis, 114
Brown, Pamela, 154

Brown, William T., 171–72
Browne family (Tolethorpe), 483
Brown Hotel Roof Garden, 154
Brown-Orleans, James, 173
Brustein, Robert, 106
Büchner, Georg, 434
Buena Vista Winery, 82
Bundshu, Jim, 81
Bungakuza Theatre (Tokyo), 492
Burford, Lord (see Charles Vere), 69
Burgess, John, 19
Burgess, Samuel, 455
Burghley, Lord, 484
Burghley House, 484
Burgtheater (Vienna), 428
Burke, Louis, 106
Burnham, Lord and Lady, 449
Burrell, John, 101
Burton, Robert, 439
Burton, Phillip, 350
Burton, Richard, 465
Burton family (Tolethorpe), 483
Busch, Frank, 428
Bushnell, Graham, 414
Business Sponsorship Incentive
    Scheme, 451
Bussert, Victoria, 262
Butler, Jerome, 333
Butterfield, Dick, 24
Bynum, Brenda Lynn, 242
Byrne, Barbara, 399

Cade, Rowena, 458–59
Cadell, Selina, 20
Cai Xiang, 411
Caisley, Robert, 142
Calderón de la Barca, Pedro, 111
Caldwell, Raymond, 337–41, 343
Caldwell, Zoe, 105, 393
California Repertory Company, 207
California Shakespeare Festival
    (Berkeley, CA), 22-28
California Theatre Center, 84, 207
Calvin, Neil B., 187
Camden Shakespeare Company
    (Camden, ME), 161–64
Cameo Theatre, 116
Cameron-Webb, Gavin, 7
Camp Shakespeare, 132

Campbell, Douglas, 384, 395
Canada Council Explora, 384
Canadian Broadcasting Corporation,
    395
Canadian Stage Company, 387–88
Canaris, Volker, 429
Canby, Vincent, 254
Canniff, Julie, 164
Canning, Heather, 19
Canterbury Hall, 249
Cao Yu, 404, 412
Cape May Playhouse, 210
Capital Theatre (Beijing), 412
Capital Theatre Company (Beijing),
    415
Capitol Repertory Theatre, 370
Capparella, Donald, 306
Carey, Denis, 101
Cariou, Len, 395
Carisbrooke Castle (Isle of Wright),
    486
Carlin, Nancy, 27
Carlin Park, 124, 126
Carlson, George, 166
Carlson, Harry, 447
Carlton, Don, 195, 197
Carmel Children's Experimental
    Theatre, 29
Carmel Shake-speare Festival
    (Carmel, CA), 28–31
Carmi, T., xiv
Carmichael, Steve, 146–47
Carnegie, David, 503
Carnovsky, Morris, 101–3, 350, 373
Carolina Playmakers, xv
Carolyn Blount Theatre, 1
Carr, Mimi, 283
Carra, Lawrence, 263
Carriage House Players, 153–54
Carrière, Jean-Claude, xiv
Carroll, Charles, 205
Carroll, Lewis, 231
Carroll, Pat, 112
Carroll, Sidney, 460
Carter Barron Amphitheatre, xviii,
    108, 112.
Cartmell, Daniel Bryan, 69
Casey, Chan, 365
Cassius Carter Centre Stage, 46, 48

Casteen, John, 105
Castiglione, John, 224
Castle, John, 451
Castorf, Frank, 429, 443–44
Catinella, Joseph, 211
Caux, Claude, 317, 339, 342
C. Douglas Ramey Amphitheatre, 153
Ceballos, Rod, 135
Cecil, William, 484
Centerstage (Toronto), 388
Center Theatre (Norfolk), 357
Central Academy of Drama, 405, 411
Central Drama Academy of Beijing, 407
Central Experimental Theatre (Beijing), 407
Central Park (New York City), xviii, 229–30, 237, 240
Cerves, Brent, 355
Chadwick, Bruce, 211–12
Chaikan, Joseph, 239
Chamberlain, Douglas, 399
Chamberlain, Richard, 124
Chambers, Steve, 306
Champlain Shakespeare Festival (Burlington, VT), 349–53, xvi
Chang Jiang Theatre, 411
Chang Yuling, 411
Chaplaincy Gardens (Isles of Falmouth), 486
Chaplin, Charlie, 307
Charles, Prince of Wales, 471
Charlip, Remy, 226
Chaurette, Normand, 389
Chautauqua, 275–76, 278
Cheaney, David, 348
Cheek by Jowl (London, England), 447–48
Chekhov, Anton Pavlovich, 373, 477
Chen Ping, 411
Cheng Bi-xian, 411
Chesley, Gene, 345
Chestnut Hill Theater, 292
Chevalier, Maurice, 414
Chicago Civic Shakespeare Society, xv, 148
Chicago Civic Theatre, xv
Chicago International Theatre Festival, 472

Chicago World's Fair, xv
Chichester Festival, 393
Children's Art Theatre (Shanghai), 411
Chiltern Shakespeare Company (Buckinghamshire, GB), 449
China Shakespeare Festival (Shanghai and Beijing), xiv, xx, 403–13
China Shakespeare Foundation, 404
China Youth Art Theatre, 405, 407, 412
Chinese Theatre Association, 404–5
Christensen, Ian, 448
Christian A. Herter Park, 182
Christman, Kermit, 124–26
Christy, James L., 298
Chrysler Museum Theatre, 357
Church, Geoffrey, 16, 20–22
Church, Tony, 12, 71, 73, 93, 94, 304
Churchill, Caryl, 239
Ciceri, Leo, 393
Cincinnati Art Institute, 153
Cincinnati Shakespeare Festival, xvi
Cincinnati Symphony Orchestra, 152
Clark, Bradford, 73
Clark, James Anthony, 337
Clark, Paul Mark, 134
Clarke, Cecil, 392
Clarke, Jennifer, 251
Clay, Jack, 93
Claypool, Joyce, 329
Clendon, Geoff, 499
Cleveland Playhouse, 266
Clifford, Mikel, 23
Cline, Casey, 216
Close, Glenn, 361
Cobb, Terry, 172
Cobin, Martin, 92
Coburg, Leopold of Saxe, 464
Coburg Theatre (Royal Coburg Theatre), 464
Coburn, Charles, xv
Coburn Shakespeare Players, xv
Cochran, Harry, 166
Coe, Peter, 105
Coe, Richard L., 122
Cohen, Alan, 454
Cohen, Jason Steven, 236
Cohen, Ralph Alan, 357–58, 360

Colas, Stella, 474
Cole, Jonathan, 205
Cole, Megan, 18, 76
Coleman, Kevin, 185, 187
Coleman, Stephen, 308
Coleman, W. Stephen, 295
Colfelt, Barry, 4
Colin, Margaret, 226
Collins, Glenn, 56
Collins, Roxanne, 315
Collins, Thomas P., 375–78
Collins, Wendy W., 375, 377–78
Colonial Theatre, 303–5
Colonial Williamsburg, 363
Colonna, Bob, 299, 301
Colorado Shakespeare Festival
    (Boulder, CO), xvi, 89–95
Colucci, Donato, 182
Columbus, Christopher, 235
Comden, Betty, 264
Committed Artists in Great Britain,
    208
Committed Artists of South Africa,
    208
Communist Party of China, 404
Company of Women (Boston, MA),
    176–78
Compañía Shakespeare de España
    (Madrid, Spain), 507–8
Compass Theatre, 496
Conley, Willy, 305
Connecticut Center for the Performing
    Arts, 104
Cons, Emma, 464
Conville, David, 415, 459–61, 463
Cook, Doug, 138
Cook, Douglas N., 344–45
Cook, John Paul, 417
Coonrod, Karin, 223
Cooper, Roberta Krensky, 104
Coppola, Francis Ford, 226
Copsey, Doug, 134–35
Coral Springs City Center, 119
Cordery, Richard, 20, 22
Corely, Elisabeth Lewis, 127
Cornelison, Gayle, 84
Cornell, Katherine, xvi, 101
Corsaro, Frank, 252
Costner, Kevin, 125

Cottle, Jack, 304
Coughlin, Beth, 194
Count Basie Theatre, 224
Coursen, Herbert, 163
Court Theatre (The Mount), 185, 188
Covent Garden, 433
Coward, Noel, 117, 137
Cox, Brian, 18
Craig, Edward Gordon, 433
Cravens, Rutherford, 317
Crescent Theatre, 154
Crinkley, Richmond, 108–9
Cronyn, Hume, 394
Crouch, J. H., 89, 90–91, 364
Crucible Theatre (Sheffield), 392
Cubiculo Experi, 234
Cuddy, Mark, 135
Cullen Trust for the Performing Arts,
    317
Culliton, Joseph, 122
Cumming, Richard, 302
Cumston, Charles, 166
Cumston Hall, 164, 166–67
Cunneen, Paddy, 447
Currier, Lesley Schisgall, 40
Currier, Robert S., 40
Curry, Christopher, 233
Curry, Julian, 18–19, 71
Curtis Theatre Collection, 299

Dakota Playmakers, xv
Dale, Jim, 487
Dale, Sam, 20–21
Dallas Theatre Center, 312–13, 322
Daly, Tyne, 37
Daniels, Ron, 106
Daphne Renaissance Festival (Daphne,
    AL), 9–10
Darjes, Hille, 424
Darkhorse Theater, 306–7
Dartlee Hall, 47
Davenport, Johnny Lee, 140, 143
David, Alan, 19
Davies, Lane, 132
Davies, Meg, 21
Davies, Robertson, 391
Davis, Ted, 165
Davis, Trvor, 293
Day, Richard Digby, 461, 463

de Barbieri, Mary Ann, 111
de Fouquières, André, 413
de Jongh, James, 253
De Vere, Edward, 29, 45, 484, 178–9
De Vries, Linda, 342
de Witt, Johannes, 32
Decker, Jay, 345
Deguchi, Norio, 492–93
DeKovic, Mark, 192
Delacorte, George T., 237
Delacorte Theater, xviii, 236–39
Delaware Park, 245
DelBuono, Jr., Robert M., 106
Demas, Carole, 351
DeMoranville, Mark, 118
Dempsey, Mark, 313
DeMunn, Jeffrey, 233
Dence, Jeffrey, 18
Dench, Judi, 358, 471, 478
Derrick, Patty S., 295
Descanso Gardens, 65, 67
Deschamps, Gail, 117–18
deShields, Henry, 356–57
DesRosiers, Anne B., 262
Dessen, Alan C., 14, 16, 73
Deutsche Shakespeare-Gesellschaft, 422, 425
Deutsches Nationaltheater (Weimar, Germany), 432
Deutsches Schauspielhaus (Hamburg, Germany), 430, 451
Deutsches Theater (Berlin), 428
Devin, Richard, 89, 91–93
Devou Park Summer Classics Theatre (Covington, KY), 151–53
DeWayne, Dan, 67–68
Dewhurst, Colleen, 239
Dexter, John, 395
Diaz, Rita, 308
Dickens, Charles, 264
Dickens, Ian, 449–50
Dickinson, Emily, 180
Dickson, Margaret Conant, 130
Dieterle, Christian, 427
Dimmick, Dana, 62–63
Dimmick, John, 63
Ding Ni, 410
Dionysus (Festival), xiii
Dishy, Bob, 104

District of Columbia Commission on the Arts and Humanities, 110
Dodd, John, 337, 339
Doehring, Carl D., 10
Doherty, Nancy N., 245, 247
Dolas, Lura, 61
Dole, Elizabeth Hanford, 111
Dolores Winningstad Theatre, 287–88
Donaldson, Peter, 399
Donat, Peter, 330, 395
Donenberg, Ben, 65–66
Donne, Jonathan, 21
Donnellan, Declan, 447–48
Donnelly, Donal, 295
Dorfman, Ariel, 118
Dorn, Dieter, 432, 442–44
Dorn, Franchelle Stewart, 112
Dorsey, Kent, 345
Dotrice, Roy, 105
Doug Anthony All-Stars, 54
Dougall, John, 21
Douglas Harris Actors' Equity Fund, 140
Dowling, Vincent, 196, 263, 264
Doyle, Kevin, 208
D. P. Productions (Nottingham, GB), 449–50
Drake, Alfred, 101
Drake, Sylvie, 67
Dream in High Park (Toronto, Ontario, Canada), xviii, 387–91
Dressler, Kevin, 10
Dreyfuss, Richard, 186
Drury Lane Theatre, 473
Dryden, Dan, 91
Dryer, Carl, 262
Dublin Theatre Festival, 56
Dudley, David H., 365
Duffy, Patrick, 226
Dunbar, Mary Judith, 72
Duncan, Isadora, xv
Duncan, Michael, 378
Dunlop, Frank, 487, 489
Dunster Castle (Somerset), 485
Dupont, Frédéric, 414
Durang, Christopher, 81
Durney, Gene, 224
Durning, Charles, 239
Duryèe, Cornelia, 367–69

Düsseldorfer Schauspielhaus
  (Düsseldorf, Germany), 429
Dyer-Bennett, Richard, 350

Earhart, Emelia, 214
Earl, Anthony, 373
Earl of Oxford (see Edward De Vere)
East River Amphitheatre, 237
Eaton, Edward, 169
Eberth, Michael, 428
E. C. Hafer Park, 270
Edelman, Richard, 304
Edgehill, Hal, 455
Edinburgh Festival (Edinburgh
  International Festival of Music and
  Drama), 54, 409
Edinburgh Fringe Festival, 184, 359
Edith Wharton Restoration Society
  (see also Wharton, Edith), 189
Edmondson, James, 283
Edwards, Michael, 71–72, 77–78
Edwards, William, 262
Egan, Robert, 40
Eisenhower Theatre, 110
Eisner, John, 303–5
El Carrusel Theatre, 118
Elizabeth I, Queen of England, 313
Elizabeth II, Queen of England, 49
Elkin, Saul, 245
Ellinger, Jeff, 308–9
Ellis, Kathi, 153
Ellson, Gary, 259, 261
Ellson, Patricia B., 259, 261
Elvgren, Gillette, 296, 298
Emmanuel Church (Boston), 178
Emmanuel Presbyterian Church, 237
Encore Players, 329
English Shakespeare Company
  (London, England), 450–54
Enters, Warren, 102
Epcot Center, 122
Epstein, Helen, 186
Epstein, Jonathan, 190
Epstein, Sabin, 131
Ernst, Lee E., 158, 373, 378
Estensen, Elizabeth, 20
Eureka Theatre, 26
European Community Cultural
  Commission, 418

Evans, Dale, 269
Evans, David, 182
Evans, Edith, 465
Evans, Maurice, 102
Evans, Sondra, 35
Evans, Stephen, 470–72
Ever Theater (Somerville, MA),
  178–79
Ewing, Scott, 55
Ewing Manor, 137, 139, 141
Eyre, Ronald, 395, 399
Ezell, John, 113–14, 262

Fair Park, 331
Fair Park Band Shell, 330
Fairfax Family Theatre, 174–75
Fairfield, Robert, 392
Fairmount Park, 293
Falls, Greg, 350, 353
Falstaff Tavern, 48
Farr, Michelle, 345
Faucit, Helen, 474
Favorini, Attilio, xviii, 294, 296–297
Fay, Richard, 222
Fechter, Charles, 474
Federal Theatre Project, xvi, 85
Fedoruk, Ronald, 384
Fee, Charles, 134
Fehling, Jürgen, 433
Feidner, Edward J., 349–50, 352–53
Feiner, Harry, 7
Fenglei Theatre (Shanghai), 411
Fenton House Garden, 486
Feore, Colm, 399
Ferraby, Clare, 466
Festival d'Avignon (France), 419
Festival Latino de Nueva York, 239
Festival Stage (Alabama), 1, 3
Festival Theatre (Stratford, Canada),
  391–92, 395, 398
Festspielhaus (Bayreuth, Germany),
  476
Feuchtwangen (Kreuzgangspiele,
  Germany), 430
Feydeau, Georges, 297, 394
Feyerabend, Paul, 443
Fields, John, 165
Finelli, Barbara, 302
Fink, Joel, 89, 94

Finnegan, Jim, 169
Finney, Albert, 465
Firbank, Ann, 17, 20
Firehouse Theatre, 10
Five-Point Pub, 127
Flanders, Earl, 167
Fleetwood, Susan, 16, 18
Fleissner, Robert F., 357
Fletcher, Allan, 102, 277
Fletcher, John, 279
Flimm, Jürgen, 430
Florida Humanities Council, 120
Florida Professional Theatre
    Association, 116, 124
Florida Shakespeare Festival (Coral
    Gables, FL), 117–18
Flower, Archibald, xiii, 474-480
Flower, Charles, xiii, 473-480
Flower, Fordham, 476-480
Flügge, Jürgen, 429–30
Flynn, Terry, 357
Foley, Geoff, 44
Folger Shakespeare Library, 108,
    110–11, 175, 226, 311, 358, 360
Folger Theatre Group, 108–9
Folly Theatre, 195
Foot, Oliver, 417
Footsbarn Travelling Theatre Company
    (Hérisson, France), 417–19
Forbes-Robertson, Johnston, 474
Ford Foundation, 102, 110
Foreman, Richard, 239
Forest Meadows Amphitheatre, 40
Forest Park Amphitheater
    (St. Louis), xv
Forest Theatre, 28–30, 79–80
Fortune Theatre, 32, 312
Forty Hall (Enfield), 485
Forward, Geoffrey G., 38–39
Foster, Donald, 356
Foster, Joanna, 21
Foster, Miranda, 21
Foster Memorial Theatre, 295
Fountain Garden (Birmingham), 485
Fountains Abbey (North
    Yorkshire), 486
Four County Players, 353
Fournier, Paul, 413
Fowler, Keith, 339, 362

Fox, Edward, 461
Fox Theatre (St. Louis), 198
Francell, Clay, 310
Francis, Decima, 184–85
Frank, David, 372, 374
Fraser, John, 21
Frayer, Brackley, 339
Freedman, Gerald, 104, 262, 264
Freeman, David, 238
Freeman, Morgan, 330
Freeman, Neil, 73
Freiman, Jonathan, 272
French, Leslie, 504–5
Fried, Erich, 422
Friedman, Kinky, 314
Friedman, Peter, 226
Friel, Brian, 48
Fringe First Award, 447
Frost Amphitheatre, 279
Fujita, Minoru, 495
Fuller, Charles, 160
Funk, Barbara Felmley, 138–39

Gadke, Susan, 321
Gaffney, Thomas, 256
Gaines, Barbara, 148–49
Gaines, Robert, 395
Gale, William, 305
Gallimaufry Players, 308
Galloway, Pat, 394
Gang, Richard P., 236
Ganz, Bruno, 440
Garner, Richard, 130–32
Garrick, David, xiii, 473
Garza Theatre, 318–19
Gasarella, Gary, 245
Gascon, Jean, 393–94
Gash, Kent, 8
Gaskill, William, 253–54, 454
Gatti, Donald C., 235
Gavignan, John, 83
Gaze, Christopher, 384
Georgia Shakespeare Festival (Atlanta,
    GA), 130–34
Geer, Ellen, 85
Geer, Herta (Herta Ware), 86
Geer, Kate, 86
Geer, Thad, 86
Geer, Will, 85–86

Gem Theatre, 34–36
Genet, Jean, 48
Genossenschaft Deutscher Bühnen-
    Angehörigen, 423
George, Colin, 458
George Hotel (Stamford), 484
George Memorial Library
    Amphitheatre, 329
Gercke, Francis J., 365
Gere, Richard, 239
German International Shakespeare
    Globe Centre (Bremen), 426
Gero, Edward, 112
Gérôme, Jean Léon, 114
Gershwin, Ira, 66
Gershwin, Lenore, 66
Gersten, Bernard, 237
Gerussi, Bruno, 393
Ghelderode, Michel de, 23
Giametti, Marcus, 214
Gibbs, Major, 481
Gibson, Jane, 447
Gielgud, John, 464, 465, 476
Gilbert, Tony, 381
Gilbert, William Schwenck, 117, 164,
    347, 395–96
Gilbert and Sullivan (see William
    Schwenck Gilbert and Arthur
    Sullivan)
Gilligan, Carol, 176–78
Gimeno, Harold, 273
Girth, Peter, 429
Givens, John, 500
Glassberg, David, xv
Glassco, Bill, 394
Glenn, Robert, 330
Glenn Hughes Playhouse, 366–67
Globe (see Tokyo Panasonic Globe)
Globe (Neuss, Germany), 426
Globe Centre (London), 426
Globe of the Great Southwest
    (Odessa, TX), 310–15
Globe Playhouse of Los Angeles (Los
    Angeles, CA), 31–34
Globe Stage (Hofstra), xvi, 225–27
Globe Theatre (London), xv, 39, 46,
    73, 151, 226, 235, 310, 346, 359,
    364, 376, 441, 495
Glover, Julian, 19

Goddard III, Robert A., 365
Godfrey, Patrick, 19
Godinez, Henry, 336
Goethe, Johann Wolfgang von, 434
Golden Bough Playhouse, 29
Golden Gate Park, 43, 59, 61
Goldenthal, Elliot, 252–53
Goldman, Judy, 230
Goldman, Michael, 358
Goldoni, Carlo, 80
Goltry, Thomas S., 375–77
Gonta, William, 248
Goodlin, John, 365
Goodman, Henry, 20
Goodman, William, 104
Goodman Theatre, 46
Goodspeed Opera House, 106
Goodwin, Philip, 114
Gordon, Bill, 358
Gorfain, Phyllis, 16
Görne, Dieter, 429
Gosch, Jürgen, 433, 441–44
Goss, Bernard, 406, 410
Gould, Harold, 345
Gounod, Charles, 497
Grace, Nicholas, 18
Gradwell, Charmian, 481
Gradwell, Elizabeth Anne, 481
Gradwell, John, 481
Graham, Billy, 436
Graham, Richard, 277
Grahame, Gloria, 33
Gramercy Park, 297
Gran Circo Teatro (Chile), xiv, 427
Grant Park (Chicago), 150
Granville-Barker, Harley, 475
Grassle, Karen, 93
Graves, Keytha, 143
Grayer, Peter, 21
Great Lakes Shakespeare Festival
    (Cleveland, OH), xvi, 262–65
Green, Adolph, 264
Green, Benny, 463
Green, Judith, 74
Greenberg, Peter, 218–19, 221
Greenspan, David, 239
Greer, Michael, 356
Greet, Ben, xv, 460
Gregg, Hubert, 460, 463

Gregory, Sam, 27
Greif, Michael, 239
Griffin, Janet, 175
Griffin, Jennifer, 323
Griffith, Hugh, 478
Grillparzer, Franz, 434
Grimaldi, Joseph, 464
Grimes, Tammy, 295, 393
Grin and Tonic Theatre Troupe
    (Clayfield, Australia), 382–83
Groenewold, Gabriele, 429
Group Theatre, 252
GroveMont Theatre, 28–30
Grove Shakespeare Festival (Garden
    Grove, CA), 34–38
Grove Theatre Company, 34, 36
Grüber, Klaus Michael, 422, 440–41,
    443
Grünig, Renato, 424
Guadeloupe Theatre Company (San
    Antonio, TX), 322
Guard, Pippa, 19
Guare, John, 238–39
Gubb, Lin, 506
Guggenheim, Daniel, 475
Guinness, Alec, 391
Guither, Peter, 138–39
Gunn, Deborah, 223
Gurney, A. R., 50–51
Gurr, Jean, 482, 484
Gussow, Mel, 254
Guthrie, Tyrone, 326, 391–93, 465
Guthrie, Woody, 85–86
Guthrie Theatre, 200, 254, 257, 392
Gwillim, David, 19
Gwilym, Mike, 16

Haigh, Kenneth, 104
Hall, Adrian, 302, 304
Hall, Mike, 446
Hall, Peter, 436, 476–77
Hall, Thomas, 46, 49
Hall Barn, 449
Halperin, Marilyn J., 148
Hamann, Karl, 55
Hamburger, Maik, 424
Hamilton, Carl, 80–81
Hamm, Carl G., 330
Hammerman, Barbara, 36

Hammerstein, Oscar, 466
Hammond, Paul B., 70, 78
Hampshire Shakespeare Company
    (Amherst, MA), 179–81
Handlen, Ruth, 415
Hands, Terry, 72, 478–79
Hangzhou Yueju Opera House
    (China), 408, 411
Hanks, Tom, 263
Hansen, John C., 174
Hapgood, Robert, 165
Hardison, O. B., 108–9, 121, 356
Hardy, Oliver, 307, 444
Hardy, Tim, 20
Hare, David, 239, 433
Harkness, Edward, 475
Harlaandt, Wilfried, 432
Harley, Jean, 482, 485
Harnes, Richard, 105
Harnick, Sheldon, 264
Harre, Beth, 365
Harris, James Berton, 348
Harris, Julie, 239, 393
Harris, Neil, 238
Harris, Rosemary, 332
Harrison, Derek, 482, 484
Harrow, Lisa, 12, 16, 19
Hartman Theatre, 110
Harvey, Cameron, 344–46
Harvey, Lady, 414
Harvey, Laurence, 476
Hassall, Craig, 381
Hathaway, Anne, 313
Hatton, Sir Christopher, 179
Hauswald, Wolfgang, 431
Havel, Václav, 239
Hawn, Goldie, 361
Haworth Shakespeare Festival
    (Haworth, NJ), 207–9
Hay, Richard, 277, 280
Hayes, Gabby, 269
Hayes, Helen, 102
Haywood, Laura, 212
Healy-Louie, Miriam, 254
Hearn, Lafcadio, 493
Heart of America Shakespeare Festival
    (Kansas City, MO), xvii, 194–98
Hebbel, Friedrich, 434
Hedge, Jr., Arthur, 105–6

Heflin, Elizabeth, 378
Heilbron, Vivien, 12, 19–20
Heinen Theatre, 330
Helbling, Niklaus, 430
Heldrich, Eva Johanna, 429
Helms, Jesse, 240
Helpmann, Max, 394
Hemingway, Ernest, 445
Hemming, Stephen, 373
Hemphill, Marie-Louise, 413–14, 416–17
Henderson, Criss, 148
Henderson, Virginia, 381
Hendrick, Allan, 20
Hennessey, David, 401
Hennigan, Sean, 93– 94
Henry, Martha, 393–95
Henry III, William A., xix
Hepburn, Katherine, 101
Hermann, Edward, 213
Hermann Park, 315
Hernandez, Roberto Javier, xiv
Heron, Herbert, 30
Herreid, Grant, 236
Herrenhausen Park (Germany), 430
Herrmann, Karl-Ernst, 439
Hessisches Staatstheater (Wiesbaden, Germany), 432
Heston, Charlton, 33, 124
Hettrick, William E., 226
Hewes, Henry, 211
Heyme, Hansgünther, 422, 441
He You, 411
Hibberd, Sue, 488
Hibbert, Jim, 62–63
Hibbert, Lady, 414
Hickle-Edwards, Allan, 258
High Park (Toronto), 387–88
High Point Theatre, 255–57
Hilgenberg, Eve, 371
Hill, Annalisa, 342
Hilo Shakespeare Festival (Hilo, HI), 134
Hinkel Park, 26
Hinkel Park amphitheatre, 25
Hinton, Peter, 390
Hirsch, John, 52, 393–96
Hitler, Adolf, 434, 436
Hodges, C. Walter, 278

Höfele, Andreas, xx, 422, 443
Hofflund, Mark, 134–35
Hoffmann, Eric, 122
Hofstra University Annual Shakespeare Festival (Hempstead, NY), 225–27
Hogg, Ima, 324
Hogg, James, 324
Hogg Foundation, 324
Holbrook, Hal, 102
Holcomb, Timothy, 180–81, 222
Holden, Stephen, 253
Holiday, Billie, 52
Hollis, Stephen, 132, 339
Hollmann, Hans, 422
Holloway, Victoria, 115–16
Holm, Ian, 478
Holt McPherson Center, 257
Holzman, Willy, 254
Holzwarth, Pit, 426–27
Homer, Sally, 452
Homewood, Bill, 17–19
Hong Kong Repertory Theatre, 92
Honolulu Youth Theatre, 374
Hood, Cynthia, 378
Hope, Barbara, 235
Horowitz, Jeffrey, 251–52, 255
Hortmann, Wilhelm, 435
Horton, Laura, 83
Hose, Marian, 190
Houseman, John, 50, 101–2, 104
Houston, 231–32
Houston, Deborah Wright, 230, 232
Houston Shakespeare Festival (Houston, TX), xviii, 315–18
Howard, Joy, 328
Howell, Yvonne, 504
Howey, David, 21
Howey, Richard, 486
Huang Yilin, 411
Hu Dao, 410
Hudd, Roy, 462
Huddle, Elizabeth, 12
Huddleston, Will, 84
Hudson Valley Shakespeare Festival (Cold Spring-on-Hudson, NY), 227–29
Huey, Kathryn, 270
Hughett, Julie, 28

Huguenet, André, 504
Humphries, Jimmy, 339
Huntington, Archer, 475
Huntington Gardens, 39
Hu Qiaomu, 404
Hu Qinshu, 407
Hurt, Mary, 312
Hurt, William, 239
Hurwitt, Robert, 59
Hutchings, Geoffrey, 18
Hutchison, Joanne, 355
Hutt, William, 226, 393–94, 396, 399
Hu Weiming, 411
Hwang, David Henry, 239
Hyland, Frances, 393
Hyman, Earle, 304, 330, 332

Iacovelli, John, 345
Ibsen, Henrik, 394, 487
Idaho Humanities Council, 135
Idaho Shakespeare Festival (Boise,
    ID), 134–37
Illinois Arts Council, 141, 144
Illinois Shakespeare Festival
    (Normal, IL), 137–43
Illinois Shakespeare Society, 141
Imura, Kimi, xiv
Ingham, Barry, 17
Inglman, Rosemary, 345
Institute of Contemporary Arts, 182
Intensive Classical Training Workshop
    for Professional Actors of Color,
    113
International Film Festival (Stratford),
    393
International Shakespeare Association,
    306
International Shakespeare Globe
    Centre, 332
Iowa Shakespeare Conservatory, 151
Iowa Shakespeare Project (West Des
    Moines, IA), 150–51
Irish Hills Shakespeare Repertory
    Festival, xvi
Irons, Jeremy, 461
Irving, Washington, 301
Isackes, Richard M., 348
Isozaki, Arata, 495
Ives, Burl, 85

Ives, Charles, 180
Ivey, Dana, 233
Iwersen, Rainer, 424–25
Izzo, Gary, 249–50
Izzo, Nancy Robbins, 249–50

Jackson, Barry, 476
Jackson, Glenda, 478
Jackson, Jill, 306
Jacobi, Derek, 471
Jacobs, Laurence H., 24
Jacobsen, Bruce C., 200
Jaczko, Caroline, 219
Jäger, Gerd, 431
Jahnke, Joel, 200–2
James, Henry, 186
Jameson, Louise, 19
Jamieson, Will, 504–5
Jarman, Derek, 370
Jarvis, Andrew, 453
Jaster, Gloria, 324
Jefferson, Thomas, 354, 361
Jenn, Stephen, 19, 21
Jenner, James, 242
Jennings, Byron, 52
Jensen, Howard, 345
Jessner, Leopold, 433
Jesuit Gardens, 202
Jiang Weiguo, 411
Jiangsu Provincial Spoken Drama, 410
Jill, Robert, 116
Jimenez, Roy, 81
Ji Zhenghua, 409
Joffet, Robert, 413
John, Elton, 314
John Anson Ford Amphitheatre, 66
John Cranford Adams Playhouse, 225
John F. Kennedy Center (see Kennedy
    Center for the Performing Arts)
John Hinkel Park, 23
John Houseman Theatre, 358
Johnson, Dan, 244
Johnson, Gregg, 100
Johnson, Jack, 154
Johnson, Jay, 367
Johnson, Jennifer, 365
Johnson, Philip E., 143
Johnson, Richard, 20
Johnson-Haddad, Miranda, 112, 114

Johnston, David, 448
Johnston, Lena, 318
Jolly, Bob, 183
Jonas, Larry, 39
Jones, Evan, 463
Jones, Gemma, 20
Jones, James Earl, 105, 239
Jones, Ken, 151
Jones, Randall L., 346
Jones, Robert Edmond, xv
Jones, Toby, 450
Jonson, Ben, 91, 279, 394, 479
Joseph, B. L., 383
Joseph, Phillip, 20
Joseph Jefferson Awards, 148
Joyce, Robert, 164–65
Juilliard School, 66, 254, 420
Julia, Raul, 239
Julia Morgan Theatre, 25
Jupiter Beach, 124

Kabuki, 203, 253, 317
Kafka, Franz, 150
Kahl, Gisela, 432
Kahn, Madeline, 226
Kahn, Michael, 92, 103, 108, 111–12,
    114, 213
Kaikkonen, Gus, 243
Kainz, Joseph, 440
Kaiser, Christian, 427
Kalakawa Park, 134
Kammerspiele (Munich, Germany),
    432, 442, 444
Kammerspiele in der Böttcherstrasse
    (Bremen, Germany), 424
Kane, John, 17, 19, 21
Kanin, Garson, 264
Kaplan, Cindy, 207–8
Karais, Karl Gabriel v., 431
Karamu Theatre, 172
Karczmar, Marian, 144
Kareda, Urjo, 395
Karen Sinsheimer and Audrey Stanley
    Festival Glen, 70
Katt, William, 125
Kaushansky, Larry, 339
Kaye, David, 338
Kazanoff, Ted, 226
Keach, Stacey, 112

Kean, Charles, xiii, 473
Kean, Edmund, 464
Kean, Tom, 213
Keating, Charles, 16, 18, 244
Kedlestone Hall (Derby), 486
Kelembar, Patricia, 345
Kelley, Sean Ryan, 94
Kelly, Maureen, 130–31
Kelly, Patrick, 41, 336
Kelly, Rachel, 216–17
Kelly, Thomas, 143
Kelly, William, 162–63
Kemper III, Rufus Crosby (Chris), 195
Kempsville Playhouse, 356
Kendal, Felicity, 461
Kenilworth Castle, 485
Kennedy Center for the Performing
    Arts, 104, 109, 173, 373
Kentrup, Norbert, 424, 426–27
Kentucky Arts Council, 152
Kentucky Shakespeare Festival
    (Louisville, KY), 153–59
Kentwell Hall (Suffolk), 486
Kerry-Rubenstein, Louisa, 321
Kesselman, Wendy, 253
Kids Fest, 125
Kiernander, Adrian, 382, 503
Kilby, John, 417
Killerton House Garden (Devon), 486
Kilmer, Val, 93
Kim, Randall Duk, 351–52, 372–73
Kimbrough, Linda, 144
Kindlon, Peter M., 251
King, David, 458
King, Floyd, 112
King, Martin Luther, 87
King, Rosemary, 458
King's County Shakespeare Company
    (Brooklyn, NY), 230–32
Kingsley, Ben, 17
Kirby Muxloe Castle, 486
Kirchner, Alfred, 428
Kirchner, Ignaz, 445
Kirkland, Sally, 37
Kirkpatrick, Melanie, 254
Kirstein, Lincoln, 100–1
Kissel, Howard, 245
Kissell, Jerry, 166
Kizziah, Casey, 162, 205

Klees, Richard, 235
Klein, Alvin, 229
Kleist, Heinrich von, 434
Klem, Alan, 202–5
Kliman, Bernice, 358
Klimt, Gustav, 283
Kline, Kevin, 195, 239
Knaub, Richard, 90
Knight, Dudley, 93–94
Knight, William, 413
Knox-Albright Art Museum, 247
Koch, Fredrick H., xv
Kochta, Karla, 429
Kohler, Estelle, 17–18
Kolb, James J., 226
Kole, Robert, 222
Komisarjevsky, Theodore, 476
Kopit, Arthur, 48
Korol, Daphne, 385–86
Kortner, Fritz, 434
Koschwitz, Andreas, 432
Koskinen, Karla, 146–47
Kostov, Kamen, xiv
Kott, Jan, 435
Kowarsky, Gerry, 199
Köweker, Kurt-Achim, 430
Kraft, Barry, 93–94
Kramer, Larry, 239
Kramer, Mimi, 228
Krämer, Günter, 431
Kratz, Barbara, 427
Krausnick, Dennis, 185–87
Krige, Alice, 505
Kröplin, Wolfgang, 431
Kuck, Gerd Leo, 433
Kümmritz, Joachim, 432
Kushlik, Taubie, 505
Kyle, Barry, 254

Labor Stage, 85
Labuda Center for the Performing
    Arts, 290–91
Lacey, Liam, 390
Lacock Abbey (Wiltshire), 485
LaGue, Michael, 318
La Jolla Museum of Contemporary
    Art, 47
La Jolla Playhouse, 56
Lake Champlain, 350

Lake Dillon Amphitheatre, 96
Lake Dillon Shakespeare Festival
    (Dillon, CO), 95–96
Lake Eola Park, 121
Lake Harriet Rose Garden, 192
Lakewood Civic Auditorium, 264
Lamb, Charles, 403
Lamb, Mary, 403
Lamb, Myrna, 238
Lamb, Thomas, 263
Lambermont, Janette, 390
Lamont, Thomas, 475
Landau, Jack, 101
Landesbühne Hannover (Germany),
    430
Landstreet, Susan, 227
Lang, Alexander, 428
Langan, E. Timothy, 1
Langham, Michael, 114
Langham, Michael, 254, 392–93, 395,
    399
Langhoff, Matthais, 433
Langhoff, Thomas, 428
Langner, Lawrence, 100–2
Langsam, Jennifer, 218, 220
Lansburgh, The, 113–14
Lansburgh (theatre), 108
Lapine, James, 50
Laughlin, Tom, 378
Laughton, Charles, 476
Laurel, Stanley, 307, 444
Laurenson, James, 18
Lázaro, Eusebio, 507
Leach, William, 345, 348
Learned, Michael, 37
Le Beauf, Sabrina, 112
Leday, Annette, 427
Lee, Anthony, 369
Lee, Ming Cho, 104, 239, 395
Lee, Paula Munier, 68
Leiber, Fritz, xv, 148
Leigh, Andrew, 464
Leigh-Hunt, Barbara, 17
Leinert, Michael, 431
Leininger, Claus, 432
Lenkiewicz, Rebecca, 364–65
Lennon, John, 487
Lenska, Rula, 461
Leon, Ruth, 240

Lepage, Robert, 402, 427
Lessing, Gotthold Ephraim,, 434
Levett, Julie G., 162
Lewis, Peter, 452
Lexington Shakespeare Festival
    (Lexington, KY), 159–61
Liaoning People's Art Theatre, 404
Liaoning Provincial People's Art
    Theatre, 407
Libbey Bowl Outdoor Theatre, 44
Liddell, Eric, 39
Li Jiayao, 411
Lilian Baylis Theatre, 55
Lilienthal, Matthais, 429
Lillich, Olivia, 411
Lincoln, Abraham, 87
Lincoln Center for the Performing
    Arts, 238, 392
Lincoln Center Institute, 252
Lincoln Center Out-of-Doors
    Festival, 66
Lindfors, Kristin, 120
Lindtberg, Leopold, 422
Lines, Sybil, 122
Linklater, Kristin, 176–78, 186
Linower, R. Robert, 111
Linwood, Jill, 59
Lithgow, Arthur, 262
Lithgow, John, 262
Little, Cleavon, 6
Liu Jiangping, 411
Liu Mudao, 411
Livermore, Michelle, 345
Li Zibai, 411
Lloyd, Bernard, 12, 16–18, 20–21
Lloyd, David, 458
London, Jack, 29
London Academy of Music and
    Dramatic Art, 252
Londré, Felicia Hardison, 194
Long, Adam, 54, 57
Long, Kay, 372
Long Wharf Theatre, 365
Looby Theatre, 307
Looman, Sara B., 131
Loper, Robert, 277
Lopez, Henry, 364
Lopez, Melinda, 190
López-Morillas, Julian, 26

Loquasto, Santo, 239
Lorca, Federico García, 50, 335
Lord Jeffery Inn, 179
Lorette, Deanne, 142–43
Los Angeles Shakespeare Company
    (Van Nuys, CA), 38–39
Louisville Shakespearean Society, 154
Love, Patti, 20
Lovell, Glen, 71
Lowell Davies Festival Stage, 46
Lowell Davies Festival Theatre, 50
Lowry, Jacqueline, 221
Lt. G. H. Bruns III Memorial
    Amphitheater, 22
Lüchinger, Peter, 427
Lucille Lortel Award, 254
Luckinbill, Laurence, 262
Ludlow Castle, 454–56, 458
Ludlow Festival (Ludlow, Shropshire,
    England), 454–58
Ludwig II (King of Bavaria), 440
LuEsther Hall, 237–38
Luken, Richard, 365
Lunghi, Cherie, 18
Lusardi, James P., 14
Luscombe, Tim, 452
Luse, James, 365
Lux, Joachim, 429
Lynner, Brian R., 150–51
Lyon, Sherry, 369
Lyric Theatre (Brisbane,
    Australia), 382

Mabou Mines, 239
MacCary, W. Thomas, 226
Macdonald, Brian, 395–96
MacKaye, Percy, xiv
MacKinnon, Cecil, 190
MaClintic, Guther, xvi
Macphee, Wendy, 485
Macy, William H., 144
Madison, James, 354
Magee, Patrick, 478
Magee, Tom, 356
Maidment, Scott, 382
Maine Arts Council, 163
Malley, Dejon Austin, 331–32
Mallinckrodt Center Drama
    Studio, 198

Maloof, Manuel, 127
Mamet, David, 144, 213
Manhattan School of Music, 419
Manitoba Theatre Center, 386, 393
Manitoga Nature Center, 227
Mann, Bruce, 504, 506
Mann, Cecile, 166
Mann, David, 293
Mann, Delbert, 33
Mann, Helen, 504, 506
Mannon, Derik R., 159
Mannville open-air theatre (South
    Africa), 504
Mantell, Robert, xv
Manuel's Tavern, 127, 129
Mapplethorpe, Robert, 240
Marcell, Joe, 19
Marcovicci, Andrea, 75
Marin Shakespeare Festival (San
    Rafael, CA), xvi, 40–42
Markey, Michael, 202–3
Marks, Gina, 131
Markus, Tom, 92
Marlowe, Edward, 479
Marlowe, Julia, xv, 86
Marowitz, Charles, 263, 330
Marsh, Brian, 180–1
Marsh, Ljuba, 180
Martha's Vineyard, 191
Martin, Karl Heinz, 433
Martin, Larry, 343
Martin, Sharon, 233
Martinson Hall, 237–38
Maruschak, Jackie, 236
Marx Brothers, 388
Mary Rippon Theatre, 89–92
Maslan, Peter, 81
Mason, Kathy, 82
Massachusetts Council on the Arts,
    185, 188
Masson, Linda, 244
Mather, Ada Brown, 419, 421
Mathis, Lynn, 336
Matt, Steven, 342
Matthaei, Konrad, 103
Matthews, Barbara, 447
Matthews, Dakin, 24–25
Mawson, Michael, 387–88
May, Walter W., 159

May Day Park, 9
Mazer, Cary M., 14
Mazzu, Gary J., 96
McAtee, Thomas, 198
McCall, Gordon, 401–2
McCalla, Allan, 322
McCallum, Diann, 330
McCally, Charles David, 313
McCarter Theatre, 103, 262
McClellan, Ted, 220
McClure, James, 81
McClure, Jon, 272
McClure, Spike, 333
McConachie, Bruce, 361
McConnell, Steve, 184
McCrary, Melinda, 196
McCrary, Will, 313, 318–20
McCready, Sam, 171–72
McCune, Marshall L., 217
McCune, Perrine D., 217
McDowell, Stuart, 243
McDowell, W. Stuart, 34, 37
McDugall, Tom, 292
McEwan, Geraldine, 471
McFerran, Patti, 89
McGee, Jay, 312
McGillis, Kelley, 112, 114
McGovern, Elizabeth, 213
McGowen, Vicki, 206
McKechnie, Donna, 37
McKellan, Ian, 357
McKie, Jim, 41–42
McKnight, Tom, 312
McLane, Derek, 114
McLaughlin, Brian, 486, 488
McLaurin, Stewart, 337
McLendon, Mark, 355
McMurry, Charles David, 314
McQuarrie, Heather, 65
McRuvie, David, 427
McVeigh, Rose, 117
Mecklenburgisches Staatstheater
    (Schwerin, Germany), 432
Medhin, Tsegaye Gabre, xiv
Meem Library Courtyard, 216–17
Meisner, Sanford, 252
Meister, Philip, 233
Mekler, Mimi, 357
Meltzer, Harlan, 303–4

Menaugh, Michael, 109
Mendes, Sam, 487
Menzer, Paul, 357
Mercury Theatre, 85
Merrill, Dina, 318
Merrill, Sharon, 216
Mesa Amphitheater, 10–11
Messersmith, Randy, 10
Messina, Cedric, 332
Metcalfe, Stephen, 51
Metropolitan Boston Arts Center, 182
Metropolitan Opera (Lincoln Center
    for the Performing Arts), 238
Metropulos, Penny, 142
MGM-Disney Studios, 122
Miami Shores Theatre, 119
Michener, James, 311
Michie, William D., 364
Micken, Patrick, 361
Middents, Jonathan, 315
Miller, Arthur, 104, 152, 487, 489
Miller, Jason, 351
Miller, Jonathan, 355, 465–66, 470
Miller, Ruth Lloyd, 45
Miller, Steven, 143
Miller Outdoor Theatre, 315–17
Millfield Theatre (London), 486
Mills-Cockell, John, 388
Milton, John, 454
Milwaukee Repertory Theatre, 302
Minack Open-Air Theatre (Penzance,
    Cornwall, England), 458–59
Mineart, Mark, 342
Minks, Wilfried, 436
Minnesota Shakespeare Company
    (Minneapolis, MN), 192–93
Minorca Playhouse, 117
Mirvish, David, 451, 464
Mirvish, Ed, 451, 464–66, 469
Missouri Arts Council, 199
Missouri Repertory Company, 196
Missouri Repertory Theatre, 27, 194
Mitchell, Adrian, 111
Mitchell, Larry, 68
Mitri, Paul T., 366–69
Mitzi E. Newhouse Theatre, 238
Moffat, Donald, 262
Moiseiwitsch, Tanya, 391
Molière (Jean-Baptiste Poquelin), 29,

224, 235, 250, 393–94, 487
Moncada, Raul, 51
Monette, Richard, 391, 394, 396, 399
Moniz, Brad, 68
Monroe, Marilyn, 336
Montana Shakespeare in the Parks
    (Bozeman, MT), xvii, 200–2
Monte, Bonnie J., 210, 213
Monterey Playhouse, 29
Montgomery Auditorium, 266, 268
Monument Valley Park, 97–98
Moody, Michael Dorn, 238
Mooney, Robert, 244
Moore, Dora Mavor, 391
Moore, Mavor, 391
Moore, Terry Edward, 366–69
Moorer, C. Alan, 161
Moorer, Stephen, 28, 30
Moran, Li, 407
Moreno, Rita, 356
Morgan, J. P., 475
Moriarty, Michael, 93, 104
Moriarty, Paul, 20
Morris, Marjorie, 311, 313–14
Morrison, Malcolm, 256
Morse, Richard V., 127
Morton H. Meyerson Symphony
    Center, 332
Moscow Art Theatre, 478
Moss, Peter, 395, 399
Moszkowicz, Imo, 430
Mottisfont Abbey, 486
Mount, The, 185, 187
Mountain View High School, 10–11
Mount Edgecumbe Country Park
    (Cornwall), 486
Moynihan, Daniel Patrick, 111
Muchmore, G. Leslie, 361
Mula, Tom, 144–145
Müller, Heiner, 422, 443
Muller, Michael, 334–35
Mullin, Bob, 174–75
Mullin, Michael, 92
Mullin, Roger W., 290
Mulvany, Joan Herbert, 144
Murney, Christopher, 304–5
Murphy, Gerard, 19, 496

Murphy, Vincent, 219

Murray, Bill, 186
Murtland, Joyce, 356
Muth, JoAnne, 146
Myers, Christine, 67
Myers, Doyle, 367
Myers, Lorre, 367
Myre, Katy, 183

Nachman, Gerald, 41
Nadeau, Albert H., 90
Nashville Shakespeare Festival
    (Nashville, TN), 306–7
Nason, Bryan, 382–83
National Arts Center (Ottawa), 392,
    394
National Endowment for the Arts, 163,
    240, 247, 359
National Endowment for the
    Humanities, 187, 350
National Governors' Association, 281
National Institute of Dramatic Art
    (Sydney), 499
National Palace (Beijing), 411
National Shakespeare Company
    (New York, NY), 232–34
National Shakespeare Conservatory,
    162, 234
National Socialism, 434
National Theatre (Washington DC),
    373
National Theatre (Great Britain), 149,
    182, 184, 186, 208, 252–53, 392,
    447, 455, 464–65, 478, 487–88
National Theatre Conservatory, 304
National Theatre for the Deaf, 305
National Theatre School (Ottawa), 387
Nattermann, Andreas, 429
Nazi (see National Socialism)
Neagle, Anna, 460
Nebraska Shakespeare Festival
    (Omaha, NE), 202–6
Needles, William, 399
Nehmer, Sherry, 235
Nehring, Michael, 69
Nelson, Brian, 339, 342
Nelson, Robert, 317
Nelson Gallery, 195
Nesbitt, Cathleen, 460
Nettles, John, 17

Neville, John, 395–96
Neville-Andrews, John, 111, 345, 347
New Jersey Shakespeare Festival
    (Madison, NJ), 210–16
New Place, xiii
New River Shakespeare Festival (Fort
    Lauderdale, FL), 118–20
New Shakespeare Company (San
    Francisco, CA), 42–44, 459, 461,
    475
New Swan Theatre, 376, 378
New Theatre Group, 85
New World Theatre, 208
New York City Ballet, 100
New York Philharmonic, 238
New York Renaissance Festival
    (Tuxedo, NY), 235–36
New York Shakespeare Festival (New
    York, NY), xvi, xviii, 236–42
New York State Council on the Arts,
    219, 224, 229–30, 247
Newhouse Theatre (see Mitzi E.
    Newhouse Theatre)
Newman, Neal, 292–93
Newman Theater, 237–38
Newport Art Museum, 300
Ngema, Mbongeni, 208
Nichols, Harriet, 297
Nicoll, Allardyce, 311
Nightcap Productions, 401
Nimrod Theatre (Sydney), 381–382
Noble, Adrian, 473, 479
Noble, Robert, 459
Noel, Craig, 46, 318
Nollen, Nancy, 82
Norman Arts and Humanities
    Council, 274
Norment, Elizabeth, 69
Norris, Lisa, 150–51
North Carolina School of the Arts, 256
North Carolina Shakespeare Festival
    (High Point, NC), 255–59
North Carolina Theatre Ensemble, 256
North Tahoe Fine Arts Council, 206
Northcott, Donna, 198–99
Nunn, Trevor, 358, 478, 487
Nye, Carrie, 102

O'Brien, Michael, 166, 169

O'Brien, Peggy, 175
O'Brien, Jack, 46, 49–50
O'Brien, Terrence, 227–29
O'Connor, Joyce, 336
O'Dea, Marcia, 22
O'Gara, Patrick, 143
O'Keefe, John, 81
O'Meara, Jack J., 270
O'Meara, Kathryn Huey, 270
O'Neill, William, 105
O'Toole, Peter, 465
Oak Park Festival Theatre
    (Oak Park, IL), 144–46
Oasis Theatre Company
    (New York, NY), 242–43
Oates, Joyce Carol, 253
Oates, Warren, 154
Occhiogrosso, Anne, 372
Octagon, The (Alabama), 1, 3
Odashima, Yushi, 493
Ogus, Carol, 4
Ohio Theatre (Cleveland), 262–63
Ohio Theatre (NY), 223
Ojai Festival Theatre Company (Ojai,
    CA), 44–46
Oklahoma Shakespeare in the Park
    (Edmond, OK), 270–73
Oklahoma Shakespearean Festival
    (Durant, OK), 266–70
Oklahoma, State Arts Council of,
    270–271
Old Arts Quad (Auckland, New
    Zealand), 498, 500
Old Globe Theatre (San Diego, CA),
    xvi, 46–53
Old Prop Shop Theater, 238
Old Vic Shakespeare Company, 464
Old Vic Theatre (London, England),
    463–70
Old Vic Theatre School, 414
Olivier, Laurence, 464–65, 478, 487
Olivier Award, 254, 447
Ollerman, Fred, 374
Oman, Timothy, 244
Omans, Stuart E., 120–21
Omer-Sherman, Randy, 64
Ontario Arts Council, 387
Open Air Theatre, New Shakespeare
    Company (London, England),
459–63
Open Air Theatre, The (Chiltern), 449
Ore-Ida Women's Challenge, 136
Oregon Shakespeare Festival
    (Ashland, OR), xvi, xvii, xviii, xix,
    275–87
Orendorf, Bruce, 93–94
Orlando - UCF Shakespeare Festival
    (Orlando, FL), 120–23
Ormerod, Nick, 447
Ornitorrinco (Brazil), xiv, 427
Osborn, Vangie, 135
Other Place, The, 473, 478
Other Stage, 238
Ouellette, Dennis T., 249
Outdoor Summer Shakespeare
    (Auckland, New Zealand),
    498–500
Ouzounian, Richard, 399
Owens, Geoffrey, 230
Oxford Dramatic Society, 414
Oxnam, Robert F., 210–11

Pacific Repertory Theatre, 28–29
Packer, Tina, 185—90
Page, Anthony, 103
Page, Patrick, 283
Palitzsch, Peter, 435
Palk, Nancy, 253
Palm, Reinhard, 433
Palm Beach County School for the
    Performing Arts, 126
Palm Beach Gardens, 123
Palm Beach Shakespeare Festival
    (Jupiter/Palm Beach, FL), 123–26
Pan Asian Repertory Theatre, 330
Papp, Joseph, 37, 104, 194, 236–40,
    252, 259
Papula, Dagmar, 424, 426–27
Parenteau, Pamela, 158
Parfitt, David, 470–71
Parkmoor Bowling Lanes, 154
Parks, Suzan-Lori, 254
Parrent, Jeanie, 330
Parrish, Maxfield, 180
Parton, Dolly, 94, 269
Paschina, Luca, 353
Pasco, Richard, 17
Pasteur, Louis, 416

Patel, Lina, 169
Patrone, Phillip, 184
Patterson, Margaret, 97
Patterson, Tom, 391
Patterson, Tom Theatre, 396
Patton, John, 455
Patton, Pat, 284, 287
Patton, William W., xix, 275, 277,
    280, 287
Paul Masson Mountain Winery, 79
Paul Masson Winery, 63
Pavilion Theatre of Performing Arts
    of Virginia Beach, 356
Payne, Ben Iden, xv, 46, 78, 276–77,
    476
Payne, Brian, 74
PBK Memorial Hall (see Phi Beta
    Kappa Memorial Hall)
Peachy, Burt, 35
Peacock, Lucy, 399
Peck, Bill, 79–80
Peel Castle (Isle of Man), 486
Pelletier, Dee, 169–70
Pendleton, Austin, 244
Pennell, Nicholas, 295, 394, 399
Pennington, Michael, 450–53
Pennsylvania Shakespeare Festival
    (Center Valley, PA), 290–92
Penshurst Place (Kent), 486
Pereira, Kim, 143
Perry, Jane, 306
Persoff, Nehemiah, 75
Peter, Jeffrey Edward, 236
Peters, Suzanna, 33
Petersen, Delores, 313
Peterson, Gary, 81
Petronius, 393
Pettigrew, John, 391, 393–94
Peymann, Claus, 422, 428, 444
Phaneuf, Cindy Melby, 202, 204–5
Phelps, Samuel, 474
Phi Beta Kappa Memorial Hall
    (Williamsburg, VA), 361
Philadelphia Shakespeare in the Park
    (Philadelphia, PA), 292–94
Phillips, R. Scott, 344–45
Phillips, Ray, 350
Phillips, Robin, 394–96, 399
Phillips, Suzanne, 315, 318

Piccolo Spoleto Festival, 360
Pickering, James H., 316
Pickle Family Circus, 42
Pinero, Arthur Wing, 238
Pinney, Robert, 97
Pinter, Harold, 48
Piñero, Miguel, 239
Pirandello, Luigi, 47
Piscator, Erwin, 433–34
Pit, The (Barbican Centre, London),
    473, 478
Pittman, Perry, 3
Pittman, Robert W., 236
Platt, Martin L., 1–3, 5
Playfair, Nigel, 475
Playground Theatre, 242
Playhouse 91 (New York City), 244
Playhouse Square, 263
Playhouse Theatre, The, 366–67
Pleasants, Philip, 8
Plummer, Christopher, 101, 105,
    392–93
Plummer, John, 218, 221
Plunkett, Mary Ann, 166
Plymouth Theatre Royal, 451
Podewell, Buzz, 268
Poel, William, 276, 327
Poertner, Tim, 339
Pogue, Kate, 329
Polak, Roman, 149
Pope, Nancy, 142
Port Elizabeth Opera House (South
    Africa), 504
Port Elizabeth Shakespeare Festival
    (Port Elizabeth, South Africa),
    504–7
Port Elizabeth Theatre Guild (South
    Africa), 505
Porter, Cole, 49, 356
Porter, Edith, 504
Porter, Eric, 466, 478
Portland Center for the Performing
    Arts, 54, 275, 281, 287–88
Portman, Jamie, 391, 393–94
Post, C. W., 318
Post Summer Shakespeare Festival
    (Garza Theatre, Post, TX), 318–21
Potter's Field Company, 104
Powell, J. Ellsworth, 311

Powell, Jan, 222, 287–90
Powell, Jeff, 312
Powis, Earl of, 456
President's Volunteer Action Award, 281
Price, Iona, 470, 472
Price, John, 451
Price, Michael, 106
Prince, Harold, 264
Prince-Jones, Jane, 318
Pritner, Cal, 138
Propfel, Michael, 430
Prospect Park (Brooklyn), 230
Public Theater, 236, 238–39, 252
Public Theatre of Greater Fort Lauderdale, 118
Publick Theatre (Boston, MA), 182–84
Puget Sound Theatre Ensemble, 370
Purkiss, Bill, 35

Quayle, Anthony, 476

Rabb, Ellis, 51, 102
Rabe, David, 238
Rackoff, Louis, 256, 258
Ragsdale, Teresa, 12
Rain, Douglas, 393–94
Raistrick, George, 21
Ramey, C. Douglas, 153–54, 156
Randall, Tony, 106
Randall L. Jones Theatre, 346–47
Randolph, Tod, 190
Ran Jie, 411
Rashbrook, Stephen, 21
Ratliff, Sally, 312
Ravenscroft, Christopher, 19
Ravinia Shakespeare Company, xvi
Rawlings, William, 458–59
Ray's Oasis, 134
Raymond, Gerard, 448
Rayne, Stephen, 208
Raz, Jeff, 42
Reade, Simon, 448, 452
Reardon, Dennis, 238
Reardon, Michael, 479
Redd, Jr., Reynolds B., 330, 332–33
Redgrave, Lynn, 104
Redgrave, Michael, 464, 476
Redgrave, Vanessa, 124, 487

Reduced Shakespeare Company (Los Angeles, CA), 53–59
Reed, David, 106
Reed, Joseph Verner, 100–2
Regent's Park, 459
Reggiardo, Carl, 69
Reid, John, 81
Reid, Kate, 396, 399
Reinhardt, Max, 42, 433
Reinhardt, Paul D., 339, 342
Renaissance Films, 472
Renaissance Theatre Company (London, England), 470–73
Renegade Shakespeare Company (Norman, OK), 273–74
Reno, Johnny, 331
Renton Howard, et al, architects, 466
Reynolds, Arthur, 455
Reynolds, Burt, 126
Reynolds, Edgar, 289
Rhode Island Shakespearean Theatre (Newport, RI), 299–303
Rhode Island State Council on the Arts, 301
Rhomberg, Vince, 118–19
Rice, Tim, 466
Rice, T. Walker, 233
Rich, Joseph, 166
Richard Basehart Playhouse, 38
Richardson, Ian, 16–17
Richardson, Ralph, 465
Richfield, Edwin, 18–19
Ricklefs, Clarence, 42–43, 60
Riddiford, Susan, 367, 369
Riegel-Ernst, Sandra, 374
Rieman, Sue Ellen, 270
Rigg, Diana, 478
Rindfleisch, Mary, 162
Ringling Bros. and Barnum & Bailey Circus, 54
Rintoul, David, 13, 19
Rippon, Mary, 90
Risso, Jogn, 268
Risso, Molly, 266
Risso, Riley, 266
Ritson, Elisabeth, 348
Riverside Park, 244
Riverside Shakespeare Company (New York, NY), 243–45

Robards, Jr., Jason, 393
Robbins, Sanford, 345
Roberge, Michele, 37
Robert Hull Fleming Museum, 351
Roberts, Eunice, 20–22
Robertson, Lanie, 52
Robertson, Toby, 404, 508
Robin, Rob, 301
Robinson, Christopher, 469
Robinson, Shaw, 61
Roche, Michelle Armstrong, 299, 301
Rock, Christopher, 164, 168–69
Rock Creek Park, xviii, 108, 112
Rockefeller, John D., 475
Rockefeller Foundation, 171
Rodriguez, Bill, 300
Roger Furman Theatre, 208
Rogers, Michael, 76
Rogers, Roy, 269
Rohmann, Chris, 180
Rolling Stones, 148, 247
Roma, Margrit, 42, 60
Rookery, The, 485
Roos, Norvid Jenkins, 73
Root, Steve, 233
Rosa Mae Griffin Foundation, 339
Rose, Bob, 455
Rose, Clifford, 20–21
Rose, Dale A. J., 194, 331
Rose, Richard, 399
Rose Court, 486
Rosen, Carol, 211
Rosenberg, Scott, 74
Rosenbush, Mark, 144
Ross, Elizabeth, 100
Ross, Murray, 97–99
Rossbander, Erik, 427
Rothe, Hans, 422
Roxbury Outreach Shakespeare
    Experience (ROSE), (Boston,
    MA), 184–85
Royal Academy of Dramatic Art, 288,
    420, 505
Royal Botanical Gardens (London),
    460
Royal Coburg Theatre, 464
Royal Court Theatre, 253
Royal National Lifeboot Institution,
    447

Royal Shakespeare Company
    (Stratford-Upon-Avon, England),
    xiii, 473–81
Royal Shakespeare Theatre, 473
Royal Victoria Coffee Music Hall, 464
Royal Victoria Theatre, 464
Royall Tyler Theatre, 349, 351
Royan, Lindsay, 485
Ruchti, Ariela, 427
Rucker, Mark, 74
Ruckhäberle, Hans-Joachim, 432
Rüdiger, Reinhold, 430
Rudman, Bill, 262
Rühle, Ursala, 431
Russell, Brian, 158
Russell, Charles, 414
Russell, Jan, 342
Russell, William, 21
Ruta, Ken, 51
Ruth Page Theater, 148–49
Rutland Open Air Theatre, 484
Ryan, Mitch, 154
Ryan, Robert, 86
Rylance, Mark, 254

Saddler, Donald, 264
Saint George's Park (South Africa),
    504
Saltz, Amy, 252
Salvante, Margaret, 251
Sam Dale, Sam, 12
Sammons Center for the Arts, 330
Sams, Eric, 356
Samuell Grand Park, 331
San Antonio Shakespeare Festival
    (San Antonio, TX), 321–24
San Diego Community Theatre, 46
San Francisco Opera, 75
San Francisco Shakespeare Festival
    (San Francisco, CA), xvi, 59–62
Sanborn-Skyline County Park, 79
Sanchez-Scott, Milcha, 254
Sand Harbor State Park, 206
Sandberg, Paul, 348
Sander, Peter, 225–26
Sandoe, James, 90, 277
Sarandon, Christopher, 105
Sarbacher, Thomas, 427
Saroyan, William, 47

Sartre, Jean-Paul, 117
Saskatchewan Tourism Award, 402
Saura, Marina, 507
Scaccia's Restaurant, 154
Scammon, Howard, 361
Scarfe, Alan, 395–96, 399
Schacter, Stephen, 144
Schade, Birge, 427
Schaubühne (Berlin), 438, 440
Schauspielhaus (Bochum, Germany),
    429
Schauspielhaus (Cologne, Germany),
    431
Schauspielhaus (Leipzig, Germany),
    431
Schauspielhaus (Zurich), 433
Scheeder, Louis, 109, 111
Scheie, Danny, 70, 76, 78
Schenk, William, 349–50, 353
Schiffman, Jean, 41, 43
Schiller, Friedrich von, 434
Schiller Park, 259–61
Schiller Theater, 428
Schlegel, A. W., 422, 435
Schlesinger, Katherine, 21
Schlueter, June, 14
Schmid, Petra, 427
Schmidt, Douglas, 51
Schmitt, Saladin, 422
Schneider, Bekki Jo, 156
Schneider, Robert Eldred, 23
Schoenberg, Deborah, 182–83
Schottleutner, Lorrie, 96
Schreck, Myron, 23
Schroeder, Bill, 266
Schubert, Gerard J., 290–91
Schutzer, Kathy, 85
Schwartz, Rita, 224
Schwartz, Steven, 217
Schweitzer Mall Outdoor Stage, 69
Scofield, Paul, 476–78
Scott, George C., 237, 239
Scott, Harold, 113–14
Scott, John, 332
Scott, Sir Walter, 24
Seale, Douglas, 102
Season Good Pavilion, 153
Seattle Repertory, 368

Seattle Shakespeare Festival (Seattle,
    WA), 366–69
Seiberling, Frank A., 266
Selby, Lorraine, 488
Sellars, Peter, 181, 186
Selling, Gunter, 432
Semple, Goldie, 399
Serban, André, 421
Serban, Andrei, 239
Sessions, John, 471
Seven Stages Theater, 127
Sewell, Marjorie, 166–68, 170
Sewell, Richard C., 164
Shaanxi People's Art Theatre, 411
Shaffer, Peter, 477
Shakespeare, John, 501
Shakespeare and Company (Lenox,
    MA), 185–91
Shakespeare Anniversary Committee,
    xvi
Shakespeare Association of America,
    358, 360
Shakespeare at Benbow Lake
    (Garberville, CA), 62–65
Shakespeare at Sand Harbor (Incline
    Village, NV), 206–7
Shakespeare at Sheldon
    (Chippenham, Wiltshire, GB),
    481–82
Shakespeare at Stan Hywet (Akron,
    OH), 265–66
Shakespeare at the Ruins
    (Barboursville, VA), 353–56
Shakespeare at Winedale (Winedale,
    TX), 324–29
Shakespeare-by-the-Book Festival
    (Houston, TX), 356–57
Shakespeare-by-the-Sea (Virginia
    Beach, VA), 356–57
Shakespeare Centre Library, 480
Shakespeare en Avignon (Avignon,
    France), 419–21
Shakespeare Festival of Dallas
    (Dallas, TX), 330–34
Shakespeare Festival/LA (Los
    Angeles, CA), 65–67
Shakespeare Globe Centre (New
    Zealand), 502

Shakespeare Globe Centre (USA), xiv, 213
Shakespeare Globe Museum (London), 359
Shakespeare in Delaware Park (Buffalo, NY), 245–49
Shakespeare in Santa Fe (Santa Fe, NM), 216–17
Shakespeare in the Park, Assiniboine Theatre (Winnipeg, Manitoba, Canada), 385–86
Shakespeare in the Park (Chico, CA), 67–68
Shakespeare in the Park (Fort Worth, TX), 334–36
Shakespeare Institute (AST), 102
Shakespeare Jubilee, xiii, 473
Shakespeare Memorial Theatre, 46, xiii, xiv, 473–480
Shakespeare on the Green (Lake Forest, IL), 146–48
Shakespeare on the Saskatchewan Festival (Saskatoon, Saskatchewan, Canada), 401–3
Shakespeare on Wheels (Baltimore, MD), xvii, 171–74
Shakespeare Orange County (Orange, CA), 68–70
Shakespeare Oxford Society, 179
Shakespeare Repertory (Chicago, IL), 148–50
Shakespeare Santa Cruz (Santa Cruz, CA), 70–79
Shakespeare Society of China, 404, 412
Shakespeare Summer Festival, xvi
Shakespeare Theatre (Tokyo, Japan), 491–95
Shakespeare Theatre (Washington, DC), xviii, 108–15
Shakespeare Theatre Arts Repertory (Campbell, CA), 79–80
Shallatt, Lee, 35, 69
Shange, Ntozake, 238–39
Shanghai Academy of Theatre, 404–5, 409–11
Shanghai Kunju Opera Troupe, 409
Shanghai People's Art Theatre, 406

Shanghai Puppet Theatre Company, 411
Shanghai Theatre Festival, 408
Shanghai Yueju Opera House, 407
Shanley, John Patrick, 81, 242
Shattuck, Charles, xv, 361
Shattuck, Scott, 339
Sha Wei, 411
Shaw, George Bernard, 102, 117, 238, 313, 347, 460, 475
Shaw, Glen Byam, 476
Shaw, Harold, 103
Shaw, Sebastian, 17
Shea, Maureen, 176
Sheen, Martin, 239
Sheldon Manor, 481
Shelley, Paul, 17, 20
Shenandoah Shakespeare Express (Dayton, VA), xvii, 357–60
Shepard, Sam, 239
Sherman Arena Company, 414
Shi Jihua, 408
Shinjuku-Nishitoyama Development Co., Ltd., 495
Shipman, Liz, 230–32
Shipp, John Wesley, 356
Shonka, Ted, 333
Shuler, Jyl, 345
Sicular, Robert, 62
Siegel, Jacqueline, 124–25
Siemens, Stephanie, 339
Sierra, Gregory, 233
Silva, Pedro M., 255–56
Simmons, Pat, 348
Simon, Eli, 348
Simon, Neil, 50
Simon Edison Centre for the Performing Arts, 46, 49
Simpson, Richard, 20
Sims, Judy, 9–10
Sinfield, Alan, xx, 477
Singer, Daniel, 53, 55
Sink, Christopher B., 185, 187
Sinsheimer, Karen, 70
Sinsheimer, Robert, 70–71
Sipes, John, 138–42
Skene, Prudence, 450
Skilbeck, Alison, 21

Skurski, Gloria, 243
Slater, Jock, 455
Smith, Auriol, 20
Smith, Cal, 312
Smith, Jamie R., 80
Smith, Maggie, 394
Smith, Oliver, 264
Smith, Sara M., 353, 355–56
Smith, Susan Harris, 295
Smith, Vicki L., 284
Smithsonian Institute Discovery
    Theatre, 111
Smits, Jimmy, 93
Smollett, Tobias, 27
Snow, Dan, 233
Sobol, Harriet, 218–19
Somerset, J. A. B., 392
Sommervill, Charles, 320
Sondheim, Stephen, 50
Sonoma Valley Shakespeare Festival
    (Sonoma, CA), 80–82
Sonoma Vintage Theatre
    (Sonoma,CA), 82–84
Sooner Shakespeare Festival (Norman,
    OK), 274–75
Sooner Theatre, 273–74
Sophocles, 213, 487
Sothern, E. H., xv, 86
South African Research Program
    (Yale University), 208
South Coast Botanical Gardens, 65, 67
South Coast Repertory, 78
South Coast Repertory Conservatory,
    420
Southeastern Shakespeare Festival, xvi
Southmoreland Park, 194
Southwest Shakespeare Festival
    (Phoenix, AZ), 10–12
Spahn, Karen S., 339
Spano, Joe, 93
Sperr, Martin, 436
Spratlan, Lewis, 304
Sprung, Guy, 387
St. Clements Church (NY), 251
St. Dogmaels Abbey, 446–47
St. George's Park (South Africa), 505
St. James Park, 59
St. Lawrence Centre, 388–89
St. Louis Shakespeare Company

(St. Louis, MO), 198–200
St. Mark's Church, 109
St. Nicholas Theatre, 144
Staats, Marilyn Dorn, 129
Staatsschauspiel (Dresden, Germany),
    429
Staatstheater (Braunschweig,
    Germany), 429
Staatstheater (Darmstadt, Germany),
    429
Staatstheater Kassel (Germany), 431
Stables (The Mount), 185
Stables Theatre, 187
Städtische Bühnen (Münster,
    Germany), 432
Staff Players Repertory Company, 29
Stagecraft Productions, 233
Staley, Mark, 82
Stalin, Joseph, 436
Stamford Arts Centre, 482
Stamford Shakespeare Company
    (Stamford, Lincolnshire, England),
    482–85
Stan Hywet Hall and Gardens, 265
Stanley, Audrey, 70, 77, 92
Stanley, Charles, 230
Stanton, Barry, 453
Starlight Theatre, 195
Starplex Amphitheatre, 331
Stauber, Sylvia, 428
Stefano, John, 138
Stein, Peter, 422, 438–40
Stein, Richard, 36
Stephen Foster Memorial Theatre, 294
Stephens, Karen, 486, 488
Steppenwolf, 138
Sterling, George, 29
Sterling Renaissance Festival
    (Sterling, NY), 249–51
Stern, Melissa, 227–29
Stevens, Christine, 180–81
Stevens, Roger, 104
Stevens, Thomas Wood, xv, 46
Stewart, Patrick, 13, 16–17
Stiers, David Ogden, 51
Stockinger, Jacob, 374
Stoddard, Joseph H., 33
Stoller, Jennie, 19
Stoppard, Tom, 81

Stotts, Michael, 210, 213
Strand Theatre, 185
Strasberg, Lee, 252
Stratford Festival of Canada (Stratford, Ontario, Canada), xvi–xvii, 391–401
Stratford Institute (CT), 105
Stratford Shakespearean Festival, xvi
Stratford Shakespeare Festival (Stratford, New Zealand), 500–2
Stratford Shakespeare Society (New Zealand), 500
Stratford-upon-the-Housatonic, Inc., 106
Strauss, Marilyn, 194, 196
Streep, Meryl, 239
Strehler, Giorgio, 436
Stríbrny, Zdenek, xiv
Strindberg, August, 23, 394
Strong, Sir Roy, 350
Stuart, Lynne, 105
Stull, William L., 32, 86
Suchet, David, 17, 487, 489
Sugar Pine Point State Park, 43
Sulka, Elaine, 233, 274
Sullivan, Arthur, 117, 164, 347, 395–96
Sullivan, Hugh, 22
Sullivan, Jeremiah, 263
Sullivan, Susan, 226
Summer Love Repertory Theatre, 375
Summers, Bill, 455
Sun Jiaxiu, 407
Sunken Garden Theatre, 321
Sunnyvale Summer Repertory (Sunnyvale, CA), 84–85
Susan Stein Shiva Theater, 237
Suthoff, Barbara, 429
Sutton, Dudley, 20
Sutton, Judith, 62
Sutton, Judith Lyn, 79–80
Suzman, Janet, 332
Swain, Howard, 27
Swan, The, 479
Swan Theatre, 32, 473
Swander, Homer, 12, 15
Swartz, John B., 79–80
Sweeney, Susan, 348
Sweet, Betsy, 164, 166

Swetz, Theodore, 373–74
Swingle, Anne Bennett, 172
Swinney, Donald H., 226
Swit, Loretta, 37
Sykes, Maureen, 458
Sykes, Ray, 454, 456–57
Sylvester, Suzan, 22

Tabori, George, 444
Tabori, Kristoffer, 35
Tackes, Ruth, 83
Taft, Ellen, 292
Takazauckas, Albert, 60
Talbot, Ian, 459, 461, 463
Tamura, Seiya, 495
Tandy, Jessica, 394
Tank Players, 308
Tate, Kamella, 69
Tatton Park Old Hall (Cheshire), 486
Taubman, Howard, 312
Tavener, Jane, 381
Taylor, Clark, 133
Taylor, C. P., 52
Taylor, R. Thad, 31–32
Taylor, Robert, 68
Taylor, Sandy, 273–74
Taymor, Julie, 252–53
Teare, Dorothy, 262–63
Teatro Due di Parma (Italy), xiv, 427
Teatro Meta, 50–51
Tebbut, Sharon, 173
Tebelak, John-Michael, 263
Temple Amphitheatre, 486
Tennon, Julius, 309
Terrace Theatre, 110
Texas Commission on the Arts, 337
Texas Shakespeare Festival (Kilgore, TX), 337–43
Thacker, David, 486–89
Thaler, Martin, 351, 353
Thalia Theater (Hamburg), 430
Thames Television, 471
Theater am Leibnizplatz (Bremen, Germany), 424
Theatre at Monmouth (Monmouth, ME), 164–70
Theatre Barn, 324–26, 328
Theatre Communications Group, 116
Théâtre du Nouveau Monde, 392–93

Théâtre et Anglais, 415
Theatre for a New Audience (New York, NY), 251–55
Theatre Guild, 100
Theatre in the Mind (ASF), 4–5
Theatre Museum (London), 469, 473
Theatre of Martin, 149
Theatre of The Enchanted Forest, 166
Théâtre Repère, 427
Theatre Royal (Bath), 451
Theatre Royal (Sydney), 382
Theatre Set-Up, Ltd. (London, England), 485–86
Theatre Workshop (Auckland, New Zealand), 499
Theatreworks Shakespeare Festival (Colorado Springs, CO), 96–100
Theodore, Madelyn, 161–62
Third Stage (Stratford), 394
Thomas, Dylan, 324
Thomas, Eberle, 196
Thomas, Gary, 391, 398, 400
Thomas, Michael, 19–20
Thomas, Tamar, 470, 472
Thompson, Kent, 1, 5–8
Thompson, Sada, 51, 395
Thornber, Robin, 471–72
Thorndike, Sue, 449
Thorndike, Sybil, 464
Thorwald, Achim, 432
Three Rivers Shakespeare Festival (Pittsburgh, PA), xviii, 294–99
Thurston, Jim, 170
Tian, Jia, 407–8
Tibbels, Marla, 173
Tichenor, Austin, 58
Tichler, Rosemarie, 236
Tieck, Ludwig, 422, 435
Tienjing People's Art Theatre, 407, 411
Timmons, John, 292
Tiwari, Atul, xiv
Tobey, Elizabeth, 169
Tofteland, Curt L., 153, 155–56
Tokyo Panasonic Globe (Tokyo, Japan), 495–98
Tolan, Robert W., 259
Tolaydo, Michael, 174–75
Toledo, Kathleen, 118

Tolethorpe Hall, 482, 484
Toliver House, 354
Tom Patterson Theatre (Stratford), 391, 396, 398
Topol, Haim, 75
Toronto Arts Council, 387
Toronto Free Theatre, 387–88
Tourneur, Cyril, 439
Tower Theatre Islington, 415
Tracy, Susan, 18
Travelling Shakespeare Company (St. Mary's City, MD), 174–76
Tree, Herbert, 474
Treetop Theatre, 10
Trenda, Robin, 67
Trewin, J. C., 460, 463
Trinity Park Playhouse, 334
Trinity Repertory Company, 299, 302
Trinity Repertory Theatre, 304
Trussell, Robert, 196
Tsoutsouvas, Sam, 345
Tubman, Harriet, 87
Tucker, Patrick, 24, 181, 222
Turner, Jerry, xviii, 92, 280, 282, 287
Turner, Scott, 335
Tuttle, Jane, 127
Tygres Heart Shakespeare Company (Portland, OK), 287–90
Tyree, Robert, 378
Tyson, John, 179

Uhley, Jay, 31
Ukiah Players Theatre, 40
Undermain Theater, 333
Union Labor Temple, 38
Universal Studios, 122
University of Bridgeport, 102
University of Bristol Theatre Collection, 469
Urkowitz, Steven, 16, 226
Ustinov, Peter, 394
Utah Shakespearean Festival (Cedar City, UT), xvi, xvii, 343–49
Utah Shakespearean Festival Center for the Performing Arts, 347

Van Cliburn Auditorium, 337, 339
Van Druten, John, 47
Van Griethuysun, Ted, 112

Van Horn, Bill, 224
Van Leishout, James A., 370–71
Van Noy, Rick, 345
Vanier Park (Vancouver), 383
Varner, Gary, 266, 268
Varon, Daniela, 176
Varsity Theatre, 279
Vaughan, Stuart, 244–45
Veloudos, Spiro, 182–83
Vere, Charles, 69, 195
Vereen, Ben, 75
Veterans Memorial Building, 24
Vickery, John, 37
Victoria Shakespeare Festival (TX),
    xvi
Victoria University of Wellington
    Summer Shakespeare (Wellington,
    New Zealand), 502–4
Victory Theatre, 254
Village Green Arts Complex, 34
Village Green Fine Arts Association,
    35
Villa Montalvo Center for the Arts, 79
Vincent, Maura, 62
Vinci, Leonardo da, 439
Vineyard Playhouse (Vineyard Haven,
    MA), 191–92
Virginia Arts Council, 355
Virginia Foundation for Humanities,
    359
Virginia Historical Society, 354
Virginia Shakespeare Festival
    (Williamsburg, VA), 361–66
Visscher, Claes Jansz, 32
Vivian Beaumont Theatre, 238, 392
Vizcaya Museum Gardens, 117
Volksbühne (Berlin), 428
Volkstheater, 425–27
Volz, Jim, 3, 5, 121
von Sydow, Max, 466
Vos, Eric, 422
Voskovec, George, 102
Voss, Gert, 445
Voss, Philip, 19
Vybiral, Frank, 143

Wachsmann, Michael, 442
Waddington, Janet, 486, 488
Wadley, Carleen, 310

Wagner, Richard, 235
Walford, Glen, 452
Walken, Christopher, 105
Walker, Jewell, 374
Walker, Margaret, 482
Walker, Nancy, 264
Wall Street Center for the Arts, 67–68
Wallace, Craig, 158
Waller, Lewis, 474
Walt Disney Amphitheater, 120–21,
    123
Walt Disney Company, 121
Walt Disney World, 122
Walter, Isabel, 500–1
Walter, Marie, 500
Waltmar Theatre, 69
Wanamaker, Sam, 332, 358, 426
Wanamaker, Zoë, 461
Wang Fum, 411
Warburton, Eileen, 299, 301
Warburton, Roger, 299
Ward, Bessye Cowden, 312
Ward, Heather, 355
Ware, Herta (Geer) 86
Warner, David, 478
Warren, Jim, 357–58, 360
Warren, Michael, 71–72
Warren, Sue, 72
Washington Center for the Performing
    Arts, 370, 371
Washington Park Parade Grounds, 218
Washington Shakespeare Festival
    Olympia, WA), 370–72
Washington Theatre Club, 109
Wasnak, Diane, 42
Waterloo Bridge, 464
Watermeier, Daniel J., 208, 357
Waters, John, 180
Watkins, Jeffrey, 126–29
Watson, Anne Thaxter, 89
Watson, Douglas, 102, 239
Watson, Julia, 20
Watson, Robert, 130–31
Weatherall, Robin, 16
Weaver, Sigourney, 186, 330
Webb, Jimmy, 125
Webber, Andrew Lloyd, 465
Weber, Harry, 199
Webster, Benjamin, 474

Webster, Bonnie, 174
Webster, John, 279, 394
Webster, Margaret, xvi
Weeden, Derrick Lee, 8
Weeks, Jerome, 331
Weicker, Jr., Lowell P., 106
Weill, Kurt, 238
Weinstein, Charles, 170
Weiss, Linus, 244
Weiss, Peter, 478
Welch, Chris, 336
Welles, Orson, 370
Wellington Botanical Gardens, 502–3
Wendrich, Fritz, 432
Wen Pulin, 411
Wesp, Patricia, 365
West, Frances, 176
West, Mae, 170
West, Steve, 355
Westbrook, John, 454
Westerly Shakespeare in the Park
    (Westerly, RI), 303–6
Westhoff Theatre, 139, 141
Whalen III, Thomas M., 218
Whalley, Ann Cook, 306
Wharton, Edith, 185
Wharton Theatre, 185, 187
Wheeler, Robert C., 224
Whitaker, Tom, 339
White, Cynthia, 136
White, Richard E. T., 24
White, Sully, 159
Whitehead, Paxton, 51
Whitener, Kim, 176
Whitford, Bradley, 345
Whitworth, Paul, 18–19, 73–74, 77
Whole Theatre Company, 252
Wiehr, Michelle, 355
Wilcox, Bob, 199
Wilcox Park, 303
Wilde Players, 415
Wilder, Katrinka, 164
Wilder, Thornton, 49, 68, 263
Wildgruber, Ulrich, 437
Wilds, Lillian, 33
Wilkins, Helen, 504
Will Geer Theatricum Botanicum
    (Topanga, CA), 85–89

William, David, 396, 399, 400, 454,
    460–61, 463
Williams, Beau, 1
Williams, Clifford, 507–8
Williams, Esther, 388
Williams, Melissa, 306
Williams, Nance, 94
Williams, Tennessee, 100
Willis, Susan, 5
Wills, Ivah, xv
Wilson, August, 50
Wilson, Eileen, 191
Wilson, Joe, 194
Wilson, Robert, 443
Wilson, Stephen D., 342–43
Winar, Gail, 235
Windelman, Mike, 339
Winedale Historical Center, 324
Winfield, J. M., 58
Winfield, Paul, 112
Wingate, Gifford W., 337
Winkworth, Patricia, 44
Winn, Steven, 41
Winston, Bobby, 59–60
Winter, Carole, 450
Winton M. Blount Cultural Park, 1, 3
Wisconsin Shakespeare Festival
    (Platteville, WI), 375–79
Wiseman, Aviva, 449
Wiseman, Joseph, 111
Wiseman, Michael, 449
Witter Bynner Foundation for Poetry,
    217
Wolfe, George C., 236, 239
Wolfinger, Kirk, 162, 164
Wolfit, Margaret, 463
Wolk, Mary, 45
Wollaton Hall, 486
Wood, Ian, 446
Woodland Park, 159
Woodman, Bill, 195–96
Woods, Mark, 256
Woodstock Opera House, 40
Woolf, Henry, 401
Woolridge Park, 308
Works Progress Administration, 90,
    276, 334
Woronicz, Henry, 275, 282, 284, 345

Worth, Irene, 391
Worthen, Laura Ann, 294
Wright, Frank Lloyd, 11, 145, 372
Wright, Jennifer, 43
Wright, Laurence, 506
Wright, Tony, 126
Wuhan Spoken Drama House, 410
Württembergische Landesbühne
    (Esslingen, Germany), 430
Wycherley, William, 100
Wyldwood, The, 251
Wyldwood Stage, 10

Xian Spoken Drama House, 410
Xiong Guodong, 410
Xiong Yuanwei, 412
Xuan Ying, 411
Xu Qiping, 406, 410

Yale Repertory Theatre, 50
Yan Bin, 411
Yang, Daniel S. P., 91–92
Yang Huizhen, 410
Yang Zongjing, 412
Yao Jinshi, 411
Yates, Frances, 495
Yeager, Michael, 161–63
Yeats, W. B., 487
Yin Ruocheng, 404
York, Susanna, 208
Yoshizawa, Ken, 493
Young, Gerald, 249
Young, Mrs. H. E., 501
Young, Stephanie, 89
Young, Virginia, 249
Young Company, The (Orlando), 123
Young Company (Stratford, Ontario),
    394–96
Young Vic Company (London,
    England), 486–91
Young Vic Theatre, 486, 488
Young Vic Youth Theatre, 488

Zachary Scott Arena Stage, 308
Zadek, Peter, 422, 436–38, 440–41,
    443–44
Zaks, Jerry, 358
Zha, Peide, 407–8
Zhang Jinglan, 409

Zhang Qihong, 411–12
Zheng Ziru, 411
Zhou Lai, 411
Zhou Lili, 408
Ziegler, Joseph, 253
Zilker Park, 308, 310
Zimmer, Steven L., 230
Zinger, Arie, 422
Zivot, Eric, 41
Zlotescu, Elena, 172

About the Editors and Contributors

THE EDITORS

RON ENGLE is the Chester Fritz Distinguished Professor of Theatre Arts at the University of North Dakota (UND) at Grand Forks. He is coeditor of *The American Stage: Social and Economic Issues from the Colonial Period to the Present*, published by Cambridge University Press, the author of *Maxwell Anderson on the European Stage*; and the founding editor of the international journal *Theatre History Studies*. He has also published widely in journals and in such books as *Foreign Shakespeare, Shakespeare Around the Globe, Theatre in the Third Reich, the Prewar Years, American Theatre Companies, Maxwell Anderson and the New York Stage*, and the *Cambridge Guide to American Theatre*. He has received grants and fellowships from such agencies as the German Academic Exchange Service, NEH, and the International Research and Exchange Board. In 1989 he was guest professor in the Institut für Theaterwissenschaft at Munich University in Germany. His research for this book was supported in part by UND Faculty Research Grants.

FELICIA HARDISON LONDRÉ is Curators' Professor of Theatre at the University of Missouri-Kansas City (UMKC) and dramaturg for the Missouri Repertory Theatre and for the Nebraska Shakespeare Festival. She is also honorary co-founder of the Heart of America Shakespeare Festival and was the founding secretary of the Shakespeare Theatre Association of America. Her books include *Tennessee Williams, Federico García Lorca, Tom Stoppard*, and *The History of World Theatre: From the English Restoration to the Present*. In 1993, she was a visiting foreign professor at Hosei University in Tokyo. In 1995, she will hold the Women's Chair in Humanistic Studies at Marquette University. She frequently lectures on the Shakespeare authorship question from an Oxfordian perspective and has given her slide presentation on a lecture tour of Hungary, as well as in Beijing, Tokyo, and Logan, Utah. Her work on this book was supported by UMKC Faculty Research Grants in 1990 and 1991.

DANIEL J. WATERMEIER is Professor of Theatre and Drama at the University of Toledo. He has published two book-length studies of the actor Edwin Booth, *Between Actor and Critic: Selected Letters of Edwin Booth and William Winter*, published by Princeton University Press, and *Edwin Booth's Performances*. He has published widely on American theatre and Shakespeare performance in *Theatre History Studies, Shakespeare Quarterly, Shakespeare Bulletin*, and in such books as the *Cambridge Guide to World Theatre* and the *Cambridge Guide to American Theatre*. He was also one of the coeditors of *Shakespeare Around the Globe: A Guide to Notable Postwar Revivals* published by Greenwood Press. In 1980-81, he was a recipient of a Guggenheim Fellowship and a Folger Shakespeare Library Fellowship. He served as a visiting professor at the University of California at Los Angeles in 1990.

THE CONTRIBUTORS

JEROME M. BIRDMAN, a theatre educator and scholar, is former Dean of the College of Fine Arts at the University of Connecticut.

PHILIP B. CLARKSON, a retired professor of theatre, is a long-time resident of Carmel, California.

KEVIN L. DRESSLER teaches theatre in Mesa, Arizona, and is associate artistic director of the Arizona Shakespeare Festival. He has also worked with Theatre for Young America in Kansas City and the Scottsdale Conservatory Theatre.

RICHARD FOTHERINGHAM is Senior Lecturer in Drama at the University of Queensland in Brisbane, Australia.

MICHAEL L. GREENWALD is Associate Professor of Theatre Arts at Texas A & M University. He is a member of the International Committee of Correspondents for the *World Shakespeare Bibliography*. His contributions to this book have led him to another project, "Shakespeare and the Director: Options and Obligations."

OSAMU HIROKAWA teaches English language courses at Hosei University in Tokyo. He frequently reviews Shakespeare productions for *Shakespeare News from Japan*.

ANDREAS HÖFELE is Professor of English at the University of Heidelberg in Germany. He has published numerous articles on German Shakespeare productions and has recently finished a documentary film on Dieter Dorn's Munich Kammerspiele production of *King Lear* for German television.

ADRIAN KIERNANDER is Senior Lecturer in Drama at the University of Queensland in Brisbane, Australia. He is currently working on a biography of Australian director John Bell.

ALAN KLEM is Coordinator of Theatre at Creighton University in Omaha, Nebraska. He is co-founder of Nebraska Shakespeare Festival, for which he has also served as co-artistic director. He was also artistic director of Fort Worth's Shakespeare in the Park for three seasons.

JENNIFER K. MARTIN is the Hall Family Foundation teacher of movement in the professional theatre-training program at the University of Missouri-Kansas City. She is also Resident Choreographer and Movement Coach for the Missouri Repertory Theatre.

PATRICIA M. McMAHON, a long-time resident of the San Francisco Bay Area, teaches theatre at Holy Names College in Oakland.

JOANNE MUTH, producer of Shakespeare on the Green in Lake Forest, Illionis, is a member of the theatre faculty at Barat College.

CINDY MELBY PHANEUF is Associate Professor and Director of Theatre at the University of Nebraska-Omaha. She is also Artistic Director of the Nebraska Shakespeare Festival, which she cofounded. Her research for this book was supported by the University of Nebraska at Omaha and the University Committee for Research and Creative Activity.

MAARTEN REILINGH is Associate Professor of Theatre and editor of the *McNeese Review* at McNeese State University in Lake Charles, Louisiana. He contributed to *Shakespeare Around the Globe* (Greenwood, 1985), to the *Cambridge Guide to World Theatre* (1988), and to the *Cambridge Guide to American Theatre* (1993).

DAVID V. SCHULZ is currently completing his dissertation in theatre history at the University of Washington.

HASSELL B. SLEDD is Professor of English at Slippery Rock University in Pennsylvania.

CHARLES VICINUS, MFA Yale School of Drama, is Professor Emeritus of Theatre, at the University of Toledo.

VICTOR WEIJIE YU assisted in the planning of the first China Shakespeare Festival. He is currently completing his dissertation at the University of Bayreuth in Germany.

ISBN 0-313-27434-7

EAN

9 780313 274343

90000>

HARDCOVER BAR CODE